Consumer Law

TEXT, CASES AND MATERIALS

David W. Oughton LLB, MPhil
Lecturer in Law
School of European Studies, University of Sussex

BLACKSTONE
PRESS LIMITED

First published in Great Britain 1991 by Blackstone Press Limited,
9-15 Aldine Street, London W12 8AW. Telephone 081-740 1173

© David W. Oughton, 1991

ISBN: 1 85431 173 5

British Library Cataloguing in Publication Data
A CIP catalogue record for this book is available from the British Library

Typeset by Style Photosetting Ltd, Mayfield, East Sussex
Printed by Ashford Colour Press, Gosport, Hampshire

Contents

6   Consumer Finance   154

Preface

My principal aim in writing this book has been to give the student of consumer law both a reasonably detailed discussion of consumer protection related issues and a selection of the main court decisions and statutory provisions relevant to those issues. It has also been possible to include a small amount of comparative material, to highlight possible deficiencies in English consumer protection law. Furthermore, it has been possible to include some European materials, particularly in relation to consumer safety, food, product liability, advertising and holiday law, given the leading role now being taken by the European Community in many of these areas.

What should be covered in a book on consumer law is always open to debate. I have chosen to include materials on the institutions of consumer protection, consumer redress, product quality, product safety, defective services, unfair contract terms and what can be roughly described as advertising law. For covenience' sake, the traditional distinction between private and public law has been maintained in the greater part of the book. However, the chapter on techniques of consumer protection seeks to provide an overview of the whole subject by examining the successes and deficiencies of the plethora of legal and non-legal controls which have been adapted as a means of protecting consumers.

While this is intended primarily as a student text and collection of materials, it is hoped that some use might be made of it by practitioners, retailers, consumer advisers and trading standards departments and others concerned with consumer protection and trading law.

In preparing the manuscript for publication, I have incurred numerous debts of gratitude. I should like to thank Alistair MacQueen, Heather Saward, Jonathan Harris and Penny Robinson at Blackstone Press for their kind assistance in bringing this work to fruition. Thanks also go to Chris Gane, Heather Keating and Rob Merkin at Sussex University and to the consumer law class of 1990/91 for helpful comments and advice given during the preparation of the text. Needless to say, the views expressed are my own and all responsibility for mistakes and infelicities rests with me. I am especially grateful for the help provided by my wife, Sue, who helped with the proof-reading and single-handedly prepared the list of contents and the list of cases. Special thanks also go to Sue and our children Gareth and Karen for their patience and good humour in the 10 months it has taken to write this book. As a good Evertonian, Gareth is delighted with the blue cover.

So far as possible, I have tried to state the law as it stands at 31 March 1991.

David Oughton
Hailsham

Acknowledgments

The author and the publishers gratefully acknowledge the authors and publishers of materials extracted in this book. In particular the following permissions are noted:

The Association of British Travel Agents for their kind permission to cite extracts from their Code of Practice.
Butterworth/Heinemann Ltd for extracts from the *All England Law Reports* and *Legal Studies*.
The Commission of the European Communities for extracts from directives and regulations.
The Consumers Association and David Tench for extracts from *Towards a Middle System of Law*.
The Glass and Glaziers' Federation for extracts from their *Code of Ethical Practice*.
W. Green & Sons Ltd for extracts from the *Scots Law Times*.
Her Majesty's Stationery Office for extracts from government publications, *Law Commission* Reports and materials published in the name of the Office of Fair Trading (see below).
The Harvard Law Review Association and Dr D. Slawson for the extract from (1971) 84 Harv L Rev 529.
The Incorporated Council of Law Reporting in England and Wales for materials extracted from the *Law Reports*, the *Weekly Law Reports* and the *Industrial Cases Reports*.
Lloyd's of London Press Ltd and Professor R. M. Merkin for extracts from *Lloyd's Maritime and Commercial Law Quarterly* and the publishers for extracts from *Lloyd's Law Reports* and *Product Liability International*. The extract from *Walton* v *British Leyland (UK) Ltd* is also to be found in Lloyd's of London Press Ltd's *Product Liability Casebook*.

Kenneth Mason Publications Ltd for extracts from the *Road Traffic Reports*.
The National Consumer Council and the authors of various commissioned
reports including, *Services and the Law – A Consumer View, Good Advice for
All, Ordinary Justice* and *The Consumer Guarantee*.
The Office of Fair Trading and the authors of various reports commissioned
by them including *Home Improvements: A Discussion Paper* and *A General
Duty to Trade Fairly*.
Barry Rose Law Periodicals Ltd and the authors of extracts from *Trading Law*
and the publishers for extracts from the *Trading Law Reports* and the *Local
Government Review*.
The Society of Public Teachers of Law and Dr Richard Tur for an extract from
Legal Studies.
Sweet & Maxwell Ltd and the authors of materials extracted from the *Journal
of Business Law* and the *Law Quarterly Review* and the publishers for extracts
from the *Common Market Law Reports* and the *European Human Rights
Reports*.

(For the most part, extracts have been reprinted without footnotes.)

Table of Cases

Table of Statutes

Table of Statutory Instruments

Table of European Legislation

CHAPTER ONE

Perspectives

1.1 WHO IS A CONSUMER?

In a book on consumer protection law, it is appropriate to consider, at the outset who it is the law purports to protect. In a literal sense, a consumer is 'one who purchases goods or services' (*Longman Dictionary of the English Language*, 1984). This would include any user of goods or services supplied by another, with the result that a construction company purchasing building materials for use in the construction of a housing estate would be acting as a consumer. However, for the purposes of consumer protection law, the term 'consumer' has a narrower meaning which is based on the capacity in which the consumer and the supplier of the goods or services supplied act.

The traditional view of a consumer, or at least that given by the thrust of modern consumer protection legislation, is of an individual dealing with a commercial enterprise. However, it is also the case that the term 'consumer' encompasses a person who makes use of the services provided by public-sector bodies or private monopolies subject to public control. On this basis, consumer protection law would also cover complaints by individuals about the services provided by British Rail, water and electricity companies and British Gas. Furthermore, in the public sector, the consumer might also have reason to complain about the way in which he has been dealt with by the Department of Social Security or he may have a legitimate complaint about the service he has received in hospital. It may also be argued that a tenant's complaint about the way in which he has been treated by his landlord should be regarded as an aspect of consumer protection law. Indeed, the American guru of consumerism, Ralph Nader, has taken the view that the term 'consumer' should be equated with the word 'citizen' and that consumer protection law should be regarded as an aspect of the protection of civic rights.

Various statutes which purport to protect consumer interests contain relevant, but limited definitions. For the most part, a direct definition of the term 'consumer' is not provided. Instead, Parliament has chosen to define phrases such as 'acting in the course of a business' or 'dealing as a consumer'. The effect of these definitions is that a person who acts in the course of a business must act or refrain from acting in a particular manner detrimental to consumer interests. Likewise, if a person deals as a consumer, the supplier may be subject to certain obligations which would not otherwise be imposed or the consumer may have entitlements not conferred on others. The difficulty presented by these statutory definitions is that some emanate from statutes imposing criminal liability and others from Acts concerned with civil liability. It may be that the emphasis in each case is different. In particular, criminal liability is not imposed lightly and it may be that the law adopts a more generous attitude towards a defendant in a criminal case. If this is so, applying the same test in criminal and civil law may not be appropriate. However, the judicial approach to the definition of the terms 'dealing as a consumer' and 'acting in the course of a business' appear to bear remarkable similarities.

In general, a consumer transaction involves three elements. First, the consumer must be an individual (Consumer Credit Act 1974, s. 189(1)) who does not act in a business capacity (Unfair Contract Terms Act 1977, s. 12(1)(a); Consumer Protection Act 1987, s. 20(6)). Secondly the supplier must act in a business capacity (Trade Descriptions Act 1968 ss. 1(1) and 14(1); Fair Trading Act 1973, s. 137(2); Unfair Contract Terms Act 1977, s. 12(1)(b); Sale of Goods Act 1979, ss. 14(2) and 14(3)). Thirdly the goods or services supplied must be intended for private, not business use (Unfair Contract Terms Act 1977, s. 12(1)(c); Consumer Protection Act 1987, s. 20(6)).

1.1.1 Individual not acting in a business capacity

The standard perception of a consumer is of an individual purchaser of goods or services and in most instances this will be the case. Indeed, most of the provisions of the Consumer Credit Act 1974 only apply where the debtor is an individual. But, the definition of an individual in s. 189(1) of the 1974 Act is drafted widely, with the result that a business debtor may still be protected by the provisions of the 1974 Act. In particular, it is clear that while a company is not an individual, a partnership or other unincorporated body of persons is regarded as an individual.

Generally, a consumer is regarded as a non-business purchaser of goods or services, but the difficulty is to decide when a purchaser acts in a business capacity. It is clear that a person who purchases at an auction sale is not to be regarded as a consumer (Unfair Contract Terms Act 1977, s. 12(2)). The Unfair Contract Terms Act 1977, s. 12(1)(a), provides that a person deals as a consumer if the other party to the contract is unable to prove (s. 12(3)) that he neither makes the contract in the course of a business nor holds himself out as doing so. The difficulty here, is to determine when a person purchases in the course of a business.

In a broad sense, every time a company enters into a contract, it does so in the course of its business because if this were not the case, the transaction would be ultra vires (*R & B Customs Brokers Co. Ltd* v *United Dominions Trust Ltd* [1988] 1 All ER 847 at p. 853 per Dillon LJ). Thus, it could be argued that where a company which runs a grocer's shop buys a new delivery van, it acts in the course of a business (ibid.).

An alternative view is that a company can be a 'consumer' purchaser where the purchase is not for some definite business purpose and is one which is not regularly made by that company. In *R & B Customs Brokers Co. Ltd* v *United Dominions Trust Ltd* [1988] 1 All ER 847 (see Brown [1988] JBL 386; Price (1989) 52 MLR 245) the plaintiff, a company carrying on the business of a freight forwarding agent, purchased a car for both business use and for the private use of its directors. It was alleged that the defendant was in breach of the implied term in the Sale of Goods Act 1979, s. 14(3), that the car would be fit for the purpose for which it was intended, namely, driving in English weather conditions, since the roof leaked. However, the defendant finance company sought to rely on an exclusion clause in the contract. Liability for breach of the implied terms in s. 14 cannot be excluded where the buyer deals as a consumer (Unfair Contract Terms Act 1977, s. 6(2)). The Court of Appeal held that since the purchase of the car was only incidental to the business of a freight forwarding agent, the transaction could not be said to be an integral part of the business carried on by the plaintiff as there was no degree of regularity in the type of purchase concerned. It therefore followed that the company had purchased as a consumer and the Unfair Contract Terms Act 1977, s. 6(2), prevented the exclusion clause from taking effect. (See also *Rasbora Ltd* v *JCL Marine Ltd* [1977] 1 Lloyd's Rep 645 and *Peter Symmons & Co.* v *Cook* (1981) 131 NLJ 758.)

The decision of the Court of Appeal may be criticised on a number of grounds. First, the interpretation of the Unfair Contract Terms Act 1977, s. 12(1)(a), may not give effect to the intention of Parliament. If s. 12(1)(a) is interpreted literally, it distinguishes between a business purchaser and a consumer purchaser and does not require the court to consider the purpose for which the goods are required. The distinction between the two approaches is one which was referred to by the Law Commission in their report which led to the enactment of the Unfair Contract Terms Act 1977 (Law Comm. No. 24 (1969) paras 90-5). The Commission concluded that legislation should impose an absolute prohibition on exclusions of liability for breach of the Sale of Goods Act implied terms in consumer sales in the strict sense and that exclusions in contracts entered into by 'business consumers' should be subject to a reasonableness test.

The second ground for criticism is that the reason for the ban on the use of exclusion clauses in consumer contracts is that the consumer is weak in terms of bargaining power, but the same cannot be said of 'business consumers'. Dillon LJ in *R & B Customs Brokers Co. Ltd* v *United Dominions Trust Ltd* considered, *obiter*, that had the purchase been in the course of a business, the exclusion clause would have satisfied the reasonableness test because the company was '*ex hypothesi* dealing in the course of a business' ([1988] 1 All ER

847 at p. 855) and that one of the directors was not devoid of commercial experience (ibid.). It seems strange that where two business contractors are of broadly similar bargaining strength, one of them is entitled to the protection of a blanket prohibition on the use of exclusion clauses.

Finally, even if the plaintiff did not contract in the course of a business, there is a strong argument to the effect that the company held itself out as acting in the course of a business (see Brown [1988] JBL 386 at p. 394). The company made the contract in its corporate name and in a section of the contractual document headed 'Business Details' the nature of the company's business, the number of years trading and the number of company employees had been stated. It is suggested that these matters taken together point to a purchase in the course of a business, not one made by a consumer devoid of commercial experience.

1.1.2 Supplier acting in the course of a business

The second requirement of a consumer transaction is that the supplier must act in the course of a business. The same requirement is to be found in both legislation imposing criminal sanctions (Trade Descriptions Act 1968, s. 1(1); Unsolicited Goods and Services Act 1971, s. 2; Business Advertisements (Disclosure) Order 1977 (SI 1977/1918), art. 2(1)) and provisions relating to civil redress in consumer transactions (Unfair Contract Terms Act 1977, s. 12(1)(b); Sale of Goods Act 1979, s. 14(2) and (3)).

The interpretation of the phrase 'in the course of a business' in this context, is not consistent. In particular, there would appear to be a difference of approach in relation to the Sale of Goods Act 1979 and the Trade Descriptions Act 1968.

So far as the Sale of Goods Act 1979 is concerned, the implied terms of fitness and quality in s. 14(2) and (3) apply only where the seller sells the goods in the course of a business. It is clear that for these purposes, a person can be regarded as a business seller if he sells by way of trade even if he does not make a habit of trading in goods of the type in question (*Ashington Piggeries Ltd* v *Christopher Hill Ltd* [1972] AC 441 at p. 494 per Lord Wilberforce; see also Final Report of the Committee on Consumer Protection (Moloney Committee) (Cmnd 1781, 1962), para. 443). Accordingly, for the purposes of this Act, the sale of stock in trade or other irregular sales by a trade seller will be regarded as sales in the course of a business and the implied terms in s. 14 will apply to the transaction.

For the purposes of the Trade Descriptions Act 1968, a different approach has emerged. This is identical to the approach adopted in *R & B Customs Brokers Co. Ltd* v *United Dominions Trust Ltd* [1988] 1 All ER 847 in relation to 'business consumers'. In *Davies* v *Sumner* [1984] 3 All ER 831, the defendant, a professional courier, sold the car he used as part of his business. Contrary to the provisions of the Trade Descriptions Act 1968, s. 1(1)(a), the defendant sold the car subject to a false statement as to the mileage covered by the vehicle. It was held by the House of Lords that the defendant had not sold the car in the course of a business since such a sale must be an integral part of the business carried on by the defendant. Furthermore, to achieve this status, the transactions concerned must have some degree of regularity. Thus the renewal of hire cars every two years by a car-hire firm can constitute a sale in the course of a business since the required degree of regularity is established (*Havering London Borough Council* v *Stevenson* [1970] 1 WLR 1375). However, it would appear that the occasional sale of a car used by a doctor for both private and professional purposes does not possess the necessary element of regularity to allow for a conviction under the Trade Descriptions Act (*Davies* v *Sumner* [1984] 1 WLR 405 at p. 410 per Robert Goff LJ; see also *Devlin* v *Hall* [1990] RTR 320). It has even been held that a postman who renovates, regularly advertises and resells cars does not sell in the course of a business, if the work is performed by way of a hobby (*Blakemore* v *Bellamy* [1983] RTR 303). The one exception to this approach arises where an isolated transaction is carried out with a view to profit (*Davies* v *Sumner* [1984] 3 All ER 831 at p. 834 per Lord Keith). Thus a person who arranges for the publication of a book of poems, supplies copies of the book to public libraries and subsequently demands payment can be said to have demanded payment in the course of a trade or business for the purposes of the Unsolicited Goods and Services Act 1971, s. 2(1) (*Eiman* v *Waltham Forest London Borough Council* (1982) 90 ITSA Monthly Review 204). Similarly, a petrol retailer who sells a car on a one-off basis with a view to profit may still be guilty of an offence under the Trade Descriptions Act 1968 (*Corfield* v *Sevenways Garage Ltd* [1985] RTR 109)

It is clear that the approach adopted in relation to the Trade Descriptions Act 1968 and other penal legislation favours the seller to a greater extent than the approach adopted in relation to the Sale of Goods Act 1979. This may be justified on the ground that in cases of doubt a penal provision should be construed in favour of the defendant. However, there may be a danger that, in the interests of consistency, the same approach may be adopted in relation to the Sale of Goods Act 1979. This danger may already be real following the application of the *Davies* v *Sumner* test to the Unfair Contract Terms Act in *R & B Customs Brokers Co. Ltd* v *United Dominions Trust Ltd*. It would be undesirable in the extreme if the implied terms in the Sale of Goods Act 1979, s. 14, were held not to apply to one-off sales by trade sellers. In any case, seeking consistency in relation to all of the statutory provisions that contain the phrase 'selling in the course of a business' is unrealistic as there are other reasons why total consistency is impossible to achieve. In particular, the Unfair Contract Terms Act 1977 has a further requirement that the goods purchased by the consumer should be of a type ordinarily supplied for private use or consumption, whereas no such restriction applies to the Sale of Goods Act 1979. Accordingly, it is suggested that there should continue to be a difference between the definition of a sale in the course of a business and a purchase in the course of a business.

1.1.3 Non-business and private use or consumption

Some statutory provisions impose a further requirement on the definition of a consumer, namely, that the goods or services acquired should be intended for non-business or consumer use (Unfair Contract Terms Act 1977, s. 12(1)(c); Consumer Protection Act 1987, ss. 10(7) and 20(6)). It is clear that in order to satisfy this requirement, goods do not need to be exclusively used by consumers.

The Unfair Contract Terms Act 1977, s. 12(1)(c), refers to goods of a type ordinarily supplied for private use or consumption. For example, it is possible that some goods could be used for both business and consumer purposes, such as a car used by a doctor for his own domestic use and for the purposes of his medical practice. Difficulties may arise where goods are of a type ordinarily purchased for private use or consumption but which are, in fact, put to business use. In such a case, s. 12(1)(c) may indicate that the buyer deals as a consumer, but it is also the case that if the buyer deals in such goods in the course of a business, the provisions of the Unfair Contract Terms Act 1977 in relation to consumer sales will not apply. Thus, if a business purchases raw materials which might also be purchased by a consumer, but uses them in its manufacturing process, clearly the purchase is not one made otherwise than in the course of a business.

The problem can also be considered in reverse. Suppose a consumer purchases material ordinarily put to a business use, such as a cement mixer. It may be that the consumer does not act in the course of a business, but if s. 12(1)(c) is not complied with, the buyer does not deal as a consumer. It may be that what is ordinarily supplied for private use will need to be considered on a case-by-case basis as consumer purchases change over a period of time. For example, the growth of the 'do-it-yourself' market may mean that articles which have been regarded, in the past, as the subject of trade purchases may come to be regarded as items ordinarily supplied for private use.

The word 'type' may also create difficulties, if it requires the court to consider merely the nature of the thing sold. For example, the purchase of a bale of peat from a garden centre would be a consumer purchase, but could the same be said of a bulk purchase of, say, 500 bales? The thing sold in each case is the same, but the quantity sold may indicate that the subject-matter of the contract is being put to something other than a purely consumer use.

Similar, but not identical provisions are contained in the Consumer Protection Act 1987, s. 20(6), in relation to the definition of a consumer for the purposes of the penal provisions of the Act concerned with misleading pricing. For these purposes a consumer of goods is one who 'might wish to be supplied with goods for his own private use or consumption' (Consumer Protection Act 1987, s. 20(6)(a)). This formulation avoids the objectivity of the Unfair Contract Terms Act 1977, s. 12(1)(c), by concentrating on the use to which the consumer might wish to put the goods. This may mean that the provisions of s. 20 apply to cases where the subject-matter is capable of being put to private use, although this is not, in fact, the case. A better formulation would have been 'might reasonably wish' (see Merkin, *A Guide to the Consumer Protection Act 1987*, para. 14.2).

In relation to misleading statements concerning the charge made for services, facilities or accommodation, the essence of the definition of a consumer is that the service etc. is not required for the purposes of a business

(Consumer Protection Act 1987, s. 20(6)(b) and (c)). Whether there is a difference between purchasing goods for private use and acquiring a service for non-business use is not clear. However, it is likely that the two provisions will be construed in a similar manner.

1.1.4 Non-contractual consumers

The foregoing discussion assumes that there is a consumer purchaser and a supplier who contracts in the course of a business. While it is the case that a consumer is often a person who has entered into a contractual relationship with a supplier, it is also true that there are many non-contractual consumers.

Until recently, the protection of such consumers was left largely to the tort of negligence in the form of the narrow rule in *Donoghue* v *Stevenson* [1932] AC 562 (see chapter 8), but in recent years, the position of the non-contractual consumer has been recognised. In particular, the provisions of part I of the Consumer Protection Act 1987 seek to give such a person a remedy in damages against the producer of a defective product. Other developments in the field of civil redress may have taken the position of the non-contractual consumer to even greater heights, had the present government been prepared to lend a more sympathetic ear. In particular, a recent attempt by the National Consumer Council (*The Consumer Guarantee* (PD29/89), September 1989) to secure the enactment of legislation in respect of consumer guarantees commanded considerable public support, but was ultimately defeated by government intervention.

Many statutory provisions creating criminal offences on the part of traders or providing for means of administrative control do not require the formation of a contractual relationship. For example, some of the offences created by the Food Safety Act 1990, the Consumer Protection Act 1987 and the Trade Descriptions Act 1968 are still committed where there is no consumer purchase at all or where the person harmed by an unsafe product is not the person who bought it from the retailer. Similarly, the Director General of Fair Trading is required by the provisions of the Fair Trading Act 1973 to review consumer trade practices and may recommend legislation (Fair Trading Act 1973, s. 14(1)). It is clear from the definition of a consumer trade practice in the Fair Trading Act 1973, s. 13(1), that certain practices will affect both contractual and non-contractual consumers. In particular, paras (c), (d) and (e) of s. 13(1) refer to methods of sales promotion, salesmanship and packaging which may affect more than just the immediate purchaser.

1.2 WHO IS A CONSUMER? – MATERIALS FOR CONSIDERATION

Unfair Contract Terms Act 1977

12. 'Dealing as consumer'
   (1) A party to a contract 'deals as consumer' in relation to another party if—
   (a) he neither makes the contract in the course of a business nor holds himself out as doing so; and

(b)   the other party does make the contract in the course of a business; and

(c)   in the case of a contract governed by the law of sale of goods or hire-purchase, or by section 7 of this Act, the goods passing under or in pursuance of the contract are of a type ordinarily supplied for private use or consumption.

(2)   But on a sale by auction or by competitive tender the buyer is not in any circumstances to be regarded as dealing as consumer.

(3)   Subject to this, it is for those claiming that a party does not deal as consumer to show that he does not.

See also the Consumer Protection Act 1987, s. 10(7), in 9.3 and s. 20(6) in 12.3.

1.2.1   Individual not acting in a business capacity

For text see 1.1.1.

R & B Customs Brokers Co. Ltd v *United Dominions Trust Ltd*
[1988] 1 All ER 847

For the facts see 1.1.1.

DILLON LJ at p. 853: It is accepted that the conditions in paras (b) and (c) in s. 12(1) [of the Unfair Contract Terms Act 1977] are satisfied. This issue turns on the condition in para. (a). Did the company neither make the contract with the defendants in the course of a business nor hold itself out as doing so?

In the present case there was no holding out beyond the mere facts that the contract and the finance application were made in the company's corporate name and in the finance application the section headed 'Business Details' was filled in to the extent of giving the nature of the company's business as that of shipping brokers, giving the number of years trading and the number of employees, and giving the names and addresses of the directors. What is important is whether the contract was made in the course of a business.

In a certain sense, however, from the very nature of a corporate entity, where a company which carried on a business makes a contract it makes that contract in the course of its business; otherwise the contract would be *ultra vires* and illegal. Thus, where a company which runs a grocer's shop buys a new delivery van, it buys it in the course of its business. Where a merchant bank buys a car as a 'company car' as a perquisite for a senior executive, it buys it in the course of its business. Where a farming company buys a Landrover for the personal and company use of a farm manager, it again does so in the course of its business. Possible variations are numerous. In each case it would not be legal for the purchasing company to buy the vehicle in question otherwise than in the course of its business. Section 12 does not require that the business in the course of which the one party, referred to in the condition in para. (a), makes the contract must be of the same nature as the business in the course of which the other party, referred to in the condition in para. (b), makes the contract, e.g. that they should both be motor dealers.

[Dillon LJ then surveyed the authorities under the Unfair Contract Terms Act 1977 and the judgment of Lord Keith in *Davies* v *Sumner* [1984] 3 All ER 831 (see 1.2.2) and continued at p. 854:]

Lord Keith emphasised the need for some degree of regularity, and he found pointers to this in the primary purpose and long title of the 1968 Act. I find pointers to a similar need for regularity under the 1977 Act, where matters merely incidental to the carrying on of a business are concerned, both in the words which I would emphasise, 'in the course of' in the phrase 'in the course of a business' and in the concept, or legislative purpose, which must underlie the dichotomy under the 1977 Act between those who deal as consumers and those who deal otherwise than as consumers.

This reasoning leads to the conclusion that, in the 1977 Act also, the words 'in the course of business' are not used in what Lord Keith called 'the broadest sense'. I also find helpful the phrase used by Lord Parker CJ and quoted by Lord Keith, 'an integral part of the business carried on'. The reconciliation between that phrase and the need for some degree of regularity is, as I see it, as follows: there are some transactions which are clearly integral parts of the businesses concerned, and these should be held to have been carried out in the course of those businesses; this would cover, apart from much else, the instance of a one-off adventure in the nature of trade where the transaction itself would constitute a trade or business. There are other transactions, however, such as the purchase of the car in the present case, which are at the highest only incidental to the carrying on of the relevant business; here a degree of regularity is required before it can be said that they are an integral part of the business carried on and so entered into in the course of that business.

Applying the test thus indicated to the facts of the present case, I have no doubt that the requisite degree of regularity is not made out on the facts. Mr. Bell's evidence that the car was the second or third vehicle acquired on credit terms was in my judgment and in the context of this case not enough. Accordingly, I agree with the judge that, in entering into the conditional sale agreement with the defendants, the company was 'dealing as consumer'. The defendants' cl. 2(a) is thus inapplicable and the defendants are not absolved from liability under s. 14(3).

Neill LJ delivered a judgment to similar effect.

Appeal dismissed.

1.2.2   Supplier acting in the course of a business

For text see 1.1.2.

The Trade Descriptions Act 1968, s. 1 (see chapter 11), and the Sale of Goods Act 1979, s. 14(2) and (3) (see chapter 7), both apply only where a person supplies or sells goods in the course of a business. The judicial approach to the effect of the phrase 'selling in the course of a business' in the Sale of Goods Act 1893 (now 1979) is explained in:

Ashington Piggeries Ltd v Christopher Hill Ltd
[1972] AC 441
House of Lords

LORD WILBERFORCE at pp. 493–4: Section 14(1) [of the Sale of Goods Act 1893] contains the words 'and the goods are of a description which it is in the course of the seller's business to supply'. The respondents relied on these words and persuaded the Court of Appeal to decide that the requirement was not satisfied because, briefly, the respondents were not dealers in mink food. A similar argument was put forward on the words in section 14(2) 'where goods are bought by description from a seller who deals in goods of that description.' The Court of Appeal decided this point, too, in the respondents' favour. The respondents, they held, did not deal in mink food, or 'King Size,' before Mr Udall placed with them the orders which produced the defective goods. I have some doubt whether this argument is even correct on the facts, because Mr Udall had been ordering 'King Size' for several months before he ordered the fatal consignment. But we must deal with the legal argument because it is clearly of general importance. It appears never previously to have been accepted and it substantially narrows the scope of both subsections. It rests, in the first place, upon a linguistic comparison of the meaning of the word 'description' in the three places where it appears and on the argument that it must mean the same in each place.

I do not accept that, taken in its most linguistic strictness, either subsection bears the meaning contended for. I would hold that (as to subsection (1)) it is in the course of the seller's business to supply goods if he agrees either generally, or in a particular case, to supply the goods when ordered, and (as to subsection (2)) that a seller deals in goods of that description if his business is such that he is willing to accept orders for them. I cannot comprehend the rationale of holding that the subsections do not apply if the seller is dealing in the particular goods for the first time or the sense of distinguishing between the first and the second order for the goods or for goods of the description. The Court of Appeal offered the analogy of a doctor sending a novel prescription to a pharmacist, which turns out to be deleterious. But as often happens to arguments of this kind, the analogy is faulty: if the prescription is wrong, of course the doctor is responsible. The fitness of the prescription is within his field of responsibility. The relevant question is whether the pharmacist is responsible for the purity of his ingredients and one does not see why not.

But, moreover, consideration of the preceding common law shows that what the Act had in mind was something quite simple and rational: to limit the implied conditions of fitness or quality to persons in the way of business, as distinct from private persons.

Compare the approach taken in relation to the penal provisions of the Trade Descriptions Act 1968, s. 1, in the following case.

Davies v *Sumner*
[1984] 1 WLR 1301
House of Lords

For the facts see 1.1.2.

LORD KEITH at p. 1304: This decision [*Havering London Borough Council* v *Stevenson* [1970] 1 WLR 1375], the correctness of which was not challenged by Mr Somerset Jones for the respondent, vouches the proposition that in certain circumstances the sale of certain goods may, within the meaning of the Act, be in the course of a trade or business, notwithstanding that the trade or business of the defendant does not consist in dealing for profit in goods of that, or indeed any other, description.

Any disposal of a chattel held for the purposes of a business may, in a certain sense, be said to have been in the course of that business, irrespective of whether the chattel was acquired with a view to resale or for consumption or as a capital asset. But in my opinion section 1(1) of the Act is not intended to cast such a wide net as this. The expression 'in the course of a trade or business' in the context of an Act having consumer protection as its primary purpose conveys the concept of some degree of regularity, and it is to be observed that the long title to the Act refers to 'misdescriptions of goods, services, accommodation and facilities provided in the course of trade'. Lord Parker CJ in the *Havering* case [1970] 1 WLR 1375 clearly considered that the expression was not used in the broadest sense. The reason why the transaction there in issue was caught was that in his view it was 'an integral part of the business carried on as a car hire firm'. That would not cover the sporadic selling off of pieces of equipment which were no longer required for the purposes of a business. The vital feature of the *Havering* case appears to have been, in Lord Parker's view, that the defendant's business *as part of its normal practice* bought and disposed of cars. The need for some degree of regularity does not, however, involve that a one-off adventure in the nature of trade, carried through with a view to profit, would not fall within section 1(1) because such a transaction would itself constitute a trade.

In the present case it was sought to be inferred that the respondent, covering as he did such a large regular mileage, was likely to have occasion to sell his car at regular intervals, so that he too would have a normal practice of buying and disposing of cars. It is sufficient to say that such a normal practice had not yet been established at the time of the alleged offence. The respondent might well revert to hiring a car, as he had previously done. Further the respondent's car was a piece of equipment he used for providing his courier service. It was not something he exploited as stock in trade, which is what the defendant was in substance doing with his cars in the *Havering* case [1970] 1 WLR 1375. Where a person carries on the business of hiring out some description of goods to the public and has a practice of selling off those that are no longer in good enough condition, clearly the latter goods are offered or supplied in the course of his business within the meaning of section 1(1). But the occasional sale of some worn-out piece of shop equipment would not fall within the enactment.

Lords Elwyn Jones, Bridge, Brandon and Templeman all agreed.
Appeal dismissed.

Contrast the view expressed by Dobson [1991] JBL 68–9:

[These cases] show up the absurdity of the whole principle of *regularity*. We already know that this principle applies to the expression 'in the course of business' in the Unfair Contract Terms Act 1977. If it also applies to the same expression in section 14 of the Sale of Goods Act 1979, then the purchaser of the Peugeot was not entitled to a car of merchantable quality or fit for its purpose. One might add that it is surely inconceivable that the same principle applies in relation to income tax. Consider the trader who occasionally buys for his business a new typewriter or who has his windows repaired following an unusually heavy storm or who replaces his office carpet after 10 years in business. The trader would not expect to be told that these expenses (whether of capital or revenue) were not 'business' expenses. It is a remarkable distortion of ordinary English to say that these transactions were not made 'in the course of a trade or business'.

1.3 THE CONTEXT OF CONSUMER PROTECTION

1.3.1 Historical context

While consumer protection law is often regarded as a modern phenomenon, typical of the 20th century, it is, in fact, the case that many of what we now regard as statutes with an emphasis on consumer protection had their origins in a much earlier age. For example, there has long been regulation in respect of essential items such as bread, meat, ale and fuel. In particular, there was early regulation in relation to prices and the provision of short measures. Whether these statutes should be properly regarded as consumer protection measures is doubtful, as much of the motivation for their enactment probably stemmed from a desire to protect honest traders from their dishonest competitors. As such, much of the earlier legislation can be regarded as being directed towards 'fair trading' rather than 'consumer protection'. For instance, the Trade Descriptions Act 1968, which is regarded as one of the earliest examples of modern regulation in the consumer interest is based, in part, on the provisions of the Merchandise Marks Acts 1887 to 1953, the avowed intent of which was to protect honest traders against their unscrupulous competitors where the latter sought to create a trading advantage by means of misdescribing the products they sold.

As trade in basic consumer commodities increased, pressure for legal controls increased. Business self-regulation by trade guilds had been employed in order to control the adulteration of food by unscrupulous traders, but this did not effectively control the abuses. The excesses of some traders were such as to involve a danger to life as well as giving them a trading advantage over their honest competitors. Reported practices included the failure to remove impurities from bread, sugar and pepper, the addition of grease to coffee and the addition of sulphuric acid to vinegar (*Butterworths Law of Food and Drugs*, para. 2). Modern food law can be traced to the Adulteration of Food and Drink Act 1860 which, amongst other provisions, prohibited the sale of food containing injurious material or ingredients. Subsequent legislation also rendered it unlawful to sell food not of the nature, substance or quality demanded by the purchaser.

Early attempts at legislating for uniform weights and measures can be found as far back as the 13th century. It was a criminal offence under the Assize of Bread and Ale of 1266 to supply these commodities in short weight. Particularly frowned upon was the deliberate use of unjust balances. Various methods of enforcement were employed, but one which proved to be effective in this particular respect was excommunication. In relation to bread and coal, legislation dating back to the 17th and 18th centuries allowed local justices to fix the price of the product according to its weight and other relevant market conditions.

Necessary in the process of regulating the supply of consumer commodities was the establishment of a set of measuring norms. Clearly, it would be intolerable to the trader to have a movable standard with which compliance was difficult or impossible. In early years, royal decrees sought to establish basic standards of measurement. For example, in 1305, Edward I enacted that '3 grains of barley, dry and round, make an inch, 12 inches make a foot and 3 feet make an *ulna*' (later to become a yard). It was common practice for monarchs to keep standard measuring rods in their treasury. Many of these early measures, particularly those relating to capacity, were crude, to say the least, often being based on the weight of materials which were likely to alter in terms of volume in different temperatures or in differing conditions.

The civil law of consumer protection was most markedly affected by developments in the 19th century, in particular the principles of freedom of contract and *caveat emptor*. The period was characterised by a general unwillingness to interfere in business affairs (see *Printing & Numerical Registering Co.* v *Sampson* (1875) LR 19 Eq 462 at p. 465 per Sir George Jessel). As a general rule, the parties to a contract were not obliged to volunteer information with the result that if a person wanted a warranty that the goods or services he purchased were of sound quality he could contract for this result and pay accordingly (see *Parkinson* v *Lee* (1802) 2 East 314). The principle of *caveat emptor* was consistent with the principles of freedom of contract and self-reliance which were features of the 19th century. This approach may well have been justified at the time since few goods would have cost enough to warrant common law protection (Atiyah, *The Rise and Fall of Freedom of Contract* (1979), p. 179). Accordingly, it was still possible to argue that the buyer could afford to learn from his mistakes and that legislative intervention in favour of the consumer was unnecessary.

Even in the 19th century, *caveat emptor* was not always blindly adhered to. Some members of the judiciary were prepared to imply warranties of fitness and quality on the part of the seller of goods (*Jones* v *Bright* (1829) 5 Bing 533) which ultimately appeared in statutory form in the Sale of Goods Act 1893. The implication of such terms in contracts can be explained by the substantial increase in manufactured goods which began to appear in the middle to late 19th century, heralding the age of the consumer which was to develop in the 20th century. If a buyer paid a sound price, he could expect his purchase to be of like quality.

1.3.2   Why protect the consumer?

See *Consumer Dissatisfaction*, Office of Fair Trading (1986) paras 7.3–7.15.

Laws intended to protect consumers, as opposed to other traders, are seen as a comparatively recent development. But it needs to be asked why such laws are necessary. The early attempts at regulation could be said to be based on discouraging fraudulent or dangerous practices. However, many modern consumer protection measures no longer require proof of fraud. Indeed, a feature of statutes such as the Trade Descriptions Act 1968, the Consumer Credit Act 1974, the Consumer Protection Act 1987 and the Food Safety Act 1990 is that, subject to the availability of statutory defences, a trader can be found guilty of a criminal offence without proof of criminal intention. It would appear to follow from this that there is some other justification for intervention in favour of the consumer.

A number of factors may be regarded as reasons for intervention in favour of consumers. Many trade practices may result in a general lack of information on the part of consumers with the result that the ability of the consumer to make a prudent shopping decision is diminished (Trebilcock (1971) 16 McGill LJ 263).

First, there were substantial changes in the nature of the consumer market after the Second World War. Articles such as televisions, synthetic fibres, processed and prepacked foods, records, magnetic tapes and more recently products based on microchip technology have come on to the market. The rate of change has been so fast that the consumer could hardly be expected to fully appreciate the operation of many of the sophisticated products he was able to purchase. Such knowledge as the consumer might have had soon became dated. Furthermore, in many cases, even the retailer had little more under-standing of the complexity of the product sold than the consumer. The same can also be said of the market for consumer services with the result that the consumer is often in no position to make a proper evaluation of the service he receives. For example, few consumers can be said to fully appreciate the nature of work carried out by a mechanic on a motor vehicle.

Other relevant factors in the growth of the consumer market included the general increase in consumers' income and the readier availability of credit in the form of hire-purchase. The increase in spending power led to a correspond-ing increase in the number of complex products purchased.

Businesses became much better organised and operated on a very large scale. The post-war years have seen a decline in the number of corner shops and a substantial increase in the number of supermarket chains. The organisation of business is a natural consequence of traders devoting their whole working day to the business and ensuring that it is profitable. By contrast, the consumer has a number of other interests to attend to. The consumer does not spend the whole day making purchases but must also consider the demands of his work, other members of his family etc.

It can be argued that modern advertising methods tend to disinform rather than to inform the consumer. In particular, it can be said that advertisements do not provide information on an objective basis. The advertiser only tells the consumer what he wants the consumer to hear and other facts which might be relevant to a prudent shopping decision tend to be omitted. A further objection to advertising techniques is that they may encourage irrational purchases, for example, it has been argued that consumer 'wants' are artificially created by advertising (Galbraith, *The Affluent Society*, 4th ed., 1984). However, it is also the case that increased consumer demand leads to increased production, which creates an expanding economy which in the long run is good for the consumer.

1.3.3   Rationales for Consumer Protection

See Ramsay, *Rationales for Intervention in The Consumer Marketplace* (OFT 1984) paras 2.1–2.3; 3.1–3.5; 3.18; 4.3 and 4.8.

Much modern consumer law can be said to be based on an attempt to rectify the inequality of bargaining power which is said to exist between the individual consumer and the more powerful supplier of goods or services with whom he deals (Law Com. No. 69 (1975); *Report of the Committee on Consumer Credit* (Crowther Committee, Cmnd 4596), 1971). It is necessary to consider how this imbalance of power has come about, how the use of common law rules and legislation has sought to combat it (see chapter 3) and whether regulation of trade practices is truly in the consumer interest.

To say that regulation in the consumer interest is justified in order to counteract inequalities of bargaining power is not helpful unless the reasons for this alleged inequality are articulated. Principally, a consumer is not in a position of equal bargaining power due to difficulties in obtaining information. The consumer does not have the ability to acquire the necessary information to be on the same level as the supplier with whom he deals. However, inequality of bargaining power may also arise for another reason, namely, that the cost of seeking redress is too great (see chapter 4).

1.3.3.1 Information problems If the market is to function in an efficient manner, consumers need to be supplied with adequate information about the price and quality of products and services available from competing traders and about the terms on which those traders are prepared to do business. Armed with this information, the consumer can make a prudent shopping decision. If the consumer is adequately informed, he can indicate his preferences which will lead to competition between traders to satisfy those preferences. However, if the necessary information on price, quality and terms is not available, little competition, if any, will follow.

If, for some reason, adequate information is not available, intervention in the market in favour of the consumer may be justified. It is important to stress that adequate, rather than perfect information is all that is required. It might be possible to stipulate that consumers should be armed with all possible information, but to do so would prove to be inefficient since the cost of intervention would outweigh any benefits derived therefrom.

A straightforward cost-benefit analysis does not provide the full answer as it is also important to consider the distributional effects of intervention or non-intervention. It may be that intervention in a particular way has the effect of benefiting one particular group of consumers to the detriment of another group. In such a case, it is important to consider whether this distribution of resources is justified. For example, the provisions of the Unfair Contract Terms Act 1977 in relation to purported exclusions of liability in respect of a breach of the implied terms of quality and fitness in a contract for the supply of goods could be said to benefit anyone who purchases goods. Since this covers the entire consumer community, the intervention is of benefit to everyone. The same might not be true of a proposal to compel manufacturers to give a five-year parts and labour warranty on new cars as this would only benefit those who were able to afford a new car. Intervention of the latter type might clearly benefit the better off, but the cost of complying with the compulsory guarantee provisions would make new cars more expensive which in turn would make second-hand cars more expensive without necessarily conferring any benefits on the purchasers of second-hand cars.

Where there is a lack of relevant information, the greatest danger is that the consumer will make a purchase for the wrong reasons. For example, but for the provisions of the Trade Descriptions Act 1968 in relation to misdescriptions of goods or the Consumer Credit Act 1974 requirements in relation to truth in lending, a consumer might make a purchase he would not otherwise make because of misleading claims about performance or rates of interest.

In determining whether legislation is required in order to ensure the availability of information, it is necessary to consider if intervention is justified. It may be that the cost of intervention is too great in comparison with the benefits it confers. Sometimes, the necessary information is readily available without the need for a detailed and costly search. In such a case, intervention to ensure the availability of the information is not needed. For example, where food is bought frequently, there is no need to provide information on taste, as this is a matter which can be assessed by experience. In contrast, there might be greater justification for intervention in order to warn of risks to health or potentially large financial losses, particularly where the commodity is infrequently purchased and experienced. For example, control of the excesses of doorstep double glazing salesmen may be justified on the ground that this is the sort of purchase which consumers infrequently make. In these circumstances there is little market pressure on the salesman to tell the truth as the consumer is unlikely to return in order to make other purchases at a later date. Similar arguments appear to lie behind the unsuccessful proposals for legislation in respect of a statutory consumer guarantee to cover new cars and expensive, infrequently purchased domestic appliances (National Consumer Council, *The Consumer Guarantee* (1989) paras 3.2.1 to 3.2.4). Since the consumer does not buy these products on a regular basis, there is no incentive on the part of the producer to give full information. However, if a producer can give a worthwhile guarantee with his product, this may be seen as giving him a competitive advantage over others who cannot provide the same sort of guarantee. In these circumstances, it is suggested that the consumer will be supplied with product information to a greater extent than would otherwise have been the case (ibid., para. 1.7).

Even where there is a competitive market, there are some types of information which may not be made available. Manufacturers of a product which contains an inherent defect are unlikely to make that information widely known, unless they are required to do so. For example, what cigarette manufacturer would voluntarily print a health warning on his product or his advertising copy? Furthermore, there is some information which is not always made available for fear of disadvantageous competition. For example, some manufacturers may decline to engage in comparative advertising on the ground that competitors may unfavourably compare a rival product with their own. The end result may be a general agreement in that sector of the market not to engage in comparative advertising.

It is sometimes argued that information will be passed to consumers by 'information brokers' such as retailers or doctors prescribing medicines. These brokers are said to have an interest in keeping the consumer properly informed as their own reputation depends on them supplying good-quality products, but retailers may be just as ignorant of the performance of complex products as is the consumer, in which case the information is not passed on.

1.3.3.2 Other factors Apart from the problem of consumer information, other rationales may also be put forward for protecting the consumer. It may be argued that consumer protection laws are based on the notion of paternalism. In some instances, there may be a distrust of the consumer's ability to protect himself. In particular, it would be reasonable to assume that where legislation has been passed in order to protect consumers against physical injury, there is a paternalist motive behind the enactment. It is not just where there is a risk of physical injury that paternalist arguments prevail. It is equally the case that where there is a high risk of considerable financial loss, intervention on paternalist grounds may be justified. For example, the enactment of the Unfair Contract Terms Act 1977 and many of the provisions of the Consumer Credit Act 1974 appear to be based on the assumption that the consumer is not always in a position to protect himself (see Crowther Committee on Consumer Credit (Cmnd 4596, 1971)).

An alternative argument in favour of consumer protection legislation is that it preserves community values, such as fair dealing and honesty. Also, some commentators claim there is a consumer right to protection, particularly where physical injury caused by unsafe products is concerned.

CHAPTER TWO

Institutions of Consumer Protection

2.1 CENTRAL GOVERNMENT

A wide range of central government departments have a role in relation to consumer protection. Some would argue that the range of departments concerned is too great and that due to the large number involved, the consumer interest is sometimes prejudiced at the hands of another interest. It might be argued that the consumer interest would be best protected by the creation of a specific department of government devoted to consumer affairs, although a proposal to this effect was dismissed by the Molony Committee on Consumer Protection (Cmnd 1781 (1962), para. 886) as a grandiose notion. In 1974 the Labour government set up a Department of Prices and Consumer Protection, but following the Conservative victory in the general election of 1979, the Department of Prices and Consumer Protection was disbanded and its functions were transferred to the Department of Trade and Industry. Other consumer protection functions are performed by the Department of Health, the Office of Fair Trading, the Home Office and the Ministry of Agriculture, Fisheries and Food.

It might be objected that the absence of a department of government with an unique consumer protection role is disadvantageous, particularly where competing interests are dealt with by the same department of government. For example, in recent years public concern has been shown over the safety of certain foods including eggs, cheese and beef. In each case, the Ministry of Agriculture, Fisheries and Food was torn between the interests of the consumer and the interests of the agricultural community, resulting in general public confusion over what was safe to eat.

Broadly speaking, the role of central government in relation to consumer protection can be described as the initiation and furtherance of legislative policy and supervising the enforcement of consumer protection measures designed to protect the economic and safety interests of consumers within the general constraints of the market.

2.1.1   Development of consumer protection policy

The two government departments most closely associated with the development of consumer policy are the Department of Trade and Industry and its satellite, the Office of Fair Trading. Other departments have a specific policy role in specialised areas which are considered below in respect of consumer economic interests and consumer health and safety.

2.1.1.1   The Department of Trade and Industry   Amongst other things, the Department of Trade and Industry is responsible for the development of policy in the fields of trading standards and fair trading, weights and measures, consumer credit and consumer safety. The Department also has important functions in relation to monopolies, mergers and restrictive practices. Much of this work devolves to agencies under the general control of the Department of Trade and Industry and, as such, is not actually performed by the Department itself.

2.1.1.2   The Fair Trading Act 1973 and the Office of Fair Trading   The Office of Fair Trading was set up under the provisions of the Fair Trading Act 1973. Broadly speaking, the Office of Fair Trading serves a dual role, namely, to protect the consumer against unfair trading practices and secondly to promote economic efficiency.

2.1.1.2.1   Consumer trade practices   The consumer protection role of the Director General of Fair Trading which most directly relates to the development of consumer policy consists of the review of commercial activities in the UK which relate to the supply of goods and services to consumers (Fair Trading Act 1973, s. 2(1)(a)). The Director is required to identify those practices which may adversely affect the economic interests of consumers. The Director also has an information collection function in respect of trading practices which affect consumer interests, whether they relate to economic, health and safety or other matters (s. 2(1)(b)). This information may be passed to the Consumer Protection Advisory Committee (CPAC), insofar as it relates to consumer economic interests (Fair Trading Act 1973, s. 14). Following such a reference, CPAC may recommend that the Department of Trade and Industry should legislate in respect of the practice, or it can modify or reject the proposals of the Director General (Fair Trading Act 1973, s. 21).

The theory behind the creation of CPAC was that it should act as a jury to assess the merits of proposed regulations and help determine whether a particular practice was detrimental to consumer economic interests or not. In the event, four references were made to CPAC. In each case, CPAC chose to modify the Director's proposals and out of those four references, only three resulted in an order being made. No references have been made since 1976 and membership of CPAC is currently suspended.

For the purposes of the reference procedure, a consumer trade practice is defined in s. 13 as a practice carried on in relation to the supply of goods or services to consumers and which relates to the terms on which they are supplied, the way in which contract terms are communicated, sales promotion and methods of salesmanship, packaging of goods or methods of seeking payment for goods or services supplied. It is evident from this that s. 13 covers practices such as purporting to exclude the consumer's inalienable rights, excessively complicated or ambiguous language used in standard-form documents, misleading advertising campaigns and doorstep selling amongst others. However, there are certain practices which would appear not to fall within the scope of s. 13. Since s. 13 is concerned with the supply of goods to consumers, transactions involving a purchase from a consumer is not within the scope of the provision. Section 13 makes no mention of the quality of goods, which is left to be dealt with by the civil law. Furthermore, since s. 13 is concerned only with practices, it would be reasonable to assume that it has no application to isolated incidents which may subsequently grow into a practice. Section 13 requires the Director to wait until a continuing and significant state of affairs has come into existence.

Under s. 17(2), where it appears to the Director that a particular practice is misleading in relation to consumer rights and obligations or is apt to put consumers under pressure to enter transactions or causes contract terms to be inequitable to consumers, he may make a reference which includes a proposal that the practice should be controlled by order by the Secretary of State. The Director's reference under s. 17 should state the effect the trade practice has and CPAC must then report on the reference, having taken into account representations from interested bodies. The mere fact that a practice has one or more of the effects listed in s. 17(2) does not automatically mean that the practice is detrimental to the interests of consumers. It must also be considered what other beneficial effects it has and the benefits and detriments have to be weighed against each other.

Unfortunately, the procedure created by the 1973 Act is subject to a number of criticisms. It is cumbersome and depends on the use of criminal sanctions as a means of implementing proposals for changes in the law. In some instances, it may be difficult and expensive to prove the necessary detriment to consumer economic interests in order to make a reference in the first place. Sometimes, it may be as easy for the Office of Fair Trading to secure a change in business attitudes by seeking to inform the public rather than to coerce them through the use of regulation.

An illustration of the defects of the s. 17 procedure can be found in comparing two methods of dealing with cases of non-compliance with statutory controls on the use of exclusion clauses. One of the references to CPAC under s. 17 concerned purported exclusion of inalienable consumer rights and resulted in the Consumer Transactions (Restriction on Statements) Order 1976 (SI 1976/1813). The reference was made to CPAC in 1974 when it was discovered that following the enactment of the Supply of Goods (Implied

Terms) Act 1973 some retailers were still displaying notices to the effect that no refunds were available should the goods purchased prove to be defective. The effect of this was that some consumers wrongly believed that they had redress in such circumstances. CPAC received the Director's recommendations and submitted their report to the Secretary of State in July 1974, but the order was not made until the end of July 1976. Quite apart from the delay in implementing the Director's proposals, which were in any event modified by CPAC, the Director's own report would have been costly to compile and in the end the Director admitted that the publicity which surrounded the s. 17 reference procedure had resulted in more people becoming aware of inalienable rights with the result that the number of 'no refund' notices had markedly decreased before the order was laid before Parliament (Director General of Fair Trading, *Annual Report*, 1975, p. 9).

In contrast to this, when the Unfair Contract Terms Act 1977 was enacted, it provided that a contract term or notice could not be used to exclude or limit liability for negligently caused death or bodily injury. It subsequently appeared that some businesses continued to display notices to the effect that they accepted no liability for injury and damage, howsoever caused. Instead of invoking the reference procedure, the Director General of Fair Trading conducted an informal information campaign through the use of press releases, articles in legal periodicals and direct communication to trade associations and individual businesses. This proved to be as effective as the drawn-out and expensive s. 17 reference procedure, and an order to ensure compliance with the requirements of the 1977 Act never proved to be necessary.

2.1.1.2.2 Codes of practice   A second important role played by the Office of Fair Trading in relation to the development of consumer policy is to encourage trade associations to publish codes of practice for their members (Fair Trading Act 1973, s. 124). This has become one of the most important weapons in the field of consumer protection. A wide range of codes have been disseminated in a number of areas of trade including the supply of motor vehicles, travel facilities, domestic electrical appliances, furniture, footwear, funeral services, some home improvement services and mail order trading services.

The areas of trade in which codes of practice have emerged have tended to be those from which the greatest number of consumer complaints have been heard. Where there is widespread consumer dissatisfaction, the role of the Office of Fair Trading is to initiate discussions with interested parties representing both consumers and the trade itself in order to identify deficiencies in the way in which the trade operates. Once the problems have been identified, the primary responsibility for preparing the code of practice lies with the trade association itself which will submit a draft code to the Office of Fair Trading for approval. Modifications to the code may follow suggestions for improvement given by the Office in order to ensure effective protection of the consumer. Following dissemination of the code, the trade association's responsibilities continue, in that it is important that the code is kept up to date in the light of changing circumstances and the identification of new consumer problems.

In some instances, it is the trade itself that initiates the procedure without initial suggestions having been made by the Office of Fair Trading. For reasons to be considered elsewhere (see 3.10.3), codes of practice have a number of important advantages over laws and these advantages are clearly appreciated by the trade associations which choose independently to prepare their own codes. This may be because during the period when most codes of practice were prepared (1973 to 1979) there was always a threat of regulation if trade associations did not get their own houses in order. Since 1979 the government has been less prepared to regulate trade practices. If the threat of regulation is removed, there is less incentive on the part of trade associations to impose further controls upon their members.

2.1.2   Protection of consumer economic interests

The Department of Trade and Industry is probably the most influential government department so far as consumer economic interests are concerned. It funds the Office of Fair Trading and has general responsibility for consumer affairs, trading standards, weights and measures, and consumer credit. Because of these general functions, the Department is responsible for, *inter alia*, the enforcement of the Consumer Credit Act 1974, the Trade Descriptions Act 1968, the Consumer Protection Act 1987, insofar as it concerns misleading pricing and orders made under the Fair Trading Act 1973.

The Department of Trade and Industry also has general responsibility for monopolies and mergers and other restrictive practices. Many of these functions are delegated to the Office of Fair Trading. This satellite of the Department of Trade and Industry, in addition to its consumer policy role, also has powers to control persistent unfair trading conduct under part III of the Fair Trading Act 1973 (see 3.8.1). Other functions served by the Office of Fair Trading which also further the economic interests of consumers include the overseeing of monopolies and mergers, the licensing of credit businesses (see 3.8.2) and the publication of consumer education materials.

The Department of Trade and Industry is also responsible for the work of other agencies, the work of which is related to both consumer economic and health and safety interests. In particular, the Department sponsors the work of the British Standards Institution and oversees the work of the National Consumer Council amongst other agencies.

Other central government departments which concern themselves with consumer economic interests include the Home Office which is responsible for legislation concerning shops and the Department of Social Security insofar as it is concerned with matters such as welfare benefits etc.

2.1.3   Protection of consumer health and safety interests

In the field of health and safety, a wide range of government departments have a role to play. Which department is responsible depends on how the threat to the consumer's health or safety comes about.

Some of the responsibilities of the Department of Trade and Industry feature in this respect since this department is responsible for general consumer safety and therefore oversees the enforcement of the Consumer Protection Act 1987 in relation to general product safety.

The Home Office has a supervisory role in relation to the control of firearms and explosives, dangerous drugs and poisons and is also responsible for the licensing of premises used for the supply of alcoholic drinks etc.

Where food is concerned, the Department of Health and the Ministry of Agriculture, Fisheries and Food (MAFF) both share the role of consumer protection watchdog. The two are responsible for the enforcement of the Food Safety Act 1990 and the Medicines Act 1968 and any regulations made under those statutes. Both the Department of Health and MAFF are partly responsible for matters of food hygiene and safety. The Department of Health will offer medical advice on possible contamination of consumer goods. MAFF has particular responsibility for laying down standards in respect of the composition of food and the labelling and advertising of products intended for human consumption. In this last respect, relevant government departments (namely the Department of Health, MAFF, the Department of Social Security and relevant departments for the purposes of food policy in Scotland, Wales and Northern Ireland) are advised by the Food Advisory Committee on matters relating to the composition, labelling and advertising of food and those relating to additives, contaminants and other substances which may be present in food.

2.2 LOCAL GOVERNMENT

Local authorities have two important roles to play in respect of consumer protection. One is to enforce the provisions of regulatory statutes concerned with the conduct of trade and the other is to provide consumer advice and information.

2.2.1 Enforcement

Local government bears the day-to-day responsibility of enforcing many statutory provisions which seek to protect the consumer. Most local authorities have created a consumer protection or trading standards department which bears responsibility, at a local level, for the enforcement of the provisions of the Trade Descriptions Act 1968, the Consumer Credit Act 1974, the Weights and Measures Act 1985, the Food Safety Act 1990 and various orders made under consumer protection legislation. In addition to bringing prosecutions for breach of these penal provisions, local authorities also have responsibility for testing equipment used by traders and sampling the products put on the consumer market by manufacturers and retailers.

Under the provisions of the Local Government Act 1972, there was a dramatic reduction in the number of enforcement authorities resulting from the creation of a middle tier of local government in the form of metropolitan authorities. The result of this was that a small number of metropolitan authorities and county councils were responsible for the enforcement of consumer protection legislation. This in turn led to a more uniform policy of enforcement and reduced the unevenness of interpretation of the law. Subsequently, the Local Government Act 1985 abolished the metropolitan authorities with the result that much of the uniformity of approach was potentially lost. The 1985 Act did allow for the creation of coordinating committees to be set up by the metropolitan districts which inherited the role of enforcement authority, but these committees have not proved to be effective. The 1985 Act also allows the Secretary of State to create a single enforcement body in metropolitan areas, but no order, so far, has been laid before Parliament to allow for this.

A major difficulty which arises from local, as opposed to national enforcement of consumer protection legislation is that local authorities may differ in their interpretation of the law, with the result that there is not a uniform policy of enforcement. For example, some local authorities may choose to enforce legislation such as the Shops Act 1950 in respect of Sunday trading and others may not. The same is equally true in respect of food and trading standards generally. Clearly, an uneven programme of enforcement is undesirable from the point of view of both the consumer and the trader, since it would be difficult to determine how the law is going to be interpreted in a given case. Consumer advisers could not predict with any certainty whether there would be a prosecution or not and manufacturers might need to produce goods to different standards according to where in the country it was proposed to sell.

Mindful of this possibility, the Association of County Councils and the Association of Metropolitan Authorities reached an agreement in 1976 to set up a body known as the Local Authorities Coordinating Body on Trading Standards (LACOTS) which was authorised to consult and negotiate with central government and trade and industry bodies with a view to establishing standards of quality. Uniformity of enforcement is achieved by asking one authority to conduct a test case in areas where the law is in doubt. Following the test case, other authorities can be advised of the outcome.

To avoid the problem of conflicting advice given by local authorities to manufacturers and retailers, LACOTS has approved the principle of the 'home authority'. If a manufacturing or retailing concern with more than one place of business requires advice on how to comply with new regulations, it is advised to approach the authority in which its principal place of business is to be found. This authority is known as the 'home authority' which will act as a coordinator in determining what advice should be given to the trader. In particular, the home authority will consult with other authorities in which the trader has a trading base before giving any significant advice. Also, should a complaint be received by an 'enforcement authority', that authority should first consult the home authority to determine what advice has been given. The fact that the home authority has advised the trader that a particular practice is lawful does not prevent the enforcement authority from taking action, but in most cases, the trader will be aware of what should be done to comply with legal requirements.

The fact that local government has gone to such trouble to set up a coordinating body such as LACOTS would seem to suggest that central government enforcement of consumer protection legislation might be more appropriate. It would certainly be an advantage to centralise enforcement of, for example, the Trade Descriptions Act 1968 in relation to the larger multi-branch businesses, but the same could not be said for small-scale businesses (see *Review of the Trade Descriptions Act 1968* (Cmd 6620, 1976), p.80). In the case of the larger business, advice to the head office or a single successful test case will produce results on a national level, whereas if the matter is left to local enforcement, there could be a large number of actions before the trader decides to alter his practices.

In contrast, local authorities would appear to be the more appropriate means of enforcement where the trader operates on a smaller scale. Moreover, local enforcement is more responsive to the needs of local consumers and businesses.

A further relevant factor in determining whether central or local enforcement is more appropriate is whether central or local authorities are more prone to 'capture' by traders and their representatives. It has been argued that regulatory bodies may start off life enthusiastically pursuing wrongful conduct, but in time, due to familiarity with the bodies with which they deal, regulators are prone to become an arm of the trade sector they were originally intended to police. In the end the regulator begins to serve the interests of trade to the detriment of the consumer he was intended to protect (Galbraith, *The Great Crash* (Houghton Mifflin, 1955) p.171).

Whether or not the 'capture theory' is accurate in practice is not entirely clear, as there are some regulatory bodies which have remained active in pursuit of the traders they were set up to police. Moreover, the capture theory is unlikely to be applicable where a regulatory body has a wide range of different types of business to police and does not become excessively familiar with the practices of one specific type of business. It would appear that the majority of local authority consumer agencies fall into this latter category and as such are less prone to capture. If the capture theory is right, it is arguable that local enforcement authorities are less likely to be captured by the traders with whom they deal than central authorities.

2.2.2   Consumer advice

Local authorities have an important role in providing advice facilities for consumers, by virtue of the Local Government Act 1972, ss. 137 and 142. In particular, it was seen as a priority to extend the availability of advice to as wide a range of consumers as possible. While the 'middle classes' who subscribed to the Consumers' Association magazine *Which?* were able to avail themselves of the services provided by that association, a large proportion of the consumer population had no ready source of advice when things went wrong. It is true that bodies such as the Citizens Advice Bureaux and some local authority weights and measures departments were prepared to advise in respect of certain matters, but there was no coordinated approach to the giving of advice generally.

Local authorities have assisted in the provision of consumer advice in two ways. They have set up consumer advice centres which may serve a preventive role by giving pre-shopping advice or a remedial role by advising on consumer problems in the event of a consumer complaint. The other important respect in which local authorities have advised consumers has been through the support of or the setting up of neighbourhood law centres in relatively deprived areas.

The role of consumer advice centres has declined in recent years since the government in 1979 decided to withdraw all funding from these bodies on the grounds of inefficiency. It was perceived that the role of advice giver could be better served by bodies such as Citizens Advice Bureaux, the central support for which was doubled. As a result of this, over half of the then operating consumer advice centres closed because local authorities were not prepared to see their operation costs become a burden on ratepayers (see Smith, *The Consumer Interest* (John Martin Publishing, 1982), p.281). Subsequent experience has shown that there is still a heavy demand for advice and that much of this is now channelled through local authority trading standards departments or high street solicitors (National Consumer Council, *Simple Justice*, p.17).

2.3   GOVERNMENT SPONSORED BODIES

Two bodies, namely, the Consumer Protection Advisory Committee (CPAC) and the National Consumer Council (NCC), are directly sponsored by the government. The role of the former in respect of consumer protection has already been considered (see 2.1.1.2.1). However, it should be observed that membership of CPAC is presently suspended and it would appear that it will probably serve little further use as a consumer protection agency.

The NCC was set up in 1975 with a view to representing consumer interests in dealings with the government, local authorities and the Office of Fair Trading and trade bodies. It also advises on consumer protection policy through the publication of reports on matters concerning consumers and through the making of representations to relevant bodies.

The range of issues taken on by the NCC is substantial as is evidenced in the reports it has published or commissioned. These include representations made concerning incomprehensible language in consumer contracts and official publications (*Gobbledegook*, 1980), public services (*Consumer Concerns*, 1990), legal services (*Ordinary Justice*, 1989; *Legal Services*, 1990), whether and how the law in respect of the quality of goods and services should be reformed (*Service Please?* 1981; *The Consumer Guarantee*, 1989) consumer credit (*Consumers and Credit*, 1980; *Consumers and Debt*, 1989) and disadvantaged consumers (*Why the Poor Pay More*, 1977). The Council also issues on a regular basis policy statements on perceived consumer problems and developments in the law over a very wide range, including not just matters related to the supply of goods and services, but also issues such as the environment, international trade, consumer education, housing, social security and health care.

In one sense, it is perhaps surprising that the NCC still exists, as it was created in the era of corporatism of the middle 1970s which was so despised by the Conservative government of 1979. The Conservative opposition party argued against the establishment of the Council, however, no attempt has been made to disband it.

2.4 PUBLIC SERVICES AND UTILITIES

Nationalised industries and 'privatised' large-scale suppliers of goods and services (such as British Gas, British Telecom and National Power) often find themselves in a position where they have a monopoly or a near-monopoly in the supply of a product or service. Because of this, it is generally regarded as necessary to oversee their operation and to subject their operations to specific regulation.

As an example, the Telecommunications Act 1984 provides for the appointment of a Director General of Telecommunications (DGT) who is empowered to review the provision of telecommunications facilities. Furthermore, the DGT or the Secretary of State is required to license bodies wishing to provide such services, The DGT heads the Office of Telecommunications (OFTEL) and has powers to ensure that, so far as is practicable, there is an adequate supply of telecommunications facilities to meet all reasonable demands (Telecommunications Act 1984, s. 3). Particular emphasis is placed on the need for emergency services, call-box facilities, maritime services and user information services. The DGT's duty is to act on behalf of the consumer.

The extent to which regulatory controls have an effect on the performance of these large utility companies may sometimes be doubted because of the monopoly position occupied by the company. For example, in 1985 OFTEL received 10,000 complaints on consumer matters, particularly in relation to tariffs, charges, quality of service and disputed accounts. A recent report commissioned by the National Consumer Council appears to take the view that, in general, the standard of service is rising in the field of telecommunications, showing that, overall, 72% of the population were satisfied with telephone services (*Consumer Concerns* (1990), p.3). However, there were areas in which performance was not good. For example, only 37% were satisfied with the cost of telephone calls, set against 45% who were dissatisfied, though it must be said that this level of dissatisfaction is an improvement on the position which prevailed in 1987 (ibid., p.8).

2.5 VOLUNTARY ORGANISATIONS

A number of other organisations offer advice or provide information for consumers or in some other way provides a service of assistance to consumers. The most important of these are the Citizens Advice Bureaux, the Consumers' Association, the National Federation of Consumer Groups and the British Standards Institution.

Citizens Advice Bureaux (CABx) can be found across the country and deal with a wide range of problems which may be brought to them. Inevitably, many of the enquiries dealt with will be consumer problems, but the work of the CABx is not exclusively consumer-protection related, for example, they will also deal with marital problems, social security claims and problems with the police.

CABx are funded by both central government, which makes a grant to the National Association of CABx, and by local authorities which provide funds on a local basis for bureaux in their area.

The Consumers' Association is a company limited by guarantee which provides consumer information on competing products and services in its magazine *Which?* It may be objected that the Consumers' Association is unrepresentative of the consumer population as it would appear that the majority of subscriptions to *Which?* come from social groups A and B (upper-middle and middle class) with very few subscriptions coming from lower social classes and that *Which?* magazine attends closely to the needs of groups A and B (Smith, *The Consumer Interest* (John Martin Publishing, 1982), p. 284).

Some would argue that the Consumers' Association's approach is subject to criticism in that its product samples are small and therefore unrepresentative; that the rate at which new brands come on to the market means that *Which?* reports are soon dated; that the testing criteria do not take account of the full range of consumer requirements and that due to the low level of subscriptions to *Which?* the test reports must have a very limited appeal (Smith, op. cit., p. 285). Much has been done in recent years to respond to the first three of these criticisms, but the fourth still remains a problem.

The National Federation of Consumer Groups (NFCG) coordinates the activities of the growing number of local consumer groups. The aim of these groups is to encourage local interest in consumer affairs. The NFCG is partly funded by grants from the Consumers' Association and the Department of Trade and Industry.

The British Standards Institution (BSI) was set up, in its present form, in 1929 and sets standards, dimensions and specifications for manufactured goods. A 'British Standard' is a document which stipulates the specifications, requirements for testing or measurements with which a product must comply in order to be suited to its intended purpose and work efficiently. Before a standard is reached, there will be a lengthy process of consultation with interested parties.

Compliance with such specifications is a matter of choice on the part of producers. However, in some instances where there is the potential for serious personal injury, as is the case with defective motor-cycle crash-helmets, compliance with BSI standards is compulsory, If a producer wishes to do so, he may apply to the BSI for certification of his product, in which case he may then display the BSI "Kitemark" on his product. Where this is the case, the producer must also be prepared for subsequent inspections by the BSI to ensure that standards are being maintained.

2.6 TRADE ASSOCIATIONS

A significant feature of many aspects of consumer protection law is the extent to which laws are supplemented with or even, in some cases, replaced by codes of practice drawn up by trade associations, often after consultation with the Office of Fair Trading. The advantages and disadvantages of codes of practice as a means of consumer protection and the contribution they can make to consumer protection are dealt with elsewhere (see 3.10).

2.7 EUROPEAN INSTITUTIONS

European Community consumer protection policy is considered in more detail elsewhere (see 3.6 et seq.) but it is also necessary to consider, briefly, the role of Community institutions in relation to consumer protection issues.

2.7.1 Introduction

The institutional framework of the European Community consists of the Council of Ministers, the Commission, the European Parliament and the European Court (see also Steiner, *Textbook on EEC Law*, 2nd ed. (Blackstone Press, 1990), part I; Lasok & Bridge, *Law and Institutions of the European Communities*, 4th ed. (1987), part II). Also of relevance to advertising law is the role of the European Court of Human Rights and its interpretation of the provisions of the European Convention for the Protection of Human Rights and Fundamental Freedoms 1953, to which all member States of the European community are now signatories, in relation to freedom of speech (see 3.6.2.5).

The EEC came into existence in 1957 following the signature of the EEC Treaty by the original six member States and by 1986 membership had risen to 12. An important development was the signing of the Single European Act (SEA) by all 12 member States in 1986. This followed an earlier paper issued by the Commission which recognised that many barriers to free trade still existed and that if a single market were to be achieved, many of these barriers would have to be removed. The SEA introduced a number of procedural changes so as to facilitate the completion of the internal market by 31 December 1992. The EEC Treaty has both social and economic aims and the SEA is an overtly political document, thereby giving the Community the aim of political cooperation.

The EEC Treaty lays down a number of broad principles which are stated to be the establishment of a common market; the approximation of the economic policies of member States and the promotion of harmonious development of economic activity, continued and balanced expansion, increased stability and an accelerated standard of living and closer relations between member States (EEC Treaty, art. 2). These general aims are accompanied by a list of the activities of the EEC which are stated in art. 3 to include:

(a)   the elimination of customs duties and quantitative restrictions on trade and other measures having an equivalent effect;
(b)   the abolition of obstacles to the free movement of persons, services and capital;
(c)   the adoption of common policies on agriculture and transport;

(d)   the avoidance of distortions in competition;
(e)   the coordination of economic policies; and
(f)   the approximation of the laws of member States to secure the working of the common market.

Additionally, following the SEA, the goals of economic and monetary cooperation, research and technological development and environmental and consumer protection, amongst others, have been added to the list.

2.7.2   The Council

The Council consists of one representative delegated by each member state. The delegate is not fixed, with the result that a different person can be sent according to the issue under consideration.

The role of the Council is to see to the implementation of EEC Treaty objectives (EEC Treaty, art.145) and is the principal decision-making body. In many cases, the Council can only act after a proposal has been made by the Commission and following the provisions of art. 100A must also consult Parliament and the Economic and Social Committee before taking action in some cases.

Decisions may be taken by a simple majority, a qualified majority or by a unanimous vote. In the case of a qualified majority, differently weighted votes are given to member States ranging from 10 votes for France, Germany, Italy and the United Kingdom down to two votes for Luxembourg. In order for a measure to be passed by a qualified majority, it must receive the support of 54 votes out of a possible 76.

In the context of consumer protection law, the qualified voting system is of importance in relation to the Treaty provisions on harmonisation. It used to be the case that attempts to harmonise the law of member States required unanimity (art. 100), but following the provisions of art. 100A, a qualified majority is sufficient in a number of important areas (see 3.6.1).

2.7.3   The Commission

The Commission consists of 17 members representing all member States. The constituent members are required to be independent and must not take instructions from a government (Merger Treaty, arts 10 and 11).

The Commission acts as the initiator of Community action and in important cases, the Council cannot act until a proposal has been received from the Commission. A proposal can be requested by the Council in order to attain the objectives of the Community (EEC Treaty, art. 152).

The Commission also acts under art. 5 to ensure that treaty obligations are complied with. Thus it is the function of the Commission to bring proceedings against member States in the case of an identified infringement (art. 169). To allow the Commission to carry out its investigative function, it is conferred with powers to obtain necessary information so as to allow it to proceed.

A further function performed by the Commission is to implement decisions which have been taken at Council level. In some instances, the necessary measures required to implement an earlier decision may have to be agreed by the Council.

2.7.4 The European Parliament

Because the predecessor of the present Parliament was not elected, it was originally given very few powers. However, since 1979 the membership of the Parliament has been determined by a democratic process of direct elections, which might suggest that greater powers may come its way in time.

Presently, the Parliament has an advisory role. It may object to proposals for new measures, but not indefinitely. Thus, the Council may still adopt a measure even though the Parliament does not agree to it. If the Parliament makes suggestions for amendment to a measure which are rejected by the Commission, the Council can implement the measure, but only by way of a unanimous vote.

The Parliament also has a supervisory function. It can require members of the Commission to explain their actions and give answers to questions. Ultimately, Parliament also has the power to dismiss the Commission by means of a vote of censure (art. 144).

CHAPTER THREE

Techniques of Consumer Protection

3.1 INTRODUCTION

The English law of consumer protection is significant for its general lack of specific direction. As consumer demand has grown in the 20th century, various aspects of English law have been adapted for the purpose of protecting consumer interests. These include adaptations of the law of contract and the law of tort, in particular, the tort of negligence. Aspects of the criminal law and the use of administrative controls have also played their part, as have self-regulating codes of practice drawn up in consultation with the Office of Fair Trading. More recently, membership of the European Economic Community has resulted in introduction of a number of specific consumer protection measures following the implementation of Community legislation. Indeed, the fact that the European Community claims to have a 'consumer protection programme' would seem to suggest that there is a more planned approach to the whole issue than is the case domestically.

For the most part, English law has developed on a haphazard basis, sometimes plugging gaps where they appear, sometimes not. Two major roles of consumer protection can be identified, namely, to prevent misleading practices and to provide redress when things go wrong. As a rough division, the criminal law, administrative control and business self-regulation fulfil the former, and common law and statutory rules relating to the civil obligations of the suppliers of goods and services satisfy the latter.

Generally, it can be said that the techniques of consumer protection fall into one of five categories:

(a) *The control of suppliers*. Statutory provisions may sometimes stipulate who may provide certain types of consumer service. Perhaps the best example of this can be found in the Consumer Credit Act 1974, which sets up a licensing system under which those deemed unsuitable to provide credit services or services ancillary to the provision of credit, may be denied a licence to operate (see 3.8.2). The licensing system operates in respect of not just prospective providers of credit, but also those who wish to engage in credit brokerage, debt adjusting, debt counselling and collecting, and the provision of credit reference services.

(b) *Seeking business.* Sometimes it may prove necessary to control methods employed by business in attracting new customers. In particular, legislation and common law rules may be employed in order to impose control on means of advertising, labelling and describing goods or services. Rules on misrepresentation, passing off, trade descriptions and sales promotion are all relevant in this context (see chapter 11).

(c) *Form and content of consumer transactions.* A common method of controlling the excesses of business is to prescribe the form of a particular type of agreement. For example, specific requirements concerning the form of contracts for the provision of credit can be found in the Consumer Credit Act 1974. In addition to these requirements, perhaps the most important means of consumer protection comes in the form of statutory rules on the content of certain types of consumer transaction. In particular, in relation to both contracts for the supply of goods and services, the common law has, for some time, implied terms relating to the obligations of the supplier. In each case, these terms are codified in the Sale of Goods Act 1979 (and related statutory provisions) and the Supply of Goods and Services Act 1982 (see chapters 7 and 10).

(d) *Broad statutory standards.* In a number of cases, Parliament has seen fit to stipulate basic standards of quality or safety. The implied terms as to quality and fitness of goods in the Sale of Goods Act 1979 (and related provisions) partially serve this purpose. A similar function is also served by legislation in respect of the safety of goods. In particular, broad statutory standards of food safety can be found in the Food Safety Act 1990 and in respect of the safety of goods generally in the Consumer Protection Act 1987 (see chapter 9). In some instances, failure to comply with safety requirements may also give rise to a civil action for damages for breach of statutory duty.

(e) *Restriction of remedies.* Where appropriate, the supplier's remedies against the consumer may be restricted. For example, under the Consumer Credit Act 1974, certain types of enforcement action are forbidden or subject to judicial control where the formalities of agreement have not been complied with. Similarly, if the consumer has paid a specified percentage of the total price for goods, the creditor's power of repossession is restricted (see 6.10.2.3).

3.2 THE CIVIL OBLIGATIONS OF SUPPLIERS AND PRODUCERS

The common law has been responsible for a number of important rules which have been adapted as consumer protection measures. Foremost amongst these are the requirements that goods supplied to a consumer must be of satisfactory quality and be fit for the purpose for which they are required and that the supplier of a service should exercise reasonable care and skill and perform the service in a workmanlike manner. Both of these requirements have since been enshrined in statutory form in the Sale of Goods Act 1979 and the Supply of Goods and Services Act 1982 respectively. The requirement of the exercise of reasonable care and skill is also one which extends to the producer of goods and services under the rule in *Donoghue* v *Stevenson* [1932] AC 562. In relation to remedies, the common law has seen the development of the award of damages for distress and disappointment (*Jarvis* v *Swans Tours* [1973] 1 All ER 71) and in relation to exclusion clauses, common law rules on communication (*Thornton* v *Shoe Lane Parking Ltd* [1971] 2 QB 163) and fundamental breach of contract (*Suisse Atlantique Société d'Armement Maritime SA* v *NV Rotterdamsche Kolen Centrale* [1967] 1 AC 361) have had important effects on the position of the consumer.

While common law rules have had some influence on consumer protection, it is true that in many respects, the common law has proved to be an inadequate tool and that statutory intervention in favour of the consumer has become necessary. A surge of consumer-protection related legislative activity was seen in the 1960s and 1970s. In particular, this period saw the enactment of the Food and Drugs Act 1955 (now the Food Act 1984 and the Food Safety Act 1990), the Consumer Protection Act 1961 (now the Consumer Protection Act 1987), the Misrepresentation Act 1967, the Unsolicited Goods and Services Act 1971, the Fair Trading Act 1973, the Supply of Goods (Implied Terms) Act 1973, the Consumer Credit Act 1974 and the Unfair Contract Terms Act 1977. All of these in some way make important provision for consumer redress and most of them were enacted to rectify deficiencies in the protection provided at common law.

While the 1960s and 1970s were important in terms of statutory development, there have been significant changes in the 1980s and 1990s, but many of these changes were inspired by European initiatives. Furthermore, some very good ideas for reform of the law have been watered down or disposed of altogether by government intervention in the period concerned.

In a period characterised by a relative lack of movement on the legislative front, an upsurge in judicial development might be expected. However, this would appear not to be the case. For example, many of the significant developments in the tort of negligence in the 1970s and early 1980s have been reversed (compare *Anns* v *Merton London Borough Council* [1978] AC 728; *Junior Books Ltd* v *Veitchi Co. Ltd* [1983] 1 AC 520 and *D & F Estates Ltd* v *Church Commissioners for England* [1988] 2 All ER 992; *Murphy* v *Brentwood District Council* [1990] 2 All ER 908). Furthermore, judicial views to the effect that the role of consumer protection watchdog is that of Parliament, not the courts, have been openly expressed (*Murphy* v *Brentwood District Council* at p. 923 per Lord Keith).

3.2.1 Contractual obligations

Some rules of the law of contract do assist consumers, but it must be said that, as a general rule, common law rules alone are inadequate as a means of consumer protection. In particular, while the consumer who has purchased a defective product will be able to pursue the seller for damages in respect of injuries to himself, harm to his property and in respect of the qualitative defectiveness of the thing purchased, the same is not true of the ultimate consumer who is not in a contractual relationship with the supplier. English law is still dominated by the doctrine of privity of contract which may prevent a contractual action in favour of the ultimate consumer. However, there are exceptions to the doctrine which will be considered below.

The consumer's position will also depend on the status of the terms of the contract he enters into. A distinction needs to be drawn between contractual conditions and warranties and between contractual terms and representations.

3.2.1.1 Privity of contract   The doctrine of privity of contract is a major restriction on consumer remedies. The doctrine can be divided into two categories, namely, 'vertical' and 'horizontal' privity. In the context of a product liability action, vertical privity is that which exists between one person and his immediate predecessor or successor in a descending chain of distribution from the producer to the retailer. In the same context, horizontal privity is that which exists between the retailer and the consumer who buys from him

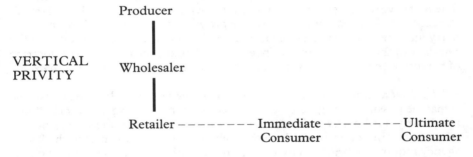

Frequently, a consumer purchase is made by one person on behalf of someone else. For example, a purchase of food may be made by one member of a family on behalf of the other members of that family or one person may buy a present for a friend. In such a case, the doctrine of privity of contract dictates that the immediate consumer can pursue a remedy in his own favour against the retailer, but cannot recover anything in respect of the harm suffered by the person for whom the purchase was made (*Preist* v *Last* [1903] 2 KB 148). The doctrine is one of a number of 19th century rules which have served to hinder the development of the law of contract to meet new conditions. On occasions, judicial ingenuity has found ways of avoiding the harsher effects of the doctrine but the doctrine has generally served to prevent the recognition of third-party contractual rights. This is particularly important in relation to an action for economic harm suffered as a result of the purchase of a defective product. Generally, the purchaser of such a product will be able to maintain an action against the retailer for breach of one of the implied terms of the supply contract, but the non-purchaser will not be in the same position. Furthermore, the purchaser is confined to an action against the immediate supplier and, accordingly, no contractual action will lie against a wholesaler or a manufacturer. Admittedly, the position of the consumer has been substantially improved by the provisions of the Consumer Protection Act 1987 (see 8.4), but only in respect of physical harm suffered as a result of the defectiveness of the product in question.

The doctrine also has adverse effects in relation to the benefits of an exclusion clause. In many instances, it may be the intention of the contracting parties that a purported exclusion of liability should extend to a person who is not a party to the contract which contains the exclusion. Where this issue does arise, it will normally involve a dispute between commercial contracting parties. However, occasionally, the problem may also involve consumers but, as a general rule, the courts will be wary of allowing a person with whom the consumer has not contracted to claim the benefit of an exclusion clause (see *Adler* v *Dickson* [1955] 1 QB 158; *Gore* v *Van der Lann* [1967] 1 All ER 360).

A number of methods of avoiding the harsher effects of the doctrine of privity of contract have been developed. Three broad methods have emerged. The first involves an expanded definition of who is to be regarded as a party to the contract. The second is to allow the promisee to sue on behalf of the third party and the third involves the use of legal principles which fall outside the province of the law of contract, since it should be appreciated that the doctrine of privity of contract merely prevents a third party from *suing on the contract*.

3.2.1.1.1   Extending the definition of a party to the contract   In some instances, it may be possible to regard a person as contracting as an agent on behalf of a third party. Ordinarily, this method of circumventing the doctrine of privity of contract will not be available to the consumer, since principles of the law of agency require the principal to have expressly authorised an agent to act on his behalf. In most consumer transactions, the purchaser is unlikely to state that he is purchasing on behalf of another person, in which case, a court is unlikely to regard the law of agency as relevant. However, in isolated cases, the court has been prepared to regard one person as having contracted as an agent on behalf of another (*Lockett* v *A.M. Charles Ltd* [1938] 4 All ER 170; *Heil* v *Hedges* [1951] 1 TLR 512).

It is more likely that the court will regard one person as contracting on behalf of another without making specific reference to an agency relationship. For example, there are certain types of contract where it is obvious that one person has made a booking on behalf of himself and other people. In such a case, it is reasonable to allow all parties to sue independently (*Lockett* v *A.M. Charles Ltd* [1938] 4 All ER 170) or to allow the person who made the contract to sue for damages on behalf of the other members of his party (*Jackson* v *Horizon Holidays Ltd* [1975] 3 All ER 92; cf. *Woodar Investment Development Ltd* v *Wimpey Construction UK Ltd* [1980] 1 WLR 227).

3.2.1.1.2 Collateral warranties If it can be shown that a manufacturer has expressly guaranteed his product to the purchaser, he may be treated as having warranted the quality or fitness of the product in question, even in the absence of an obvious contractual relationship. In *Wells (Merstham) Ltd* v *Buckland Sand & Silica Ltd* [1965] 2 QB 170 the plaintiff purchased a particular type of sand from a retailer in reliance upon the manufacturer's express assertion that it was fit for the purchaser's required purpose. It was held that the purchaser could succeed in an action against the manufacturer, based on a collateral warranty of fitness for purpose (see also *Shanklin Pier Ltd* v *Detel Products Ltd* [1951] 2 KB 854). It is important that the manufacturer expressly warranted the fitness of his product and that the parties were in direct contact with each other. At present, it would appear unlikely that the collateral warranty doctrine will be used in relation to implied warranties of fitness and satisfactory quality in circumstances where the consumer has relied on the national advertising of the manufacturer of a product. In some instances, if the product is extravagantly described, this may give rise to liability on the part of the manufacturer, but such cases will probably be rare. However, in *Wood* v *Letrik Ltd* (1932) *The Times*, 12 January 1932, the defendant had advertised an electric comb for sale, stating that it was guaranteed to dispose of the problem of grey hair within 10 days. Further, the advertisement also guaranteed a payment of £500 if the device did not work. The plaintiff purchased one of the combs, used it as directed but instead of remedying his problem, it scratched the plaintiff's scalp and caused him discomfort. Rowlatt J held that the use of the word 'guarantee' was about as emphatic as could be imagined and that any ordinary sensible person would take this to mean that the defendant had offered to bind himself according to the terms of the advertisement (see also *Carlill* v *Carbolic Smokeball Co.* [1893] 1 QB 256).

A major restriction on the application of the collateral warranty doctrine to consumer transactions is that the courts may assert that there should be consideration for the making of the collateral contract (*Heilbut Symons & Co.* v *Buckleton* [1913] AC 30; *Lambert* v *Lewis* [1980] 1 All ER 978, reversed on other grounds [1981] 1 All ER 1185). However, the search for consideration prior to the finding of a collateral contract has not always been deep (*De Lassalle* v *Guildford* [1901] 2 KB 215; *Dick Bentley Productions Ltd* v *Harold Smith (Motors) Ltd* [1965] 2 All ER 65).

3.2.1.1.3 Promisee sues on behalf of the third party The person to whom a promise has been made may be able to sue for damages for a breach of that promise. However, an award of damages is intended, in theory, to compensate the person who brings the action. If the promise is intended for the benefit of a third party, the promisee will have suffered no loss and any award of damages ought to be nominal only. In some instances, this problem can be avoided by regarding the loss of the third party as the loss of the promisee. In *Jackson* v *Horizon Holidays Ltd* [1975] 1 WLR 1468, the distress suffered by the plaintiff's family as a result of a disastrous holiday was regarded as harm suffered by the plaintiff himself (at p. 1474 per James LJ).

As an alternative to an action for damages, it may be possible for the promisee to seek an order for specific performance of the contractual promise in favour of a third party. This option is most likely to be fruitful in circumstances in which the promisor would be unjustly enriched if his promise were not to be enforced. By enforcing the promise, the unjust enrichment would be reversed (*Beswick* v *Beswick* [1968] AC 58).

Even where the possibility of an action by the promisee on behalf of the third party exists, there remains the problem that the third party must rely on the promisee to bring the action. Clearly, this means that the relationship between the two is crucial. If the promisee is unwilling to sue on behalf of the third party, there appears to be little that can be done. In *Beswick* v *Beswick* [1968] AC 58 this problem did not arise as the promisee was also the third party. However, the position is different where the two are separate individuals. In the Court of Appeal in *Beswick* v *Beswick* [1966] Ch 538, Lord Denning MR suggested that it might be possible for the third party to sue the promisor and join the promisee as a co-defendant, but this was a view not shared by the other members of the court.

3.2.1.1.4 Non-contractual evasion of the doctrine of privity Since the doctrine of privity of contract merely prevents a person from suing on a contract to which he is not a party, there is nothing to prevent other rules of law from being used to circumvent the harsher effects of the doctrine. Most important in this context is the tort of negligence under which a defendant may be under a duty to exercise reasonable care in relation to the third party. This may involve a duty not to break a contract with A negligently so as to cause foreseeable harm to B.

3.2.1.2 The effect of statements made to the consumer When a consumer enters into a contract a number of statements may be made to him. Some of these statements may become terms of the contract whereas others may be regarded as pre-contractual representations only. The classification of a particular statement as a term or as a representation may affect the consumer's remedies against the person with whom he deals. If a term of the contract made by the consumer is broken, he will have an action for repudiation of the contract or for damages. If the statement is classified as a misrepresentation, the standard remedy is that of rescission of the contract, but damages may also be recovered for fraud in the tort of deceit or damages may be recoverable under the Misrepresentation Act 1967, s. 2(1), if the misrepresentation was made negligently.

Whether or not a statement will be treated by the court as a term or a representation is often difficult to ascertain. It has been argued that if the maker of the relevant statement is not 'at fault', the statement will be regarded as a representation rather than as a term of the contract (*Dick Bentley Productions Ltd* v *Harold Smith (Motors) Ltd* [1965] 2 All ER 65; cf. *Oscar Chess Ltd* v *Williams* [1957] 1 All ER 325). However, this is difficult to reconcile with *Beale* v *Taylor* [1967] 3 All ER 253 in which a seller who was said not to be at fault in his misdescription of a motor vehicle was nonetheless considered to be in breach of a term of the contract relating to the description of the goods supplied. Perhaps a better approach is to consider the expertise of the person making the statement. Generally, a tradesman dealing with a consumer will be regarded as having the greater expertise. In such a case, it is more likely that a statement made by the trader to the consumer will be treated as a term of the contract than is the case if the statement had been made by the consumer to the trader (see *Esso Petroleum Co. Ltd* v *Mardon* [1976] QB 801). Other factors which may be relevant are whether the statement was of particular importance to the consumer, whether it was made at a crucial stage of negotiations and whether the consumer has been asked by the trader to verify the truth of a statement (*Ecay* v *Godfrey* (1974) 80 Ll L Rep 286).

3.2.1.2.1   Representations as statements of fact   A representation is generally regarded as a statement of fact that induces a person to enter into a contract, but does not amount to a term of the contract. A factual statement may sometimes give rise to contractual liability if it is classified as a collateral warranty. However, in such circumstances it is normally said that the parties must show an intention to enter into contractual relations (*Lambert* v *Lewis* [1981] 1 All ER 1185).

Factual statements need to be distinguished from mere puffs, statements of opinion and statements of intention. Mere puffs are most frequently encountered in advertising material. They are statements which are not intended to be relied upon and do not have any legal effect. A claim that a certain brand of lager refreshes parts of the body not reached by competing brands is a typical example. No one can seriously claim that a statement of this kind should be believed and relied upon. While the law does not control such statements, there is a degree of voluntary control in the form of the Code of Advertising Practice.

A misrepresentation should also be distinguished from a statement of opinion. The latter, if honestly expressed, does not give rise to liability. Thus if the seller of land not previously used for sheep farming honestly expresses the opinion that the land is capable of supporting a specified number of sheep, he will not be liable if the statement later proves to be inaccurate (*Bisset* v *Wilkinson* [1927] AC 177). However, it is not true that the maker of a statement can avoid liability in every case by prefacing his remarks with the words, 'I believe'. If it appears that the maker of the statement could not possibly have held the opinion he expresses (*Smith* v *Land & House Property Corporation* (1884) 28 ChD 7) or if the 'opinion' is expressed by a person with a particular skill in the matter referred to (*Esso Petroleum Co. Ltd* v *Mardon* [1976] QB 801) the statement is likely to be treated as one of fact, thereby giving rise to liability for misrepresentation or for breach of a collateral contract. Alternatively, if the statement by the expert is reasonably relied upon by the consumer, an action may lie in the tort of negligence under the rule in *Hedley Byrne & Co. Ltd* v *Heller & Partners Ltd* [1964] AC 465 (see 11.2.2).

A representation should also be distinguished from a statement of intention. If the latter is not a contractual promise, it will generally not give rise to liability on the part of its maker. However, in some instances, what appears to be a statement of intention may give rise to liability for misrepresentation if it is clear that the maker has no intention of making the statement come true (*Edgington* v *Fitzmaurice* (1885) 29 ChD 459). For example, if an airline confirms the availability of a seat on a specified flight, but due to a deliberate overbooking policy is unable to transport the passenger on that flight, it could be argued that the airline has merely expressed an intention to make a seat available. However, due to the deliberate policy of overbooking, the airline knows there may be circumstances in which the passenger cannot be carried because all available seats will be taken. In such a case, it could be said that the airline has represented the availability of a seat on the flight in circumstances in which they know that the statement cannot be made to come true (see *British Airways Board* v *Taylor* [1976] 1 WLR 13, a case decided under the Trade Descriptions Act 1968, s. 14; see now European Community Regulations on denied boarding considered in chapter 10).

3.2.1.2.2   Contractual terms   Terms of a contract may be express or implied. In consumer transactions, the consumer will often buy goods or contract for services without specifying in detail what he wants. In such a case there may not be any express terms of the contract. Clearly, this would be an unsatisfactory state of affairs and it is common to find that the law implies terms into consumer contracts which favour the consumer. Many of these are dealt with in more detail in other parts of this book (see chapters 7 and 10).

If a statement is regarded as a contractual term, traditional classification distinguishes between conditions and warranties. The breach of a condition will allow the consumer to treat the contract as being at an end, whereas a breach of warranty gives rise to an action for damages only. The courts have also developed the notion of the 'innominate term' whereby a term is classified according to the effect of its breach upon the contract as a whole. The result of this is that a term may be a condition in name, but if the effect of its breach is not sufficiently serious to go to the substance of the contract, only an action for damages may be allowed. This approach is more likely to be found in commercial contracts than in dealings between consumers and businesses. For the most part, terms in consumer contracts will be classified as either conditions or as warranties. Indeed, there is considerable doubt whether it is possible to regard a statutory term as anything other than that which it has been defined as by Parliament. An amendment to the Sale of Goods Act 1979 has been proposed in the Consumer Guarantees Bill 1990 creating a new s. 15A(1) which will allow the court to treat a slight breach of one of the implied conditions as to description, quality and fitness as breaches of warranty in a non-consumer transaction, but no similar provision applies to consumer contracts.

3.2.1.3   Consumer remedies   The consumer's principal remedies for a breach of contract are those of repudiation of the contract in the case of a serious breach of contract or an action for damages in less serious cases. In a contract for the supply of goods, repudiation will involve rejection of the goods and recovery of the price paid. In a contract for the supply of services repudiation will mean that the consumer is no longer required to pay for the service.

3.2.1.3.1 Repudiation If the supplier of goods or services is in breach of a condition of the contract, the consumer may treat his contractual obligations as being at an end, thereby allowing him to decline to pay or to recover the price and sue for damages in respect of any additional, foreseeable loss suffered by him as a result of the breach of contract.

The main difficulties encountered by the consumer arise where he has accepted goods supplied to him. In this case, rejection of the goods supplied is not possible and the consumer is required to treat the breach of condition as a breach of warranty (Sale of Goods Act 1979 (hereafter SGA), s. 11(4)). In certain instances, whether or not the consumer has accepted goods is subject to his having been given a reasonable opportunity to inspect them (SGA, s. 34).

The concept of acceptance is closely associated with the common law rules on affirmation of the contract, waiver and estoppel. However, there are differences between the different doctrines. A person, generally, will not be treated as having affirmed a contract unless he knows of the other party's breach and is aware of his right to terminate. However, a buyer of goods may be held to have accepted goods in those circumstances. In some instances, a buyer may be treated as having waived his right to reject the goods. This will normally arise where the buyer has made clear representations to the effect that he will not reject goods (or services) on the ground of late performance. This approach is most likely to be adopted in commercial contracts and is unlikely to be employed against a consumer.

In a contract for the supply of services, whether or not the consumer can treat his contractual obligations as being at an end will depend largely on whether he has been deprived substantially of the benefit it was intended he should receive. The mere fact that the service provided is qualitatively defective does not automatically mean that the consumer can decline to pay, particularly if it can be said that the consumer has derived some benefit from the supplier's performance (see chapter 10).

For the purposes of a contract for the sale of goods, it is necessary to consider when a consumer has accepted the goods supplied to him. For these purposes, SGA, s. 35, provides for three methods of acceptance. The first is where the buyer, subject to s. 34, intimates to the seller that he has accepted the goods (SGA, s. 35(1); proposed amendment s. 35(1)(a)). This could arise in a consumer transaction where the buyer signs a delivery note which contains an express provision to the effect that the buyer has waived his right to reject the goods. Since all the law requires is that the intimation should be clear and unequivocal (*Varley* v *Whipp* [1900] 1 QB 513) it is possible that something short of an express intimation will suffice. It follows that in appropriate circumstances, retention of goods may amount to an intimation of acceptance.

The second method of acceptance specified in SGA arises where the buyer, subject to s. 34, has done some act in relation to the goods which is inconsistent with the seller's ownership (s. 35(1); proposed amendment s. 35(1)(b)). An example of this method of acceptance arises where the buyer disposes of the goods to another person. The same would be true of a buyer who advertises a car for sale after he has taken delivery of it. It has even been held that the use of a motor vehicle after sale is an act inconsistent with the ownership of the seller (*Lee* v *York Coach & Marine* [1977] RTR 35), but it may be better to regard this as an example of the third variety of acceptance considered below.

The third method of acceptance arises where the buyer retains the goods without intimating to the seller whether he has accepted them or not (SGA s. 35(1); proposed amendment s. 35(4)). If the buyer delays before registering his complaint or if it takes some time to discover that there is a complaint, the consumer may discover that he is deemed to have accepted the goods supplied to him. The longer the consumer delays and continues to use the goods, the more difficult it will be for him to show that he has not done some act inconsistent with the ownership of the seller. The difficulty this provision creates is that some defects are less discoverable than others. While it seems perfectly reasonable to regard a person as having accepted goods when he has failed to discover a reasonably discoverable defect, the same is not true of a well hidden defect. The present law does not take this into account with the result that both types of defect are subject to the same rule. An alternative approach might be to require time to run from the date of discovery of a hidden defect, but maintain the present rule in relation to more obvious defects (Brown [1988] JBL 56 at p. 63).

It might be possible for a consumer to refrain from using goods pending the outcome of future litigation, but if the thing purchased is particularly expensive, few consumers would be able to absorb the cost of purchasing a replacement in order to show that they had no intention of doing an act inconsistent with the seller's ownership. It is clear from *Bernstein* v *Pamson Motors (Golders Green) Ltd* [1987] 2 All ER 220 (see Brown [1988] JBL 56) that the purchaser of a motor car will lose his right to reject soon after he begins to make use of it. In that case, the plaintiff bought a car which suffered from major engine defects. He had owned the car for three weeks prior to its breakdown. Due to the owner's illness, the car had been driven only 140 miles, but it was held by Rougier J that the right to reject had been lost through the lapse of a reasonable time. It was considered important that the seller should be able to 'close his ledger reasonably soon after the transaction is complete' (at p. 230). This may well be a relevant factor in a commercial transaction, where the parties are roughly equal in terms of bargaining strength (see Law Com. No. 160, (1987), paras 5.6-5.13), but the same cannot be said where the buyer is a consumer.

Decisions based on hire-purchase legislation (see Mullan [1990] JBL 231) have tended to be more favourable to the consumer, though it should be appreciated that in this respect, s. 35 does not apply and the position is governed by common law rules on affirmation of the contract. The cases in this area seem to allow the right to reject to survive for weeks or even months after the date on which delivery was taken by the consumer. A contract of hire-purchase involves a bailment of goods to the consumer. Therefore, the supplier will continue to have an interest in the goods up to the point at which the consumer exercises his option to purchase the goods. Because of this it can be said that the supplier does not have the same interest as a seller of goods in 'closing his ledger'. Furthermore, since the relationship between the debtor and the creditor is continuing in nature, the courts appear to have concluded that the goods supplied should be of merchantable quality during the continuance of the agreement.

In the light of the foregoing, the courts have been prepared to adopt a more flexible approach in determining whether the debtor can reject the goods. In particular, factors such as the conduct of the parties (*Yeoman Credit Ltd v Apps* [1961] 2 All ER 281), attempts at repair (*Farnworth Finance Facilities Ltd v Attryde* [1970] 1 WLR 1053), negotiations for a settlement, depreciation in value between agreement and rejection (*Porter v General Guarantee Corporation Ltd* [1982] RTR 384) and the discovery of hidden defects (*Laurelgates Ltd v Lombard North Central Ltd* (1983) 133 NLJ 720) have been taken into account.

If the buyer of goods seeks a cure for defective goods, it is not entirely clear whether this will affect his right to reject. In relation to hire-purchase transactions, it would appear that the time taken by the consumer in seeking a cure can be discounted in determining whether a reasonable time has elapsed (*Farnworth Finance Facilities Ltd v Attryde* [1970] 1 WLR 1053) but whether the same approach can be adopted in relation to a contract for the sale of goods in view of the interpretation of s. 35 in *Bernstein v Pamson Motors (Golders Green) Ltd* [1987] 2 All ER 220 would appear to be questionable. The proposed SGA, s. 35(5)(b), does provide that the buyer is not deemed to have accepted goods by virtue of the fact that he agrees to their repair, but it is still possible that such a considerable period of time will have elapsed since the date of delivery that it would be unreasonable to allow rejection.

The principal difference between the sale and the hire-purchase cases is that the courts are able to use the monthly instalment so as to achieve a fair result. If it is considered that the debtor has derived some benefit from his use and enjoyment of the goods, it is possible to require him to pay instalments up to the value of that benefit (*Porter v General Guarantee Corporation Ltd* [1982] RTR 384). In sale of goods cases, the position is not so simple and the courts, so far, have been unable to develop principles to deal with the buyer's use of the goods after delivery.

Some of the provisions of s. 35 are subject to s. 34 which provides that the buyer must be given a reasonable opportunity to examine the goods. It is clear that before a buyer will be considered to have intimated to the seller that he accepts and before he is deemed to have done an act inconsistent with the ownership of the seller, he must have been given this reasonable opportunity (proposed amendment s. 35(2)). However, acceptance by retention is not subject to a similar requirement. Since the act of retaining goods may fall into all three categories of acceptance, it is possible that the consumer's position will depend on how the court construes his conduct. This is particularly so since the right to an opportunity to inspect, where it applies, cannot be excluded by agreement, waiver or otherwise (proposed amendment s. 35(3)).

Whether these provisions assist the consumer is doubtful since many defects in consumer goods will be discoverable on a reasonable examination in which case the buyer will not be able to complain that the goods are not of merchantable quality (SGA, s. 14(2)(b); proposed amendment s. 14(2C)(b)). Where defects are not discoverable on a reasonable examination, ss. 34 and 35 do not help since the defect will remain hidden. In these circumstances, a reasonable time may still be deemed to have elapsed and the consumer will then be confined to his remedy in damages alone, assuming that he is not out of time for the purposes of the Limitation Act 1980.

3.2.1.3.2   *Damages*   Where a consumer claims damages for either a breach of a contractual condition or warranty, the award is supposed to put him in the position he would have been in had the contract been performed. Thus in a sale of goods contract the buyer is entitled to damages representing the difference between the value of the goods as they were at the date of delivery and their value had they fulfilled the term of the contract (SGA, s. 53(3)). Determining this diminished value can be difficult and may involve guesswork on the part of the court. It is necessary to consider what the market value of the goods would have been had the consumer and the seller been aware of the defects at the time of delivery (*Jackson* v *Chrysler Acceptances Ltd* [1978] RTR 474 at p. 481).

A particular problem in consumer cases is that the goods are bought for use, not for resale and s. 53(3) does not distinguish between the two. Since the consumer requires the goods for use, it will be possible to have them repaired so as to bring them up to his requirements. In such a case, the obvious measure of damages is the cost of repair rather than the difference between the values stated above (*Bernstein* v *Pamson Motors (Golders Green) Ltd* [1987] 2 All ER 220).

A consumer may also complain of losses consequent on the seller's breach of contract. If goods are not of the required quality, they may cause personal injury or property damage. Such harm may be regarded as a loss arising naturally, in the usual course of events from the breach of contract (*Hadley* v *Baxendale* (1854) 9 Exch 341; SGA, s. 53(2)). For example, if the seller sells a smokeless fuel mixed with explosives which results in damage to the consumer's house (*Wilson* v *Rickett Cockerell & Co. Ltd* [1954] 1 QB 598) or if a hot-water bottle bursts depositing its contents on the consumer (*Preist* v *Last* [1903] 2 KB 148), the physical harm suffered by the consumer is recoverable as natural losses arising in the usual course of things from the breach of contract. Similarly, it would appear that if the consumer suffers inconvenience or disappointment as a consequence of the breach of contract, damages may be recovered in this respect. Thus the consumer who buys a defective car and suffers a ruined holiday or day out, damages may be recovered in this respect (*Jackson* v *Chrysler Acceptances Ltd* [1978] RTR 474; *Bernstein* v *Pamson Motors (Golders Green) Ltd* [1987] 2 All ER 220).

Difficulties may arise where the harm suffered by the consumer is not a natural consequence of the breach of contract. The second limb of *Hadley* v *Baxendale* (1854) 9 Exch 341, as qualified by *The Heron II* [1969] 1 AC 350 requires the loss to have been foreseen, at the time of contracting, as a serious possibility. In relation to physical harm, the courts have on occasion (see *H. Parsons (Livestock) Ltd* v *Uttley, Ingham & Co. Ltd* [1978] QB 791), resorted to a test which more closely resembles the reasonable foresight test applied in tort cases (see *Hughes* v *Lord Advocate* [1963] AC 837; cf. *Tremain* v *Pike* [1969]

1 WLR 1556) under which the general kind of harm suffered should be foreseeable even though the precise extent of damage could not have been foreseen.

In the case of a contract for the supply of services, difficulties may arise in deciding what the appropriate measure of damages should be. This problem is dealt with below in relation to specific types of service (see chapter 10). The harm suffered by the consumer must be a foreseeable consequence of the supplier's breach of contract. It would appear that judicial views on what is foreseeable may be less sympathetic to the consumer than is the case where contracts for the sale of goods are concerned and that a strict interpretation of the rule in *Hadley* v *Baxendale* (1854) 9 Exch 341 may be employed. Thus in *Kemp* v *Intasun Holidays Ltd* (1987) 7 Tr LR 161, the defendant tour operator was not liable for specific discomfort suffered by the plaintiff where a casual remark had been made to the booking agent to the effect that the plaintiff suffered from a specific medical condition. The condition had not been specifically identified at the time of contracting, therefore the harm suffered by the plaintiff was not foreseeable.

3.2.2 Tortious obligations

Rules of the law of tort have been adapted in a number of ways as a consumer protection technique. The immediately obvious example is the adaptation of the tort of negligence in relation to the liability of producers for defective products and the liability of the supplier of a service, but tortious principles are also relevant in other respects. In particular, the law of tort may be of some limited use in the field of advertising law and in relation to the misuse of property belonging to another by both the consumer and the trader with whom he deals.

3.2.2.1 Product safety The decision of the House of Lords in *Donoghue* v *Stevenson* [1932] AC 562 represents a landmark in the field of consumer protection law, providing that a manufacturer owes a duty of care in respect of the safety of his product. The development of the law in this respect is pursued in more detail elsewhere (see chapter 8), but for present purposes it should be observed that difficulties have arisen in determining how far the duty extends. In particular, it would now appear that the manufacturer does not owe the consumer of a defective product any extensive duty in respect of pure economic loss (*D & F Estates Ltd* v *Church Commissioners for England* [1988] 2 All ER 992; *Murphy* v *Brentwood District Council* [1990] 2 All ER 908; and see chapter 8).

Apart from the problem of economic loss, the difficulties of establishing causation and proving fault on the part of the manufacturer have led to calls for reform of the law, culminating in the enactment of the Consumer Protection Act 1987. Whether this provides for substantially greater protection from unsafe products is a matter of some doubt.

In certain instances, manufacturers and retailers are under a statutory duty to comply with basic safety standards. Failure to comply with these standards may give rise to a civil action for breach of statutory duty. Satisfying the requirements of the tort of breach of statutory duty is often difficult (see 8.6) and as a result, successful civil actions in this respect are rare.

3.2.2.2 Defective services The tort of negligence has proved a useful, if not wholly adequate tool in relation to the liability of the supplier of a service (see chapter 10). Doctors, lawyers, architects and surveyors are required to exercise reasonable care in their dealings with their clients and, in some cases, third-party consumers. Some would argue that the service industries should be subject to greater liability, in particular, there is a view expressed by consumer groups to the effect that the supplier of a service should guarantee the result required by the consumer. Such an obligation would go well beyond the present requirement of the exercise of reasonable care and skill (see 10.4.2).

Negligence is not the only relevant tort for the purposes of the supply of services. In relation to medical services, a limited role may also be played by the tort of battery, particularly where non-consensual medical treatment is concerned.

The tort of trespass also plays a part in respect of the misuse of consumer goods. If a consumer leaves his property with another for the purposes of repair or safe-keeping and the repairer manages to wrongly dispose of the goods to another, the consumer may have an action for conversion (see 10.8.1). The same equally applies where the consumer has temporary possession of goods belonging to the supplier, as is the case under a contract of hire. Wrongful disposition of the hired goods may render the consumer liable for conversion.

3.2.2.3 Advertising law The principal controls on misleading advertising in favour of the consumer lie in the criminal law and in self-regulating codes of practice. However, principles of the law of tort may have some minor significance (see 11.2.2).

Statements made to a consumer in the form of advertisements may be construed as negligent or fraudulent misrepresentations. In the former case, an action will lie under the Misrepresentation Act 1967, if the advertisement induces the consumer to make a contract with the advertiser. If the advertisement induces the consumer to contract with a retailer independent of the advertiser, it is possible that an action may lie under the rule in *Hedley Byrne & Co. Ltd* v *Heller & Partners Ltd* [1964] AC 465, provided the necessary relationship of proximity can be established. If the misrepresentation is made without regard for its truth or falsity, an action may lie in the tort of deceit, but the burden of proof in this respect lies on the person to whom the statement has been made and is very difficult to discharge.

Where a retailer or producer engages in comparative advertising, he may make some disparaging reference to a rival's product. This may amount to slander of goods if the statement is untrue, disparaging and has an adverse effect on the trade of the person whose goods are disparaged. It should be noted that this does not relate directly to the issue of consumer protection since the obvious plaintiff is not the consumer but the rival trader.

3.3 CIVIL OBLIGATIONS OF SUPPLIERS AND PRODUCERS – MATERIALS FOR CONSIDERATION

3.3.1 Contractual obligations

3.3.1.1 Privity of contract   For text see 3.2.1.1.

While the doctrine of privity of contract is potentially destructive of consumer avenues of redress against those with whom he has no direct contractual relationship, methods have been adopted to avoid the harsher effects of the doctrine. Examples include the use of the law of agency, the notion of the collateral warranty and allowing the promisee to sue on behalf of the consumer third party.

Lockett v *A. & M. Charles Ltd*
[1938] 4 All ER 170
King's Bench Division

The plaintiff's husband placed an order for a meal at the defendant's restaurant. Mrs Lockett suffered from food poisoning as a result of what she ate.

TUCKER J at pp. 171–3: With regard to the female plaintiff's position in respect of breach of warranty, every proprietor of a restaurant is under a duty to take reasonable care to see that the food which he supplies to his guests is fit for human consumption. If he does not take such reasonable steps, and if he is negligent, a person who buys the food which he supplies can recover damages from him based on his negligence. As, however, there is no allegation of such negligence in this case, it must be assumed that the proprietor of the hotel and his servants could not be at fault in any way, and either plaintiff can recover only if he or she establishes that there was a contract between him or her and the proprietor of the hotel.

Counsel for the plaintiffs is, in my opinion, right when he submits that, when persons go into a restaurant and order food, they are making a contract of sale in exactly the same way as they are making a contract of sale when they go into a shop and order any other goods. I think that the inference is that the person who orders the food in a hotel or restaurant prima facie makes himself or herself liable to pay for it, and when two people — whether or not they happen to be husband and wife — go into a hotel and each orders and is supplied with food, then, as between these persons and the proprietor of the hotel, each of them is making himself liable for the food which he orders, whatever may be the arrangement between the two persons who are eating at the hotel. On the facts in this case, it is, in my opinion, right to hold that there was a contract implied by the conduct of the parties between the plaintiff, Mrs Lockett, and the defendants when she ordered and was supplied with the whitebait at the Hotel de Paris.

This matter was discussed in *Regensteiner* v *Canuto's Restaurant Ltd (Hales and Piper, Third Parties)* (1938) *The Times*, 6 May 1938, in which it appears that Hilbery J, although not finding it necessary to make the matter actually the basis of his decision (because he held that it was not open to a third party to raise the point, since it had not been raised by the actual defendant in that case), nonetheless expressed the view that, on the facts of the case before him (it was a case of husband and wife), there being no special or unusual circumstances, the wife was entitled to recover in contract. I respectfully concur in the view which he expressed that each case depended on its own circumstances. However, where there is no evidence to indicate to the proprietor of the hotel what the relationship between the parties is, and where there is no evidence that one or the other is in charge of the proceedings, and yet one or the other takes on himself the position of a host entertaining his guests, the proper inference of law is that the person who orders and consumes the food is liable to pay for it as between himself and the proprietor of the restaurant. If that is so, it follows beyond all doubt that there is an implied warranty that the food supplied is reasonably fit for human consumption.

Notes

(1)   What is the basis of this decision? Is it that the restaurateur directly contracts with all who enter his premises, whether they pay for the goods or not? How does this affect a family trip to a supermarket to make the weekly purchase of food and household items?

(2)   Does the reference to Mr Lockett as the 'host entertaining his guests' raise an inference of an agency relationship?

Where a manufacturer gives an express assertion that his product is fit for a particular use and the consumer, in reliance on that assertion, purchases that product from an independent supplier, the courts are prepared to infer a collateral warranty on the part of the manufacturer.

Wells (Merstham) Ltd v *Buckland Sand & Silica Ltd*
[1965] 2 QB 170
Queen's Bench Division

For the facts see 3.2.1.1.1.

EDMUND DAVIES J at p. 178: [The plaintiffs] rely, in other words, upon what has, in many of the reported cases, been called a collateral contract, and they base themselves on the well-known words of Lord Moulton in *Heilbut, Symons & Co.* v *Buckleton* [1913] AC 30 that, 'It is evident, both on principle and on authority, that there may be a contract the consideration for which is the making of some other contract. "If you will make such and such a contract I will give you £100", is in every sense of the word a complete legal contract. It is collateral to the main contract, but each has an independent existence, and they do not differ in respect of their possessing to the full the character and status of a contract.'

As between A (a potential seller of goods) and B (a potential buyer), two ingredients, and two only, are in my judgment required in order to bring about a collateral contract containing a warranty: (1) a promise or assertion by A as to the nature, quality or quantity of the goods which B may reasonably regard as being made *animo contrahendi*, and (2) acquisition by B of the goods in reliance on that promise or assertion. As K.W. Wedderburn expresses it in 'Collateral contracts' [1959] CLJ at p. 79: '. . . the consideration given for the promise is no more than the act of entering into the main contract. Going ahead with that bargain is a sufficient price for the promise, without which it would not have gone ahead at all.' And a warranty may be enforceable notwithstanding that no specific main contract is discussed at the time it is given, though obviously an *animus contrahendi* (and, therefore, a warranty) would be unlikely to be inferred unless the circumstances show that it was within the present contemplation of the parties that a contract based upon the promise would shortly be entered into.

The decision in *Wells (Merstham) Ltd* v *Buckland Sand & Silica Ltd* is based on an express warranty, but would the same approach be adopted in respect of an implied warranty of fitness? The following extract suggests this is not likely.

Lambert v *Lewis*
[1980] 1 All ER 978
Court of Appeal

STEPHENSON LJ at pp. 1002–3: The construction of these documents in the circumstances of this case leads us to the same conclusion as the judge, that the claims in them 'were not intended to be, nor were they acted on as being express warranties and (though this further finding, if it adds anything, is not strictly necessary) the [suppliers] did not purchase the coupling in reliance on such warranties'.

Nor do we think that the development of the law in *Shanklin Pier Ltd* v *Detel Products Ltd* [1951] 2 KB 854 (and, it may be, in the unreported case of *Independent Broadcasting Authority* v *EMI Electronics Ltd* [subsequently reported 14 BLR 1]) helps the suppliers to a different result. The effect and ratio of the former decision are correctly stated by the judge in his judgment in these terms:

> In that case the defendant paint company made certain express representations as to the quality of its paint and its suitability for use on the plaintiffs' pier which was then to be repaired by contractors. On the strength of that representation the plaintiffs caused the specification for their works to be carried out by contractors to be amended by substituting the defendants' paint for that previously specified. The contractors bought and used the paint, which was unsatisfactory and unsuitable for use on the pier. It was held that the plaintiff company could recover damages on the warranty from the defendant paint company despite the fact that there was no contract other than a collateral one between the plaintiff pier company and the defendant paint company. In my judgment the basis of this decision was that consideration for the representation was the procurement by the plaintiffs of a contract of sale by their contractors with the defendants.

There the express representation was clearly an express warranty, for which the consideration was the procurement of a particular contract, as the judge pointed out; but here was no warranty and we find it unnecessary to consider whether that decision could be extended to the contract of purchase made by the suppliers, or the contract of resale made by them, and to hold that in consideration of either of those contracts, both in fact unknown to the manufacturers, they are promising or warranting, either expressly or by implication, that their claims for their hitch are true, and they are prepared to stand by their warranties and pay the suppliers and any other distributors in their position damages for breach of them, as long (counsel for the suppliers was constrained to add) as the user of the hitch is reasonable.

The Court of Appeal's decision in *Lambert* v *Lewis* was reversed by the House of Lords on other grounds [1981] 1 All ER 1185.

In some instances, the court may conclude that the promisee can sue on behalf of a third party and recover damages in respect of the third party's loss.

Jackson v Horizon Holidays Ltd
[1975] 3 All ER 92
Court of Appeal

LORD DENNING MR at p. 95: We have had an interesting discussion as to the legal position when one person makes a contract for the benefit of a party. In this case it was a husband making a contract for the benefit of himself, his wife and children. Other cases readily come to mind. A host makes a contract with a restaurant for a dinner for himself and his friends. The vicar makes a contract for a coach trip for the choir. In all these cases there is only one person who makes the contract. It is the husband, the host or the vicar, as the case may be. Sometimes he pays the whole price himself. Occasionally he may get a contribution from the others. But in any case it is he who makes the contract. It would be a fiction to say that the contract was made by all the family, or all the guests, or all the choir, and that he was only an agent for them. Take this very case. It would be absurd to say that the twins of three years old were parties to the contract or that the father was making the contract on their behalf as if they were principals. It would equally be a mistake to say that in any of these instances there was a trust. The transaction bears no resemblance to a trust. There was no trust fund and no trust property. No, the real truth is that in each instance, the father, the host or the vicar, was making a contract himself for the benefit of the whole party. In short, a contract by one for the benefit of third persons.

What is the position when such a contract is broken? At present the law says that the only one who can sue is the one who made the contract. None of the rest of the party can sue, even though the contract was made for their benefit. But when that one does sue, what damages can he recover? Is he limited to his own loss? Or can he recover for the others? Suppose the holiday firm puts the family into a hotel which is only half built and the visitors have to sleep on the floor? Or suppose the restaurant is fully booked and the guests have to go away, hungry and angry, having spent so much on fares to get there? Or suppose the coach leaves the choir stranded halfway and they have to hire cars to get home? None of them individually can sue. Only the father, the host or the vicar can sue. He can, of course, recover his own damages. But can he not recover for the others? I think he can. The case comes within the principle stated by Lush LJ in *Lloyd's v Harper* (1880) 16 ChD 290 at p. 321.

... I consider it to be an established rule of law that where a contract is made with A for the benefit of B, A can sue on the contract for the benefit of B, and recover all that B could have recovered if the contract had been made with B himself.

Notes

(1) While Lord Denning stated that Lush LJ was a common lawyer, speaking of the common law, his view has been strongly criticised in *Woodar Investment Development Ltd v Wimpey Construction UK Ltd* [1980] 1 All ER 571 on the ground that *Lloyd's v Harper* is a case concerned with the law of trusts (which Lord Denning rejected as irrelevant to this case).

(2) The proper view of *Jackson v Horizon Holidays Ltd* preferred by the House of Lords in *Woodar Investment Development Ltd v Wimpey Construction UK Ltd* was that expressed by James LJ that this was a 'contract . . . made by Mr Jackson for a family holiday' and that 'he did not get a family holiday' [1975] 3 All ER 92 at p. 96. If this is the case did the damages awarded cover

only Mr Jackson's distress or that of the whole family? Can the same reasoning be applied to all consumer purchases obviously intended to be consumed by the whole family?

3.3.1.2   Consumer remedies   For text see 3.2.1.3.

3.3.1.3.1   Repudiation

Sale of Goods Act 1979

11.   When condition to be treated as warranty
   (4)   Where a contract of sale is not severable and the buyer has accepted the goods or part of them, the breach of a condition to be fulfilled by the seller can only be treated as a breach of warranty, and not as a ground for rejecting the goods and treating the contract as repudiated, unless there is an express or implied term of the contract to that effect.

34.   Buyer's right of examining the goods
   (1)   Where goods are delivered to the buyer, and he has not previously examined them, he is not deemed to have accepted them until he has had a reasonable opportunity of examining them for the purpose of ascertaining whether they are in conformity with the contract.

35.   Acceptance
   (1)   The buyer is deemed to have accepted the goods when he intimates to the seller that he has accepted them, or (except where section 34 above otherwise provides) when the goods have been delivered to him and he does any act in relation to them which is inconsistent with the ownership of the seller, or when after the lapse of a reasonable time he retains the goods without intimating to the seller that he has rejected them.

Consumer Guarantees Bill 1990

The Bill is based on the recommendations of the Law Commission (Law Com. No. 160 (Cm 137), 1987).

17.—(1)   In section 35 of the Sale of Goods Act 1979 (acceptance) for the words from 'when he intimates' to '(2)' there is substituted—
   'subject to subsection (2) below—
      (a)   when he intimates to the seller that he has accepted them, or
      (b)   when the goods have been delivered to him and he does any act in relation to them which is inconsistent with the ownership of the seller.
   (2)   Where goods are delivered to the buyer, and he has not previously examined them, he is not deemed to have accepted them under subsection (1) above until he has had a reasonable opportunity of examining them for the purpose—
      (a)   of ascertaining whether they are in conformity with the contract and,
      (b)   in the case of a contract for sale by sample, of comparing the bulk with the sample.
   (3)   Where the buyer deals as consumer or (in Scotland) the contract of sale is a consumer contract, the buyer cannot lose his right to rely on subsection (2) above by agreement, waiver or otherwise.

(4)   The buyer is also deemed to have accepted the goods when after the lapse of a reasonable time he retains the goods without intimating to the seller that he has rejected them.

(5)   The questions that are material in determining for the purposes of subsection (4) above whether a reasonable time has elapsed include whether the buyer has had a reasonable opportunity of examining the goods for the purpose mentioned in subsection (2) above.

(6)   The buyer is not by virtue of this section deemed to have accepted the goods merely because (for example)—

(a)   he asks for, or agrees to, their repair by or under an arrangement with the seller, or

(b)   the goods are delivered to another under a subsale or other disposition.

(7)   Where the contract is for the sale of goods making one or more commercial units, a buyer accepting any goods included in a unit is deemed to have accepted all the goods making the unit.

In this subsection, 'commercial unit' means a unit division of which would materially impair the value of the goods or the character of the unit.

In a contract for the sale of goods, the right to reject is lost where the consumer has accepted the goods supplied. The problem is to determine when acceptance occurs.

Bernstein v *Pamson Motors (Golders Green) Ltd*
[1987] 2 All ER 220
Queen's Bench Division

For the facts see 3.2.1.3.1.

ROUGIER J quoted the Sale of Goods Act 1979, s. 11(4), and continued at p. 229: Clearly this contract was not severable, so the inquiry shifts to whether or not the plaintiff accepted the car. For this question assistance is to be derived from s. 35(1) of the 1979 Act, which defines three sets of circumstances in which the buyer of goods is deemed to have accepted them.

ROUGIER J then quoted the Sale of Goods Act 1979, ss. 34 and 35, and continued at p. 230: However, this subsection [s. 34(1)] it will be seen, only provides an exception to the second set of circumstances included in s. 35(1), namely those wherein the buyer does not act in relation to the goods inconsistently with the continued ownership of the seller. That situation does not arise in this case any more than does an express intimation to the seller that the buyer has accepted the goods. Therefore the only situation to be considered is the one when, after the lapse of a reasonable time, the buyer has retained the goods without intimating to the seller that he has rejected them. This in turn prompts the inquiry: what is a reasonable time in the circumstances? And here the 1979 Act ceases to be helpful. By s. 59 'a reasonable time' is defined as a question of fact, no more, as if it could be anything else.

The submission made on behalf of the defendants is that in the context of the sale of new motor car a reasonable time must entail a reasonable time to inspect and try out the car *generally* rather than with an eye to any specific defect, and that to project the period further would be artificial and contrary to the general legal proposition that there should, whenever possible, be finality in commercial transactions. At first I regret to say this proposition got a hostile reception on the ground that a mere 140-odd miles, and some three weeks, part of which were occupied by illness, were not nearly enough to afford the plaintiff any opportunity of discovering this wholly latent defect.

However, it was pointed out, and in my view rightly, that the whole concept of discovery of any *particular* defect and subsequent affirmation of the contract was only material in contracts of hire-purchase and that there was nothing in the Sale of Goods Act 1979 to justify any analogous approach. This distinction was clearly stated by Webster J in the recent case of *Laurelgates Ltd* v *Lombard North Central Ltd* (1983) 133 NLJ 720.

In effect, it was argued, the wording of s. 35 of the 1979 Act creates its own implied affirmation, as it were, by stating merely that once a buyer has had the goods for a reasonable time, *not*, be it noted, related to the opportunity to discover any particular defect, he is deemed to have accepted them. I think that this submission is correct.

In my judgment, the nature of the particular defect, discovered *ex post facto*, and the speed with which it might have been discovered, are irrelevant to the concept of reasonable time in s. 35 as drafted. That section seems to me to be directed solely to what is a reasonable practical interval in commercial terms between a buyer receiving the goods and his ability to send them back, taking into consideration from his point of view the nature of the goods and their function, and from the point of view of the seller the commercial desirability of being able to close his ledger reasonably soon after the transaction is complete. The complexity of the intended function of the goods is clearly of prime consideration here. What is a reasonable time in relation to a bicycle would hardly suffice for a nuclear submarine.

Turning to the facts of the present case one asks whether some three weeks and 140-odd miles constitute a reasonable time after taking delivery of a new motor car? I am bound to say that I think the answer is yes. Adopting, as I do, the suggestion of counsel for the defendants that a reasonable time means reasonable time to examine and try out the goods in general terms, the evidence persuades me that such a time had elapsed by 3 January 1985. I discount the period when the plaintiff was ill because reasonable seems to me to be referable to the individual buyer's situation as well as to that of the seller. But the plaintiff after recovering, had taken two or three short trips in his car for the express purpose of trying it out, and had opportunity to make more trips had he wished to do so. In the circumstances I consider he must be deemed to have accepted the goods within the meaning of s. 35 so that he is compelled to treat his claim under s. 14 as a claim for breach of warranty and thereby to limit his remedy to damages rather than to rescission of the entire contract.

In contracts for the supply of goods to which the Sale of Goods Act 1979 does not apply, the position is governed by the common law rule on affirmation of the contract. The common law rule appears to be more sympathetic to the consumer, particularly in hire-purchase transactions, in which the periodic payments can be taken into account to recognise the fact that the consumer has had use of the goods during the period of hire.

Farnworth Finance Facilities Ltd v *Attryde*
[1970] 1 WLR 1053
Court of Appeal

LORD DENNING MR at pp. 1059–60: The next question is whether Mr Attryde affirmed the contract. Mr Hamilton points out that Mr Attryde had ridden this bicycle for 4,000 miles. Even after he got it back from the makers on 15 October he had used it for five or six weeks till 23 November and had ridden 3,000 miles on it. Mr Hamilton said that by using it all that time Mr Attryde had affirmed the contract and it was too late for him to repudiate it. But as the argument proceeded, I think that Mr Cazalet gave the right answer. He pointed out that affirmation is a matter of election. A man only affirms a contract when he knows of the defects and by his conduct elects to go on with the contract despite them. In this case Mr Attryde complained from the beginning of the defects and sent the machine back for them to be remedied. He did not elect to accept it unless they were remedied. But the defects were never satisfactorily remedied. When the rear chain broke, it was the last straw. It showed that the machine could not be relied upon. This knowledge was not brought home to him until this last final incident. Mr Attryde was entitled to say then: 'I am not going on with this machine any longer. I have tried it long enough.' After all, it was a contract of hiring. The machine was not his until the three years had been completed, and the price paid. Owing to the defects, Mr Attryde was entitled to throw up the hiring: to say he would have no more to do with it; and to claim damages. The judge found that Mr Attryde did not affirm the contract and I agree with him.

I may add that even if Mr Attryde had affirmed the contract (so that he would be liable to pay the instalments), nevertheless Mr Hamilton conceded quite rightly that Mr Attryde would still have been able to claim damages for the fundamental breach. The exception clauses would not protect the finance company. But I need not go into that question because in my view there has ben no affirmation. Mr Attryde was entitled to reject the machine and claim damages against the finance company. I may say that the finance company supported Mr Attryde. They were quite ready to admit that this machine was unroadworthy, but they claimed to be indemnified by the dealers.

There is one other point, and that is on damages. Mr Hamilton said that Mr Attryde ought to give credit for the use which he had of the bicycle for some 4,000 miles. He relied on *Charterhouse Credit Co. Ltd* v *Tolly* [1963] 2 QB 683 where such a credit was allowed. But it seems to me that the value of any use had by Mr Attryde is offset by the great amount of trouble he had. So no credit need be given for the use. I see no reason for interfering with the award of the judge on damages.

So the finance company are liable to Mr Attryde. But they are entitled to claim over against the dealers on the express promise that the machine was in a roadworthy condition. They can recover against them the full amount of £149 1s., and for the £195 9s. 10d. they have to pay Mr Attryde. The judge so ordered. I find that there is no fault to be found with the judgment of the judge in this case, and I would dismiss the appeal.

3.3.1.3.2   Damages

Sale of Goods Act 1979

53.   Remedy for breach of warranty

(2)   The measure of damages for breach of warranty is the estimated loss directly and naturally resulting, in the ordinary course of events, from the breach of warranty.

(3)   In the case of breach of warranty of quality such loss is prima facie the difference between the value of the goods at the time of delivery to the buyer and the value they would have had if they had fulfilled the warranty.

Kemp v *Intasun Holidays Ltd*
(1988) 7 Tr LR 161
Court of Appeal

For facts see 3.2.1.3.2 and see extracts from this case quoted in 10.8.6.2.

3.3.2 Tortious obligations

For text see 3.3.2.1.

For materials on consumer safety see chapter 8. For materials on consumer services see chapter 10. For materials on advertising law see chapter 11.

3.4 THE CRIMINAL LAW AS A MEANS OF CONSUMER PROTECTION

While the civil law serves to provide a means of compensation for harm suffered by consumers, the criminal law serves to deter manufacturers and retailers from specified forms of trading abuse. The principal means of control is the strict liability criminal offence which is employed as a means of encouraging the business community to reach high standards.

Examples of the use of the criminal law as a means of consumer protection include the Trade Descriptions Act 1968, the Consumer Credit Act 1974, the Consumer Protection Act 1987, parts II and III, and the Food Safety Act 1990, which between them seek to create broad statutory standards designed to safeguard the consumer's interests in economic well-being and safety.

The statutory offences created by these statutes are enforced by public officials at public expense and thus avoid one of the failings of the civil law which, for the most part, can only be enforced by the private initiative of the individual consumer.

3.4.1 The use of the strict liability criminal offence as a means of consumer protection

If a criminal offence is said to be one of strict liability, this means that the prosecution is relieved of the responsibility of proving that the offender has the necessary *mens rea* as to one or some of the elements of the *actus reus* of the crime. Sometimes, the phrase 'absolute' liability is used to describe this phenomenon, but this is a misleading description as the defendant must be aware of his act or failure to act before he can be convicted of an offence.

Due to the presence of a number of statutory defences, it is sometimes said that offences of strict liability will involve an element of negligence on the part of the offender, but in the context of consumer protection, the nature of the wrong may need to be considered. In particular, it would appear that very high standards are required where food for human consumption is concerned, and it is possible for a food producer to be convicted where it appears that he has done virtually everything in his power to avoid the commission of an offence (*Parker* v *Alder* [1899] 1 QB 20; *Smedleys Ltd* v *Breed* [1974] AC 839). Arguably, this approach conflicts with the approach adopted, *obiter*, by four members of the House of Lords in *Alphacell Ltd* v *Woodward* [1972] AC 824 that a person charged with an offence of strict liability should not be convicted if the commission of the offence was due to the act of a stranger or an act of nature and where no reasonable precautions could have been taken to prevent the act in question.

3.4.1.1 When is strict liability imposed by consumer protection legislation? Ordinarily, there is a presumption in favour of *mens rea*, but this may be displaced by the wording of the statute creating the offence or by the subject-matter with which the statute deals (*Sherras* v *De Rutzen* [1895] 1 QB 918, at p. 921 per Wright J). Furthermore, in some instances, it may be necessary to go outside the words of the statute and examine the context in which the statutory words are used and the mischief aimed at by the Act (*Sweet* v *Parsley* [1970] AC 132).

3.4.1.1.1   Reading the words of the statute   Some statutory provisions contain clear words to the effect that proof of *mens rea* is a requirement. For example, if the statute provides that an offence is committed where a person knowingly or recklessly makes a false statement of a prohibited nature, it would seem to follow that the offence is not one of strict liability. The Trade Descriptions Act 1968, s. 14(1), contains these words, yet the reference to 'knowingly' has been construed by the House of Lords in *Wings Ltd* v *Ellis* [1984] 3 All ER 577 to create an offence of 'semi-strict liability'. It was held that a person can make a false statement innocently, but if he later discovers its falsity and takes insufficient precautions to correct the false impression created by it, he commits an offence.

If the statute contains provisions which require an offence to be committed knowingly and others which make no reference to that word, it can normally be assumed that the latter are offences of strict liability. In *Pharmaceutical Society of Great Britain* v *Storkwain Ltd* (1986) 83 Cr App R 359, the question arose whether the Medicines Act 1968, s. 58(2)(a), created an offence of strict liability. The relevant provision prohibits the sale by retail of specified substances except in accordance with a medical practitioner's prescription. Other provisions of the same Act require the offences they create to be committed knowingly, but s. 58(2)(a) was silent on the matter. It was held that the offence created was one of strict liability. Since Parliament had gone to the trouble of identifying those offences which required proof of *mens rea* it could be assumed that where it remained silent, the intention was to create an offence of strict liability.

A further aid to the interpretation of consumer legislation lies in the presence or absence of 'no negligence' defences, such as may be found in the Trade Descriptions Act 1968, the Fair Trading Act 1973 and the Consumer Protection Act 1987. It may be assumed that if Parliament has gone to the trouble of providing an escape route for the person who has offended without negligence, then there is an intention to punish the negligent offender (*Clode* v *Barnes* [1974] 1 All ER 1166).

Consumer protection legislation often makes use of certain words some of which have been interpreted to imply that proof of mens rea is a requirement. For example, it would be unusual for an offence of 'permitting' something to happen to be treated as one of strict liability, since a person cannot permit something without knowing this. However, a person can unwittingly 'cause' an event with the result that the offence of causing the sale of a short measure of whisky is a crime of strict liability (*Sopp* v *Long* [1970] 1 QB 518). Similarly, since the acts of sale or supply can be performed by a person other than the contractual seller, the presence of the words 'selling' or 'supplying' imply the existence of a strict liability offence.

3.4.1.1.2   The context and subject-matter of the statutory provision   If the mischief aimed at by the statute is one which public policy demands should be kept under control, the imposition of strict liability may be justified.

The social purposes served by consumer protection legislation fall into two broad categories, namely, to protect public health and safety (Food Safety Act 1990 and the Consumer Protection Act 1987) and to protect consumer economic interests (Trade Descriptions Act 1968; Fair Trading Act 1973; Consumer Credit Act 1974). Considering the social purpose of an enactment is not the only relevant factor. Other matters which should also be considered include the nature of the crime, the punishment, the absence of social obloquy, the particular mischief and the field of activity in which it occurs (*Sweet* v *Parsley* [1970] AC 132 at p. 156 per Lord Pearce).

Consideration of these matters in the context of consumer protection legislation has led the courts to the view that if there is something a business can do to improve its operations, this justifies the imposition of strict liability (*Tesco Supermarkets Ltd* v *Nattrass* [1972] AC 153 at p. 194 per Lord Diplock). This is not to say that liability is imposed in every case, because a conviction might not serve any useful purpose. It is important that strict liability should only be imposed if it assists in the enforcement of the statute by promoting greater vigilance (*Gammon (Hong Kong) Ltd* v *Attorney-General of Hong Kong* [1984] 2 All ER 503 at p. 508 per Lord Scarman) and that the impression of searching for a luckless victim should not be given. It could be said that this principle went astray in *Smedleys Ltd* v *Breed* [1974] AC 839 where it appears that there was little the defendants could have done to improve their business so as to avoid the presence of a well sterilised caterpillar in one of their tins of processed peas. Since the case involved food intended for human consumption the decision might have been justified on the basis that it operated as a salutary warning to food processors that they had to reach the highest possible standards, but the doubt remains whether there was anything more Smedleys could have done.

3.4.1.2   Critique of strict liability   It has been argued by some that the imposition of strict criminal liability involves the punishment of the morally blameless and is therefore at variance with the basic purpose of the criminal law. In some instances, this criticism is borne out, particularly where there appears to be little that the defendant can do to avoid liability (see *Smedleys Ltd* v *Breed* [1974] AC 839). In cases of this kind, the exercise of prosecutorial discretion can avoid the unnecessary expenditure of public money, and on occasions enforcement authorities have been urged by the courts to be more discriminatory in selecting their targets for prosecution (*Wings Ltd* v *Ellis* [1984] 3 WLR 965 at p. 975 per Lord Hailsham LC). It should always be appreciated that the criminal law should not be used to bring upon respectable traders who have acted honestly, the unjustified reputation of having acted fraudulently (ibid., loc. cit.). In contrast, if the statute is passed in order to protect the public, that protection should not be undermined in any way (*Wings Ltd* v *Ellis* at p. 978 per Lord Scarman), particularly if the enactment is concerned with maintaining trading standards.

The view expressed by Lord Scarman in *Wings Ltd* v *Ellis* can be justified on the ground that the role of the criminal law in the field of trading standards is preventive rather than punitive and the deterrent effect of the statutory provision lies in the stigma of criminal liability. It may be argued that these statutes are regulatory and do not create 'real' crimes, with the result that there is no need to talk of the 'innocent' defendant as Lord Hailsham did in the same case.

A further objection to the use of the criminal sanction in the field of trading law is that it may create a disrespect for the law (see Tench, *Towards a Middle System of Law* (Consumers' Association, 1981)). This argument is based on the premise that since the crimes created are not regarded as morally reprehensible, it becomes easy to ignore them. Indeed, in some instances, it would appear that a commercial decision has been taken by some retailers to ignore the law. In *Stoke-on-Trent City Council* v *B & Q Retail Ltd* [1984] 2 All ER 332, the problem which faced the enforcement authority was that the defendants appeared to regard the criminal penalties imposed by the Shops Act 1950, s. 47, as insufficient to deter them from opening their do-it-yourself stores on a Sunday. In the event, the city council was able to enforce the law by obtaining a civil injunction, but it is clear that the presence of criminal penalties was outweighed by the defendants' ability to make a profit by ignoring the law.

It may also be argued that offences of the type under consideration are man-made evils which may be bitterly resented if they are regarded as unjust by the trading community (see Williams, *Textbook of Criminal Law*, 2nd ed. (1983) p. 931). Furthermore, there may be a tendency on the part of business to regard fines under consumer protection legislation as 'tiresome pinpricks' which may be shrugged off as an inevitable inconvenience (Borrie [1980] JBL 315 at p. 320). It would appear to follow from this that larger retail organisations, at least, will regard conviction as inevitable and will write the fines off as business overheads. Even the judiciary do not regard strict liability, regulatory offences in the same light as 'real' crimes. They have been described as acts 'which are not criminal in the real sense' (*Sherras* v *De Rutzen* [1895] 1 QB 918 at p. 922 per Wright J) and as 'quasi-criminal' offences which do not involve the disgrace of criminality (*Sweet* v *Parsley* [1970] AC 132).

It has been suggested that crimes which are not criminal in the real sense should not be treated as crimes at all and that civil penalties should be introduced to cover inadvertent transgressions (see Tench, *Towards a Middle System of Law* (Consumers' Association, 1981); Justice, *Breaking the Rules — The Problem of Crimes and Contraventions* (1980). In this way, large sections of the criminal law might be decriminalised and replaced by a middle system between the criminal and the civil law. It is argued that if the stigma of criminality is removed, there would be a greater respect for the law in that a business paying a civil penalty to the victim of the transgression would see this as serving a purpose by compensating someone rather than paying a pointless fine which gets lost in the State machinery.

It should be emphasised that the proposal to decriminalise consumer protection law would not, and should not cover all the present offences. There is a case for retaining the criminal conviction for the purposes of those cases where the offender is clearly at fault. For example, the car dealer who deliberately turns back the odometer reading on a motor vehicle in order to enhance its retail value at the expense of consumers should still be guilty of an offence under the Trade Descriptions Act 1968, s. 1(1)(a), and the supplier of services who knowingly or recklessly misdescribes his product should remain subject to the offences created by the Trade Descriptions Act 1968, s. 14.

While the use of the criminal law as a means of consumer protection has its critics, it should be appreciated that it does serve a useful enforcement role. Enforcement authorities argue that it would be too difficult and time-consuming to prove fault in every case. Moreover, where it is clear that there is little an offender could have done to avoid the commission of the offence in question, enforcement authorities may exercise their discretion not to prosecute. It has been demonstrated that a non-prosecution policy may be adopted where there is insufficient evidence to proceed and where there is evidence of absence of fault on the part of the offender (Smith and Pearson [1969] Crim LR 5). In this respect, the enforcement authority is not merely the instigator of penal proceedings, but is also an adviser and an educator in trading practices.

There are areas in which the use of the penal sanction may be justified. In particular, the law cannot, as a matter of policy, entertain pleas of no fault in areas where very high standards are required. For example, where public health and safety are concerned, there is a strong argument in favour of tight control on the retailing and manufacturing community in order to ensure high standards. Furthermore, it may be argued that in a period of tight regulatory control over particular trading practices, the continued prohibition of such acts through the use of the criminal law has the effect of persuading the public to regard those practices as wrong (Kadish (1963) 30 U Chi L Rev 423).

3.4.2 Statutory defences

While many consumer protection measures impose strict criminal liability, the truly innocent offender will often be able to escape liability where he can show that one of the statutory defences applies to his case. By far the most important of these is the defence that the person charged has taken reasonable precautions and has acted with due diligence in order to avoid the commission of an offence (Trade Descriptions Act 1968, s. 24(1)(b); Fair Trading Act 1973, s. 25(1)(b); Consumer Credit Act 1974, s. 168(1)(b); Weights and Measures Act 1985, s. 34(1); Consumer Protection Act 1987, s. 39(1); Food Safety Act 1990, s. 21(1)). In addition to this, some Acts require the person charged to show that the commission of the offence was also due to a mistake, reliance on information supplied by another, the act or default of another person, an accident or some other event beyond his control.

3.4.2.1   Reasonable precautions and due diligence   It is necessary for the person charged to prove that he has both taken reasonable precautions *and* exercised due diligence in order to avoid the commission of an offence by himself or any person under his control.

The defence contains two distinct elements. It is first necessary for the person charged to show that the initial precautions he has taken are sufficient, but he must also show that he has continued to act diligently thereafter in order to secure compliance with the regulatory scheme.

3.4.2.1.1   Reasonable precautions   What is reasonable is a question of fact which will vary according to the circumstances of each case. Factors which may be relevant are the nature of the establishment operated by the alleged offender, the sort of goods sold and the extent to which a reasonable person would think it right to take the precautions which are being canvassed (*Ashurst* v *Hayes & Benross Trading Co.* (1974 unreported) per Lord Widgery CJ). In particular cases, it may be relevant for the person charged to show that he has obtained supplies from a reputable source (*Sherratt* v *Geralds The American Jewellers Ltd* (1970) 114 SJ 147) or that where there is doubt about the truth of a particular description, a retailer has taken steps to verify it (*Sutton London Borough Council* v *Sanger* (1971) 135 JP 239). In relation to the supply of a second-hand car, the odometer of which has been turned back, a number of reasonable precautions may be taken. The car can be checked over by a mechanic to ensure that its condition roughly corresponds with the mileage reading on the odometer (*Lewis* v *Maloney* [1977] Crim LR 436). Alternatively, a previous owner can be consulted to discover what the mileage reading was when he disposed of the car (*Wandsworth London Borough Council* v *Bentley* [1980] RTR 429; cf. *Crook* v *Howell's Garages (Newport) Ltd* [1980] RTR 434). Where it is not possible to discover the truth a suggested precaution is that the supplier should seek to disclaim responsibility for the accuracy of the mileage reading (*Zawadski* v *Sleigh* [1975] RTR 113) but the extent to which a disclaimer is effective is subject to fairly stringent requirements (see 11.3.1.7). If a retailer supplies goods which are capable of causing injury, it is a reasonable precaution to make random safety checks (*Garrett* v *Boots the Chemist* (1980) 88 ITSA Monthly Rev 238; *Rotherham MBC* v *Raysun (UK) Ltd* (1988) 8 Tr LR 6). Where, as is commonly the case, the alleged offender is a corporate body which employs a large number of people, it must be shown that an adequate training programme has been put into effect (*Tesco Supermarkets Ltd* v *Nattrass* [1972] AC 153). In these circumstances, it would be unreasonable to expect the 'directing mind and will' of the company to exercise personal control over all employees within the organisation, but it is necessary for the company to show that it has set up a tiered structure to ensure that employees at all levels of the company do what is necessary to comply with legal requirements.

Explanations of the reason for committing an offence should not be confused with the taking of reasonable precautions. If a retailer offends due to staff shortages, for example, he is still guilty of an offence, but the explanation may be pleaded in mitigation of penalty (*Marshall* v *Herbert* [1963] Crim LR 506).

3.4.2.1.2 Due diligence Even if the alleged offender can show that he has taken reasonable initial precautions, it is also necessary for him to go further and establish that those precautions have been diligently carried out. For example, in *Tesco Supermarkets Ltd* v *Nattrass* [1972] AC 153, it was not sufficient for the defendants to show that they had a system of training on paper, they also had to show that they had diligently put that system into effect. A requirement of this kind is easy to state, but it is far more difficult to apply in practice. For example, when there has been a major aircraft or passenger ship disaster, a public inquiry into the corporate precautions for avoiding accidents can take months or even years, possibly involving many visits to the company head office and local offices to inspect and sample procedures. In contrast, in a case like *Tesco Supermarkets Ltd* v *Nattrass* the same feat has to be achieved in a much shorter period.

3.4.2.2 Other aspects of the general defences The modern tendency has been to enact defences based on the requirements of due diligence and reasonable precautions without any further requirement of proof. However, some older consumer protection measures also require the offender to show that the commission of the offence was due to some specific act or omission. These include the following.

3.4.2.2.1 Mistake Trade Descriptions Act 1968, s. 24(1)(a); Fair Trading Act 1973, s. 25(1)(a); Consumer Credit Act 1974, s. 168(1)(a).
If the defence of mistake is to succeed, the mistake must be that of the person charged and no one else. The effect of this is that a corporate offender will not be able to rely on the mistake of one of its employees (*Birkenhead Co-operative Society Ltd* v *Roberts* [1970] 1 WLR 1497; *Hall* v *Farmer* [1970] 1 All ER 729), although in these circumstances the defence of act or default of another may be available, subject to the satisfaction of certain procedural requirements.
If the mistake is to be operative, it must be a mistake of fact, thus it would not be open to the person charged to plead that he was unaware that acting in a particular way constitutes the commission of an offence (*Stone* v *Burn* [1911] 1 KB 927).
There appears to be little authority on what sort of mistake will satisfy this requirement, but it would appear reasonable to assume that an inadvertent misdescription might suffice or mistakenly reading a price list (*Butler* v *Keenway Supermarkets Ltd* [1974] Crim LR 560). Possibly, a person could mistakenly believe a description to be correct (cf. contra *Kat* v *Diment* [1951] 1 KB 34 under the Merchandise Marks Act 1887, s. 2).

3.4.2.2.2 Reliance on information supplied by another Trade Descriptions Act 1968, s. 24(1)(a); Fair Trading Act 1973, s. 25(1)(a); Consumer Credit Act 1974, s. 168(1)(a); Food Safety Act 1990, s. 21(3)(a).
The presumed purpose of this defence is to protect the likes of advertising agencies and publishers who may rely on information supplied to them by their clients. The defence will also extend further to cover retailers who rely on information supplied to them by others (*Sherratt* v *Geralds The American*

Jewellers Ltd (1970) 114 SJ 147; Food Safety Act 1990, s. 21(3)). In order to avail himself of this defence, it is necessary for the person charged to show that the source of the information is one on which it is reasonable for him to rely (*Barker* v *Hargreaves* [1981] RTR 197; *Sutton London Borough Council* v *Sanger* (1971) 135 JP 239). Thus it would not be reasonable to rely on an MOT certificate as evidence of roadworthiness since the certificate specifically states that it should not be treated in this way. Furthermore, if a person relies on suspect information, it can hardly be said that he has taken reasonable precautions to guard against the commission of an offence.

It would appear that a mileage reading on a car's odometer can be regarded as information supplied by the previous owner. Similarly, information printed on the packaging in which goods are supplied could also fall within the scope of this defence. However, it may be objected that the true purpose of this defence is to allow the offender to rely only on that information which is supplied exclusively to him and that it was not intended to cover information intended for general consumption (see Mickleburgh, *Consumer Protection* (1979) p. 306).

Where the defence is relied upon, it is necessary for the person charged to give seven days' notice to the prosecution. Furthermore, all available information relating to the identity of the supplier must be disclosed in order to assist the prosecution should they decide to pursue him instead (Trade Descriptions Act 1968, s. 24(2); Fair Trading Act 1973, s. 25(2); Consumer Credit Act 1974, s. 168(2); Consumer Protection Act 1987, s. 39(2); Food Safety Act 1990, s. 21(5)).

3.4.2.2.3 Act or default of another   Trade Descriptions Act 1968, s. 24(1)(a); Fair Trading Act 1973, s. 25(1)(a); Consumer Credit Act 1974, s. 168(1)(a); Consumer Protection Act 1987, s. 39(1); Food Safety Act 1990, s. 21(3))

If the person charged gives seven days notice of an intention to rely upon this defence in order to allow for the identification of the person concerned (Trade Descriptions Act 1968, s. 24(2); Fair Trading Act 1973, s. 25(2); Consumer Credit Act 1974, s. 168(2); Consumer Protection Act 1987, s. 39(2); Food Safety Act 1990, s. 21(5)), that person may be proceeded against directly, under what is known as the bypass procedure (Trade Descriptions Act 1968, s. 23; Fair Trading Act 1973, s. 24; Consumer Protection Act 1987, s. 40(1); Food Safety Act 1990, s. 20). The effect of this is that a retailer who technically offends against the Trade Descriptions Act 1968, for example, may be able to set up the defence that the commission of the offence was due to the act or default of another, and it may be determined by the enforcement authority that the policy of the Act is best served by prosecuting that other person. Ordinarily, this will involve the prosecution of a corporate offender, for example where a manufacturer is proceeded against instead of the retailer. However, on occasions, the by-pass procedure has been used against individual employees within a large organisation (*Whitehead* v *Collett* [1975] Crim LR 53), although this is not possible under the Consumer Protection Act 1987, since the employee does not act in the course of a business (Consumer Protection Act 1987, s. 40(1)).

The act or default defence raises three important issues. First, it is necessary for the person charged to give sufficient information to allow the other person to be identified. It is not sufficient for the person seeking to set up the defence to argue that an unidentified person is to blame for the commission of the offence. Thus a corporate offender cannot avoid liability by saying that one of a number of employees must have been at fault. Instead, a particular employee must be identified (*McGuire* v *Sittingbourne Co-operative Society Ltd* [1976] Crim LR 268). Secondly, it must be decided what constitutes an act or default and thirdly, it must be established that the act or default is that of a person other than the person first charged with the commission of an offence under the relevant legislation.

It is necessary for there to be a causal connection between the offence committed by the person charged and the act or default of the other party. Thus if the act or default of the other does not cause the person charged to commit an offence, the defence cannot be pleaded (*Tarleton Engineering Co. Ltd* v *Nattrass* [1973] 1 WLR 1261). Furthermore, it would appear to be the case that the act or default of the other must be wrongful. Thus if a manufacturer supplies to a retailer material which complies with legal requirements and the retailer subsequently supplies the same material to a consumer at a time when new regulations render its supply unlawful, there is no wrongful act or default on the part of the manufacturer (*Noss Farm Products* v *Lillico* [1945] 2 All ER 609 see also *Lill Holdings Ltd* v *White* [1979] RTR 120). However, on a literal interpretation of the wording of the defence, there is no specific requirement that there should be a negligent or wrongful act or default. Therefore, it may be argued that the innocence of the offender is a matter relevant only to sentence if that person is proceeded against under the bypass procedure (*Lindley* v *Horner & Co. Ltd* [1950] 1 All ER 234).

Once it has been decided that there is an act or default, it must then be determined whether it is that of another person. In the case of individual offenders this will be a simple process, but problems may arise where a corporate offender wishes to set up the act or default of an employee as the basis for a defence. In *Tesco Supermarkets Ltd* v *Nattrass* [1972] AC 153, it was held that it is necessary to distinguish between the corporate identity of a company and mere employees. An official who forms part of the directing mind and will of the company is identified with the company itself and an act or default on the part of such a person is treated as the act or default of the company. In such a case, the official, such as a director, senior manager or company secretary may be liable as well as the company (Trade Descriptions Act 1968, s. 20; Fair Trading Act 1973, s. 132; Consumer Credit Act 1974, s. 169; Consumer Protection Act 1987, s. 40(2); Food Safety Act 1990, s. 36). A wrong committed by a junior employee or even a branch manager is an act or default of another person, with the result that the corporate offender may set this up as a defence, if it can be shown that reasonable precautions have been taken and due diligence exercised. The effects of this identification doctrine can be criticised on the ground that a person such as a branch manager of a supermarket is surely acting on behalf of the company in supervising the workforce and carrying out the wishes of directors and area managers.

3.4.2.2.4   Accident or some other cause beyond the defendant's control   Trade Descriptions Act 1968, s. 24(1)(a); Fair Trading Act 1973, s. 25(1)(a); Consumer Credit Act 1974, s. 168(1)(a).

The word 'accident' must be read in the light of the words 'beyond the defendant's control'. This means that where an employee accidentally causes the commission of an offence, this defence is not available (*Hall* v *Farmer* [1970] 1 All ER 729). In this case, the employer must plead act or default of another and satisfy the requirement of seven days' written notice in this respect.

What does constitute an accident is not entirely clear, but it would appear that an unforeseen mechanical breakdown may fall into this category (*Bibby-Cheshire* v *Golden Wonder Ltd* [1972] 1 WLR 1487). However, it is essential to show that reasonable precautions have also been taken to avoid the commission of an offence.

3.5   CRIMINAL LAW AS A MEANS OF CONSUMER PROTECTION – MATERIALS FOR CONSIDERATION

3.5.1   The use of the strict liability criminal offence as a means of consumer protection

For text see 3.4.1.

The reason for construing consumer protection legislation as creating strict liability criminal offences are numerous, but the most important are public policy related.

Tesco Supermarkets Ltd v *Nattrass*
[1972] AC 153
House of Lords

LORD DIPLOCK [speaking of the now repealed Trade Descriptions Act 1968, s. 11(2)] said at p. 194: Consumer protection, which is the purpose of statutes of this kind, is achieved only if the occurrence of the prohibited acts or omissions is prevented. It is the deterrent effect of penal provisions which protects the consumer from the loss he would sustain if the offence were committed. If it is committed he does not receive the amount of any fine. As a tax-payer he will bear part of the expense of maintaining a convicted offender in prison.

The loss to the consumer is the same whether the acts or omissions which result in his being given inaccurate or inadequate information are intended to mislead him or are due to carelessness or inadvertence. So is the corresponding gain to the other party to the business transaction with the consumer in the course of which those acts or omissions occur. Where, in the way that business is now conducted, they are likely to be acts or omissions of employees of that party and subject to his orders, the most effective method of deterrence is to place upon the employer the responsibility of doing everything which lies within his power to prevent his employees from doing anything which will result in the commission of an offence.

This, I apprehend, is the rational and moral justification for creating in the field of consumer protection, as also in the field of public health and safety, offences of 'strict liability' for which an employer or principal, in the course of whose business the offences were committed, is criminally liable, notwithstanding that they are due to acts or omissions of his servants or agents which were done without his knowledge or consent or even were contrary to his orders. But this rational and moral justification does not extend to penalising an employer or principal who has done everything that he can reasonably be expected to do by supervision or inspection, by improvement of his business methods or by exhorting those whom he may be expected to control or influence to prevent the commission of the offence (see *Lim Chin Aik* v *The Queen* [1963] AC 160, 174; *Sweet* v *Parsley* [1970] AC 132, 163). What the employer or principal can reasonably be expected to do to prevent the commission of an offence will depend upon the gravity of the injury which it is sought to prevent and the nature of the business in the course of which such offences are committed. The Trade Descriptions Act 1968 applies to all businesses engaged in the supply of goods and services. If considerations of cost and business practicability did not play a part in determining what employers carrying on such business could reasonably be expected to do to prevent the commission of an offence under the Act, the price to the public of the protection afforded to a minority of consumers might well be an increase in the cost of goods and services to consumers generally.

My lords, I approach the question of construction of the Trade Descriptions Act 1968 in the expectation that Parliament intended it to give effect to a policy of consumer protection which does have rational and moral justification.

Since the imposition of strict liability can be justified if it promotes greater vigilance on the part of traders, it follows that it should not be imposed where nothing more can be done by the trader.

Smedleys Ltd v *Breed*
[1974] AC 839
House of Lords

For the facts see 3.4.1.1.2.

VISCOUNT DILHORNE at p. 856: In deciding whether or not to prosecute are they not to have regard to the general interests of consumers? I do not find anything in the Act imposing on them the duty to prosecute automatically whenever an offence is known or suspected and I cannot believe that they should not consider whether the general interests of consumers were likely to be affected when deciding whether or not to institute proceedings.

In this case when full information was given by the appellants before the information was laid, I am, I must confess, entirely at a loss to see on what grounds it could have been thought that a prosecution was desirable to protect the general interests of consumers.

The exercise by food and drugs authorities of discretion in the institution of criminal proceedings and the omission to do so where they consider that a prosecution will serve no useful purpose is no more the exercise of a dispensing power than the omission of the law officers, the Director of Public Prosecutions and the police to prosecute for an offence. I have never heard it suggested that the failure of the police to prosecute for every traffic offence which comes to their notice is an exercise by them of a dispensing power.

No duty is imposed on them to prosecute in every single case and although this Act imposes on the food and drugs authorities the duty of prosecuting for offences under section 2 it does not say — and I would find it surprising if it had — that they must prosecute in every case without regard to whether the public interest will be served by a prosecution.

What this litigation has cost I dread to think. A great deal of the time of the courts has been occupied. I cannot see that any advantage to the general body of consumers has or will result, apart, perhaps, from the exposition of the law.

In cases where it is apparent that a prosecution does not serve the general interests of consumers, the justices may think fit, if they find that the Act has been contravened, to grant an absolute discharge.

In similar vein see also *Wings Ltd* v *Ellis* [1984] 3 WLR 965 at pp. 973-4 per Lord Hailsham.

3.5.1.1 Critique of the use of strict liability criminal offences as a means of consumer protection   For text see 3.4.1.2.

Some people argue that confusing regulatory offenders with 'real criminals' is counter-productive and that an alternative to the use of the criminal law should be found.

Tench, *Towards a Middle System of Law*
(Consumers' Association, 1981), pp. 20-21.

The result of the growth of crimes of strict liability is that people convicted of them and members of the public who hear of them, no longer regard them as 'criminal in any real sense'.

Crimes which are not crimes in any real sense have no business being crimes at all. The answer is to transform their character, so that they continue to be forbidden and remain unlawful, but that they cease to be crimes. Sanctions — in the form of civil penalties — could be introduced for such transgressions. If they were, Parliament, the courts, enforcement agencies, the public, to say nothing of the transgressors themselves, would have an altogether more appropriate attitude to the law.

Many of the problems that arise from enacting offences of strict liability would be eased by adopting civil penalties as the sanction. One of the deficiencies of the present system is the 'all or nothing at all' approach. A trader who has committed a technical infringement (the canners in the case concerning the caterpillar in the tin of peas, for instance) either gets prosecuted, convicted and fined, with all the rigmarole of the criminal law, or he gets away with it completely. In marginal cases, the prosecuting authority decides, behind closed doors, and according to criteria which are neither publicly accounted for, nor uniform throughout the land, whether or not to prosecute. In fairness to him, as well as to the trader, there ought to be a third option. This is what the middle system of law would provide.

Those at present prosecuted and convicted for technical offences would cease to feel a sense of grievance or outrage at being branded criminals for acts which were not 'criminal in any real sense'. Most, however, recognise the need for a law on the subject, and that this necessarily entails some sanction. The payment of a civil penalty for such infringements would generally feel quite different from the payment of a fine, although the cost may be the same.

. . . the actual fine is sometimes nominal. Under the new system, the court may well feel much more at ease in awarding a civil penalty that really hurts, once the obloquy of a criminal conviction is removed from the transgression. So far as prosecution policy is concerned, enforcement agencies may well feel more relaxed about proceeding with a claim for an infringement of the law, when the outcome will be the award of a civil penalty.

The criminal law will always be there to deal with cases which are 'criminal in any real sense': for matters involving fraud, for instance, in the area of consumer affairs. The introduction of a middle system of law, with civil penalties as the sanction,would provide nothing more than an additional option to enforcing agencies. They could still prosecute for a crime, where they were dealing with crooks, and could prove it. One of the disadvantages of the present system is that the distinction between real crooks and technical offenders is not clear.

3.5.2 Statutory defences

For text see 3.4.2.

Trade Descriptions Act 1968

24. Defence of mistake, accident, etc.

(1) In any proceedings for an offence under this Act it shall, subject to subsection
(2) of this section, be a defence for the person charged to prove—

(a) that the commission of the offence was due to a mistake or to reliance on information supplied to him or to the act or default of another person, an accident or some other cause beyond his control; and

(b) that he took all reasonable precautions and exercised all due diligence to avoid the commission of such an offence by himself or any person under his control.

(2) If in any case the defence provided by the last foregoing subsection involves the allegation that the commission of the offence was due to the act or default of another person or to reliance on information supplied by another person, the person charged shall not, without leave of the court, be entitled to rely on that defence unless, within a period ending seven clear days before the hearing, he has served on the prosecutor a notice in writing giving such information identifying or assisting in the identification of that other person as was then in his possession.

Food Safety Act 1990

21.—(1) In any proceedings for an offence under any of the preceding provisions of this part (in this section referred to as 'the relevant provision'), it shall, subject to subsection (5) below, be a defence for the person charged to prove that he took all reasonable precautions and exercised all due diligence to avoid the commission of the offence by himself or by a person under his control.

For subsections (3) and (4) see 9.6.4.

3.5.2.1 Reasonable precautions and due diligence   For text see 3.4.2.1.

The purpose of the statutory defences is, so far as possible, to relieve the non-negligent offender of liability.

Tesco Supermarkets Ltd v *Nattrass*
[1972] AC 153
House of Lords

A branch manager employed by the defendants had allowed a misleading indication of the sale price of packets of soap powder to be displayed in the store he managed. The defendants were charged with the commission of an offence under the (now repealed) Trade Descriptions Act 1968, s. 11(2), but claimed that they had set up a proper system of education and training with the result that they had taken reasonable precautions and acted with due diligence to avoid the commission of an offence.

LORD MORRIS at p. 179–81: How, then, does a company take all reasonable precautions and exercise all due diligence? The very basis of section 24 involves that some contraventions of the Act may take place and may be contraventions by persons under the control of the company even though the company itself has taken all reasonable precautions and exercised all due diligence and that the company will not be criminally answerable for such contraventions. How, then, does a company act? When is some act the act of the company as opposed to the act of a servant or agent of the company (for which, if done within the scope of employment, the company will be civilly answerable)? Within the scheme of the Act now being considered an indication is given (which need not necessarily be an all-embracing indication) of those who may personify 'the directing mind and will' of the company. The question in the present case becomes a question whether the company as a company took all reasonable precautions and exercised all due diligence. The magistrates so found and so held. The magistrates found and held that 'they' (i.e. the company) had satisfied the provisions of section 24(1)(b). The reason why the Divisional Court felt that they could not accept that finding was that they considered that the company had delegated its duty to the manager of the shop. The manager was, they thought, 'a person whom the appellants had delegated in respect of that particular shop their duty to take all reasonable precautions and exercise all due diligence to avoid the commission' of an offence. Though the magistrates were satisfied that the company had set up an efficient system there had been 'a failure by someone to whom the duty of carrying out the system was delegated properly to carry out that function'.

My lords, with respect I do not think that there was any feature of delegation in the present case. The company had its responsibilities in regard to taking all reasonable precautions and exercising all due diligence. The careful and effective discharge of those responsibilities required the directing mind and will of the company. A system had to be created which could rationally be said to be so designed that the commission of offences would be avoided. There was no delegation of the duty of taking precautions and exercising diligence. There was no such delegation to the manager of a particular store. He did not function as the directing mind or will of the company. His duties as the manager of one store did not involve managing the company. He was one who was being directed. He was one who was employed but he was not a delegate to whom the company passed on its responsibilities. He had certain duties which were the result of the taking by the company of all reasonable precautions and of the exercising by the company of all due diligence. He was a person under the control of the company and on the assumption that there could be proceedings against him, the company would by section 24(1)(b) be absolved if the company had taken all proper steps to avoid the commission of an offence by him. To make the company automatically liable for an offence committed by him would be to ignore the subsection. He was, so to speak, a cog in the machine which was devised: it was not left to him to devise it. Nor was he within what has been called the 'brain area' of the company. If the company had taken all reasonable precautions and exercised all due diligence to ensure that the machine could and should run effectively then some breakdown due to some action or failure on the part of 'another person' ought not to be attributed to the company or to be regarded as the action or failure of the company itself for which the company was to be criminally responsible. The defence provided by section 24(1) would otherwise be illusory.

Note
Is it fair to say that Tesco was lucky and that more could have been done to avoid the commission of an offence? How does the decision in *Tesco Supermarkets Ltd* v *Nattrass* compare with that in *Smedleys Ltd* v *Breed* [1974] AC 839? Were Smedleys unfairly convicted because the wording of the statutory defences, at the time, was inadequate? How would Smedleys fare under the defences provided by the Food Safety Act 1990, s. 21?

3.5.2.2   Act or default of another   For text see 3.4.2.2.3.
   One effect of a successful plea of act or default of another is that 'the other' can be prosecuted under the 'bypass procedure'.

Trade Descriptions Act 1968

23.   Offences due to fault of other person
Where the commission by any person of an offence under this Act is due to the act or default of some other person that other person shall be guilty of the offence, and a person may be charged with and convicted of the offence by virtue of this section whether or not proceedings are taken against the first-mentioned person.

Consumer Protection Act 1987

40.   Liability of persons other than principal offender
   (1)   Where the commission by any person of an offence to which section 39 above applies is due to an act or default committed by some other person in the course of any business of his, the other person shall be guilty of the offence and may be proceeded against and punished by virtue of this subsection whether or not proceedings are taken against the first mentioned person.

The 'bypass procedure' raises the question whether there is a causal connection between the act or default of the other and the commission of the offence by the person first charged.

Tarleton Engineering Co. Ltd v *Nattrass*
[1973] 1 WLR 1261
Queen's Bench Division

WIEN J at pp. 1269–70: They [the magistrates] further find that at the time of the auction of the defendants' car on 10 September 1971, a vendor who wished to guarantee the mileage was specifically required to write 'guaranteed' against the mileage figure on the entry form. A possible inference from that is that in the absence of the word 'guaranteed' it was not to be assumed that the mileage recorded was correct. That is getting very near to a possible disclaimer. There was no finding that the defendants themselves turned back the mileometer.

That was an entirely erroneous approach by the justices to the question whether the commission of the offence by Thornton Car Sales was due to the act or default of the defendants. One can sympathise with the justices who were doubtless led astray by a close examination of the contractual position as between the defendants and the auctioneers. They were misled largely by the submissions made on behalf of the prosecutor. It was a submission made that Mr Obrusik on behalf of the defendants was applying a false trade description to the car and thus had failed to observe condition 18(a). Whilst not guaranteeing the accuracy of the mileage, the failure to disclaim its accuracy was, it was said, an act or default due to which the offence by Thornton Car Sales was committed; but there was no causal connection that was relied upon in that submission.

In effect, in this court, the submission on behalf of the prosecutor was that the acts or defaults of the defendants were equal to and coextensive with those of Thornton Car Sales. To regard the case in such a light involves ignoring the justices' findings and conclusions. On the facts as found the commission of the offence by Thornton Car Sales was quite independent of and was unrelated to anything done or omitted by the defendants.

The final difficulty is to determine who is another person.

Tesco Supermarkets Ltd v *Nattrass*
[1972] AC 153
House of Lords

VISCOUNT DILHORNE at pp. 184–8: If the chain of supermarkets owned and run by the appellants, some 800 we were told, were owned and run by an individual or partnership, then it could not be disputed that Mr Clement was another person within the meaning of the subsection. Does he cease to be 'another person' because the stores are owned by a limited company?

Further, if the stores were owned and run by an individual or partnership and that individual or the partners had themselves exercised all due diligence, is it right that they should be held not to have done so because a shop manager of theirs has not done so? And has the statute here to be interpreted differently where a company is accused than where the accused is an individual?

Prima facie one would have thought it unlikely that Parliament intended 'another person' to have a different meaning in relation to a company from that in relation to an individual or that the ambit of section 24(1)(b) should differ depending on whether the owner of the shop was a company or individual.

If an offence under section 11(2) is committed by a company, the acts necessary to constitute the offence must have been done by individuals in their employ. Here the question is not whether the company is criminally liable and responsible for the act of a particular servant but whether it can escape from that liability by proving that it exercised all due diligence and took all reasonable precautions and that the commission of the offence was due to the act or omission of another person. That, in my view, is a very different question from that of a company's criminal responsibility for its servants' acts.

The Act dos not exclude a person in the employ of a company from being 'another person'. In *Beckett* v *Kingston Bros (Butchers) Ltd* [1970] 1 QB 606, it was argued that it did. That argument was rejected by Bridge J, and rightly, in my opinion. If it had prevailed, the statutory defence would seldom avail an accused company for seldom would it be possible to prove that the act or default was that of someone not employed by the company. . . .

That an employer, whether a company or an individual, may reasonably appoint someone to secure that the obligations imposed by the Act are observed cannot be doubted. Only by doing so can an employer who owns and runs a number of shops or a big store hope to secure that the Act is complied with, but the appointment by him of someone to discharge the duties imposed by the Act in no way relieves him from having to show that he has taken all reasonable precautions and had exercised all due diligence if he seeks to establish the statutory defence.

He cannot excuse himself if the person appointed fails to do what he is supposed to do unless he can show that he himself has taken such precautions and exercised such diligence. Whether or not he has done so is a question of fact and while it may be that the appointment of a competent person amounts in the circumstances of a particular case to the taking of all reasonable precautions, if he does nothing after making the appointment to see that proper steps are in fact being taken to comply with the Act, it cannot be said that he has exercised all due diligence.

. . . one has in relation to a company to determine who is or who are, for it may be more than one, in actual control of the operations of the company, and the answer to be given to that question may vary from company to company depending on its organisation. In my view, a person who is in actual control of the operations of a company or of part of them and who is not responsible to another person in the company for the manner in which he discharges his duties in the sense of being under his orders, cannot be regarded as 'another person' within the meaning of sections 23 and 24(1)(a).

Section 20 provides that where an offence under the Act has been committed by a body corporate and is proved to have been committed with the consent or connivance or to be attributable to any neglect on the part of any director, manager, secretary or other similar officer of the body corporate or any person who was purporting to act in any such capacity, he, as well as the company, is to be guilty of the offence. Parliament by this section may have attempted to identify those who normally constitute the directing mind and will of a company and by this section have sought to make clear that although they are not other persons coming within sections 23 and 24(1)(a), they may still be convicted.

However this may be, shop managers in a business such as that conducted by the appellants — and their number may be of the order of 800 if the appellants have that number of shops — cannot properly be regarded as part of the appellants' directing mind and will and so can come within the reference to 'another person' in sections 23 and 24(1)(a).

3.6 EUROPEAN COMMUNITY OBLIGATIONS

A large body of consumer protection law now emanates from the institutions of the European Community. Positive Community laws may be 'self-executing' or may be of a type which expects member States of the Community to take appropriate action to ensure compliance. Self-executing laws, which include regulations and treaty obligations, take direct effect as part of domestic law and override existing and future Acts of Parliament. Other Community legislation is of a harmonising nature which requires member States to take appropriate action to ensure compliance and does not take effect until such action has been taken.

Most activity, to date, in respect of consumer protection, has been of a harmonising nature. For the future, it is intended to complete the internal market by 1992 and if after that date, the necessary steps to ensure the freedom of movement of goods, services and capital have not been taken by member States, relevant Community obligations may take direct effect in member States if they are not subject to the harmonisation measures taken under art. 100 or 100A of the EEC Treaty.

3.6.1   European Community consumer protection policy

The European Community consumer protection policy has had a chequered history. When the Community was first set up, it is probably fair to say that a consumer protection policy was not envisaged. Article 2 of the EEC Treaty states the mission of the Community to be to promote, *inter alia*, a harmonious development of economic activities and an accelerated raising of the standard of living. To this end the Commission proposed the setting up of a Consumers' Consultative Committee (OJ L283/10.10.73, p. 18) which was required to advise on the development of consumer policy and to represent consumer interests.

Initially, the absence of a clear reference to a consumer protection policy led to some difficulty in justifying the later development of such a policy (see 3.6.1.2), but a policy has nonetheless been promoted. Furthermore, the future development of a consumer protection policy has been substantially enhanced by the provisions of art. 100A of the EEC Treaty, which by way of derogation from art. 100, gives high priority to proposals concerning health, safety, environmental protection and consumer protection in seeking to implement the objectives stated in art. 8A in relation to the establishment of the internal market by 1992.

The early stages of the development of the consumer protection policy have been unspectacular and at one stage the 'action programmes' constituting the first two stages of the consumer protection policy were criticised on the ground that they were singularly lacking in any sort of action (Ken Collins, Chairman, European Parliament Committee on the Environment, Public Health and Consumer Protection, reported in *Consumer Affairs*, vol. 61 (January/February 1983, pp. 61-2).

3.6.1.1   The Community programmes   The First Consumer Protection Programme (annexe to Council Resolution of 14 April 1975; OJ 1975, C92/1) had as its broad objectives the right to safety, the right to choose, the right to be heard and the right to be informed. It addressed issues such as consumer information, education, redress and representation, consumer health and safety, and the legal and economic interests of consumers. Of these issues, the health and safety of consumers was the subject of the greatest number of Directives and Regulations. The object of many of these was to secure the safety of basic foodstuffs such as fruit and vegetables. Other consumer goods affected by the early programme included solvents, food packaging, cosmetics and motor vehicles.

In relation to consumer information and education, Community policy was to ensure that the consumer should be provided with sufficient information to enable him to assess the basic features of goods or services available to him and to be able to make a rational choice between competing products and services. Furthermore, it was the expressed policy of the Community to ensure satisfactory redress for the consumer in respect of any injury or damage caused by defective goods or services.

Laudable though these policies were, it remained the case that little was done during the currency of the first programme to implement them. One Directive on the labelling of the energy consumption of domestic appliances was adopted by the Council in 1979, but little else can be said of the rest of the programme in these respects.

With a view to the protection of consumer economic interests, draft Directives on doorstep selling and producers' liability for defective products were submitted to the Council by the Commission, but it took some time before finalised legislation on these matters was eventually adopted. Directives on misleading advertising and consumer credit were also developed.

In 1981, the Council approved a Second Programme on Consumer Protection Policy (OJ 1971 C133) which reiterated the objectives stated in the first programme and added a new direction for the programme, namely the field of consumer services.

In 1985, the Commission published a critique of the First and Second Programmes (*A New Impetus for Consumer Protection Policy* (COM(85) 314 Final 23.07.85)) which pointed to the dilatory pace at which reform had been achieved and recommended action in respect of health and safety, consumer economic interests and the coordination of consumer policy with other Community policies. One of the principal reasons for the slow pace of change was seen to be the requirement of unanimity under art. 100 of the EEC Treaty, under which the majority of consumer protection measures had been previously promoted. The importance of art. 100A in this respect is that it allows the Council to act by way of a qualified majority (see chapter 2) on a proposal from the Commission in cooperation with the European Parliament. Other reasons for the slow pace of change cited by the Commission in *A New Impetus* included the effects of the deep economic recession of the late 1970s and the early 1980s and that member states may have regarded consumer protection as an internal matter.

Some of the early developments at a Community level have been criticised. In particular, the present Director General of Fair Trading has described the early Directives as falling within three broad categories, namely, irritating and irrelevant; retrograde and well intentioned but damaging to national interests (Borrie, *The Development of Consumer Law and Policy* (1984), p. 106 et seq.).

Those policies regarded as irritating and irrelevant include the consumer credit Directive (OJ L042/12.8.87, p. 48). It was said that since the Directive was based almost wholly on the provisions of the Consumer Credit Act 1974, it was irrelevant on a domestic level. However, it is also the case that legislation similar to the Consumer Credit Act 1974 did not exist in some member States. Accordingly, with a view to harmonisation on a community level, the Directive is to be welcomed.

In its original form, the proposed Directive on misleading advertising was regarded as retrograde in that it did not allow for implementation of its provisions by means of self-regulating codes of practice. This defect was not present in the finalised legislation (OJ L250/19.9.84, p. 17) with the result that the criticism is unfounded.

The third criticism of Community legislation was that some initiatives were damaging to proposed domestic reforms. In particular, it was said that the Directive on product liability (OJ L210/7.8.85 p. 29) may have acted as a barrier to the early implementation of what is now part I of the Consumer Protection Act 1987. However, it may also be argued that proposals for reform of the law in this area had been around for a long time and that it was only concerted effort on the part of the Community that found an element of consensus sufficient to justify legislation. Had the matter been left to individual member states, no change would necessarily have been forthcoming.

Following the criticisms of the earlier policies on consumer protection, in particular, the slow rate of change, the Council has issued a Resolution (OJ C294/22.11.89, p. 1) on Future Priorities for Relaunching Consumer Protection Policy. In particular, it requires the Commission to produce a three-year plan on Community objectives in seeking to protect and promote consumer interests and stipulates a number of priorities in this respect in the light of the intention to move towards the completion of the internal market. It is provided that the consumer protection policy should be integrated into all other common policies; that consumer representation should be improved at a Community level; that general priority should be given to promoting the safety of goods and services and that better information should be made available concerning the quality of goods and services.

3.6.1.2 The legal basis of the consumer protection policy   At one stage, there was some doubt about the legality of the consumer protection policy and it was arguable that such measures were beyond the powers of the Community (see Close, 'The legal basis for the consumer protection programme of the EEC' in *Consumer Law in the EEC*, ed. Woodroffe (1984);(1983) 8 Euro L. Rev 221). However, in the early stages, two provisions of the EEC Treaty were cited as reasons for intervention. Article 100 allows for the issue of Directives for the purpose of the approximation of the laws of member States in relation to the establishment and functioning of the common market. Furthermore, art. 235 of the EEC Treaty allows intervention to secure one of the objectives of the Community where the Treaty itself has failed to provide the necessary powers to achieve that objective (see Indication of Prices of Foodstuffs (OJ 1979/L/158/19)).

For the most part, measures designed to improve the position of consumers have been justified under art. 100. These include Directives concerned with the health and safety of consumers such as those on the packaging and labelling of dangerous substances (see OJ L196/16.8.67, p. 1; OJ L262 27.9.76, p. 201), low-voltage electrical equipment (see OJ 0777 26.3.79, p. 29), the packaging and labelling of solvents (see OJ L189 11.7.73, p. 7; OJ L303 28.11.77, p. 23), cosmetic products (see OJ L262 29.7.76, p. 169), and articles which come into contact with food (see OJ L277 20.10.84, p. 12). Some measures concerned with the economic interests of consumers were also justified under art. 100. These included the product liability Directive (OJ L210 7.8.85, p. 29), the misleading advertising Directive (OJ L250 19.9.84, p. 17), the Directive on contracts negotiated away from business premises (OJ L372 31.12.85, p. 31) and the consumer credit Directive (OJ L042 12.2.87, p. 48).

The difficulty which arose in relation to art. 100 was that in order for harmonising legislation to be justified under that provision, existing laws were required to have a direct effect on the functioning of the common market. It was not always clear that activities legislated against under art. 100 necessarily had such a direct effect (see Close, 'The legal basis for the Consumer Protection Programme of the EEC', in *Consumer Law in the EEC*, ed. Woodroffe (1984)). If this is the case, it is arguable that some of the legislation based on the subsequently developed consumer protection policy had no legal basis.

Subsequently, with a view to the completion of the internal market by 1992, art. 100A(3) made consumer protection an objective of Community measures, with the result that recent legislation is now based on that provision rather than art. 100. Examples include Directives and proposed Directives in respect of toy safety (OJ L187 16.7.88, p. 1), general product safety (OJ C156 27.6.90, p. 8), packaging and labelling of dangerous preparations (OJ L187 16.7.88, p. 14), price indications on goods other than food (OJ L142 9.6.88, p. 19), unfair contract terms in consumer contracts (OJ C243 28.9.90, p. 2) and holidays and package tours (OJ L158 23.6.90, p. 59).

3.6.2 Specific application of European Community law

Community legislation and proposals for change affect a wide range of issues relevant to consumer protection law. In particular Community policy has high regard for the consumer's economic and health and safety interests. Moreover, aspects of Community law are also relevant to advertising and marketing practices and to the issue of consumer information.

In addition to Community legislation and proposals for change, there are also certain fundamental principles of Community law which must be heeded by member States when legislating for certain trading activities. In particular, it is possible that some consumer legislation may restrict the free movement of goods and the right to supply and receive services with the result that it may be unlawful under other aspects of European Community policy.

In relation to the importation of goods, art. 30 of the EEC Treaty seeks to defeat quantitative restrictions and all measures having equivalent effect on imports of goods. Article 34 contains similar provisions in respect of the export of goods. Both these provisions are subject to art. 36 which provides that certain restrictions will be permitted where they are justified on the grounds of public morality, public policy, public security, the protection of the health and life of humans, animals or plants, the protection of national treasures or the protection of industrial and commercial property.

In relation to the supply of services, art. 59 of the EEC Treaty provides that restrictions on the freedom to supply services shall be progressively abolished. However, the freedom to provide services is subject to a number of limitations based on the grounds of public policy, public security or public health (arts 56 and 66). Furthermore, the freedom to supply services in another member State is also limited to the extent that the national conditions for the provision of such services must be satisfied (art. 52(2)). Thus an English lawyer wishing to practise in France must satisfy French professional practice requirements.

3.6.2.1 Quantitative restrictions on the import of goods

A quantitative restriction is one which amounts to a total or partial restriction on imports or exports. Thus a ban by a member State on the import of certain products will contravene art. 30 of the EEC Treaty unless it is justified. In *Commission v United Kingdom* (case 261/85) [1988] 2 CMLR 11, a blanket ban on the import of pasteurised milk from other member States contravened art. 30. A claimed justification under art. 36 on the grounds of public health was dismissed because a blanket ban was not proportionate. Measures less disruptive to Community trade could have been adopted, such as a system for monitoring milk imported into the country. Similarly, if a member State imposes a licensing system upon those who wish to deal in certain types of product, such measures may amount to a quantitative restriction or a measure with equivalent effect (*International Fruit Co. NV v Produktschap voor Groenten en Fruit (No. 2)* (cases 51-4/71) [1971] ECR 1107).

Even if a particular measure does not amount to a quantitative restriction, it may be treated as having equivalent effect. This includes both overtly protective or 'distinctly applicable' measures and 'indistinctly applicable' measures. The latter include apparently justifiable provisions in respect of size and weight or other provisions intended to ensure that goods conform to national standards.

The meaning of a measure having equivalent effect, is amplified in Directive 70/50 (see also *Procureur du Roi v Dassonville* (case 8/74) [1974] ECR 837) which provides that such measures include those which hinder imports or make importation more difficult or costly than the disposal of a domestic product. Also included are those indistinctly applicable measures which fail to satisfy the principle of proportionality invoked in *Internationale Handelsgesellschaft mbH* (case 11/70) [1970] ECR 1125. Thus an absolute ban on the use of additives in beer will contravene art. 30 if the objective of protecting public health can be achieved by less restrictive means (*Commission v Germany* (case 178/84) [1988] 1 CMLR 780). In the circumstances, the ban was not proportionate.

In order to contravene art. 30 it is not necessary to show that there is actually an effect on trade. It is sufficient that the measure is capable of affecting trade between member States. Thus in *Procureur du Roi v Dassonville* (case 8/74) [1974] ECR 837 a Belgian requirement that goods should carry a certificate of origin issued by the State in which goods were manufactured was held to be capable of breaching art. 30 where a French supplier of Scotch whisky was unable to provide such a certificate. The Belgian importer attached a home-made certificate and was prosecuted for forgery, but successfully pleaded the illegality of the certification requirement. The provision was held to be capable of hindering intra-Community trade because it was equivalent to a quantitative restriction.

If a measure is of purely domestic application, it will not contravene art. 30, even if it is restrictive in relation to the sale of goods. Thus provided the measure does not affect intra-Community trade, it will not contravene art. 30. In *Jongeneel Kaas BV* v *Netherlands* (case 237/82) [1982] ECR 483 regulations concerning permitted ingredients in Dutch cheese which applied only to Dutch manufacturers were held to be lawful even though other member States might choose to apply less stringent measures.

A further restriction on the broad *Dassonville* test was laid down in *Rewe-Zentrale AG* v *Bundesmonopolverwaltung für Branntwein* (case 120/78) [1979] ECR 649 (the *Cassis de Dijon case*) in which the court took account of the proportionality principle and sought to make a clearer distinction between distinctly and indistinctly applicable measures. On the facts, the result of the *Cassis de Dijon* case was that there had been a breach of art. 30, but it was also stated that hindrances to the free movement of goods had to be tolerated if they resulted from disparities between national laws relating to the marketing of goods and those laws were necessary to satisfy mandatory requirements relating to the effectiveness of fiscal supervision, the protection of public health, the fairness of commercial transactions and the defence of the consumer. This 'rule of reason' applies to indistinctly applicable measures, but not to distinctly applicable measures which will fall foul of art. 30 unless they are justified under art. 36.

The decision in the *Cassis de Dijon* case is important since the range of permitted restrictions under that rule is wider than the range of lawful restrictions under art. 36. Furthermore, art. 36 contains an exhaustive list of permitted derogations from art. 30, whereas the rule of reason contains a non-exhaustive list of reasons for permitting restrictions on the free movement of goods. However, in the light of the actual result in the *Cassis de Dijon* case, it is essential that the restriction is necessary to protect the interest concerned. Thus, in the *Cassis de Dijon* case a German law which laid down a minimum alcohol content of 25% for certain drinks effectively amounted to a ban on the importation of the French liqueur, cassis, which had an alcohol content of 15-20%, and therefore contravened art. 30. The restriction was defended on the grounds that it was intended to protect public health and to ensure the fairness of commercial transactions, but it was held that these ends could be achieved by other means, such as clear labelling of the product which would not constitute the same hindrance to free trade.

The court also laid down a second principle to the effect that it can be presumed that where goods have been lawfully produced and sold in one member State, they may also be sold in another member State without having to satisfy additional requirements. The presumption is rebuttable where it can be shown that additional requirements are necessary in order to protect an interest covered by the rule of reason.

The presumption arising from the second principle in the *Cassis de Dijon* case is particularly difficult to rebut with the result that very strong evidence will be required to justify a restriction on trade in one member State where another member State does not impose a similar restriction (*Criminal Proceedings against Karl Prantl* (case 16/83) [1984] ECR 1299).

While the way in which art. 30 has been interpreted suggests that restrictions on the free movement of goods will be permitted only where necessary, there is recent evidence that the European Court is prepared to allow certain restrictions and to recognise the interests of individual member States. For example, in *Torfaen Borough Council* v *B & Q plc* (case 145/88) [1990] 1 All ER 129, the restrictions on Sunday trading imposed by the Shops Act 1950, s. 47, were held to be a legitimate part of economic and social policy consistent with the objectives of public interest. Furthermore, it was considered that s. 47 reflected political and economic choices in that it arranged working hours in such a way as to accord with national or regional socio-cultural characteristics. Accordingly, s. 47 was not subject to the provisions of art. 30 and it was for the national court to decide if the measures exceeded what was necessary to achieve the aims of the member State's policy objectives.

3.6.2.2   Permitted derogation from Article 30   Apart from the 'rule of reason' which applies in relation to indistinctly applicable measures, directly applicable measures which constitute a quantitative restriction on trade may still be allowed under art. 36 of the EEC Treaty. This permits such restrictions on the grounds of public morality, public policy, public security, the protection of the health and life of humans, animals and plants, the protection of national treasures and the protection of industrial and commercial property. Of these, the most relevant to the issue of consumer protection would appear to be the protection of the health and life of humans.

To succeed on this ground, it will be necessary to establish a real risk to health. Accordingly, if other member States have adopted methods of assuring the quality of certain types of food, additional restrictions limiting those who can supply that food, purportedly on the ground that such controls ensure freedom from contamination, will not be justified under art. 36 (*Commission* v *United Kingdom (re UHT Milk)* (case 124/81) [1983] ECR 203). However, if there is a risk to the health of consumers from imported produce which does not affect similar domestic produce, restrictions on imports may be justified under art. 36 (*Rewe-Zentralfinanz* v *Landwirtschaftskammer* (case 4/75) [1975] ECR 843).

It is clear that the court will pay high regard to the proportionality test in determining whether an art. 36 justification is made out. Thus if the objective of the restriction can be achieved by other less restrictive means, it is unlikely that an art. 36 justification will be made out. In particular, if the measure adopted by a member State unduly prejudices imports from other member States without subjecting domestic supplies of the same product to similar controls, it is unlikely that the measure will be justified, even if the controls appear to be designed to ensure high product standards.

3.6.2.3 Remaining lawful barriers to trade It is clear from art. 36 and 'the rule of reason' that some lawful barriers to trade will remain, and these may have the effect of preventing the completion of the single market. Accordingly, they have to be dealt with through a programme of harmonisation. It has been seen that the process of harmonisation under art. 100 was hampered by the requirement of unanimity. However, with the advent of art. 100A and the process of qualified majority voting (see chapter 2) there would appear to be a greater chance of harmonisation, particularly since it is clear from art. 8A that the new procedure applies to the free movement of goods, capital and services. It follows that restrictions on trade which fall outside the provisions of art. 30 can be the subject of the harmonisation provisions of the EEC Treaty.

While the use of qualified majority voting is the most important aspect of art. 100A, it also represents a departure from art. 100 in one other important respect. Article 100 only allowed the adoption of Directives, with which member States had to comply by a specified date by means of implementing legislation. However, art. 100A refers to harmonising *measures*, which would appear to include Regulations taking direct effect.

3.6.2.4 Freedom to supply and receive services The issue of supply of services appears to have received less attention than that of the supply of goods. Nevertheless, there are relevant provisions of the EEC Treaty which affect both the supplier and the recipient of a service. In particular, art. 59 of the EEC Treaty provides for the progressive abolition of restrictions on the freedom to supply services, though restrictions on the supply of services may be justified on the grounds of public policy, public security and public health (arts 56 and 66).

With a view towards completing the internal market, the Commission has made the establishment of a common market in services a priority for the future (Commission White Paper, June 1985, COM(85) 310 final). Accordingly, harmonisation of existing laws on the provision of services can be expected.

The freedom to supply services carries with it a complementary right to receive services (*Luisi* v *Ministero del Tesoro* (case 286/82) [1984] ECR 377). Thus a holiday-maker in another member State can claim to be entitled to equal treatment to that offered to nationals in respect of the risk of assault (*Cowan* v *French Treasury* (case 186/87) *The Times*, 13 February 1989). This right was seen as a corollary to the right to receive services. This does not appear to mean that the consumer has complete freedom to receive all services provided by other member States as there are permitted restrictions on the availability of services provided out of public funds (*Belgian State* v *Humbel* (case 236/86) [1989] 1 CMLR 393).

3.6.2.5 Advertising law and freedom of expression General principles of international law are often invoked by the European Court as the basis for principles of Community law. Of particular importance in this respect are the principles contained in the European Convention for the Protection of Human Rights and Fundamental Freedoms 1953. All member States of the European

Community are signatories to this convention and are bound by the principles it lays down. Also of some significance is the fact that the major European Community institutions regard themselves as bound by the fundamental freedoms enshrined in the Human Rights Convention and will take them into account as general principles of law.

In the context of consumer protection law, one of the most important principles established by the Human Rights Convention is that of freedom of expression contained in art. 10, particularly since this appears to extend to 'commercial speech' (*Markt Intern Verlag GmbH & Beerman* v *Germany* [1990] 12 EHRR 161). It follows from this that a number of advertising restrictions apparently imposed for the protection of consumers may infringe art. 10 and may be declared unlawful on the ground that they unnecessarily restrict the advertiser's freedom to put across his message.

Article 10(1) provides that everyone has the right to freedom of expression, including the right to receive and impart information and ideas without interference by public authorities. However, this right is subject to restrictions prescribed by law which are necessary in a democratic society, in the interests of national security, territorial integrity or public safety, for the prevention of disorder or crime, for the protection of health or morals, for the protection of the reputation and rights of others, for preventing the disclosure of information received in confidence, or for maintaining the authority and impartiality of the judiciary (art. 10(2)).

It follows from art. 10(2) that a government wishing to place restrictions on advertising will have to show that the interference is prescribed by law, justified under art. 10(2) and necessary in a democratic society in the sense that there is a pressing social need for control.

3.6.2.5.1 Prescribed by law Article 10 of the European Human Rights Convention applies only where the restriction is prescribed by law. Some of the controls placed upon English advertisers take the form of voluntary codes of practice (see 12.1) and as such are not prescribed by law. While it is the case that 'laws' include unwritten rules such as those developed at common law, it would be difficult, at the present time, to regard codes of practice as laws. However, if Parliament was to impose a duty to trade fairly (see 3.12), one feature of which might be to require compliance with the provisions of a relevant code of practice, the position might then be different.

3.6.2.5.2 Legitimate aims Where freedom of expression is concerned there is a general social interest which justifies its protection. In the case of advertising, competing interests have to be taken into account. While the advertiser should have the freedom to promote his product, the consumer interest and the interests of competitors have to be balanced against this. Thus, if the restriction is legitimately aimed at the protection of the reputation and rights of others, it may not infringe art. 10 (*Markt Intern Verlag GmbH & Beerman* v *Germany* [1990] 12 EHRR 161 at p. 173). However, it may be argued that by giving precedence to one particular interest, the law may unfairly restrict the right to communicate information to others. Accordingly, a heavy burden should fall on the government wishing to impose a restraint on advertising freedom to show that the restriction is not just reasonable, but relevant and sufficient (*Markt Intern Verlag GmbH & Beerman* v *Germany* at p. 176 (joint dissenting opinion); *Handyside* v *United Kingdom* [1979] 1 EHRR 737). If the necessity for the restraint is not convincingly established, then the restriction should be regarded as an infringement of art. 10.

3.6.2.5.3 Necessary in a democratic society Whether a particular restriction is necessary in a democratic society appears to involve a variety of cost-benefit analysis. The court must weigh the requirements of the protection of the reputation and rights of others against the right of the publisher to impart information. While it is the case that consumers deserve protection from misleading and less than objective advertising, the advertiser also has to be given the opportunity to put across his message. In seeking to balance these competing interests, the court will have to take into account the principle of proportionality. In *Markt Intern Verlag GmbH & Beerman* v *Germany* [1990] 12 EHRR 161 a restraining order was placed on the publication of an article in a trade journal which described a consumer complaint against a mail order firm and requested evidence of other such complaints. The restriction was justified, at a national level, on the ground that the statement was contrary to 'honest practices'. A bare majority of the European Court of Human Rights held that the restriction was justified and that there was no infringement of art. 10 because the restraint served to protect the reputation and rights of others (at p. 173). However, it may be objected that the principle of proportionality was not adhered to. While regard should be had to the rights of others, an outright ban on publication might be said to go too far. For example, a more appropriate control might have been to allow the institution of civil or criminal proceedings (at p. 178 per Judge Pettiti (dissenting)).

3.7 EUROPEAN COMMUNITY OBLIGATIONS – MATERIALS FOR CONSIDERATION

3.7.1 European Community consumer protection policy

For text see 3.6.1.

EEC Treaty

100. The Council shall, acting unanimously on a proposal from the Commission, issue Directives for the approximation of such provisions laid down by law, regulation or administrative action in member States as directly affect the establishment or functioning of the common market.

Note
Contrast the position under art. 100A which allows the adoption of measures by a favourable qualified majority vote.

The Assembly and the Economic and Social Committee shall be consulted in the case of Directives whose implementation would, in one or more member States, involve the amendment of legislation.

235.   If action by the Community should prove necessary to attain, in the course of the operation of the common market, one of the objectives of the Community and this Treaty has not provided the necessary powers, the Council shall, acting unanimously on a proposal from the Commission and after consulting the Assembly, take the appropriate measures.

The new art. 100A of the EEC Treaty dispels any fears which might have existed about the legality of the consumer protection programme.

EEC Treaty

100A.   1.   By way of derogation from Article 100 and save where otherwise provided in this Treaty, the following provisions shall apply for the achievement of the objectives set out in Article 8A. The Council shall, acting by a qualified majority on a proposal from the Commission in cooperation with the European Parliament and after consulting the Economic and Social Committee, adopt the measures for the approximation of the provisions laid down by law, regulation or administrative action in member States which have as their object the establishment and functioning of the internal market. . . .
      3.   The Commission, in its proposals envisaged in paragraph 1 concerning health, safety, environmental protection and consumer protection, will take as a base a high level of protection.

3.7.2   Specific application of European Community law

For text see 3.6.2.

3.7.2.1   Quantitative restrictions on imports   Since domestic consumer protection law is capable of amounting to a quantitative restriction on the importation of goods, it is capable of contravening the EEC Treaty art. 30.

EEC Treaty

30.   Quantitative restrictions on imports and all measures having equivalent effect shall, without prejudice to the following provisions, be prohibited between member States.

Some potentially restrictive provisions are permitted under the EEC Treaty, Art. 36.

EEC Treaty

36.   The provisions of articles 30 to 34 shall not preclude prohibitions or restrictions on imports, exports or goods in transit justified on grounds of public morality, public policy or public security; the protection of health and life of humans, animals or plants;

the protection of national treasures possessing artistic, historic or archaeological value; or the protection of industrial and commercial property. Such prohibitions or restrictions shall not, however, constitute a means of arbitrary discrimination or a disguised restriction on trade between member States.

A total ban on imports is clearly a quantitative restriction and may be declared unlawful under art. 30 unless permitted under art. 36. But the action taken must satisfy the proportionality test.

Commission v *United Kingdom* (case 261/85)
[1988] 2 CMLR 11
European Court of Justice

United Kingdom regulations banned the import of pasteurised milk and unfrozen pasteurised cream from other member States. It was argued that the restriction was necessary for the protection of human life and health and was justified under art. 36 of the EEC Treaty.

JUDGMENT at pp. 26–9

(9)   The Commission maintains that the rules in force in the United Kingdom are contrary to article 30 of the Treaty and are not justified under article 36, in so far as the total prohibition of imports is disproportionate in relation to the health objectives adopted by the United Kingdom. In the first place, it has not been shown in what way the legislation of the other member States offers only inadequate guarantees as to the quality of the milk. In the second place, the United Kingdom should, rather than imposing a general and absolute prohibition, allow the importation of milk found to comply with the United Kingdom standards. There is no reason for claiming that milk from other member States never complies with those standards. Certain tests make it possible to verify this within a sufficiently short time and it is incumbent upon the United Kingdom to set up an organisation capable of carrying out the necessary checks. Finally, the Commission states that it would be excessive to prohibit, for reasons for public health, the importation of milk which already satisfied the rules laid down in Directive 85/397.

(10)   The United Kingdom concedes that the rules in question are contrary to article 30 of the Treaty. It considers, however, that they are justified under article 36. It states, in the first place, that pasteurisation offers less substantial guarantees regarding health than ultra-high-temperature treatment. . . .

(11)   It must be observed that, as is recognised by both the parties, the contested rules fall within the scope of article 30 of the Treaty and of Regulation 804/68, the purpose of which is to achieve a single market in milk and milk products. The only question to be resolved therefore is whether or not the measures in question are justified under article 36 of the Treaty for reasons relating to the protection of human life and health.

(12)   It must be borne in mind in that connection that, as the Court has consistently held, whilst human life and health are among the matters protected by article 36 and whilst, as a result, it is for the member States to decide within the limits of the Treaty as to the level of protection which they wish to ensure, national rules restricting imports are compatible with the Treaty only insofar as they are necessary for the effective protection of human life and health and only if that objective cannot be achieved by measures less restrictive of intra-Community trade (*De Peijper* (Case 104/75) [1976]

ECR 613; *Commission* v *United Kingdom* (case 124/81) [1983] ECR 203; *CMC Melkunie BV* (case 97/83) [1984] ECR 2367). . . .

(15)   It appears, in that connection, that the contested rules, whose purpose is to impose a general and absolute prohibition on all imports of the products concerned, on the ground that they could not, in any event, satisfy the United Kingdom health inspection requirements, are disproportionate in relation to the objectives pursued. Until such time as common standards enter into force, the United Kingdom could achieve those objectives whilst permitting the importation from other member States of pasteurised milk and unfrozen pasteurised cream which met its own requirements.

(16)   Even assuming it were true, as the United Kindom contends — a contention not substantiated by the documents before the Court or at the hearing — that at the present time no system for the production of pasteurised milk which complies with the requirements of the United Kingdom legislation exists in any member State, the fact nevertheless remains that the absolute prohibition of imports imposed by the United Kingdom would from the outset, discourage producers in the other member States from making adjustments so as to conform to those requirements and would, at least potentially, obstruct intra-Community trade.

(17)   In those circumstances, it is for the United Kingdom to establish a system enabling the importers in question to prove that the imported milk products comply with the national standards in force. As the Court has already held (see in particular *Commission* v *United Kingdom* (case 124/81) [1983] ECR 203), the United Kingdom would be able to ensure such compliance by asking importers to produce certificates issued for that purpose by the competent authorities in the exporting countries. As stated in the same judgment, it would also be able to carry out controls to ensure observance of the standards which it has laid down and to prevent the entry of consignments found not to conform with those standards, whilst at the same time addressing itself to the question whether cooperation with the authorities in the other member States might make it possible to facilitate and simplify such controls.

3.7.3   Advertising law and freedom of expression

For text see 3.6.2.5.

European Convention on Human Rights and Fundamental Freedoms (1953)

10.   1.   Everyone has the right to freedom of expression. This right shall include freedom to hold opinions and to receive and impart information and ideas without interference by public authority and regardless of frontiers. This article shall not prevent States from requiring the licensing of broadcasting, television or cinema enterprises.

2.   The exercise of these freedoms, since it carries with it duties and responsibilities, may be subject to such formalities, conditions, restrictions or penalties as are prescribed by law and are necessary in a democratic society, in the interests of national security, territorial integrity or public safety, for the prevention of disorder or crime, for the protection of health or morals, for the protection of the reputation or rights of others, for preventing the disclosure of information received in confidence, or for maintaining the authority and impartiality of the judiciary.

This freedom appears to extend to 'commercial speech' with the result that advertising material may be protected.

Markt Intern Verlag GmbH and Beerman v *Germany*
[1990] 12 EHRR 161
European Court of Human Rights

Judgment pp. 172–176.

B. *Compliance with Article 10*

27. In the Court's view, the applicants clearly suffered an interference by public authority in the exercise of the right protected under article 10, in the form of the injunction issued by the Federal Court of Justice restraining them from repeating the statements appearing in the information bulletin of 20 November 1975. Such an interference infringes the Convention if it does not satisfy the requirements of article 10(2). It should therefore be determined whether it was 'prescribed by law,' whether it pursued one or more of the legitimate aims set out in that paragraph and whether it was 'necessary in a democratic society' to achieve such aims. . . .

3. *'Necessary in a democratic society'*

32. The applicants argued that the injunction in question could not be regarded as 'necessary in a democratic society.' The Commission agreed with this view. . . .

35. In a market economy an undertaking which seeks to set up a business inevitably exposes itself to close scrutiny of its practices by its competitors. Its commercial strategy and the manner in which it honours its commitments may give rise to criticism on the part of consumers and the specialised press. In order to carry out this task, the specialised press must be able to disclose facts which could be of interest to its readers and thereby contribute to the openness of business activities. . . .

It cannot be said that the final decision of the Federal Court of Justice — confirmed from the constitutional point of view by the Federal Constitutional Court — went beyond the margin of appreciation left to the national authorities. It is obvious that opinions may differ as to whether the Federal Court's reaction was appropriate or whether the statements made in the specific case by *Markt Intern* should be permitted or tolerated. However, the European Court of Human Rights should not substitute its own evaluation for that of the national courts in the instant case, where those courts, on reasonable grounds, had considered the restrictions to be necessary.

38. Having regard to the foregoing, the court reaches the conclusion that no breach of article 10 has been established in the circumstances of the present case.

But did the decision of the majority comply with the principle of proportionality? Were there other measures which could have been taken? The dissenting judgment of Judge Pettiti at p. 178 (footnotes omitted) is instructive:

In this field the States have only a slight margin of appreciation, which is subject to review by the European Court. Only in rare cases can censorship or prohibition of publication be accepted. This has been the prevailing view in the American and European systems since 1776 and 1789.

This is particularly true in relation to commercial advertising or questions of commercial or economic policy, in respect of which the State cannot claim to defend the general interest because the interests of consumers are conflicting. In fact, by seeking to support pressure groups — such as laboratories — , the State is defending a specific interest. It uses the pretext of a law on competition or on prices to give precedence to one group over another. The protection of the interests of users and consumers in the face of dominant positions depends on the freedom to publish even the harshest criticism of products. Freedom must be total or almost total except where an offence is committed or where an action is brought for unfair competition, but in those circumstances the solution is not censorship but criminal prosecution or civil proceedings between the undertakings. The arsenal of laws caters for the punishment of misleading advertising.

The limitation of the freedom of expression in favour of the States' margin of appreciation, which is thereby given priority over the defence of fundamental rights, is not consistent with the European Court's case law or its mission. Such a tendency towards restricting freedoms would also run counter to the work of the Council of Europe in the field of audiovisual technology and trans-frontier satellites aimed at ensuring freedom of expression and protecting the rights of others including those of users and consumers of communication media.

Note
Is a ban on the use of the following advertising material 'legitimately aimed at the protection of the rights of consumers'?

(a)   Worth £50 — now only £25.
(b)   Oughton's beer refreshes the parts of the body other beers cannot reach.

See further chapters 11 and 12.

3.8   ADMINISTRATIVE CONTROL

A domestic alternative to the use of the criminal and civil law as a means of consumer protection is to place powers of regulation in the hands of an administrative agency. In this respect, the role of the Office of Fair Trading is most important. The role of the Office of Fair Trading in respect of the formulation of consumer protection policy is considered above (see chapter 2), but the same body also has administrative powers, particularly in relation to the licensing of credit businesses and the control of trading practices.

The attraction of administrative control is that it appears to keep matters relevant to the issue of consumer protection out of the courts, except in extreme cases. In many instances, the actions of the administrative agency may achieve the desired effect of dissuading a trader from engaging in unfair practices. Moreover, if the licensing of credit businesses is effective, it will prevent traders who might act against the best interests of consumers from entering the consumer market in the first place.

In contrast to these claimed advantages, it should also be observed that setting up a centrally organised administrative body is expensive and it is always possible that this cost may outweigh the benefits to be derived from having a back-up to existing civil and criminal laws.

3.8.1   Unfair trading conduct

Under the Fair Trading Act 1973, s. 34, the Director General of Fair Trading may act so as to prevent a person from acting in a manner which is detrimental to the economic, health or safety interests of consumers and which is unfair to consumers.

3.8.1.1 Unfair conduct In order to be unfair, the trader's conduct must amount to a breach of existing civil or criminal law (Fair Trading Act 1973, s. 34(2) and (3)). It is not the case that civil or criminal proceedings must have been brought in respect of the trader's conduct (s. 34(2) and (3)), since the Director General can also take into account complaints received from individuals, from consumer advice agencies and from local authority trading standards departments.

Examples of unfair conduct include persistent infringements of the Trade Descriptions Act 1968 or failures to comply with the requirements of the Unfair Contract Terms Act 1977 in relation to the exclusion of liability for negligently caused death or bodily injury, thereby allowing the Director General to take action. Similarly, repeated supplies of food injurious to health (*Director General of Fair Trading* v *Smiths Bakeries (Westfield) Ltd* (1978) *The Times*, 12 May 1978) or the supply of services not in accordance with contract specifications would also constitute unfair trading conduct. However, a failure to comply with provisions contained in a voluntary code of practice would appear not to come within the definition since the failure is not prohibited by law.

3.8.1.2 Consumer interests There is no requirement in the Fair Trading Act 1973, s. 34, that the trader's conduct should specifically relate to consumers, thus a nuisance which does not directly affect consumers could be said to amount to unfair trading conduct. However, s. 34(1)(a) provides that the conduct must be detrimental to consumer interests, with the result that this part of the Fair Trading Act 1973 is effectively confined to consumer problems.

3.8.1.3 Control of unfair trading conduct There is a two-tier procedure for dealing with unfair trading conduct. If the Director General identifies unfair conduct on the part of a trader, the Fair Trading Act 1973, s. 34(1), empowers him to seek a written assurance from the trader that the conduct will not be repeated. This may be sufficient to dissuade the trader from further transgressions, in which case no further action need be taken. Furthermore, since many offenders will be companies which may go out of business, there is provision for seeking an assurance from senior company officers or persons with a controlling interest in a company (Fair Trading Act 1973, ss. 38 and 39). It follows that if a person promotes a company which engages in unfair conduct, subsequently closes down that business and sets up a similar business in a new name, a written assurance obtained from that individual will still be effective.

If the trader gives an assurance but subsequently breaks it or if he refuses to give a written assurance, the matter can be taken further by the Director General. It is open to the Director General to seek an order in the Restrictive Practices Court that the trader should refrain from engaging in a particular practice. Alternatively, the court can seek a binding assurance from the trader.

In either event, if the trader fails to comply with the court order he may be held to be in contempt of court and punished accordingly (Fair Trading Act 1973, s. 35).

One view of the part III procedure is that it constitutes additional punishment of the trader in that the request for a written assurance may come on top of a conviction for the commission of a strict liability criminal offence or an action for damages brought by an affected consumer. However, it would appear that the procedure is intended to operate in a rehabilitative fashion, seeking to avoid future detrimental conduct (*R* v *Director General of Fair Trading, ex parte F.H. Taylor & Co. Ltd* [1981] ICR 292). This is particularly the case in the light of the practice of the Office of Fair Trading in publishing details of assurances obtained from individual traders (see FTA 1973, s. 124(1) and s. 133(1) and (2)).

3.8.2   Licensing of traders

See Borrie [1982] JBL 91.

An alternative administrative control on trading practices can be found in the licensing powers of the Director General of Fair Trading under the Consumer Credit Act 1974.

The licences granted under the 1974 Act may be either standard licences or group licences. A standard licence is issued to a single person, company or partnership, lasts for ten years and specifies the activity permitted by the licence. A group licence may be issued to legitimate the activities of the group of businesses named in the licence. For example, a group licence has been granted to the Law Society to cover all solicitors holding current practising certificates. Such a licence will specify the activities which are permitted, with the result that if an individual firm of solicitors wishes to engage in a credit business not covered by the group licence, it will be necessary to obtain a standard licence for the purposes of that individual firm.

3.8.2.1   Factors relevant to the grant of a licence   Licences to engage in a credit business may be refused or revoked with the result that, in theory, less than scrupulous credit businesses may be weeded out before they cause a problem or at least before they cause too much damage. It is not just primary credit providers who are subject to the licensing requirement, since the net extends to cover ancillary credit businesses including dealers or brokers, debt adjusters, debt counsellors, debt collectors and credit reference agencies (Consumer Credit Act 1974, s. 145(1)). It is even the case that those who indirectly engage in a credit business are subject to the licensing requirement. Thus an unlicensed dealer who sells cars to a licensed dealer so as to facilitate finance arrangements commits an offence because he is indirectly engaged in credit brokerage (*Hicks* v *Walker* (1984) 148 JP 636; Consumer Credit Act 1974, s. 39(1)).

The Director General is permitted to grant a licence to a 'fit person' (Consumer Credit Act 1974, s. 25(1)(a)). A number of factors can be considered in determining whether a person is fit to engage in a credit business. These include whether the applicant has been found guilty of fraud or dishonesty, whether he has contravened any provisions in respect of credit, whether he has committed acts constituting sex or race discrimination and whether he has engaged in oppressive or deceitful business practices (s. 25(2)).

The burden of proving fitness is placed on the applicant (s. 25(1)) and that application may be subject to a 'minded to refuse notice' issued by the Director (s. 27(1)(a)). Alternatively, the Director can invite the applicant to make representations in support of his application (s. 27(1)(b)).

If the Director does issue a minded to refuse notice, it will refer to any of the matters specifically listed in s. 25(2), but other factors will also be relevant to the Director's decision and some matters listed in s. 25(2) will be more relevant than others, depending on the nature of the application. For example, a conviction for an offence of violence would be of particular relevance to an application for the licensing of a debt-collecting service, whereas a similar conviction might not be so relevant to an application for the licensing of a credit reference agency where there is likely to be less face-to-face contact with consumers. Similarly, offences of dishonesty will be of great relevance wherever the applicant is likely to come into contact with money.

While previous convictions are a relevant factor, other matters may also be taken into consideration. In particular, the Director will have to take account of complaints received from members of the public and local authority trading standards departments which have not resulted in a successful prosecution. The problem here is that such complaints only give one side of the story and since the matter has not been tested in court, the applicant will not have had a chance to explain his actions. Because of this, it is likely that the Director General will grant a licence even if there appears to be some cause for concern.

3.8.2.2 The purposes served by licensing
At first sight, licensing is a very powerful means of controlling trade practices since it serves to deny the opportunity to engage in business and therefore spreads a much wider net than is possible with specific controls concerned with individual transactions (see Crowther Committee on Consumer Credit (Cmnd 4596, 1971), vol. 1, p. 255). Moreover, the administrative body in charge of the licensing programme has a flexible tool with which it can act in relation to activities which are not strictly controlled by law and can dissuade businesses from engaging in undesirable, but lawful practices. Licensing as a means of control of business practices also appears to allow for consistency of approach to the standards of conduct required of licensees.

The licensing system also has other useful side-effects. In particular, it will provide a considerable amount of information on the area of business subject to the licensing requirement. The licensing authority will be able to identify emerging practices which may require legislative action in the interests of consumers.

The advantages of a licensing system have to be set against its disadvantages, perhaps the most important of which is that of cost. In order to set up a licensing system on the scale of that envisaged under the 1974 Act, it has become necessary to create a huge administrative machine. This cost can be borne by the public purse, but it is also possible to make a licensing system self-financing by charging a fee for the grant of a licence.

Where the scale of the licensing scheme is substantial, it is more likely to give rise to problems of cost. For example, the Consumer Credit Act 1974 scheme is a system of positive licensing, under which anyone who wishes to engage in a credit business must be granted prior approval. Some would argue that the system set up under the 1974 Act goes too far, particularly since it also requires dealers or credit brokers to be licensed. A result of this is that by the end of 1987, the number of licences granted totalled 217,378, of which the largest category was that of credit brokerage (Annual Report of the Director General of Fair Trading, 1987, Appendix I, section 6).

In contrast, other licensing schemes have fallen short of a requirement of positive licensing. For example, the licensing scheme adopted under the Estate Agents Act 1979, ss. 22 and 23, can be better described as a negative system under which any person can operate as an estate agent until it is shown that he is unfit to do so.

Apart from problems of size and cost, a licensing system can lead to unfair decisions on the matter of refusal to grant or renew a licence. In this respect, it is important that the challenge procedure works properly and that appropriate administrative law measures are developed in order to deal with possible abuses of the system.

3.9 ADMINISTRATIVE CONTROL – MATERIALS FOR CONSIDERATION

3.9.1 Unfair trading conduct

For text see 3.8.1.

Fair Trading Act 1973

34. Action by Director with respect to course of conduct detrimental to interests of consumers

(1)   Where it appears to the Director that the person carrying on a business has in the course of that business persisted in a course of conduct which—

(a)   is detrimental to the interests of consumers in the United Kindom, whether those interests are economic interests or interests in respect of health, safety or other matters, and

(b)   in accordance with the following provisions of this section is to be regarded as unfair to consumers,

the Director shall use his best endeavours, by communication with that person or otherwise, to obtain from him a satisfactory written assurance that he will refrain from continuing that course of conduct and from carrying on any similar course of conduct in the course of that business.

(2)   For the purposes of subsection (1)(b) of this section a course of conduct shall be regarded as unfair to consumers if it consists of contraventions of one or more enactments which impose duties, prohibitions or restrictions enforceable by criminal proceedings, whether any such duty, prohibition or restriction is imposed in relation to

consumers as such or not and whether the person carrying on the business has or has not been convicted of any offence in respect of any such contravention.

(3)   A course of conduct on the part of the person carrying on a business shall also be regarded for those purposes as unfair to consumers if it consists of things done, or omitted to be done, in the course of that business in breach of contract or in breach of a duty (other than a contractual duty) owed to any person by virtue of any enactment or rule of law and enforceable by civil proceedings, whether (in any such case) civil proceedings in respect of the breach of contract or breach of duty have been brought or not.

(4)   For the purpose of determining whether it appears to him that a person has persisted in such a course of conduct as is mentioned in subsection (1) of this section, the Director shall have regard to either or both of the following, that is to say—

(a)   complaints received by him, whether from consumers or from other persons;

(b)   any other information collected by or furnished to him, whether by virtue of this Act or otherwise.

35.   Proceedings before Restrictive Practices Court.

If, in the circumstances specified in subsection (1) of section 34 of this Act,—

(a)   the Director is unable to obtain from the person in question such an assurance as is mentioned in that subsection, or

(b)   that person has given such an assurance and it appears to the Director that he has failed to observe it,

the Director may bring proceedings against him before the Restrictive Practices Court.

Is the procedure under part III of the Fair Trading Act 1973 a further punishment additional to any fine imposed in earlier proceedings or is some other purpose served?

R v *Director General of Fair Trading, ex parte F.H. Taylor & Co. Ltd*
[1981] ICR 292
Queen's Bench Divisional Court

The company had been convicted on 13 occasions of offences contrary to safety regulations. The Director sought a written assurance which was given, but the Director also proposed to publish details of the assurance. The applicants sought a declaration that this course of action was beyond the Director's powers.

DONALDSON LJ at pp. 296-8: Sections 124 and 133 [of the Fair Trading Act 1973] seem to me to constitute a clear warning and direction to the Director General and the Office of Fair Trading that, so far as practicable, they are to avoid disclosing matters which would seriously and prejudicially affect the interests of named or identifiable individuals. Furthermore, the purpose of part III of the Act is, as I read it, to provide additional punishment for those who have persisted in a course of conduct which is detrimental to the interest of consumers. In particular, it is not intended to drive them out of business. Rather it is intended to provide additional deterrence to the continuance of this course of conduct in the hope that there may be reform and that the offender will rehabilitate himself. . . .

I think that the Director General should ask himself some questions.

First, who necessarily should be informed that assurances have been given? The answer is probably 'all who may be expected to let the Director General know if there has been a breach'. . . .

Second, what should be the form in which the information is disseminated? Of course, the Office of Fair Trading is seeking a dissemination of information without cost to itself. The more colourful it makes its handout, the more likely it is to achieve this object. But the Director General and the Office of Fair Trading have obligations towards the individual. They must always be asking themselves 'Are we being fair to him? Are we giving him a fair chance to mend his ways?' In the present instance I have deliberately refrained from setting out the draft press release in full, but I think that it certainly goes to the limit of what is fair and may perhaps go further. . . .

Third, is it really relevant to say, however accurately, that the assurances were only given after a threat of legal proceedings? It may have been necessary to emphasise the threat in this case, but such a threat is implicit in any request for written assurances made under section 34 of the Act and is virtually explicit in the standard form of letter of request.

Fourth, why is it appropriate to publish an expression of gratitude to the trading standards departments of the three local authorities? Would not a letter have sufficed? Or is this intended to increase the likelihood of obtaining a reference in the local press to the fact that assurances have been given? If so, this comes back to the question of the extent to which the performance of the Director General's functions will be facilitated by informing the general public or whether the result may not simply be to make it more difficult for the company to carry on its business.

3.9.2   Licensing of traders

For text see 3.8.2.

Consumer Credit Act 1974

25.   Licensee to be a fit person

(1)   A standard licence shall be granted on the application of any person if he satisfies the Director that—

(a)   he is a fit person to engage in activities covered by the licence, and

(b)   the name or names under which he applies to be licensed is or are not misleading or otherwise undesirable.

(2)   In determining whether an applicant for a standard licence is a fit person to engage in any activities, the Director shall have regard to any circumstances appearing to him to be relevant, and in particular any evidence tending to show that the applicant, or any of the applicant's employees, agents or associates (whether past or present) or, where the applicant is a body corporate, any person appearing to the Director to be a controller of the body corporate or an associate of any such person, has—

(a)   committed any offence involving fraud or other dishonesty, or violence,

(b)   contravened any provision made by or under this Act, or by or under any other enactment regulating the provision of credit to individuals or other transactions with individuals.

(c)   practised discrimination on grounds of sex, colour, race or ethnic or national origins in, or in connection with, the carrying on of any business, or

(d)   engaged in business practices appearing to the Director to be deceitful or oppressive, or otherwise unfair or improper (whether unlawful or not).

(3)   In subsection (2), 'associate', in addition to the persons specified in section 184, includes a business associate.

3.10   BUSINESS SELF-REGULATION

In addition to legal and administrative controls on business activities, a further important source of consumer rights and redress can be found in codes of practice drawn up for the guidance of the particular area of business to which they apply. Generally, codes of practice are not intended to supplant the law, but merely to complement existing legal rules.

Codes of practice can take one of two forms. There are 'statutory' codes drawn up under a legally created power or duty and there are 'non-statutory' codes, generally drawn up by trade associations for the guidance of their members.

In the field of consumer protection, examples of both types of code can be found. One of the most recent examples of a statutory code of practice can be found in the form of the Code of Practice for Traders on Price Indications, made under the Consumer Protection Act 1987, s. 25 (see further chapter 12). Such codes provide important guidance on how to comply with the requirements of a statutory prohibition to which they relate.

Non-statutory codes of practice generally take the form of voluntary controls prepared by trade associations for the guidance of their members. Such codes may be prepared entirely voluntarily by particular areas of business, such as the Code of Advertising Practice prepared by the advertising industry, but other areas of business may require prompting. In this last respect, an important function of the Director General of Fair Trading is to encourage trade associations to prepare codes of practice to be sent to their members with a view to safeguarding and promoting the interests of consumers (FTA, 1973 s. 124(3)).

3.10.1   The role of the Office of Fair Trading

The Office of Fair Trading can guide trade associations in such a way as to require them to address issues of consumer concern. Without pressure from a body which has the consumer interest in mind, there is always the danger that self-regulation on the part of a trade association will merely address the interests of traders. For example, it has been said that where people of the same trade meet together there is likely to be a conspiracy against the public or some contrivance to raise prices (Adam Smith, *The Wealth of Nations* (1937), p. 128).

The Office of Fair Trading has involved itself in a bargaining process with relevant trade associations under the powers conferred by the Fair Trading Act 1973. If it is not satisfied with the proposals drawn up by a trade association, suggestions for change may be passed on and, ideally, amendments will be introduced with a view to advancing the position of consumers.

If the bargaining position of the Office of Fair Trading is to remain strong, there has to be the possible threat of regulation should the trade association fail to meet the requests for alterations to a code of practice. It would appear that such a threat was present in the period between 1973 and 1979 with the result that a considerable number of trade association codes were developed. However, since 1979 there has not been a strong political desire to advance the consumer interest in the form of government regulation. One consequence of this is that since the threat of regulation is not present, trade associations have been less willing to agree to voluntary controls on trade practices (Borrie (1984) 7 J Consum Policy 197).

3.10.2   The features of codes of practice

Codes of practice may be particularly useful in dealing with possible trading abuses which may not be susceptible to legal controls, but it is also the case that the advantages of codes of practice need to be weighed against their disadvantages, which in some instances may be substantial. In formulating a code of practice, it is important that the duties of traders and the rights of consumers are clearly outlined. Mere expressions of good will towards consumers are insufficient and it is important that codes are kept up to date in the light of changing circumstances (Director General of Fair Trading, *Annual Report* 1975 p. 10). Furthermore, a code of practice should be designed to encourage higher trading standards, remove trading abuses and provide a suitable means of handling consumer complaints (Director General of Fair Trading, *Annual Report* 1976 p. 9).

The essence of a trade association code of practice is that it is designed specifically to meet the problems encountered in a particular area of trade. Because of this, the content of one code may differ substantially from that of another. However, there are certain features which appear to be common to most of the codes of practice developed in recent years. For example, there may be statements concerning the standard of service to be expected of members of the association, restrictions on advertising and promotion techniques, provisions in respect of the exclusion or limitation of liability to consumers, provision for a customer complaint service, including in some cases an arbitration scheme, provision for full price information and provision for refunds to be given to dissatisfied customers.

For the most part, the codes of practice which have been developed, in conjunction with the Office of Fair Trading, have been concentrated in those areas which have given rise to the greatest number of consumer complaints. Thus codes regulate the practices of suppliers of motor vehicles (joint code of the Society of Motor Manufacturers and Traders (SMMT), the Motor Agents Association (MAA) and the Scottish Motor Trade Association (SMTA)), domestic electrical appliances (codes produced by the Association of Manufacturers of Domestic Electrical Appliances (AMDEA), the Electricity Council, and the Electrical and Television Retailers Association (RETRA)), footwear (code of the Footwear Distributors Federation), furniture and holiday caravans. In the service industries, there are also codes of practice which have appeared in those sectors of trade most closely associated with consumer dissatisfaction. In particular codes have been developed to deal with the practices of funeral directors (code of the National Association of Funeral

Directors) and the suppliers of home improvement services, particularly double glazing contractors (code of Ethical Practice of the Glass and Glazing Federation). Codes also cover the servicing of motor vehicles (joint code of SMMT, MAA & SMTA; Vehicle Builders and Repairers Association code) and domestic electrical appliances (AMDEA, RETRA and Electricity Council codes), postal services (Post Office Code of Practice for Postal Services), photographic processing services, domestic laundry and cleaning services (code of the Association of British Laundry, Cleaning and Rental Services) and package holiday services (Association of British Travel Agents Codes of Conduct and see chapter 10).

3.10.3   Advantages and disadvantages of codes of practice

See Office of Fair Trading, *A General Duty to Trade Fairly* (1986), pp. 14–17.

Provided a code of practice does deal adequately with the causes of consumer dissatisfaction and is kept up to date in the light of changing practices, it can be argued that codes of practice can deal with matters which are not regulated by law. For example, some codes of practice are well ahead of the law in that they allow cancellation of contracts where no similar legal remedy exists. Moreover, codes of practice are particularly useful in controlling practices which would be difficult to regulate by law. For example, the code of practice of the National Association of Funeral Directors provides for what should happen if two funeral directors arrive at the home of a bereaved consumer — a matter that is hardly conducive to legislative regulation.

In general, it can be argued in favour of codes of practice that they are more flexible than laws in that they can be tailored to the needs of a particular trade or industry. Furthermore, since responsibility for drafting and enforcement rests with those who have a close knowledge of the trade, it can be said that codes are often more successful in dealing with likely consumer problems.

While codes of practice can claim to have advantages when compared with legislation, it is also the case that they suffer from a number of apparent disadvantages. In particular, it can be said that there are problems of implementation, structural deficiencies, motivation and enforcement.

So far as the matter of implementation is concerned, one of the features of all trade association codes is that they apply only to members of the association. It follows from this that traders who have chosen not to belong to a relevant trade association will not be subject to any sanctions the association may wish to impose in the event of a breach of one of the requirements of the code. Moreover, since non-members are more likely to engage in conduct detrimental to the consumer interest, the only constraints on their activities would appear to emanate from legislative or judicial controls. The problem of unfair practices amongst non-members of a trade association is also likely to lead to resentment amongst those traders who have voluntarily submitted themselves to the rules of the association, particularly if the non-member is seen to derive a competitive advantage from engaging in such practices without being punished.

A further problem of implementation is that trade associations can sometimes appear to be slow to enforce the terms of the code against their members.

Against this, it should be observed that codes of practice are not like rules of law and that a process of encouragement rather than compulsion is sometimes beneficial. Having said this, it remains the case that trade associations are dependent for their survival on members' subscriptions and there may be some substance to the view that there is a tendency not to look at possible cases of abuse from a truly independent position.

A further argument against codes of practice is that they sometimes appear to be structurally deficient on the ground that consumer views are not considered prior to their formulation and that rules contained in the code may tend to be based on current business practice. However, in the case of codes of practice drawn up in consultation with the Office of Fair Trading, there is ample evidence that appropriate consumer organisations will have been consulted. Moreover, in the case of the British Code of Advertising Practice, there is also a process of full consultation with representatives of consumer groups (see Thompson, 'Self-regulation in advertising' in *Consumer Law in the EEC* (ed. Woodroffe, 1984), pp. 53-68).

The problem of motivation is based on the argument that codes of practice generally tend to come into existence as a means of averting a threat of legal control. Furthermore, some would suggest that the provisions of some codes of practice may provide a form of insulation from competitive forces. However, there are good examples of code provisions which provide useful means of consumer redress in excess of anything the law could do, which would seem to suggest that it is not just business that benefits from their provisions.

Some codes of practice suffer from problems of enforcement in the sense that they appear to possess few 'real' sanctions. While it is the case that some trade associations are prepared to impose fines in the event of an infringement, others merely provide for a reprimand or for the publication of adverse reports in a trade journal. Ultimately, there is always the sanction of dismissal from membership of the trade association, but this is only an effective measure if the trade association claims a very high proportion of traders of the type under consideration as members. If there is a high proportion of 'fringe' operators who are not members of the trade association concerned, dismissal will not always be effective. In the end, the extent to which trade association sanctions are effective depends on the vigilance of the trade association itself and it would appear that some are more vigilant than others.

Some of the problems of enforcement have been addressed by the present Director General of Fair Trading (Borrie, *The Development of Consumer Law and Policy* (1984), ch. 4) who suggests that the requirements laid down by codes of practice could be enforced by means of the procedure in the Fair Trading Act 1973, part III, in respect of unfair trading conduct (see 3.8.1.3). This would necessitate a change in the law since at present part III of the 1973 Act applies only to a breach of existing requirements of the criminal or civil law. If a failure to comply with trade association requirements were to be subject to the written assurance provisions of ss. 34 and 35 of the 1973 Act, a powerful means of enforcement would lie in the hands of an agency with consumer interests in mind.

This proposal is not without its difficulties since there are many require-ments laid down by trade associations which would be difficult to enforce by such means and it might become necessary to review the wording of many codes if such a power were to be introduced. Furthermore, the proposal as it stands would not address the problem of unfair practices engaged in by non-members of a trade association. To meet this problem, it would be necessary to introduce a mandatory requirement of membership of a relevant trade association.

3.11   BUSINESS SELF-REGULATION - MATERIALS FOR CONSIDERATION

For text see 3.10.

Borrie, 'Consumer protection laws for the 1990s' [1988] JBL 116 at p. 121

It would however be unwise to dismiss the value of codes of practice. May I give four reasons:

(i)   The Parliamentary timetable is such that it cannot be sensible to dismiss ways of improving consumer rights and redress possibilities that are not dependent on finding a slot in the legislative programme.

(ii)   Low-cost methods of redress for consumers have been made available through codes of practice, not only conciliation facilities and independent facilities for arbitration (under the aegis of the Chartered Institute of Arbitrators or otherwise) but also such devices as the Footwear Testing Centre.

(iii)   Where a code bans certain types of contractual terms or requires certain terms to be inserted into contracts, the codes help to rewrite standard-form contracts so that they are less one-sided than before. Clearly, a code can be more than self-regulation — it can have an indirect effect on people's *legal rights* — if consumers' contract rights are improved as a result of the code. Thus, if a tour operator adheres to the code agreed with the Association of British Travel Agents, he will not seek to avoid his contractual obligation to exercise due diligence in making travel arrangements for his client.

The most recent code to be approved by the OFT concerns the selling of caravans. All members of the British Holiday and Home Parks Association (BH and HPA) and the National Caravan Council (NCC) are required to offer a written agreement to all persons buying a caravan and placing it on a pitch in a caravan park. This agreement will be for an initial fixed term of five years and must contain other matters comprised in the code of practice which cover, *inter alia*, a minimum three months' notice of any increase in pitch fees, provision for arbitration at the instance of two-thirds of the caravan owners affected by a proposed increase, services available to the pitch and the caravan owner's right to sell the caravan and assign the contract for occupation of the pitch. In effect the code provisions become contract terms and enforceable through arbitration or through the courts.

(iv)   Codes of practice can be evolved so that they are harnessed to the kind of broad statutory provision I was favouring earlier in this lecture. They can represent guidance as to how the statutory provision may be complied with, but would not be exhaustive of its meaning and, by being contained in a code, would be that much more easily alterable. It is important that the status of such a code is made clear in the legislation. I am of course thinking again of the general prohibition of misleading price indications provided for in the Consumer Protection Act [1987] and the attached code. Section 20 of the Act says in simple general terms:

> a person shall be guilty of an offence if, in the course of any business of his, he gives (by any means whatever) to any consumers an indication which is misleading as to the price at which any goods, services, accommodation or facilities are available. . . .

It is important to say that the code (to be approved by the Secretary of State after consulting myself) is not meant to detract in any way from the broad sweep of the new offence. The code is not intended to give a more detailed description of the offence. If it is sought to do that, it would need to be written in a different style of English with a precision of wording suitable to the description of criminal offences, and it could land us back with the disadvantages of listing specific detailed offences and once more opening the way for loopholes to be found. The code is intended instead to give clear practical guidance in plain English to traders to enable them to avoid being misleading.

I have described the proposals in the Act as an instructive example of how a code, harnessed to a broad legislative statement of principle, can avoid some of the disadvantages of the detailed legislation of the past and create a more sensible balance between certainty and flexibility. But there is one provision in the Act as it stood during the debates in the Lords that was strongly criticised by the National Consumer Council and others, and that is the provision that compliance with the code would be an absolute defence. They wanted instead something similar to the status of the Highway Code — compliance would simply tend to negative liability and contravention tend to prove the offence. The government justified its tilt towards greater certainty by the fact that criminal sanctions are at issue. However, if the wording of the code is meant to create absolute defences, then that wording ought to be just as precise as the government has said would be necessary if the code gave detailed descriptions of offences. The government's view of the status of the code has been somewhat confused. I agree with the government that the code should seek to give clear guidance in plain English to help traders avoid being misleading. But, rather than allow reliance on the code to be an absolute defence, I would provide in the legislation that either the prosecution or the defence may refer to the code as evidence that an offence has been committed or has not been committed. Further, I would take out of the code and put into regulations certain matters where recent experience had demonstrated that particular types of price indications are definitely misleading. Where they can be specified with a clarity suitable for prohibitions, backed by criminal sanctions, (such as 'worth' and 'value' claims) they should be prohibited in a non-exhaustive list that should be contained in regulations. Flexibility is taken too far if it is left uncertain how the general provision is to apply to those types of price indications that have already been prohibited since the Price Marking (Bargain Offers) Order 1979 (SI 1979/364).

3.12   A GENERAL DUTY TO TRADE FAIRLY

In the light of the various criticisms of different aspects of English consumer protection law, it has been suggested, on a number of occasions, that there should be a general duty to trade fairly. While it can be said that the combined effect of the Consumer Protection Act 1987, part II, and the proposed EC General Product Safety Directive (when implemented) create a duty to trade safely (see 9.2), it is doubtful whether there is a general duty in English law not to mislead consumers.

3.12.1 Current aspects of the duty to trade fairly

It is arguable that in certain respects there is already a partial duty to trade fairly, insofar as the Director General of Fair Trading has powers under the Fair Trading Act 1973 to seek assurances from traders to the effect that they will not engage in practices detrimental to the consumer interest (see 3.8.1.3). However, the power to seek assurances is presently confined to trading conduct amounting to the breach of existing civil and criminal law obligations.

In addition to this general power, there are also specific areas in which fair trading is required as a matter of law. For example, the licensing provisions of the Consumer Credit Act 1974 (see 3.8.2) mean that if a credit business engages in conduct detrimental to consumers, there is the possibility that his licence to deal may be revoked.

In recent years, there has also been a general move away from specifically defined criminal offences in consumer legislation. At one stage, the Parliamentary draftsman would seek to define in very specific terms the constituent elements of a statutory criminal offence. For example, the Trade Descriptions Act 1968, s. 2, contains a long list of the types of statement which are capable of amounting to trade descriptions and the now repealed provisions of s. 11 of the same Act in respect of price indications sought to prohibit those types of price comparison which were recognised as misleading in 1968. The difficulty with long lists is that over a period of time advertisers are likely to develop practices which comply with the letter of the law, but not necessarily its spirit (see *A General Duty to Trade Fairly* (OFT, 1986), para. 2.5). In relation to price comparisons, it is interesting to compare the regime introduced by the Consumer Protection Act 1987, s. 20(1) which makes it an offence to give, by whatever means, a misleading indication as to the price at which goods, services, accommodation and facilities are available (see also 12.2.2). Of course one of the difficulties of such a generally worded prohibition is that, without qualification, it would be difficult to know when a particular statement about prices is lawful or not. In order to meet this problem, a statutory code of practice has been issued under s. 25 of the 1987 Act which gives general guidance on misleading and permitted price comparisons. If this can be done for prices, presumably there would be no great difficulty in doing the same for other potentially misleading statements. A further important development in similar vein can be found in the form of the Control of Misleading Advertisements Regulations (SI 1988/915), introduced to comply with the EC Misleading and Unfair Advertising Directive (84/450 EEC, OJ L250 19.9.84, p. 17) which introduce a general restriction on misleading and unfair statements in advertisements, supported by a power on the part of the Director General of Fair Trading to seek injunctive relief in respect of contraventions (see 11.5).

A similar direction has also been taken in relation to food following the enactment of the Food Safety Act 1990, which provides for a general food safety requirement in s. 8. Under this it is an offence for a person to supply, offer to supply, expose for supply or have in possession for the purposes of supply any food which is injurious to health, unfit for human consumption or so contaminated that it would not be reasonable to expect it to be used for human consumption (Food Safety Act 1990, s. 8, see also 9.5.2 and cf. the even broader general product safety requirement in the Consumer Protection Act 1987, s. 10, considered at 9.2.2).

In addition to the use of the criminal law and administrative provisions as means of securing basic standards of fair trading, aspects of the civil law may also be seen in the same light. For example, the consumer who has been persuaded to enter a credit agreement as a result of doorstep salesmanship may in certain circumstances cancel the agreement during a 'cooling-off' period (Consumer Credit Act 1974, ss. 67 and 68 and see 6.3.2).

At one stage, it appeared that certain members of the judiciary were willing to allow the development of a general principle of inequality of bargaining power which would permit a contracting party in an unequal bargaining position to escape the consequences of a contract he had entered into. According to *Lloyd's Bank Ltd* v *Bundy* [1975] QB 326, this general principle is based on four essential requirements, namely lack of advice, disparity of consideration, exploitability and pressure or influence by the stronger party. The fortunes of this general principle appear to have been short-lived, since the House of Lords has subsequently taken the view that the task of providing a general principle of relief against inequality of bargaining power is a matter for Parliament, not the courts (*National Westminster Bank plc* v *Morgan* [1985] AC 686 at p. 708 per Lord Scarman). Moreover, it was the view of the House of Lords that such a task had been partly undertaken in the form of modern consumer protection legislation, in particular, the power conferred on the courts to reopen extortionate credit bargains under the Consumer Credit Act 1974, ss. 137 to 139 (see also 6.8.3.4).

3.12.2 The need for a general duty to trade fairly

Given the range of current provisions which may be described as aspects of a duty to trade fairly, the question arises whether it is necessary to go further. One feature of the changes which have occurred to date is that they have been introduced on a piecemeal basis, dealing with particular issues when the need has arisen. No attempt has been made to overhaul the basis of consumer protection law by imposing a general duty on all traders to refrain from deceptive and misleading trade practices.

Whether there is a need for such a duty depends on whether there are trade practices which remain unregulated. The view of the Office of Fair Trading appears to be that there are still areas of doubt, with the result that there is still ample evidence of consumer dissatisfaction with the way in which consumer protection laws are implemented (*A General Duty to Trade Fairly* (OFT 1986), paras 1.13 to 1.17; *Consumer Dissatisfaction* (OFT 1986)).

There are misleading statements in respect of goods and services which do not presently fall within the provisions of the Trade Descriptions Act 1968, ss. 1 and 14 (see 11.3.1 and 11.3.2). Some of these practices may be policed by self-regulating codes of practice, but it has already been observed that such codes are only fully effective if the trade association promoting them can command the membership of all traders in the line of business to which their code of practice applies.

3.12.3 Advantages and disadvantages of a general duty

Whether or not the imposition of a general duty to trade fairly is an advantageous move will depend very much on the form in which it is implemented (see 3.12.4 for the alternatives). However, in general terms, it can be argued that a general duty to trade fairly avoids a case-by-case approach to trading malpractice and concentrates, instead, on general patterns of trading practice. Moreover, a general duty is a flexible tool, particularly taken in conjunction with a published list of recognised forms of misleading conduct. This last requirement is important in order to counteract the criticism of general duties that they tend to produce uncertainty in trading circles about what is regulated conduct. By virtue of the generality of a duty to trade fairly, the law provides a safety-net for the protection of consumers. Furthermore, a general duty to trade fairly also provides an opportunity to overcome the limitations of the civil law and the criminal law as a means of consumer protection. In particular, it avoids some of the problems of enforcement currently associated with consumers having to pursue a civil action in order to seek redress and may answer the critics of the use of the criminal penalty as a means of enforcement (see Thomas (1985) 4 Tr L 74 at pp. 74-5).

3.12.4 The form of a duty to trade fairly

A number of possible approaches could be taken in formulating a duty to trade fairly. But in seeking the most desirable solution, it is necessary to consider the criticism of a general duty that it tends to produce uncertainty. The problem of uncertainty can be met if the approach adopted in the Trade Descriptions Act 1968, s. 2, is employed, namely, Parliament should seek to define in an exhaustive list those practices which are regarded as misleading. However, such an approach inevitably raises the problem of under-inclusion. Furthermore, while it is possible to add to the list of forbidden practices, the inflexibility of the legislative machine may prevent new forms of trading abuse from being speedily added to the list.

One possible approach would be to impose a general prohibition on all forms of deceptive, misleading or unconscionable conduct (see the United States Federal Trade Commission Act 1970, s. 45(a)(1)). While this approach has the effect of catering for all forms of trading abuse, it has the unfortunate effect of leaving traders, enforcement authorities and consumers in the dark as to when a trader has infringed the duty. Furthermore, experience of the Federal Trade Commission Act has shown that a general duty of this kind tends to produce endless litigation, seeking to determine what is deceptive, misleading or unconscionable.

A way of avoiding the defects of the two approaches so far considered is to combine elements of both. For example, it would be possible to lay down a general duty to refrain from deceptive, misleading or unconscionable trading practices, but supplement the general duty with a list of conduct defined as misleading etc. (see British Columbia Trade Practices Act 1979, ss. 2, 3 and 4; Australian Trade Practices Act 1974, ss. 52 to 64). Furthermore, in order to provide for new practices, it would be necessary to allow for additions to the list by means of subordinate legislation.

The combined approach appears to be that which has been adopted recently in the Consumer Protection Act 1987, ss. 20 to 22, in relation to misleading statements as to the price of goods and services. While there is a general prohibition on any form of misleading price statement, there is also a more specific definition of what statements are acceptable in the form of a code of practice issued under s. 25 of the Act (see further chapter 12). If a general duty is considered necessary, this sort of combined approach is to be preferred.

A final consideration in relation to a general duty to trade fairly is how it is to be enforced. Clearly, the use of criminal sanctions as a means of enforcement may not be the best way ahead, particularly if a person is branded as a criminal for some act which is not clearly defined as illegal. The preferred view of the Office of Fair Trading is that local authority trading standards departments should have a major role in enforcement and that they should secure enforcement by means of written assurances under a regime similar to that which presently exists under the Fair Trading Act 1973, part III (*A General Duty to Trade Fairly* (OFT 1986), paras 5.28 to 5.36).

3.13   A GENERAL DUTY TO TRADE FAIRLY – MATERIALS FOR CONSIDERATION

For text see 3.12.

If it is decided to impose a duty to trade fairly, what form would it take?

A General Duty to Trade Fairly
Office of Fair Trading (1986)

5.13   The Office has considered carefully the many points which have been put to it on this topic. While recognising that it will be necessary to exercise judgment over the appropriate balance when the objectives are in conflict to some extent, the Office suggests that a new general duty should aim to meet the following criteria:

(a)   it should have the twin overall objectives of raising trading standards generally and providing cheaper and readily accessible means for consumers to obtain redress;

(b)   it should be structured to facilitate a rolling back of the criminal law where possible and appropriate;

(c)   compliance costs to businessmen should be minimised;

(d)   it should provide a range of sanctions;

(e)   enforcement should be quick and primarily local;

(f)   there should be reasonable certainty as to what in the context of any business would constitute fair trading practice;

(g)   the law should be flexible and adaptable to deal with new trading practices as they arise;

(h) it must be capable of dealing uniformly with unfair trading practices in particular sectors, and therefore apply to traders whether or not they are members of trade associations.

Form of a general duty to trade fairly
5.14 Without prejudice to the requirements of the existing general law, legislation would provide for the introduction in the United Kingdom of a general duty to trade fairly, which would be a broad statutory duty. It might alternatively be framed in terms such as a general prohibition on deceptive and misleading practices. Arguably this could be supplemented by specific prohibitions of particular unacceptable practices.

5.15 The question arises whether obligations under the general duty to trade fairly should be limited to transactions between trader and consumer or should extend also to transactions at an earlier stage in the cycle of production and distribution, that is between trader and trader. On the one hand, it could be argued that if there were to be established a general duty to trade fairly it ought to apply whether a customer is a business or a private consumer. On the other hand those in business are normally better equipped than consumers to look after their own interests. There may also be a basic difficulty in determining what, as between traders, constitutes fair or unfair trading. If unfair trading is taken in the sense of advantage being taken of a relatively weaker position, much in trader-trader relationships can be held to be of its nature 'unfair'. The Office consequently does not consider that a general duty should extend to trader-trader relationships. Thus the law would need to distinguish for this purpose between 'consumer' and 'non-consumer' transactions: a 'consumer' might be defined to include acting on behalf or in the interest of other individual consumers. There appears no case for setting an upper value limit on consumer transactions in this context. The general duty would apply to all sectors of industry, trade and services including manufacturers but only in their dealings with consumers.

Codes of practice
5.16 The Office envisages that legislation would make provision for the general duty to be supported by codes of practice both vertical (by trading practice) and horizontal (by sector) setting out the trading practices which were regarded as acceptable (or unacceptable) in the sectors concerned. The Office proposes that such new-style codes should be introduced, taking account of discussions with the interests concerned, by the Director General of Fair Trading; it would seem appropriate for the codes to have the endorsement of the Secretary of State and be laid before Parliament.

5.17 The existing codes of practice which the Office has endorsed could provide the starting-point for discussion of the sectoral codes which would be needed to supplement the general duty to trade fairly. Existing Office-endorsed codes are only partial in their coverage of consumer transactions. . . .

5.20 The Office envisages approved codes containing a statement of general principles of fair trading pertinent to the sector but not being excessively detailed. Thus for example traders' obligations in respect of the provision of appropriate information, written estimates, spare parts, servicing or the features of extended warranties would be included in relevant sectors. As a further instance approved codes should provide a means of banning arbitration clauses in some traders' standard contracts which oblige consumers to go to arbitration and deprive them of their rights of access to the court including the small claims procedure or, in Scotland, to the sheriff court.

Implementation
5.23   There are various ways in which a general duty could be implemented. One option would be for the obligations under a general duty to trade fairly to apply only to the extent spelt out in approved codes of practice. Under this approach a general duty would in effect be introduced sector by sector. If no approved codes existed for a particular sector or trading practice, the ordinary law would prevail and the general duty would not apply. It would take time for codes to be introduced, and consequently consumers would have different rights, and traders different responsibilities in different sectors. On the other hand once approved codes were in place they would have statutory backing and would apply to all traders in the sector, not only to members of trade associations.

5.24   Alternatively it is arguable that a general duty might apply to all consumer transactions, whether or not approved codes were in place. With this approach codes would amplify the general duty as and when they are negotiated. That duty would be framed in general terms but might be accompanied by some basic definitions or illustrations of what is involved in unfair trading and, in the absence of codes specifically approved in this context, it would be for the courts over time to develop an interpretation of what is required and to define the relationship of the duty to existing law. The courts would in this way be given overriding power to reinterpret bargains between traders and consumers and to consider contractual obligations in the light of the general obligation to trade fairly, if appropriate varying the contract to ensure that its terms were fair. In doing so, account would be taken not only of the letter of the contract and the provisions of the existing general law but of the fairness of the contractual terms and of the circumstances in which it was entered. One option would be to produce guidelines to aid interpretation. Such an approach would have the advantage of an immediate impact but would be subject to the criticism that there may be unavoidable confusion and uncertainty to traders, consumers and the courts over the meaning of a general duty in a particular transaction pending the development of case law, and the negotiation of codes. In this framework it would be open to a trader to adduce as a defence in proceedings that he observed the terms of a code which although not formally approved in connection with the general duty did in fact satisfy its requirements.

Enforcement
5.28   Local authority trading standards departments (and environmental health departments as appropriate) should be given a major role in enforcement. Without such a role for local enforcement agencies, which can act quickly on the basis of local information, a general duty would be unlikely to be effective in raising trading standards or improving redress. The Office proposes that in the event of a trading standards officer becoming aware, through complaint or otherwise, of instances of trading practices which he considers to be a breach of the relevant code, it would be open to the officer to make an informal approach asking the trader to comply with the code and, in a suitable case, ask the trader to give redress to aggrieved consumers. If the informal approach failed it would be open to the trading standards officer to serve the trader with a formal notice. This would set out the alleged breach of the code and invite the trader to propose a remedy which would include an undertaking to comply with the relevant code provisions and an offer to give suitable redress. If the trader complied with the formal notice, that would be the end of the matter. If, however, the trading standards officer were unable to obtain a satisfactory response, he could take action in the local county or sheriff court seeking a court order requiring the trader to comply with the

relevant sections of the code and, where appropriate, to give suitable redress. If the trading standards officer's case were successful the court would grant a mandatory injunction or interdict ordering the trader to refrain from breach of the relevant sections of the code and would order redress to any consumers who had been injured by the breach of the code. Ultimately the sanctions for breach of the injunction would be a fine or imprisonment for contempt of court. In instances where financial compensation was not appropriate, an alternative sanction open to the court could be to declare the contract unenforceable. The above procedure could also be applied to breaches of the existing civil and criminal law.

CHAPTER FOUR

Consumer Redress

The fact that the consumer has legal rights in respect of defective goods and services is little compensation if there is not a suitable and inexpensive means of enforcing those rights. This chapter seeks to examine sources of consumer advice and assistance and the various avenues of consumer redress in both civil and criminal proceedings and those arising out of trade association codes of practice.

4.1 CONSUMER ADVICE AND ASSISTANCE

4.1.1 Consumer advice

Even where a consumer does have grounds for complaining about goods or services supplied to him, it does not always follow that he will be aware of his grounds for redress. Accordingly, there is a strong argument in favour of national publicity campaigns to ensure that the necessary information is made available to consumers to allow complaints to be taken further. Organisations such as the National Consumer Council and the Consumers' Association have played their part in publicising matters of consumer concern, seeking to explain in simple terms the rights of the consumer when things go wrong. Moreover, recent years have seen the codification of a number of common law rules affecting consumers, based on the generally held view that if matters related to consumer redress are conveniently stated in an Act of Parliament, people are more likely to be aware of those rights than if they are hidden in obscure common law rules. Clearly a campaign to increase consumer awareness of rights is essential, for without this basic information, there is no prospect of matters being taken further.

In addition to the information provided by specific consumer organisations, consumer advice is also made available through local authority consumer advice centres (see 2.2.2) and trading standards departments and Citizens Advice Bureaux (see 2.5). The advice given by these organisations may sometimes result in the settlement of a dispute, but frequently the matter may go further with the result that the complaint is referred to a solicitor with the possibility of legal action in mind. However, it is often the case that matters go no further since the prospect of pursuing a complaint through the court system may deter the consumer for a number of reasons (see 4.3.1). But, in any case, there is evidence that the present system fails the consumer since lawyers generally show little interest in consumer complaints on the grounds of cost, and advice centres are hard pressed to deal with the social welfare problems that come their way. Accordingly, the consumer may find himself in a position where informed advice is only available from Citizens Advice Bureaux, consumer organisations and the national and local media (Cranston, *Consumers and the Law* 2nd edn, (1984), pp. 83-5).

It has been argued that a national consumer agency might be in the best position to provide the necessary 'competent and accessible national network of generalist advice agencies' (Royal Commission on Legal Services (Cmnd 7648, 1979)). However, it has subsequently been observed that while progress has been made, the aim of the Royal Commission has been nowhere near achieved (National Consumer Council, *Good Advice for All* (1986), para 1.3). The particular problems identified in the field of consumer advice appear to be a lack of any sort of centralised government policy, disparities in advice provision at a local level, in particular the availability of advice services in rural areas and inadequate provision for funding of advice services (National Consumer Council, *Information and Advice Services in the UK* (1983)).

In order to improve provision for consumer advice, it has been suggested that there should be a comprehensive network of local advice centres capable of dealing with a wide range of matters such as social security, housing, fuel, consumer, money, employment, immigration and family matters, geared to the particular needs of the local area (National Consumer Council, *Good Advice for All* (1986), para. 1.12). In addition to this basic provision, it is also recommended that there should be access to a wider specialist service which is capable of providing, *inter alia*, representation services, debt advice services, research and legal casework services (ibid., para. 1.13).

4.1.2   Legal aid and advice

Where the consumer considers taking matters further, a means of obtaining legal advice and some means of financial support for the less well-off is necessary. It has been observed that the principle that everyone should have access to the law is meaningless if those who are unable to afford the services of a lawyer cannot use it (National Consumer Council, *Ordinary Justice* (1989), p. 73).

The present legal aid and advice system for the purposes of civil matters manifests itself in three main forms, namely full legal aid, the 'green form' scheme and advice by way of representation, although the latter tends to be used mainly for matrimonial matters rather than consumer disputes.

4.1.2.1 Full civil legal aid Where full civil legal aid is given, it will provide financial assistance in respect of the consumer's own legal costs and will cushion the recipient against the full financial consequences of an unsuccessful action since he is only required to pay the other party's costs so far as is reasonable, having regard to the means available to the parties (Legal Aid Act 1974, s. 8(1)(e)). In one sense, only unsuccessful litigants are legally aided since if the consumer is successful, the cost to the legal aid fund is recoverable from the costs awarded to the legally aided party.

Not every applicant for legal aid will be successful since both a merit test and a means test will have to be endured before a legal aid certificate is granted. Thus, the consumer may fail at the first hurdle, if the legal aid area office decides that there are not reasonable grounds for taking or defending the action. Moreover, unless a proposed action is particularly important, full civil legal aid is not normally granted in small claims proceedings. Since the majority of consumer complaints will fall within this category, the availability of legal aid is severely restricted.

Even where the merit test is satisfied, the consumer may also be turned down on the ground that his means are sufficient to render him ineligible for civil legal aid. The means test covers both the disposable income and capital of the applicant and his or her spouse. If the applicant's income is considered to fall within the specified upper and lower income levels, he will be required to make a contribution, which may be paid in instalments. Only those with very low incomes are entitled to free legal aid.

4.1.2.2 The green form scheme Under the green form scheme, the consumer can obtain initial legal advice on any matter. A solicitor may provide up to £50 worth of advice without seeking approval. Only those with less than average incomes are eligible for free advice, although applicants with higher incomes may qualify on condition that they make a contribution.

4.1.2.3 Critique of the legal aid and advice system One of the earliest criticisms of the system was that few people were aware of its existence. There is evidence that many litigants in personal injury actions had consulted a solicitor but were still unaware that financial assistance was available to them (Harris et al., *Compensation and Support for Illness and Injury* (1984)). Attempts have been made in more recent years to give greater publicity to the scheme by circulating an explanatory booklet to advice centres, libraries and the courts. In order to reach a wider audience, the booklet has also been translated into a number of different languages.

Other criticisms include the administrative delays in approving applications for legal aid and the inadequate payments made to those solicitors participating in the scheme. One consequence of insufficient remuneration is that the number of solicitors now carrying out legal aid work is falling significantly.

Perhaps most importantly, the number of people eligible for legal aid has also fallen in recent years due to the fact that means test limits have not been kept in line with rises in the value of State benefits and average earnings with the result that possibly 25% of the population was ineligible for legal aid by 1986 and since then matters appear to have deteriorated (Glasser, LS Gaz, 9 March, 1988, p. 11).

In the light of these criticisms, the Lord Chancellor's Department carried out a survey of the legal aid system, which recommended a closer relationship between solicitors in private practice and organisations such as advice centres. The other principal recommendations of the survey were that green form advice should only be available for a limited range of legal problems, which include the normal range of consumer complaints. Furthermore, there was a general recommendation that all initial advice should be given by advice centres, and cases should only be referred to a solicitor when it becomes clear that legal action should be taken, thereby releasing public money for generalist advice centres.

The survey and a white paper which followed it (*Legal aid in England and Wales* (Cm 118, 1987)) resulted in the Legal Aid Act 1988 which creates a Legal Aid Board conferred with powers to administer the legal aid scheme and advise on possible improvements, still leaving overall control of the scheme in the hands of the Lord Chancellor's Department.

4.2 CONSUMER ADVICE AND ASSISTANCE – MATERIALS FOR CONSIDERATION

4.2.1 Consumer Advice

For text see 4.1.1.

National Consumer Council, *Good Advice for All*
(1986)

A comprehensive advice network: our model
1.12   The core of the network is a neighbourhood-based advice service able to offer enquirers — irrespective of race, religion, sex or political persuasion — advice, practical assistance and mediation on all subjects. . . .

1.13   In addition to this core of neighbourhood-based advice services, each community should have access to a wider network of more specialised services able to provide:

*   detailed and expert casework in the fields of social security, housing, fuel, consumer, money, employment, immigration and family matters. These represent the major areas of work at present, and will need to be amended and added to as new needs arise;
*   representation at tribunals;
*   representation at county courts;
*   legal casework and assistance for community groups;
*   an independent public health inspection service;
*   debt/money advice and negotiation services;
*   research, education and project work designed to meet the inarticulated needs for advice and legal services;
*   resources which enable people to participate in decisions and policy-making which affect their community.

This will require advice or legal workers who specialise in each of these areas and who will work from, for example, law centres, housing aid, consumer and money advice centres, and citizens advice bureaux.

Consumer principles applied to local advice services
1.26   When the NCC investigates the way goods and services are being provided — anything from buying a kettle to choosing a home, from using the health service to catching a bus — we focus particularly on: *access* — can consumers actually get the goods, service or information they need?
choice — does the consumer have any?
information — is it adequate to enable consumers to make a sensible choice? *quality* — are standards as high as they can reasonably be?
redress — is there any, when things go wrong?

1.27   The strand running through this list of basic consumer interests — and through much of our work — is to make it easier for consumers to make better decisions for themselves and in so doing help themselves and their families give and get their dues as citizens.

1.28   In terms of advice this policy framework has been interpreted as follows:
  *   *access*: is there a centre within easy reach of the consumer?

are local centres open at appropriate times?

are they sufficiently well staffed to avoid long periods of waiting?

are the premises physically accessible, particularly for those with limited mobility or sensory impairment?

does the style of work of the centres make the service psychologically accessible to all sections of the community?

are outreach services provided to meet the needs of isolated and housebound consumers?

  *   *choice*: is there a sufficient range of specialist services to meet the specific needs of consumers?

are consumers offered a choice of styles of advice provision, sufficient to meet the diversity of needs?

  *   *information*: are services well publicised and signposted?

do services go beyond advice-giving to individuals and provide educational services and information materials?

do centres possess sufficient information resources to enable them to provide accurate and up-to-date assistance to consumers?

  *   *quality*: is the advice which consumers receive appropriate, accurate and up to date?

are there sufficient staff to allow consumers to receive the full extent of assistance required?

are staff adequately trained and experienced? do centres possess sufficient information materials?

are services free to act in the best interests of consumers?

are services free of party political interests?

   *   *redress*: are the services accountable to the local community?

is there a complaints procedure?

are centres covered by adequate indemnity insurance?

4.2.2   Legal aid

For text see 4.1.2.

National Consumer Council, *Ordinary Justice*
(1989), pp. 98–101

Strengths and weaknesses of the present system
Along with other Western European countries, Britain has adopted what the Americans call a 'judicare' system of legal aid. In their international survey of access to justice, Cappelletti and Garth describe 'judicare' as:

> a system whereby legal aid is established as *a matter of right* for all persons eligible under the statutory terms, with *the State paying the private lawyer* who provides those services. The goal of judicare systems is to provide the same representation for low income litigants that they would have if they could afford a lawyer. The idea is to make a distinction only with respect to the billing: the State, rather than the client, is charged the cost.

. . . Although legal aid aims to overcome the cost barrier, it does not overcome any of the other barriers which people encounter in using lawyers. It does very little to inform people of their legal rights, and it does not prevent them from being intimidated by the idea of going into a solicitor's office. Few solicitors' offices are located in deprived areas where the poor have most need of them, and solicitors receive little training in social welfare law. The problem is circular — the poor do not think of using a lawyer for advice with their problems, hence lawyers do not develop skill and expertise in these areas, and a service is not available for those wishing to use it.
. . . The legal aid scheme is dominated by traditional areas of lawyers' practice such as matrimonial and personal injuries work. Although welfare benefit and debt cases are growing fast, the numbers of people helped in social welfare law under the green form scheme are tiny in comparison with those helped by advice centres.
The problem is compounded by the fact that legal aid does not cover representation before the majority of tribunals, including industrial tribunals, and both first and second tier tribunals dealing with social security and immigration. Solicitors'

experience in this area is likely to be confined to representing employers in unfair dismissal and redundancy cases. Without the experience of seeing cases through, they rarely give advice about these matters under the green form scheme. The idea is perpetuated that social security and immigration are not proper 'legal work'. In preliminary research carried out into the green form scheme one solicitor commented on this dilemma:

> 'The issue was raised in 1984 about whether welfare benefit work or immigration work was proper solicitors' work. It's related to the question of why solicitors don't do certain types of work. It becomes a self-defining and self-perpetuating definition which rests entirely upon the *status quo*: it's proper solicitor's work because solicitors do it.'

In 1977, the National Consumer Council published *Why the Poor Pay More* which looked at ways in which the poor received less value for money from both private and public services. We concluded that despite the legal aid scheme, legal services were not readily available to the poor. The poor lived in neighbourhoods with a smaller choice of solicitor, and solicitors had less knowledge of the areas of law that most concern them. The poor had little access to information about their legal rights, and were unlikely to be familiar with using a solicitor's office. There was little empirical evidence on whether legally aided clients received a service of equivalent standard to fee-paying clients, but it was likely that the ignorant and inarticulate demanded and received less from their solicitors. The legal aid scheme of itself did little to address inequalities in knowledge or use, or to encourage solicitors to provide new services. We concluded that there was a need to make lawyers more accessible through salaried services in law centres and community agencies.

Although the detail has changed in the last 12 years, we consider that the essential analysis of *Why the Poor Pay More* continues to apply to legal services provision.

4.3 CONSUMER REDRESS IN CIVIL PROCEEDINGS

Where the legal advice given to the consumer is that he stands a reasonable chance of success in legal proceedings, he may decide to take the matter further. Where the consumer decides to sue, it is likely to be in contract or tort and dependent on the value of the action will be heard in the High Court or the county court, although the latter is now the more likely venue, for reasons to be considered below.

The jurisdiction of the county court is defined in the County Courts Act 1984, s. 15 (as amended), as including any action founded on contract or tort in respect of an amount not in excess of £15,000 or any greater sum by agreement of the parties. Furthermore, the county court may also hear actions in respect of extortionate credit bargains up to the £15,000 limit (Consumer Credit Act 1974, s. 139(5)(a)). Where the action involves an amount in excess of £15,000, it falls within High Court jurisdiction, but this does not necessarily mean that it will be heard in the High Court. New procedures have been introduced in the Courts and Legal Services Act 1990, s. 1, which allow for the transfer of business between the High Court and the county court by order of the Lord Chancellor. Included in the list of powers available to the Lord Chancellor is the power to confer jurisdiction on the county courts in relation to proceedings in which the High Court has jurisdiction (Courts and Legal Services Act 1990, s. 1(1)(b)). In coming to a decision to make an order of this kind, the Lord Chancellor may take into account criteria such as the value of actions, the nature and complexity of the proceedings and the parties to those proceedings (Courts and Legal Services Act 1990, s. 1(3)). The effect of these provisions is to avoid the criticism voiced in the Civil Justice Review (Cm 394, 1988), para. 71, that too many cases are dealt with at an unnecessarily high level.

4.3.1   The problems of civil litigation

There are a number of considerations which may deter the consumer from instituting civil proceedings. A general feature of civil law rights is that the consumer must take the initiative in commencing proceedings - no one is going to do this for him. The opening assumption, therefore, is that the consumer knows his rights and is prepared to take action to enforce them, but this is frequently not the case since adequate consumer advice is not always available. There also appear to be other reasons why consumers do not take the initiative, for example, they may lack the motivation to take the matter further; the cost may appear too great; the formality and remoteness of the courts may appear too daunting and the amount the consumer stands to recover, if successful, may not make litigation worthwhile (see generally Cranston, *Consumers and the Law*, 2nd ed. (1984), pp. 81-3).

The response to many of these problems has been the introduction of a small claims procedure in the county court designed to reduce the cost of litigation and cut out much of the formality associated with court proceedings.

4.3.2   County court litigation

More than 90% of all civil proceedings commence in the county courts and for the purposes of consumer complaints, this means that virtually all claims by or against consumers of goods and services will be subject to the rules of procedure which apply to county courts.

It has been noted that very few consumers who have a complaint actually use the county court. Indeed on one assessment it would appear that only 2% of consumers who believed that they had grounds for complaint actually took the step of threatening action in the county court (Office of Fair Trading, *Consumer Dissatisfaction* (1986)).

4.3.2.1   Small claims procedure   In order to simplify matters and in an attempt to provide an accessible cheap and easy procedure for resolving the likes of consumer disputes, an automatic small claims arbitration procedure was introduced in 1973. The basis for the procedure is contained in the County Court Rules 1981, ord. 19, part I, which provides for defended claims of not less than £1,000 to go to arbitration before a registrar, or exceptionally a circuit judge or outside arbitrator. Under the scheme one of the parties can apply to the registrar to have the case heard in full court. However, this will only be allowed where a difficult point of law or fact is in issue, where a charge of fraud

has been made or where it would be unreasonable for the matter to be heard by the arbitrator.

In theory, the principal advantages of the arbitration scheme are that strict rules of the law of evidence are inapplicable and that proceedings are much less formal than full court proceedings. The County Court Rules 1981 provide that there should be a preliminary hearing before a registrar to consider the dispute and try to find a way of resolving it (ord. 19, r. 5(2)). Should this not be possible, a date is fixed for the hearing at which the arbitrator may adopt such procedure as he considers appropriate to allow each party to present his case. Legal representation is permitted, but is generally not encouraged since there is a rule to the effect that costs of representation are only recoverable where incurred through the unreasonable conduct of the other party (County Court Rules 1981, ord. 19, part I).

4.3.2.2 Critique of the small claims system

A number of deficiencies in the small claims arbitration scheme have come to be identified in the light of the experience of its operation. In particular, while the scheme was intended to open up the courts to the likes of consumers, statistics show that only a small proportion of plaintiffs bringing actions in the county courts are consumers whereas a substantial number of defendants are consumers. In other words the small claims procedure is being used to a substantial extent by businesses to recover debts from consumers. Recent statistics show that private citizens represented 38% of plaintiffs and 58% of defendants whereas the percentage of business plaintiffs was 52% and business defendants 40% (Report of the Review Body on Civil Justice (Cm 394, 1988), p. 89, table 12).

The fact that so few consumers use the small claims procedure also seems to suggest that there may be a publicity problem. While there is useful information published by the Lord Chancellor's Department which explains the nature of the arbitration scheme on a national level, the same level of information is not always available on a local level. For example, it has been suggested by the National Consumer Council that information provided by local courts is frequently not understandable because it is written in legal jargon and in some cases important information is omitted such as how long proceedings will take and what papers ought to be brought to court (*Ordinary Justice* (1989), p. 288). Moreover, while information on the procedure taken is available, little is said about how to enforce a judgment. While it may be fairly easy to secure judgment against a trader, it is not so easy to make him pay.

A further matter of concern was the £500 limit on cases subject to automatic referral to arbitration. This limit has now been raised to £1,000 on the suggestion of the Civil Justice Review, which will substantially improve matters, by including a large number of consumer complaints in respect of relatively expensive items such as holidays, home improvement work, furniture, carpets, domestic appliances and motor vehicles.

While the small claims procedure is supposed to be informal, much depends on the attitude of the registrar hearing the dispute. There is evidence that some registrars have found it difficult to break away from their formal legal training and still adhere to the ordinary rules of evidence (National Consumer Council,

Ordinary Justice (1989), p. 295). For example, the informal procedure has not prevented an unrepresented consumer plaintiff from being cross-examined by a solicitor acting on behalf of the defendants (*Chilton* v *Saga Holidays plc* [1986] 1 All ER 841). Since the rule-making body has decided that legal representation is not forbidden, it follows that the registrar cannot prevent a party from making proper use of the services of his solicitor (*Chilton* v *Saga Holidays plc* at p. 843 per Lord Donaldson MR).

For the most part, it would appear that registrars who take a more formal line are more inclined to hold a preliminary hearing than those who approach the arbitration scheme on an informal level. The objection to the preliminary hearing is that it takes up valuable time and is a substantial cause of lost wages resulting from enforced attendance at court.

4.3.3 Alternative arbitration schemes

Because of deficiencies in the county court arbitration scheme when it was first introduced, a number of alternative schemes have grown up, particularly those operated by trade associations. Many codes of practice contain provisions to the effect that consumer disputes should be referred to arbitration, should an initial conciliation process instigated by the trade association itself fail to achieve results. For the most part, such arbitrations are based on documentary evidence, with the result that costs are substantially reduced and the consumer avoids the problem of having to take time off work in order to attend a hearing.

One of the main difficulties with such schemes is that the way in which arbitration clauses in consumer contracts have been worded in the past suggests that they are a method of ousting the jurisdiction of the courts. However, the answer to this complaint is that arbitration clauses of this kind also tend to provide that where the matter is agreed to be referred to an arbitrator his decision on the matter is to be treated as final. As such, there is an agreement to go to arbitration and the arbitration clause cannot be treated as a unilateral attempt by one of the parties to the contract to oust the jurisdiction of the courts (*Ford* v *Clarksons Holidays Ltd* [1971] 1 WLR 1412).

While the reduction in costs brought about by arbitration provisions is often an advantage to the consumer, it cannot always be said that arbitration is an ideal solution to consumer disputes. Often, the complaint may be sufficiently serious for the consumer to wish to consider litigation. Unfortunately, the effect of an agreement to go to arbitration is to prevent the consumer from asserting his right to use the courts. In order to meet this criticism, the Consumer Arbitration Agreements Act 1988 (CAAA) provides that where a person deals as a consumer, an agreement that a dispute between the parties shall be referred to arbitration cannot be enforced against him in respect of a cause of action to which the Act applies (CAAA 1988, s. 1(1)). However, s. 1(1) specifies three instances in which the consumer is bound by an agreement to go to arbitration, namely, where he has agreed in writing to go to arbitration after a dispute has arisen (s. 1(1)(a)); where he has submitted to arbitration in pursuance of the agreement (s. 1(1)(b)) and where a court order is made to the effect that the dispute shall be referred to arbitration (s. 1(1)(c)).

The provisions of s. 1(1)(b) may cause some difficulty, in that it will be necessary to decide when the consumer has submitted to arbitration in pursuance of the agreement. It may be that before a consumer is deemed to have submitted to arbitration, he must be fully informed of the consequences of his actions, with the result that agreement cannot be inferred from an acceptance by a third party. There may also be an onus on the party wishing to enforce the arbitration provision to show that there has been an attempt to explain to the consumer the effect of accepting an arbitration provision as part of the contract.

CAAA, s. 1(1)(c), allows the High Court or county court to order that the matter be referred to arbitration where it would not be detrimental to the consumer to do this (CAAA 1988, s. 4(2)) and so long as the dispute falls outside the small claims jurisdiction of the county courts (CAAA 1988, s. 4(4)(a)). Whether or not it is detrimental to the consumer's interests is determined by reference to matters such as the availability of legal aid, and likely expense to the consumer (CAAA 1988, s. 4(3)).

4.3.4 Class actions

It has been observed that one of the difficulties of the civil justice system is that, for the most part, it is left to the individual consumer to pursue the trader who has caused the damage of which the consumer complains. In many instances, the consumer may be deterred from taking matters further because of the cost and difficulty involved in doing so. However, in some instances, particularly in product liability cases involving design defects (see 8.2.3.2) a wide range of consumers may be affected by a single act on the part of a manufacturer. For example, in recent years the manufacture of the drugs thalidomide and opren resulted in widespread harm to consumers and the actions of the South Western Water Authority in allowing harmful chemicals to be deposited in domestic water supplies have resulted in extensive harm. In such cases, there is clearly some merit in pursuing consumer complaints on a class basis, whereby representatives of the consumer group sue on behalf of the rest.

If a number of different plaintiffs have been injured in the same accident as a result of a single defendant's alleged negligence, there is nothing to stop the actions of all plaintiffs from being joined. However, where there is no common accident, joinder of actions is not possible, but the use of a test case may be an alternative. For example, an individual plaintiff may be singled out as representing the whole class of plaintiffs affected by the defendant's action (Rules of the Supreme Court 1965, ord. 15, r. 12). However, there is a major obstacle to such actions in that it has been held that damages cannot be recovered on the part of the class in a representative action because the merits of each individual plaintiff's case might differ (*Markt & Co. Ltd* v *Knight Steamship Co. Ltd* [1910] 2 KB 1021; cf. Federal Rules of Civil Procedure for the United States District Courts (1966), r. 23). Furthermore, it has been observed by the present Master of the Rolls that, in his view, the concept of the class action is, as yet, unknown to the English courts. However, he has gone on to say that the desirability of such actions is something that ought to be considered and that, in the meantime, courts must be flexible and adaptable in applying existing procedures with a view to reaching a decision quickly and economically where large numbers of plaintiffs are involved (*Davies* v *Eli Lilly & Co.* [1987] 3 All ER 94 at p. 96 per Sir John Donaldson MR).

In some instances, the courts have appeared to be more lenient. For example, it has been held that where a representative action is brought, it is open to a member of that class to treat the decision in the representative action as *res judicata*, but it will still be necessary for him to prove damage in a separate action (*Prudential Assurance Co. Ltd* v *Newman Industries Ltd* [1979] 3 All ER 507 at p. 521 per Vinelott J).

As an alternative to individual actions brought on behalf of a representative group of potential plaintiffs, it might also be possible to allow an action to be brought on behalf of consumers generally by a representative agency (see Tur (1982) 2 J Legal Stud 135 at pp. 162-3). Clearly, such actions would be public-interest based rather than being geared towards the needs of individual consumers who may have suffered specific harm at the hands of a particular defendant. For example, action might be taken in respect of a particular practice which is potentially harmful to consumer interests generally. To a certain extent this power already exists in other areas of English law. For example, action may be brought by the Commission for Racial Equality or the Equal Opportunities Commission to eradicate persistent discriminatory practices. Similarly, the Director General of Fair Trading has powers under the Restrictive Trade Practices Act 1976 in respect of registrable restrictive trading agreements.

In cases involving the consumer interest, bodies such as the Consumers' Association appear to have some role to play. The Association's magazine *Which?* regularly runs a consumer advice column, requesting consumers to submit their legal problems and on occasions, the Association is prepared to commit resources to assisting a particular consumer if the case has a significant bearing on consumer interests generally. For example, in *Woodman* v *Photo Trade Processing Ltd* (May 1981 unreported) the Association's chief legal officer appeared in the county court to argue one of the first cases to be heard under the Unfair Contract Terms Act 1977. But this is a long way from the type of representative action which may be brought in some other jurisdictions (cf. British Columbia Trade Practices Act 1979, ss. 18 and 24).

4.4 CONSUMER REDRESS IN CIVIL PROCEEDINGS – MATERIALS FOR CONSIDERATION

4.4.1 Small claims procedure

For text see 4.3.2.1.

National Consumer Council, *Ordinary Justice*
(1989), pp. 301-4

A system of justice which meets the needs of unrepresented litigants is a radical step, needing major departures from traditional court practices and a new attitude from court staff and judges. Over the last 15 years, England and Wales have gained considerable experience of how a small claims procedure can work, and there are many examples of good practice. It is now time to build on good practice to ensure a nationally consistent procedure, which is simple, cheap, quick and fair, and can be used by ordinary people without lawyers.

The main changes which need to be introduced are:

1.   Improving the identity of the small claims procedure
In *Simple Justice* we found that individual litigants often did not know the difference between the county court, the small claims court, or arbitration. We agree with the Civil Justice Review that rules, forms and signs within county courts should specifically refer to 'small claims' and 'the small claims court'. An entry should be placed under 'small claims court' in the telephone directory.

We recommend that the Lord Chancellor's Department takes steps to publicise the small claims court as a place for resolving consumer disputes.

2.   More advice from court staff
We are very pleased that the Review has recommended that court staff should be trained to advise litigants on the procedure and to give help completing forms. Where possible, small claims should have their own staff, trained to help individuals enforce small claims decisions.

3.   A separate arbitration code
We agree that the small claims procedure should have its own short code, written in simple English. It should be self-contained, and other county court rules shuld not apply. Small claims litigants should not have to deal with lawyers brandishing copies of the green book.

4.   Court forms
The Review recommends that the Lord Chancellor's Department should produce well designed forms written in plain English for use throughout the country. These should be piloted before being introduced. The explanatory small claims booklet should also be updated and simplified. We agree.

We wish to see standard claim forms covering the most common consumer disputes, together with leaflets on how to complete them. There should also be a short leaflet on how to prepare for the hearing sent to litigants with the notice of hearing.

5.   Serving the claim
It is often difficult for consumers to find the address of the registered office of the company they are suing. We consider that consumers bringing claims for faulty products or services obtained from a shop should be able to serve the claim on the shop rather than on the company's registered office. In order that corporate defendants are not inconvenienced, the time for filing a defence could be extended from 14 to 21 days in such cases.

6.   Dispensing with the preliminary hearing
We agree with the Review that a preliminary hearing should only be held in a limited number of cases. Normally, court staff would look through the claim form and defence and clarify matters by telephone or post. Court staff will then set a date and send a notice to the litigants, enclosing advice on preparing for trial. The notice should include a

phone number and contact name so that litigants can contact staff if they are unsure about the procedure or need to ask for another date.

7. Legal jargon in court documents

We wish to discourage lawyers from writing documents in legalese, especially in small claims proceedings. Where claims or defences have been written by lawyers in language which is incomprehensible to lay people, the court should have the power to return their documents and ask that they be rewritten.

8. Conduct of hearings

We agree with the Review's recommendation that the arbitration code should provide the outline of how hearings should be conducted. Registrars should try to set the parties at ease, explain the procedure and law, and take the initiative in finding the facts. They should explain why they have reached their decisions. The object is to make lawyers unnecessary. The way in which hearings are conducted should not change when lawyers are present.

We are plesed that the Review has recommended that witnesses should not be cross-examined directly by lawyers and that questions should be asked through the registrar. The ruling in *Chilton* v *Saga Holidays plc* needs to be reversed.

9. Training for registrars

We agree with the Review's proposals for improving training for registrars in conducting small claims. The training could include videos of hearings, discussion, and practical exercises, and should be supplemented by a manual on the conduct of hearings. We wish to see the manual made public but it should not have any official status. Registrars will also need regular updates on the substantive law.

10. The time and place of hearings

We endorse the Civil Justice Review's recommendation that evening courts should be established on an experimental basis. Hearings should be in small informal rooms, and need not always be on court premises. Hearings should be in private, but, if litigants agree, interested onlookers should be allowed to sit in.

11. Expert evidence

The court should have the power to ask for expert reports out of public funds, as in Northern Ireland. We would like to see the Institute of Trading Standards Administration provide the courts with details of where test reports can be obtained at reasonable cost.

12. Expenses

We agree with the Review that the arbitration code should spell out the standard approach to travel expenses and lost earnings. The registrar should ask the successful party about these as a matter of course at the end of the hearing, and should award them against the loser. Other expenses, such as expert reports, should be a matter of discretion.

13. Advice and representation

The greater use of small claims proceedings will increase rather than diminish the need for free, independent advice from an advice centre. People thinking of using the small claims court should be able to seek advice about the merits of their case and the procedure. In a few cases, which involve complex points or where individuals have particular difficulties expressing themselves, litigants will need to be accompanied to the hearing.

We agree with the Review's proposal that litigants should be able to be accompanied by the representatives of their choice. Representatives should only be excluded if they are unruly, and registrars should give reasons for excluding anyone.

The rule that legal costs may only be awarded in exceptional circumstances should continue. Lawyers should not be necessary and the risk of having to pay high legal costs would deter people from using the court.

14. Link officers

The Review recommends that courts should appoint a link officer, from whom advice agencies can obtain information and guidance about court proceedings. The link officer should ensure that litigants are aware of sources of advice and that forms and leaflets about the small claims scheme are prominently displayed in the locality.

15. Increasing the small claims limit

In 1979 we recommended that the small claims limit should cover the purchase price of most major consumer durables, with the exception of new cars, and we urged that it be increased to £500. We endorse the Review's recommendation that the limit should now be raised to £1,000. This would also cover minor personal injury claims, including pavement trips.

There may be a case for a further increase in the limit if the changes we have recommended prove effective. But we do not wish to restrict the availability of legal aid for claims over £1,000 until it is shown that consumers can use the procedure comfortably without lawyers.

16. Appeals

Simple justice need not necessarily be rough justice. As the small claims limit is increased and the system grows in importance, we recommend that rights of appeal should be extended.

4.4.2   Class actions

For text see 4.3.4.

R. H. S. Tur, 'Litigation and the consumer interest; the class action and beyond',
(1982) 2 J Legal Stud 135, pp. 148-9, 153, 161-3

In some areas of law there is little need to stimulate litigation. In other areas of law, however, there are significant restraints which are susceptible of manipulation in order to facilitate access to the courts. The restraints are well-known. They include the disproportion of loss and costs although the total unjust enrichment may be considerable where many individuals each suffer modest loss. That is clearly a matter of public concern. Legal aid may not be available or, if it is, the vast majority of victims may enjoy incomes which take them out of the scope of such aid without placing them in a financial position to contemplate litigation. Victims may lack the knowledge and skills necessary to an assertion of right, or potential litigants may perceive themselves as weak and isolated in comparison to well organised defendants. Aggressive plaintiffs may be bought off by way of settlement to avoid an embarrassing precedent in the courts and a succession of like actions. . . .

Such considerations point to the conclusion that the challenge facing the consumer movement is that of devising appropriate means to facilitate access to the courts, not only to provide remedies for injured parties but also to deter breaches of and encourage conformity to the law. The 'test case' is such a device but its impact is limited in that the losing defendant is under no legal obligation to treat other potential plaintiffs in like fashion to that determined by the court in the case of the 'test' plaintiff. . . .

Consumer law has failed to deliver; consumer rights go by default; enforcement agencies have limited impact, especially upon civil remedies; regulatory agencies are neither equipped nor designed to assert the consumer interest by way of the judicial process. In such circumstances, the class action appears an attractive recourse. 'Mass injuries represent a characteristic feature of our epoch' (M. Capelletti, *Access to Justice*, vol. 3, p. 519). Given the collective nature of defendants a collectivity of plaintiffs seems an appropriate counter-balance. The class action meets one of the most obvious restraints upon litigation by pooling the interests and possibly the resources of many plaintiffs, each of whom may have suffered modest loss. If A defrauds B of £5,000,000 the law provides a remedy; if A has the wit to defraud one million individuals of £5 each, absent any class action procedure, he runs little risk of civil action on the motion of any one of them; 'By the simple device of committing numerous small wrongs, law breakers might escape the aim of justice as long as they stay clear of criminal sanctions and the reach of repressive administrative action' (Homburger (1971) 71 Colum L Rev 609 at 641). This is unsatisfactory, not only in that individuals are in fact denied remedies to which they are legally entitled, but also in that the purpose of the law, namely securing conduct in conformity with legal rules, is thwarted. The class action is also defended as a means of upholding the law, the threat of mass damages restraining the potential defendant from breaches of law in pursuit of profit.

However, the class action alone is a limited reform and steps beyond the class action call for consideration, steps which if implemented would establish 'public interest actions' or actions on behalf of the 'consumer interest'. We are well reminded of the alleged 'law of non-transferability of law (Seidman (1970) 5 Law Soc Rev 161 at 200–1). Transplanting legal institutions and procedures calls for detailed consideration of the conditions which contribute to their successful functioning in their native environment. By its very nature the class action raised difficulties of initiative and management. In America the public interest lawyer, contingent fees and treble damages secure external management and initiative. 'Perhaps the aspect of the American class action for damages which is most notable to European eyes is the role of the lawyer, in developing, managing and often financing the lawsuit' (Fisch (1979) 27 Am J Comp Law 51 at 58). Without functional equivalents of that role, the implementation of the class action may not produce all the perceived advantages. 'Class actions are not a universal panacea . . . they still require consumers to take the initiative' (Cranston, *Consumers and the Law*, p. 98).

Commentators such as Professor Fisch draw attention to what they see as functional equivalents or analogues of the class action operative in Continental jurisdictions. Broadly speaking, these exhibit the common feature of giving selected groups and associations standing to pursue actions in the courts on behalf of particular interests such as those of consumers or environmentalists where such groups are regarded as serving the public interest. In France, by permitting these groups to be constituted *partie civile* actions for damages on behalf of the collective interest fostered by the group becomes a procedural possibility. The comparable process in Germany is the *Adhäsionprozess* which is more restrictive, contemplating only material and not moral interest and consumer groups specifically authorised by statute to sue on behalf of the consumer interest can seek only injunctive relief. In France more significance is attached to securing observance of the law than to obtaining damages. As Professor Fisch observes, 'In France [when] a group is permitted to claim damages for collective injury the amounts recovered have usually been small or even nominal [*un franc de dommages-intérêts*] and the main purpose of the action has been to ensure the enforcement of the law' (Fisch (1979) 27 Am J Comp Law 51 at 79). The statutes in France qualifying group actions are chiefly concerned with intangible interests of a diffuse and fragmented kind such as moral opposition to racialism or prostitution or a commitment to environmentalism or consumerism where damages necessarily assume low priority. In France consumer groups can sue for damages but generally only on the basis of injury to the collective interest they foster and not on behalf of individual consumers. In Germany consumer groups are authorised to sue only for injunctive relief and cannot obtain damages on behalf of individual consumers. It is, therefore, misleading to regard the French or German processes as functional equivalents of the class action which emphatically seeks to redress the individual losses of a collectivity of plaintiffs.

There are apparent virtues in combining the class action, increasingly characteristic of common law jurisdictions, and the role of groups developed in Continental systems, most particularly in France. Two types of class actions would then be possible; first, the class action *simpliciter* or the 'internal plaintiff class action' in which one or several individuals take action on behalf of themselves and all other members of the class on the basis of a cause of action which he or they share with all other members; secondly, a type of group action which is taken on behalf of the consumer interest or the public interest by a group or association granted statutory standing to sue wherein, quite apart from injunctive or declarative relief and quite separate from damages in its own right for injury to the interest it fosters, damages on behalf of affected individuals may be sought and awarded. To distinguish this latter type of class action it may be called a 'public interest class action' or an 'external plaintiff class action'. Given the problems of management and initiative and the need to secure conformity between conduct and legal rules there would be a place for such external plaintiff class actions even where provision had been made in a legal system for the class action *simpliciter*. The external plaintiff class action would meet many of the difficulties of management and initiative and ensure that collective, knowledgeable, repeat playing defendants were met by collective, well-informed, experienced plaintiffs, to the betterment of the enforcement of the law. It would meet the point, as true today as when uttered 20 years ago that 'the rights which the law gives to the consumer too often go by default (Cmd 1781 (1962), para. 403). And it meets, in part, the observation that 'what is really needed in Britain is a procedure . . . whereby consumer protection agencies can take proceedings on behalf of consumers affected by a breach of the civil law' (Cranston, *Consumers and the Law*, p. 100) albeit by substituting private, voluntary, extra-governmental groups for the regulatory agencies or governmental bodies originally contemplated by Ross Cranston.

Consequently, the first step beyond the class action suggested by a consideration of developments on the Continent is the external plaintiff class action wherein consumer groups could take action on behalf of individual consumers and obtain damages on their behalf. This could meet the potential gap as regards initiative and management caused by the absence of any functional equivalent of the public interest lawyer and the contingent fee.

4.5   CONSUMER REDRESS IN CRIMINAL PROCEEDINGS

A significant part of consumer protection law is to be found in the form of statutory provisions imposing criminal liability on the part of traders (see chapters 9, 11 and 12). While some of these statutes confer a right of civil action for breach of statutory duty (see 8.6) others do not. Moreover, the main purpose of the criminal law is not to provide compensation for individuals who may suffer at the hands of a wrongdoer, but to encourage improved trading standards.

Despite these general observations on the role of the criminal law as a means of consumer protection, ss. 35 to 38 of the Powers of Criminal Courts Act 1973 now give a criminal court the power to award compensation to the victim of a crime provided civil proceedings have not been concluded before the date of conviction of the offender (*Hammertons Cars Ltd* v *Redbridge London Borough Council* [1974] 2 All ER 216). If civil proceedings are subsequently successful, the amount of compensation awarded under the 1973 Act must be deducted from the subsequent award of damages (Powers of Criminal Courts Act 1973, s. 38).

In order for the compensation provisions to apply there must be a conviction and the victim must be able to show that he has suffered loss in the form of 'personal injury, loss or damage' (Powers of Criminal Courts Act 1973, s. 35(1)); *R* v *Horsham Justices, ex parte Richards* [1985] 2 All ER 1114). However, in some cases proof of the value of the harm suffered may be very difficult to provide, for example, where the victim suffers distress or anxiety. In such cases, it would appear that such proof is unnecessary where the court is able to assume that the victim must have been terrified or frightened (*Bond* v *Chief Constable of Kent* [1983] 1 All ER 456).

While there must be a conviction, it is no longer the case that there must be a punishment in the form of a fine or imprisonment, since it is now provided that a compensation order may be made instead of punishment (Powers of Criminal Courts Act 1973, s. 35(4A)). Furthermore, general encouragement in favour of making compensation orders is given by the requirement that if a court decides not to make an order for compensation, it should give its reasons for doing so (Criminal Justice Act 1988, s. 104(1)).

Certain matters limit the court's decision on the matter of compensation. In particular, regard must be had to the defendant's ability to pay (Powers of Criminal Courts Act 1973, s. 35(1A)) and the court is able to give the offender time in which to pay the compensation or order payment by instalments (Powers of Criminal Courts Act 1973, s. 34).

CHAPTER FIVE

Exclusion Clauses and Other Unfair Terms in Consumer Contracts

5.1 REASONS FOR THE CONTROL OF EXCLUSION CLAUSES

The principle of freedom of contract suggests that it should be open to the parties to a contract to agree to whatever terms they see fit. However, where one of the parties is a consumer, the courts and Parliament have taken a stand against the indiscriminate use of exclusion and limitation clauses, particularly where they are contained in standard-form documents.

5.1.1 Inequality of bargaining power and paternalism

One view of these standard-form contracts containing exclusion clauses is that they have developed out of the concentration of business in a relatively small number of hands (*Schroeder Music Publishing Co. Ltd* v *Macaulay* [1974] 3 All ER 616 at p. 624 per Lord Diplock). It may also be objected that such contracts are not the subject of negotiation between the parties and that they may be described as weapons of consumer oppression (Yates, *Exclusion Clauses*, 2nd ed., p. 2). These arguments are consistent with the 'exploitation theory' of exclusion clauses in consumer contracts (see Kessler (1943) 43 Colum L Rev 629; Slawson (1971) 84 Harv L Rev 529).

The exploitation theory may not fully explain the Unfair Contract Terms Act 1977 which seeks to prevent or limit to a reasonable extent the use of exclusion clauses in consumer contracts. The use of exclusion clauses in relation to certain types of contract term, such as the implied terms as to quality in contracts for the supply of goods, is prohibited altogether. It is doubtful whether the use of exclusion clauses in this context is any more exploitative than in the context of the supply of services. But in the latter case, an exclusion of liability in a consumer contract is permitted where reasonable. In these circumstances, it may be that Parliament has acted out of paternalist motives to protect what may be perceived as inalienable rights which should never be subject to an exclusion of liability.

5.1.2 Transaction costs

Arguments based on the notion of inequality of bargaining power assume a monopoly or near-monopoly situation in which the consumer is faced with little or no choice but to take the terms offered to him if he wishes to make use of the goods or services on offer. Sometimes it may be argued that the standard-form contract is not the instrument of consumer oppression outlined above, but a means of reducing transaction costs with the result that goods and services may be made available to consumers at lower cost than would otherwise be the case. For example, in relation to the sale of insurance, there is a wide choice of policies available, if the consumer cares to look, but there appears to be little or no negotiation over the terms of those policies. It has been argued that the fact that there is no negotiation over terms is not that insurance companies wish to browbeat consumers but because it is not cost-effective to negotiate individual contracts with each consumer (Posner, *Economic Analysis of Law*, 2nd ed., p. 84; see also Trebilcock in *Studies in Contract Law* (eds Reiter and Swan, 1981), p. 381). If the consumer compares competing policies, he will find what he wants and the insurer with the least attractive terms will be compelled by market forces to produce something more attractive.

5.1.3 Information

While it may be true that the consumer can shop around in the market-place, it would appear that this is not always done. There are rules at common law which require a business seeking to rely on an exclusion clause to communicate its existence to the consumer. However, the consumer may not read the terms of the standard-form contract thrust at him by the other party. Accordingly, it may be that the objection to the use of exclusion clauses in standard-form consumer contracts is to be based on the notion of information asymmetry. The consumer can only make an effective choice if he has the necessary information at his fingertips. In this respect, it may sometimes be necessary for Parliament to legislate for the form and content of certain contract terms.

5.2 REASONS FOR THE CONTROL OF EXCLUSION CLAUSES – MATERIALS FOR CONSIDERATION

For text see 5.1.

Slawson, 'Standard form contracts and democratic control of lawmaking power'
(1971) 84 Harv L Rev 529, pp. 530-2, 565-6

The predominance of standard forms is the best evidence of their necessity. They are characteristic of a mass production society and an integral part of it. They provide information and enforce order. A typical automobile insurance policy, for example, informs the policyholder how to conduct himself should he become involved in an accident or other kind of occurrence from which liability of the kind covered may arise. It enforces all or a part of such conduct by the sanction of denying insurance protection unless it is performed. These services are essential, and if they are to be provided at reasonable cost, they must be standardised and mass-produced like other goods and services in an industrial economy. The need for order could, in theory, be fully satisfied by officially drafted rules — by laws in the traditional sense. One of the beliefs by which our society is organised, however, is that at least some lawmaking is better accomplished in a decentralised manner. We therefore prefer that the economy be controlled privately to a large extent, and private control today means control largely by standard form. . . .

The prevalence of uncontrollable standard forms also has unfortunate economic results. The effect of mass production and mass merchandising is to make all consumer forms standard, and the combined effect of economics and the present law is to make all standard forms unfair. Mass production and mass merchandising work to make all forms standard because a nonstandard form is characteristically just as expensive for a seller to make and sell as is a nonstandard tangible product. In either case he loses the ability to spread his costs of 'production' — legal or mechanical — over a large number of products. The rational decision is therefore normally either not to offer nonstandard products or to charge much higher prices for them. The much higher price for a nonstandard tangible product may not be too high to discourage its sale entirely — custom-made automobiles still have some market, for example — but two additional factors make it unlikely that a form will ever be 'custom-made'. First, the buyer of a nonstandard form would normally have to pay the expenses of his own attorney in negotiating it, in addition to the extra costs of the seller. Second, whatever benefits a buyer could obtain from a seller by negotiating a nonstandard form could normally be obtained more easily and less expensively in other ways. If he wanted increased warranty protection, for example, a buyer could probably obtain the same protection less expensively by purchasing insurance to cover the risks which would be covered by an expanded warranty. Even more simply, he could just pay the extra unreimbursed repair costs himself. . . .

It would be unrealistic to try to make the law of contract fair and legitimate by insisting that a standard form, to be enforceable, must be an uncoerced, informed agreement. The extreme specialisation of function of modern life requires that we contract with each other too frequently to take the time to reach even a mildly complicated agreement every time we do, and the complexity of modern life and modern law combine to demand that even minor agreements usually be complicated. There are other situations, moreover, in which even if we were willing to devote the time, any agreement reached would be without the consent of one of the parties because the other would have possessed the power to dictate the terms without question. To obtain other benefits which we consider sufficient, we have created or tolerated monopolies in many areas of life. The power to contract in this situation is the power of one party to impose whatever terms he likes on the other. . . .

Conclusion

If contract law is to provide the basis for a democratic system of private law and for a competitive economy which works in the interests of consumers — indeed, if it is to meet the minimal requirements of rationality — it must take into account the two pervasive conditions under which modern contracting takes place. Most contracts today are made quickly, often without thought as to any but their major terms, and many contracts are made without one party having any real alternative but to accept the terms which the other party sets. The first condition is adequately taken into account if we restore the principle that a contract includes only those terms which *both* parties can reasonably be expected to understand. Quick contracts are then necessarily simple, and the issuers of standard forms are required in every situation to make the contents of their forms reasonably understood by the recipient or the forms will not be considered contracts. A form which is not a contract can nevertheless be enforced, if its terms can be justified by reference to standards which do appear in the contract or to public standards imposed or approved judicially. The second condition can be adequately taken into account by recognising that contracts of adhesion gain no legitimacy from the supposed consent of the party for whom they are adhesive, since manifestations which are known to be the product of adhesion do not express consent. Contracts of adhesion therefore gain whatever legitimacy they have from their capability of justification by reference to the same public standards as are needed to support those parts of every standard form which cannot be supported by reference to an actual contract. There being no private consent to support a contract of adhesion, its legitimacy rests entirely on its compliance with standards in the public interest. The individual who is subject to the obligations imposed by a standard form thus gains the assurance that the rules to which he is subject have received his consent either directly or through their conforming to higher public laws and standards made and enforced by the public institutions that legitimately govern him.

5.3 COMMUNICATION TO THE CONSUMER

Since an exclusion clause is a contract term, it is subject to ordinary principles of contract law. In particular, before a consumer can be said to have contracted on terms which are unfair to him, it must be shown that the other party, or *proferens* has adequately communicated the effect of the exclusion to the consumer.

In most consumer contracts, the *proferens* will make use of a standard-form document containing the terms on which he wishes to contract. In some instances the consumer will not sign the document and may not even read it. In the latter event, it is for the *proferens* to show that he has done sufficient to convey his intention to rely on the term as part of his contract with the consumer.

5.3.1 The requirement of reasonable notice

The *proferens* must show that he has taken steps to give reasonably sufficient notice of the existence of an exclusion clause to the other party to the contract (*Parker* v *South Eastern Railway Co.* (1877) 2 CPD 416). Where the other party is a consumer, it would appear that the *proferens* may need to take special steps to ensure that the consumer not only knows that there are purported exclusions of liability but also how far they go (*Thornton* v *Shoe Lane Parking Ltd* [1971] 2 QB 163). The difficulty this creates is that if the requirement is applied to all terms in consumer contracts, contract documents may become excessively bulky. In some instances, communication of all of the terms on which the consumer is expected to contract is feasible, as where the consumer books a holiday and is supplied with a brochure containing the terms of contracting of the tour operator (*Hollingworth* v *Southern Ferries Ltd* [1977] 2 Lloyd's Rep 70). However, in other cases this is not so. For example, it would not be possible to print all the terms on which British Rail contracts on a standard railway ticket. Accordingly, reference to the document in which those terms can be found on the ticket is permitted, provided this is clear (*Sugar* v *London, Midland & Scottish Railway Co.* [1941] 1 All ER 172).

What is reasonable depends on the circumstances of each case. Thus if the consumer possesses peculiar characteristics, it may be that additional steps must be taken to adequately communicate the intention to rely on the exclusion of liability. Thus it may be that where the *proferens* frequently deals with consumers who do not speak English, it may be necessary to provide a translation of the terms in question (*Geier* v *Kujawa* [1970] 1 Lloyd's Rep 364; cf. *Saphir* v *Zissimos* [1960] 1 Lloyd's Rep 490).

The nature of the purported exclusion is also important. It would appear that in addition to the reasonable notice rule a further 'red hand' rule has also developed (see Macdonald [1988] JBL 375) which applies to individual terms as opposed to all of the proposed terms of the contract. Some terms are so onerous in effect that before notice could be said to be sufficient, they would need to be printed in red ink with a red hand pointing towards them (*J. Spurling Ltd* v *Bradshaw* [1956] 1 WLR 461 at p. 466 per Denning LJ). It can follow from this that the majority of the terms proposed by the *proferens* satisfy the reasonable notice test, but one or two may be subject to the more onerous 'red hand' test because of what they purport to do. Thus it has been said that some exclusions may be so unreasonably wide and destructive of rights that only the most explicit reference to them will suffice (*Thornton* v *Shoe Lane Parking Ltd* [1971] 1 QB 163 at p. 170 per Lord Denning MR). How far the rule extends is not entirely clear. Alternative formulations apply it to unreasonable contract terms (ibid.); to terms which are unusual in the class of contract under consideration (ibid. at p. 172 per Megaw LJ); or to terms which are onerous or unusual (*Interfoto Picture Library Ltd* v *Stiletto Visual Programmes Ltd* [1988] 1 All ER 348 at p. 350 per Dillon LJ).

5.3.2 Signed contractual documents

Where the consumer signs a document which contains contractual terms, he is bound by those terms even where the contractual document has not been read (*L'Estrange* v *Graucob Ltd* [1934] 2 KB 394). The signature of the consumer is regarded, in law, as the clearest objective evidence of acceptance of the terms proposed in the document. Exceptionally, a signed document is not binding, for example where the signature has been obtained by fraud or misrepresentation (*Curtis* v *Chemical Cleaning & Dyeing Co. Ltd* [1951] 1 KB 805) or where an express oral statement overrides the terms of the written agreement (*J. Evans & Son (Portsmouth) Ltd* v *Andrea Merzario* [1976] 1 WLR 1078).

5.3.3 Implied communication

In some instances it will not be possible for the *proferens* to show that the consumer has actual knowledge of an exclusion clause. For example, a notice refering to a purported exclusion of liability may have fallen down, or the notice may be displayed where it can be read only after the contract has been entered into (*Olley* v *Marlborough Court Hotel Ltd* [1949] 1 KB 532). Where this is the case, the court may be prepared to infer awareness of the relevant term by reference to a previous course of dealing between the parties.

Normally, this inference of awareness is made in the case of business transactions where the parties have consistently dealt with each other over a long period of time. The nature of many consumer transactions is such that a consistent course of dealing will rarely be encountered except in the case of the frequent use of travel services and possibly consistent use of the same garage for the purposes of maintaining the family car (see also *Mendelssohn* v *Normand* [1970] 1 QB 177 at p. 182 per Lord Denning MR).

Where knowledge of a contract term is implied, two conditions must be satisfied. First, the *proferens* must show that there is a consistent course of dealing between the parties. If there are inconsistencies in business practice, it is unlikely that a course of dealing will be established (*McCutcheon* v *David Macbrayne Ltd* [1964] 1 WLR 125). Secondly, if the course of dealing is sporadic, the element of consistency is not satisfied and knowledge of the exclusion will not be inferred (*Hollier* v *Rambler Motors (AMC) Ltd* [1972] 2 QB 71). Furthermore, where the plaintiff is a consumer, there may be the problem of inequality of bargaining power, which may justify a restrictive approach to the inference of knowledge of contract terms (*British Crane Hire Corporation Ltd* v *Ipswich Plant Hire Ltd* [1975] QB 303 at p. 310 per Lord Denning MR).

5.3.4 Exclusion clauses and third parties

Sometimes it is necessary to decide if an exclusion clause can affect the liability of a person who is not a party to the contract with the consumer. Problems of this kind have been encountered more frequently in business transactions where the question has arisen whether C can claim the protection of an exclusion clause contained in a contract between A and B where A, B and C are all parties to a chain of related contracts. In these cases, whether or not the exclusion can be relied on by C has depended on how clearly it has been stated by A that the term of the contract protects C (*New Zealand Shipping Co. Ltd* v *A. M. Satterthwaite & Co. Ltd* [1975] AC 154).

Ordinarily, where consumer contracts are concerned, the courts are likely to apply the doctrine of privity of contract strictly so as to prevent the *proferens* from broadening the scope of the exclusion of liability to include employees, agents and subcontractors. Thus a passenger on board a ferry may proceed against members of the crew whose alleged negligence has caused harm to the passenger's property, even though the ferry operator has excluded his own liability and purported to extend that exclusion to include employees (*Adler* v *Dickson* [1955] 1 QB 158).

5.3.5 Non-contractual exclusions

Where an exclusion of liability does not form part of a contract between the consumer and the person seeking to rely on it, it will not affect the contractual liability of the parties, but it could serve as a disclaimer in respect of tortious liability. Thus if a purported exclusion of liability is contained in a document regarded as a receipt rather than a contractual document (*Chapelton v Barry Urban District Council* [1940] 1 KB 532) or where the manufacturer of a product purports to exclude his liability in respect of certain losses by means of a statement on the packaging of his product, there may not be a contractual relationship, but it must be considered whether the disclaimer affects the defendant's liability.

For the purposes of disclaiming tortious liability, the reasonable notice rule still applies in that the disclaimer must be sufficiently clearly worded and displayed in a prominent position so that the plaintiff can take precautions for his own safety (*Ashdown v Samuel Williams & Sons Ltd* [1957] 1 QB 409). Furthermore, any ambiguity in the disclaimer will be construed *contra proferentem* in the same way as a contractual exclusion clause (*Vacwell Engineering Co. Ltd v BDH Chemicals Ltd* [1971] 1 QB 88 and see 8.2.3.3).

Where the disclaimer relates to negligently caused death or bodily injury, it will have no effect (Unfair Contract Terms Act 1977, s. 2(1)), but if it relates to negligently inflicted economic loss or property damage, it will be permitted, but only insofar as it complies with the reasonableness test laid down by the Unfair Contract Terms Act 1977, s. 11, which may be particularly difficult to satisfy where the other party to the contract is a consumer (see 5.7.4.1 and *Smith v Eric S. Bush* [1989] 2 All ER 514).

5.4   COMMUNICATION TO THE CONSUMER – MATERIALS FOR CONSIDERATION

5.4.1   The requirement of reasonable notice

For text see 5.3.1.

It is an essential requirement that a person wishing to rely on an exclusion clause must have given reasonable notice of the exclusion to the other party to the contract. However, whether this means reasonable notice of the existence of the clause or, more importantly, its precise effect is not entirely clear.

The decision in *Thornton v Shoe Lane Parking Ltd* [1971] 2 WLR 585 Court of Appeal, suggests that communication of the effect of the purported exclusion of liability is desirable.

Thornton v Shoe Lane Parking Ltd
[1971] 2 WLR 585
Court of Appeal

LORD DENNING MR at p. 589: Assuming, however, that an automatic machine is a booking clerk in disguise — so that the old-fashioned ticket cases still apply to it. We then have to go back to the three questions put by Mellish LJ in *Parker v South Eastern Railway Co.* (1877) 2 CPD 416, 423, subject to this qualification: Mellish LJ used the word 'conditions' in the plural, whereas it would be more apt to use the word 'condition' in the singular, as indeed the lord justice himself did on the next page. After all, the only condition that matters for this purpose is the exempting condition. It is no use telling the customer that the ticket is issued subject to some 'conditions' or other, without more: for he may reasonably regard 'conditions' in general as merely regulatory, and not as taking away his rights, unless the exempting condition is drawn specifically to his attention. (Alternatively, if the plural 'conditions' is used, it would be better prefaced with the word 'exempting', because the exempting conditions are the only conditions that matter for this purpose.) Telescoping the three questions, they come to this: the customer is bound by the exempting condition if he knows that the ticket is issued subject to it; or, if the company did what was reasonably sufficient to give him notice of it.

Mr Machin admitted here that the company did not do what was reasonably sufficient to give Mr Thornton notice of the exempting condition. That admission was properly made. I do not pause to inquire whether the exempting condition is void for unreasonableness. All I say is that it is so wide and so destructive of rights that the court should not hold any man bound by it unless it is drawn to his attention in the most explicit way. It is an instance of what I had in mind in *J. Spurling Ltd v Bradshaw* [1956] 1 WLR 461, 466. In order to give sufficient notice, it would need to be printed in red ink with a red hand pointing to it — or something equally startling.

Contrast *Parker* v *South Eastern Railway Co.* (1877) 2CPD 416 at p. 423 per Mellish LJ.

5.4.2 Implied communication

Where reasonable notice has not been given to the consumer, he may be deemed to have implied knowledge of the terms of contracting resulting from a consistent course of past dealings.

Mendelssohn v *Normand Ltd*
[1970] 1 QB 177
Court of Appeal

LORD DENNING MR at pp. 182–183: Secondly, there was a condition on the ticket. The attendant gave Mr Mendelssohn a ticket with printed conditions on it. Mr Mendelssohn had been to this garage a hundred times and he had always been given a ticket with the selfsame wording. Every time he had put it into his pocket and produced it when he came back for the car. He may not have read it. But that does not matter. It was plainly a contractual document: and, as he accepted it without objection, he must be taken to have agreed to it. That appears from *J. Spurling Ltd v Bradshaw* [1956] 1 WLR 461, 467. As Lord Devlin said in *McCutcheon* v *David Macbrayne Ltd* [1964] 1 WLR 125 at p. 134: 'when a party assents to a document forming the whole or a part of his contract, he is bound by the terms of the document, read or unread, signed or unsigned, simply because they are in the contract'.

The conditions on that ticket were, therefore, part of the contract.

In terms of consumer contracts, this is probably unrepresentative, since the majority of consumer purchases are infrequently made with the result that there is unlikely to be the necessary regularity of dealing for knowledge of the effect of an exclusion clause to be implied.

Hollier v Rambler Motors (AMC) Ltd
[1972] 2 QB 71
Court of Appeal

SALMON LJ at pp. 77–8: The *Hardwick Game Farm* Case [*Henry Kendall & Sons* v *William Lillico & Sons Ltd* [1969] 2 AC 21] seems to be a typical case where a consistent course of dealing between the parties makes it imperative for the court to read into the contract the condition for which the sellers were contending. Everything that the buyer had done, or failed to do, would have convinced any ordinary seller that the buyer was agreeing to the terms in question. The fact that the buyer had not read the term is beside the point. The seller could not be expected to know that the buyer had not troubled to acquaint himself with what was written in the form that had been sent to him so often, year in and year out during the previous three years, in transactions exactly the same as the transaction then in question.

The sellers in that case sought to rely on *McCutcheon* v *David Macbrayne Ltd* [1964] 1 WLR 125, which was also a decision of the House of Lords. They relied on that authority chiefly for a passage in the speech of Lord Devlin, at p. 134, which taken literally would mean that no term can be implied into a contract by a course of dealing unless it can be shown that the party charged has actual and not only constructive knowledge of the term, and with such actual knowledge has in fact assented to it. *McCutcheon* v *David Macbrayne Ltd* is an example of a case in which dealings between the parties prior to the contract in question cannot be relied upon to import a term into the relevant contract.

In that case the appellant had asked his brother-in-law to have a car shipped from Islay to the mainland. The appellant had personally consigned goods on four previous occasions. On three of them he was acting on behalf of his employer; on the other occasion he sent his own car; and each time he signed what was called a 'risk note'. The risk note made it plain that the respondents were accepting the goods on their ship on the condition that they would not be responsible for any damage by negligence that the goods might suffer during the course of the voyage. In that case, through negligence, the ship sank and the car was lost. The appellant's brother-in-law, who took the car to be shipped on the occasion in question, had himself consigned goods of various kinds on a number of previous occasions. He said that sometimes he had signed a note, and sometimes he had not. On one occasion he sent his own car. He said that on the occasion in question no risk note was put before him. Apparently, unknown to him, the purser, by mistake, had taken the car on board without asking him to sign the risk note. The House of Lords held, as I have already indicated, that there was no previous course of dealing from which the term of exclusion could be implied into the contract which had been made on behalf of the appellant by his brother-in-law. The appellant himself, as I have already said, had only consigned goods on some four previous occasions, but he, the appellant, had always signed a risk note. His brother-in-law had done so many times, sometimes after signing the risk note and sometimes not.

It seems to me that if it was impossible to rely on a course of dealing in *McCutcheon* v *David MacBrayne Ltd*, still less would it be possible to do so in this case, when the so-called course of dealing consisted only of three or four transactions in the course of five years. As I read the speeches of Lord Ried, Lord Guest and Lord Pearce, one, but only one among many, of the facts to be taken into account in considering whether there had been a course of dealing from which a term was to be implied into the contract was whether the consignor actually knew what were the terms written on the back of the risk note. Lord Devlin said that this was a critical factor. Even on the assumption that Lord Devlin's dictum went further than was necessary for the decision in that case, and was wrong — which I think is the effect of the *Hardwick Game Farm* case [1969] 2 AC 31 — I do not see how that can help the defendants here. The speeches of the other members of the House on the decision itself in *McCutcheon's* case [1964] 1 WLR 125 make it plain that the clause upon which the defendants seek to rely cannot in law be imported into the oral contract they made in March 1970.

5.5 JUDICIAL CONSTRUCTION OF EXCLUSION CLAUSES

Before the advent of statutory controls on exclusion clauses, where a term was said to have been adequately communicated to the other party, the greatest excesses of the business community were controlled through a process of judicial construction of the terms of the contract.

5.5.1 The *contra proferentem* rule

If a term of the contract is intended to benefit one party to the contract, it will be construed against the person seeking to rely on it in the case of any ambiguity. This process of construction would seek to identify whether the exclusion clause was sufficiently clearly worded so as to cover the breach of contract under consideration. Thus if the supplier of goods purported to exclude liability for breach of an implied term, this would not cover the breach of an express term of the contract (*Andrews Bros Ltd* v *Singer & Co. Ltd* [1934] 1 KB 17) and the purported exclusion of liability for a breach of warranty would be ineffective in relation to a breach of condition (*Wallis, Son & Wells* v *Pratt & Haynes* [1911] AC 394).

The courts came to look very closely at the wording of the contract and very often engaged in a hostile approach to the construction of contract terms perceived to be unreasonable. Generally, terms which purported to exclude liaiblity altogether were treated more harshly than those which sought to limit liaibility to a reasonable level. This led to the view that limitation clauses would normally be construed literally whereas it might be appropriate to construe an exclusion clause in a hostile manner (*Ailsa Craig Fishing Co. Ltd* v *Malvern Fishing Co. Ltd* [1983] 1 All ER 101 at p. 124 per Lord Wilberforce). Thus in *George Mitchell (Chesterhall) Ltd* v *Finney Lock Seeds Ltd* [1983] 2 AC 803 the House of Lords held that cabbage seed which produced cabbages with no heart had to be regarded a qualitatively defective cabbage seed and could not be treated as being something other than cabbage seed. This literal interpretation of the wording of a limitation of liability was more appropriate than the strained construction adopted by the majority of the Court of Appeal.

It would appear that whether the term is a limitation clause or an exclusion clause, it will continue to be construed against the person seeking to rely upon it where it derogates from common law rights (*Ailsa Craig Fishing Co. Ltd* v *Malvern Fishing Co. Ltd* [1983] 1 All ER 101 at p. 105 per Lord Fraser).

A further aspect of the *contra proferentem* rule is the extent to which a term can be used to restrict liability for negligence. The courts have taken the view that if the *proferens* would have been liable for his negligence but for the provision in the contract, he will still be so liable unless the clause is very clearly worded (*Alderslade* v *Hendon Laundry Ltd* [1945] 1 All ER 244). Thus generally worded provisions such as 'no liability accepted for damage howsoever caused' could be struck out on the ground that they did not cover liability for negligence.

5.5.2   The doctrine of fundamental breach of contract

A particular aspect of the *contra proferentem* rule which developed in the 1950s and 1960s was that the *proferens* could not rely on an exclusion or limitation clause where it sought to restrict liability in respect of the breach of terms which were fundamental to the contract. Thus if a person delivered a thing which was different in kind from the thing ordered, the *proferens* would not be able to rely on a term of the contract which purported to restrict the supplier's liability in that respect (*Karsales (Harrow) Ltd* v *Wallis* [1956] 2 All ER 866; see also the 'peas and beans' cases, e.g., *Chanter* v *Hopkins* (1838) 4 M & W 399).

The development of this doctrine involved a process of identifying those breaches which were fundamental to the contract. In particular, it was said that there would be such a breach if the party not in default is deprived of substantially the whole benefit it was intended that he should obtain from the contract.

With a view to consumer protection the doctrine of fundamental breach came to be regarded as a rule of law with the result that every time there was such a breach of contract, an exclusion clause in the contract would automatically fail (*Karsales (Harrow) Ltd* v *Wallis* [1956] 2 All ER 866). Whilst this provided a useful tool in respect of consumer protection, the general principle also applied to commercial contracts with the result that sensible business allocations of risk might be upset on the ground that there had been a serious breach of contract.

Ultimately, the rule of law approach was abandoned (*Photo Production Ltd* v *Securicor Transport Ltd* [1980] AC 827). Instead, the doctrine of fundamental breach was regarded as laying down nothing more than a rule of construction which required the court to consider whether the exclusion clause as worded was sufficiently clear to cover the particular breach under consideration. As such, it is merely an aspect of the *contra proferentem* rule.

5.6   JUDICIAL CONSTRUCTION OF EXCLUSION CLAUSES – MATERIALS FOR CONSIDERATION

5.6.1   The *contra proferentem* rule and the doctrine of fundamental breach

For text see 5.5.1 and 5.5.2.

The need to resort to a strained construction of the meaning of an exclusion clause is not so great as used to be the case because the courts may now strike down an unreasonable exclusion of liability under the Unfair Contract Terms Act 1977.

George Mitchell (Chesterhall) Ltd v *Finney Lock Seeds Ltd*
[1983] 2 AC 803
House of Lords

LORD BRIDGE at pp. 813-14: My lords, it seems to me, with all due deference, that the judgments of the learned trial judge and of Oliver LJ on the common law issue come dangerously near to reintroducing by the back door the doctrine of 'fundamental breach' which this House in *Photo Production Ltd* v *Securicor Transport Ltd* [1980] AC 827, had so forcibly evicted by the front. The learned judge discusses what I may call the 'peas and beans' or 'chalk and cheese' cases, sc. those in which it has been held that exemption clauses do not apply where there has been a contract to sell one thing, e.g. a motor car, and the seller has supplied quite another thing, e.g. a bicycle. I hasten to add that the judge can in no way be criticised for adopting this approach since counsel appearing for the appellants at the trial had conceded 'that if what had been delivered had been beetroot seed or carrot seed, he would not be able to rely upon the clause': [1981] 1 Lloyd's Rep. 476, 479. Different counsel appeared for the appellants in the Court of Appeal, where that concession was withdrawn.

In my opinion, this is not a 'peas and beans' case at all. The relevant condition applies to 'seeds'. Clause 1 refers to seeds 'sold' and 'seeds agreed to be sold'. Clause 2 refers to 'seeds supplied'. As I have pointed out, Oliver LJ concentrates his attention on the phrase 'seeds agreed to be sold'. I can see no justification, with respect, for allowing this phrase alone to dictate the interpretation of the relevant condition, still less for treating clause 2 as 'merely a supplement' to clause 1. Clause 2 is perfectly clear and unambiguous. The reference to 'seeds agreed to be sold' as well as to 'seeds sold' in clause 1 reflects the same dichotomy as the definition of 'sale' in the Sale of Goods Act 1979 as including a bargain and sale as well as a sale and delivery. The defective seeds in this case were seeds sold and delivered, just as clearly as they were seeds supplied, by the appellants to the respondents. The relevant condition, read as a whole, unambiguously limits the appellants' liability to replacement of the seeds or refund of the price. It is only possible to read an ambiguity into it by the process of strained construction which was deprecated by Lord Diplock [1980] AC 827, 851C in *Photo Production Ltd* v *Securicor Transport Ltd* and by Lord Wilberforce in *Ailsa Craig Fishing Co. Ltd* v *Malvern Fishing Co. Ltd* [1983] 1 WLR 964, 966G.

5.7   CONTROL OF EXCLUSION CLAUSES UNDER THE UNFAIR CONTRACT TERMS ACT 1977

5.7.1   Background

While common law rules on the communication and construction of exclusion clauses in contracts served to curb some of the excesses of business, it became appparent that those rules alone were not wholly capable of protecting the consumer interest. A widespread practice had evolved of excluding liability for breach of the implied terms in the Sale of Goods Act 1893. Exclusion clauses were also prevalent in other consumer contracts such as contracts with railway operators and other providers of consumer services.

The issue was passed to the Law Commission for consideration and in two reports (Law Com. No. 24 (1969); Law Com. No. 69 (1975)), legislation was recommended first in relation to the exclusion of liability for breach of the implied terms in supply of goods contracts and later in respect of the use of exclusion clauses in standard-form contracts generally. In particular, the Law Commission believed that in many instances the consumer was unaware of how he was being treated, but even where he was, he was often powerless to do anything but accept the terms offered because alternative, more favourable terms were not available (Law Com. No. 24 (1969), para. 68). Furthermore, the effect of some exclusions of liability was to deprive the consumer of certain specific rights which social policy required that he should have (Law Com. No. 69 (1975), para. 146).

One of the underlying assumptions of the Law Commission appears to be that consumers are not in a position of equal bargaining strength in comparison with the business with which they deal. However, the reasons for this inequality have to be closely examined (see 1.3.3) and there are cost reasons for the use of standard-form contracts which contain exclusions and limitations of the supplier's liability to the consumer.

Since the passing of the Unfair Contract Terms Act 1977, the European Community has also taken an interest in unfair terms in consumer contracts and the Commission has published a proposed Directive in this regard (COM(90) 322 fin OJ C243/2, 28.9.90) which contains many provisions similar to those contained in the Unfair Contract Terms Act 1977. The proposed Directive is concerned with terms which cause a significant imbalance in the parties' rights and obligations; terms which cause the contract to be unduly detrimental to the consumer; terms which cause performance of the contract to be significantly different from what the consumer could legitimately expect and terms which are incompatible with the requirements of good faith (proposed Directive, art. 1). The proposed Directive gives further guidance on unfair terms in a detailed annexe and requires member States to prohibit the use of such terms by a person acting in the course of a trade, business or profession where he deals with a consumer, but the fact that such terms are void will not affect the remaining terms of the contract (art. 3).

5.7.2   The scope of the Unfair Contract Terms Act 1977

The Unfair Contract Terms Act 1977 applies to purported exclusions of both contractual liability and liability under the tort of negligence. It covers unilateral exclusions of liability such as notices displayed by the occupier of premises which do not necessarily form part of a contractual relationship. The regime created by the 1977 Act comprises of two principal means of controlling exemption clauses. In some instances an exclusion clause is rendered statutorily invalid on the ground that it impinges on some inalienable right on the part of the consumer. In other cases, an exclusion clause may be treated as valid only if it satisfies a test of reasonableness.

5.7.2.1   Business liability   Subject to an exception in respect of supply of goods contracts (see 5.7.3.2), exemptions of liability in private transactions are not covered by the provisions of the Act. This follows from the assertion that the Act applies only to the purported exclusion of business liability (s. 1(3)).

The Act defines a business as including a profession and the activities of government departments or local or public authorities (s. 14), but it is clear that a person who grants access to premises for recreational or educational purposes does not fall within the regime created by the Act unless this is done as part of the business activities of the occupier (s. 1(3)(b)).

5.7.2.2 Primary and secondary obligations The Unfair Contract Terms Act 1977 is concerned with contract terms or notices which exclude or restrict liability. On a literal interpretation this might suggest that the Act only applies to the secondary obligations of the parties which follow from the breach of a primary obligation. On this basis, the Act is concerned mainly with provisions which exclude or limit the liability of the *proferens* where he has admitted a breach of duty. However, it is also possible for an exclusion clause to be drafted in such a way that it defines the primary obligations of the parties. For the most part, the Act will not apply to terms of the contract which operate in this way since this would involve an interference with the root of the contract. Thus if the consumer buys a car and the seller expressly states that the vehicle is guaranteed fit for all use other than for competitive racing, the seller is not excluding his liability should the car be raced, he is stating that he is selling a car suitable for purposes other than racing.

To this general rule there are two exceptions. First, the ability of a person to exclude the duty of care giving rise to liability in negligence is substantially limited (ss. 2, 5 and 13(1)). Secondly, the supplier of goods is not allowed to exclude his duties to a consumer which arise out of the terms implied by the Sale of Goods Act 1979 and related legislation.

5.7.2.3 Application to liability for negligence The Unfair Contract Terms Act 1977 clearly applies to an attempt by the *proferens* to exclude or restrict his liability for negligently caused harm. For the purposes of the 1977 Act negligence is defined as including the breach of a contract term requiring the exercise of reasonable care and skill, the breach of a common law duty of care and a breach of the common duty of care owed under the provisions of the Occupiers' Liability Act 1957 (s. 1(1)). Furthermore, for the purposes of the Act it does not matter that the breach of duty was inadvertent or intentional (s. 1(4)), which would seem to include the commission of any tort which requires the exercise of reasonable care. This would appear to include torts such as trespass to the person (see *Fowler* v *Lanning* [1959] 1 QB 476) and nuisance (see *Bolton* v *Stone* [1951] AC 850; *Goldman* v *Hargrave* [1967] 1 AC 645) insofar as they require the exercise of reasonable care.

So far as the provisions as to negligence liability are concerned, it will not be open to the *proferens* to argue that an exclusion clause prevents a duty of care from coming into existence where but for the exclusion, he would have been guilty of a failure to exercise reasonable care (s. 13(1)). Thus a building surveyor cannot provide a valuation report on a domestic dwelling which is qualified by a statement to the effect that the surveyor accepts no responsibility for the contents of the report (*Smith* v *Eric S. Bush* [1989] 2 All ER 514). In this respect, it is important to distinguish between the compilation of the report itself and the work which leads up to its compilation (*Smith* v *Eric S. Bush* p. 524 per Lord Templeman).

5.7.3   Statutory invalidity

5.7.3.1   Death and bodily injury caused by negligence   Any attempt to exclude or restrict liability for death or bodily injury resulting from negligence is void (Unfair Contract Terms Act 1977, s. 2(1); see also EC proposed Directive annexe (a)). Thus it is not open to a carrier of passengers to display a notice on a bus to the effect that passengers travel at their own risk (see also Public Passenger Vehicles Act 1981, s. 29). Where the defendant is in breach of a strict duty with the result that the consumer suffers bodily injury, s. 2(1) of the 1977 Act will not apply. However, other statutory provisions may serve to restrict the *proferens*'s ability to exclude his liability (see Defective Premises Act 1972, s. 1(1); Consumer Protection Act 1987, s. 7).

The EC proposed Directive differs in one very important respect in that it renders void any exclusion of liability for death or bodily injury resulting from an act or omission. As worded, this covers more than just negligence on the part of the *proferens* and will also cover acts or omissions which give rise to a strict liability on the part of the *proferens*.

5.7.3.2   Implied terms in consumer contracts for the supply of goods
Where the recipient of goods deals as a consumer (see 1.1) and the supplier seeks to exclude or restrict his liability in respect of a breach of the implied terms in the Sale of Goods Act 1979 or related legislation, the exclusion will be regarded as void (Unfair Contract Terms Act 1977, s. 6(1), (2); s. 7(2), (3A); see also EC proposed Directive, annexe (c)). If the recipient of the goods deals otherwise than as a consumer, liability for breach of the implied terms as to title (Sale of Goods Act 1979, s. 12; Supply of Goods (Implied Terms) Act 1973, s. 8; Supply of Goods and Services Act 1982, s. 2) cannot be excluded (s. 6(1), (2)). In relation to the remaining implied terms as to description, quality and fitness, liability for breach may be excluded in non-consumer transactions provided the exclusion clause satisfies the statutory test of reasonableness. An important point of distinction between the EC proposed Directive and the 1977 Act is that the latter applies to all types of supply, whereas, strangely, the proposed Directive is concerned only with the sale of goods (annexe (c)), which is not defined as including other forms of supply.

As a general rule, the 1977 Act applies only to business liability, but s. 6 applies to any contract of hire-purchase or sale of goods (s. 6(4)). Since the total invalidity provisions of s. 6 apply only where the buyer or hirer deals as a consumer and since a requirement of dealing as a consumer is that the supplier should act in the course of a business (see 1.1.2), it follows that the invalidity provisions will not apply to private supplies. However, where the goods are sold privately, a purported exclusion of the supplier's liability will be subject to the reasonableness test. This extension will only be relevant for the purposes of the implied terms as to description (Sale of Goods Act 1979, s. 13) and sample (Sale of Goods Act 1979, s. 15) since the implied terms as to quality and fitness only apply where the seller sells in the course of a business (Sale of Goods Act 1979, s. 14(2), (3)).

5.7.3.3 Guarantees of consumer goods A particular form of abuse which once adversely affected the consumer arose out of the use of exclusions of liability in guarantees provided by the manufacturer of consumer goods. The unfortunate effect of such guarantees was that on closer examination they gave the consumer fewer rights than he already possessed at law. If appropriately worded, the guarantee could negative the consumer's rights against both the retailer and the manufacturer himself, by confining the consumer's 'rights' to those provided by the guarantee itself.

The position in respect of such guarantees is now regulated by the Unfair Contract Terms Act 1977 which provides that where goods of a type ordinarily put to private use or consumption cause loss or damage either as a result of the defectiveness of the goods themselves or as a result of negligent manufacture or distribution, liability for such loss or damage cannot be excluded or restricted by reference to a guarantee of such goods (s. 5). For these purposes, a guarantee is anything in writing which purports to contain some promise or assurance that defects in the goods will be made good in some way (s. 5(2)(b)).

Section 5 does not affect the relationship between the consumer and the retailer (s. 5(3)), it merely applies to the relationship between the consumer and the producer. Since the 1977 Act applies to notices as well as to contract terms, it does not matter that there is no contractual relationship between the manufacturer and the consumer.

5.7.4 Exclusion clauses subject to the requirement of reasonableness

While some exclusion clauses are rendered totally invalid by virtue of the operation of the Unfair Contract Terms Act 1977, a variety of others are permitted provided they are regarded as reasonable. The onus of proving reasonableness rests on the *proferens* rather than the consumer being required to establish its unreasonableness (s. 11(5)).

5.7.4.1 Damage other than death or bodily injury caused by negligence If the *proferens* seeks to exclude or restrict liability for negligently inflicted harm other than death or personal injury, the relevant term or notice must satisfy the test of reasonableness (Unfair Contract Terms Act 1977, s. 2(2)). Thus a purported exclusion of liability in respect of property damage or economic loss resulting from the failure of a supplier of services to exercise reasonable care may be struck down on the ground that it is unreasonable for the *proferens* to rely upon it. Section 2(2) is not confined to contract terms as it also applies to notices which purport to exclude or restrict liability. Thus a notice displayed in a multi-storey car park to the effect that the owner accepts no responsibility for damage to property, howsoever caused, will be ineffective unless regarded as reasonable.

It might be argued that it is undesirable to allow a person to restrict his liability for any form of negligently caused damage, since this might encourage people to behave carelessly. However, in relation to property damage and economic losses, the insurance position must be considered. It may be that the consumer is sometimes in the best position to insure his property against the risk of loss, in which case it may be reasonable to allow the defendant to restrict his liability in some way (see Law Com. No. 69 (1975), para. 56). Conversely, where personal injury and death are concerned, it would be unacceptable to regard the consumer as the best insurer or least cost avoider and place the risk of loss on the consumer.

5.7.4.2 Residual consumer contracts While exclusion clauses in respect of the implied terms in consumer contracts for the supply of goods are widely catered for by the invalidity provisions of the Unfair Contract Terms Act 1977, there still remains a residual category of consumer contracts. Exclusion clauses in such contracts are subject to a requirement of reasonableness (s. 3(1)). It follows that in consumer contracts for the supply of services and other consumer contracts not otherwise provided for by the 1977 Act, a purported exclusion or limitation of the liability of the *proferens* must be reasonable.

For the purposes of s. 3(1), the Act further provides that the *proferens* cannot exclude or restrict liability in respect of his own breach of contract (s. 3(2)(a)) or claim to be entitled to give a contractual performance substantially different to that which could be reasonably expected of him (s. 3(2)(b)(i); see also EC proposed Directive, annexe (b)) or claim to be able to offer no performance at all in respect of any part of his contractual obligations (s. 3(2)(b)(ii)) , unless to do so satisfies the test of reasonableness.

Where the *proferens* is in breach of contract, s. 3(2)(a) provides that he cannot exclude or restrict liability in respect of his own breach unless the exclusion or restriction is reasonable. Thus, a provision in a consumer contract which attempts to limit the liability of the *proferens* to a particular amount or one which requires notification of damage within a specified period in the event of a breach of contract will have to satisfy the test of reasonableness.

Section 3(2)(a) refers specifically to liability, therefore there must be a breach of contract on the part of the *proferens*. Accordingly, if the term of the contract is worded in such a way as to define the primary obligations of the parties, s. 3(2)(a) will have no application since there will be no breach of contract if the *proferens* has clearly defined what he is prepared to provide under the terms of the contract.

Under s. 3(2)(b)(i) the *proferens* cannot claim to be entitled to render a performance substantially different from that which was reasonably expected of him, unless the relevant contract term satisfies the requirement of reasonableness. This provision would appear to take on board the majority of cases which were previously dealt with by means of the doctrine of fundamental breach of contract since the failure to do what can reasonably be expected will ordinarily go to the root of the contract.

If this is to add anything to s. 3(2)(a), it must cover something other than a breach of contract. Thus it would appear to cover a contract term which specifies that a particular method of performance is not to be regarded as a breach of contract. In the context of travel services, if a tour operator states that he is free to change itineraries, the advertised route or the nature of the accommodation initially advertised, it would appear that such provisions would have to satisfy the test of reasonableness (see *Anglo-Continental Holidays Ltd* v *Typaldos Lines (London) Ltd* [1967] 2 Lloyd's Rep 61; Law Com. No. 69 (1975), paras. 143-146; see also EC proposed Directive, annexe (c)). In the case of consumer contracts, certain expectations of performance arise independently of the contract itself (see Downes, *Textbook on Contract* 1987), p. 216) in which case those expectations may be defeated by a contract term which seeks to define the obligations of the tour operator. Acccordingly, it may be reasonable to expect a performance on the part of the tour operator in excess of that which he purports to provide.

Section 3(2)(b)(i) assumes that it is possible to identify a reasonably expected performance. However, the 1977 Act does not specify whose view of the matter should be taken into account. One possible approach is to consider the expectations of the unreasonably suspicious person who reads all small print in every document before committing himself to anything (see Beale, Bishop and Furmston, *Contract Cases and Materials*, 2nd ed. (1990), p. 717). However, if this were to be the case, s. 3(2)(b)(i) would be totally ineffective. Instead, it would be preferable if courts were to consider the matter from the position of the person who is aware of what the contract provides, but expects the exclusion clause to be applied fairly. This would amount to something similar to the 'main purpose of the contract' rule applied at common law under the doctrine of fundamental breach of contract. On this basis, if a carrier agrees to transport the consumer from A to B, but reserves the right to depart from the agreed route, any deviation must be in accordance with the main purpose of the contract, namely to transport the consumer from A to B. Thus if the deviation takes the consumer wildly off-course, the deviation clause would probably be struck down as unreasonable (*Glynn* v *Margetson & Co.* [1893] AC 351). Similarly, a provision in a holiday contract which allows the tour operator to change destinations and itineraries must be fairly applied so as not to place the holidaymaker in accommodation which could not have been reasonably expected at the time the contract was entered into.

By virtue of s. 3(2)(b)(ii) the *proferens* cannot claim to be entitled to render no performance at all in respect of any part of his contractual obligations. This would appear to cover partial or total cancellation of the contract and would therefore include a provision in a holiday contract to the effect that the tour operator may refuse to comply with his contractual obligations on economic grounds. Similarly, it would also seem to cover the cancellation at short notice, of a dramatic production at a theatre.

So far as total non-performance is concerned, it can be argued that s. 3(2)(b)(ii) adds nothing to the position at common law since if a person renders no performance at all there would appear to be a total failure of consideration. Furthermore, if the *proferens* claims to be entitled to offer a partial non-performance, there is a danger that what is offered may be substantially different from that which could reasonably be expected, in which case s. 3(2)(b)(i) might apply.

5.7.4.3 **Indemnity clauses in consumer contracts** A consumer cannot

be made to indemnify another in respect of liability arising due to negligence or breach of contract, except where it is reasonable for that other to rely on the indemnity clause (Unfair Contract Terms Act 1977, s. 4).

Indemnity clauses may be of two kinds, namely reflexive indemnities and insurance indemnities (see Adams and Brownsword [1982] JBL 200). A reflexive indemnity is one whereby a contracting consumer is required to indemnify another party to the contract in respect of that other's liability to the consumer. Thus if a consumer engages a removal firm to transport his personal property to a new house, the contract may provide that the consumer shall indemnify the contractor against all claims and demands in excess of £500 in the event of damage to the consumer's effects resulting from negligence or other breach of contract on the part of the removal firm (see *Gillespie Bros & Co. Ltd* v *Roy Bowles Transport Ltd* [1973] QB 400). Such indemnity clauses can be described as being the obverse of an exclusion clause (*Smith* v *South Wales Switchgear Co. Ltd* [1978] 1 All ER 18 at p. 22 per Viscount Dilhorne).

An insurance indemnity requires the consumer to indemnify the other party to the contract in respect of his liability to a third party for negligence or breach of contract. This would appear to cover a provision in a contract with a removal firm whereby the consumer agrees to indemnify the contractor in respect of liability he might incur to a third party in the course of unloading the consumer's personal effects. For example, it would apply where the consumer's dining-room table is dropped on the foot of his next-door neighbour or where one of the contractor's employees stands on the neighbour's prize rose bush. That both types of indemnity clause (see s. 4(2)(b)) and that the vicarious liability of the contractor (see s. 4(2)(a)) are covered is clear from the provisions of s. 4.

5.7.4.4 Exclusion of liability for misrepresentation
Section 8 of the Unfair Contract Terms Act 1977 amends the Misrepresentation Act 1967, s. 3, which also requires a purported exclusion of liability for misrepresentation to satisfy a test of reasonableness.

A number of difficulties surround the interpretation of the Misrepresentation Act 1967, s. 3. In particular it refers to liability by reason of any misrepresentation made by a party before the contract was made. If the misrepresentation is incorporated as an express term of the contract, it would appear not to be subject to the provisions in respect of excluding liability for misrepresentation and since express terms not contained in standard-form documents, for the most part, fall outside the provisions of the Unfair Contract Terms Act 1977, the innocent party might be prejudiced.

Furthermore, s. 3 of the Misrepresentation Act 1967 is intended to cover clauses which exclude liability and restrict remedies. However, if the term can be drafted in such a way that it does neither of these things, it would appear to escape statutory control (*Overbrooke Estates Ltd* v *Glencombe Properties Ltd* [1974] 1 WLR 1335). Thus if the relevant term provides that the representee does not rely on the statement of the representor, there would appear to be no actionable misrepresentation due to the absence of reliance or inducement unless the reference to the absence of reliance is a pure sham (*Cremdean Properties Ltd* v *Nash* (1977) 244 EG 547 at p. 551 per Bridge LJ).

5.7.5   The tests of reasonableness

5.7.5.1   The general test   Section 11(1) of the Unfair Contract Terms Act 1977 provides that the appropriate test to apply is to ask whether an exclusion or limitation clause is fair and reasonable having regard to the circumstances which were or ought reasonably to have been known to the parties at the time the contract was entered into. The onus of proving reasonableness lies on the *proferens* who seeks to rely upon the exclusion clause (s. 11(5)).

Because the test is applied at the time of contracting, subsequent events which might influence the court's decision are not to be taken into account in deciding whether the relevant term is reasonable or not. Accordingly, the nature of the breach of contract and its seriousness in relation to the contract as a whole should not be taken into account, unless such matters were within the contemplation of the parties at the time of contracting.

What is reasonable is not defined in the Act since this is bound to be a factual issue, thereby giving the courts considerable scope for the exercise of discretion (see Adams and Brownsword (1988) 104 LQR 94). The factors relevant to the question of reasonableness will change from case to case, but some guidelines have been judicially indicated.

In a number of cases, the courts have openly considered which of the parties could have best insured against the risk of loss under consideration (*Photo Production Ltd* v *Securicor Transport Ltd* [1980] AC 827 at p. 843 per Lord Wilberforce; *Smith* v *Eric S. Bush* [1989] 2 All ER 514 at p. 531 per Lord Griffiths). This may be a relevant factor in consumer transactions, particularly where property damage is concerned. The consumer may be in the best position to insure against the risk of loss at minimal cost, in which case, the use of an exclusion or limitation clause on the part of the *proferens* could be justified.

In some instances, the court may be forced to consider the complexity and comprehensibility of the purported exclusion of liability in order to determine whether it is reasonable (*Stag Line Ltd* v *Tyne Shiprepair Group Ltd* [1984] 2 Lloyd's Rep 211 at p. 222 per Staughton J). This matter would be particularly relevant to consumer transactions in which the consumer rarely has access to independent legal advice and may not be in a position to understand a particularly complex exclusion or limitation of liability (see also *Levison* v *Patent Steam Carpet Cleaning Co. Ltd* [1978] QB 69).

There has been a growing tendency to resort to the list of guidelines contained in sch. 2 to the 1977 Act, even though these are specifically relevant only to supply of goods transactions between business contracting parties (see 5.7.5.3). Clearly, some of the factors listed in those guidelines will be relevant in other contexts (see *Phillips Products Ltd* v *Hyland* [1987] 2 All ER 620). Accordingly, it will be relevant to consider the relative bargaining strength of the parties and whether the goods or services contracted for could have been acquired elsewhere and at what cost (*Smith* v *Eric S. Bush* [1989] 2 All ER 514 at p. 531; see also *Woodman* v *Photo Trade Processing Ltd* (7 May 1981 unreported, Exeter County Court)). In particular, it will be necessary to consider whether the consumer has received any sort of representation.

Sometimes, the content of a standard-form contract will have been negotiated in consultation with a trade association (see *R. W. Green Ltd* v *Cade Bros Farms* [1978] 1 Lloyd's Rep 602; cf. *George Mitchell (Chesterhall) Ltd* v *Finney Lock Seeds Ltd* [1983] 2 AC 803). In some instances, it may be the case that the consumer interest is considered through consultation with consumer bodies. The difficulty this may present is that contract terms may represent the wish of the majority with the result that some individual preferences may not be catered for (cf. *Woodman* v *Photo Trade Processing Ltd*).

Other factors which may also be taken into account include an assessment of the difficulty of the task undertaken by the *proferens* and a consideration of the practical consequences of the court's decision on the reasonableness issue. Thus if the supplier of a service has undertaken to perform a particularly simple task, it is unlikely that an exclusion of liability would be appropriate. The court would also need to consider the sum of money at stake, including the possibility of the consumer being faced with a financial catastrophe or a loss of an emotional kind (see *Woodman* v *Photo Trade Processing Ltd*).

5.7.5.2 Limitation clauses Where the contract term purports to limit the liability of the *proferens* to a specified sum of money, the Unfair Contract Terms Act 1977 gives specific guidance. It is provided that the court should have particular regard to the insurance position by considering whether insurance was available to the *proferens* and whether he had sufficient resources to meet liability should it arise (s. 11(4)).

5.7.5.3 Statutory reasonableness guidelines A list of guidelines relevant to the issue of the reasonableness of exemption clauses in non-consumer contracts for the supply of goods is contained in sch. 2 to the Unfair Contract Terms Act 1977. While not specifically applicable to consumer transactions, it is no doubt the case that these factors will be taken into account where appropriate. The relevant factors include the relative bargaining strengths of the parties; whether there was any inducement to agree to the exemption clause; whether any condition as to the enforcement of liability could practicably be complied with; whether the buyer could have bought elsewhere without being subject to the exclusion or limitation of liability and whether the goods were made to the special order of the buyer.

The list of guidelines is not exclusive, and other factors may be considered according to the factual circumstances of the case. Because of this, it is probably unlikely that an appellate court will readily interfere with the decision reached at first instance since there is considerable scope for the exercise of discretion on the part of the courts and there may be room for differences of judicial opinion (*George Mitchell (Chesterhall) Ltd* v *Finney Lock Seeds Ltd* [1983] 2 AC 803 at pp. 815-16 per Lord Bridge).

5.7.6 Secondary evasion of liability

In order to prevent secondary evasion of the provisions of the Unfair Contract Terms Act 1977, s. 10 provides that a person is not bound by any terms of a contract which seek to prejudice or take away rights which arise under or in connection with the performance of another contract. Thus if a consumer contracts to purchase a television and at the same time enters a separate service agreement in respect of the television, the terms of the service agreement will be ineffective if they purport to limit the supplier's liability in respect of the quality or fitness of the television.

5.8   STATUTORY CONTROL OF EXCLUSION CLAUSES – MATERIALS FOR CONSIDERATION

5.8.1   Statutory materials

The Unfair Contract Terms Act 1977

PART I AMENDMENT OF LAW FOR ENGLAND AND WALES
AND NORTHERN IRELAND

Introductory

1.   Scope of part I

  (1)   For the purposes of this Part of this Act, 'negligence' means the breach—

  (a)   of any obligation, arising from the express or implied terms of a contract, to take reasonable care or exercise reasonable skill in the performance of the contract;

  (b)   of any common law duty to take reasonable care or exercise reasonable skill (but not any stricter duty);

  (c)   of the common duty of care imposed by the Occupiers' Liability Act 1957 or the Occupiers' Liability Act (Northern Ireland) 1957.

  (2)   This part of this Act is subject to part III; and in relation to contracts, the operation of sections 2 to 4 and 7 is subject to the exceptions made by schedule 1.

  (3)   In the case of both contract and tort, sections 2 to 7 apply (except where the contrary is stated in section 6(4)) only to business liability, that is liability for breach of obligations or duties arising—

  (a)   from things done or to be done by a person in the course of a business (whether his own business or another's); or

  (b)   from the occupation of premises used for business purposes of the occupier; and references to liability are to be read accordingly but liability of an occupier of premises for breach of an obligation or duty towards a person obtaining access to the premises for recreational or educational purposes, being liability for loss or damage suffered by reason of the dangerous state of the premises, is not a business liability of the occupier unless granting that person such access for the purposes concerned falls within the business purposes of the occupier.

  (4)   In relation to any breach of duty or obligation, it is immaterial for any purpose of this part of this Act whether the breach was inadvertent or intentional, or whether liability for it arises directly or vicariously.

Avoidance of liability for negligence, breach of contract, etc.

2.   Negligence liability

  (1)   A person cannot by reference to any contract term or to a notice given to persons generally or to particular persons exclude or restrict his liability for death or personal injury resulting from negligence.

(2)   In the case of other loss or damage, a person cannot so exclude or restrict his liability for negligence except insofar as the term or notice satisfies the requirement of reasonableness.

(3)   Where a contract term or notice purports to exclude or restrict liability for negligence a person's agreement to or awareness of it is not of itself to be taken as indicating his voluntary acceptance of any risk.

3.   Liability arising in contract

(1)   This section applies as between contracting parties where one of them deals as consumer or on the other's written standard terms of business.

(2)   As against that party, the other cannot by reference to any contract term—

(a)   when himself in breach of contract, exclude or restrict any liability of his in respect of the breach; or

(b)   claim to be entitled—

(i)   to render a contractual performance substantially different from that which was reasonably expected of him, or

(ii)   in respect of the whole or any part of his contractual obligation, to render no performance at all,

except insofar as (in any of the cases mentioned above in this subsection) the contract term satisfies the requirement of reasonableness.

4.   Unreasonable indemnity clauses

(1)   A person dealing as consumer cannot by reference to any contract term be made to indemnify another person (whether a party to the contract or not) in respect of liability that may be incurred by the other for negligence or breach of contract, except insofar as the contract term satisfies the requirement of reasonableness.

(2)   This section applies whether the liability in question—

(a)   is directly that of the person to be indemnified or is incurred by him vicariously;

(b)   is to the person dealing as consumer or to someone else.

Liability arising from sale or supply of goods

5.   'Guarantee' of consumer goods

(1)   In the case of goods of a type ordinarily supplied for private use or consumption, where loss or damage—

(a)   arises from the goods proving defective while in consumer use; and

(b)   results from the negligence of a person concerned in the manufacture or distribution of the goods,

liability for the loss or damage cannot be excluded or restricted by reference to any contract term or notice contained in or operating by reference to a guarantee of the goods.

(2)   For these purposes—

(a)   goods are to be regarded as 'in consumer use' when a person is using them, or has them in his possession for use, otherwise than exclusively for the purposes of a business; and

(b)   anything in writing is a guarantee if it contains or purports to contain some promise or assurance (however worded or presented) that defects will be made good by complete or partial replacement, or by repair, monetary compensation or otherwise.

(3)   This section does not apply as between the parties to a contract under or in pursuance of which possession or ownership of the goods passed.

6.   Sale and hire-purchase

(1)   Liability for breach of the obligations arising from—

    (a)   section 12 of the Sale of Goods Act 1979 (seller's implied undertakings as to title, etc.);

    (b)   section 8 of the Supply of Goods (Implied Terms) Act 1973 (the corresponding thing in relation to hire-purchase)

cannot be excluded or restricted by reference to any contract term.

    (2)   As against a person dealing as consumer, liability for breach of the obligations arising from—

    (a)   section 13, 14 or 15 of the 1979 Act (seller's implied undertakings as to conformity of goods with description or sample, or as to their quality or fitness for a particular purpose);

    (b)   section 9, 10 or 11 of the 1973 Act (the corresponding things in relation to hire-purchase),

cannot be excluded or restricted by reference to any contract term.

    (3)   As against a person dealing otherwise than as consumer, the liability specified in subsection (2) above can be excluded or restricted by reference to a contract term, but only insofar as the term satisfies the requirement of reasonableness.

    (4)   The liabilities referred to in this section are not only the business liabilities defined by section 1(3), but include those arising under any contract of sale of goods or hire-purchase agreement.

7.   Miscellaneous contracts under which goods pass

    (1)   Where the possession or ownership of goods passes under or in pursuance of a contract not governed by the law of sale of goods or hire-purchase, subsections (2) to (4) below apply as regards the effect (if any) to be given to contract terms excluding or restricting liability for breach of obligation arising by implication of law from the nature of the contract.

    (2)   As against a person dealing as consumer, liability in respect of the goods' correspondence with description or sample, or their quality or fitness for any particular purpose, cannot be excluded or restricted by reference to any such term.

    (3)   As against a person dealing otherwise than as consumer, that liability can be excluded or restricted by reference to such a term, but only insofar as the term satisfies the requirement of reasonableness.

    (3A)   Liability for breach of the obligations arising under section 2 of the Supply of Goods and Services Act 1982 (implied terms about title etc. in certain contracts for the transfer of the property in goods) cannot be excluded or restricted by reference to any such term.

    (4)   Liability in respect of—

    (a)   the right to transfer ownership of the goods, or give possession; or

    (b)   the assurance of quiet possession to a person taking goods in pursuance of the contract,

cannot (in a case to which subsection (3A) above does not apply) be excluded or restricted by reference to any such term except insofar as the term satisfies the requirement of reasonableness.

Proposal for a Council Directive on unfair terms in consumer contracts (COM(90) 322 fin. OJ C243/2 28.9.90)

Article 1

The purpose of this Directive is to approximate the laws, regulations and administrative provisions of the member States relating to unfair terms in consumer contracts.

Article 2

For the purposes of this Directive:

1.   A contractual term is unfair if, of itself or in combination with another term or terms of the same contract, or of another contract upon which, to the knowledge of the person or persons who conclude the first-mentioned contract with the consumer, it is dependent:

— it causes to the detriment of the consumer a significant imbalance in the parties' rights and obligations arising under the contract, or

— it causes the performance of the contract to be unduly detrimental to the consumer, or

— it causes the performance of the contract to be significantly different from what the consumer could legitimately expect, or

— it is incompatible with the requirements of good faith.

2.   The annexe contains a list of types of unfair terms.

3.   'The consumer' means a natural person who, in transactions covered by this Directive, is acting for purposes which can be regarded as outside his trade, business or profession.

4.   'Trade' and 'business' shall be taken to include the activities of suppliers, whether publicly owned or privately owned, and those expressions also cover the sale, hiring out or other provision of appliances by those suppliers.

5.   The fairness or unfairness of a contractual term is to be determined by reference to the time at which the contract is concluded, to the surrounding circumstances at that time and to all the other terms of the contract.

Article 3

Member States shall:

— prohibit the use of unfair terms in any contract concluded with a consumer by any person acting in the course of his trade, business or profession; this prohibition shall be without prejudice to the seller's right to obtain compensation from his own supplier,

— provide that if, notwithstanding this prohibition, unfair terms are used in such a contract they shall be void, and that the remaining terms of the contract shall continue to be valid and that the contract shall continue to bind the parties upon those terms if it is capable of continuing in existence without the void provisions.

Annexe

The following types of terms are unfair if they have the object or effect of:

(a)   excluding or limiting the liability of a contracting party in the event of death or personal injury to the consumer resulting from an act or omission of that contracting party;

(b)   providing that a seller or supplier of goods or services may alter the terms of contract unilaterally, or terminate unilaterally a contract of indeterminate duration by giving an unreasonably short period of notice. This prohibition shall not prevent a supplier of financial services:

(i)   from altering the rate of interest on a loan or credit granted by him or the amount of other charges therefor; or

(ii)   from terminating unilaterally a contract of indeterminate duration,

provided the contract confers the power to do so and also requires suitable notice of the alteration or termination to to be given to the other contracting party or parties.

Moreover, this paragraph (b) shall not affect:

(i)   the application of price indexation clauses where these are lawful;

(ii)   stock exchange transactions;

(iii)   contracts for the purchase of foreign currency;

(c)   1.   denying the consumer the right, as purchaser under a contract for the sale of goods:

— to receive goods which are in conformity with the contract and are fit for the purpose for which they were sold,

— to complain that the goods contain hidden defects,

— to require the seller (in the event that the goods supplied are not in conformity with the contract or are not fit for the purpose for which they were sold):

(i)   to reimburse the whole of the purchase price; or

(ii)   to replace the goods; or

(iii)   to repair the goods at the seller's expense; or

(iv)   to reduce the price if the consumer retains the goods,

— to require the seller (whichever of the foregoing options the consumer chooses) to compensate the consumer for damage sustained by him which arises out of that contract,

— (in cases where the seller transmits to the consumer the guarantee of the manufacturer of the goods) to benefit from the manufacturer's guarantee for a period equal, at the least, to the normal life of the goods or 12 months, whichever is the shorter; and to enforce payment, either by the seller or by the manufacturer, of the costs incurred by the consumer in obtaining implementation of that guarantee;

2.   denying the consumer the right, as purchaser under a contract for the supply of services:

— to be supplied with those services at the agreed time and efficiently from his point of view,

— to have the supplier's warranty that the supplier has the requisite skill and expertise to supply the services in the manner specified in the foregoing indent;

(d)   providing for the price of goods to be determined at the time of delivery or allowing a seller or supplier of goods to increase their price, notwithstanding that in these various cases the consumer buyer has no corresponding right to cancel the contract if the final price is too high in relation to the price he expected when concluding the contract; but the application of price indexation clauses where lawful shall not hereby be affected;

(e)   excluding or limiting the liability of the seller or supplier or of another party in the event of total or partial non-performance by him;

(f)   imposing on the consumer a burden of proof which, according to the applicable law, should lie on another party to the contract;

(g)   in relation to a 'contract' for the purchase of a time-share interest in a building, fixing the date of conclusion of the contract in such a way as to deny to the consumer the possibility of withdrawing from the contract within seven clear days after making it.

5.8.2   Application of the Unfair Contract Terms Act 1977 to negligence

Smith v Eric S. Bush
[1989] 2 All ER 514
House of Lords

LORD TEMPLEMAN at pp. 523–4: In *Harris* v *Wyre Forest District Council* [1988] 1 All ER 691, (1988) QB 835 the Court of Appeal (Kerr, Nourse LJJ and Caulfield J) accepted an argument that the [Unfair Contract Terms Act 1977] did not apply because the council by their express disclaimer refused to obtain a valuation save on terms that the valuer would not be under any obligation to Mr and Mrs Harris to take reasonable care or exercise reasonable skill. The council did not exclude liability for negligence but excluded negligence so that the valuer and the council never came under a duty of care to Mr and Mrs Harris and could not be guilty of negligence. This construction would not give effect to the manifest intention of the 1977 Act but would emasculate the Act. The construction would provide no control over standard-form exclusion clauses which individual members of the public are obliged to accept. A party to a contract or a tortfeasor could opt out of the 1977 Act by declining, in the words of Nourse LJ, to recognise 'their own answerability to the plaintiff's' (see [1988] 1 All ER 691 at 697, [1988] QB 835 at 845). Caulfield J said that the Act 'can only be relevant where there is on the facts a potential liability' (see [1988] 1 All ER 691 at 704, [1988] QB 835 at 850). But no one intends to commit a tort and therefore any notice which excludes liability is a notice which excludes a potential liability. Kerr LJ sought to confine the Act to 'situations where the existence of a duty of care is not open to doubt' or where there is 'an inescapable duty of care' (see [1988] 1 All ER 691 at 702, [1988] QB 835 at 853). I can find nothing in the 1977 Act or in the general law to identify or support this distinction. In the result the Court of Appeal held that the Act does not apply to 'negligent misstatements where a disclaimer has prevented a duty of care from coming into existence' (see [1988] 1 All ER 691 at 699–700, [1988] QB 835 at 848 per Nourse LJ). My lords, this confuses the valuer's report with the work which the valuer carries out in order to make his report. The valuer owed a duty to exercise reasonable skill and care in his inspection and valuation. If he had been careful in his work, he would not have made a 'negligent misstatement' in his report.

Section 11(3) of the 1977 Act provides that, in considering whether it is fair and reasonable to allow reliance on a notice which excludes liability in tort, account must be taken of 'all the circumstances obtaining when the liability arose or (but for the notice) would have arisen'. Section 13(1) of the Act prevents the exclusion of any right or remedy and (to that extent) s.2 also prevents the exclusion of liability 'by reference to . . . notices which exclude . . . the relevant obligation or duty'. Nourse LJ dismissed s. 11(3) as 'peripheral' and made no comment on s.13(1). In my opinion both these provisions support the view that the 1977 Act requires that all exclusion notices which would in common law provide a defence to an action for negligence must satisfy the requirement of reasonableness.

5.8.3 The reasonableness tests

Unfair Contract Terms Act 1977

11.   The 'reasonableness' test
(1)   In relation to a contract term, the requirement of reasonableness for the purposes of this part of this Act, section 3 of the Misrepresentation Act 1967 and section 3 of the Misrepresentation Act (Northern Ireland) 1967 is that the term shall have been a fair and reasonable one to be included having regard to the circumstances which were, or ought reasonably to have been, known to or in the contemplation of the parties when the contract was made.

(2)   In determining for the purposes of section 6 or 7 above whether a contract term satisfies the requirement of reasonableness, regard shall be had in particular to the matters specified in schedule 2 to this Act; but this subsection does not prevent the court or arbitrator from holding, in accordance with any rule of law, that a term which purports to exclude or restrict any relevant liability is not a term of the contract.

(3) In relation to a notice (not being a notice having contractual effect), the requirement of reasonableness under this Act is that it should be fair and reasonable to allow reliance on it, having regard to all the circumstances obtaining when the liability arose or (but for the notice) would have arisen.

(4) Where by reference to a contract term or notice a person seeks to restrict liability to a specified sum of money, and the question arises (under this or any other Act) whether the term or notice satisfies the requirement of reasonableness, regard shall be had in particular (but without prejudice to subsection (2) above in the case of contract terms) to —

(a) the resources which he could expect to be available to him for the purpose of meeting the liability should it arise; and

(b) how far it was open to him to cover himself by insurance.

(5) It is for those claiming that a contract term or notice satisfies the requirement of reasonableness to show that it does.

SCHEDULE 2 'GUIDELINES' FOR APPLICATION OF REASONABLENESS TEST

The matters to which regard is to be had in particular for the purposes of sections 6(3), 7(3) and (4), 20 and 21 are any of the following which appear to be relevant—

(a) the strength of the bargaining positions of the parties relative to each other, taking into account (among other things) alternative means by which the customer's requirements could have been met;

(b) whether the customer received an inducement to agree to the term, or in accepting it had an opportunity of entering into a similar contract with other persons, but without having to accept a similar term;

(c) whether the customer knew or ought reasonably to have known of the existence and extent of the term (having regard, among other things, to any custom of the trade and any previous course of dealing between the parties);

(d) where the term excludes or restricts any relevant liability if some condition is not complied with, whether it was reasonable at the time of the contract to expect that compliance with that condition would be practicable;

(e) whether the goods were manufactured, processed or adapted to the special order of the customer.

Smith v *Eric S. Bush*
[1989] 2 All ER 514
House of Lords

LORD GRIFFITHS at pp. 530-2: Finally, the question is whether the exclusion of liability contained in the disclaimer satisfies the requirement of reasonableness provided by s. 2(2) of the [Unfair Contract Terms Act 1977]. The meaning of reasonableness and the burden of proof are both dealt with in s. 11(3), which provides: 'In relation to a notice (not being a notice having contractual effect), the requirement of reasonableness under this Act is that it should be fair and reasonable to allow reliance on it, having regard to all the circumstances obtaining when the liability arose or (but for the notice) would have arisen.' It is clear, then, that the burden is on the surveyor to establish that in all the circumstances it is fair and reasonable that he should be allowed to rely on his disclaimer of liability.

I believe that it is impossible to draw up an exhaustive list of the factors that must be taken into account when a judge is faced with this very difficult decision. Nevertheless, the following matters should, in my view, always be considered.

(1)   Were the parties of equal bargaining power? If the court is dealing with a one-off situation between parties of equal bargaining power the requirement of reasonableness would be more easily discharged than in a case such as the present where the disclaimer is imposed on the purchaser who has no effective power to object.

(2)   In the case of advice, would it have been reasonably practicable to obtain the advice from an alternative source taking into account considerations of costs and time? In the present case it is urged on behalf of the surveyor that it would have been easy for the purchaser to have obtained his own report on the condition of the house, to which the purchaser replies that he would then be required to pay twice for the same advice and that people buying at the bottom end of the market, many of whom will be young first-time buyers, are likely to be under considerable financial pressure without the money to go paying twice for the same service.

(3)   How difficult is the task being undertaken for which liability is being excluded? When a very difficult or dangerous undertaking is involved there may be a high risk of failure which would certainly be a pointer towards the reasonableness of excluding liability as a condition of doing the work. A valuation, on the other hand, should present no difficulty if the work is undertaken with reasonable skill and care. It is only defects which are observable by a careful visual examination that have to be taken into account and I cannot see that it places any unreasonable burden on the valuer to require him to accept responsibility for the fairly elementary degree of skill and care involved in observing, following up and reporting on such defects. Surely it is work at the lower end of the surveyor's field of professional expertise.

(4)   What are the practical consequences of the decision on the question of reasonableness? This must involve the sums of money potentially at stake and the ability of the parties to bear the loss involved, which, in its turn, raises the question of insurance. There was once a time when it was considered improper even to mention the possible existence of insurance cover in a lawsuit. But those days are long past. Everyone knows that all prudent, professional men carry insurance, and the availability and cost of insurance must be a relevant factor when considering which of two parties should be required to bear the risk of a loss. We are dealing in this case with a loss which will be limited to the value of a modest house and against which it can be expected that the surveyor will be insured. Bearing the loss will be unlikely to cause significant hardship if it has to be borne by the surveyor but it is, on the other hand, quite possible that it will be a financial catastrophe for the purchaser who may be left with a valueless house and no money to buy another. If the law in these circumstances denies the surveyor the right to exclude his liability, it may result in a few more claims but I do not think so poorly of the surveyors' profession as to believe that the floodgates will be opened. There may be some increase in surveyors' insurance premiums which will be passed on to the public, but I cannot think that it will be anything approaching the figures involved in the difference between the Abbey National's offer of a valuation without liability and a valuation with liability discussed in the speech of my noble and learned friend Lord Templeman. The result of denying a surveyor, in the circumstances of this case, the right to exclude liability will result in distributing the risk of his negligence among all house purchasers through an increase in his fees to cover insurance, rather than allowing the whole of the risk to fall on the one unfortunate purchaser.

I would not, however, wish it to be thought that I would consider it unreasonable for professional men in all circumstances to seek to exclude or limit their liability for negligence. Sometimes breathtaking sums of money may turn on professional advice against which it would be impossible for the adviser to obtain adequate insurance cover and which would ruin him if he were to be held personally liable. In these circumstances it may indeed be reasonable to give the advice on a basis of no liability or possibly of liability limited to the extent of the adviser's insurance cover.

In addition to the foregoing four factors, which will always have to be considered, there is in this case the additional feature that the surveyor is only employed in the first place because the purchaser wishes to buy the house and the purchaser in fact provides or contributes to the surveyor's fees. No one has argued that if the purchaser had employed and paid the surveyor himself, it would have been reasonable for the surveyor to exclude liability for negligence, and the present situation is not far removed from that of a direct contract between the surveyor and the purchaser. The evaluation of the foregoing matters leads me to the clear conclusion that it would not be fair and reasonable for the surveyor to be permitted to exclude liability in the circumstances of this case. I would therefore dismiss this appeal.

It must, however, be remembered that this is a decision in respect of a dwelling-house of modest value in which it is widely recognised by surveyors that purchasers are in fact relying on their care and skill. It will obviously be of general application in broadly similar circumstances. But I expressly reserve my position in respect of valuations of quite different types of property for mortgage purposes, such as industrial property, large blocks of flats or very expensive houses.

CHAPTER SIX

Consumer Finance

The period immediately following the end of the Second World War saw an increase in the availability of credit. The increase in the amount of credit available caused an increase in the number of problems encountered by consumers in dealing with their creditors. To meet this widespread dissatisfaction, the Crowther Committee on Consumer Credit was set up to examine the existing law and come up with proposals for reform. Their final report (Cmnd 4596, 1971) resulted in the passing of the Consumer Credit Act 1974 which replaced earlier piecemeal legislation in respect of specific types of credit transaction.

The control of credit provision has existed for some time. Examples can be found in the Moneylenders Acts 1900 to 1927 and the Pawnbrokers Acts 1872 to 1960 in relation to the lending of money and in the Hire-Purchase Acts 1938 to 1965 in relation to lending connected to the supply of goods. The most comprehensive statutory control of credit provision has come in the form of the Consumer Credit Act 1974. More recently, the European Community has intervened in the form of the Directive on the approximation of the laws of Community States in respect of consumer credit (OJ L42/48 (87/102/EEC) 12.2.87). However, the Directive appears to be based on the Consumer Credit Act 1974 and contains little in excess of the provisions of that Act. Accordingly, there has been no additional subordinate legislation in the United Kingdom to implement the requirements of the Directive.

6.1 TYPES OF CREDIT

The Consumer Credit Act 1974 does not dispose of the terminology employed prior to its enactment, accordingly the types of credit available remain the same. The three principal types of credit transaction are contracts of hire-purchase, conditional sales and credit sales.

6.1.1 Hire-purchase, conditional sale and credit sale

A hire-purchase agreement is defined as one in which goods are bailed in return for periodic payments by the person to whom they are bailed and passing of ownership is delayed pending compliance with certain conditions which will normally involve the exercise of an option to purchase the goods (Consumer Credit Act 1974, s. 189). Thus if the bailee is under no obligation to purchase goods hired to him, the contract is likely to be regarded as one of hire-purchase rather than one of sale (*Helby* v *Matthews* [1895] AC 471). But if the buyer is obliged to make a specified number of deferred payments after which ownership in the goods will pass to him, the contract is one of conditional sale (*Lee* v *Butler* [1893] 2 QB 318 and see also Consumer Credit Act 1974, s. 189). A conditional sale agreement is governed by the provisions of the Sale of Goods Act 1979 although insofar as it involves the provision of credit, it is also subject to the provisions of the Consumer Credit Act 1974. Where the contract is one of credit sale, ownership in the goods will pass to the buyer at or before the time of delivery, in which case the buyer will have the right to transfer title to another person. Such credit sales are nonetheless regulated under the provisions of the Consumer Credit Act 1974 despite the fact that very few of the restrictions imposed by the Hire-Purchase Acts 1938 to 1965 applied to such transactions.

6.1.2 The terminology of the Consumer Credit Act 1974

The Consumer Credit Act 1974 introduces terminology of its own, distinguishing between the debtor, the supplier and the creditor. A consumer credit agreement is defined as a personal credit agreement by which the creditor provides the debtor with credit not exceeding £15,000 (s. 8(2)). For these purposes, the debtor must be an individual, although this includes a partnership, but not a company (s. 189).

The types of credit identified by the Act include running-account credit, fixed-sum credit, restricted-use credit and unrestricted-use credit.

6.1.2.1 Running-Account and Fixed-Sum Credit A running account credit is a revolving credit under which the debtor may make withdrawals up to an agreed credit limit, subject to an understanding that the debtor will top up his account with payments to the creditor (Consumer Credit Act 1974, s. 10(1)(a)). Examples include the main types of credit card agreement under which the consumer can choose how much of his debt to repay at the end of each month.

For the purposes of such transactions, the credit limit is defined as the maximum debit balance allowed under the agreement (s. 10(2)). So as to allow for the identification of the credit limit in the case of a running-account credit, s. 10(3) provides that the overall £15,000 limit is deemed not to be exceeded where the specified credit limit under the agreement is not in excess of £15,000; where the debtor cannot draw more than £15,000 in one transaction; where there is provision for an increase in credit charges should the debt ever exceed an amount specified in the agreement; and where it appears unlikely that the credit limit will ever exceed £15,000 even though it is technically possible under the agreement. The main purpose of s. 10(3) is to prevent evasion of the regulatory regime imposed under the 1974 Act.

A fixed-sum credit agreement is any personal credit agreement which is not a running-account credit agreement (s. 10(1)(b)). This type of credit includes loans made for a specific purpose, such as the acquisition of goods on hire-purchase or conditional sale and which are limited to a specified amount.

6.1.2.2 Restricted-use and unrestricted-use credit   Section 11(2) of the Consumer Credit Act 1974 provides that any agreement not covered by s. 11(1) is one for unrestricted-use credit. By virtue of s. 11(1) a restricted-use credit agreement is one which performs one of three possible functions.

First, a restricted-use credit may finance an agreement between the debtor and the creditor whether forming part of that agreement or not (s. 11(1)(a)). This will include contracts of hire-purchase, credit sale and conditional sale since in such transactions the creditor is also the legal supplier of the goods even though they may have been physically supplied by someone else (see s. 56 and 6.4.2.2).

Secondly, a restricted-use credit agreement includes one which finances a transaction between the debtor and a supplier other than the creditor (s. 11(1)(b)). This will include retail purchases using credit cards and voucher-trading agreements where the goods or services are purchased from a person distinct from the creditor.

Thirdly, credit agreements which refinance any existing indebtedness of the debtor (whether to the creditor or some other person) are classified as restricted-use credit agreements (s. 11(1)(c)). This will cover what are called 'consolidation' loans whereby the consumer's debts to a range of creditors may be settled by taking out a single loan from a further creditor.

In general terms, a restricted-use credit is one in which the debtor can use the credit only in a prescribed manner and an unrestricted-use credit is one in which the debtor is free to use the credit as he chooses (s. 11(3)).

If the supplier is not known at the time the credit agreement is made but the creditor refuses to make the credit available until the supplier is identified, this is still a restricted-use credit (s. 11(4)).

6.1.2.3 Exempt agreements   Only regulated agreements are covered by the Consumer Credit Act 1974. Certain agreements which would otherwise be regarded as regulated are treated as exempt under the provisions of the Act. These are covered by s. 16 and include, for the most part, loans for the purposes of house purchase given by 'reputable' lenders.

Small agreements, namely those where the credit provided does not exceed £50 (s. 17), and non-commercial agreements (s. 189), such as a loan made by one friend to another and which is not made in the course of a business, are also exempt from the provisions of certain parts of the 1974 Act. In particular, the provisions of part V of the Act governing the formalities of entry into credit agreements do not apply to such transactions.

6.1.2.4 Debtor-creditor-supplier agreements and debtor-creditor agreements
There are generally three ways in which goods can be acquired on credit. In the first instance the goods and the credit may be obtained from the creditor himself, in which case, the creditor is also the supplier. Alternatively, the goods may be acquired from a supplier who is connected to the creditor, or in some instances from a supplier who is not connected with the creditor.

Where one person fulfils the roles of supplier and creditor, as is the case where there is a hire-purchase or credit-sale contract, the credit transaction is a debtor-creditor-supplier (DCS) agreement. Similarly, where there is a link between the creditor and the supplier there is a debtor-creditor-supplier agreement because of the connection between the supplier and the creditor.

Where there is no link between the creditor and supplier, for example, where the consumer is lent money to spend in whatever way he likes, there is a debtor-creditor (DC) agreement.

The principal difference between the two is that in the case of a DCS agreement, the creditor is responsible for the supplier's misrepresentations and breaches of contract (s. 75). Furthermore, canvassing DC agreements is prohibited off trade premises whereas canvassing of a DCS agreement is permitted (s. 49).

A connected loan is one made by a person who is also the supplier or by a person who has business connections with the supplier and will normally be for restricted-use credit. Under the 1974 Act there are three varieties of DCS agreement (s. 12). First, there is a restricted-use credit agreement which falls within s. 11(1)(a) (s. 12(1)(a)). This would include hire-purchase, conditional sale and credit-sale agreements.

Secondly, a DCS agreement will comprise a restricted-use credit agreement which falls within s. 11(1)(b) which is made by the creditor under pre-existing arrangements, or in contemplation of future arrangements, between himself and the supplier (s. 12(1)(b)). This will cover a situation in which a supplier refers customers to a specific finance house following arrangements between the creditor and the supplier. Similarly, where a customer uses an Access or Visa card to make a purchase, the credit transaction between the customer and the bank will fall within s. 12(1)(b) because arrangements will have been made between the creditor and the supplier.

A third form of DCS agreement can be found where there is an unrestricted-use credit agreement made by the creditor under pre-existing arrangements between himself and an independent supplier in the knowledge that the credit is to be used to finance an agreement between the debtor and the supplier (s. 12(1)(c)). This appears to cover the situation in which a creditor makes a cash advance to a debtor who has been referred to the creditor by an identified supplier with whom the creditor has made pre-existing arrangements.

A DC agreement is defined in s. 13 and can take one of three forms. First, it may consist of a restricted-use credit agreement under s. 11(1)(b) which is not made under pre-existing arrangements nor in contemplation of future arrangements (s. 13(a)). This would cover a situation in which the debtor obtains goods or services from a supplier who has no connection with the creditor and the creditor is approached directly by the debtor to provide finance which is tied to the purchase of those goods or services.

Secondly, it may be a restricted-use credit agreement made under s. 11(1)(c) (s. 13(b)), for example, where one creditor lends money which is tied to repaying debts owed by the debtor to another creditor.

Thirdly, there is a DC agreement where there is an unrestricted-use credit agreement not made under pre-existing arrangements (s. 13(c)). For the most part, this will cover personal loans made to the debtor provided he is left free to use the finance facility in whatever way he pleases (see sch. 2, examples 8, 16, 17 and 21).

6.1.2.4.1 Pre-existing arrangements It is clear that it is important to identify what will be regarded as pre-existing arrangements so as to be able to recognise a DCS agreement. By virtue of s. 187(1) and (4) pre-exisiting arrangements are those previously made between the creditor and the supplier (or their associates). These will include an arrangement between a retailer and banks offering Access or Visa facilities whereby the retailer will accept the use of these credit cards in his shop (see sch. 2, example 21) and an arrangement whereby a supplier is paid a commission for introducing customers to a finance company (see sch. 2, example 8).

Where the creditor is an associate of the supplier, for example, where the creditor and supplier are part of the same group of companies, there is a presumption that there are pre-existing arrangements between the two companies unless the contrary can be proved by the creditor (s. 187(5)).

For the purposes of s. 12, the mere fact that there is or will be an arrangement for the making of payments to suppliers by the creditor is not to be treated as a pre-existing or future arrangement (s. 187(3)). Thus an arrangement entered into by a bank to honour cheque payments supported by a cheque guarantee card will not, of itself, constitute a pre-existing or a future arrangement.

6.1.2.4.2 Future arrangements Future arrangements are those which the creditor or one of his associates expects to make with the supplier or one of the supplier's associates (s. 187(2)). For these purposes, it would appear that there need only be an expectation of arrangements. Thus if a creditor issues a credit card to a customer and the supplier only agrees to honour such cards after they have been issued, there is an expectation of future arrangements when the supplier and the creditor reach their agreement.

At first sight, these provisions might lead to the conclusion that an arrangement between a high street supermarket and a bank in respect of electronic transfer of funds from a current account is one made in contemplation of future arrangements. However, it is clear from an amendment to the 1974 Act brought about by the Banking Act 1986 that this is not the case (s. 187(3A)).

6.1.2.5 Linked transactions It is not just the credit agreement which is affected by the provisions of the Consumer Credit Act 1974: linked or related transactions are also governed (s. 19). Thus a contract of supply associated with the credit agreement or an insurance contract which the lender requires the debtor to enter into so as to protect the goods subject to the credit agreement are subject to some of the provisions of the Act.

6.1.2.5.1   Varieties of linked transaction   Contracts for the provision of security are excluded from the definition of a linked transaction (s. 19(1)) and are dealt with under separate provisions of the Act.

A transaction is linked if it is entered into between the debtor (or a relative of his) and another person and the agreement is entered into in compliance with a term of the credit agreement (s. 19(1)(a)). A compulsory requirement in a hire-purchase agreement that the debtor should insure the goods bailed would fall within this category. However, the same would not be true of an optional offer of insurance since it is not entered into in compliance with a term of the credit agreement.

If the credit arrangement is a DCS agreement and a further transaction is financed by it, that additional transaction is linked (s. 19(1)(b)). Thus the supply of goods financed by a loan facility made under pre-existing arrangements between the creditor and the supplier will be linked. Similarly, a contract to provide travel facilities where a flight is paid for by a credit card would be linked under s. 19(1)(b). However, the same is not true of the supply element in a hire-purchase contract since the supply forms part of the regulated agreement and is excluded from the definition of a linked transaction in s. 19(1).

If the agreement has been entered into to induce the creditor to enter into the principal agreement, it is linked (s. 19(1)(c)(i)). Thus if the consumer takes out life assurance in order to persuade the creditor to make a loan facility available, the assurance policy will be a linked transaction. Furthermore, similar treatment is accorded to an agreement which is entered into for some other purpose relevant to the principal agreement (s. 19(1)(c)(ii)). For example, where credit is provided by a skiing tour operator and, at the operator's suggestion, the debtor takes out accident insurance, the insurance contract is linked. Finally, where the principal agreement is a DCS agreement, and a further contract is made for a purpose related to a transaction financed by that agreement, that additional transaction is linked (s. 19(1)(c)(iii)). This would appear to cover a maintenance contract entered into with the supplier of electrical equipment which has been supplied on credit provided by a creditor who has made pre-existing arrangements with the supplier.

In all of the cases covered by s. 19(1)(c), it is a requirement that a person associated with the creditor or someone who is, at least, aware that the principal agreement may be entered into (s. 19(2)) has suggested entry into the linked transaction.

6.1.2.5.2   The effect of treating a transaction as linked   Where a transaction is linked, charges paid under it are treated as part of the total charge for credit (s. 20(2)), a linked transaction has no effect until the principal agreement has been concluded (s. 19(3)) and if the debtor withdraws from or cancels the principal agreement, the linked transaction is also terminated (ss. 57(1) and 69(1)). Furthermore, any sums paid under a linked transaction will also be taken into account in computing the appropriate rebate to be granted to the debtor on early settlement (s. 95(1)).

6.2   TRUTH IN LENDING

6.2.1   Pre-contract disclosure

One purpose of the Consumer Credit Act 1974 is to ensure that the debtor is given sufficient information regarding the proposed transaction, before it becomes binding. Thus a creditor will be required to give adequate information to the debtor in advertisements (s. 44) and quotations (s. 52) to allow him to be aware of the commitment he might be taking on. Adverse consequences for the contract follow if the creditor fails to provide the necessary information.

Regulations (SI 1983/1553) pursuant to s. 55(1) require the document containing the terms of the agreement to be signed, legible and to provide financial information, for example, the annual percentage rate of charge (APR), the required deposit, the amount of credit provided, a comparison of the cash price and the credit price, the total charge for credit and the total amount payable.

Failure to comply with these requirements renders the agreement improperly executed (s. 55(2)) with the result that the agreement is unenforceable against the debtor in the absence of a court order (s. 65). The Act gives no definition of the word unenforceable, but for the purposes of the Hire-Purchase Acts 1938 to 1965 it has been held that it means that the debtor may enjoy possession of the property without having to pay for it (*Eastern Distributors Ltd* v *Goldring* [1957] 2 QB 600).

Under s. 60(1) of the Consumer Credit Act 1974, regulations may be made regarding the form and content of agreements (see SI 1983/1553 above). The Act also requires the debtor to be supplied with copies of the unexecuted and the executed agreement and with notice of cancellation rights (ss. 62 and 64). Failure to comply with these requirements in respect of copies and cancellation notices renders the agreement improperly executed (ss. 62(3) and 64(5)).

If the relevant document is posted to the debtor, a copy of the agreement must be sent at the same time along with any other document referred to in it, for example, an insurance contract or a legal charge.

If the unexecuted agreement is presented to the debtor personally for his signature and, at that stage, the agreement becomes executed, he must be given a copy of the executed agreement immediately (s. 63(1)). This will probably be an unlikely occurrence as the agreement will normally be sent to the creditor for signature, in which case the agreement remains unexecuted until signature on behalf of the creditor.

In normal cases, s. 63(2) provides that a copy of the executed agreement must be sent to the debtor within seven days of the making of the agreement. If the agreement is subject to the cancellation provisions of the Act, s. 63(3) provides that a copy of the executed agreement must be sent by post. Since the sending of the copy constitutes acceptance, the postal acceptance is subject to contractual rules on this method of acceptance.

Before the agreement can be said to be properly executed, it must be contained in a document which embodies the terms of the contract in legible form and is signed by both the debtor, in person, and the creditor, or someone acting on his behalf (s. 61(1)). It is also essential that all blank spaces on the standard form are filled in. It is not sufficient that the debtor signs the contract, leaving the details to be filled in by the dealer at a later stage. In such a case, there is no agreement about essential terms of the contract such as the price of the goods supplied (*Campbell Discount Co. Ltd* v *Gall* [1961] 1 QB 431).

6.2.2 Disclosure of information during the currency of the agreement

A key feature of the 1974 Act is that the debtor is entitled to be kept aware of the state of his indebtedness. Thus, if the debtor under a fixed-sum credit agreement makes a request in writing concerning the amount he owes, the creditor must respond within 12 days of the request by providing the debtor with a statement of the total amount he has paid under the agreement and the amount which remains to be paid or will become due (s. 77(1)). It is in the interests of the creditor to ensure that the information he gives is correct, since the statement is binding on him (s. 172(1)).

In the case of a running-account credit agreement, there is a similar provision, except that the type of information which the creditor must supply differs. Section 78(1) provides that the debtor must be informed, within 12 days of his written request of the state of the account, of the amount presently payable and amounts which will become payable and the dates on which they are to be paid. In addition to the required response to a written request from the debtor, the creditor is also required to provide periodic statements of account under a running-account credit agreement whether these have been requested or not (s. 78(4)). These statements should be sent out at least once every 12 months.

6.3   WITHDRAWAL AND CANCELLATION

6.3.1   Withdrawal

The debtor is permitted to withdraw from a prospective agreement. The provisions of the Consumer Credit Act 1974, s. 57, are in addition to the common law rule which allows a person to revoke an offer before acceptance.

Section 57 operates only in favour of the debtor and allows notice of withdrawal to be given to persons other than the offeree. The notice of withdrawal extends to linked transactions. In the event of withdrawal, the parties should be returned to their prior position.

6.3.2   Cancellation

In addition to the right of withdrawal from a prospective agreement, the debtor may also cancel certain concluded agreements (s. 67), although this will depend on where the contract is made.

6.3.2.1 Cancellable agreements A cancellable agreement is one made off trade premises (Consumer Credit Act 1974, s. 67(b)) as a result of oral representations made to the debtor (or a relative) in the course of antecedent negotiations. The representations may be made by the creditor, any party to a linked transaction or the negotiator in the antecedent negotiations. The general effect of this provision is to strike at unsolicited 'door-to-door' salesmanship which may involve remarks made to a consumer in his own home.

The withdrawal and cancellation provisions of the Act and the requirements in respect of copies of the agreement do not apply to non-commercial agreements, small agreements, most agreements for the provision of a current account and agreements providing for payments to be made on death (s. 74).

It is important for the purposes of the cancellation provisions that there have been antecedent negotiations which include oral representations. These representations must have been made in the presence of the debtor or a relative of his, although not necessarily to him. For example, antecedent negotiations could consist of passing remarks made by a salesman to someone other than the debtor which the debtor overhears. However, because of the requirement that the representations should be made in the presence of the debtor, mail-shot and telephone representations will not fall within the cancellation provisions of the Act.

Antecedent negotiations are defined in s. 56 (see 6.4.2.2.2), but it is possible for these negotiations to commence before the creditor is aware of the debtor's identity, since s. 56(4) provides that negotiations can include communication by means of an advertisement, although there must also be an oral representation.

The debtor may give notice of cancellation to the creditor or his agent or any person specified in the notice of cancellation rights (s. 69(1) and (6)).

Cancellation is permitted during the cooling-off period specified in s. 68. The debtor has five days in which to exercise his right and the relevant period runs from the day after the second copy of the agreement or notice of cancellation has been received (s. 68(a)).

Alternatively, if the creditor is exempt from delivering a separate cancellation notice under s. 64(4), the debtor has a cooling-off period of 14 days from the date of signing the agreement (s. 68(b)).

6.3.2.2 The effects of cancellation If an agreement is cancelled, it and any linked transaction (s. 69(1)) are treated as if they had never been entered into (s. 69(4)). Thus payments made by the debtor can be recovered and goods delivered to the debtor must be redelivered. The debtor's right of cancellation is only lost if he fails to deliver the required cancellation notice within the period specified in s. 68.

6.3.2.2.1 Money paid by the debtor Any money paid by the debtor as part of the total charge for credit can be recovered (s. 70(1)(a)). Thus deposits and interest payments made to the creditor are recoverable. Furthermore, the debtor also ceases to be responsible for sums of money due after cancellation (s. 70(1)(b)). The dealer is also required to pay back to the creditor any sum he has received where there is a DCS agreement under s. 12(b).

As a general rule, the debtor's claim for repayment will be made to the person to whom the charge for credit was paid (s. 70(3)). However, where there is a DCS agreement under s. 12(b), the dealer and the creditor are jointly and severally liable for the amount due (s. 70(3)). Thus the debtor may hold the creditor liable under a purchase-loan agreement arranged by the dealer and where payment has been made to the dealer alone. However, in such cases, the creditor may be entitled to an indemnity against the dealer (s. 70(4)).

6.3.2.2.2 *Continuation of unrestricted-use loan agreements*

After cancellation, an unrestricted-use credit agreement remains in force so far as it relates to the repayment of credit and and the payment of interest (s. 71(1)).

The motive behind this is to prevent a creditor from advancing a cash loan in anticipation of an executed agreement, since by s. 71(2), if the debtor repays the credit, or any part of it, within one month of service of the notice of cancellation, or before the first repayment is due, no interest is payable on the loan. However, if the credit is not repaid in time, the terms of the agreement remain in force and by virtue of s. 71(3) the interest then payable is calculated by reference to the terms of the cancelled agreement.

6.3.2.2.3 *Return of goods by the debtor*

The general effect of the cancellation provisions of the Consumer Credit Act 1974 is that the parties should be returned to their position before entering the contract. Thus, goods in the possession of the debtor are returnable (s. 72).

Under s. 72(3) the debtor is under a duty to retain possession of the goods during the cancellation period and to take reasonable care of them during that period. The duty only applies to a restricted-use, DCS agreement and to a transaction linked to such an agreement (s. 72(1)). Thus the duty to return does not apply to an unrestricted-use credit agreement, or to a debtor-creditor agreement since the supply of goods in such cases is independent of the credit agreement.

While the duty to return the goods implies that they should be returned to the creditor, in fact, it is sufficient that the debtor makes the goods available for recollection at his own premises (s. 72(5)). Furthermore, the notice of cancellation can be sent to anyone specified in the cancellation notice, with the result that return to the supplier will suffice (s. 72(6)).

When return is effected, the debtor's duty to take care of the goods comes to an end (s. 72(7)). However, if the debtor refuses to surrender the goods after receipt of a reasonable request, he exposes himself to an action for damages for breach of statutory duty (s. 72(11)). Furthermore, if the debtor receives a notice requiring him to redeliver the goods within 21 days of cancellation, and he refuses to comply, the duty of care which rests on him continues until actual redelivery (s. 72(8)). Conversely, if no such notice is received, the debtor's duty to take care of the goods in his possession terminates 21 days after the notice of cancellation was received by an authorised person.

Certain types of agreement are exempt from the provisions of s. 72, namely those which relate to perishable goods, goods which are consumed by use and have been consumed before cancellation, goods supplied to meet an emergency and goods which have been incorporated in land (s. 72(9)).

6.3.2.2.4 *Return of goods given in part–exchange*   Goods given in part-exchange by the debtor are returnable (s. 73). Under s. 73(2), unless part-exchange goods are returned to the debtor within 10 days of cancellation, the debtor is entitled to a cash equivalent of the cost of those goods.

6.4   CONTINUANCE OF THE AGREEMENT

6.4.1   The terms of the contract

During the currency of the agreement, the debtor may have cause to complain that the goods supplied are defective. In this event, the debtor's remedies will be based on the express terms of the contract or the implied terms arising out of the provisions of the Sale of Goods Act 1979, the Supply of Goods (Implied Terms) Act 1973 or the Supply of Goods and Services Act 1982 (see chapter 7).

6.4.2   Creditor's liability for the acts of the supplier

6.4.2.1   The effect of the form of credit provision   Against whom the debtor should proceed when he has a complaint concerning the goods supplied will depend on the type of credit made available to him. In some instances, the supplier will have provided the credit himself ('vendor credit') in the form of a conditional or credit-sale agreement, or there might be separate contracts of sale and loan. In these circumstances, the lender and the supplier are the same person and the consumer will be able to proceed against him as a seller in respect of the quality of the thing supplied.

In other instances the credit will be provided by a person other than the physical supplier of the goods. One way in which this can be done is through the medium of 'lender credit' or 'sales financing' under which the supplier enters into a contract of sale with the consumer and the creditor lends the consumer the money to make that purchase. In these circumstances, the consumer would have his normal sale of goods remedies against the supplier, and the loan agreement would be subject to the requirements of the Consumer Credit Act 1974. In the past, such arrangements were unpopular since they fell within the restrictive provisions of the Moneylenders Acts 1900 to 1927, but these Acts have now been repealed and it may be that a growth in the number of lender credit arrangements will increase.

Because of the difficulties encountered under the Moneylenders Acts 1900 to 1927, the more familiar type of credit arrangement has involved a system of 'direct financing'. In the typical hire-purchase contract, the dealer sells the goods to the creditor for their cash price, less the amount of any deposit paid to the dealer. The creditor then enters into an instalment contract with the consumer debtor. The advantage of such an arrangement under the old law was that the creditor was not engaged in a business which had as its primary object the lending of money (Moneylenders Act 1900, s. 6) and thereby avoided the provisions of the Moneylenders Acts 1900 to 1927. The effect of such an arrangement is that the creditor also becomes the legal supplier of the goods subject to the instalment contract and is primarily responsible for the quality of the goods supplied. It is also the case that no contract exists between the dealer and the consumer. However, it is possible that a collateral contract may be found to exist (*Brown* v *Sheen & Richmond Car Sales Ltd* [1950] 1 All ER 1102; *Andrews* v *Hopkinson* [1957] 1 QB 229).

A number of problems arose due to the fact that there was no contract between the dealer and the consumer. In particular, the deposit was paid to the dealer, but the contract was made with the creditor and it became necessary to decide if the dealer was an agent for one or other of the parties to the instalment contract.

6.4.2.2   The dealer as an agent

6.4.2.2.1   The position at common law   The normal common law rule is that a person is only liable for his own breaches of contract. Thus it follows that the creditor should not be made responsible for the acts or omissions of the dealer who supplies the goods subject to the credit agreement, unless the dealer is the creditor's agent.

At common law, there was a divergence of opinion on this issue. On one view, the dealer is not an agent for the finance company where he receives a deposit paid by the consumer. In such a case, he is a party in his own right, acting primarily on his own behalf (*Mercantile Credit Ltd* v *Hamblin* [1965] 2 QB 242 at p. 388 per Pearson LJ, adopted by the House of Lords in *Branwhite* v *Worcester Works Finance Ltd* [1969] 1 AC 552). It would appear that the mere fact that a dealer holds stocks of a finance company's standard forms will not be sufficient to give rise to an agency relationship. To reinforce this view, the finance company can put the matter beyond doubt by stipulating in the hire-purchase contract that the dealer has no authority to commit the finance company in any respect. Furthermore, if the creditor expressly takes steps to notify the consumer of this, there is unlikely to be any apparent or ostensible authority to bind the creditor on the part of the dealer (*Overbrooke Estates Ltd* v *Glencombe Properties Ltd* [1974] 3 All ER 511).

There may be circumstances in which the dealer is authorised to deal as an intermediary. For example, in the absence of any indication to the contrary, the dealer may have an ostensible authority to receive communication of the revocation of an offer on behalf of the finance company (*Financings Ltd* v *Stimson* [1962] 3 All ER 386).

6.4.2.2.2   Agency under the Consumer Credit Act 1974   Where the credit agreement is regulated under the provisions of the Consumer Credit Act 1974 the position is different. The Act refers to the dealer as a negotiator in antecedent negotiations and further provides that an agreement is void if it purports to treat a negotiator as an agent for the debtor (s. 56(3)(a)). This avoids the problem which surfaced under the Hire-Purchase Acts 1938 to 1965 whereby a clause in the hire-purchase contract deemed the dealer to be the debtor's agent rather than that of the creditor.

Under s. 56(2), a person other than the creditor who conducts 'antecedent negotiations' leading to the making of a regulated agreement is deemed to be the agent of the creditor.

According to s. 56(1)(a), antecedent negotiations include any negotiations with the debtor conducted by the creditor in relation to the making of a regulated agreement (see sch. 2, examples 1 and 4). This will cover the case where the negotiations are led by a dealer who finances the transaction himself under a conditional sale agreement or where an employee of a moneylender leads the negotiations.

By virtue of s. 56(1)(b) antecedent negotiations also include those conducted by a credit broker in respect of goods sold or proposed to be sold by the credit broker to the creditor before the goods become the subject of a DCS agreement under s. 12(a) (see sch. 2, examples 2 and 4). Thus if a hire-purchase contract is entered into after the consumer debtor has read a poster describing the goods in question and displayed on the dealer's premises, there have been antecedent negotiations, provided there is a business relationship between the dealer and the creditor.

Additionally, negotiations conducted by the supplier in relation to a transaction financed or proposed to be financed by a DCS agreement within s. 12(b) or (c) are antecedent negotiations for the purposes of s. 56(1)(c) (see sch. 2, example 3). This would cover a conversation between a shop assistant and the customer concerning the merits and demerits of goods the customer proposes to purchase using a credit card.

The effect of s. 56 is to treat the negotiator as the creditor's agent, but it is important that statements made in the course of negotiations are related to the credit transaction. In *United Dominions Trust Ltd* v *Whitfield* [1986] CLY 375 the defendant traded in a car which was still subject to a hire-purchase contract with UDT and wished to acquire a further vehicle on credit. The dealer had promised the defendant that he would pay off UDT using credit provided by a second finance company (FNS). The dealer failed to pay UDT and the defendant elected to pay FNS. Accordingly, he was sued by UDT, who brought in FNS as third parties claiming that the dealer's promise to pay UDT bound FNS. It was held that the promise was sufficiently related to the purchase of the car to form part of antecedent negotiations. It followed that FNS were required to pay UDT as they were bound by their agent's promise.

Before the statutory agency provisions operate, there must have been representations in respect of the provision of credit or other financial accommodation. Since a consumer hire agreement does not involve the provision of credit, it would appear that s. 56 will not allow the consumer to hold the hirer responsible where a dealer makes representations about goods which are the subject of a lease-back arrangement (*Moorgate Mercantile* v *Isobel Gell & Ugolini* [1986] CLY 371).

6.4.2.3 The vicarious liability of the creditor

Under s. 75 of the Consumer Credit Act 1974 the debtor has a remedy against the creditor in respect of the supplier's breaches of contract or misrepresentations. This provision overlaps with the statutory agency provisions of s. 56 (see 6.4.2.2.2) insofar as both sections cover DCS agreements falling within s. 12(b) and (c). The effect of this is that all consumer hire contracts, debtor-creditor loans are not covered by s. 75. Furthermore, if the agreement falls within s. 12(a), as does a hire-purchase contract, s. 56 is the appropriate provision to apply (cf. *Porter v General Guarantee Corporation Ltd* [1982] RTR 384 - incorrectly decided?). For the relationship between ss. 75 and 56 see Fairest and Rudkin (1978) 128 NLJ 243; Lowe (1981) 97 LQR 532; Dobson [1983] JBL 312; Hill-Smith (1983) 133 NLJ 1012 and 1063. For other problems of s. 75 see Dobson [1981] JBL 179; Lowe (1981) 97 LQR 533.

An important effect of s. 75 and s. 56(1)(c) is that they cover the typical three-party credit card agreement, whereby goods are paid for with the use of a credit card, provided the credit card agreement was entered into after 1 April 1977 (SI 1977/802).

The effect of s. 75 is to give the debtor a 'like claim' against the creditor. Thus any action he would have had against the supplier for damages for breach of contract or misrepresentation may be asserted against the creditor.

A broad interpretation of s. 75 would extend this right to rescission of the contract, and such an interpretation was given to s. 75 in *United Dominions Trust Ltd* v *Taylor* (1980) SLT 28 (cf. Davidson (1980) 96 LQR 343). Conversely, it can be argued that the word 'claim' suggests a claim for money.

Section 75 also refers to 'a like claim *in relation to*' the supply agreement, thus the claim must refer to the supply agreement and not to the credit agreement.

Where the creditor is liable to the debtor under s. 75(1), he has a right of recourse against the supplier in respect of his breach, with the result that the creditor can claim an indemnity against the supplier (s. 75(2)). In this respect, the creditor can make the supplier a party to any proceedings which may be brought against him by the debtor. However, there always remains the danger that the supplier is insolvent, in which case the creditor will have to accept full responsibility for the supplier's misrepresentation or breach of contract.

Some types of agreement are exempt from the provisions of s. 75. In particular, non-commercial agreements and ones in which the cash price is less than £100 or more than £30,000 are exempt (s. 75(3) and SI 1983/1878).

6.4.3 Variation of the agreement

The ability to vary the terms of an agreement may be conferred in one of two ways. There may be an express term of the contract which permits this, most commonly found in long-term arrangements such as running-account credit agreements, under which the creditor will wish to alter the rate of interest applied to the debtor's account in the light of changes in the prevailing base rate of interest. In such a case, the variation will not take effect until a notice in the prescribed form has been delivered to the debtor (s. 82(1) and SI 1977/328 as amended by SI 1979/661 and 667).

Alternatively, the right to vary may arise from a subsequent agreement between the parties, for example, where the debtor has experienced difficulty in keeping up repayments and asks for his debt to be rescheduled over a longer period.

In some instances, the original agreement will leave the matter of variation to the absolute discretion of the creditor. In such a case, the creditor can unilaterally modify the rate of interest under the agreement, although he should not use this power in a capricious manner so as to treat old customers less favourably than potential customers (*Lombard Tricity Finance Ltd* v *Paton* [1989] 1 All ER 918).

6.5 CONTINUANCE OF THE AGREEMENT – MATERIALS FOR CONSIDERATION

6.5.1 The dealer as the creditor's agent

For text see 6.4.2.2.

The position at common law is summed up in the following extract.

Branwhite v ***Worcester Works Finance Ltd***
[1969] 1 AC 552
House of Lords

The appellant arranged to purchase a car under a hire-purchase contract arranged with the respondents. A dealer took the plaintiff's car (valued at £130) in part exchange. Subsequently, the respondents refused to proceed with the agreement on the ground that there were irregularities in the way in which the hire-purchase forms had been completed. The appellant argued that the dealer was an agent for the respondents and held the £130 deposit on their behalf, thereby rendering the contract complete.

LORD MORRIS OF BORTH-Y-GEST at p. 573: A dealer may in some circumstances be held out by a finance company as their agent. A dealer may in express terms be made an agent. A dealer may for some *ad hoc* purpose be the agent of a finance company. I agree with what was said by Pearson LJ (as he then was) in *Mercantile Credit Co. Ltd* v *Hamblin* [1965] 2 QB 242, 269:

There is no rule of law that in a hire-purchase transaction the dealer never is, or always is, acting as agent for the finance company or as agent for the customer. In a typical hire-purchase transaction the dealer is a party in his own right, selling his car to the finance company, and he is acting primarily on his own behalf and not as general agent for either of the other two parties. There is no need to attribute to him an agency in order to account for his participation in the transaction. Nevertheless, the dealer is to some extent an intermediary between the customer and the finance company, and he may well have in a particular case some *ad hoc* agencies to do particular things on behalf of one or the other or it may be both of those two parties. For instance, if the car is delivered by the dealer to the customer after the hire-purchase agreement has been concluded, the dealer must be making delivery as agent of the finance company.

In the present case the only oral evidence at the hearing was that given by the appellant. There was little to support a contention that Raven were held out as agents and on the facts of this case I do not consider that the mere possession by Raven of the respondents' forms was enough to constitute agency. Nor do I consider that the terms of the master agreement were such as to constitute Raven the agents of the respondents so far as concerned the events which actually took place in this case.

The position under the Consumer Credit Act 1974 is different.

Consumer Credit Act 1974

56. Antecedent negotiations

(1)   In this Act 'antecedent negotiations' means any negotiations with the debtor or hirer—

(a)   conducted by the creditor or owner in relation to the making of any regulated agreement, or

(b)   conducted by a credit-broker in relation to goods sold or proposed to be sold by the credit-broker to the creditor before forming the subject-matter of a debtor-creditor-supplier agreement within section 12(a), or

(c)   conducted by the supplier in relation to a transaction financed or proposed to be financed by a debtor-creditor-supplier agreement within section 12(b) or (c),
and 'negotiator' means the person by whom negotiations are so conducted with the debtor or hirer.

(2)   Negotiations with the debtor in a case falling within subsection (1)(b) or (c) shall be deemed to be conducted by the negotiator in the capacity of agent of the creditor as well as in his actual capacity.

(3)   An agreement is void if, and to the extent that, it purports in relation to an actual or prospective regulated agreement—

(a)   to provide that a person acting as, or on behalf of, a negotiator is to be treated as the agent of the debtor or hirer, or

(b)   to relieve a person from liability for acts or omissions of any person acting as, or on behalf of, a negotiator.

(4)   For the purposes of this Act, antecedent negotiations shall be taken to begin when the negotiator and the debtor or hirer first enter into communication (including communication by advertisement), and to include any representations made by the negotiator to the debtor or hirer and any other dealings between them.

6.5.2   The vicarious liability of the creditor

Consumer Credit Act 1974

75. Liability of creditor for breaches by supplier

(1)   If the debtor under a debtor-creditor-supplier agreement falling within section 12(b) or (c) has, in relation to a transaction financed by the agreement, any claim against the supplier in respect of a misrepresentation or breach of contract, he shall have a like claim against the creditor, who, with the supplier, shall accordingly be jointly and severally liable to the debtor.

(2)   Subject to any agreement between them, the creditor shall be entitled to be indemnified by the supplier for loss suffered by the creditor in satisfying his liability under subsection (1), including costs reasonably incurred by him in defending proceedings instituted by the debtor.

(3)   Subsection (1) does not apply to a claim—
   (a)   under a non-commercial agreement, or
   (b)   so far as the claim relates to any single item to which the supplier has attached a cash price not exceeding £100 or more than £30,000.

(4)   This section applies notwithstanding that the debtor, in entering into the transaction, exceeded the credit limit or otherwise contravened any term of the agreement.

(5)   In an action brought against the creditor under subsection (1) he shall be entitled, in accordance with rules of court, to have the supplier made a party to the proceedings.

Does the reference to a 'like claim' in s. 75(1) disclose only an action for money or does it also allow rescission of the contract or recovery of the contract price?

United Dominions Trust Ltd v *Taylor*
1980 SLT (Sh Ct) 28
Sheriff Court

SHERIFF PRINCIPAL ROBERT REID QC at pp. 30–1: The pursuers made a loan to the defender for the purchase of a motor car from a supplier, who is not a party to the action. The defender avers that the car was represented to him as being in good condition, roadworthy and fit for use on public roads and that it was none of these things. He has intimated the alleged misrepresentation and breach of contract to the supplier and the pursuers and has refused to pay the monthly instalments of loan repayment as they fall due. In the present action the pursuers sue for the balance of the loan and interest. The defender has pleaded the supplier's misrepresentation and breach of contract as a defence to the action and contends that he is entitled to do so under the terms of s. 75(1) of the Consumer Credit Act 1974. . . . The pursuers admit that the agreement with them is covered by the Consumer Credit Act 1974 and the parties' agents were agreed that the whole transaction was a debtor-creditor-supplier agreement in terms of s. 11(1)(b) and 12(b) of the Act.

In opening the appeal the defender argued that he had relevantly averred that the contract had been rescinded on the ground of the supplier's misrepresentation and breach of contract and that, by virtue of s. 75(1), the rescission affected both the contract of sale with the supplier and the contract of loan with the pursuers. The question, according to the appellant, was whether the words 'any claim against the supplier' included a claim of rescission of the contract with the supplier and the answer he proposed was that, as a matter of ordinary English usage, they plainly did. The pursuers' reply to this argument was that there were two contracts and that the grounds of rescission of the contract with the supplier, namely, misrepresentation and breach of contract, could only apply to that contract. These grounds could not constitute 'a like claim against the creditor' because there was no question of the contract of loan having been induced by misrepresentation or of there being a breach of contract in relation to it. The pursuers' agent also presented the wider argument that s. 75(1) was intended to enable the debtor to exercise claims against the creditor, such as claims for restitution or damages, but not to plead a right as a defence to an action by a creditor because the claims referred to in the subsection were limited to those whose enforcement would make the creditor jointly and severally liable with the supplier to the pursuer. The pursuers' agent accepted that there would be anomalous results if these limited rights were exercised while the loan contract remained operative but he contended that these difficulties arose from the wording of the subsection.

I do not agree with the pursuers' argument. The subject-matter of the section is 'any claim against the supplier in respect of a misrepresentation or breach of contract'. The claims which leap to mind as being open in these circumstances are claims to rescind the contract, to claim restitution of any sums paid to the supplier and to claim any damage which the debtor has sustained. It would be odd, to say the least, if the right to rescind was not available against the creditor and the right to restitution, which depends on rescission, was available. The section goes on to provide that, where such claims against the supplier exist, the debtor shall have 'a like claim against the creditor'. The section does not require that the claim against the creditor shall be justifiable on like grounds to the claim against the supplier, merely that it shall be the same sort of claim. The words 'a like claim' are thus wide enough to include a claim for rescission although the creditor has given no grounds for rescission of the loan contract.

This view of the subsection has been confirmed by a consideration of other provisions of the Act, particularly as they relate to debtor-creditor-supplier agreements. The long title of the Act narrates *inter alia* that the Act establishes a new system of licensing and other control of traders concerned with the provision of credit and their transactions. A reading of the Act discloses that it has created a completely new system of classifications and remedies to take effect whenever consumer credit is associated with the contracts of sale and hire. These statutory remedies have been superimposed on existing contractual remedies. One of the innovations of the Act is to treat two or more contracts which are economically part of one credit transaction as transactions which are legally linked. Where these linked transactions contain two contracts the fate of each contract depends on the other, even where the parties to the contracts are different. This approach leaves no room for the idea of privity of contract which is fundamental to the common law of contract. It is for that reason that I am unable to agree with the learned sheriff's use of the principle of privity of contract to throw light on the meaning of the subsection.

6.6   TERMINATION OF THE CONTRACT BY THE DEBTOR

6.6.1   Early settlement of the debt

The debtor is not obliged to wait for the agreement to run its course. He has an inalienable right to demand early settlement under s. 94 of the Consumer Credit Act 1974 at any time. Any attempt to exclude this right is void under s. 173(1).

Where there is an early settlement, the principal agreement and linked transactions are discharged (s. 96(1)), except where the linked transaction itself provides credit (s. 96(2)).

In the event of such early settlement, the debtor is entitled to be provided with settlement information. This includes a statement of the total amount repayable and any rebate due on early settlement. The amount of the rebate is calculated according to the provisions of the Consumer Credit (Rebate on Early Settlement) Regulations 1983 (SI 1983/1562).

One difficulty which arises under s. 94 is how to calculate the settlement rebate to which the debtor is entitled under the rebate regulations. In particular, problems may arise where the creditor brings proceedings for default. In such a case, ordering payment of the full amount might give the creditor an advantage because the rebate on early settlement would have been ignored. But if the full rebate at the date of judgment is given, the creditor might lose out if payment of the judgment debt is deferred.

One view is that judgment for the full debt should be given, subject to a deduction in respect of the applicable rebate at the time of judgment (*Forward Trust* v *Robinson* [1987] BTLC 12). However, a different view has been taken in *Forward Trust* v *Whymark* [1989] 3 All ER 915, where it was held that judgment should be made for the full amount without deduction if the case is heard in the county court, since the rebate represents future interest on the loan. However, if the case is heard in the High Court, judgments in that court bear interest and the early settlement rebate can be deducted.

A further complication is that the date for assessing the rebate under the regulations is the date of payment by the debtor. Since at the date of judgment, the full amount was still outstanding in *Forward Trust Ltd* v *Whymark*, judgment was entered for the full amount. However, when the debtor does pay, he may pay the amount ordered, less any rebate due to him at the time payment is tendered.

This still leaves the problem that a judgment debt of £100 can only be satisfied by the payment of £100 (*Foakes* v *Beer* (1884) 9 App Cas 605), but it appears that the rebate regulations are an exception to this rule following the decision in *Forward Trust Ltd* v *Whymark*.

6.6.2 Termination of hire-purchase agreements

In the case of a hire-purchase agreement, special provision is made in the Consumer Credit Act 1974 for voluntary termination of the contract. Under s. 99(1), the debtor may give written notice terminating the contract at any time before full performance. Notice may be given to anyone entitled to receive payments under the agreement (effectively the creditor or the dealer). For the reasons considered below, termination of the contract is not in the debtor's interest, as he will be subject to liabilities and will lose possession of the goods subject to the agreement.

6.6.2.1 Events constituting termination

6.6.2.1.1 Mutual agreement A contract can be terminated by mutual agreement between the parties. Ordinarily, this agreement will be followed by the substitution of a new agreement, for example, one which allows the debtor to spread payments over a longer period than that allowed by the earlier agreement. Where a later agreement modifies or varies an earlier arrangement between the parties, the Consumer Credit Act 1974 provides that the earlier agreement is to be treated as revoked and the new agreement is deemed to contain provisions reproducing the combined effect of both agreements (s. 82(2)).

6.6.2.1.2   Exercise of a power to terminate   An agreement will often provide for voluntary termination of the contract on the part of the debtor. However, the contract may also stipulate that the debtor is required to make some payment in addition to outstanding instalments. Such a stipulation is known as a minimum payment clause and may give rise to problems concerning the doctrine of penalties where it operates in the event of the debtor's breach of contract (see 6.10.4). If the contract allows the debtor to terminate, his exercise of that right is not a breach of contract, but the minimum payment clause may require him to make what appears to be an excessive payment. The justification for such provisions is that they protect the creditor's investment by ensuring that he gets a minimum return from the contract.

If the agreement is not regulated under the 1974 Act, common law rules will apply and the minimum payment clause will be treated as an agreement to pay the amount stipulated in return for the right to terminate at an early date (*Associated Distributors Ltd* v *Hall* [1938] 2 KB 83). This may not always be a satisfactory solution, since the amount required of the debtor may be excessive, in which case the court may be inclined to place a strained construction on the conduct of the debtor by regarding it as a breach of contract, thereby bringing the common law doctrine of penalties into play (*Bridge* v *Campbell Discount Ltd* [1962] AC 600). In particular, the court is not likely to hold that the debtor has voluntarily terminated the contract unless he is fully aware of the consequences of his actions (*United Dominions Trust Ltd* v *Ennis* [1968] 1 QB 54).

Where the agreement is regulated under the 1974 Act, the provisions of ss. 99 and 100, considered below, apply with the result that a term of the contract will only be enforceable if it provides for a payment of less than that stipulated under the Act or for no payment at all (ss. 100(1) and 173).

6.6.2.1.3   Debtor's breach of contract   A particularly serious breach of contract on the part of the debtor may give rise to a right on the part of the creditor to terminate the contract. This matter is considered in more detail below (see 6.10.2).

6.6.2.2   Effects of termination   In the event of the termination of a hire-purchase contract, title in the goods remains vested in the creditor. Furthermore, the debtor must discharge all outstanding liabilities (Consumer Credit Act 1974, s. 99(2)). Thus, any sums already due under the agreement will remain payable and the creditor will be able to sue for damages in respect of breaches of contract on the part of the debtor prior to termination.

The rights of termination and cancellation coexist for a brief period at the commencement of a hire-purchase agreement. Because of s. 99(2), it is better for the debtor to cancel rather than terminate, if he has the option, since s. 69(4) provides that the agreement is treated as if it had never been entered into and the debtor will be able to recover all payments made by him.

Where the debtor terminates the agreement, the goods must be returned to the creditor. Furthermore, he may also be liable to pay sums of money in accordance with the provisions of s. 100 (see 6.10.3.4.1).

6.6.3   Termination of credit sale and conditional sale agreements

In the case of a credit-sale agreement, ownership of the goods passes to the debtor when the contract is made, but liability to pay for the goods is staggered. Thus, the buyer will be the owner of the goods before he has fully paid for them. If the debtor defaults, the creditor or seller, where the agreement is regulated, will be able to sue for the amount still outstanding, subject to the requirements of the Consumer Credit Act 1974 in relation to default (see 6.8.1).

Since the debtor under a credit-sale agreement is the owner of the goods from the outset, there is no right on the part of the creditor to recover possession of the goods subject to the agreement. Furthermore, the matter of 'protected goods' considered below (6.10.2.3.2) is irrelevant for the purposes of credit-sale agreements for the same reason.

Where there is a conditional sale agreement the date on which property passes to the debtor may be deferred until payment of the price, but the contract is still one of sale in that the debtor has committed himself to purchase the goods subject to the agreement. In these circumstances, a disposition to a third party will pass a good title, which will ordinarily prevent the creditor from recovering the goods. Where the debtor is in breach of contract, becomes bankrupt or dies, the contract may provide for recovery of the goods by the creditor. In such a case, the term of the contract will be enforceable subject to the operation of the common law rules on damages and penalties.

Despite the fact that at common law there is no general right to terminate a conditional sale agreement, it is clear from the provisions of s. 99(1) that the statutory right does extend to the debtor under a regulated conditional sale agreement. The consequences of termination are generally the same as those which apply to hire-purchase contracts considered above (see 6.6.2.2), but special provisions apply so as to prevent the debtor from terminating a conditional sale agreement where there has been a valid disposition of the goods to a third party (s. 99(4)).

Under s. 99(5), goods revest in the 'previous owner' (or his successor in title or trustee in bankruptcy) where the debtor terminates a regulated conditional sale agreement and property in the goods has already passed to him. Thus the creditor will become, once more, the owner of the goods.

6.7   TERMINATION OF THE CONTRACT BY THE DEBTOR - MATERIALS FOR CONSIDERATION

6.7.1   Early settlement by the debtor

Consumer Credit Act 1974

94.   Right to complete payments ahead of time

(1)   The debtor under a regulated consumer credit agreement is entitled at any time, by notice to the creditor and the payment to the creditor of all amounts payable by the debtor to him under the agreement (less any rebate allowable under section 95), to discharge the debtor's indebtedness under the agreement.

(2) A notice under subsection (1) may embody the exercise by the debtor of any option to purchase goods conferred on him by the agreement, and deal with any other matter arising on, or in relation to, the termination of the agreement.

96. Effect on linked transactions

(1) Where for any reason the indebtedness of the debtor under a regulated consumer credit agreement is discharged before the time fixed by the agreement, he, and any relative of his, shall at the same time be discharged from any liability under a linked transaction, other than a debt which has already become payable.

(2) Subsection (1) does not apply to a linked transaction which is itself an agreement providing the debtor or his relative with credit.

(3) Regulations may exclude linked transactions of the prescribed description from the operation of subsection (1).

Where the debtor settles early, he is entitled to a rebate, but difficulties may arise where the early settlement becomes due after a default judgment.

Forward Trust Ltd v *Whymark*
[1989] 3 All ER 915
Court of Appeal

LORD DONALDSON MR at pp. 918, 920–2:

The commercial problem
Forward Trust do not seek any windfall profit as a result of suing to recover the indebtedness under the loan agreement. They do, however, object strongly to being placed at any significant disadvantage. This, they claim, is exactly what happens if they can only obtain judgment for the outstanding amount less the statutory rebate. The rebate represents future interest which, if they sued in the High Court, would be replaced by interest on the judgment debt. They are, however, required by s. 141 of the 1974 Act to sue in the county court, whose judgments do not bear interest unless and until rules are made under s. 74 of the County Courts Act 1984, which has not yet occurred.

Their preferred solution was that they should obtain judgment for the full amount without reduction to take account of the rebate, leaving the rebate to be calculated and taken into account when the judgment is met. This could be unjust to the debtor. No doubt if he tendered the full amount of the judgment less whatever rebate was due at that time, Forward Trust would accept it in discharge of the judgment debt. However, if it was necessary to enforce the judgment by execution against the debtor's goods, the bailiffs would be seeking to raise the full amount of the outstanding judgment debt and would be in no position to calculate the amount of any rebate which would become due on the footing that at some future date following the sale of the goods cash would be available to satisfy the judgment. Furthermore, in the event of any dispute as to the amount of the rebate, the debtor would have to sue the lender in order to obtain recovery of any overpayment. . . .

The solution
It is quite clear from ss. 94 and 95 of the 1974 Act that Parliament has intended that a debtor should be free to discharge his indebtedness before the expiration of the term fixed under the regulated consumer credit agreement and that, should he do so, he should be entitled to a rebate reflecting the unearned interest element. It is also clear

that Parliament intended that a rebate might also be required on refinancing or where, as a result of breach of the agreement or for any other reason, the indebtedness of the debtor became payable before the time fixed by the agreement. In principle one would have expected that the rebate would have reflected the advantage to the creditor of expedited payment and would only have been available if there was such payment, since an expedited liability, unaccompanied by payment, is of no benefit to the creditor who is called on to allow the rebate. However, whether or not this expectation is realised depends not on the Act, but on the 1983 rebate regulations made under s. 95.

The underlying assumption which has bedevilled the recovery through the courts of debts due under consumer credit agreements has been that a judgment for £100 can only be satisfied by the payment of £100. This is the normal rule, but there are exceptions. Thus there is statutory authority for discharging a debt, including a judgment debt, by paying the full amount of that debt less a rebate calculated by deducting income tax for which the debtor has accounted to the Inland Revenue: see *Riches* v *Westminster Bank Ltd* [1947] 1 All ER 469, [1947] AC 390. In my judgment the Consumer Credit Act 1974 and the Consumer Credit (Rebate on Early Settlement) Regulations 1983 produce a further exception. When the debtor decides, or is forced, to discharge the judgment debt, he can do so by payment of the amount stated in the judgment *less* any rebate which is applicable in respect of such discharge at that date.

This may be, and I consider that it is, a correct answer to the problem from a technical point of view, but it still leaves practical problems to be resolved. They include the following.

(1)   If a debtor applies to be allowed to discharge the judgment debt by instalments, no question of rebate arises until the payment of the final instalment which discharges the judgment debt. In most cases in which the debtor seeks to discharge the judgment debt by instalments this discharge will not occur sufficiently early for any question of a rebate to arise, but in fixing the amount of the instalments, registrars and judges should bear in mind that, if they order an initial instalment of a large amount, perhaps because the debtor has some available savings but not enough, followed by a large number of small instalments, the creditor may be getting the advantage of expedited payment without having to give the debtor the compensating advantage of a rebate.

(2)   A judgment for the full outstanding amount of the indebtedness under a consumer credit agreement should never be ordered to be enforced as a judgment of the High Court, since this would create problems of interest on interest.

(3)   If and when the Lord Chancellor makes any order under s. 74 of the County Courts Act 1984 whereby county court judgments would bear interest, an exception should be made for judgments in respect of sums due in respect of consumer credit agreements to which the rebate provisions apply, although there would be no injustice in such a judgment bearing interest as from the expiry date of the original period for which credit was given and paid for.

(4)   Means must be found for informing the judgment debtor that in some circumstances he may be able to discharge the judgment debt by a payment of less than 100p in the pound and for informing bailiffs that their right and duty to execute against goods will not extend to taking more goods than are sufficient to satisfy the judgment debt *less* any rebate which will apply.

6.7.2   Voluntary termination by the debtor

Consumer Credit Act 1974

99.   Right to terminate hire-purchase etc. agreements

(1)   At any time before the final payment by the debtor under a regulated

hire-purchase or regulated conditional sale agreement falls due, the debtor shall be entitled to terminate the agreement by giving notice to any person entitled or authorised to receive the sums payable under the agreement.

(2)   Termination of an agreement under subsection (1) does not affect any liability under the agreement which has accrued before the termination. . . .

(4)   In the case of a conditional sale agreement relating to goods, where the property in the goods, having become vested in the debtor, is transferred to a person who does not become the debtor under the agreement, the debtor shall not thereafter be entitled to terminate the agreement under subsection (1).

(5)   Subject to subsection (4), where a debtor under a conditional sale agreement relating to goods, terminates the agreement under this section after the property in the goods has become vested in him, the property in the goods shall thereupon vest in the person (the 'previous owner') in whom it was vested immediately before it became vested in the debtor:

Provided that if the previous owner has died, or any other event has occurred whereby that property, if vested in him immediately before that event, would thereupon have vested in some other person, the property shall be treated as having devolved as if it had been vested in the previous owner immediately before his death or immediately before that event, as the case may be.

6.8   ENFORCEMENT OF THE CONTRACT BY THE CREDITOR

There is always the danger that, for a number of reasons, a consumer debtor cannot keep up payments under an instalment credit agreement. The creditor may have provided for such an event in the contract. Some of these provisions may be designed to protect the creditor's investment by ensuring that he receives a specified amount or is paid in full at an earlier date than originally agreed. For example, it is common to find minimum payment clauses in hire-purchase contracts under which the creditor claims to be entitled to a minimum amount in the event of the debtor's breach of contract. In conditional sale and credit-sale agreements, a commonly found term is an accelerated payment clause under which the debtor may be required to pay the balance of any remaining indebtedness in the event of default or some other specified occurrence.

The use of such provisions in instalment credit contracts is understandable since creditors view the goods subject to the contract as security for the credit which has been made available. Where minimum payment clauses are concerned, the sort of goods normally subject to credit arrangements are of a type that rapidly depreciate in value. The creditor will want to pass on the cost of this depreciation to the consumer, since he has had the benefit of the use of the goods. Furthermore, where the debtor's default results in repossession of the goods supplied, the creditor is left with a second-hand article on his hands which he will find more difficult to dispose of than an article which is brand new.

Where the creditor relies on a minimum payment clause or an accelerated payment clause, it is important that its effect is not to entitle the creditor to more than he would have received had the agreement gone its full course. In particular, accelerated payment clauses should provide for a rebate to the consumer since the debt is being paid off at an earlier date than would otherwise have been the case. Similarly, a minimum payment clause must not amount to a penalty, intended to punish the consumer for his breach of contract — to be valid, it must be a genuine estimate of the loss likely to flow from the debtor's breach of contract.

6.8.1 Procedure on default where the agreement is regulated

Where the debtor is in breach of a regulated agreement, the creditor may wish to pursue one of a number of avenues. He may wish to sue for debt in respect of instalments due but not paid; he may wish to recover damages in respect of specific losses suffered as a result of the debtor's breach; he may wish to treat his own obligations of performance as terminated where there is a serious breach of contract; he may wish to repossess goods in the debtor's possession, or he may wish to demand early payment of a sum of money, for example, under the provisions of an accelerated payment clause.

Where, in the event of the debtor's default, the creditor seeks to take a course of action which would involve the debtor in doing more than just honour the agreement, the debtor must be served with a default notice (Consumer Credit Act 1974, s. 87(1)). Thus, such a notice must be served where the creditor wishes to terminate the agreement, demand early payment, recover possession of goods, terminate or restrict a right of the debtor or enforce any security since all of these courses of action can be viewed as a kind of threat designed to induce the debtor to honour the agreement.

Where the debtor's breach of contract consists of overdrawing on credit facilities made available to him, the creditor may immediately restrict the availability of further credit facilities. Such action is not subject to the requirement of service of a default notice (s. 87(2)). Thus, if the consumer exceeds the credit limit stipulated under his agreement with the issuer of a credit card, steps may be taken by the creditor to prevent any further overrun on the credit facility.

The Act stipulates in s. 88(1) the required form of a default notice. It must identify the nature of the debtor's breach, state what action is necessary to remedy the breach and by when this must be done. Thus if the debtor has failed to pay a number of instalments or has broken a covenant to keep the goods maintained in a satisfactory state of repair, the default notice should specify what should be done to remedy the breach.

Furthermore, if the breach is not capable of remedy, the default notice must specify the sum of money required to be paid by the debtor and the date by which it should be paid. For example, if the debtor has sold goods subject to a credit-sale or conditional sale agreement and has thereby conferred a good title on the third party, the default notice will have to specify the amount required from the debtor to pay for the goods in question.

There must also be a statement of the consequences for the debtor if he fails to comply with the default notice (s. 88(4)). For example, the creditor must state that he proposes to repossess the goods and terminate the agreement in the event of the default not being remedied by the debtor.

If the debtor complies with the requirements of the default notice by remedying the breach or by paying the amount specified in the default notice, the breach is to be treated as if it had never occurred (s. 89).

Special provision is made for the situation in which breach of one term of the contract brings into force another term. An example of this arises in the case of an accelerated payment clause, which requires the debtor to pay the full outstanding debt due under the agreement if he has failed to pay one or more instalments due to the creditor. The Act provides that failure to comply with the second term is not to be treated automatically as a breach of contract for the purposes of the default notice (s. 88(3)). Instead, if the first breach (non-payment of the instalment) is not remedied within seven days of service of the default notice, only then can the failure to comply with the second term (non-payment of the outstanding balance) be treated as a breach of contract. If this stage is reached, the creditor must serve a second default notice and start the default procedure once more.

6.8.2 Enforcement of regulated agreements in the absence of default

6.8.2.1 Enforcement of the agreement on death Where the debtor dies, his rights and liabilities will pass to his personal representatives, with the result that the creditor could serve a default notice in the event of non-payment. However, it is normal practice for the credit agreement to contain a term to the effect that the death of the debtor will terminate the agreement or that on death any outstanding balance shall become due.

Where the agreement is regulated, the Consumer Credit Act 1974 provides that the creditor cannot claim to be entitled to do any of the acts which trigger the default procedure (see 6.8.1) in the event of the debtor's death if the agreement is fully secured (s. 86(1)). In the case of an unsecured or partially secured agreement, for a period specified in the contract, which has not yet expired (s. 86(3)), the creditor may do one of the acts listed in s. 87(1) if he seeks a court order (s. 86(2)). It follows that the requirement of seeking a court order does not extend to an agreement of unlimited duration, with the result that such credit agreements can be enforced at any time after the death of the debtor.

6.8.2.2 Non-default enforcement In certain circumstances, the creditor may wish to enforce a term of the contract at a time when the debtor is not in breach of contract. For example, the contract may provide that the creditor is entitled to immediate payment of any outstanding balance or that he may repossess the goods subject to the agreement in the event of the debtor's bankruptcy. Similar provisions may also apply where the debtor changes his address, becomes unemployed or is convicted of an offence of dishonesty. In these circumstances, there may be a risk to the creditor, but there is no default on the part of the debtor.

To deal with enforcement in the absence of default, ss. 76 and 98 of the Consumer Credit Act 1974 provide for a procedure similar to that which applies to enforcement in the event of default (see 6.8.1. and ss. 87 and 88), although these provisions only apply to agreements of specific duration (ss. 76(2) and 98(2)). It follows that if a bank overdraft agreement allows the bank to demand immediate payment, s. 76 will have no application.

Section 76(1) requires the creditor to serve notice on the debtor if he proposes to demand early payment of any sum, recover possession of the goods or treat any right of the debtor's as restricted. If the creditor proposes to terminate the agreement, he must give the debtor at least seven days' notice of his intention (s. 98(1)).

6.8.3 Judicial powers in enforcement proceedings

6.8.3.1 Enforcement orders Where the creditor applies for an enforcement order, the court must determine whether there has been a fatal or a non-fatal irregularity. A fatal irregularity is one which leaves the court with no option but to refuse the application for an enforcement order (see Consumer Credit Act 1974, s. 127(3) and (4)). Examples of such irregularities include failure to secure the signature of the debtor (s. 61(1)(a)); failure to specify the prescribed terms of the agreement (s. 60(1)) and failure to supply notice of cancellation rights (s. 64(1)).

Non-fatal irregularites do not render the agreement unenforceable, but a discretion rests in the court to determine whether or not enforcement is appropriate. There is a non-fatal infringement where the contractual document is not legible (s. 61(1)) or where not all the terms of the contract are expressed in writing (s. 61(1)). Similarly, the court has such a discretion where the agreement is not in the form set out in the Agreements Regulations (SI 1983/1553) or where there is a failure to supply copies of the agreement (ss. 62(3) and 63(5)).

The county court has jurisdiction over enforcement orders and may exercise one of three options in the event of an application for an enforcement order. It may enforce the agreement according to its terms or subject to modifications or decline to make any order at all.

6.8.3.2 Time orders If it appears just to do so, the court may make a time order in favour of the debtor (Consumer Credit Act 1974, s. 129). The effect of such an order is to allow the debtor more time to comply with his obligations under his contract with the creditor.

The debtor has a limited right to apply for a time order after a default notice under s. 87 or a non-default notice under s. 76 or s. 98 has been served upon him. There is also a wider right where the creditor has applied to the court for enforcement of the agreement.

The court's powers consist of giving time to pay sums due, giving time to rectify a breach and conferring the right to continued possession after making a time order.

6.8.3.3 Other orders So as to protect the creditor's position pending a claim for repossession, the court may issue a protection order under s. 131, so that the goods are preserved until trial.

Other orders which may be made include return orders (s. 133) and transfer orders (s. 133) in the case of proceedings in relation to hire-purchase and conditional sale agreements.

6.8.3.4   Power to reopen extortionate credit bargains   One of the most important court powers relates to extortionate credit bargains. If a contract (regardless of value) requires the payment of grossly exorbitant sums or otherwise grossly contravenes ordinary principles of fair dealing (Consumer Credit Act 1974, s. 138(1)), the bargain may be reopened (s. 137(1)). The creditor bears the onus of proving that the bargain is not extortionate (*Bank of Baroda* v *Shah* [1988] 3 All ER 24) once the debtor or a surety has first raised the issue (s. 139(1)).

Where a credit bargain is considered to be extortionate, the debtor may be relieved of his obligations under the contract, and sums paid may be ordered to be repaid by the creditor. The power relates not only to the credit agreement but also to any related agreement and to both the primary and secondary obligations of the debtor. Thus, these provisions will apply to terms of the contract which operate on default and linked transactions (s. 138(5)).

A number of factors are specified in s. 138 as being relevant to the question whether a credit bargain is extortionate or not. In particular s. 138(2) provides that regard should be had to matters such as interest rates at the time of making the agreement (see *Ketley Ltd* v *Scott* [1981] ICR 241; *Davies* v *Direct Loans Ltd* [1986] 2 All ER 783); personal factors such as the age, experience, business capacity and health of the debtor; the degree of risk undertaken by the creditor; the relationship of creditor and debtor and whether an inflated cash price has been quoted to the debtor.

The meaning of 'extortionate' is not fettered by percentage limits as used to be the case under the Moneylenders Acts 1900 to 1927, with the result that seemingly high rates of interest can be justified where the circumstances permit.

6.9   ENFORCEMENT OF THE CONTRACT BY THE CREDITOR – MATERIALS FOR CONSIDERATION

6.9.1   Duty to serve notice before taking certain courses of action

For text see 6.8.1 and 6.8.2.

Consumer Credit Act 1974

76.   Duty to give notice before taking certain action
(1)   The creditor or owner is not entitled to enforce a term of a regulated agreement by—
    (a)   demanding earlier payment of any sum, or
    (b)   recovering possession of any goods or land, or
    (c)   treating any right conferred on the debtor or hirer by the agreement as terminated, restricted or deferred,

except by or after giving the debtor or hirer not less than seven days' notice of his intention to do so.

(2)   Subsection (1) applies only where—

(a)   a period for the duration of the agreement is specified in the agreement, and

(b)   that period has not ended when the creditor or owner does an act mentioned in subsection (1),

but so applies notwithstanding that, under the agreement, any party is entitled to terminate it before the end of the period so specified.

(3)   A notice under subsection (1) is ineffective if not in the prescribed form.

(4)   Subsection (1) does not prevent a creditor from treating the right to draw on any credit as restricted or deferred and taking such steps as may be necessary to make the restriction or deferment effective.

(5)   Regulations may provide that subsection (1) is not to apply to agreements described by the regulations.

(6)   Subsection (1) does not apply to a right of enforcement arising by reason of any breach by the debtor or hirer of the regulated agreement.

87. Need for default notice

(1)   Service of a notice on the debtor or hirer in accordance with section 88 (a 'default notice') is necessary before the creditor or owner can become entitled, by reason of any breach by the debtor or hirer of a regulated agreement,—

(a)   to terminate the agreement, or

(b)   to demand earlier payment of any sum, or

(c)   to recover possession of any goods or land, or

(d)   to treat any right conferred on the debtor or hirer by the agreement as terminated, restricted or deferred, or

(e)   to enforce any security.

(2)   Subsection (1) does not prevent the creditor from treating the right to draw upon any credit as restricted or deferred, and taking such steps as may be necessary to make the restriction or deferment effective.

(3)   The doing of an act by which a floating charge becomes fixed is not enforcement of a security.

6.9.2   Judicial powers in enforcement proceedings

One of the most important powers available to the court is to reopen an extortionate credit bargain.

Consumer Credit Act 1974

137.   Extortionate credit bargains

(1)   If the court finds a credit bargain extortionate it may reopen the credit agreement so as to do justice between the parties.

(2)   In this section and sections 138 to 140,—

(a)   'credit agreement' means any agreement between an individual (the 'debtor') and any other person (the 'creditor') by which the creditor provides the debtor with credit of any amount, and

(b)   'credit bargain'—

(i)   where no transaction other than the credit agreement is to be taken into account in computing the total charge for credit, means the credit agreement, or

(ii)   where one or more other transactions are to be so taken into account, means the credit agreement and those other transactions, taken together.

138.   When bargains are extortionate

(1)   A credit bargain is extortionate if it—

(a)   requires the debtor or a relative of his to make payments (whether unconditionally, or on certain contingencies) which are grossly exorbitant, or

(b)   otherwise grossly contravenes ordinary principles of fair dealing.

(2)   In determining whether a credit bargain is extortionate, regard shall be had to such evidence as is adduced concerning—

(a)   interest rates prevailing at the time it was made,

(b)   the factors mentioned in subsection (3) to (5), and

(c)   any other relevant considerations.

(3)   Factors applicable under subsection (2) in relation to the debtor include—

(a)   his age, experience, business capacity and state of health; and

(b)   the degree to which, at the time of making the credit bargain, he was under financial pressure, and the nature of that pressure.

(4)   Factors applicable under subsection (2) in relation to the creditor include—

(a)   the degree of risk accepted by him, having regard to the value of any security provided;

(b)   his relationship to the debtor; and

(c)   whether or not a colourable cash price was quoted for any goods or services included in the credit bargain.

(5)   Factors applicable under subsection (2) in relation to a linked transaction include the question how far the transaction was reasonably required for the protection of debtor or creditor, or was in the interest of the debtor.

139.   Reopening of extortionate agreements

(1)   A credit agreement may, if the court thinks just, be reopened on the ground that the credit bargain is extortionate—

(a)   on an application for the purpose made by the debtor or any surety to the High Court, county court or sheriff court; or

(b)   at the instance of the debtor or a surety in any proceedings to which the debtor and creditor are parties, being proceedings to enforce the credit agreement, any security relating to it, or any linked transaction; or

(c)   at the instance of the debtor or a surety in other proceedings in any court where the amount paid or payable under the credit agreement is relevant.

(2)   In reopening the agreement, the court may, for the purpose of relieving the debtor or a surety from payment of any sum in excess of that fairly due and reasonable, by order—

(a)   direct accounts to be taken, or (in Scotland) an accounting to be made, between any persons,

(b)   set aside the whole or part of any obligation imposed on the debtor or a surety by the credit bargain or any related agreement,

(c)   require the creditor to repay the whole or part of any sum paid under the credit bargain or any related agreement by the debtor or a surety, whether paid to the creditor or any other person,

(d)   direct the return to the surety of any property provided for the purposes of the security, or

(e)   alter the terms of the credit agreement or any security instrument.

(3)   An order may be made under subsection (2) notwithstanding that its effect is to place a burden on the creditor in respect of an advantage unfairly enjoyed by another person who is a party to a linked transaction.

6.10   THE CREDITOR'S REMEDIES ON DEFAULT BY THE DEBTOR

Where the debtor is in default, certain remedies are conferred on the creditor by law. He is entitled to sue for each instalment payable under the agreement as it falls due. He may be able to sue for damages in respect of losses suffered as a result of the debtor's breach. If the debtor's breach is so serious as to amount to repudiation at common law, the creditor may be able to treat the contract as being at an end and recover damages in respect of the breach.

The agreement itself may also confer remedies on the creditor, such as a power to demand immediate payment of the outstanding balance or a power to terminate the agreement in specified circumstances. Likewise, the agreement may allow the creditor to take possession of the goods subject to the agreement or may empower him to remedy a breach and charge the cost to the debtor. Sometimes the contract contains a liquidated damages clause which specifies a fixed sum to be paid in the event of certain breaches of contract on the part of the debtor.

6.10.1   Actions for sums due under the agreement

Where the debtor has failed to make payments required by the agreement he has entered into, the creditor can recover each payment as it becomes due (*Yeoman Credit Ltd* v *Apps* [1962] 2 QB 508). It is important to distinguish this action from one for damages for breach of contract, as they are quite different in nature (*Overstone* v *Shipway* [1962] 1 All ER 52). The action for instalments due is one for debt in respect of the hire-rent due as a result of the hirer's use of the goods subject to the agreement. In contrast, the action for damages is based on some specific breach on the part of the debtor which has caused additional loss to the creditor over and above any debt due under the agreement.

Since the action for debt is based on hire-rent becoming due under the agreement, it is essential that the hiring period has commenced. If the debtor has refused to take delivery, hiring has not commenced, in which case, there will be no action for debts due, although an action for damages for failure to take delivery may be available (*National Cash Register Co. Ltd* v *Stanley* [1921] 3 KB 292). Similarly, if no agreement is reached, hire-rent is not due and no action will lie for debt (*Campbell Discount Ltd* v *Gall* [1961] 1 QB 431 (overruled on other grounds)).

Once the hiring period has commenced, the debtor is liable to make payments according to the terms of the agreement, while-ever he remains in possession of the goods. However, if the debtor gives up possession of the goods, the hire-rent ceases to be payable by him (*Belsize Motor Co.* v *Cox* [1914] 1 KB 244).

If the contract contains an accelerated payment clause, its effect may be to convert into debts sums which would otherwise be due in the future. Whether the acceleration clause is valid or not depends on a number of factors. If the agreement is regulated, the creditor has to give the debtor at least seven days' notice of an intention to invoke the clause and demand full payment earlier than was originally agreed (Consumer Credit Act 1974, s. 76(1) (non-default) and s. 87(1) (default)). If the notice is served on the debtor following his default and the debtor subsequently complies with the requirements of the default notice (for example, by paying an outstanding instalment) the breach is treated as if it had never occurred (s. 89).

If the acceleration clause merely requires payment of the cash price of the goods, there can be no question of its validity since all it serves to do is to bring forward the date on which the debtor must pay for the subject-matter of the contract. But in most cases, the creditor will want to recover the interest due in respect of the period of credit. In these circumstances, it is important that the contract provides the debtor with a rebate for early settlement, otherwise it could be struck down on the ground that it is penal (see *Wadham Stringer Finance Ltd* v *Meaney* [1980] 3 All ER 789 and 6.10.4).

If the agreement is regulated, the creditor cannot rely on a term which subjects the debtor to a rise in interest rate following his default under the agreement (s. 93).

6.10.2   Termination and repossession by the creditor

In the event of the debtor's repudiation or a breach of condition, the creditor may wish to terminate the contract and in a case where owenership in the goods has not passed to the debtor, the creditor may wish to retake possession. It is important to distinguish between termination after the debtor's repudiation and termination under a term of the contract. In some instances, a term of the contract allows the creditor to bring the contract to an end in the event of the debtor's breach of contract or upon some other specified occurrence. Where this is the case and the breach does not amount to a repudiation, the creditor is treated as the cause of the termination of the contract. Where there is a repudiation, the debtor is regarded as the cause of termination, which could have adverse consequences for him if the creditor also sues for damages.

6.10.2.1   Repudiation   The debtor will be treated as having repudiated the contract where he does some act which is totally repugnant to the agreement. Thus if the debtor sells goods which are subject to a hire-purchase contract (*Bowmakers Ltd* v *Barnet Instruments Ltd* [1945] KB 65) or indicates that he has no intention of proceeding with the hiring (*Overstone Ltd* v *Shipway* [1962] 1 WLR 117), he may be treated as having repudiated the agreement. While it is possible for the court to infer repudiation from a person's conduct, it is clear that such an inference will not be lightly made. For example, repeated failure to pay instalments punctually, as required by the agreement does not necessarily amount to repudiation (*Lombard North Central plc* v *Butterworth* [1987] 1 All ER 267). However, failure to pay any instalments at all is likely to be construed as repudiatory conduct (*Yeoman Credit Ltd* v *Waragowski* [1961] 1 WLR 1124).

6.10.2.2 Non-repudiatory breaches of contract Some breaches of contract may not be sufficiently serious to amount to repudiation but may give the creditor a contractual right to terminate the contract. This may be the case where the debtor fails to pay instalments on time or fails to take reasonable care of the goods which are the subject of the agreement. Where the agreement is regulated, the Consumer Credit Act 1974 provides that the debtor must be given the chance to remedy his default (see s. 87(1) and 6.8.1) and that if he does so, the default is treated as if it had never occurred (s. 89).

6.10.2.3 Recovery of the goods on termination Where an agreement has been terminated, the common law rule is that the debtor no longer has a right to possession of the goods. Accordingly, the creditor is entitled to retake possession whether the contract specifically allows this or not (*Bowmakers Ltd* v *Barnet Instruments Ltd* [1945] KB 65). Thus the creditor can either commence proceedings for damages for conversion or physically take possession of the goods. The difficulty with the latter option is that if the goods are on the debtor's premises, the creditor will be guilty of trespass if he enters those premises without the debtor's permission. This problem could be avoided where the contract contains a term which authorises the creditor to enter the debtor's premises for the purpose of retaking possession.

6.10.2.3.1 Restriction on repossession In the case of regulated agreements, the Consumer Credit Act 1974 limits the repossession option by providing that the creditor cannot enter premises to take possession of goods or land without leave of the court (s. 92). A creditor who fails to comply with s. 92 is guilty of a breach of statutory duty and may be liable in damages (s. 92(3)).

6.10.2.3.2 Protected goods status Where the goods are classified as 'protected' under s. 90 of the Consumer Credit Act 1974, the creditor in a regulated hire-purchase or conditional sale agreement may not recover them without a court order. Goods are protected if the debtor is in breach of the agreement (s. 90(1)(a)), has paid more than one third of the total price of the goods (s. 90(1)(b)) and property in the goods remains with the creditor (s. 90(1)(c)).

It follows from this that goods are not protected where the debtor exercises his right of voluntary termination. Accordingly, it is important to determine whether a debtor's communication constitutes breach or voluntary termination, since in the case of voluntary termination by the debtor, the creditor will be able to take possession of the goods, provided the necessary notice has been given to the debtor. In these circumstances, the court will order the debtor to deliver the goods to the creditor and will not give the debtor the option of paying for them except where it would not be just to make such an order (s. 100(5)). For this reason, the debtor who finds himself in financial difficulties is advised not to be precipitate in returning the goods to the creditor. Instead, he is in a better position if he defaults and waits for the creditor to act against him. The courts are mindful of the debtor's position in the event of a voluntary termination and may be reluctant to regard his conduct as amounting to such a termination, particularly if its consequences have not been fully explained (*United Dominions Trust (Commercial) Ltd* v *Ennis* [1968] 1 QB 54).

The effect of s. 90(1)(c) is that goods subject to a conditional sale agreement under which the debtor is obliged to purchase will not be protected since property in the goods must remain with the creditor.

The definition of protected goods requires the debtor to have paid one third or more of the total price of the goods. It will be necessary to total the amounts paid by the debtor including any deposit, instalments paid prior to default and the option fee. If this comes to more than one third of the total price for the goods, they are protected. However, s. 90(2) provides that any amount paid by the debtor by way of an installation charge is to be deducted from the amount paid by the debtor. If the debtor has paid £200 of the total price of a £600 gas cooker, but that £600 includes a £60 installation charge, it is necessary that he should have paid the whole of the installation charge and one third of the remainder. In this example the cooker is not protected because in order to achieve protected goods status the debtor would be required to have paid the installation charge of £60 plus one third of the price of the cooker ignoring the installation charge, i.e., one third of £600 − £60, or one third of £540, which is £180. The debtor has paid £200 but £60 + £180 = £240.

6.10.2.3.3 Effect of ignoring protected goods status Where a creditor wrongly takes possession of protected goods, he commits no crime, but the agreement is automatically terminated and no further liabilities on the part of the debtor arise under it (s. 90(3)). Furthermore, the debtor can recover all sums paid to the creditor in an action for moneys had and received (s. 91(b)). In *Capital Finance Co. Ltd* v *Bray* [1964] 1 All ER 603, the creditor wrongly took possession of a car subject to a hire-purchase agreement. The debtor asked for return of all sums paid by him so the creditor returned the car to the debtor. The debtor used the car on a number of occasions but paid no further instalments. In a subsequent action by the creditor it was held that the initial repossession without a court order meant that the creditor had no defence to a counterclaim by the debtor for the return of all sums paid by him under the agreement.

6.10.2.3.4 Loss of protected goods status If the debtor or his agent has consented to repossession, s. 91 of the Consumer Credit Act 1974 will not apply (s. 173(3)). Thus if the debtor has failed to read his copy of the agreement, does not realise that the goods are protected and agrees to repossession, he cannot later claim repayment of sums paid under the agreement because of his consent (*Mercantile Credit Co. Ltd* v *Cross* [1965] 2 QB 194). It is essential, in this respect, that the debtor's consent is fully informed (*Chartered Trust plc* v *Pitcher* [1988] RTR 72). Thus, consent given by a third party will not suffice (*Peacock* v *Anglo Auto Finance Ltd* (1968) 112 Sol Jo 746).

Similarly, if the debtor has abandoned the goods or if he has sold the goods to a third party, s. 91 will not apply because s. 90(1) refers to *recovering possession from the debtor*. In the case of a disposition to a third party, the rights of the third party will have to be considered, but the right to seize the goods would appear to be available (see *Bentinck Ltd* v *Cromwell Engineering Co.* [1971] 1 QB 324).

6.10.3   Damages for breach of contract

Where the debtor is in breach of contract, he may have caused loss to the creditor which is remediable in the form of an award of damages. Ordinarily, the principal cause of loss to the creditor will be the fact that the debtor has fallen into arrears, in which case it will be necessary to decide whether the default amounts to a repudiation of the contract or not.

The creditor may also have a legitimate claim where the debtor has wrongly failed to take delivery of the goods subject to the agreement or where the debtor has failed to take care of goods in his possession. Furthermore, if the debtor wrongly refuses to give up possession of the goods when properly asked to do so, he may be liable in damages for conversion.

6.10.3.1   Failure to take delivery   Provided the goods delivered are in accordance with the contract, the debtor is under an obligation to accept them. If the debtor fails to take delivery, the creditor's action is not one for instalments due, because hire-rent does not become due until the hiring has commenced (*National Cash Register Co. Ltd* v *Stanley* [1921] 3 KB 292). Instead, the appropriate action is one for damages for non-acceptance. Ordinary principles of contract damages will apply in these circumstances. Thus the creditor will be able to recover any loss arising naturally from the breach of contract. This will include the difference between the price paid for the goods by the creditor and the market value of the goods on resale and the creditor's lost finance charges. However, in quantifying the award, the court will have to take into account the fact that the creditor is being paid back earlier than would have been the case had the agreement run its course.

6.10.3.2   Failure to take care of the goods   Where the debtor is not the owner of the goods, he owes a duty to the creditor to take reasonable care of the goods in his possession. Ordinarily, the creditor will take no chances and there will be express terms of the contract defining the nature of the debtor's responsibility. But even in the absence of such terms, the debtor is a bailee and is therefore responsible for harm caused to the goods by his negligence (see *Brady* v *St Margaret's Trust Ltd* [1963] 2 QB 494).

6.10.3.3   Refusal to give up possession   If the hiring terminates for some reason, the creditor may be entitled to retake possession of the goods, subject to certain restrictions (see 6.10.2.3). If the debtor wrongly refuses to give up possession, he may be liable in the tort of conversion. The measure of damages will normally be the value of the converted goods at the date of conversion, with the result that an award of damages in such a case will amount to a compulsory sale of the goods concerned. Account will be taken of any instalments already paid under the agreement, but the debtor will be required to pay the amount which would have become payable under the agreement had it not been terminated (*Wickham Holdings Ltd* v *Brooke House Motors Ltd* [1967] 1 WLR 295). This does not mean that account will not also be taken of the fact that the creditor may receive accelerated payment, in which case a reduction in the award will be made.

6.10.3.4 Damages for breach of instalment payment obligations

Where the debtor fails to pay instalments due under a conditional sale or credit-sale agreement, the creditor will be able to sue for the price or for damages for loss of profit, but not for both. In the case of a hire-purchase, the creditor will be able to recover the goods subject to the agreement and hire-rent due in respect of the period of hire. This double recovery on the part of the creditor may be added to where the contract contains a minimum payment clause which requires a payment by the debtor in respect of future instalments due under the agreement.

In seeking to find a solution to the problem created by minimum payment clauses in conjunction with apparent default on the part of the debtor, it is necessary to determine whether the debtor's default amounts to a voluntary termination of the contract, a repudiation of the contract or a breach not amounting to repudiation.

6.10.3.4.1 Voluntary termination If the debtor's conduct is construed as a voluntary termination of the contract, no question of damages for breach of contract will arise, assuming the agreement or statute confers such a right (see Consumer Credit Act 1974, s. 99). However, a minimum payment clause may still provide for payment of future hire-rent in such a case. At common law the position appears to be that the minimum payment clause is to be construed as an agreement to pay the amount stipulated as compensation for loss of future interest. Furthermore, since there is no breach of contract, the doctrine of penalties, considered below, has no application (see *Associated Distributors Ltd* v *Hall* [1938] 2 KB 83 and 6.6.2.1.2).

If the agreement is regulated by the Consumer Credit Act 1974, the debtor is given some protection against what might otherwise be a requirement to pay an exorbitant amount. In particular, the debtor will be required to pay no more than half of the total price (s. 100(1)). Thus if the debtor's payments including the deposit and sums due but not yet paid come to that amount, the creditor can expect to be paid nothing more. If the debtor's payments have not reached the 50% threshold, the court can require him to pay up to that amount, subject to a discretion to reduce the sum payable in accordance with the actual loss suffered by the creditor (s. 100(3)).

In addition to any payment made under s. 100(1), the debtor will also be liable to the creditor for his failure to take care of the goods in his possession (s. 100(5)). This liability is superimposed on any payment made under s. 100(1).

The provisions of s. 100(1) apply only where the terms of the contract concerning payment are less favourable than those stipulated in the Act. Thus, if the contract provides for no payment, or payment of a sum less than half of the total price, the relevant term will be applied (s. 100(1)).

6.10.3.4.2 Default amounting to repudiation Where the debtor's default amounts to a repudiation, that default is regarded as the cause of the termination of the contract and the amount the creditor receives by way of damages may exceed the amount payable under a minimum payment clause. The repudiation may come in the form of an express statement (*Overstone Ltd v Shipway* [1962] 1 All ER 52), or it may be inferred from a substantial failure to perform (*Yeoman Credit Ltd v Waragowski* [1961] 1 WLR 1124).

In *Yeoman Credit Ltd v Waragowski* [1961] 1 WLR 1124, the creditor could have relied on a minimum payment clause which would have allowed him a 50% payment, but sought damages for repudiation instead. He recovered damages which put him in the position he would have been in had the agreement run its course even though the agreement was terminated after six months of the envisaged three-year period. This element of over-compensation has since been recognised and the court is likely to reduce damages so as to take into account the earlier settlement date (*Overstone Ltd v Shipway* [1962] 1 All ER 52).

6.10.3.4.3 Non-repudiatory default If the debtor's default does not go to the root of the contract, the decision of the creditor to terminate the contract cannot be attributed to the breach. Accordingly, termination in such a case is caused by the creditor rather than the debtor and the latter is then treated more favourably. In these circumstances, the creditor cannot claim damages for loss of future payments and is limited to the arrears outstanding at the time of termination (*Financings Ltd v Baldock* [1963] 2 QB 104).

In the light of the decision of the Court of Appeal in *Financings Ltd v Baldock*, there has been a judicial tendency to regard the debtor's conduct as not amounting to repudiation, given the adverse consequences that follow from the decision in *Yeoman Credit Ltd v Waragowski* [1961] 1 WLR 1124. Thus a creditor cannot write to the debtor saying that unless payment is received within a specified period it is to be assumed that the debtor no longer wishes to continue with the agreement (*Eshun v Moorgate Mercantile Co. Ltd* [1971] 1 WLR 722). Generally, it cannot be assumed from the failure to pay two instalments that a person has repudiated the contract.

While the courts may be reluctant to hold that a debtor has repudiated the contract, the creditor may be able to get round the decision in *Financings Ltd v Baldock* by making prompt payment of the essence of the contract (*Lombard North Central plc v Butterworth* [1987] 1 All ER 267). Where this is the case, default in the form of persistent late payment may go to the root of the contract, with the result that the creditor can rely on a minimum payment clause in the contract. Where there is no time of the essence clause and no repudiation, any purported termination of the contract cannot be blamed on the debtor with the result that the creditor will be confined to recovery of outstanding instalments.

6.10.4   Application of the doctrine of penalties to minimum payment clauses

It is clear from the decision in *Financings Ltd* v *Baldock* [1963] 2 QB 104 that a minimum payment clause may be struck down on the ground that it is penal, in the sense that the clause operates *in terrorem* over the head of the debtor (see *Dunlop Pneumatic Tyre Co. Ltd* v *New Garage & Motor Co. Ltd* [1915] AC 79; *Landom Trust Ltd* v *Hurrell* [1955] 1 WLR 391). In particular, a minimum payment clause will be penal if it requires the payment of an extravagant or unconscionable amount which is out of proportion to the greatest possible loss that the creditor could suffer. In particular, if a minimum payment clause requires the debtor to pay more than the amount he would have paid had the contract run its full course, it will be struck down as penal (*Lombard Ltd* v *Excell* [1964] 1 QB 415).

In considering the application of the penalty doctrine, it is necessary to distinguish between the operation of a minimum payment clause in the event of breach of contract by the debtor, voluntary termination by the debtor and the death or bankruptcy of the debtor. As the law stands at present, the doctrine only applies where there has been a breach of contract on the part of the debtor and not where the contract comes to an end by virtue of a voluntary termination or by virtue of the death or bankruptcy of the debtor (cf. Law Commission, *Penalty Clauses and Forfeiture of Moneys Paid* (Working Paper 61, 1975) para. 26).

Where there is a default in the form of a late payment the contract may provide that it shall terminate automatically thereby immediately triggering the minimum payment clause. In such a case, the clause is penal and will be struck down (*Cooden Engineering Co. Ltd* v *Stanford* [1953] 1 QB 86). The problem with most minimum payment clauses is that they cannot be regarded as a genuine estimate of the loss likely to be suffered by the creditor in the event of the debtor's breach of contract.

If the clause requires payment of the same amount regardless of the number of payments made by the debtor before breach, it will be struck down as penal, since it operates in relation to one of a number of different events which may be of differing importance (*Landom Trust Ltd* v *Hurrell* [1955] 1 WLR 391).

Finance companies have sought to get round the problem of the doctrine of penalties by drawing up a scale of compensation, providing for payment of a variable percentage of the total price at each stage of the repayment period. Such minimum payment clauses have been held to be genuine liquidated damages clauses (*Phonographic Equipment (1958) Ltd* v *Muslu* [1961] 1 WLR 1379), but it now appears that following the decision of the House of Lords in *Bridge* v *Campbell Discount Co. Ltd* [1962] AC 600, these too can be regarded as penal.

The typical minimum payment clause is claimed to operate as a means of securing compensation for depreciation, but depreciation in the value of a motor vehicle increases as time passes by, whereas the amount required under a variable percentage minimum payment clause gets smaller as time passes. Accordingly, the majority of minimum payment clauses do work on a sliding scale, but one which operates in the wrong direction.

In order to comply with the requirements of *Bridge* v *Campbell Discount Co. Ltd* a minimum payment clause will have to give the debtor due allowance for the value of repossessed goods, make allowance for early payment, produce a scale of compensation sliding in an upward direction and take account of the condition of the goods at the time of breach, thereby compensating the creditor for his true loss. In *Anglo Auto Finance Co. Ltd* v *James* [1963] 1 WLR 1042 these requirements were satisfied except that no allowance was made for early payment. Accordingly, the clause was regarded as penal.

Where a minimum payment clause is held to be a penalty, it will not be enforceable against the debtor. Instead, the creditor will be confined to an action for unliquidated damages in respect of the debtor's breach (see 6.10.3).

6.11 THE CREDITOR'S REMEDIES ON DEFAULT BY THE DEBTOR – MATERIALS FOR CONSIDERATION

6.11.1 Actions for money due under the agreement

For text see 6.10.1.

Yeoman Credit Ltd v *Apps*
[1962] 2 QB 508
Court of Appeal

A car subject to a hire-purchase agreement proved to be unfit for use on the roads. The debtor had chosen not to reject the vehicle until after he had made payments under the agreement.

HOLROYD PEARCE LJ at pp. 521–2: The defendant, therefore, kept the car, and was entitled to £100 damages to make good the car for the use for which he was paying, and which he had an ultimate right to buy which he has now lost. In my view that is damage which he has suffered, and to which he is entitled. On this point the judge said:

> Later, however, owing to the strong view he had formed about the condition of the vehicle, and his inability to get satisfaction from either the dealer or the plaintiffs, the defendant declined to make further payments. Stereotyped formal reminders were sent, but he still failed to pay. The defendant tells me that he rang the plaintiff company telling them that the car was not roadworthy, that he was not going to pay any more, and that they could take the car away. The plaintiffs have no record of this, but I think some such remark was made to some officer of the plaintiffs. The defendant made no serious effort to return the car, and I do not think I can find that he terminated the hiring as he was entitled to do under clause 5 of the agreement.

> That seems to show that the defendant allowed the August instalment to fall due before he sought to repudiate the agreement. In my view he is, therefore, liable for the August instalment. Thereafter he rejected the car. Was he entitled to do so? Had this been a sale of goods on instalment payments, he could not, of course, have done so after payment of instalments and acceptance of the goods. Had this been a simple hiring, say, of a gas stove which did not work at all, and which the owners, after frequent requests over some months, had declined to put in order, he would have been entitled to reject

it and end the hiring since the owner's breach was a continuing one. The owner's conduct would constitute a continuing repudiation. This hire-purchase agreement was, at the material time, more analogous to a simple hiring than to a purchase. It had a contingent option to purchase of which the defendant might have availed himself in two years' time; but in September the defendant could, as a hirer, refuse to go on with the transaction since the plaintiffs, in spite of repeated requests, were still consistently refusing to honour their obligations.

The defendant, therefore, is entitled to £100 damages; but he must pay the instalment that fell due on August 21, namely, £14 19s 1d.

6.11.2   Termination and repossession by the creditor

For text see 6.10.2.

Where the creditor seeks to repossess goods subject to a regulated agreement, there are restrictions on the extent to which this is possible.

Consumer Credit Act 1974

90.   Retaking of protected hire-purchase etc. goods

(1)   At any time when—

   (a)   the debtor is in breach of a regulated hire-purchase or a regulated conditional sale agreement relating to goods, and

   (b)   the debtor has paid to the creditor one third or more of the total price of the goods, and

   (c)   the property in the goods remains in the creditor,

the creditor is not entitled to recover possession of the goods from the debtor except on an order of the court.

(2)   Where under a hire-purchase or conditional sale agreement the creditor is required to carry out any installation and the agreement specifies, as part of the total price, the amount to be paid in respect of the installation (the 'installation charge') the reference in subsection (1)(b) to one third of the total price shall be construed as a reference to the aggregate of the installation charge and one third of the remainder of the total price.

(3)   In a case where—

   (a)   subsection (1)(a) is satisfied, but not subsection (1)(b), and

   (b)   subsection (1)(b) was satisfied on a previous occasion in relation to an earlier agreement, being a regulated hire-purchase or regulated conditional sale agreement, between the same parties, and relating to any of the goods comprised in the later agreement (whether or not other goods were also included),

subsection (1) shall apply to the later agreement with the omission of paragraph (b).

(4)   If the later agreement is a modifying agreement, subsection (3) shall apply with the substitution, for the second reference to the later agreement, of a reference to the modifying agreement.

(5)   Subsection (1) shall not apply, or shall cease to apply, to an agreement if the debtor has terminated, or terminates, the agreement.

(6)   Where subsection (1) applies to an agreement at the death of the debtor, it shall continue to apply (in relation to the possessor of the goods) until the grant of probate or administration, or (in Scotland) confirmation (on which the personal representative would fall to be treated as the debtor).

(7)   Goods falling within this section are in this Act referred to as 'protected goods'.

6.11.3   Damages for breach of contract

For text see 6.10.3.

While a number of different breaches of contract may render the debtor liable in damages, one of the most common is the failure to comply with payment obligations. In these circumstances, it may also be the case that the creditor wishes to rely on a minimum payment clause which operates on the occurrence of one of a number of events which may be specified in the contract.

If a hire-purchase or conditional sale agreement is regulated and the debtor's non-payment is regarded as a voluntary termination of the contract rather than as a breach of contract, the matter is governed by the following provision.

Consumer Credit Act 1974

100.   Liability of debtor on termination of hire-purchase etc. agreement

(1)   Where a regulated hire-purchase or regulated conditional sale agreement is terminated under section 99 the debtor shall be liable, unless the agreement provides for a smaller payment, or does not provide for any payment, to pay to the creditor the amount (if any) by which one half of the total price exceeds the aggregate of the sums paid and the sums due in respect of the total price immediately before the termination.

(2)   Where under a hire-purchase or conditional sale agreement the creditor is required to carry out any installation and the agreement specifies, as part of the total price, the amount to be paid in respect of the installation (the 'installation charge') the reference in subsection (1) to one half of the total price shall be construed as a reference to the aggregate of the installation charge and one half of the remainder of the total price.

(3)   If in any action the court is satisfied that a sum less than the amount specified in subsection (1) would be equal to the loss sustained by the creditor in consequence of the termination of the agreement by the debtor, the court may make an order for the payment of that sum in lieu of the amount specified in subsection (1).

(4)   If the debtor has contravened an obligation to take reasonable care of the goods or land, the amount arrived at under subsection (1) shall be increased by the sum required to recompense the creditor for that contravention, and subsection (2) shall have effect accordingly.

(5)   Where the debtor, on the termination of the agreement, wrongfully retains possession of goods to which the agreement relates, then, in any action brought by the creditor to recover possession of the goods from the debtor, the court, unless it is satisfied that having regard to the circumstances it would not be just to do so, shall order the goods to be delivered to the creditor without giving the debtor an option to pay the value of the goods.

6.11.4   The doctrine of penalties and minimum payment clauses

Where the non-payment does amount to a breach of contract, s. 100 does not apply, but a minimum payment clause may still purport to operate in the event of breach. If the clause provides for the payment of excessive amounts, it may be struck down under the common law doctrine of penalties.

Bridge v *Campbell Discount Co. Ltd*
[1962] AC 600
House of Lords

The debtor had made an initial payment of £105 and had paid one instalment out of a total price of £482 10s but then informed the creditor that he could not keep up payments. Clause 6 of the agreement gave the debtor the right to terminate in writing, upon which event clause 9 of the agreement came into operation. Clause 9 provided for payment, by way of compensation for depreciation, to the creditor of a sum necessary to make up the payments received to two thirds of the purchase price.

LORD MORTON OF HENRYTON at pp. 614–616: My Lords, the Court of Appeal allowed the appeal and gave judgment for the present respondents for £206 3s 4d with costs. The court, holding that the present appellant had exercised his option to terminate the hiring under clause 6 of the agreement followed the decision of the Court of Appeal in *Associated Distributors Ltd* v *Hall* where Slesser LJ said that:

here the hirer, not the owner, terminated the hiring. He has exercised an option and the terms on which he may exercise that option are those set out in clause 7. The question therefore whether these payments constitute liquidated damages or a penalty . . . does not arise in the present case.

My Lords, in my opinion the case of *Associated Distributors Ltd* v *Hall* was rightly decided and, if I had thought that in the present case the appellant exercised his option under clause 6 of the agreement of July 20, 1959, I should have agreed with the decision of the Court of Appeal in the present case. In that event the present appellant would have been bound to pay the stipulated sum of £206 3s 4d, not by way of penalty or liquidated damages but simply because payment of that sum was one of the terms upon which the option could be exercised.

I am of the opinion, however, that the appellant never had the slightest intention of exercising the option contained in clause 6, and the terms of his letter show that he did not have clause 6 in mind. He frankly and simply informs the respondents that 'I will not be able to pay any more payments on the Bedford Dormobile.'

My Lords, if I am right so far, the appellant has clearly committed a breach of the hire-purchase agreement by failing to pay the subsequent instalments, and it becomes necessary to consider whether the payment stipulated in clause 9(b) of the agreement was a penalty or liquidated damages. 'The essence of a penalty is a payment of money stipulated as in terrorem of the offending party; the essence of liquidated damages is a genuine covenanted pre-estimate of damage.' See per Lord Dunedin in *Dunlop Pneumatic Tyre Co. Ltd* v *New Garage and Motor Co. Ltd* [1915] AC 79, 86; 30 TLR 625, HL.

I find it impossible to regard the sum stipulated in clause 9 as a genuine pre-estimate of the loss which would be suffered by the respondents in the events specified in the same clause. One reason will suffice, though others might be given. This was a second-hand car when the appellant took it over on hire-purchase. The depreciation in its value would naturally become greater the longer it remained in the appellant's hands. Yet the sum to be paid under clause 9(b) is largest when, as in the present case, the car is returned after it has been in the hirer's possession for a very short time, and gets progressively smaller as time goes on. This could not possibly be the result of a genuine pre-estimate of the loss. Further, in my view, the provisions of clause 9 were 'stipulated as in terrorem' of the appellant. As counsel for the appellant put it: 'They are intended to secure that the hirer will not determine the agreement until at least two-thirds of the price has been paid.'

CHAPTER SEVEN

Product Quality

7.1 THE RESPECTIVE ROLES OF CONTRACTUAL AND TORTIOUS PRINCIPLES

The issue of product quality is regarded as largely a matter falling within the province of the law of contract. If a product is not qualitatively up to standard, it is not worth as much as the consumer expected when he bought it. In other words, the type of loss suffered is economic loss and is not to be confused with personal injury to the consumer himself or damage to property other than the defective product itself. However, it is also the case that if a product is not of the quality desired by the consumer and as a consequence of those qualitative defects it causes foreseeable physical harm to the consumer or his property, that harm is remediable in an action for damages against the retailer (*Godley* v *Perry* [1960] 1 WLR 9; *Wilson* v *Rickett Cockrell & Co. Ltd* [1954] 1 QB 598).

The consumer's principal remedies lie against the retailer and not against the manufacturer since there is unlikely to be a relationship of privity of contract between the consumer and the manufacturer of the product (see chapter 3).

Exceptionally, the law of tort, principally the tort of negligence, may assist the consumer by allowing an action for economic loss. However, it would appear that the circumstances in which the necessary proximity of relationship required to exist between the parties for the purposes of a successful negligence action are very few. Indeed, it may be the case that as between the consumer and the producer of a qualitatively defective product the necesary relationship of proximity simply does not exist (see 7.5.2).

7.2   CONTRACTS OF SALE AND RELATED TRANSACTIONS

It used to be important to distinguish between a contract of sale and other contracts in which ownership in goods passed to the consumer, since the Sale of Goods Act 1893 implied terms into a contract of sale which favoured the purchaser. It was not always entirely clear whether these terms now contained in the Sale of Goods Act 1979, relating to title to sell (s. 12), description (s. 13), merchantable quality (s. 14(2)), fitness for purpose (s. 14(3)) and sales by sample (s. 15) also applied to analogous contracts in which property in, or possession of goods passed to a consumer. Such contracts included contracts of hire purchase, contracts under which trading stamps are redeemed for goods, contracts for work and materials, contracts of hire and 'free' supplies of goods made for the purposes of sales promotion.

The problem stemmed from the fact that there is a specific definition of the requirements of a contract of sale and if these requirements are not met, the implied terms in the Sale of Goods Act 1979 are inapplicable. It was always possible that similar terms could be found to exist at common law, but in consumer terms, it was far more comforting to see the relevant implied terms printed in black and white in an Act of Parliament.

The principal differences between a contract of sale and other analogous contracts are that in a contract of sale there has to be a money consideration called the price (Sale of Goods Act 1979, s. 2(1)), and the purpose of the contract must be to transfer property in the goods at the time of the contract (s. 2(1)).

Because of the requirement of a money consideration, contracts of barter or exchange (*Harrison* v *Luke* (1845) 14 M & W 139) and contracts under which 'free' goods are transferred (*Esso Petroleum Co. Ltd* v *Customs & Excise Commissioners* [1976] 1 All ER 117) are not contracts of sale. On the other hand, if the goods transferred are paid for partly in kind and partly in cash, as in the case of a contract of part-exchange, the contract is one of sale (*Aldridge* v *Johnson* (1857) 7 E & B 885).

If the contract involves the transfer of possession but not ownership in goods, as in the case of contracts of bailment, the contract falls outside the scope of the Sale of Goods Act 1979. Thus contracts of hire and hire-purchase clearly fall outside the scope of the Act. Since the primary purpose of a contract for the sale of goods is the transfer of property in the goods, if the contract serves some other, more important purpose, it is possible that this takes the contract outside the scope of the Sale of Goods Act 1979. Thus if the object of the contract is the exercise of skill on the part of a person who also incidentally supplies a finished product, the contract is not one for the sale of goods. But if the primary purpose of the contract is the transfer of ownership in the goods then the Sale of Goods Act 1979 applies (see further chapter 10). The important difference between the two types of contract is that the implied terms of quality and fitness which apply to the supplier of goods impose obligations which must be strictly complied with, whereas in a contract for work and materials, the obligations which attach to the supplier of the service impose only a fault-based duty to exercise reasonable care and skill. It follows that in the case of contracts for work and materials, it is necessary to determine whether the consumer's complaint arises out of the defectiveness of the service provided or whether it is based on the defectiveness of the goods ultimately supplied.

It is clear that terms identical to those which apply to sale of goods contracts are implied in contracts of hire-purchase by virtue of the provisions of the Supply of Goods (Implied Terms) Act 1973, ss. 8 to 11 and in trading stamp transactions by virtue of the Trading Stamps Act 1964, s. 4. In the case of other contracts involving the transfer of ownership or possession of goods, it was not until ss. 2 to 5 of the Supply of Goods and Services Act 1982 were enacted that it was made clear in a statute that similar implied terms also form part of a contract for work and materials and any other contract involving the transfer of ownership or possession of goods (see further 10.3.1.2). If the contract is one of hire, different considerations apply since in a contract of hire there is no intention that ownership of the goods should ever be transferred. Accordingly, a modified version of the terms implied in a sale of goods contract apply by virtue of the Supply of Goods and Services Act 1982, ss. 6 to 10.

7.3 THE STATUTORY IMPLIED TERMS AS TO QUALITY AND FITNESS

In a contract for the supply of goods, there are a number of implied terms which relate directly to the issue of product quality. These include an implied term that the goods supplied will comply with any description which has been given of the goods by the seller, an implied term that the goods will be of merchantable (or satisfactory) quality and a term to the effect that the goods supplied will be fit for the particular purpose for which they are intended to be used.

7.3.1 The status of the implied terms

The Sale of Goods Act 1979, the Supply of Goods (Implied Terms) Act 1973 and the Supply of Goods and Services Act 1982, ss. 2 to 5 and 7 to 10 refer to these implied terms as conditions of the contract (see Sale of Goods Act 1979, s. 12(2); Supply of Goods (Implied Terms) Act 1973, s. 8(1)(b); Supply of Goods and Services Act 1982, ss. 2(2) and 7(2) in relation to freedom from encumbrances). However, the Supply of Goods and Services Act 1982, insofar as it relates to the supply of services, refers to the 'implied terms' of the contract which impose obligations on the parties.

If a term is classified as a condition, breach of it will give rise to the option to treat contractual obligations of performance as terminated. A breach of a warranty gives rise to an action for damages only and will not permit repudiation of the contract. In the context of a consumer contract, this represents a difference between being able to reject the goods supplied and claim a refund of the price paid and being confined to an action for damages in respect of specific harm suffered as a result of the breach of contract. As an exception to this general rule, if the buyer has accepted goods supplied under a non-severable contract of sale, a breach of one of the implied conditions will be treated as giving rise only to an action for damages for breach of warranty (see chapter 3). In the case of contracts which are not for the sale of goods, the common law rules on affirmation of the contract may likewise prevent rejection of the goods supplied, even where they are defective (see chapter 3).

Since Parliament has gone to the trouble of classifying these terms as conditions, it would seem that the courts have no power to regard them in any other light. This is particularly important since at common law the courts have developed the notion of the innominate term. This notion requires the courts to consider the effect of a breach of contract in the light of the seriousness of its consequences in relation to the contract as a whole (*Hongkong Fir Shipping Co. Ltd* v *Kawasaki Kisen Kaisha Ltd* [1962] 1 All ER 474; *Cehave NV* v *Bremer Handelsgesellschaft mbH* [1975] 3 All ER 739; cf. *Bunge Corporation* v *Tradax Export SA* [1980] 1 Lloyd's Rep 294). The result is that even if the parties have called a term a condition, the court may treat the consequences of its breach as insufficiently serious to justify rejection of the goods supplied. Consequently, the buyer will be confined to an action for damages.

Whether a breach of one of the conditions of the contract relating to the quality of the goods supplied is always sufficiently serious to justify rejection is doubtful. If the court wishes to avail itself of the development at common law in relation to innominate terms, it must contrive to find an express term of the contract which relates to the quality of the thing supplied (see *Cehave NV* v *Bremer Handelsgesellschaft mbH* [1975] 3 All ER 739).

The developments referred to above have all occurred in relation to commercial contracts and have resulted in proposals to amend the Sale of Goods Act 1979 so as to allow the court to treat a breach of one of the implied terms as giving rise only to an action for damages in cases where the buyer does not deal as a consumer (proposed s. 15A). It is clear from the proposed amendment that consumer contracts will not be affected with the result that where the Sale of Goods Act 1979 (or any comparable legislation) refers to a condition of the contract, breach of that term will still give the consumer the right to reject the goods, subject to the rules on acceptance and affirmation.

7.3.2   Correspondence with a description

The Sale of Goods Act 1979, s. 13(1) (see also Supply of Goods (Implied Terms) Act 1973, s. 9(1); Supply of Goods and Services Act 1982, ss. 3(2) and 8(2)) provides that in a contract for the sale of goods by description, there is an implied condition that the goods will correspond with that description. It should be emphasised that this condition applies whether or not the seller sells in the course of a business and is useful to consumer purchasers insofar as the implied term as to description also covers statements relating to the quality of the goods, which might not be covered by s. 14 considered below.

The implied term about description covers both statements about quantity and quality. So far as quantitative matters are concerned, if the buyer orders goods of a certain size or gauge or orders a specific quantity of goods and the seller fails to comply with the buyer's requirements, there would appear to be a breach of s. 13, subject to the operation of the principle *de minimis non curat lex*. The requirement that the seller should deliver the right amount seems to be construed very strictly in favour of the buyer (see *Arcos Ltd* v *E.A. Ronaasen & Son* [1933] AC 470; *Re Moore & Co. Ltd and Landauer & Co. Ltd* [1921] 2 KB 519 and Sale of Goods Act 1979, s. 30).

7.3.2.1 Meaning of sale by description The phrase 'sale by description' covers a wide range of transactions. It will cover transactions in which the buyer does not see the goods but relies on a written or oral description of the thing ordered, as in the case of mail order transactions. Likewise it will apply where a consumer orders something yet to be made or where the goods are stored in bulk and sold in small quantities, as in the case of draught beer sold in a public house.

It is even possible for a sale to be by description where the consumer has seen the goods before purchase (Sale of Goods Act 1979, s. 13(3)). Even where the goods are identified (or specific), it is still possible for the sale to be by description where they are sold under a descriptive label. Thus, if a consumer orders 'woollen undergarments' or a 'hot-water bottle', the sale is by description (*Grant* v *Australian Knitting Mills Ltd* [1936] AC 85 at p. 100 per Lord Wright). Even the sale of a second-hand motor car can be a sale by description where the buyer has relied on a document which describes what is purchased (*Beale* v *Taylor* [1967] 1 WLR 1193). Following this, it would appear that there are not many transactions which cannot be regarded as sales by description. It has been suggested that provided there is some sort of descriptive label on goods supplied in a supermarket the sale will be by description, but if the consumer buys unlabelled fruit or vegetables which he selects himself from a retailer's display and no assistance is given by the retailer, the sale will not be by description (Harvey and Parry, *Law of Consumer Protection and Fair Trading*, 3rd ed. (1987), pp. 80-1). Likewise, it would appear that there is no sale by description where the goods supplied are unique and are purchased on a 'take it or leave it basis' (see *Smith* v *Lazarus* (1981) (unreported)). Similarly, if it is clear that the buyer places no reliance, at all, on the seller's description, there will be no sale by description (*Harlingdon & Leinster Enterprises Ltd.* v *Christopher Hull Fine Art Ltd* [1990] 1 All ER 737).

7.3.2.2 Should matters of description be the subject of an implied term? By designating s. 13 of the Sale of Goods Act 1979 as an implied term, Parliament has treated as a legally imposed obligation something which may go to the root of the agreement between the parties. As such, matters relating to the description of the thing supplied should be treated as express terms of the contract instead (cf. UCC, § 2-313(1)(b)).

If a person fails to supply the very thing he has contracted to supply, the breach goes to the root of the contract. Yet if the obligations in s. 13 are contained in implied terms, but for the provisions of the Unfair Contract Terms Act 1977, ss. 6(2) and 7(2), the seller might be able to exclude liability for failing to supply the thing contracted for. At common law, the courts have treated the obligation imposed by s. 13 as fundamental and have refused to allow it to be easily defeated by an exclusion clause (see *Vigers Bros* v *Sanderson Bros* [1901] 1 KB 608).

If the supplier has failed to make his intentions entirely clear, the exclusion clause will be construed *contra proferentem*. In determining the extent to which a supplier can exclude or limit liability for breach of a term describing the thing sold, it is necessary to distinguish between specific and unascertained goods. In the case of the former, the consumer is aware of the attributes of the thing he buys, but in the case of unascertained goods, the consumer must rely on the supplier's description, in which case a purported exclusion of liability is less likely to be successful since the exclusion would render the subject-matter of the contract uncertain. It follows from this that where the goods sold are specific and the supplier stipulates that they are purchased as seen, even though there may be a supply by description, the exclusion of liability may still be effective, provided it satisfies the Unfair Contract Terms Act 1977 test of reasonableness (*Cavendish-Woodhouse Ltd* v *Manley* (1984) 82 LGR 376; *Hughes* v *Hall* [1981] RTR 430). Where the goods are unascertained, the supplier cannot exclude liability in respect of a breach which relates to the identity of the thing sold, but he may be able to exclude liability for trivial breaches of contract which are not covered by the *de minimis* principle.

7.3.2.3   The status of descriptive statements   Not every descriptive word will take effect as a term of the contract. There are some descriptive words which have no legal effect at all (see *Reardon Smith Line Ltd* v *Yngvar Hansen-Tangen* [1976] 1 WLR 989) and others which take effect as misrepresentations. In some instances the statement will be a term of the contract, but will not amount to a condition, because the court does not view the consequences of its breach particularly seriously. However, for the reasons considered in 7.3.1, it would appear that this approach cannot be adopted in relation to a statutory implied term of the contract, although it can apply to express terms (*Ashington Piggeries Ltd* v *Christopher Hill Ltd* [1972] AC 441 at p. 503 per Lord Diplock).

Where a descriptive statement is made, it is necessary to determine whether it is a term of the contract or a representation. A literal reading of s. 13 of the Sale of Goods Act 1979 would suggest that any descriptive statement may be the subject of the implied term in s. 13 but this is clearly not the case, and some descriptive statements will take effect as representations only (see *Oscar Chess Ltd* v *Williams* [1957] 1 WLR 370). However, there are also cases which appear to have ignored the common law distinction and applied s. 13 where the rule on representations ought to have been applied. In *Beale* v *Taylor* [1967] 1 WLR 1193 the defendant advertised his car for sale as a 'Herald convertible, white, 1961'. The car was in fact an amalgam of parts from two different cars which had been welded together. Part of the car was from a 1961 model but the rest was not. It was held that the words '1961 Herald' formed part of the description of the car. However, the statement could have been treated as an external inducement to enter the contract and not as a term as in *Oscar Chess Ltd* v *Williams* [1957] 1 WLR 370. Perhaps the difference lies in the fact that *Beale* v *Taylor* involved a statement by a seller and the courts tend to construe statements by sellers as terms of the contract, whereas *Oscar Chess Ltd* v *Williams* involved a statement by a consumer to a trade purchaser. It may also have been relevant that *Beale* v *Taylor* was based on the law which applied before the Misrepresentation Act 1967 came into force, and treating a statement as a term of the contract was one way of ensuring that the buyer was compensated for what was essentially a qualitative defect.

In order to amount to a contractual description, the words have to identify the goods supplied (*Ashington Piggeries Ltd* v *Christopher Hill Ltd* [1972] AC 441 at pp. 503-4 per Lord Diplock). The test to apply is to ask whether the buyer has got what he bargained for according to the standards of the relevant market (ibid. at p. 489 per Lord Wilberforce). The problem this test creates is that it can result in apparently contradictory decisions presumably because the standards of different markets will vary. Thus a mixture of hemp and rape oil did not satisfy the description 'foreign refined rape oil' (*Nicol* v *Godts* (1854) 10 Exch 191), but herring meal contaminated by a toxin generated by an internal chemical reaction can still be described as herring meal (*Ashington Piggeries Ltd* v *Christopher Hill Ltd* [1972] AC 441).

In seeking to determine whether words identify the goods in question, it is necessary that those words identify an essential part of the description of the goods. Thus words which merely say where goods are to be found are not sufficient to amount to words of description (*Reardon Smith Line Ltd* v *Yngvar Hansen-Tangen* [1976] 1 WLR 989), but words which identify the very nature of the thing the consumer buys will form part of the description. Thus if the buyer purchases 'a silk scarf', the seller cannot get away with supplying one made of an artificial silk substitute, because the words identify a substantial ingredient in the goods.

7.3.2.4 The importance of reliance

A further requirement which appears to apply to descriptive words is that they should have been relied upon by the consumer in entering into the transaction. Strictly, this requirement is at odds with the general rule that if a statement is a condition of the contract, breach of the condition, no matter how slight, should give rise to a right to reject the goods supplied. However, the requirement of reliance was seen as crucial by a majority of the Court of Appeal in *Harlingdon & Leinster Enterprises Ltd* v *Christopher Hull Fine Art Ltd* [1990] 1 All ER 737. It was considered that in the absence of reliance by the buyer, the descriptive statement would not be incorporated into the contract (at p. 744 per Nourse LJ). Alternatively, it was also stated that the presence or absence of reliance on the part of the buyer was a powerful indication of the incorporation of the description as a term of the contract (at p. 752 per Slade LJ). In contrast, Stuart-Smith LJ took the view that a pre-contractual statement would form part of the description of the goods sold unless its effect was expressly negatived prior to the formation of the contract (at p. 748).

The importance of reliance is also underlined by contrasting *Oscar Chess Ltd* v *Williams* [1957] 1 WLR 370 and *Beale* v *Taylor* [1967] 1 WLR 1193. It can be said that it was totally unreasonable for a trader with expert knowledge of motor vehicles to rely on the statement of the consumer wishing to trade in his own vehicle in *Oscar Chess Ltd* v *Williams*. However, it was probably reasonable for the buyer to rely on the seller's statement in *Beale* v *Taylor* as he was not buying just a car, but a car of a particular type identified by the seller's description of it in a newspaper advertisement.

7.3.3   Merchantable or satisfactory quality

The Sale of Goods Act 1979, s. 14(2) (see also Supply of Goods (Implied Terms) Act 1973, s. 10(2); Supply of Goods and Services Act 1982, ss. 4(2) and (3) and 9(2) and (3)) provides that where the seller sells goods in the course of a business (see 1.1.2) there is an implied condition that the goods supplied will be of merchantable quality.

The use of the term 'merchantable quality' in consumer transactions has been the subject of much criticism, particularly because the word 'merchantable' dates from the Sale of Goods Act 1893 and carries connotations of a commercial nature, ill-suited to the needs of the modern consumer transaction. As a result, the Law Commission (Law Comm No. 160, Cm 137, 1987), has made recommendations for change, suggesting that the requirement of merchantable quality should be replaced by a requirement that the goods should be of satisfactory or acceptable quality. These changes were incorporated in a private member's, Consumer Guarantees Bill (Bill 16, 1990), which failed to gain the support of the government and was lost at the end of the 1989-90 Parliamentary session, but are to be reintroduced as part of the Government's 'Citizens' Charter'.

When the proposed changes are given statutory effect, they will apply to all contracts for the supply of goods. Accordingly the proposed definition of 'satisfactory' quality will apply to contracts for the sale of goods, credit transactions and supply contracts governed by the Supply of Goods and Services Act 1982.

7.3.3.1   Goods to which the condition applies   Both the requirements of merchantable and satisfactory quality apply to 'the goods supplied under the contract'. This wording has been interpreted to mean that the condition applies to anything supplied pursuant to the contract. Thus anything supplied under the contract must satisfy the condition, with the result that 'free' goods supplied by way of a promotional offer (see *Esso Petroleum Co. Ltd* v *Commissioners of Customs & Excise* [1976] 1 All ER 117) and packaging in which goods are supplied (*Geddling* v *Marsh* [1920] 1 KB 668) must be of the desired quality. Similarly, the seller cannot avoid liability by claiming that impurities in goods supplied were not contracted for and therefore are not covered by the implied condition. Thus in *Wilson* v *Rickett Cockrell & Co. Ltd* [1954] 1 QB 598, the seller supplied a quantity of smokeless fuel which contained a detonator. It was not open to the seller to argue that the detonator was not contracted for and that, the detonator apart, the fuel supplied was of merchantable quality. The detonator was supplied pursuant to the contract and was covered by the words 'goods supplied under the contract'.

It is also arguable that these words will cover defective instructions for use which render the goods supplied unfit for normal use. If the instructions are such that the goods cannot be used for the buyer's particular intended use there is a possibility that the goods fail to comply with the requirement of fitness for purpose under s. 14(3) (see *Wormell* v *RHM Agriculture (East) Ltd* [1987] 3 All ER 75 and see also MacLeod (1981) 97 LQR 550). If the goods cannot be used for their normal purpose for the same reason, it would seem to follow that the defective instructions can also render the goods unmerchantable.

7.3.3.2 Circumstances in which the implied term is inapplicable

The Sale of Goods Act 1979, s. 14(2)(a), and the proposed amendment provide that the implied condition of merchantable or satisfactory quality does not apply where the seller has specifically drawn the buyer's attention to defects in the goods prior to the making of the contract. Thus, if a seller points to defects in a second-hand car and the buyer purchases the vehicle knowing of these defects, he cannot later claim that those defects render the car unmerchantable (*Bartlett* v *Sidney Marcus Ltd* [1965] 1 WLR 1013).

Under s. 14(2)(b) and the proposed amendment, the condition of merchantable quality is also inapplicable where the buyer has examined the goods and that examination ought to have revealed a defect in the goods. It is clear from the present wording of the Act that there must have been an examination, but if there is present an obvious defect, the buyer purchases subject to that defect. However, s. 14(2)(b) will not affect the buyer in relation to latent defects, which by their nature are not reasonably discoverable on any examination (see *Wren* v *Holt* [1903] 1 KB 610).

It has become apparent that the wording of s. 14(2)(b), which is not covered by the proposed amendments, is defective in one respect. In *R & B Customs Brokers Co. Ltd* v *United Dominions Trust Ltd* [1988] 1 All ER 847 the plaintiff bought a car on conditional sale, which was delivered immediately. Before the contract was legally concluded the plaintiff discovered a defect which the car dealer agreed to repair. Despite numerous attempts, the defect was not remedied and the plaintiff subsequently purported to reject the car. It was argued by the defendants that because the plaintiff took delivery of the car before the contract was made, he had had a chance to inspect it with the result that the condition of merchantable quality was inapplicable. In the event, the defendants were liable under s. 14(3), and the court did not express an opinion on the wording of s. 14(2)(b). However, if the defendant's argument is correct, the position of the consumer under a conditional sale agreement is unenviable.

One way in which the problem might be resolved is by resort to the inference of a collateral contract. If the supplier is told of a defect before the contract is made and he undertakes to repair it, he will be liable for a breach of a collateral undertaking if he fails to effect those repairs. In such a case, the finance company may also be liable for the supplier's breach of contract under the provisions of the Consumer Credit Act 1974, s. 56 (see chapter 6).

7.3.3.3 The meaning of merchantable and satisfactory quality

The current statutory definition of merchantable quality in the Sale of Goods Act 1979, s. 14(6), requires goods to be fit for the purpose or purposes for which goods of that kind are commonly used, as is reasonable to expect, having regard to matters such as the price of the goods, their description and any other relevant factor.

This definition contains elements of the two judicial tests applied before the introduction of the statutory definition in 1973. These tests examined the 'usability' and the 'acceptability' of the goods.

The judicial test of 'usability' which commended itself to the minority of the House of Lords in *Henry Kendall & Sons* v *William Lillico & Sons Ltd* [1969] 2 AC 31 required the court to consider whether the goods could be used for at least one of the purposes for which goods of that kind could commonly be put. In contrast, the majority adopted a test of acceptability which required the court to consider whether the goods were in such a state that a buyer fully acquainted with all relevant facts would buy them without substantial abatement in the price which could be obtained for such goods in reasonable condition (see also *Bristol Tramways Co. Ltd* v *Fiat Motors Ltd* [1910] 2 KB 831 at p. 841 per Farwell LJ; *Australian Knitting Mills Ltd* v *Grant* (1933) 50 CLR 387 at p. 418 per Dixon J).

It is clear from these definitions that merchantability does not merely connote saleability. This is particularly important in the context of a consumer transaction, since the consumer does not buy for resale, he buys for use and enjoyment. Accordingly an acceptability test or a usability test is more appropriate to the needs of the consumer.

It would appear that the requirement of merchantable quality will ordinarily relate to physical characteristics of the goods supplied, but not exclusively so. For example, goods may be unmerchantable because their legal state is such that they cannot be used as intended (*Niblett Ltd* v *Confectioners' Materials Co. Ltd* [1921] 3 KB 387; cf. *Sumner Permain & Co.* v *Webb & Co.* [1922] 1 KB 55).

The Court of Appeal was divided on the application of the requirement of merchantable quality to non-physical defects in *Harlingdon & Leinster Enterprises Ltd* v *Christopher Hull Fine Art Ltd* [1990] 1 All ER 737. Nourse LJ was of the opinion that a mistake as to authorship of a painting rendered it defective, but was not sufficient to make the painting unsaleable (at p. 745). Accordingly, the painting was of merchantable quality. Slade LJ went even further, expressing the opinion that since the complaint related to the identity of the artist, s. 14 had no application (at p. 753). However, Stuart-Smith LJ differed in his approach holding that the requirement of merchantable quality does extend to factors other than the physical characteristics of the goods supplied. In particular, it is necessary to consider the description of the goods supplied, and if a painting is said to be by a particular artist, this is a factor relevant to the quality of the work of art (at p. 750).

7.3.3.3.1 Fitness for purpose or purposes Under the statutory definition of merchantable quality in s. 14(6), it is sufficient that the goods supplied are fit for any of the purposes for which goods of that kind are commonly used (*Henry Kendall & Sons* v *William Lillico & Sons Ltd* [1969] 2 AC 31); *B.S. Brown & Son Ltd* v *Craiks Ltd* [1970] 1 All ER 823; *Aswan Engineering Establishment Co.* v *Lupdine Ltd* [1987] 1 WLR 1).

The proposed amendments which would introduce a requirement of satisfactory quality purport to reverse the effect of these cases and will require goods to be fit for all common purposes. If a court holds that the purpose for which the goods are required is uncommon, the new provision will not apply and the buyer will be required to show that he has informed the seller of the purpose to which he intends to put the goods so that s. 14(3) may apply. However, where this is the case, the buyer must show that he has relied on the seller's skill and judgment.

What is a 'common' purpose is difficult to define since the decision will depend on the context in which the case arises. What is clear is that the goods supplied do not need to be fit for immediate use if it is clear that something has to be done to them in order to render them fit for use, e.g., food that has to be cooked or furniture sold in kit form which has to be assembled at home (cf. *Grant* v *Australian Knitting Mills Ltd* [1936] AC 85).

One difficulty which may arise from the requirement that goods should be fit for all common purposes is that if goods of a particular kind can be used for a number of different purposes, the price may differ according to which purpose is intended by the buyer. Suppose food can be used for both human and animal consumption and the buyer expressly purchases it cheaply for the purposes of feeding to his cattle. It would be unreasonable to allow the buyer to reject the goods on the ground that they are unfit for human consumption. The price paid for the food would be some indication of the purpose for which the buyer required it, but under the proposed amendment the food might still be regarded as unsatisfactory. In such a case, it would be necessary for the court to treat food for human consumption and food for animal consumption as goods which are not of the same kind.

This problem does not arise under s. 14(6) as goods are required to be fit for any of their normal purposes. Accordingly, it does not matter that goods might be sold for another normal purpose at a different price.

7.3.3.3.2 Safety The definition of merchantable quality in the Sale of Goods Act 1979, s. 14(6), does not make it entirely clear whether or not goods have to be safe in order to satisfy its requirements. It has been held that a car which cannot be safely used is not of merchantable quality (*Bernstein* v *Pamson Motors (Golders Green) Ltd* [1987] 2 All ER 220). Safety is now specifically referred to in the proposed amendment as a relevant factor in determining whether goods are of satisfactory quality.

If goods are defective because of a hidden defect it must be assumed that both the buyer and the seller are aware of the defect in order to determine whether the goods are merchantable. Difficulties can arise where goods are dangerous unless information about the use of the goods is given, e.g., medicines which must be diluted before consumption. It would appear sensible to conclude that goods which are supplied with inadequate instructions for use are not of merchantable quality. However, the decision of the House of Lords in *Henry Kendall & Sons* v *William Lillico & Sons* [1969] 2 AC 31 raises difficulties in this regard. Groundnut extraction was held to be merchantable because it was fit for its most common use, namely for compounding into animal feed. A feed manufactured using the extraction was fit for use as a cattle feed, but was dangerous if fed to poultry. Had the buyer known this fact, no damage would have been suffered as a warning could have been passed on to his customers. However, the fact remained that the buyer was not made aware of the toxicity of the extraction.

The basis for the House of Lords decision appears to be that the goods were acceptable in that if the buyer had been aware of all material facts he would still have bought the extraction and would have labelled it accordingly.

This decision does raise substantial problems since it is the very fact that the relevant information has not been given that causes the goods to be unsuitable. The problem is one which is not covered by the definition of satisfactory quality, therefore doubts will remain in relation to the need for safety warnings on goods supplied.

7.3.3.3.3 Reasonable fitness   Section 14(6) of the Sale of Goods Act 1979 requires the goods to be reasonably fit for normal use. This does not mean that they must be *perfectly* fit for use. As a result goods may be partly defective but still merchantable, e.g., a second-hand car does not have to be in perfect condition. Recent decisions show that in the case of new goods, minor defects can still render them unmerchantable (*Rogers* v *Parish (Scarborough) Ltd* [1987] QB 933; *Shine* v *General Guarantee Corporation Ltd* [1988] 1 All ER 911; *Bernstein* v *Pamson Motors (Golders Green) Ltd* [1987] 2 All ER 220).

The proposed definition of satisfactory quality requires goods to be free from minor defects, which would appear to confirm the position in *Rogers* v *Parish (Scarborough) Ltd*. However, the factors listed in the definition of satisfactory quality are stated to be merely aspects of the quality of goods. It would seem to follow that if goods suffer from minor defects, but are still reasonably satisfactory in quality, having regard to other factors, the seller will not be in breach of s. 14(2).

The definition of satisfactory quality implies that the goods should be reasonably acceptable, since what a reasonable person would regard as satisfactory is that which he would be prepared to accept. It should be appreciated, however, that the reference to reasonableness relates to the quality of the goods not their acceptability. It may be the case that defects in goods are not sufficiently serious for a buyer to want to reject. For example, the buyer might choose to keep goods suffering from minor defects and seek to recover damages. The fact that the goods are 'acceptable' does not mean that there is no breach of s. 14(2) if the standard of quality is deemed to be unreasonable. It follows that if the buyer gets exactly what he ordered, there may still be a breach of s. 14(2) if the standard of quality remains unreasonable (see Atiyah, *Sale of Goods*, 8th ed. 1990), pp. 168-9).

7.3.3.3.4 Durability   A matter which has given rise to controversy is whether the seller impliedly contracts to supply goods which are durable. In *Lambert* v *Lewis* [1982] AC 225 (see also *Crowther* v *Shannon Motors Co.* [1975] 1 All ER 139) it was held that the implied condition of fitness for purpose in s. 14(3) amounts to a continuing warranty that goods will continue to be fit for a reasonable period after the making of the contract. What is a reasonable time will clearly depend on the circumstances of the case, for example, something bought very cheaply cannot be expected to last for ever.

The requirement of durability is a matter specifically listed in the proposed amendment to s. 14(2) as a factor to consider in determining whether goods are of satisfactory quality. The effect of this addition may not make a great deal of difference due to the provisions of ss. 35 and 11(4) (see 3.2.1.3.1) since the buyer will be confined to an action for damages where he is deemed to have accepted the goods. If the defect in the goods is reasonably discoverable, the buyer is deemed to purchase subject to that defect if he has examined the goods (s. 14(2)(b)). If the defect is not reasonably discoverable, the requirement of merchantable or satisfactory quality applies, but if it does not manifest itself until some time after delivery, the buyer may be deemed to have accepted the goods by virtue of the lapse of an unreasonable length of time. In these circumstances, a requirement that the goods should be durable may not make any difference at all to the purchaser who wishes to reject the goods and recover the purchase price.

7.3.3.3.5 Relevance of the price Section 14(6) of the Sale of Goods Act 1979 expressly stipulates that the price paid for goods is a relevant factor in determining whether goods are of merchantable quality. The same is equally true of the proposed requirement of satisfactory quality. The effect of this is that the buyer is entitled to value for money (*Rogers* v *Parish (Scarborough) Ltd* [1987] QB 933; cf. *Harlingdon & Leinster Enterprises Ltd* v *Christopher Hull Fine Art Ltd* [1990] 1 All ER 737).

The price paid is also a relevant factor in relation to second-hand motor vehicles, since the older the car, the cheaper the buyer expects it to be. At the same time, if the car is second-hand, the buyer can presumably expect a lower standard of quality, although he can reasonably expect it to be roadworthy and perhaps more. If the buyer has paid a substantial price for an up-market second-hand vehicle, he can expect it to do more than move from A to B and can expect it to satisfy his aesthetic requirements (*Shine* v *General Guarantee Corporation Ltd* [1988] 1 All ER 911; cf. *Business Applications Specialists Ltd* v *Nationwide Credit Corporation Ltd* [1988] RTR 332).

7.3.4 Fitness for purpose

The Sale of Goods Act 1979, s. 14(3) (see also Supply of Goods (Implied Terms) Act 1973, s. 10(3); Supply of Goods and Services Act 1982, ss. 9(4) and (5) and 4(4) and (6)), provides that where the seller sells goods in the course of a business there is an implied condition that the goods sold are reasonably fit for any purpose expressly or impliedly made known to the seller by the buyer, provided it is reasonable for the buyer to rely on the seller's skill and judgment in selecting goods suited to that purpose. In the case of sales which involve the provision of credit, such as a conditional sale agreement, it is sufficient that the buyer makes known to the dealer the purpose for which the goods are required.

Like the provisions in respect of quality in s. 14(2), s. 14(3) only applies to sales made by the seller in the course of a business (see 1.1.2) and does cover all goods supplied pursuant to the contract of sale (see 7.3.3.1).

7.3.4.1   The purpose   Section 14(3) of the Sale of Goods Act 1979 requires the goods to be fit for the purpose for which the consumer requires them. It may be the case that the goods are required for their normal purpose, in which case, there will be an overlap between the provisions of the Act in relation to quality and fitness. This overlap is inevitable given that merchantable quality is defined in s. 14(6) in terms of fitness for the purpose for which goods of that kind are commonly used. Thus, catapults which break in normal use (*Godley* v *Perry* [1960] 1 WLR 9) and injure the user or hot-water bottles that burst when used according to the manufacturer's instructions (*Preist* v *Last* [1903] 2 KB 14) are neither of merchantable quality nor fit for the purpose for which they are required. Conversely, there are circumstances in which the two provisions do not overlap. For example, a car which suffers from a range of minor defects may be unmerchantable (*Rogers* v *Parish (Scarborough) Ltd* [1987] 2 All ER 232), but if it can be driven, it will probably still be fit for the purpose for which it is intended. Similarly, an animal feed may be fit for feeding to animals generally without being fit for feeding to the particular type of animal which the buyer had in mind (*Ashington Piggeries Ltd* v *Christopher Hill Ltd* [1972] AC 441). In such a case there may be a breach of s. 14(3) without there being a breach of s. 14(2).

If goods can be put to one purpose only, there will be a breach of the requirement of fitness for purpose if they cannot be used for that purpose. In such a case, it is pointless to require the buyer to expressly make that purpose known to the seller and it will be assumed that the seller is aware that the buyer requires the goods for that purpose.

There are circumstances in which goods can be put to one of a number of purposes. If this is the case, it cannot be assumed that the goods are fit for the particular use to which the buyer wishes to put them. Instead, it is necessary for the buyer to show that he has communicated to the seller the particular purpose for which he requires them (see *Sumner Permain & Co.* v *Webb & Co.* [1922] 1 KB 55). Thus in *Griffiths* v *Peter Conway Ltd* [1939] 1 All ER 685 the buyer required a tweed coat, but failed to inform the seller that she had an unusually sensitive skin and was therefore prone to dermatitis. Had the seller been aware of this fact he would have advised the buyer against purchasing a garment made of such a coarse material. It was held that the seller was not in breach of the implied term as to fitness for purpose. The buyer's abnormal sensitivity was a matter which should have been communicated to the seller before liability could attach.

7.3.4.2   Reliance on the seller's skill and judgment   Even where the buyer has made known the particular purpose for which he requires goods, it does not automatically follow that the condition of fitness applies to the transaction. It is also a requirement that the buyer has reasonably relied on the seller's skill and judgment in selecting goods suited to that purpose. The burden of proof in this respect lies on the supplier who must show that the consumer did not rely on his skill and judgment (cf. *Aswan Engineering Establishment Co.* v *Lupdine Ltd* [1987] 1 All ER 135). This burden can be discharged by showing that the buyer has not relied on the seller or that the buyer's reliance is unreasonable.

If the seller knows of the purpose for which the goods are required, as is the case where the goods are purchased for a single, normal purpose, reliance will be readily assumed. Thus in *Grant* v *Australian Knitting Mills Ltd* [1936] AC 85 it was stated that the consumer can assume that the seller has selected his stock with skill and judgment (at p. 99 per Lord Wright), thereby satisfying the requirement of reliance.

If the buyer has relied solely on his own skill and judgment, he cannot avail himself of the protection afforded by s. 14(3), but there is nothing to prevent the buyer from relying, in part, on the seller's skill and judgment. However, it must be established that the loss suffered by the buyer results from the reliance he has placed on the seller (*Ashington Piggeries Ltd* v *Christopher Hill Ltd* [1972] AC 441). Thus if the buyer has inspected goods prior to purchase, it does not necessarily follow that there is no reliance on the seller's skill and judgment.

Factors which may be relevant in determining whether the consumer does reasonably rely on the seller's skill and judgment include the relative expertise of the parties (cf. *Henry Kendall & Sons* v *William Lillico & Sons Ltd* [1969] 2 AC 31) whether instructions for use have been supplied either before or after the making of the contract (*Wormell* v *RHM Agriculture (East) Ltd* [1987] 3 All ER 75) and whether the supplier is also the manufacturer (*Henry Kendall & Sons* v *William Lillico & Sons Ltd* [1969] 2 AC 31 at p. 84 per Lord Reid).

7.3.4.3 The duration of the duty Strictly, the duties of the seller to supply goods which are merchantable and fit for the purpose for which they are required apply only at the time of the contract. Thus if a defect manifests itself some time after sale and it is shown that that defect was not present at the time of contracting, the implied conditions would appear not to apply. However, it has subsequently been held that the implied condition of fitness for purpose also implies a warranty of durability (*Crowther* v *Shannon Motor Co.* [1975] 1 All ER 139; *Lambert* v *Lewis* [1982] AC 225). If there is any doubt in this matter in relation to the requirement of merchantable quality, it has been suggested that a statutory amendment should make it clear that durability is a factor to consider in determining whether the goods comply with the requirements of s. 14(2).

7.3.4.4 The strictness of the duty The duty imposed by s. 14(3) of the Sale of Goods Act 1979 is strict in the sense that where the goods prove not to be reasonably fit for the purpose for which they are required, the seller is liable even where no amount of care on his part could have avoided the presence of the defect rendering them unfit for the buyer's intended use (see *Frost* v *Aylesbury Dairy Co. Ltd* [1905] 1 KB 608).

The fact that s. 14(3) requires the buyer to have reasonably relied on the seller's skill and judgment does not import a requirement of fault into the implied condition of fitness. It follows that s. 14(3) applies to latent defects (*Henry Kendall & Sons* v *William Lillico & Sons Ltd* [1969] 2 AC 31 at p. 84 per Lord Reid).

It is important that s. 14(3) requires the goods to be reasonably fit for the purpose for which the buyer requires them, since this negates the view that the implied condition imposes a form of absolute liability. The standard required of the seller will depend on the preciseness with which the buyer has specified his requirements. In the ordinary consumer supply contract, it is unlikely that the buyer will have spelt out in detail what his requirements are. Accordingly, the seller will be required to supply goods which are reasonably fit for the normal purpose for which the goods are used. Furthermore, if the buyer fails to reveal facts which are exclusively within his own knowledge, the seller cannot be expected to anticipate these and s. 14(3) will not come to the buyer's aid (*Griffiths* v *Peter Conway Ltd* [1939] 1 All ER 685 at p. 691 per Lord Greene MR).

7.3.5   The difference between sections 13, 14(2) and 14(3)

Where the consumer is faced with qualitatively defective goods, the success of his action against the supplier will depend on whether his case fits s. 13 or s. 14 of the Sale of Goods Act 1979. There are differences between the various provisions of the Act which may fashion the consumer's choice.

Prima facie, the difference between the three provisions would appear to be simple to identify – s. 13 applies where the buyer has not received that which he contracted to buy and s. 14 applies where he got what he contracted for but, due to defects in the goods, he cannot put them to their normal use or some special, but identified use. However, the distinction is not that simple. Sometimes, matters of quality will creep into the description of the goods contracted for. For example, a sale of food will also imply that the food is fit for human consumption. While food which cannot be eaten is not of merchantable quality, it is probably also the case that fitness for consumption would also form part of the description of the goods (*see Ashington Piggeries Ltd* v *Christopher Hill Ltd* [1969] 3 All ER 1496 at p. 1512). In these circumstances, the distinction between s. 13 and s. 14(2) is purely academic, as the consumer would have an action under both provisions.

In other cases, the difference between description, quality and fitness may be more important. For example, goods may be merchantable, in the sense that they are both of acceptable quality and can be resold without substantial abatement in price, but at the same time are not what the buyer asked for. In such a case, s. 13 must be relied upon. Alternatively, goods may comply generally with their description but, due to some defect they may not be fit for the particular use to which the buyer wishes to put them. This problem may arise where goods are contaminated by some extraneous matter and it becomes necessary to determine whether the presence of that matter destroys the mercantile character of the thing supplied (*Ashington Piggeries Ltd* v *Christopher Hill Ltd* [1972] AC 441 at p. 489 per Lord Wilberforce and see also *Gill & Duffus SA* v *Berger & Co. Inc.* [1981] 2 Lloyd's Rep 233; *Gill & Duffus SA* v *Berger & Co. Inc. (No. 2)* [1983] 1 Lloyd's Rep 622).

7.3.5.1   Sale in the course of a business   Perhaps the most important difference between s. 13 of the Sale of Goods Act 1979 and both limbs of s. 14 of the Act is that the latter apply only where the supplier acts in the course of

a business, whereas s. 13 applies to all sales by description. Thus, if the consumer wishes to proceed against a private seller in respect of a qualitative defect in the goods he has purchased, he must show that there is an express term of the contract which relates to his complaint or that the qualitative defect relates to a matter concerned with the identity of the thing supplied. Thus in *Beale* v *Taylor* [1967] 1 WLR 1193, the plaintiff had to show that the car he purchased had been wrongly described even though his complaint was one which related to the quality of the thing supplied. An action under s. 14(2) or (3) was denied because the seller did not act in the course of a business.

7.3.5.2 The relevance of reliance The requirement of reliance is a central feature of an action under s. 14(3) of the Sale of Goods Act 1979 in that it must be reasonable for the buyer to rely on the seller's skill and judgment in selecting goods suited for the particular purpose the buyer has in mind.

Reliance also appears to be an important factor in determining the liability of the supplier under s. 13 in the sense that the consumer must rely on the supplier's description of the thing supplied (*Varley* v *Whipp* [1900] 1 QB 513 at p. 516 per Channell J). It is the description that goes to the root of the contract and has such an influence on the buyer that it becomes an essential term of the contract (*Harlingdon & Leinster Enterprises Ltd* v *Christopher Hull Fine Art Ltd* [1990] 1 All ER 737 at p. 744 per Nourse LJ). It is the fact of reliance by the buyer that throws light on the intention of the parties to treat a descriptive statement as an essential term of the contract (ibid. at p. 752 per Slade LJ).

So far as s. 14(2) is concerned, it would appear that reliance is not an essential requirement in that the condition is broken if the goods are not fit for the purpose for which goods of that kind are normally bought. However, on closer examination, reliance may be a factor in dertermining liability. Because of the provisions of s. 14(2)(a) and (b), the condition of merchantability does not apply where the buyer has been told of a defect in the goods or where he has examined the goods and that examination ought to have revealed a defect. In both cases, if the buyer purchases the goods, he has no recourse against the seller because he has relied on his own judgment in purchasing the goods despite the presence of the defect in question.

7.4 THE STATUTORY IMPLIED TERMS ABOUT QUALITY AND FITNESS – MATERIALS FOR CONSIDERATION

7.4.1 Correspondence with a description

For text see 7.3.2.

Sale of Goods Act 1979

13. Sale by description

(1) Where there is a contract for the sale of goods by description, there is an implied condition that the goods will correspond with the description.

(2)   If the sale is by sample as well as by description it is not sufficient that the bulk of the goods corresponds with the sample if the goods do not also correspond with the description.

(3)   A sale of goods is not prevented from being a sale by description by reason only that, being exposed for sale or hire, they are selected by the buyer.

The phrase 'sale by description' covers a wide range of transactions, since goods are capable of describing themselves. It follows that there will be very few transactions which do not involve a description of the goods.

Beale v *Taylor*
[1967] 1 WLR 1193
Court of Appeal

For the facts see para. 7.3.2.3.

SELLERS LJ at pp. 1196–7: We were referred to a passage in the opinion of Lord Wright in *Grant* v *Australian Knitting Mills Ltd* [1936] AC 85 at p. 100, which I have read to the seller and which I think is apt as far as this case is concerned:

> It may also be pointed out that there is a sale by description even though the buyer is buying something displayed before him on the counter; a thing is sold by description, though it is specific, so long as it is sold not merely as the specific thing but as a thing corresponding to a description, e.g., woollen undergarments, a hot water bottle, a second-hand reaping machine, to select a few obvious illustrations (and, I might add, a second-hand motor car.)

I think that on the facts of this case the buyer when he came along to see this car was coming along to see a car as advertised, that is, a car described as a 'Herald convertible, white, 1961'. When he came along he saw what ostensibly was a Herald convertible, white, 1961, because the evidence shows that the '1200' which was exhibited on the rear of the car is the first model of the '1200' which came out in 1961: it was on that basis that he made the offer to purchase it and in the belief that the seller was advancing his car as that which his advertisement indicated. Apart from that, the selling of a car of that make, I would on the face of it rather agree with the submission of the seller that he was making no warranties at all and making no contractual terms. But fundamentally he was selling a car of that description. The facts, as revealed very shortly afterwards, show that that description was false. It was unfortunately not false to the knowledge of the seller nor of the buyer because no one could see from looking at the car in the ordinary sort of examinaton which would be made that it was anything other than that which it purported to be. It was only afterwards that on examination it was found to be in two parts.

See also 3.2.1.2.1)

Both s. 14(2) and s. 14(3) require reasonable reliance on the part of the buyer, but there is no specific mention of reliance in s. 13. But given its close relation to misstatements, reliance would appear to be a requirement.

Harlingdon & Leinster Enterprises Ltd v *Christopher Hull Fine Art Ltd*
[1990] 1 All ER 737
Court of Appeal

NOURSE LJ at pp. 743–4: . . . one must look to the contract as a whole in order to identify what stated characteristics of the goods are intended to form part of the description *by* which they are sold.

We were also referred to the decision of Sellers J in *Joseph Travers & Sons Ltd* v *Longel Ltd* (1947) 64 TLR 150, where it was held that, since the buyers had placed no reliance on a descriptive name for rubber boots, the sale was not one by description. The decision is chiefly of value for Sellers J's approval (at 153) of the following passage in *Benjamin on Sale* (7th ed., 1931), p. 641:

> Sales by description may, it seems, be divided into sales: 1. Of unascertained or future goods, as being of a certain kind or class, or to which otherwise a 'description' in the contract is applied. 2. Of specific goods, bought by the buyer in reliance, at least in part, upon the description given, or to be tacitly inferred from the circumstances, and which identifies the goods. So far as any descriptive statement is a mere warranty or only a representation, it is no part of the description. It is clear that there can be no contract for the sale of unascertained or future goods except by some description. It follows that the only sales not by description are sale of specific goods *as such*. Specific goods may be sold as such when they are sold without any description, express or implied; or where any statement made about them is not essential to their identity; or where, though the goods are described, the description is not relied upon, as where the buyer buys the goods such as they are (*Benjamin's* emphasis.)

It is suggested that the significance which some of these authorities attribute to the buyer's reliance on the description is misconceived. I think that that criticism is theoretically correct. In theory it is no doubt possible for a description of goods which is not relied on by the buyer to become an essential term of a contract for their sale. But in practice it is very difficult, and perhaps impossible, to think of facts where that would be so. The description must have a sufficient influence in the sale to become an essential term of the contract and the correlative of influence is reliance. Indeed, reliance by the buyer is the natural index of a sale by description. It is true that the question must, as always, be judged objectively and it may be said that previous judicial references have been to subjective or actual reliance. But each of those decisions, including that of Judge Oddie in the present case, can be justified on an objective basis. For all practical purposes, I would say that there cannot be a contract for the sale of goods by description where it is not within the reasonable contemplation of the parties that the buyer is relying on the description. For those purposes, I think that the law is correctly summarised in these words of *Benjamin*, p. 641, which should be understood to lay down an objective test:

> Specific goods may be sold as such . . . where, though the goods are described, the description is not relied upon, as where the buyer buys the goods such as they are.

7.4.2 Merchantable or satisfactory quality

For text see 7.3.3.

Sale of Goods Act 1979

14.   Implied terms about quality or fitness

(1)   Except as provided by this section and section 15 below and subject to any other enactment, there is no implied condition or warranty about the quality or fitness for any particular purpose of goods supplied under a contract of sale.

(2)   Where the seller sells goods in the course of a business, there is an implied condition that the goods supplied under the contract are of merchantable quality, except that there is no such condition—

(a)   as regards defects specifically drawn to the buyer's attention before the contract is made; or

(b)   if the buyer examines the goods before the contract is made, as regards defects which that examination ought to reveal.

The provisos to s. 14(2) make it clear that the implied condition does not apply in the circumstances specified, but there appears to be another possible exception.

R & B Customs Brokers Co. Ltd v United Dominions Trust Ltd
[1988] 1 All ER 847
Court of Appeal

For the facts see 7.3.3.2.

DILLON LJ at pp. 850–1: So far as subsection (2) (of s. 14 of the Sale of Goods Act 1979) is concerned, the relevant date is the date when the contract was made. With the usual tripartite arrangement between a dealer, a finance company and a purchaser, that is likely to be the entirely fortuitous date when the relevant documents are countersigned by the finance company, just as in the present case the contract was made on 3 November 1984. That is not satisfactory for the working of the 1979 Act because if, as here, the purchaser is allowed interim possession of the car (or other goods) in question he may well by the experience of use become aware of defects, without appreciating their gravity, before the date on which the contract happens to be made. So in the present case the company was, through Mr Bell, aware by experience before 3 November that the roof of the car leaked, though it had no idea that the leak was incurable.

The question therefore that arises under subsection (2) is whether, even though the car was in fact not of merchantable quality at 3 November, the company is precluded from relying on the condition in subsection (2) by virtue of the exception in para. (b) because the company knew there was a leak in the roof even though it did not know that the leak was incurable. The judge held that the company was precluded from relying on the condition in subsection (2) because the company had knowledge that there was a leak in the roof; in effect, *caveat emptor* once the purchaser has notice of a defect, however apparently slight. If that is right then, in the usual tripartite case involving a finance company, subsection (2) is something of a trap for a purchaser; he may lose his rights under the subsection if he fails to return the car or goods, or renegotiate the proposed contract, on the first appearance of an apparently slight defect.

However, in the circumstances of the present case I find it unnecessary to express a concluded view on whether the company can rely on the condition in subsection (2).

One of the principal difficulties with the implied condition of merchantable quality has been to determine what is meant by merchantable quality.

Sale of Goods Act 1979

14. Implied terms about quality or fitness
(6)   Goods of any kind are of merchantable quality within the meaning of subsection (2) above if they are as fit for the purpose or purposes for which goods of that kind are commonly bought as it is reasonable to expect having regard to any description applied to them, the price (if relevant) and all the other relevant circumstances.

'Merchantable' is a businessman's word, possibly indicating saleability (see 7.3.3.3). A more appropriate test from the point of view of a consumer is acceptability. A proposal to amend the definition of the standard of quality required was contained in the Consumer Guarantees Bill 1990.

Consumer Guarantees Bill 1990

16.—(1)In section 14 of the Sale of Goods Act 1979 (implied terms about quality or fitness) for subsection (2) there is substituted—

(2)   Where the seller sells goods in the course of a business, there is an implied term that the goods supplied under the contract are of satisfactory quality.

(2A)   For the purposes of this Act, goods are of satisfactory quality if they meet the standard that a reasonable person would regard as satisfactory, taking account of any description of the goods, the price (if relevant) and all the other relevant circumstances.

(2B)   For the purposes of this Act, the quality of goods includes their state and condition and the following (among others) in appropriate cases aspects of the quality of goods—

(a)   fitness for all the purposes for which goods of the kind in question are commonly supplied,

(b)   appearance and finish,

(c)   freedom from minor defects,

(d)   safety, and

(e)   durability.

(2C)   The term implied by subsection (2) above does not extend to any matter making the quality of goods unsatisfactory—

(a)   which is specifically drawn to the buyer's attention before the contract is made,

(b)   where the buyer examines the goods before the contract is made, which that examination ought to reveal, or

(c)   in the case of a contract for sale by sample, which would have been apparent on a reasonable examination of the sample.

The proposed amendment specifically includes safety as a requirement, but this was probably already the case.

Bernstein v *Pamson Motors (Golders Green) Ltd*
[1987] 2 All ER 220
Queen's Bench Division

ROUGIER J at p. 226: First and foremost it is perhaps self-evident that the court must look not only at the nature of the defect itself, considered in isolation, but also its likely

effect on the performance of the car. In *Bartlett* v *Sidney Marcus Ltd* [1965] 2 All ER
753, [1965] 1 WLR 1013 the Court of Appeal decided that the two basic requirements
of any car, certainly a second-hand car, were, first, that it should be capable of being
driven and, second, that it should be capable of being driven in safety, and that
statement I respectfully adopt. A car that will not move is useless; a car that will move
as intended but is a death trap to its occupants is worse than useless. In my judgment
it would be only in the most exceptional case (of which I cannot for the moment imagine
an example) that a new car which on delivery was incapable of being driven in safety
could ever be classed as being of merchantable quality.

At this stage it is necessary to discuss the question of whether the fact that the defect
under review is easily discoverable is relevant to the question of merchantability. It was
argued that if a defect existed which prevented the car being driven in safety, but which
was perfectly obvious, for example the absence of a wheel, that would not render the
car unmerchantable. On reflection, however, I do not think that the question of
discoverability by itself affects the issue; in other words, the question of whether the
defect is latent or patent is immaterial. A car minus one of its wheels cannot be driven,
certainly cannot be driven in safety, and while it remains in that condition it remains
unmerchantable. Since the absence of a wheel is a defect so quickly and easily rectified
(always assuming the missing wheel, or a substitute, is available) it might be thought
that to declare a wheel-less car unmerchantable and entitling its purchaser to rescission
is somewhat drastic. The practical reality of the matter, however, is that any glaringly
obvious defect which renders the car either inoperative or manifestly dangerous is one
whose existence will prevent the *delivery* of the car taking place, and will therefore be
dealt with at the pre-delivery stage. Nobody is going to accept delivery of a car with a
wheel missing, or some similar defect. Merchantability, however, is to be tested by
reference to the condition of the car *at the time of delivery*. In practice the argument
whether a car was of merchantable quality only arises when, after accepting delivery,
the buyer becomes aware of some defect. To that extent, therefore, there will always be
an element of latency in any particular defect which is the subject of a claim for
rescission such as the present.

A large number of minor defects may render goods unacceptable, but do they
also mean that goods are unmerchantable? The proposed amendment covers
this, but there have been moves in this direction already.

Rogers v *Parish (Scarborough) Ltd*
[1987] 2 WLR 353
Court of Appeal

The plaintiff purchased a new Range Rover for £14,000 which suffered from
a number of minor defects including a defective gearbox and oil seals. The
plaintiff drove the car more than 5,500 miles, but frequently made complaints
about its performance. Eventually, he sought to reject the vehicle on the
ground that it was not of merchantable quality.

MUSTILL LJ at pp. 359–60: . . . the judge applied the test of whether the defects had
destroyed the workable character of the car. No doubt this echoed an argument similar
to the one developed before us that if a vehicle is capable of starting and being driven
in safety from one point to the next on public roads and on whatever other surfaces the
car is supposed to be able to negotiate, it must necessarily be merchantable. I can only

say that this proposition appears to have no relation to the broad test propounded by section 14(6) (of the Sale of Goods Act 1979) even if, in certain particular circumstances, the correct inference would be that no more could be expected of the goods sold.

This being so, I think it legitimate to look at the whole issue afresh with direct reference to the words of section 14(6). Starting with the purpose for which 'goods of that kind' are commonly bought, one would include in respect of any passenger vehicle not merely the buyer's purpose of driving the car from one place to another but of doing so with the appropriate degree of comfort, ease of handling and reliability and, one might add, of pride in the vehicle's outward and interior appearance. What is the appropriate degree and what relative weight is to be attached to one characteristic of the car rather than another will depend on the market at which the car is aimed.

To identify the relevant expectation one must look at the factors listed in the subsection. The first is the description applied to the goods. In the present case the vehicle was sold as new. Deficiencies which might be acceptable in a second-hand vehicle were not to be expected in one purchased as new. Next, the description 'Range Rover' would conjure up a particular set of expectations, not the same as those relating to an ordinary saloon car, as to the balance between performance, handling, comfort and resilience. The factor of price was also significant. At more than £14,000 this vehicle was, if not at the top end of the scale, well above the level of the ordinary family saloon. The buyer was entitled to value for his money.

With these factors in mind, can it be said that the Range Rover as delivered was as fit for the purpose as the buyer could reasonably expect? The point does not admit of elaborate discussion. I can only say that to my mind the defects in engine, gearbox and bodywork, the existence of which is no longer in dispute, clearly demand a negative answer.

Note

It is clear from what Mustill LJ said in *Rogers v Parish (Scarborough) Ltd* that the price paid was an important consideration in determining whether goods are of merchantable quality. This may be so for the purposes of a new car, but may not always be relevant to the purchase of a second-hand vehicle.

Business Applications Specialists Ltd v Nationwide Credit Corporation Ltd
[1988] RTR 333
Court of Appeal

A second-hand Mercedes car was let to the plaintiffs by the defendants. After 800 miles of driving, the car broke down because it had burnt-out valves and valve seals were badly worn. £635 worth of repairs were necessary to the car, which was valued at £14,850.

PARKER LJ at pp. 335–7: The independent expert . . . said that he would not expect defects of this kind to manifest themselves after 800 miles of driving from the date of purchase and that it would be very unusual for such defects to manifest themselves in a car of this kind as early as 38,000 miles. There was other evidence, not by an independent expert under subpoena, to the effect that such defects could not be regarded as unusual. The car continued to be roadworthy and a safe car up to 13 January when repairs costing some £635 had to be carried out. The price of the car was a little short of £15,000 and it is a material consideration that the cost of repair was, in comparison with the overall cost of the car, not particularly great. . . .

I have no hesitation in saying that I am wholly unable to accept that the old tests necessarily apply in the case of every second-hand car. It appears to me that if a Rolls Royce motor car, with no more than perhaps 1500 miles on the clock, is being sold for the sort of price that such a car might reasonably command, it would be insufficient for that car to be driven in safety on the road and nothing else would matter. Having said that, it follows that the judge may have applied the wrong test because, although he was referred to both *Rogers* v *Parish (Scarborough) Ltd* [1987] QB 933 and *Bernstein* v *Pamson Motors (Golders Green) Ltd* [1987] 2 All ER 220 he does not mention them in his judgment. I proceed on the basis that he did apply the wrong test. . . .

I am satisfied that the judge, had he applied the correct test — that is to say, had he taken into account all the circumstances — would have been perfectly justified in reaching the conclusion of fact that this car was reasonably fit for the purpose and was of merchantable quality. I would myself have come to the same conclusion. The car as driven away exhibited no defects for some 800 miles, by which time it was two and a half years old and had 37,800 miles on the clock. Some degree of wear must therefore have been expected. The degree of wear involved repairs to the tune of £600-odd. There is no evidence whatever that at the time this vehicle was sold its compression and oil consumption were not satisfactory. The fact that within 800 miles and two months it had become unsatisfactory is no doubt some evidence that at the time of sale the valves and the valve guides of this car were worn. But I do not regard that as being sufficient evidence to conclude that this vehicle was not of merchantable quality.

The proposed amendment also includes a reference to durability, which may or may not have been a requirement of the Sale of Goods Act 1979, s. 14(6).

Lambert v *Lewis*
[1981] 1 All ER 1185
House of Lords

LORD DIPLOCK (at p. 1191): The implied warranty of fitness for a particular purpose relates to the goods at the time of delivery under the contract of sale in the state in which they were delivered. I do not doubt that it is a continuing warranty that the goods will continue to be fit for that purpose for a reasonable time after delivery, so long as they remain in the same apparent state as that in which they were delivered, apart from normal wear and tear. What is a reasonable time will depend on the nature of the goods, but I would accept that in the case of the coupling the warranty was still continuing up to the date, some three to six months before the accident, when it first became known to the farmer that the handle of the locking mechanism was missing. Up to that time the farmer would have had a right to rely on the dealers' warranty as excusing him from making his own examinaton of the coupling to see if it were safe; but, if the accident had happened before then, the farmer would not have been held to have been guilty of any negligence to the plaintiff. After it had become apparent to the farmer that the locking mechanism of the coupling was broken, and consequently that it was no longer in the same state as when it was delivered, the only implied warranty which could justify his failure to take the precaution either to get it mended or at least to find out whether it was safe to continue to use it in that condition would be a warranty that the coupling could continue to be safely used to tow a trailer on a public highway notwithstanding that it was in an obviously damaged state. My lords, any implication of a warranty in these terms needs only to be stated to be rejected. So the farmer's claim against the dealers fails *in limine*. In the state in which the farmer knew the coupling to be at the time of the accident, there was no longer any warranty by the dealers of its continued safety in use on which the farmer was entitled to rely.

Note

These comments were not directed at the effect of the Sale of Goods Act 1979, s. 14(2), but at the predecessor of s. 14(3) in relation to fitness for purpose. However, there is little doubt that they can also be applied to s. 14(2). The proposed s. 14(2B) is capable of imposing a condition as opposed to the warranty referred to in this case.

7.4.3 Fitness for purpose

For text see 7.3.4.

Sale of Goods Act 1979

14. Implied terms about quality or fitness

(3)   Where the seller sells goods in the course of a business and the buyer, expressly or by implication, makes known—

(a)   to the seller, or

(b)   where the purchase price or part of it is payable by instalments and the goods were previously sold by a credit-broker to the seller, to that credit-broker,

any particular purpose for which the goods are being bought, there is an implied condition that the goods supplied under the contract are reasonably fit for that purpose, whether or not that is a purpose for which such goods are commonly supplied, except where the circumstances show that the buyer does not rely, or that it is unreasonable for him to rely, on the skill or judgment of the seller or credit-broker.

Ordinarily there will be an overlap between s. 14(2) and s. 14(3) where the goods are used for their normal purpose, but if the consumer wishes to put the goods to a special use, he should inform the supplier, so that the latter can use his judgment as to suitability.

Griffiths v Peter Conway Ltd
[1939] 1 All ER 685
Court of Appeal

For the facts see 7.3.4.1.

GREENE MR at p. 691: On the basis of that finding, which is not challenged, Mr Morris says: 'Take the language of the section, and the present case falls within it'. He says that the buyer, Mrs Griffiths, expressly made known to the defendants the particular purpose for which the coat was required — that is to say, for the purpose of being worn by her, Mrs Griffiths, when it was made. Once that state of affairs is shown to exist, Mr Morris says that the language of the section relentlessly and without any escape imposes upon the seller the obligation which the section imports.

It seems to me that there is one quite sufficient answer to that argument. Before the condition as to reasonable fitness is implied, it is necessary that the buyer should make known, expressly or by implication, first of all the particular purpose for which the goods are required. The particular purpose for which the goods were required was the purpose of being worn by a woman suffering from an abnormality. It seems to me that, if a person suffering from such an abnormality requires an article of clothing for his or her use, and desires to obtain the benefit of the implied condition, he or she does not make known to the seller the particular purpose merely by saying: 'The article of clothing is for my own wear'. The essential matter for the seller to know in such cases with regard to the purposes for which the article is required consists in the particular abnormality or idiosyncrasy from which the buyer suffers. It is only when he has that knowledge that he is in a position to exercise his skill or judgment, because how can he decide and exercise skill or judgment in relation to the suitability of the goods that he is selling for the use of the particular individual who is buying from him unless he knows the essential characteristics of that individual?

Reliance is an important feature of the requirements of the Sale of Goods Act 1979, s. 14(3), but it can often be assumed.

Grant v *Australian Knitting Mills Ltd*
[1936] AC 85
Privy Council

LORD WRIGHT at p. 99: The first exception, if its terms are satisfied, entitles the buyer to the benefit of an implied condition that the goods are reasonably fit for the purpose for which the goods are supplied, but only if that purpose is made known to the seller 'so as to show that the buyer relies on the seller's skill or judgment'. It is clear that the reliance must be brought home to the mind of the seller, expressly or by implication. The reliance will seldom be express: it will usually arise by implication from the circumstances: thus to take a case like that in question, of a purchase from a retailer, the reliance will be in general inferred from the fact that a buyer goes to the shop in the confidence that the tradesman has selected his stock with skill and judgment: the retailer need know nothing about the process of manufacture: it is immaterial whether he be manufacturer or not: the main inducement to deal with a good retail shop is the expectation that the tradesman will have bought the right goods of a good make: the goods sold must be, as they were in the present case, goods of a description which it is in the course of the seller's business to supply: there is no need to specify in terms the particular purpose for which the buyer requires the goods, which is nonetheless the particular purpose within the meaning of the section, because it is the only purpose for which any one would ordinarily want the goods. In this case the garments were naturally intended, and only intended, to be worn next the skin. . . . The conversation at the shop in which the appellant discussed questions of price and of the different makes did not affect the fact that he was substantially relying on the retailers to supply him with a correct article.

7.5   THE TORT OF NEGLIGENCE AND PRODUCT QUALITY

Because of the apparent defects in the law of contract emanating, in particular, from a strict application of the doctrine of privity of contract, the question has arisen whether the tort of negligence can be used to compensate for those deficiencies (see Markesinis (1987) 103 LQR 354). The principal way in which this can be done is through the expansion of the circumstances in which a duty of care is owed by a manufacturer to a consumer of a defective product.

7.5.1 Economic loss and physical harm

See generally, Cane (1979) 95 LQR 117.

The main problem with the issue of product quality is that the consumer's complaint is that the product is not worth as much as he expected when he made his purchase. In some way the product is less valuable due to the presence of qualitative defects and it is that diminution in value which the consumer seeks to recover.

The implications of the House of Lords decision in *Anns v Merton London Borough Council* [1978] AC 728 were that in certain circumstances, economic loss such as the damage caused by a defective building to itself was remediable in an action for negligence if the defectiveness of the building was such as to create a present or imminent danger to the occupant of the building. By analogy, if a defective product gave rise to such a danger, damages representing the cost of rectifying the defect could be awarded.

The conceptual difficulty this gave rise to was that the harm complained of in *Anns v Merton London Borough Council* was pure economic loss - the plaintiff was given damages to compensate for the diminution in value of the building concerned, and this was not the province of the tort of negligence. Accordingly, the decision in *Anns v Merton London Borough Council* was overruled in *Murphy v Brentwood District Council* [1990] 2 All ER 908 on the ground that it represented an unwarranted extension of the tort of negligence into an area it was never intended to cover.

The effect of overruling *Anns v Merton London Borough Council* is that if the only damage suffered is to the defective product itself, the manufacturer of that product will owe the consumer no duty of care. Similarly if the consumer discovers a defect before it becomes dangerous and replaces or repairs the product, the loss he has suffered is purely economic and, generally, no duty of care is owed. Apparently, once the defect has been discovered, the product is no longer dangerous and the manufacturer's duty of care ceases to exist when this is the case (*D & F Estates Ltd v Church Commissioners for England* [1988] 2 All ER 992 at p. 1006 per Lord Bridge).

In some cases, what appeared to be economic loss was remediable as a variety of physical damage where the 'complex structure' theory applied. This was a theory which had been put forward in *D & F Estates Ltd v Church Commissioners for England* [1988] 2 All ER 992 which suggested that in the case of a complex structure, one part of such a structure could cause damage to another part of the same structure and that damage was remediable in the tort of negligence as physical harm. Unfortunately, the theory suffered from inadequate explanation (see Wallace (1989) 105 LQR 46; Cane (1989) 52 MLR 200), but since Lord Bridge in *D & F Estates Ltd v Church Commissioners for England* equated defective buildings with other defective products ([1988] 2 All ER 992 at p. 1006, cf. Lord Oliver at p. 1012), the theory is capable of being applied to products such as defective motor cars and domestic electrical appliances, if these can be described as complex structures.

In *Murphy v Brentwood District Council* three members of the House of Lords sought to explain this concept further. It was said that the complex structure theory cannot apply to a product or building which is wholly erected and equipped by the same contractor ([1990] 2 All ER 908 at p. 922 per Lord Keith). The whole package is to be regarded as a single unit which is rendered unsound by a defect in part of it. Each part of such a structure is interdependent on the other parts (at p. 928 per Lord Bridge). The theory is applicable to structures which are erected by more than one contractor and the work of one results in damage to another part of the structure as a whole. Thus, damage to a building owned by A caused by defective electrical wiring installed by B in the same structure might satisfy the requirements of the theory (per Lord Keith). Similarly, damage caused to the same building by a defective central heating boiler negligently installed by C or negligently manufactured by D might also be classified as physical harm under the theory (at p. 928 per Lord Bridge). However, it would appear that an aeroplane which is fitted with a defective engine is not subject to the complex structure theory (*Trans World Airlines Inc.* v *Curtiss-Wright Corporation* (1955) 148, N&S 2d 284, 1 Misc 2d 477).

If a consumer suffers extensive damage to his new car because a tyre bursts when the car is being driven at speed, his likelihood of success in a negligence action will depend on who manufactured the tyre. If the manufacturer of the car is also the manufacturer of the tyre, the complex structure theory suggests that the consumer will be unable to maintain a negligence action. However, if the manufacturers of the tyre and the car are distinct, the consumer will be able to recover damages in tort from the tyre manufacturer.

7.5.2 The requirement of proximity

The House of Lords in *Murphy* v *Brentwood District Council* [1990] 2 All ER 908 did admit to the existence of exceptional cases in which economic loss was remediable in a negligence action, namely, where the rule in *Hedley Byrne & Co.* v *Heller & Partners Ltd* [1964] AC 465 applied and where the relationship of proximity was so great as to fit within the principle laid down in *Junior Books Ltd* v *Veitchi Co. Ltd* [1983] 1 AC 520. Thus if the manufacturer gives information or advice concerning his product which is relied on by the consumer who subsequently suffers economic loss as a result of that reliance, the *Hedley Byrne* principle seems to apply.

A feature of both these cases is the very close relationship of proximity which exists between the plaintiff and the defendant. It is very unlikely that this necessary relationship will be found to exist between the manufacturer and consumer of a qualitatively defective product which results in economic loss to the consumer. This much was clear from the decision of the House of Lords in *Junior Books Ltd* v *Veitchi Co. Ltd* [1983] 1 AC 520 in which it was considered that, in most cases, the consumer will have relied on the retailer (rather than the manufacturer) to provide goods of the desired quality (at p. 533 and 547 per Lords Fraser and Roskill; see also *Muirhead* v *Industrial Tank Specialities Ltd* [1985] 3 All ER 705). To the contrary, it can be argued that in some instances the primary reliance of the consumer is on the manufacturer rather than the retailer, particularly where the consumer has relied on the general reputation of the manufacturer or where he has been influenced by a national advertising campaign (see Oughton [1987] JBL 370; Palmer and Murdoch (1983) 46 MLR 213). In such a case, from whom the product is purchased would appear to be immaterial, thereby negating the possibility of reliance on the retailer.

The reluctance to allow the tort of negligence to be used in respect of qualitative defects is based on the fact that it is difficult to ascertain the appropriate standard to which the goods supplied should conform. The *Donoghue* v *Stevenson* [1932] AC 562 duty is one to take reasonable care to ensure that goods supplied are not dangerous, but to extend that duty to include quality would pose substantial problems since the desired standard of quality in each case will depend on the standard of quality contracted for. It has been seen already that the standard of quality under a contract for the supply of goods will depend on a range of factors including the price paid for the goods and any description applied to them. Where the defendant is a manufacturer, there is no contractual relationship with the consumer, and the courts, at present, see it as too difficult a task to ascertain the standard of quality required. Accordingly, the buyer is presently required to enter into his contract with the retailer with care and to specify what he requires in the way of quality. While this is a fair argument to employ in relation to business contracts, the same is not necessarily applicable where the buyer is a consumer who does not possess the business expertise to determine in advance what he requires from the supplier.

7.6   THE TORT OF NEGLIGENCE AND PRODUCT QUALITY – MATERIALS FOR CONSIDERATION

For text see 7.5.

Product quality is concerned with the value of the thing supplied. In some instances, negligence on the part of a manufacturer may result in the product itself being worth less than was anticipated by the consumer. One must not hide from the fact that this is pure economic loss, which is not recoverable in an action for negligence, as a general rule.

D & F Estates Ltd v *Church Commissioners for England*
[1988] 2 All ER 992
House of Lords

LORD BRIDGE at p. 1006: If the hidden defect in the chattel is the cause of personal injury or of damage to property other than the chattel itself, the manufacturer is liable. But if the hidden defect is discovered before any such damage is caused, there is no longer any room for the application of the *Donoghue* v *Stevenson* [1932] AC 562 principle. The chattel is now defective in quality, but is no longer dangerous. It may be valueless or it may be capable of economic repair. In either case the economic loss is recoverable in contract by a buyer or hirer of the chattel entitled to the benefit of a relevant warranty of quality, but is not recoverable in tort by a remote buyer or hirer of the chattel.

If the same principle applies in the field of real property to the liability of the builder of a permanent structure which is dangerously defective, that liability can only arise if the defect remains hidden until the defective structure causes personal injury or damage to property other than the structure itself. If the defect is discovered before any damage is done, the loss sustained by the owner of the structure, who has to repair or demolish it to avoid a potential source of danger to third parties, would seem to be purely economic. Thus, if I acquire a property with a dangerously defective garden wall which is attributable to the bad workmanship of the original builder, it is difficult to see any basis in principle on which I can sustain an action in tort against the builder for the cost of either repairing or demolishing the wall. No physical damage has been caused.

The overriding difficulty in defective product cases is that the House of Lords has consistently said that there is an insufficient relationship of proximity between the manufacturer of a defective product and a consumer who alleges that the product is not worth the amount he paid for it.

Junior Books Ltd v *Veitchi Co. Ltd*
[1982] 3 All ER 201
House of Lords

LORD FRASER at pp. 206–7: Having thus reached a conclusion in favour of the respondents on the somewhat narrow ground which I have indicated, I do not consider this to be an appropriate case for seeking to advance the frontiers of the law of negligence on the lines favoured by certain of your lordships. There are a number of reasons why such an extension would, in my view, be wrong in principle. In the first place, I am unable to regard the deterioration of the flooring which is alleged in this case as being damage to the respondents' property such as to give rise to a liability falling directly within the principle of *Donoghue* v *Stevenson* [1932] AC 562. The flooring had an inherent defect in it from the start. The appellants did not, in any sense consistent with the ordinary use of language or contemplated by the majority in *Donoghue* v *Stevenson*, damage the respondents' property. They supplied them with a defective floor. Such an act can, in accordance with the views I have expressed above, give rise to liability in negligence in certain circumstances. But it does not do so merely because the flooring is defective or valueless or useless and requires to be replaced. So to hold would raise very difficult and delicate issues of principle having a wide potential application. I think it would necessarily follow that any manufacturer of products would become liable to the ultimate purchaser if the product, owing to negligence in manufacture, was, without being harmful in any way, useless or worthless or defective in quality so that the purchaser wasted the money he spent on it. One instance mentioned in argument and adverted to by Stamp LJ in *Dutton* v *Bognor Regis United Building Co. Ltd* [1972] 1 All ER 462 at 489, [1972] 1 QB 373 at 414 was a product purchased as ginger beer which turned out to be only water, and many others may be figured. To introduce a general liability covering such situations would be disruptive of commercial practice, under which manufacturers of products commonly provide the ultimate purchaser with limited guarantees, usually undertaking only to replace parts exhibiting defective workmanship and excluding any consequential loss. There being no contractual relationship between manufacturer and ultimate consumer, no room would exist, if the suggested principle were accepted, for limiting the manufacturer's liability. The policy considerations which would be involved in introducing such a state of affairs appear to me to be such as a court of law cannot properly assess, and the question whether or not it would be in the interests of commerce and the public generally is, in my view, much better left for the legislature. The purchaser of a defective product normally can proceed for breach of contract against the seller who can bring his own supplier into the proceedings by third-party procedure, so it cannot be said that the present state of the law is unsatisfactory from the point of view of available remedies.

While it may not be important to the consumer that he cannot recover the diminished value of a bottle of ginger beer from the manufacturer, when the retailer has gone out of business, it may be very important that he cannot recover the decreased value of a motor car, particularly if he has relied on the manufacturer's advertising material.

Oughton, 'Liability in tort for economic loss suffered by the consumer of defective goods
[1987] JBL 370 at p. 375

In contrast, there are undoubtedly circumstances in which the buyer of a defective product does rely on the manufacturer rather than his supplier. For example, the consumer may rely on the general reputation of the manufacturer for producing reliable goods. Such reliance may be referred to as 'brand loyalty'. In other cases, a manufacturer of a new line of goods may conduct his own 'pre-launch' advertising campaign in such a way that the only person who can be said to have been relied upon is the manufacturer himself. Furthermore, in some cases commercial buyers of specialist materials will consult the manufacturer and rely on his skill and experience before purchasing from a retail outlet. Finally, in the case of finance-leasing agreements, the hirer may consult and rely upon the manufacturer of expensive plant or machinery before it is sold to a bank and then leased back to the hirer. In all these cases the notion of reliance on the immediate supplier is unreal. Such reliance as there is, is upon the manufacturer.

An exception to the general rule of non-recovery exists where one part of a complex structure damages another part of the same complex structure. In such a case, the damage is characterised as physical harm. Is a car a complex structure? Can a defective oil seal or a leaking battery damage the rest of the vehicle?

Murphy v *Brentwood District Council*
[1990] 2 All ER 908
House of Lords

LORD KEITH at p. 922: In *D & F Estates Ltd* v *Church Commissioners for England* [1988] 2 All ER 992, [1989] AC 177 both Lord Bridge and Lord Oliver expressed themselves as having difficulty in reconciling the decision in *Anns* v *Merton London Borough Council* [1978] AC 728 with pre-existing principle and as being uncertain as to the nature and scope of such new principle as it introduced. Lord Bridge suggested that in the case of a complex structure such as a building one element of the structure might be regarded for *Donoghue* v *Stevenson* purposes as distinct from another element, so that damage to one part of the structure caused by a hidden defect in another part might qualify to be treated as damage to 'other property' (see [1988] 2 All ER 992 at 1006, [1989] AC 177 at 206). I think that it would be unrealistic to take this view as regards a building the whole of which had been erected and equipped by the same contractor. In that situation the whole package provided by the contractor would, in my opinion, fall to be regarded as one unit rendered unsound as such by a defect in the particular part. On the other hand, where, for example, the electric wiring had been installed by a subcontractor and due to a defect caused by lack of care a fire occurred which destroyed the building, it might not be stretching ordinary principles too far to hold the electrical subcontractor liable for the damage. If in the *East River* case [*East River Steamship Corporation* v *Transamerica Delaval Inc.* (1986) 476 US 858] the defective turbine had caused the loss of the ship the manufacturer of it could consistently with normal principles, I would think, properly have been held liable for that loss.

7.7   MANUFACTURERS' GUARANTEES OF QUALITY

The protection afforded the consumer under the Sale of Goods Act 1979 and related legislation assumes the existence of a contractual relationship between the consumer buyer and the retailer. However, all too often, the ultimate consumer of a product is not the person who has purchased the qualitatively defective product. As an alternative, the consumer might wish to pursue the manufacturer of the defective product, but this can present almost insurmountable hurdles where the complaint is that the product is merely qualitatively defective.

The difficulties of establishing a contractual relationship between the consumer and the manufacturer of a product are substantial and have been discussed elsewhere (see 3.2.1.1). The present alternative to a contractual action is one based on the tort of negligence, but it has been seen already that the necessary relationship of proximity will rarely exist between the consumer and a manufacturer where the consumer's complaint is that the product is qualitatively defective as opposed to being unsafe (see 7.5.2).

As an alternative to the conventional contractual and tortious remedies of the consumer, it is frequently the case that the consumer is given a guarantee of the quality of the product he uses. If fully effective, guarantees are a highly desirable means of consumer protection as they operate as a means of prevention rather than as a cure after things have already gone wrong. The consumer is not left to pursue his remedies through the courts, but has a simple remedy against the person who gives the guarantee. However, the question remains whether these guarantees are worth any more than the paper they are written on.

7.7.1   The features of and purposes served by guarantees

A wide range of guarantees are presently available. These include short-term gauarantees provided by some suppliers of goods and services which may last for approximately one year after the date of supply. In addition to original guarantees, some retailers will also offer extended warranties, usually backed by insurance, for a period of about four years on top of the original guarantee, under which defective workmanship and materials are covered. However, these extended warranties tend, for the most part, to exclude liability for general wear and tear.

In other cases, particularly in the home improvements sector, longer-term guarantees, sometimes backed by insurance, are available for periods of 25 or 30 years.

Some manufacturers will also give guarantees or warranties with their product, which are in addition to the statutory rights of the consumer under the Sale of Goods Act 1979 and related legislation. Most often, these manufacturer's guarantees are to be found in relation to the more expensive consumer purchases such as motor vehicles and 'white' goods such as domestic kitchen appliances. It is common to find that certain parts of the product are guaranteed for longer periods than others and in some cases, certain parts, particularly of motor vehicles, are excluded from the guarantee altogether. In some instances, the guarantee is subject to a servicing requirement, with the result that a guarantee may be invalidated if the consumer does not have his motor car serviced on a regular basis at an approved garage.

Guarantees do not only serve the consumer, they also provide the manufacturer with useful product information and act as a promotional device. In particular, it appears to be accepted by manufacturers and retailers that information about complaints is essential to effective quality management (see National Consumer Council, *Competing in Quality* (1989) para. 5.1). Unless a producer knows how well his product is performing in use, it is virtually impossible to gauge consumer satisfaction and improve the quality of products. Guarantees and consumer responses associated with guarantees can help to provide the information required by producers in this respect.

Given the various roles served by guarantees, there are a number of competing theories concerning the reasons for giving guarantees with consumer goods and services (see Priest (1980-81) 90 Yale LJ 1297; Whitford (1982) 91 Yale LJ 1371).

One view is that guarantees are essentially exploitative devices imposed by retailers and manufacturers on consumers because they are aware of the consumer's inequality of bargaining power. This is borne out by those guarantees which seek to exclude or limit the liability of the guarantee-giver to a level below that provided by the Sale of Goods Act 1979. The exploitative nature of guarantees has been recognised by Parliament and measures have been taken to deal with guarantees that operate in this fashion (see 7.7.2).

An alternative view is that guarantees provide a signal of the reliability of the product. The search costs which face consumers who wish to compare rival products before making a purchase are substantial, but the presence of a wide-ranging guarantee may signal to the consumer that the producer has confidence in his product. In this way the consumer may cut down his search costs by comparing the warranty provisions of competing manufacturers and ignoring other matters. However, with any product, there are likely to be parts which are more prone to suffer from defects and it is likely that the manufacturer will use small print in the guarantee to exclude or limit his liability in these respects. Accordingly, the consumer still has the search costs associated with reading each guarantee to discover how the exclusions of one producer differ from those of another. Given that few consumers ever read the small print in contractual documents, this would seem to destroy the signal theory. Furthermore, in many cases, the guarantee is not discovered until after purchase, because it is contained in the packaging surrounding the goods, in which case, it cannot have figured in the consumer's decision to purchase.

A further theory is the investment theory developed by Priest ((1980-81) 90 Yale LJ 1297) which seeks to identify which of the consumer or producer is in the best position to insure against a particular risk of loss. In particular, Priest points to the fact that if a particular defect is best avoided by the producer taking precautions at the design stage or by adopting quality control techniques, he is more likely to give a warranty that covers such defects. On the other hand, there may be defects which are best covered by private insurance taken out by the consumer, in which case, such defects are likely to be excluded from the guarantee by the producer. The investment theory is therefore based on the notion of the least-cost avoider. On this basis, it is argued that the manufacturer of a motor vehicle ought to be allowed to exclude liability in respect of the unmerchantability of his product, because the consumer can obtain alternative insurance elsewhere. Furthermore, if the manufacturer is obliged to provide extensive cover beyond that given in his warranty, this will reduce the consumer's incentives to maintain his vehicle or obtain insurance elsewhere, with the result that the number of product defects will increase. Accordingly, less careful consumers will be cross-subsidised by those who are more careful with their purchases. This might seem to suggest that provisions such as the Unfair Contract Terms Act 1977, s. 5 (see 7.7.2) are inefficient measures insofar as they prevent the use of exclusions of liability in manufacturers' guarantees.

7.7.2   The problems of guarantees

All of these guarantees, if enforceable, provide the consumer with rights of considerable value, but quite often the guarantee is nothing more than a marketing ploy or a means of diverting the consumer's attention from his legal rights.

In some instances in the past, manufacturers' guarantees have even been used to take away rights which the consumer enjoyed under statute or at common law (see *Adams* v *Richardson & Starling Ltd* [1969] 1 WLR 1645 at pp. 1648-9 per Lord Denning MR). Arguments of this type are consistent with the exploitation theory considered above, but it also needs to be considered whether countermeasures are efficient in the light of the investment theory.

Exploitation abuses were recognised and the Unfair Contract Terms Act 1977, s. 5, now provides that liability for loss or damage caused by a defective product cannot be excluded by reference to a guarantee if the product is of a type ordinarily supplied for private use or consumption and the damage etc. arises from the product proving to be defective whilst in consumer use and is caused by the negligence of a person concerned with the manufacture or distribution of the product. Accordingly, where a guarantee is now given, it adds to the remedies of the consumer without taking away his existing legal rights. Furthermore, it is also a criminal offence for a person acting in the course of a business to make a statement to the effect that the consumer's rights under the Sale of Goods Act 1979, related legislation or the Unfair Contract Terms Act 1977 are in any way restricted or excluded (Consumer Transactions (Restrictions on Statements) Order (SI 1976/1813), art. 3). Furthermore, it is also a criminal offence for a person to publish a statement which relates to consumer rights, for example, a guarantee, without also clearly stating that the statutory rights of the consumer are unaffected (SI 1976/1813, art. 4).

Whether or not guarantees are used in an exploitative fashion, data collected by the Office of Fair Trading and the National Consumer Council suggest that many consumers are still highly dissatisfied with guarantee provisions. It has been reported that much consumer dissatisfaction emanates from the failure of guarantees to cover labour costs and from the lack of clarity in the language used in guarantee disclaimers of liability (OFT, *Consumer Guarantees* (1986), para. 5.9). The extent of consumer dissatisfaction also appears to be increasing. For example, in 1988 it was estimated that 38% of the adult population was dissatisfied with a purchase made by them (OFT, *Beeline*, issue 88/4, pp. 22-4) whereas in 1986, the relevant figure was 28% (OFT, *Consumer Dissatisfaction* (1986)). Even given trade suggestions that the OFT data were suspect, it has still been conservatively estimated that at least one million people each year fail to resolve complaints concerning faulty new goods (NCC, *The Consumer Guarantee* (1989), para. 3.1.4) It is also uncontroversial that the greatest level of dissatisfaction emanates from the purchase of cars and household appliances (ibid., para. 3.1.5).

7.7.3 Proposals for reform

The level of consumer dissatisfaction indicated above has led the National Consumer Council to propose a regime of consumer product guarantees based on the notions of competition and increased consumer information (NCC, *The Consumer Guarantee*, (1989)). Their proposals were taken up in the private member's Consumer Guarantees Bill (Bill 16, 1990) which was lost due to absence of Parliamentary time in summer 1990 and now stands no chance of reintroduction.

Had the NCC proposals become law, they would have permitted producers to give a free consumer guarantee which would have been enforceable as a variety of statutory contract. While producers would not have been compelled to give a guarantee, those who chose not to do so would have been placed at a competitive disadvantage through the operation of consumer choice in the market-place. The theoretical underpinning of the regime was that market forces could be employed as a means of consumer protection, by allowing those producers who stood by their products to say so by complying with the statutory requirements of the consumer guarantee.

It was proposed that producers be entitled to offer no consumer guarantee, a consumer guarantee for a minimum period of 12 months, or a consumer guarantee plus which should provide for benefits, not legally required, in excess of the minimum consumer guarantee. The principal targets of the report were motor cars and expensive domestic electrical appliances, but it was also proposed that the producer of any other product should be allowed to give a guarantee, if he so chose.

The proposed guarantee would have entitled the consumer to free repairs to defective goods and compensation or a loaned replacement in the event of delays in the repair process. It was also proposed that where repairs proved to be ineffective, the consumer should be entitled to a similarly guaranteed replacement or his money back.

The guarantee would not have been applicable to defects caused by consumer misuse, including failure to maintain and by the act or default of a person or thing unconnected with the guarantor. Furthermore, to protect the guarantor, it was recommended that a deduction for consumer use should be made where a guarantee on a motor vehicle has run for longer than six months.

By way of enforcement, the Consumer Guarantees Bill would also have made it a criminal offence for a person to offer a guarantee in contravention of the provisions about the content of guarantees.

7.8   MANUFACTURERS' GUARANTEES OF QUALITY – MATERIALS FOR CONSIDERATION

For text see 7.7.

The Consumer Guarantees Bill

PART I THE CONSUMER GUARANTEE

1.   Definition of Consumer Guarantee

For the purposes of this Act, a Consumer Guarantee is a guarantee whose minimum terms, as regards any product in relation to which it is given, are as follows.

(a)   The guarantor will repair any defect in the product unless he shows that the defect was caused by—

(i)   misuse of the product by a consumer;

(ii)   failure to maintain or service the product reasonably; or

(iii)   an act or default of any person (not being the guarantor or a servant or agent of the guarantor), or a cause independent of human control, occurring after the product has left the control of the guarantor.

(b)   If the product is defective, the guarantor will either—

(i)   provide the consumer with the use of a comparable replacement product; or

(ii)   compensate the consumer for any loss of the use of the product,

if the guarantor does not repair the product within four relevant days (or, in the case of a motor vehicle, two relevant days).

(c)   In exchange for the product, the guarantor will, at the option of the consumer, either—

(i)   subject to section 2, pay the consumer a refund, consisting of the sum paid for the product on its supply to the consumer and any related part-exchange allowance; or

(ii)   provide the consumer with a replacement product, if the number of relevant days applying to a product (whether in respect of the same defect or two or more different defects) during any one 12 month period of the Consumer Guarantee exceeds 21.

(d) The guarantor will provide these remedies free of charge, for a period of at least 12 months beginning with the date on which the product was first supplied to a consumer within the terms of the guarantee.

(e) The guarantor will not make these remedies subject to unreasonable conditions.

(f) When making a refund or providing a replacement product under subsection (c) above, the guarantor may make a charge for use of the product, subject to the following conditions—

(i) the charge must be reasonable having regard to the nature of the product and all other relevant circumstances;

(ii) except in the case of a motor vehicle, the charge may be made only in relation to a Consumer Guarantee given for more than the minimum period of 12 months, and must be directly attributable to any use of the product after that period and not before;

(iii) in the case of a motor vehicle, the charge may relate to any use of the motor vehicle after the first six months of the Consumer Guarantee or after the first 6,000 miles of use.

(g) When making a refund or providing a replacement product under subsection (c) above, the guarantor may make a reasonable charge for any significant physical damage to the product other than damage resulting from normal use.

(h) If the consumer shows that the product was under or awaiting repair by or on behalf of the guarantor for any length of time, the period of the guarantee will be extended by that length of time.

(i) The consumer may notify a defect orally or in writing, and may do so either to the guarantor, or to the person who first supplied the product to a consumer.

(j) 'Relevant' days applying to a product are days after the date of notification of a defect in the product up to and including the day on which the product is made available to the consumer after repair, not counting—

(i) any day lost for the purposes of repair as a result of the unreasonable behaviour of the consumer; and

(ii) any Saturday, Sunday, Christmas Day, Good Friday or a day which is a bank holiday under the Banking and Financial Dealings Act 1971 in the part of the United Kingdom where the product is to be made available to the consumer after repair.

2. Special provisions in relation to finance agreements

(1) This section applies where a product covered by a Consumer Guarantee is supplied to a consumer under a credit agreement or a consumer hire agreement.

(2) Where a consumer within subsection (1) chooses to be paid a refund under a Consumer Guarantee, in accordance with section 1(c), the guarantor—

(a) shall, as agent of the consumer, give notice to and pay the creditor such amounts as would be necessary under sections 94 to 96 of the Consumer Credit Act 1974 to discharge the consumer's indebtedness; and

(b) shall pay to the consumer any sum paid by the consumer, or his relative, under or in contemplation of the consumer credit agreement or any linked transaction, including any item in the total charge for credit, and any part-exchange allowance.

(3) Where a guarantor has satisfied subsection (2), he shall be entitled to recover the product.

PART II PROVISIONS RELATING TO THE CONSUMER GUARANTEE
3. Existence or otherwise of Consumer Guarantee to be stated

(1) Every producer of a specified product shall, in accordance with this section, state in relation to that product either—

    (a)   that the product is covered by a Consumer Guarantee and whether its duration is the minimum period of 12 months or longer; or

    (b)   that the product is not covered by a Consumer Guarantee.

   (2)   The statement required by subsection (1) shall be:

    (a)   in writing;

    (b)   in, upon or attached to the product, or its labelling or in packaging in a manner which will make it obvious to consumers at the time of first supply to a consumer;

    (c)   included in every non-media advertisement for the product;

    (d)   easily legible and of a colour which is readily distinguishable from the colour of the background; and

    (e)   afforded no less prominence (whether by capital letters, underlining, large or bold print or otherwise) than any other statements apart from the name of the producer or supplier, trade names and the name of the product.

   (3)   The statement required by subsection (1)(b) shall be immediately followed by a statement in the form shown in schedule I to this Act, and subsections 2(a), (b) and (d) shall apply to the latter statement. . . .

4.   Consumer Guarantees by producers and suppliers

   (1)   Any producer or supplier of a product may, in accordance with this section, state in relation to that product that it is covered by a Consumer Guarantee.

   (2)   Any person who issues or causes to be issued a statement under subsection (1), must also state whether the duration of the Consumer Guarantee is the minimum period of 12 months or longer.

   (3)   A statement issued under subsection (1) above must be preceded by the name of the supplier where that person is supplying the product to consumers.

5.   Consumer Guarantees Plus

   (1)   Any producer or supplier of a product may state that a Consumer Guarantee given by him in relation to a product is a Consumer Guarantee Plus.

   (2)   For the purposes of this Act, a Consumer Guarantee Plus is a guarantee under which consumers will receive benefits additional to the minimum terms of a Consumer Guarantee, not being benefits required by law, provided that they are substantial and that a prominent indication is given of their nature.

   (3)   A Consumer Guarantee is not a Consumer Guarantee Plus by reason only that it duration exceeds 12 months.

The benefits of a guarantee in these terms are explained by the National Consumer Council in:

National Consumer Council, *The Consumer Guarantee* (1989)

1.2   When consumers go shopping they want value for money. Value for money is a combination of price and quality. For most products, quality is something that is assessed by use. For items in the weekly shopping basket, such as detergent or food, consumers can act on their experience. It is relatively easy to switch to another brand or another shop. In this way the right signals are sent to manufacturers about what consumers want.

1.3   Our main concern is with expensive items which are not bought regularly, such as cars and household appliances. Here full competition can only flourish if there is reliable information for customers about the guarantees, after-sales service and reliability of the product. With these expensive products, information gained by consumers through experience is often gained too late. The endless introduction of 'new improved' models and the infrequency of the purchase can mean that businesses which produce low-quality goods can escape penalties in the market-place.

1.4   This is a problem not just for thousands of individual consumers every week but for society at large. We all have to pay for the production and marketing of goods which are faulty or useless.

1.5   In this country there is little law requiring the disclosure of information about the quality of products. One way consumers try to gauge the reliability of a product is by the guarantee offered with it. Yet there are no laws that help to distinguish a good guarantee from a worthless one. This distorts competition and misleads consumers.

1.6   Competition is not just about price, it should also be about the reliability and quality of the product and about after-sales service. Our research into north American markets suggests that UK consumers, particularly car buyers, are badly served — we pay far more and we get far less for the same products. One of the main reasons for this is that in the USA there is a legal framework for competing in quality.

1.7   We therefore propose a clear and simple guarantee, backed by legislation. This will allow consumers to choose a product by reference to its quality, reliability and after-sales service, and not simply by its price.

We do not recommend that businesses should be required by law to give these guarantees. However, we do recommend that manufacturers of motor vehicles and major household appliances should be obliged to state whether or not they offer this protection.

In this way, consumers will be able to see which manufacturers are prepared to stand by their products. This in turn we believe will force manufacturers to address the issues of product quality and customer service diligently.

CHAPTER EIGHT

Product Safety I – The Civil Obligations of the Producer and Retailer

In addition to product quality, the consumer also has an interest in product safety. Product safety is a matter which goes beyond the quest for compensation when things go wrong. There is a general social interest in ensuring that consumer goods and, to a lesser extent, consumer services reach general standards of safety. For the most part, the criminal law is used to this end and will be considered in chapter 9). It is also the case that where the consumer suffers physical harm to his person or to his property, that harm may be the subject of a civil action for compensation. The principal means by which this harm is compensated is through the operation of the law of tort in the form of an action for negligence, an action under the Consumer Protection Act 1987, part I, or an action for damages for breach of statutory duty. It is also the case that where goods supplied to a consumer fail to reach the required standard of merchantability or fitness for purpose and as a consequence cause physical harm, that harm may be taken into account in an award of damages for breach of contract.

8.1 CONTRACTUAL DUTIES AND PRODUCT SAFETY

While the implied terms of merchantable quality and fitness for purpose considered above in chapter 7 are generally concerned with the quality of the goods supplied, it is undoubtedly the case that if the goods supplied are unsafe they will fail to reach the required qualitative standard and the retailer will be liable for their lack of safety (see 7.3.3.3.2). Where the consumer suffers harm to his person or damage to property other than the defective product itself, such harm is remediable in an action for consequential loss provided it satisfies the contractual principles of remoteness of damage (see 3.2.1.3.2; cf. Waddams (1974) 37 MLR 154).

If the consumer purchases food which cannot be eaten safely (*Heil* v *Hedges* [1951] 1 TLR 512) or if he buys clothes which cause a skin complaint (*Grant* v *Australian Knitting Mills Ltd* [1936] AC 85), the goods concerned are neither of merchantable quality nor fit for the purpose for which they are required. The same applies equally to the packaging in which goods are supplied. Thus if a glass bottle in which a soft drink is supplied causes an injury to the consumer (*Geddling* v *Marsh* [1920] 1 KB 668) it, too, fails to satisfy the Sale of Goods Act 1979, s. 14. Similarly, solid fuel or other material which causes an unexpected explosion, thereby resulting in property damage (*Wilson* v *Rickett Cockrell & Co. Ltd* [1954] 1 QB 598; *Vacwell Engineering Co. Ltd* v *BDH Chemicals Ltd* [1969] 3 All ER 1681), fails to satisfy the requirements of merchantability and fitness.

8.2 MANUFACTURERS' LIABILITY FOR NEGLIGENCE

The manufacturer of a product is expected to exercise reasonable care in the preparation and putting up of his product so as to ensure the safety of the product he puts into circulation.

According to the 'narrow' rule in *Donoghue* v *Stevenson* [1932] AC 562:

> A manufacturer of products, which he sells in such form as to show that he intends them to reach the ultimate consumer in the form in which they left him with no possibility of intermediate examination and with the knowledge that the absence of reasonable care in the preparation or putting up of the products will result in an injury to the consumer's life or property, owes a duty to the consumer to take reasonable care (at p. 599 per Lord Atkin).

The rule is based on the notion of fault which must be proved by the consumer. Accordingly, it is not so favourable to the consumer-purchaser as the implied terms in contracts of supply (see chapter 7) which impose strict liability on the supplier. However, the duty of care owed by the manufacturer of a product does extend to anyone whom he can foresee as likely to be affected by his acts or omissions. Accordingly, a wider range of plaintiffs is embraced by the 'narrow' rule.

8.2.1 Parties to the action

8.2.1.1 Manufacturers The term 'manufacturer' is given a very wide definition with the result that it includes not just the producer of an end-product but also the supplier of a service and a retailer. A better way of stating the rule is that it covers any person who fails to take reasonable care when he puts a product into circulation. Thus it has been held that the rule extends to include retailers (*Andrews* v *Hopkinson* [1957] 1 QB 229) and wholesalers (*Watson* v *Buckley, Osborne, Garrett & Co. Ltd* [1940] 1 All ER 174) who have failed to inspect or test goods, repairers (*Haseldine* v *C.A. Daw*

& Son Ltd [1941] 2 KB 343), assemblers (*Malfroot v Noxal Ltd* (1935) 51 TLR 551) and those who hire products to consumers (*White v John Warwick & Co. Ltd* [1953] 2 All ER 1021). It is also the case that a donor (*Griffiths v Arch Engineering Co. (Newport) Ltd* [1968] 3 All ER 217), the builder of a house (*Dutton v Bognor Regis Urban District Council* [1972] 1 QB 319; cf. *D & F Estates Ltd v Church Commissioners for England* [1988] 2 All ER 992) and possibly a local authority building inspector (*Murphy v Brentwood District Council* [1990] 2 All ER 908) fall within the rule.

8.2.1.2 Consumers Unlike the position of the retailer under the Sale of Goods Act 1979, the manufacturer is liable to any person foreseeably affected by his defective product. There is no requirement that the person affected should have contracted to purchase the product. Accordingly, the rule will extend to cover a purchaser (*Grant v Australian Knitting Mills Ltd* [1936] AC 85), or a borrower (*Griffiths v Arch Engineering Co. (Newport) Ltd* [1968] 3 All ER 217) and members of his family and invited guests. Similarly a manufacturer may also owe a duty of care to a donee (*Donoghue v Stevenson* [1932] AC 562), an employee of the purchaser (*Davie v New Merton Board Mills Ltd* [1959] AC 604), or even a mere bystander (*Stennett v Hancock* [1939] 2 All ER 578).

8.2.2 Products

While the rule in *Donoghue v Stevenson* [1932] AC 562 applied specifically to food and drink, it was not long before it was extended to cover the full range of manufactured products. Thus it has been held to extend to clothing (*Grant v Australian Knitting Mills Ltd* [1936] AC 85), motor cars (*Herschtal v Stewart & Ardern Ltd* [1940] 1 KB 155), cleaning fluids (*Fisher v Harrods Ltd* [1966] 1 Lloyd's Rep 500), hair dyes (*Holmes v Ashford* [1950] 2 All ER 76), buildings (*Dutton v Bognor Regis Urban District Council* [1972] 1 QB 373; cf. *D & F Estates Ltd v Church Commissioners for England* [1988] 2 All ER 992) and the packaging in which products are supplied (*Hill v James Crowe (Cases) Ltd* [1978] 1 All ER 812).

8.2.3 Failure to take reasonable care

The rule requires the manufacturer to take reasonable care. In general, absence of reasonable care can be established by the consumer of the product if he can point to a breakdown in the production process, a defective design, defective instructions for use or a failure to warn of a known danger.

8.2.3.1 The production process An end-product may be defective because of the introduction of impurities which should have been removed before the product was put into circulation (*Donoghue v Stevenson* [1932] AC 562; *Grant v Australian Knitting Mills Ltd* [1936] AC 85). Alternatively, the impurities may have been naturally present and not removed by the manufacturer. Thus, a caterer who leaves a bone in a chicken sandwich may be in breach of his duty of care to the consumer (*Tarling v Nobel* [1966] ALR 189).

In other cases, inadequate construction may be the cause of complaint, whether it be the construction of the product itself (*Walton* v *British Leyland (UK) Ltd* (1978) Product Liability International (August 1980) pp. 156-60) or the packaging in which it is supplied (*Hill* v *James Crowe (Cases) Ltd* [1978] 1 All ER 812). In other cases, the product may be defective if the manufacturer has used inadequate component parts supplied by someone else. In such a case, the manufacturer of the finished product may be liable if there was something he could have done to avoid the presence of the defect in the product, for example, testing it.

8.2.3.2 Design defects   A breakdown in the production process tends to produce 'one-off' defective products, however, defective design produces a whole range of defective products. It may be that a range of products has been designed with the use of insufficiently strong or durable materials or that the whole range creates a health hazard or lacks essential safety features (*Griffiths* v *Arch Engineering Co. (Newport) Ltd* [1968] 3 All ER 217).

The difficulty in design cases is that the manufacturer may be at the forefront of technology, with the result that he may not be aware of the potential of a prototype product for causing injury. In such a case, it cannot be said that the manufacturer has failed to comply with the requirement of reasonable care. The reasonable man who sets the standard of reasonable care could not expect a manufacturer to be aware of a potential for harm if the state of scientific and technological development is not sufficient to allow the defect to be discovered.

8.2.3.3 Warnings and instructions for use   The presence or absence of a warning or instructions is important in two respects. If the manufacturer gives a warning, this may serve to divert liability elsewhere on the ground of causation (see 8.2.5). Alternatively, if the manufacturer is aware of a possible defect in his product or if he is aware that a product may be misused in some way by the consumer, and he fails to give a warning, this may be evidence of negligence on his part (*Andrews* v *Hopkinson* [1957] 1 QB 229).

Even where a warning is issued, it may be inadequate for what it says or fails to say. Thus, a warning which contains false representations may give rise to liability (*Watson* v *Buckley, Osborne, Garrett & Co. Ltd* [1940] 1 All ER 174). Similarly, it is no use to warn that a chemical gives off a harmful vapour when it also has a tendency to react violently in contact with water (*Vacwell Engineering Co. Ltd* v *BDH Chemicals Ltd* [1971] 1 QB 88 and 111).

In order to decide whether a failure to give a warning amounts to negligence on the part of a manufacturer, a number of factors will have to be considered. Generally, it can be said that in the case of known latent defects, a warning is a practicable step to take. Thus it is reasonable to expect a warning to be given with products which possess explosive and flammable qualities. The obviousness of the danger should also be considered. Thus, there would be no need to warn of a danger that all consumers would be expected to know of (*Farr* v *Butters Brothers & Co.* [1932] 2 KB 606).

If the product has been put into circulation before its defectiveness can reasonably be discovered, the manufacturer must apply his knowledge of the defect to future supplies (*Wright* v *Dunlop Rubber Co. Ltd* (1972) 13 KIR 255), but it is doubtful whether the negligence principle requires him to recall products already in circulation (cf. *Walton* v *British Leyland (UK) Ltd* (1978) Product Liability International (August 1980) pp. 156-60).

8.2.4 Proof of Negligence

The burden of proof generally lies on the person seeking to establish a particular point. As a result, the consumer of a defective product must prove that the manufacturer is negligent. This requires proof that the product was defective; that the injury was caused by that defect and that the injuries suffered by the consumer were caused by the manufacturer's failure to exercise reasonable care.

This appears to place a heavy burden on the consumer, however, there is a rule to the effect that the consumer does not have to identify the exact person responsible for the defect in the product (*Grant* v *Australian Knitting Mills Ltd* [1936] AC 85 at p. 101 per Lord Wright). Negligence can be inferred from the fact that the product leaves the manufacturer in a defective state. The effect of this is that the manufacturer is required to show that he was not negligent in using an improper system and that his employees have not been careless. This would appear to amount to something very close to an application of the doctrine of *res ipsa loquitur* (cf. *Donoghue* v *Stevenson* [1932] AC 562 at p. 622 per Lord McMillan) and has been described by one commentator as making the manufacturer an insurer of his own product (Fleming, *The Law of Torts*, 7th ed. (1987), p. 469).

In addition to the doctrine of *res ipsa loquitur*, the Civil Evidence Act 1968, s. 11, provides that the burden of disproving negligence rests on the defendant where he has been convicted of a criminal offence arising out of the facts which also form the basis of the product liability action. It follows that if the manufacturer has committed a criminal offence under the Consumer Protection Act 1987, part II, or the Food Safety Act 1990, the Civil Evidence Act 1968, s. 11 could asssist the consumer in a civil action against the manufacturer.

8.2.5 Causation

The manufacturer's negligence must be the cause of the injury suffered by the consumer. It may be that there is some other independent cause of the consumer's injuries or it may be that someone else is expected to examine the product before it reaches the consumer. In either event, the manufacturer may be relieved of responsibility for the defective product.

8.2.5.1 Alternative cause The manufacturer is only responsible for defects caused by his own conduct. Thus if the defect results from wear and tear or the consumer has used the product in an unforeseeable way or if another person in the chain of distribution is responsible for the defect, the manufacturer may escape liability. But if the product reaches the consumer subject to the same defect as when it left the manufacturer, this will be evidence that the defendant has caused the harm which flows from the defective product.

It is important that the burden of proof rests on the consumer since it may be the case that there are two plausible explanations of the accident, in which case negligence on the part of the manufacturer is not proved. This can be a particular problem in consumer transactions where there is a lengthy chain of distribution and where the product is assembled using components supplied by a number of different manufacturers. In the latter event, it is often difficult to establish which component was the cause of the accident, particularly if the accident does not occur until some time after the finished product was put into circulation (*Evans* v *Triplex Safety Glass Co. Ltd* [1936] 1 All ER 283).

In other cases, the consumer may be the cause of his own injury. Thus if the consumer is aware of a danger, but continues to use the product, he cannot later complain (*Farr* v *Butters Brothers & Co.* [1932] 2 KB 606), although simple knowledge of a defect is not sufficient to divert responsibility if there is nothing the consumer can do to avoid the danger (*Denny* v *Supplies & Transport Co. Ltd* [1950] 2 KB 374).

It can be argued that if the manufacturer has created a danger, he should not be excused merely because another person has failed to remove it. However, in some cases, the manufacturer will have given explicit instructions for the use of his product and if these are ignored, the resultant injury cannot be said to be due to the manufacturer's fault (*Kubach* v *Hollands* [1937] 3 All ER 907).

The problem with a causation argument is that there is no room for apportioning blame. Either the manufacturer is the cause of the consumer's injury or he is not. Since the passing of the Law Reform (Contributory Negligence) Act 1945, the position is different in that the court may now apportion damages by reference to the plaintiff's degree of blameworthiness.

Where the consumer misuses a product in an unforeseeable manner, the manufacturer will not be liable because his responsibility only extends to injury suffered as a result of the contemplated use of his product. In these circumstances, it cannot be said that the product is defective. Had the product been used in the manner intended, no harm would have been suffered (*Aswan Enginering Establishment Co.* v *Lupdine Ltd* [1987] 1 All ER 135 at p. 154 per Lloyd LJ).

8.2.5.2 Intermediate examination In some instances it may be reasonable to expect someone other than the manufacturer to inspect the product before use. Whether or not there is an opportunity to examine goods before they reach the consumer is essentially a matter of causation, since the person who is required to examine and fails to discover a defect in the product can be regarded as the cause of the harm suffered by the consumer.

The fact that someone other than the manufacturer has had an opportunity to examine the goods is not sufficient to exonerate the manufacturer. It must also be shown that the manufacturer can reasonably expect the other person to take up the opportunity to examine (*Griffiths* v *Arch Engineering Co. (Newport) Ltd* [1968] 3 All ER 217 at p. 222 per Chapman J). For this reason, the fact that the consumer could have washed clothing before wearing it for the first time will not excuse the manufacturer if that clothing is likely to cause a skin disease unless washed before use (*Grant* v *Australian Knitting Mills Ltd* [1936] AC 85).

An examination by another person can be expected where the manufacturer has issued a warning that tests should be carried out before use (*Kubach* v *Hollands* [1937] 3 All ER 907; *Holmes* v *Ashford* [1950] 2 All ER 76). In these circumstances the failure by the other person to heed the warning may break the chain of causation, thereby relieving the manufacturer of liability. If the failure of the intermediary to inspect is, itself, negligent, the consumer may be able to sue the intermediary.

8.2.6 Damage

The *Donoghue* v *Stevenson* [1932] AC 562 principle refers to negligence on the part of the manufacturer resulting in an injury to the consumer's life or property. This is consistent with the general rule that tortious rules are concerned with physical damage. Thus the negligence principle compensates the consumer for death, personal injury and property damage.

So far as property damage is concerned, it would appear that if the 'complex structure theory' advanced in *D & F Estates Ltd* v *Church Commissioners for England* [1988] 2 All ER 992 (see 7.5.1) applies to defective products, one part of a complex product may cause damage to another part of the same product. That damage is regarded as damage to other property. The difficulty in these circumstances is that it may be difficult to say when one part of a product is distinct from the rest of the product.

If the defective product causes damage to other property belonging to the consumer, that property damage is actionable in a negligence action on ordinary principles. But, it may be the case that the property damage also results in additional, consequential losses, which may be financial in nature. It appears that these losses are recoverable in a tort action even if they amount to no more than pure economic loss (*Spartan Steel & Alloys Ltd* v *Martin & Co. (Contractors) Ltd* [1973] QB 27; *Muirhead* v *Industrial Tank Specialities Ltd* [1986] QB 507).

In some instances, a defective product may also suffer from qualitative defects as well as those which render it unsafe to use. Accordingly the question has arisen whether the tort of negligence can be used as a means of recovering these economic losses. This matter is considered in more detail in 7.5 in relation to the qualitative defectiveness of a product but it would appear that a successful action by a consumer in this respect is now very unlikely.

8.3 MANUFACTURERS' LIABILITY FOR NEGLIGENCE – MATERIALS FOR CONSIDERATION

It might appear that the 'narrow rule' in *Donoghue* v *Stevenson* [1932] AC 562 is less significant, in terms of manufacturers' liability for defective products, than it once was due to the enactment of the Consumer Protection Act 1987 (see 8.4). However, the 1987 Act does not apply to certain products, such as primary agricultural produce. Moreover, it has no application to economic loss. The tort of negligence may be of some use to the consumer in those circumstances. (But as to economic loss see 7.5).

8.3.1   Failure to take reasonable care

For text see 8.2.3.

Product defects resulting from a failure to take reasonable care may arise for a number of reasons including a breakdown in the production process, design defects and a failure to give an adequate warning of known defects.

Grant v *Australian Knitting Mills Ltd*
[1936] AC 85
Privy Council

LORD WRIGHT at p. 105: The presence of the deleterious chemical in the pants, due to negligence in manufacture, was a hidden and latent defect, just as much as were the remains of the snail in the opaque bottle: it could not be detected by any examination that could reasonably be made. Nothing happened between the making of the garments and their being worn to change their condition. The garments were made by the manufacturers for the purpose of being worn exactly as they were worn in fact by the appellant: it was not contemplated that they should be first washed. It is immaterial that the appellant has a claim in contract against the retailers, because that is a quite independent cause of action, based on different considerations, even though the damage may be the same. Equally irrelevant is any question of liability between the retailers and the manufacturers on the contract of sale between them. The tort liability is independent of any question of contract.

Griffiths v *Arch Engineering Co. (Newport) Ltd*
[1968] 3 All ER 217
Newport Assizes

CHAPMAN J at pp. 220–1: But this machine was not properly set up, and, because it was improperly set up, it was in fact explosive. Why should it not be regarded as a thing dangerous in itself?

The basic questions nowadays are always the same, namely: (i) was there a reasonably foreseeable risk that the person in fact injured would sustain injury if no precautions were taken to guard against that risk?; and (ii) was the defendant so situated that it was incumbent on him to take reasonable precautions to guard against that risk? On question (i), it seems to me clear that the answer must be yes. In the light of the knowledge which I have from a competent engineer, no other answer is possible. And I think that the viewpoint from which the question must be approached is the viewpoint of a reasonably competent engineer when one is dealing with a piece of mechanical engineering. If a person professing to handle or control such a machine does not in fact have the engineering knowledge to enable him to appreciate whether the machine is correctly set up, so much the worse for him. He can hardly be heard to say, 'Although I profess to be an engineer, in fact I am an ignoramus and simply did not know that it was dangerous'. If he does not know, then his duty must, in my view, extend to enquiring so as to find out.

Walton v *British Leyland (UK) Ltd*
(1978) Product Liability International, August 1980, p. 156
Queens Bench Division

WILLIS J at pp. 156–60: The facts and tragic results of the accident which gave rise to this claim are not in dispute and can be shortly stated. Mr and Mrs Victor Walton, the plaintiffs, were on holiday in this country from Australia. During the evening of April 22, 1976 they were travelling northwards on the M1 motorway as passengers in an Austin Allegro motor car, owned and driven by the first plaintiff's brother, Mr Albert Walton. At a point near Newport Pagnell when the car was travelling at 50–60 m.p.h. the *rear nearside wheel* came off, the driver lost control and the vehicle collided with the central crash barrier. . . .

It is now necessary to go back somewhat in the history of the Allegro. A significant alteration in its design compared with e.g. the Maxi and 1300 range was the introduction of tapered roller bearings in the rear hub assembly which had to be adjusted in a different way from earlier models fitted with roller bearings. The Marina was designed in a similar way. This was a bearing designed by the well-known firm of Timken, and it is fitted to a great many makes of car worldwide; it is a tried method and no criticism is sought to be made of Leyland for using it in the Marina and Allegro. Its proper adjustment involves what is technically described as 'end float', to produce a certain amount of play in the wheel which is apparent upon its rotation and rocking after it has been properly adjusted.

According to the documents I have seen, the first rumblings that all was not well with the rear hub assembly of the Allegro had been heard by Leyland by at least October 1973, and probably earlier. On the 17th of that month, Leyland circulated a Product Bulletin to the service managers of (*inter alios*) all their accredited dealers, with a request to pass the information therein to all workshop personnel. This drew attention to the change in the method of adjusting the new rear hub bearing and emphasised the importance of correct end float and the risk of bearings seizing up if enough end float was not provided.

I only propose to select entries to illustrate the scale of the problem as it was presented to Leyland.

In the month to August 22, not less than 10 cases of bearing failures, some with wheels adrift, had been reported from the Continent.

By September 5, a total of 50 cases of failure had been reported to Leyland.

By October 26, no less than '100 cases of wheel adrift to date' are recorded as having been reported, i.e. 50 more than in seven weeks.

In January 1975, three further failures were reported 'thought to be due to corrosion'. A further case from this cause is entered on February 7.

What then of Leyland's responsibility in the matter? In my judgment, it is total. It is not being wise after the event to state that had the larger washer been fitted to Mr Walton's car the accident would, in all probability, not have happened. Over a period of about a year, until October 1974, Leyland were faced with mounting and horrifying evidence of Allegro wheels coming adrift. Any of the cases reported to them could have had fatal results for the occupants of the cars concerned and other road users. They assumed, rightly or wrongly, that apart from isolated cases of corrosion, human error on the part of mechanics was the cause of the bearing failures. The deputy chairman was gravely disturbed; the view of the chief engineer by September 16, 1974 was that the design, not being 'idiot proof', would continuously involve risk, a risk which he thought would have been tolerable had the larger washer been fitted from the start.

Some steps, in my view totally inadequate, were taken to give instructions on the lines of what Dutton Forshaw were recommended to do but only to dealers. Outside this limited safety net were left, in ignorance of the risk to which Leyland knew they were subject, a very large number of Allegro owners, including Mr Walton and his passengers. In my view, the duty of care owed by Leyland to the public was to make a clean breast of the problem and recall all cars which they could, in order that the safety washers could be fitted. I accept, of course, that manufacturers have to steer a course between alarming the public unnecessarily and so damaging the reputation of their products, and observing their duty of care towards those whom they are in a position to protect from dangers of which they and they alone are aware. The duty seems to me to be the higher when they can palliate the worst effects of a failure which, if Leyland's view is right, they could never decisively guard against. They knew the full facts; they saw to it that no one else did. They seriously considered recall and made an estimate of the cost at a figure which seems to me to have been in no way out of proportion to the risks involved. It was decided not to follow this course for commercial reasons. I think this involved a failure to observe their duty to care for the safety of the many who were bound to remain at risk, irrespective of the recommendations made to Leyland dealers and to them alone. . . . It was, in my view, their duty to ensure that all cars still in stock and unsold by the time the washer palliative was proven were fitted with this safety feature before sale. It is sufficient for Mr Walton's purposes that the duty is put no higher than that. This would have saved Mr Walton and his passengers and, in my judgment, Leyland were negligent in having failed to do so.

8.3.2 Causation

For text see 8.2.5.

Even if negligence is established, the manufacturer will not be liable if that negligence is not the cause of the harm suffered by the consumer.

Evans v *Triplex Safety Glass Co. Ltd*
[1936] 1 All ER 283
King's Bench Division

The plaintiff was injured when a car windscreen manufactured by the defendants shattered while the car to which it was fitted was in normal use.

PORTER J at p. 285: The plaintiff must prove negligence and there must not be an opportunity for examination by an intermediate party or an ultimate purchaser. The article must reach the purchaser in the form in which it left the manufacturer. Now in this case I do not propose to make new law or to lay down exact limits and so far as this case is concerned the negligence has been put in this way. . . .

According to the evidence given by the defendants it would need a good deal more than a scratch to cause the glass to disintegrate. They say that it will stand up to ordinary heat and a light blow will not cause disintegration. They point out that the glass is carefully manufactured and properly examined. It is heated up to 600 degrees and they say that this glass would stand up to an ordinary blow from a non-cutting instrument better than ordinary glass and that the usual cause of disintegration was a breakage of the outside surface. In those circumstances am I to infer that properly made glass would never disintegrate without fault?

8.4   THE CONSUMER PROTECTION ACT 1987, PART I

Part I of the Consumer Protection Act 1987 is intended to supplement common law rules (s. 2(6)) by imposing a strict liability regime (s. 2(1)) on the producer of a defective product. It applies to producers rather than manufacturers and the intention is that a producer should insure his product against its potential for causing harm to consumers.

Section 1(1) of the Act states that it shall have effect so as to make such provision as is necessary in order to comply with the product liability Directive (Directive 85/374/EEC (25 July 1985)) and shall be construed accordingly. This wording is important since if problems arise over the interpretaion of the Act, reference may be made to the Directive as an aid to interpretation, particularly in cases where the wording of the 1987 Act differs from the wording of the Directive. Furthermore, since it is for the European Court to determine the scope of the Directive, principles of interpretation may differ from those employed by English courts in relation to domestic statutory provisions (see Whittaker (1989) 105 LQR 125, 130).

8.4.1 Producers

Primary liability under the Consumer Protection Act 1987 in respect of a defective product rests with the producer rather than the retail supplier. In ideal circumstances there would be only one producer of a product and he would be expected to insure his product against its potential for causing harm to the consumer. This avoids the position which obtains under the 'enterprise liability' system whereby all businesses in the chain of supply are potentially liable for the defectiveness of the product and will take out insurance accordingly.

If the Act succeeds in identifying one producer for each product, this may serve to avoid wasteful multiple insurance (see Merkin, *A Guide to the Consumer Protection Act 1987,* p. 10). However, it would appear that under the 1987 Act there is the possibility that more than one producer will be found to exist and where this is the case, potential defendants are jointly and severally liable (s. 2(5)). Furthermore, in limited circumstances, liability may pass down the chain of supply, in which case a number of participants in the supply chain may decide it is in their interests to insure. If this is the case, the effect may be to increase the cost of consumer goods.

Included in the definition of a producer in s. 2(2) and s. 1(2) is the manufacturer of a finished product (s. 1(2)(a)), the manufacturer of a component part (Product Liability Directive, art. 3), the producer of raw materials (s. 1(2)(b)), a person who has subjected a product to an industrial or other process (s. 1(2)(c)), the seller of an own-brand product (s. 2(2)(b)) and a person who imports goods into the EEC from elsewhere (s. 2(2)(c)). In exceptional circumstances where the primary producer cannot be identified, the retailer or any other supplier of the product will be liable (s. 2(3)).

8.4.1.1 Supply In order that a person may be held liable under the Consumer Protection Act 1987, he must have supplied a defective product (s. 4(1)(b)) and that supply must be in the course of a business (s. 46(5) and see 1.1.2). It follows that a supply by one member of a family to another will not be covered by the Act. Also, it is a defence for the producer who does act in the course of a business to show that the product was not supplied so as to make a profit (s. 4(1)(b)). Accordingly, produce made for charitable purposes such as bring and buy sales will fall outside the scope of the Act, provided the 'producer' can satisfy the burden of proof.

It is also important to emphasise that the supply does not need to be directly to the ultimate consumer. It is sufficient that the producer has voluntarily put the product into circulation.

For these purposes, supply includes selling, hiring, lending, supply pursuant to a hire-purchase agreement and a contract for work and materials, exchange for any consideration, provision pursuant to a statutory function, voluntary transfer by way of gift and the provision of a service by which gas or water is made available (s. 46(1)). For the purposes of credit transactions, the dealer and not the finance company is deemed to be the supplier (s. 46(2)).

In the light of this definition, there is little by way of voluntary transfer which will not amount to a supply. However, the transfer or disposal of an interest in land does not bring the supply of the building within the scope of the product liability provisions of the Act (s. 46(4)).

Difficulties may arise in determining who is liable for the supply of a finished product which is defective because of inadequate component parts supplied by another. In these circumstances, the manufacturer of the finished product has supplied the finished product but the component manufacturer has supplied the component part. Ordinarily, the manufacturer of the finished product will be liable in respect of his supply of that product, provided it is covered by the provisions of the Act, but where the finished product is exempt from the provisions of the Act, the manufacturer of that product is not liable for its defectiveness if this results solely from a defect in a component part (s. 1(3)). An exception to this rule exists in the case of a builder who is not liable in respect of his supply of the building (the finished product) but is deemed to be liable for the defectiveness of components used to construct the building (s. 46(3)).

8.4.1.2 Producers other than manufacturers Liability under the Consumer Protection Act 1987 is not confined to those who manufacture a finished product. By virtue of s. 1(2) liability also extends to those who have won or abstracted a raw material and to those who have processed a natural product where the essential characteristics of the product are due to that process. In relation to processing, s. 1(2) is not entirely clear. The product liability Directive proposed that a processor should be liable for a defect arising from initial processing (art. 2). The difficulty created by s. 1(2) is that it will be necessary for the courts to determine the essential characteristics of each product so as to determine whether the provisions of the Act apply.

By virtue of s. 2(2)(b) a person who puts his own name on a product, thereby holding himself out as the producer will be treated as a producer. Typically, this will cover the high street supermarket chain that sells its 'own-brand' products without revealing the identity of the actual producer. One who, in the course of a business, imports a product into the European Community from outside is also deemed to be a producer under s. 2(2)(c).

Where it is not possible to identify the producer or importer of a product, the Act provides for secondary liability on the part of another supplier of the product (s. 2(3)). This person is not necessarily the retail supplier, although in practice the person who supplies to the consumer is most likely to have to accept responsibility, in addition to his liability under the Sale of Goods Act 1979.

In order that a supplier may be liable for harm suffered by the consumer, four requirements must be satisfied. First, the consumer must have asked the supplier to identify the producer (s. 2(3)(a)). Secondly, the request by the consumer must be made within a reasonable time of the occurrence of damage (s. 2(3)(b)). Thirdly, it must have become impracticable for the consumer to identify the actual producer (s. 2(3)(b)). Fourthly, the supplier must have failed, within a reasonable time of the request, to comply with it or to identify the person who supplied him with the product (s. 2(3)(c)). These provisions make it important for retailers to keep records of purchases for some considerable time after initial supply to the consumer, so that they can identify their own supplier, the producer or importer so as to avoid liability themselves.

If the supplier does identify the producer of the product or the person who supplied him with the product, he has satisfied the requirements of s. 2(3) with the result that he will be no longer liable to the consumer. If it happens to be the case that the person or persons identified are insolvent, the consumer may still be left with no practical remedy under the Act.

A difficulty presented by the provisions of s. 2(3) is to determine what is meant by a reasonable time. If the consumer's request is not made within a reasonable time of the occurrence of the damage, the supplier will not be liable. Likewise, if the supplier fails to comply with the consumer's request within a reasonable time of it having been made, he will face liability under s. 2(3).

The Act does not define a reasonable time, but what is reasonable will depend on the circumstances of each case. For the purposes of the initial request by the consumer, it will be necessary to determine when damage occurs. This is defined for the purposes of property damage as the earliest date on which a person having an interest in the property had knowledge of the material facts concerning the loss or damage (s. 5(5)). This knowledge test is further qualified in s. 5(6) and (7) with the result that it amounts to a test of objective discoverability with subjective qualifications. It is necessary to ask, first, whether *this* particular plaintiff was aware of the damage suffered and secondly, whether he would have been reasonable in reaching the particular conclusion he reached.

There is no parallel provision in respect of personal injury, but it would be reasonable to assume that a discoverability test also applies. Thus a consumer who suffers latent personal injury, for example, through consuming pharmaceutical products, will not be deemed aware of the harm he has suffered until it is reasonably discoverable. This may require the consumer's reasonable suspicions to be confirmed through seeking medical advice. In these circumstances, the request will still be made within a reasonable time even though it may come some years after the initial purchase of the product.

8.4.2 Products

The term 'product' is defined in very wide terms in the Consumer Protection Act 1987, subject to a number of specific exclusions. Generally, a product covers any goods, or electricity, and includes any component part or raw material included in another product (s. 1(2)). Furthermore, goods are defined as including substances, growing crops, things comprised in land by virtue of being attached to it, ships, aircraft and vehicles (s. 45(1)). These provisions, if unqualified, mean that virtually anything movable or immovable is capable of being a product for the purposes of the Act. However, the product liability Directive defines a product as something movable, accordingly there will be certain 'products' which do not fall within the scope of the Act. Included amongst these are some building work, some forms of agricultural produce and products governed by the provisions of the Nuclear Installations Act 1965 (Consumer Protection Act 1987, s. 6(8)).

8.4.2.1 Buildings and fittings If a building is supplied by way of the creation or disposal of an interest in land, the supply is not subject to the provisions of the Consumer Protection Act 1987, (s. 46(4)). However, this does not prevent the disposal of goods incorporated in a building from being treated as goods (s. 46(3)). Thus if a building collapses due to a defect in one of the constituent parts employed in its construction, an action under the 1987 Act may lie in respect of personal injury or damage to property other than the building itself.

8.4.2.2 Agricultural produce Article 2 of the product liability Directive also excludes from its definition of a product any primary agricultural produce and game. Primary agricultural products are defined as products of the soil, stock farming and of fishing (Consumer Protection Act 1987, s. 1(2)), excluding products which have undergone initial processing. The intention to include agricultural produce which has been subject to an initial process is given effect in ss. 1(2) and 2(4), but the wording of the Act differs significantly from that of the main body of the Directive in that it refers to an industrial or other process which changes the essential characteristics of the product. On the other hand, the third recital to the Directive refers to an industrial process.

Arguably, an initial process includes crop-spraying with chemicals or hormone treatment of cattle prior to slaughter, which might serve to bring such agricultural produce within the scope of the Act. Whether these could be described as an industrial process is a different matter. Accordingly, it will remain to be seen whether the wording of the Act achieves what appears to have been intended in the Directive. The terms 'initial' and 'industrial' process appear to include large-scale processes such as pre-cooking and packaging, canning and possibly freezing. However, the requirement of s. 1(2) that the process should change the essential characteristics of the produce must also be considered. The fact that a chicken has been frozen, does not change the fact that it is still essentially a chicken. This particular requirement appears nowhere in the Directive, accordingly, the justification for its inclusion is suspect, to say the least.

Where processed food is subject to the provisions of the Act, the processor appears to be strictly liable for the consequences of his process and for defects introduced at an earlier stage. The wording of s. 1(2) is such that if a person has subjected produce to an industrial process which changes its essential characteristics, he is a producer. Accordingly, he is liable for the defectiveness of the product, even though it may not be attributable to his process. Thus, a commercial food processor will be responsible for defects in meat used to make a pie filling where those defects are caused by a farmer giving his cattle infected animal feed.

Why agricultural produce should be exempt from the provisions of the Act and the Directive is difficult to understand. From the point of view of the consumer, food poisoning is a matter of considerable concern. However, the interests of the farming community appear to have been given priority on the grounds that the imposition of liability might place farmers at a competitive disadvantage.

If it transpires that the consumer has been injured as a result of consuming unprocessed food, whether or not he has any remedy will depend on whether he bought the food himself or whether someone in the chain of supply can be said to be at fault. If there is a contractual relationship, the implied terms in the Sale of Goods Act 1979 will apply, in which case liability may pass up the chain of supply and eventually reach the producer of the agricultural produce, who is protected from the application of the provisions of the 1987 Act.

8.4.2.3 Other products   The use of the word 'substance' in the definition of goods in s. 45(1) of the Consumer Protection Act 1987 opens up the possibility of the application of the 1987 Act to a wide range of products. It can be argued that human blood and organs fall within the definition of a product (see Clark (1987) 50 MLR 614), although it would appear that they are not goods for the purposes of the Sale of Goods Act 1979. Furthermore, it may also be necessary to decide whether 'intellectual' products, such as the ideas that go into a book or computer software can be regarded as products (see Whittaker (1989) 105 LQR 125). So far as computer software is concerned, it would appear that a distinction should be made between software which is commercially produced and sold 'off the shelf' and that which has been tailored to the specific needs of an individual client (Prince (1980) 33 Okla L Rev 848 cited in Whittaker op. cit.). In the former case, the product has been placed in the stream of commerce and the producer is in the best position to control risks. In the latter case, the matter is best equated with the liability of a supplier of professional advisory services, which generally only attracts fault-based liability. So far as books are concerned, it is generally the case that information given by the author will result in economic losses which are excluded from the provisions of the 1987 Act (s. 5(1) and (2)). However, the author and the publishers of a book of recipes may need to consider if they have published a product, where reliance on a defective recipe results in food poisoning (see Whittaker op. cit., pp. 133-5). Policy arguments based on protecting freedom of speech may justify a decision not to impose liability, but it may be difficult to raise a freedom of expression issue in relation to a mass-produced recipe book.

8.4.3 Defectiveness

The basis of the producer's liability under the Consumer Protection Act 1987 is that his product is defective. For these purposes, s. 3(1) provides that a product is defective if it is not as safe as persons generally are entitled to expect. Accordingly, the Act applies only to unsafe products and not to useless products. Thus a product which is perfectly safe but useless, such as a firework which contains no explosive, is not covered by the provisions of the 1987 Act. Instead, such complaints about quality are dealt with under the provisions of the Sale of Goods Act 1979 (see 7.3) and the common law rule on negligence, to the extent that qualitative complaints are covered by the rule in *Donoghue* v *Stevenson* [1932] AC 562 (see 7.5).

So far as the incidence of the burden of proof is concerned, the product liability Directive is clear. It states in art. 4 that the consumer must prove damage, defectiveness and a causal link between the two. This having been established, it is then for the producer to prove that he is covered by one of the defences to liability. On the issue of the burden of proof, the 1987 Act is silent, but applying the rule that he who affirms must prove, general principles of English law require the consumer to bear the burden of proving defectiveness.

8.4.3.1 Statutory guidelines as to defectiveness Section 3(2) of the Consumer Protection Act 1987 identifies a number of factors which can be considered in order to determine the safety of a product. These include the marketing of the product, its get-up and the provision of instructions or warnings about use, expectations about use of the product and the time of supply.

8.4.3.1.1 Marketing, get-up etc. Due to s. 3(2)(a) of the Consumer Protection Act 1987 the court may consider the reason for manufacture, the way the product has been advertised, the sort of instructions supplied with the product and any warnings about misuse which may have been supplied by the producer. By including this wide range of factors for consideration, the Act is more complex than the simple requirement of the Directive that the presentation of the product should be considered (art. 6(1)(a)).

It will be important to identify the producer's intended market, as safety considerations will be affected by the group of people targeted. For example, it might be reasonable to expect higher standards where a product is intended for use by children rather than adults. Similarly, food products primarily intended for consumption by the infirm or the aged might be expected to reach higher standards of safety than food aimed at the ordinary adult population who might be less prone to illness.

In the context of marketing, s. 3(2)(a) also allows the court to consider the purposes for which a product has been marketed. This would appear to allow the court to engage in a cost-benefit analysis based on the objective of the producer in putting the product into circulation balanced against the risk it creates. Accordingly, the court may be able to treat as sufficiently safe, a beneficial pharmaceutical product which contains certain inherent safety defects provided the risks to the user are not too substantial.

Also relevant in the context of a defective product is whether or not it has been supplied along with adequate instructions for use and appropriate warnings in respect of known dangers (see generally, MacLeod (1981) 97 LQR

550; Clark [1983] JBL 130). If the producer provides suitable instructions for use or appropriate warnings, this may prevent the product from being defective. It has been seen already that an appropriate warning can relieve the manufacturer of liability under the rule in *Donoghue* v *Stevenson* [1932] AC 562 and a similar regime applies under the 1987 Act. Accordingly, the fact that a producer supplies an inherently dangerous product does not automatically subject him to the strict liability regime of the Act, since he can negative the danger created by his product if he warns the consumer in a suitable fashion.

It may be that considerations similar to those which apply to the liability of an occupier of premises under the Occupiers' Liability Act 1957 may be appropriate to the 1987 Act in relation to the adequacy of warnings about product use. It is clear that a warning will not be of any use unless it enables a visitor to be safe on the occupier's premises (Occupiers' Liability Act 1957, s. 2(4)(a); *White* v *Blackmore* [1972] 3 All ER 158). Furthermore, account is taken of the fact that children are less likely to heed warnings than adults. Thus in the context of the 1987 Act, it will need to be considered whether a product is intended to be used by a supervised or an unsupervised child in determining whether the producer's warning suffices to render the product safe for its expected use.

8.4.3.1.2 Expectations about use By virtue of s. 3(2)(b) of the Consumer Protection Act 1987 the court may also consider what may reasonably be expected to be done with or in relation to the product in deciding whether it is defective. The Act does not specify whose reasonable expectations should be considered, but since s. 3(1) refers to the expectations about safety of persons generally, it can be assumed that all relevant expectations can be taken into account. These would appear to include the expectations of the producer and the consumer.

It has been seen that in the context of the common law negligence liability of a manufacturer, a product can be defective due to a breakdown in the production process, a design defect and a failure to give adequate warnings about use (see 8.2.3). In the case of a production process defect which renders a product unsafe, it is likely that the product will be defective under the 1987 Act since it fails to reach the standard expected by the producer himself. Design defects present a different problem, since a whole range of products is produced according to the producer's intentions. Deciding whether the end-product satisfies the reasonable expectations of persons generally in such a case may be difficult, since persons generally may not have any expectations at all until they have had a chance to test the product.

It would appear that in relation to design defects, a test similar to the 'expectations' test in s. 3(2)(b) has been abandoned in favour of a cost-benefit test similar to the approach adopted at common law in deciding whether there has been a breach of the duty of care. Factors considered by the courts include the difficulty or otherwise of eliminating the defect, balanced against the benefits to society which would have been lost had introduction of the product been delayed pending further tests etc. (see *Barker* v *Lull Engineering Co. Inc.* (1978) 573 P 2d 443).

Another relevant factor arising under the heading of expectations about use is that the court may consider whether the consumer has used the product in an unexpected fashion for which the product was not intended. For example, it is unlikely that a producer would be held responsible for the death of a poodle warmed in a microwave oven on a cold day. Similarly the manufacturer of industrial alcohol clearly labelled as a fuel would not be responsible for its use as the base for a party cocktail (*Barnes* v *Litton Industrial Products* (1976) 409 F Supp 1353). In less extreme cases, the producer would be well advised to issue a warning about the use of his product, if there is a danger that it might be misused. For example, it is common to see warnings concerning inhalation on solvent-based products such as certain types of glue and cigarette lighter fluid. The giving of the warning should serve to exonerate the producer, but it could also be argued that, even in the absence of a warning, the product has not been used in the manner expected by the producer in particular and by persons generally.

8.4.3.1.3 Time of supply   Section 3(2)(c) of the Consumer Protection Act 1987 specifies the time of supply as a relevant factor in determining when a product is defective. It would appear that this provision protects the producer against later developments in terms of product safety. Thus it is further provided by the concluding words of s. 3(2) that nothing is to be inferred from the fact that the safety of later products is greater than that of the product supplied by the producer in question.

The time of supply is also relevant in relation to the 'shelf-life' of certain products. It is quite possible that certain products will remain unsold for a considerable period of time. In these circumstances, the producer is judged according to the standards of safety which prevailed at the time he put the product into circulation, not when the product is eventually supplied to the consumer.

8.4.3.2 Defects which do not attract liability under the Act

8.4.3.2.1 Compliance with Community or statutory obligations   Where proceedings are brought against a person under the Consumer Protection Act 1987, he may plead compliance with a mandatory requirement as a defence (s. 4(1)(a)). Thus if the goods supplied comply with the requirements of a Community obligation or a domestic statutory provision, an action against the producer will fail.

8.4.3.2.2 Defects arising after the date of supply   Since the producer is only responsible for the defectiveness of the product at the time he put it into circulation, he will have a defence if the defect in the product only came about after the time of supply (Consumer Protection Act 1987, s. 4(1)(d); 4(2)(a)). Thus if the defect arises due to wear and tear or misuse by the consumer or some other person, the producer may be able to rely on this defence. Where the producer seeks to rely on this defence, he bears the burden of proving that the product was not defective at the time he put it into circulation.

It is important to emphasise that the defence does not apply to defects which existed in the product at the time of supply but which did not come to the attention of the producer until a later date. In these circumstances, the producer might be able to rely on the scientific and technological development defence (see 8.4.3.2.3).

Where the defendant is a supplier liable under s. 2(3) (see 8.4.1.2) he will not be responsible for defects which came about after the last date on which the product was supplied by a producer or importer (s. 4(2)(b)).

8.4.3.2.3 *Scientific and technological development*

It is a defence under s. 4(1)(e) for the defendant to show that the state of scientific and technological development at the time the product was put into circulation was not such that a producer of a product of the same description as the product in question might be expected to have discovered the defect if it had existed in his products while they were under his control.

The wording of the defence in s. 4(1)(e) does not exactly follow the wording employed in art. 7(e) of the product liability Directive with the result that it can be argued that the 1987 Act provides for a much wider defence than was envisaged in the Directive (see Merkin, *A Guide to The Consumer Protection Act 1987*, pp. 32-4). If this is the case, the United Kingdom is in breach of the EEC Treaty, and the Directive rather than the 1987 Act will be the relevant law on this matter.

The defence is one which member States were permitted to include if they wished. Accordingly, there is not a consistent practice throughout the Community. One possible consequence of this is that those States which have chosen to include the defence may become testing grounds for newly developed products, and that supplies to States which have not made use of the defence will be delayed until trials have shown that the product is safe for use.

The principal arguments employed to justify the inclusion of the defence were that without it research into the development of new products might be stifled and that the potential liability of producers might be so great as to render their activities uninsurable.

The effect of the defence is that if a product is still on trial and that a defect in it is not discoverable at the time of its being put into circulation, the defendant will not be liable. The main problem is to identify what is discoverable, and it is this that lies at the root of the wording of s. 4(1)(e). The argument which convinced the UK government to adopt the more detailed wording of s. 4(1)(e) rather than that of the Directive is that the defect must be reasonably discoverable. It would not be reasonable to make a defendant liable if research which had identified a possible defect was not widely available (see Newdick [1988] C LJ 455).

If the approach adopted in s. 4(1)(e) is correct, products developed with the use of new technology are subject to little more than a fault-based regime since the producer will only be liable if he has failed to take care in keeping abreast of reasonably discoverable relevant research, although the burden of proof, in this respect, will rest on the producer.

8.4.3.2.4 Contributory negligence The Law Reform (Contributory Negligence) Act 1945 applies to an action brought under part I of the Consumer Protection Act 1987, (s. 6(4) of the 1987 Act). Accordingly, it will be open to the court to apportion the plaintiff's damages having regard to his responsibility for the harm he has suffered. If liability under the 1987 Act is viewed as strict, there might be a problem in comparing the blameworthy conduct of the plaintiff against the apparently non-blameworthy conduct of the defendant. However, in some instances under the Act the defendant's liability will be effectively based on fault (see 8.4.3.2.3). Even if the defendant's liability is said to be strict, the courts have faced similar problems in relation to actions for breach of a statutory duty and problems are unlikely to arise.

8.4.4 Causation

The essential requirements of the Consumer Protection Act 1987 are that the producer has put the product into circulation, that the product is defective and that the defectiveness of the product has caused damage within the meaning of the Act. While it is the case that fault on the part of the producer does not have to be proved, the problematic issue of causation still remains and is subject to ordinary principles.

It is clear from the wording of s. 2(1) that the consumer bears the onus of proving that the defect in the product wholly or partly caused the damage he complains of. The wording of s. 2(1) appears to solve one of the problems faced by the consumer in a negligence action, namely, what is the cause of damage resulting partly from a defect in the finished product and partly from a defect in a component used in its manufacture. It is sufficient that a producer is partly responsible for the damage suffered.

While a blameworthy consumer may have his damages reduced by virtue of an application of the contributory negligence 'defence', it is also the case that the 'extremely blameworthy' consumer may be regarded as the cause of the harm he suffers. For example, a person who uses a microwave oven to warm a pet poodle on a cold day can hardly be heard to complain. In these circumstances, the producer may be able to escape liability on the grounds of causation. The issue of causation in this type of case is closely bound up with the meaning of defectiveness considered above. For example, even without an appropriate warning on the microwave oven, it is probably fair to assume that persons generally would not reasonably expect to use the appliance in that way. In these circumstances, the producer can argue either that he is not the cause of the harm suffered or that the appliance is not defective.

8.4.5 Damage

The losses recoverable under the Consumer Protection Act 1987 are fairly clearly defined. By virtue of s. 5(1) damage includes death or personal injury and any loss of or damage to property, including land.

8.4.5.1 Death and personal injury   So far as death and personal injury are concerned, the main deficiency of the Act, if it can be considered such, is that it does not specify how damages are to be assessed. It may be assumed that ordinary principles of the law of tort apply, in which case the plaintiff will be able to recover consequential losses such as lost earnings, and that an award may be made in respect of pain and suffering (see product liability Directive, art. 9).

8.4.5.2 Property damage   Section 5(3) qualifies the meaning of property damage for the purposes of the Act. It is provided that a producer will not be liable for damage to property which at the time of damage is not intended for private use, occupation or consumption (s. 5(3)(a)). Furthermore, the person suffering the damage must also intend to put the property mainly to private use, occupation or consumption (s. 5(3)(b)).

The effect of this is that a producer will not be liable for damage to business property. The provisions of s. 5(3)(b) mean that the plaintiff must intend to put the property to private use, accordingly, property used by a company in the course of business will be excluded. However it is possible under s. 5(3) for a person to use property for both business and private purposes and so long as it is mainly put to private use, it will be covered by the Act.

In respect of trivial property damage, it is provided that no award of damages shall be made where the claim is for an amount less than £275.

As a result of the definition of damage, economic loss is not recoverable, except insofar as consequential economic losses are recoverable if ordinary tort principles apply. Furthermore, s. 5(2) specifically provides that damage to or loss of the defective product itself (or anything supplied with or comprised in it) is not remediable (s. 5(2)). This might mean that the damage caused by the explosion of a defective battery fitted to a car manufactured by the defendant is not remediable. However, that conclusion might be questioned on the ground that the battery was not comprised in the car.

8.4.6 Limitation of actions

The limitation period for the purposes of an action under part I of the Consumer Protection Act 1987 runs for three years from the date on which damage was caused by the defective product or for three years from the date on which the damage could reasonably have been discovered (Limitation Act 1980, s. 11A(4)).

The first of these alternatives will apply to patent damage. In the case of latent damage, it is quite possible that the normal three-year period will have expired before the consumer is aware that he has suffered any damage at all. Accordingly, the discoverability test is more likely to be applied in these circumstances.

By virtue of the Limitation Act 1980, s. 11A(3), there is a long-stop on the liability of the producer which runs for 10 years from the date on which the product was first put into circulation. Accordingly, if a product first put into circulation in 1985 causes undetectable damage in 1986, which becomes discoverable by the consumer in 1996, the consumer will not be permitted to commence his action because of the long-stop provision.

Where the action is one for personal injuries, the court has a discretion under the Limitation Act 1980, s. 33, to extend the time during which an action may be commenced. This discretion is subject to the long-stop provision in s. 11A(3) with the result that s. 33 cannot be used to extend the time available to the consumer beyond 10 years from the time the product was put into circulation.

8.5   CONSUMER PROTECTION ACT 1987, PART I – MATERIALS FOR CONSIDERATION

For text see 8.4.

Consumer Protection Act 1987

PART I PRODUCT LIABILITY

1.   Purpose and construction of part I

(1)   This part shall have effect for the purpose of making such provision as is necessary in order to comply with the product liability Directive and shall be construed accordingly.

(2)   In this part, except insofar as the context otherwise requires—

'agricultural produce' means any produce of the soil, of stock-farming or of fisheries;

'dependant' and 'relative' have the same meaning as they have in, respectively, the Fatal Accidents Act 1976 and the Damages (Scotland) Act 1976;

'producer', in relation to a product, means—

(a)   the person who manufactured it;

(b)   in the case of a substance which has not been manufactured but has been won or abstracted, the person who won or abstracted it;

(c)   in the case of a product which has not been manufactured, won or abstracted but essential characteristics of which are attributable to an industrial or other process having been carried out (for example, in relation to agricultural produce), the person who carried out that process;

'product' means any goods or electricity and (subject to subsection (3) below) includes a product which is comprised in another product, whether by virtue of being a component part or raw material or otherwise; and

'the product liability Directive' means the Directive of the Council of the European Communities, dated 25th July 1985, (No. 85/374/EEC) on the approximation of the laws, regulations and administrative provisions of the member States concerning liability for defective products.

(3)   For the purposes of this part a person who supplies any product in which products are comprised, whether by virtue of being component parts or raw materials or otherwise, shall not be treated by reason only of his supply of that product as supplying any of the products so comprised.

2.   Liability for defective products

(1)   Subject to the following provisions of this part, where any damage is caused wholly or partly by a defect in a product, every person to whom subsection (2) below applies shall be liable for the damage.

(2)   This subsection applies to—

(a)   the producer of the product;

(b)   any person who, by putting his name on the product or using a trade mark or other distinguishing mark in relation to the product, has held himself out to be the producer of the product;

(c)   any person who has imported the product into a member State from a place outside the member States in order, in the course of any business of his, to supply it to another.

(3)   Subject as aforesaid, where any damage is caused wholly or partly by a defect in a product, any person who supplied the product (whether to the person who suffered the damage, to the producer of any product in which the product in question is comprised or to any other person) shall be liable for the damage if—

(a)   the person who suffered the damage requests the supplier to identify one or more of the persons (whether still in existence or not) to whom subsection (2) above applies in relation to the product;

(b)   that request is made within a reasonable period after the damage occurs and at a time when it is not reasonably practicable for the person making the request to identify all those persons; and

(c)   the supplier fails, within a reasonable period after receiving the request, either to comply with the request or to identify the person who supplied the product to him.

(4)   Neither subsection (2) nor subsection (3) above shall apply to a person in respect of any defect in any game or agricultural produce if the only supply of the game or produce by that person to another was at a time when it had not undergone an industrial process.

(5)   Where two or more persons are liable by virtue of this Part for the same damage, their liability shall be joint and several.

(6)   This section shall be without prejudice to any liability arising otherwise than by virtue of this part.

3.   Meaning of 'defect'

(1)   Subject to the following provisions of the section, there is a defect in a product for the purposes of this part if the safety of the product is not such as persons generally are entitled to expect; and for those purposes 'safety', in relation to a product, shall include safety with respect to products comprised in that product and safety in the context of risks of damage to property, as well as in the context of risks of death or personal injury.

(2)   In determining for the purposes of subsection (1) above what persons generally are entitled to expect in relation to a product all the circumstances shall be taken into account, including—

(a)   the manner in which, and purposes for which, the product has been marketed, its get-up, the use of any mark in relation to the product and any instructions for, or warnings with respect to, doing or refraining from doing anything with or in relation to the product;

(b)   what might reasonably be expected to be done with or in relation to the product; and

(c)   the time when the product was supplied by its producer to another;

and nothing in this section shall require a defect to be inferred from the fact alone that the safety of a product which is supplied after that time is greater than the safety of the product in question.

4.   Defences

(1)   In any civil proceedings by virtue of this part against any person ('the person proceeded against') in respect of a defect in a product it shall be a defence for him to show—

    (a)   that the defect is attributable to compliance with any requirement imposed by or under any enactment or with any Community obligation; or

    (b)   that the person proceeded against did not at any time supply the product to another; or

    (c)   that the following conditions are satisfied, that is to say—

      (i)   that the only supply of the product to another by the person proceeded against was otherwise than in the course of a business of that person's; and

      (ii)   that section 2(2) above does not apply to that person or applies to him by virtue only of things done otherwise than with a view to profit; or

    (d)   that the defect did not exist in the product at the relevant time; or

    (e)   that the state of scientific and technical knowledge at the relevant time was not such that a producer of products of the same description as the product in question might be expected to have discovered the defect if it had existed in his products while they were under his control; or

    (f)   that the defect—

      (i)   constituted a defect in a product ('the subsequent product') in which the product in question had been comprised; and

      (ii)   was wholly attributable to the design of the subsequent product or to compliance by the producer of the product in question with instructions given by the producer of the subsequent product.

    (2)   In this section 'the relevant time', in relation to electricity, means the time at which it was generated, being a time before it was transmitted or distributed, and in relation to any other product, means—

    (a)   if the person proceeded against is a person to whom subsection (2) of section 2 above applies in relation to the product, the time when he supplied the product to another;

    (b)   if that subsection does not apply to that person in relation to the product, the time when the product was last supplied by a person to whom that subsection does apply in relation to the product.

5. Damage giving rise to liability

    (1)   Subject to the following provisions of this section, in this part 'damage' means death or personal injury or any loss of or damage to any property (including land).

    (2)   A person shall not be liable under section 2 above in respect of any defect in a product for the loss of or any damage to the product itself or for the loss of or any damage to the whole or any part of any product which has been supplied with the product in question comprised in it.

    (3)   A person shall not be liable under section 2 above for any loss of or damage to any property which, at the time it is lost or damaged, is not—

    (a)   of a description of property ordinarily intended for private use, occupation or consumption; and

    (b)   intended by the person suffering the loss or damage mainly for his own private use, occupation or consumption.

    (4)   No damages shall be awarded to any person by virtue of this part in respect of any loss of or damage to any property if the amount which would fall to be so awarded to that person, apart from this subsection and any liability for interest, does not exceed £275.

    (5)   In determining for the purposes of this part who has suffered any loss of or damage to property and when any such loss or damage occurred, the loss or damage shall be regarded as having occurred at the earliest time at which a person with an interest in the property had knowledge of the material facts about the loss or damage.

(6)   For the purposes of subsection (5) above the material facts about any loss of or damage to any property are such facts about the loss or damage as would lead a reasonable person with an interest in the property to consider the loss or damage sufficiently serious to justify his instituting proceedings for damages against a defendant who did not dispute liability and was able to satisfy a judgment.

(7)   For the purposes of subsection (5) above a person's knowledge includes knowledge which he might reasonably have been expected to acquire—

(a)   from facts observable or ascertainable by him; or

(b)   from facts ascertainable by him with the help of appropriate expert advice which it is reasonable for him to seek;

but a person shall not be taken by virtue of this subsection to have knowledge of a fact ascertainable by him only with the help of expert advice unless he has failed to take all reasonable steps to obtain (and, where appropriate, to act on) that advice.

6.   Application of certain enactments etc.
. . .

(4)   Where any damage is caused partly by a defect in a product and partly by the fault of the person suffering the damage, the Law Reform (Contributory Negligence) Act 1945 and section 5 of the Fatal Accidents Act 1976 (contributory negligence) shall have effect as if the defect were the fault of every person liable by virtue of this part for the damage caused by the defect.

(5)   In subsection (4) above 'fault' has the same meaning as in the said Act of 1945.

(7)   It is hereby declared that liability by virtue of this part is to be treated as liability in tort for the purposes of any enactment conferring jurisdiction on any court with respect to any matter. . . .

Compare the Consumer Protection Act 1987 Part I with the provisions of the EC Directive on Product Liability (Directive 85/374/EEC, 25 July 1985).

Article 1

The producer shall be liable for damage caused by a defect in his product.

Article 2

For the purpose of this Directive 'product' means all movables, with the exception of primary agricultural products and game, even though incorporated into another movable or into an immovable. 'Primary agricultural products' means the products of the soil, of stock-farming and of fisheries, excluding products which have undergone initial processing. 'Product' includes electricity.

Article 3

1.   'Producer' means the manufacturer of a finished product, the producer of any raw material or the manufacturer of a component part and any person who, by putting his name, trade mark or other distinguishing feature on the product presents himself as its producer.

2.   Without prejudice to the liability of the producer, any person who imports into the Community a product for sale, hire, leasing or any form of distribution in the course of his business shall be deemed to be a producer within the meaning of this Directive and shall be responsible as a producer.

3.   Where the producer of the product cannot be identified, each supplier of the product shall be treated as its producer unless he informs the injured person, within a reasonable time, of the identity of the producer or of the person who supplied him with

the product. The same shall apply, in the case of an imported product, if this product does not indicate the identity of the importer referred to in paragraph 2, even if the name of the producer is indicated.

Article 4
The injured person shall be required to prove the damage, the defect and the causal relationship between defect and damage.

Article 5
Where, as a result of the provisions of this Directive, two or more persons are liable for the same damage, they shall be liable jointly and severally, without prejudice to the provisions of national law concerning the rights of contribution or recourse.

Article 6
1.   A product is defective when it does not provide the safety which a person is entitled to expect, taking all circumstances into account, including:
  (a)   the presentation of the product;
  (b)   the use to which it could reasonably be expected that the product would be put;
  (c)   the time when the product was put into circulation.

2.   A product shall not be considered defective for the sole reason that a better product is subsequently put into circulation.

Article 7
The producer shall not be liable as a result of this Directive if he proves:
  (a)   that he did not put the product into circulation; or
  (b)   that, having regard to the circumstances, it is probable that the defect which caused the damage did not exist at the time when the product was put into circulation by him or that this defect came into being afterwards; or
  (c)   that the product was neither manufactured by him for sale or any form of distribution for economic purpose nor manufactured or distributed by him in the course of his business; or
  (d)   that the defect is due to compliance of the product with mandatory regulations issued by the public authorities; or
  (e)   that the state of scientific and technical knowledge at the time when he put the product into circulation was not such as to enable the existence of the defect to be discovered; or
  (f)   in the case of a manufacturer of a component, that the defect is attributable to the design of the product in which the component has been fitted or to the instructions given by the manufacturer of the product.

Article 8
1.   Without prejudice to the provisions of national law concerning the right of contribution or recourse, the liability of the producer shall not be reduced when the damage is caused both by a defect in the product and by the act or omission of a third party.
2.   The liability of the producer may be reduced or disallowed when, having regard to all the circumstances, the damage is caused both by a defect in the product and by the fault of the injured person or any person for whom the injured person is responsible.

Article 9

For the purpose of Article 1, 'damage' means:

(a)   damage caused by death or by personal injuries;

(b)   damage to, or destruction of, any item of property other than the defective product itself, with a lower threshold of 500 ECU, provided that the item of property:

(i)   is of a type ordinarily intended for private use or consumption, and

(ii)   was used by the injured person mainly for his own private use or consumption.

This Article shall be without prejudice to national provisions relating to non-material damage.

Article 10

1.   Member States shall provide in their legislation that a limitation period of three years shall apply to proceedings for the recovery of damages as provided for in this Directive. The limitation period shall begin to run from the day on which the plaintiff became aware, or should reasonably have become aware, of the damage, the defect and the identity of the producer.

2.   The laws of Members States regulating suspension or interruption of the limitation period shall not be affected by this Directive.

Article 11

Member States shall provide in their legislation that the rights conferred upon the injured person pursuant to this Directive shall be extinguished upon the expiry of a period of 10 years from the date on which the producer put into circulation the actual product which caused the damage, unless the injured person has in the meantime instituted proceedings against the producer.

Article 12

The liability of the producer arising from this Directive may not, in relation to the injured person, be limited or excluded by a provision limiting his liability or exempting him from liability.

Article 13

This Directive shall not affect any rights which an injured person may have according to the rules of the law of contractual or non-contractual liability or a special liability system existing at the moment when this Directive is notified.

Article 14

This Directive shall not apply to injury or damage arising from nuclear accidents and covered by international conventions ratified by the Member States.

Article 15

1.   Each Member State may:

(a)   by way of derogation from Article 2, provide in its legislation that within the meaning of Article 1 of this Directive 'product' also means primary agricultural products and game;

(b)   by way of derogation from Article 7(e), maintain or, subject to the procedure set out in paragraph 2 of this Article, provide in this legislation that the producer shall be liable even if he proves that the state of scientific and technical knowledge at the time when he put the product into circulation was not such as to enable the existence of a defect to be discovered.

2.   A Member State wishing to introduce the measure specified in paragraph 1(b) shall communicate the test of the proposed measure to the Commission. The Commission shall inform the other Member States thereof.

The Member State concerned shall hold the proposed measure in abeyance for nine months after the Commission is informed and provided that in the meantime the Commission has not submitted to the Council a proposal amending this Directive on the relevant matter. However, if within three months of receiving the said information, the Commission does not advise the Member State concerned that it intends submitting such a proposal to the Council, the Member State may take the proposed measure immediately.

If the Commission does submit to the Council such a proposal amending this Directive within the aforementioned nine months, the Member State concerned shall hold the proposed measure in abeyance for a further period of 18 months from the date on which the proposal is submitted.

3.   Ten years after the date of notification of this Directive, the Commission shall submit to the Council a report on the effect that rulings by the courts as to the application of Article 7(e) and of paragraph 1(b) of this Article have on consumer protection and the functioning of the common market. In the light of this report the Council, acting on a proposal from the Commission and pursuant to the terms of Article 100 of the Treaty, shall decide whether to repeal Article 7(e).

Article 16

1.   Any Member State may provide that a producer's total liability for damage resulting from a death or personal injury and caused by identical items with the same defect shall be limited to an amount which may not be less than 70 million ECU.

2.   Ten years after the date of notification of this Directive, the Commission shall submit to the Council a report on the effect on consumer protection and the functioning of the common market of the implementation of the financial limit on liability by those Member States which have used the option provided for in paragraph 1. In the light of this report the Council, acting on a proposal from the Commission and pursuant to the terms of Article 100 of the Treaty, shall decide whether to repeal paragraph 1.

Article 17

This Directive shall not apply to products put into circulation before the date on which the provisions referred to in Article 19 enter into force.

Article 18

1.   For the purposes of this Directive, the ECU shall be that defined by Regulation (EEC) No. 3180/78, as amended by Regulation (EEC) No. 2626/84. The equivalent in national currency shall initially be calculated at the rate obtaining on the date of adoption of this Directive.

2.   Every five years the Council, acting on a proposal from the Commission, shall examine and, if need be, revise the amounts in this Directive, in the light of economic and monetary trends in the Community.

Article 19

1.   Member States shall bring into force, not later than three years from the date of notification of this Directive, the laws, regulations and administrative provisions necessary to comply with this Directive. They shall forthwith inform the Commission thereof.

2.   The procedure set out in Article 15(2) shall apply from the date of notification of this Directive.

8.6   BREACH OF STATUTORY DUTY

Consumer protection legislation makes wide-ranging use of the strict liability criminal offence in order to regulate trading conduct. Ordinarily, such regulations are regarded as deterrent in effect or at least to encourage businesses to seek to achieve the highest trading standards possible (see chapter 9). However, it may be the case that the breach of a statutory duty also gives rise to a civil action for damages in tort where the consumer can show that he has suffered particular damage as a result of the trader's breach of statutory duty.

8.6.1   The intention of Parliament

In relation to product safety, there are two principal statutes which impose duties on producers and retailers, namely the Food Safety Act 1990 and the Consumer Protection Act 1987, part II. In order to determine whether these statutes allow a civil action for breach of statutory duty, the courts must ascertain the intention of Parliament in this respect. This task is simple where Parliament has expressed its intention, as in the case of the Consumer Protection Act 1987, which provides that an action for breach of statutory duty will lie in the event of the breach of a safety regulation (s. 41(1)). However, the matter is more difficult where no such intention has been expressed, as is the case with the Food Safety Act 1990.

Factors which the courts will consider in seeking to identify the intention of Parliament include the size of the class of people protected by the action for breach of statutory duty, the nature of the penalty provided for by the statute and whether there is an adequate alternative remedy available to the consumer.

If the class of people to whom the action for breach of statutory duty might extend is particularly large, it becomes less likely that the court will find in favour of the plaintiff. Consumers may be regarded as too wide a class of people to be afforded the luxury of a further cause of action in civil law. It is generally thought that if a statutory provision is passed for the protection of the general public and not for the protection of a more closely defined group of people, no action for breach of statutory duty will lie (*Solomons* v *R. Gertzenstein* [1954] 2 QB 243). However, it has also been argued that it would be strange if an unimportant duty owed to a defined group of people could be enforced by civil action when a comparatively more important duty owed to persons generally could not be so enforced (*Phillips* v *Britannia Laundry Ltd* [1923] 2 KB 832 at p. 841 per Atkin LJ). So far as food legislation is concerned, the courts have generally taken the view that consumers of food constitute such a large group of people that they can be identified with the whole community only (*Buckley* v *La Reserve* [1959] Crim LR 451).

The availability of alternative remedies has also proved to be a stumbling-block for the consumer seeking to establish a civil remedy for breach of statutory duties in respect of food. The judicial view appears to be that most breaches of food safety regulations will also give rise to an available civil action under the Sale of Goods Act 1979, with the result that there is no need to create a further civil action (*Square* v *Model Farm Dairies (Bournemouth) Ltd* [1939] 2 KB 365). However, it should be observed that the existence of common law duties on the part of employers has not prevented the courts from finding new civil actions for breach of statutory duty.

8.6.2   The Consumer Protection Act 1987, part II

The Consumer Protection Act 1987 makes it clear that a civil action will lie for breach of a duty imposed by product safety regulations (s. 41(1)). Part II of the Act (see chapter 9) creates a range of obligations which may be based on regulations in respect of the safety of goods generally or particular products (s. 11(1)). The Act also imposes a general safety requirement (s. 10(1)) and allows for the service of prohibition notices and notices to warn (s. 13(1)) and suspension notices (s. 14(1)). Failure to comply with any of these amounts to the commission of a criminal offence, but it is only in respect of the breach of a safety regulation that a civil action for breach of statutory duty will lie (s. 41(1)). No such civil action will be available in respect of the breach of the general safety requirement, a prohibition notice, a notice to warn or a suspension notice (s. 41(2)).

8.6.3   The incidents of an action for breach of statutory duty

In any action for breach of statutory duty, it must be shown that the duty is owed to the plaintiff. Section 41(1) of the Consumer Protection Act 1987 provides that the duty is owed by the person in breach to any other person who may be affected by a contravention of the safety regulation. The consumer must also be able to show that he has been affected by the failure to comply with the safety regulation and in particular that the injury he has suffered is one which the regulation was intended to guard against. Thus, economic losses suffered by a retailer would not be remediable because the Act is concerned with the safety of goods and because the retailer is not a consumer. However, on the latter point the wording of s. 41(1) may be wide enough to cover a physically injured retailer as he could be regarded as a person affected by a contravention of the safety regulation. Other relevant factors in an action for breach of statutory duty are whether there has been a breach of the duty and whether that breach has caused the injury complained of. Important in this last respect might be consumer misuse of a product supplied in breach of safety regulations.

Some actions for breach of statutory duty create torts of strict liability whereas others are construed by the courts as giving rise to fault-based liability on the part of the defendant. The fact that the 1987 Act provides for a due diligence defence (s. 39(1)) might suggest that a breach of safety regulations would be construed as giving rise to fault-based liability only. In these circumstances, it would be for the defendant to discharge the onus of proof on the no-negligence issue.

CHAPTER NINE

Product Quality and Safety Under the Criminal Law

9.1 PRODUCT QUALITY AND SAFETY GENERALLY

Civil law rules in respect of product safety form an important part of consumer protection law, but they cannot satisfy all the requirements of a modern consumer society. In particular, while rules of the law of contract and the law of tort can provide consumers with valuable individual rights in respect of harm caused by one-off defects, the criminal law performs an important preventative role. On the basis that prevention is better than cure, a range of statutes have attempted to introduce broad standards of safety in respect of consumer goods generally and specific items such as food, medicines and poisons.

These broad statutory standards apply mainly to the matter of safety, and the enforcement of the law in respect of qualitative defects in consumer products is left to the individual consumer. However, where food and medicines are concerned, Parliament has chosen to legislate with the result that it is a criminal offence for a person to sell food or medicinal products which are not of the nature or quality demanded by the consumer (Medicines Act 1968, s. 64; Food Safety Act 1990, s. 14). Furthermore, in relation to food, the Food Safety Act 1990, ss. 16–19, permits regulations to be made in respect of the quality and composition of specified food items.

9.1.1 Rationales for consumer safety legislation

No one would dispute the need for a regime which seeks to promote the safety of consumer goods, but it is necessary to consider how far such a regime should go and what it should seek to achieve. It might be possible to aim for absolute safety, but some would argue that the cost of doing so would be prohibitive. As an alternative, Parliament could seek an acceptable standard of safety, whereby the benefits of regulation do not exceed the costs imposed by it. (see *Safety of Goods* (Cmnd 9302, 1984), para. 10; *Building Businesses . . . not Barriers* (Cmnd 9794,1986)). For example, excessive safety measures could easily make some consumer goods so expensive that they fall out of the reach of poorer consumers. Enforcement costs also have to be considered. A regime enforced by means of the criminal law or through some administrative agency has to be paid for and the more elaborate the scheme, the greater those enforcement costs are likely to be.

Generally, certain risks of harm may be viewed more seriously than others. Thus, in balancing the benefits created by a particular activity against the costs it creates, it is necessary to place a value on those social costs. Some risks, such as death and serious bodily injury may be regarded as so great that a substantial level of intervention is justified even where the cost of compliance is also great.

As in other areas of consumer law, the issue of consumer information is a primary consideration in regard to product safety. In some instances, the consumer will be unaware of any risk at all and in others he may not be able to appreciate the risks created by purchasing goods of a particular type because the scientific information available is too complex for the ordinary consumer to understand. Accordingly, one of the rationales for a consumer safety regime is that the consumer should be provided with sufficient information to allow him to assess those risks. For example, regulations may require the producer of processed foods to give comprehensible information about the composition of the food he produces.

Consumer safety legislation may also be justified on the ground that persons other than the immediate purchaser may be affected by unsafe goods. While the immediate purchaser will be able to pursue a civil action for breach of contract against his immediate supplier this does not provide a full response to the problem. First, prevention is surely better than cure and a consumer safety regime involving the use of penalties for contravention will go some way towards cutting out the problem of unsafe consumer goods, rather than simply providing for the payment of damages for breach after the event. Secondly, persons other than the immediate purchaser have no contractual action in their favour, but an injury to such a person will impose considerable social costs. Avoidance or reduction of these costs can be achieved by means of a safety regime directed at those consumer goods presenting the greatest risk.

Consumer safety regulation may also be justified on paternalist grounds. It would appear that in some instances there may be a social distrust of the ability of the consumer to protect himself against risks created by unsafe products.

9.1.2 The legislative background

The need to regulate the safety and quality of food in the interests of both consumer protection and public health has been recognised for some time. The modern legislative framework in the form of the Food Safety Act 1990 contains a number of provisions of considerable antiquity. In particular, the offence of selling food not of the nature, quality or substance demanded by the purchaser dates back to the Sale of Food and Drugs Act 1875. In addition to this, there is also a range of controls in respect of injurious food, food hygiene, food labelling and food composition (see 9.5.4. and 1.3).

Public regulation of the safety of products other than food has progressed slowly since the early 1960s. The most important legislation in this field is now the Consumer Protection Act 1987, part II, which replaces the provisions of the Consumer Protection Acts 1961 and 1971 and the Consumer Safety Acts 1978 and 1986. Tracing the history of the earlier legislation shows a gradual awareness of the problems surrounding the issue of general product safety and reveals a range of different techniques designed to meet those problems.

The Consumer Protection Act 1961, the Consumer Safety Act 1978 and the Consumer Safety (Amendment) Act 1986 progressively introduced a number of means of regulating product safety. Both the 1961 and the 1978 Acts provided for regulation-making powers, but the 1961 Act was largely defective in that regulations were very slow in being formulated. Even where regulations did exist, local authorities were not obliged to enforce them and only a limited range of suppliers were subject to the provisions.

The 1978 and the 1986 Acts sought to remedy a number of the perceived criticisms of the earlier legislation. Local authorities became obliged to enforce regulations; a wider range of regulations could be made; new enforcement powers were introduced, including prohibition notices, prohibition orders and notices to warn. The 1986 Act improved the position under the 1978 Act by allowing imported goods to be detained at the point of entry to the country and new enforcement powers including the issue of suspension and forfeiture orders were created. The beneficial features of the earlier legislation are now to be found in part II of the Consumer Protection Act 1987.

9.2   SAFETY OF GOODS UNDER THE CONSUMER PROTECTION ACT 1987, PART II

The law in respect of consumer safety is now contained in the Consumer Protection Act 1987, part II, which comprises most of the features of the earlier law, but adds a general safety requirement, breach of which will amount to the commission of a criminal offence. Some of the matters dealt with by the 1987 Act may need to be amended in the light of a proposed EC Directive on general product safety (COM(90) 259 final, OJ C156/8, 27.6.90) when it achieves full Directive status.

9.2.1   Safety regulations

9.2.1.1   Powers of the Secretary of State   The Consumer Protection Act 1987 allows the Secretary of State to make safety regulations so as to ensure that goods are safe (s. 11(1)(a)) and that, where goods are unsafe, whether generally or to a specific group of people, they are not made available to the consumer market (s. 11(1)(b)). Furthermore, regulations may also be made so as to ensure that appropriate information about goods is made available to consumers or that inappropriate information is withheld (s. 11(1)(c)).

For the purposes of s. 11, safety would appear to be subject to the same definition as applies to the general safety requirement considered in 9.2.2.1).

While the Secretary of State may make regulations in respect of consumer goods, he can only do so in respect of those products which fall within the scope of the Act. Some products are already subject to a separate regime and are therefore excluded from the provisions of the 1987 Act (see 9.2.2.2).

Like its predecessors, the 1987 Act contains a list of the matters in respect of which the Secretary of State may make regulations. The list is similar in content to that contained in the Consumer Safety Act 1978 and includes matters such as composition, contents, design and construction, approval requirements, requirements as to testing and inspection, requirements as to warnings or instructions given with goods, prohibitions on supply and information requirements (s. 11(2) and (3)).

Where safety regulations are made by the Secretary of State, he is under a duty to consult any person or organisation whom he considers appropriate (s. 11(5)). It follows from this that it is likely that relevant trade associations and consumer organisations will be involved in the regulation-making process, however, it appears from the wording of s. 11(5) that it is a matter for the Secretary of State to determine which bodies or persons are appropriate to consult.

In addition to the power to make regulations under the 1987 Act, the Secretary of State also has the power to order that regulations made under the Consumer Protection Act 1961 shall take effect as if made under s. 11 of the 1987 Act (s. 50(5)). Due to this provision the defects in the enforcement procedure applicable to the 1961 Act are avoided once the provisions of the 1987 Act apply to such regulations.

9.2.1.2 Consequences of a breach of safety regulations Where a safety regulation has been made, it does not of itself create a new criminal offence (Consumer Protection Act 1987, s. 11(4)), but an offence is committed where the provisions of s. 12 apply. This states that if a safety regulation prohibits a person from supplying, offering to supply, agreeing to supply or exposing for supply, a person commits an offence if he contravenes the regulation (s. 12(1)). An offence is also committed by a person who, having been required by regulations to test goods, fails to comply with the testing requirement (s. 12(2)(a)) or fails to deal properly with goods that fail to satisfy the test (s. 12(2)(b)). Where a regulation requires a person to mark goods in a particular way or to give specified information, failure to comply with that requirement will amount to the commission of an offence (s. 12(3)). In order to assist enforcement of the safety provisions of the Act, it is an offence for a person to fail to provide information required to be supplied by a safety regulation or to knowingly or recklessly give false information when so required (s. 12(4)).

Where the breach of a safety regulation causes death or personal injury, it will give rise to an action in tort for breach of statutory duty (s. 41(1) and see also 8.6.3). Since the purpose of part II of the 1987 Act is to guard against death and bodily injury only, it follows that no civil action for breach of statutory duty will lie in respect of property damage or economic loss, and that in such a case, the consumer will have to pursue his alternative remedies under the Sale of Goods Act 1979 or under part I of the Consumer Protection Act 1987.

9.2.2 The general safety requirement

One of the major problems of consumer safety law prior to 1987 was that it was tied to limited categories of goods covered by existing regulations. The only means of dealing with new hazards was by means of the prohibition notices and orders provided for by the Consumer Safety Act 1978. In order to meet this problem, the 1987 Act makes it an offence for a person to supply, offer to supply, agree to supply, expose for supply or possess for the purposes of supply any consumer goods which are not reasonably safe.

The duty to trade safely, as the general safety requirement may be described, is couched in negative terms. In this respect, the duty differs from that contained in the proposed EC Product Safety Directive (COM (90) 259 final, OJ C156/8, 27.6.90, art. 3.1) which is couched in positive terms, requiring suppliers to place only safe goods on the market.

9.2.2.1 Safety Goods must be reasonably safe (Consumer Protection Act 1987, s. 10(2)), and for these purposes this means that there must be no risk or a risk reduced to a minimum of death or personal injury (s. 19(1)). Thus, unlike the product liability provisions of the 1987 Act (see 8.4.5), goods which only pose a danger to other property or which are merely defective in the sense that they are not fit for use do not fall within the regime provided for by part II of the Act.

It is clear from the definition of safety that regard must be had not only to the intended use of the goods, but also to the condition in which they are kept and the way they are assembled or supplied (s. 19(1)). Thus goods may be unsafe if supplied in defective packaging or stored in an unsuitable environment.

Since goods must be reasonably safe, regard must be had to all the circumstances in which the goods are made available. Whilst this does not preclude the consideration of any relevant factor, the Act does specify three matters which should be taken into account (s. 10(2)). These are the way in which the goods are marketed (s. 10(2)(a)), published safety standards (s. 10(2)(b), and means of making the goods safe (s. 10(2)(c)).

9.2.2.1.1 Marketing etc. The reference to the way in which the goods have been marketed is based on wording identical to that used in s. 3(2)(a) in defining defectiveness for the purposes of the product liability provisions of the Act (see 8.4.3.1.1.) and therefore raises the same considerations. This approach may be criticised on the ground that it is not necessarily appropriate to apply an identical test of safety to both matters of civil compensation and criminal prosecution in the interests of consumer health and safety. The latter is surely a matter of great concern, in respect of which very high standards can be expected.

9.2.2.1.2 Safety standards Regard is also to be had to published safety standards. If an enforcement authority fails to take account of standards which are in force at the time of the alleged contravention of the general safety requirement, this may prove fatal to any subsequent action the authority might choose to pursue (*R v Birmingham City Council, ex parte Ferrero Ltd* (1990) 9 Tr LR 148 at pp. 157-8 per Hutchison J). Conversely, regulations which have been prepared but are not yet in force should be disregarded (ibid. at p. 160 per Hutchison J).

On the wording of s. 10(2)(b) the standards which may be considered can be published by anyone with the result that there is always the possibility of what has been described as 'window dressing' (*Rotherham MBC v Raysun (UK) Ltd* (1989) 8 Tr LR 6 at p. 12 per Woolf LJ), namely, the preparation of bogus standards by some private body and an appearance of reliance upon such standards. However, it seems that the courts are unwilling to allow a trader to rely on standards which carry no weight and which have not been prepared with care and precision (ibid.).

9.2.2.1.3 Means by which goods could be made safer The third relevant criterion is the existence of means by which the goods could have been made safer. Since the standard is one of reasonable safety, we are not concerned with methods of making goods totally safe. Factors such as cost and the likelihood and extent of improvement have to be considered. For example, motor cars could be made much safer by fitting a control device which prevents the vehicle from travelling faster than 10 m.p.h., but the social cost would be too great to bear. Similarly, if the proposed safety measure would push the purchase price of certain domestic appliances out of the reach of most consumers, it could hardly be regarded as reasonable, unless there was some unacceptable danger to consumers. The express reference to cost might lead consumers to believe that cheap goods need not be safe. If this is the case, the 1987 Act is defective in that there must be certain minimum expectations of safety for all goods.

So far as the issue of cost is concerned, the proposed EC Directive defines safety in different terms. It specifies that a safe product is one which does not present any risk, or only those reduced to such a level as is acceptable and consistent with a high standard of protection for the safety and health of consumers (art. 2(b)). Noticeably absent from this definition is any express reference to the cost of the product. This does not mean that cost is irrelevant under the EC proposal. For example, when the risks presented by a particular product are acceptable, but nonetheless not insignificant and not immediately obvious, a supplier must provide the consumer with the necessary information to allow him to assess those risks (art. 3.2.). Where the necessary information has been supplied, the consumer will be able to assess the safety of a product in line with its cost. Secondly, in the absence of more specific rules, the safety of a product is to be assessed by reference to the state of scientific and technical knowledge, *having regard to practical feasibility* and to the safety which users or consumers may reasonably expect (art. 4.3). The reference to practical feasibility would seem to suggest that the cost of compliance is a matter which can be considered in determining whether goods comply with the general safety requirement.

9.2.2.1.4 Compliance with safety requirements In determining whether goods are safe, regard must be had to safety requirements laid down by any enactment or European Community obligation, since compliance with such requirements will mean that the goods cannot be found to be unsafe (s. 10(3)). The effect of this is to place a very heavy burden on legislators to ensure that no lacunae are to be found in safety legislation (National Consumer Council, *Response to the Proposed EC Product Safety Directive* (PD31/89, October 1989) para. 3.2). The approach adopted in the proposed EC general product safety Directive appears to differ slightly in this respect in providing that goods which comply with EC or national requirements shall be deemed to satisfy the general safety requirement (art. 4.1), but that conformity with such rules shall not prevent competent authorities of a member State from taking action where it appears that goods are dangerous (art. 4.4).

9.2.2.1.5 Liability of retail suppliers The main thrust of the 1987 Act and the EC proposal is against the producer of goods, but this should not detract from the important role which may be played by a supplier in ensuring product safety. In particular, the general safety requirement applies to possession of goods for the purposes of supply (s. 10(1)(c)) and to the keeping of goods (s. 19(1)). The role of the supplier is important, since the way in which he deals with goods can render them unsafe. For example, he may store food at the wrong temperature or supply a number of apparently safe products which when used together are unsafe. Similarly, a retailer may supply a product such as a solvent-based glue or butane gas which when improperly used by a youthful purchaser can present a grave danger of death or physical injury. In this last instance, if the retailer is aware of the likelihood of solvent abuse, it is arguable that he breaches the general safety requirement.

The 1987 Act provides the retail supplier with a defence where he is unaware that goods do not comply with the general safety requirement or where he does not have reasonable grounds for believing that the safety requirement has been broken (s. 10(4)(b)). Moreover, the general defence of taking reasonable precautions and acting with due diligence (s. 39) will exonerate the truly innocent retailer. The 1987 Act does not give any guidance on what is a reasonable precaution or what constitutes due diligence, although the courts have developed guidelines on this matter (see 3.3.2) and it would appear that making random safety checks on goods intended for retail supply is some evidence of taking reasonable precautions (*Garrett* v *Boots the Chemist* (1980) 88 ITSA Monthly Review 238; *Rotherham MBC* v *Raysun (UK) Ltd* (1988) 8 Tr LR 6).

The proposed EC Directive introduces a requirement that suppliers should monitor the safety of products (art. 3.2). Monitoring may take the form of marking products for the purposes of later identification, sample testing and a complaints assessment procedure (art. 3.2). Assuming the proposal achieves Directive status, the adoption of such measures would presumably be good evidence of the taking of reasonable precautions. Simply imposing a monitoring requirement alone is not sufficient, in the absence of a requirement of action should the monitoring process reveal a risk of death or physical injury.

Accordingly, the proposed Directive also requires appropriate action to be taken, including, where necessary, the recall or withdrawal of the product (art. 3.2).

9.2.2.2 Consumer goods It is clear from the wording of the Consumer Protection Act 1987 that the general safety requirement and the power of the Secretary of State to make safety regulations do not apply to all goods. Safety regulations cannot be made in respect of growing crops and things comprised in land, food, water, feeding stuffs and fertilisers, gas, and controlled drugs and medicinal products (s. 11(7)). The general safety requirement applies only to consumer goods which are defined as those intended for private use or consumption (see 1.1.3), but not including the products referred to in s. 11(7) and in addition, aircraft, motor vehicles and tobacco (s. 10(7)). In contrast, the proposed European Community Directive on general product safety does include food and any other manufactured or processed product within its remit (art. 2(a)).

The fact that different products are subject to different regimes is a matter which may be criticised, since fundamentally different rules may apply according to the type of product under consideration (National Consumer Council, *Response to the Proposed EC Product Safety Directive* (PD31/89, October 1989), para. 2.6.). For example, different rules apply to injuries caused by defective transport equipment or by the consumption of food and drugs and medicines. Instead, it is preferable that there should be a general safety net which applies to all products used by consumers.

Further omissions from the 1987 Act relate to goods which are not new (s. 10(4)(c)) and goods intended for export (s. 10(4)(a)). The policy of the 1987 Act in relation to goods intended for export was that domestic criminal law should not be used to protect the world in general and that other countries should develop their own laws in this regard. Moreover, if United Kingdom exporters were to be required to comply with the provisions of the 1987 Act, they would be placed at a competitive disadvantage if they exported to a country which did not have equivalent laws in respect of the safety of consumer goods. The proposed product safety Directive intends to introduce a principle of equivalence in respect of basic standards of consumer safety, with which all member States will have to comply, with the result that all exporters based in the European Community will be subject to the requirements of the proposed Directive.

So far as goods which are not new are concerned the reasons for the inapplicability of the 1987 Act are less clear. The danger to the consumer from a second-hand car is just as great, if not greater, than that presented by a new car. For these purposes, there may be some difficulty in determining when goods are new, since it is always possible that goods may have been manufactured some time before they are first supplied to a consumer or may have been repaired following factory damage (see *R* v *Ford Motor Co. Ltd* [1974] 3 All ER 489 and see also 11.5.1.6). For the purposes of the 1987 Act, it would appear that the principal issue for the purposes of s. 10(4)(c) is whether the goods have previously been sold to a business or private user (Merkin, *A Guide to the Consumer Protection Act 1987*, p. 63).

The proposed EC Directive takes a different view of second-hand goods, providing that goods subject to the safety requirement shall include goods whether new, used or reconditioned (art. 2(a)).

9.2.3   Follow-up powers of enforcement

The Consumer Protection Act 1987 re-enacts a number of provisions found in earlier legislation concerning powers of enforcement. These powers include the issue of prohibition notices, notices to warn, suspension notices and forfeiture orders. Failure to comply with a prohibition notice, a notice to warn or a suspension notice constitutes the commission of a criminal offence (s. 13(4); s. 14(6)).

Unlike the Consumer Safety Act 1978, the 1987 Act does not allow for the service of a prohibition order preventing all traders from dealing in a particular type of goods considered to be unsafe. These orders have been rendered unnecessary following the introduction of the general safety requirement in s. 10, since if a range of goods is considered to be unsafe, a criminal offence is committed by a supplier even where no specific regulations exist.

Under the Consumer Safety Act 1978, a breach of one of these follow-up powers gave rise to an action for damages for breach of statutory duty. The same position no longer prevails under the 1987 Act, since only a breach of safety regulations made under s. 11 will give rise to an action for breach of statutory duty (s. 41(2)).

9.2.3.1   Prohibition notices   A prohibition notice may be served on a specific trader, requiring him not to supply, offer or agree to supply, expose for supply or possess for the purposes of supply any goods specified in the notice as being dangerous (s. 13(1)(a)).

Where such a notice is served, it may be subject to such conditions as are considered appropriate by the Secretary of State (s. 13(3)). Thus, a prohibition notice may direct the trader not to supply the goods referred to in the notice to a specific group of consumers such as children or pensioners while leaving him free to supply to others not specified in the notice.

Goods subject to such a notice are restricted to those in respect of which safety regulations may be made (s. 13(6)(a)). Thus, it follows that a prohibition notice cannot be served in respect of goods such as food, water, gas, medicines and things attached to or forming part of land.

Where a prohibition notice is served on a named trader, it is incumbent on the Secretary of State to give his reasons for imposing the restriction on the goods concerned. In doing so, he must state why he considers the goods to be unsafe. He must also state the date on which the prohibition is to take effect and he must inform the trader that he may make written representations seeking to establish that the goods covered by the notice are safe (sch. 2, para. 1). Moreover, where representations are made, the Secretary of State must either revoke the notice or appoint an expert to consider the representations and report on the matter within 21 days, after having considered the evidence. After the consultation process, the Secretary of State may revoke, confirm or vary the notice, but in the case of a variation, the notice cannot be strengthened (sch. 2, paras. 2, 3, 4, and 5).

9.2.3.2 Notices to warn A notice to warn may be served on a trader requiring him, at his own expense, to publish a warning about goods considered by the Secretary of State to be unsafe (Consumer Protection Act 1987, s. 13(1)(b)). It follows that in circumstances such as those which arose in *Walton* v *British Leyland (UK) Ltd* (1978) Product Liability International (August 1980), 156 (see 8.3.1) where a serious defect was discovered in a range of the defendant's cars after they had been put into circulation, it would now be possible to require the manufacturer to warn consumers of the danger.

The range of goods to which notices to warn apply is wider than that applicable to prohibition notices. While the latter may be made only in respect of goods subject to the issue of safety regulations under s. 11, notices to warn may be served in respect of all such goods, growing crops and things comprised in land by virtue of being attached to it (s. 13(6)(b)).

As in the case of prohibition notices, the service of a notice to warn is also subject to certain procedural requirements. These require the service of a draft notice specifying the Secretary of State's reasons for regarding the goods as unsafe and allowing for written representations (sch. 2, para. 6). The Act also provides for a 28-day consultation period, during which time evidence in respect of the proposed notice may be considered and at the end of which the Secretary of State must decide whether to withdraw the notice or issue it in its final form (sch. 2, paras 8 and 9).

9.2.3.3 Suspension notices The power to issue a suspension notice was first created by the Consumer Safety (Amendment) Act 1986 and is re-enacted in the Consumer Protection Act 1987. Where an enforcement authority has reasonable grounds for suspecting that there has been a breach of the general safety requirement, a safety regulation, a prohibition notice or another suspension notice, it may serve a suspension notice on the person considered to be in breach, requiring him to retain possession of the goods and not to supply them without the consent of the enforcement authority (s. 14(1)). If such consent is given, it may be conditional (s. 14(5)).

A suspension notice may not continue in force for longer than six months, but after service, it may prevent the trader from supplying, offering or agreeing to supply or exposing for supply any goods referred to in the notice (s. 14(1)).

The importance of such a power is that, during the currency of the notice, tests may be carried out on goods and additional time is made available to allow a prosecution to be brought. At the same time the public are protected from potentially dangerous goods as a result of the suspension.

Generally, a suspension notice cannot be renewed after the expiry of the initial six-month period unless proceedings have been instituted against the trader for forfeiture of the goods or in respect of a breach of a safety provision other than a contravention of a suspension notice (s. 14(4)).

Since the service of a suspension notice is based on suspicion that there has been a breach of a safety requirement, it is always possible that it may later be revealed that there has been no such breach. In these circumstances, the enforcement authority is liable to pay compensation in respect of loss or damage caused by virtue of service of the notice (s. 14(7)). Since the most likely loss to be suffered by the trader is loss of profit which would otherwise have been made, it may be argued that the basis of assessment should be similar to that adopted in relation to the award of contractual damages (Cardwell and Kay (1990) 7 Tr L 212, 215-16). It is also possible that in the course of testing, goods may have suffered damage in which case the diminution in value of the goods ought to be recoverable.

The Act also provides for an appeals procedure in s. 15 under which the trader can apply for an order setting aside a suspension notice. The magistrates' court may set aside the order only if it is satisfied that there has been no contravention of a safety provision (s. 15(3)). In addition to the s. 15 appeal procedure, it is also open to a person who has been served with a suspension notice to seek an order to the effect that the notice be quashed on the ground that proper procedures have not been properly complied with. Thus if an enforcement authority fails to consider relevant safety standards in force at the time of the commission of the alleged contravention or if it takes into account irrelevant considerations, such as regulations which are not in force at the relevant time, a notice may be quashed (*R* v *Birmingham City Council, ex parte Ferrero Ltd* (1990) 9 Tr LR 148 at p. 162 per Hutchison J).

9.2.3.4 Forfeiture orders   Where there has been a contravention of a safety provision, an enforcement authority can apply to a magistrates' court for a forfeiture order (s. 16(1)). For these purposes, it is not necessary that the trader should have been convicted of an offence, since no offence is committed where a suspension notice has been issued and complied with, yet a suspension notice is a safety provision for the purposes of the 1987 Act (Cardwell (1987) 50 MLR 622, 632).

It is not necessary for all goods in a consignment to be inspected and tested before an order for forfeiture is made since all goods in a given batch can be assumed not to comply with safety requirements where it is shown that a representative sample is dangerous (s. 16(4)).

Where a forfeiture order is made, goods are to be destroyed in accordance with the instructions of the court (s. 16(6)), although, if it is appropriate to do so, the goods may be released to a person specified by the court, provided the goods are not supplied to another other than as scrap or to a person who carries on a business of repair or reconditioning (s. 16(7)(a) and s. 46(7)) and that the costs of the enforcement authority in bringing the proceedings are paid by that person (s. 16(7)(b)).

9.2.3.5 Other possible powers   One power which exists elsewhere but has not been provided for in the Consumer Protection Act 1987 is the ability to serve a 'recall' notice. While the Act does enable the Secretary of State to issue a notice to warn (see 9.2.3.2) the only obligation of the person served with such a notice is to warn of a specified danger. In certain circumstances it might be appropriate to order a producer to recall consumer goods which are known to be dangerous.

In relation to motor vehicles, members of the Society of Motor Manufacturers and Traders are subject to the provisions of the SMMT Code of Practice, which operates a recall procedure in association with the Department of Transport. However, experience of this has shown that a surprisingly low percentage of consumers actually return their vehicle for repair (Miller, *Product Liability & Safety Encyclopaedia*, div. VI, 'Note' after para. 1093).

It appears that the government's view at the time the 1987 Act was passed was that manufacturers could be relied on to voluntarily recall dangerous goods and that, in practice, the service of a notice to warn would achieve the same purpose (Merkin, *A Guide to the Consumer Protection Act 1987*, p. 69).

9.2.4 Defences

Where a person is charged with the commission of an offence under ss. 10, 12, 13 or 14 of the Consumer Protection Act 1987 it is a defence for him to show that he took all reasonable precautions and exercised all due diligence to avoid the commission of an offence (s. 39(1) and see 3.3.2.1).

Where, in addition to raising the s. 39(1) defence, it is also alleged that the commission of the offence is due to the act or default of another person or due to reliance on information supplied by another, the person first charged must give seven days' notice to the prosecution, which should provide the necessary information identifying or assisting in the identification of the other person (s. 39(2) and (3)).

If an offence is shown to have been committed as a result of the act or default of another person, that person is taken to be guilty of the offence and may be proceeded against and punished accordingly (s. 40(1)). Thus it may be possible for an individual employee to be prosecuted where his act or default has caused the commission of an offence by his employer.

9.3 CONSUMER PROTECTION ACT 1987, PART II – MATERIALS FOR CONSIDERATION

For text see 9.2.

Consumer Protection Act 1987

10.   The general safety requirement
    (1)   A person shall be guilty of an offence if he—
    (a)   supplies any consumer goods which fail to comply with the general safety requirement;
    (b)   offers or agrees to supply any such goods; or
    (c)   exposes or possesses any such goods for supply.
    (2)   For the purposes of this section consumer goods fail to comply with the general safety requirement if they are not reasonably safe having regard to all the circumstances, including—

(a)   the manner in which, and purposes for which, the goods are being or would be marketed, the get-up of the goods, the use of any mark in relation to the goods and any instructions or warnings which are given or would be given with respect to the keeping, use or consumption of the goods;

(b)   any standards of safety published by any person either for goods of a description which applies to the goods in question or for matters relating to goods of that description; and

(c)   the existence of any means by which it would have been reasonable (taking into account the cost, likelihood and extent of any improvement) for the goods to have been made safer.

(3)   For the purposes of this section consumer goods shall not be regarded as failing to comply with the general safety requirement in respect of—

(a)   anything which is shown to be attributable to compliance with any requirement imposed by or under any enactment or with any Community obligation;

(b)   any failure to do more in relation to any matter than is required by—

(i)   any safety regulations imposing requirements with respect to that matter;

(ii)   any standards of safety approved for the purposes of this subsection by or under any such regulations and imposing requirements with respect to that matter;

(iii)   any provision of any enactment or subordinate legislation imposing such requirements with respect to that matter as are designated for the purposes of this subsection by any such regulations.

(4)   In any proceedings against any person for an offence under this section in respect of any goods it shall be a defence for that person to show—

(a)   that he reasonably believed that the goods would not be used or consumed in the United Kingdom; or

(b)   that the following conditions are satisfied, that is to say—

(i)   that he supplied the goods, offered or agreed to supply them or, as the case may be, exposed or possessed them for supply in the course of carrying on a retail business; and

(ii)   that, at the time he supplied the goods or offered or agreed to supply them or exposed or possessed them for supply, he neither knew nor had reasonable grounds for believing that the goods failed to comply with the general safety requirement; or

(c)   that the terms on which he supplied the goods or agreed or offered to supply them or, in the case of goods which he exposed or possessed for supply, the terms on which he intended to supply them—

(i)   indicated that the goods were not supplied or to be supplied as new goods; and

(ii)   provided for, or contemplated, the acquisition of an interest in the goods by the persons supplied or to be supplied.

(5)   For the purposes of subsection (4)(b) above goods are supplied in the course of carrying on a retail business if—

(a)   whether or not they are themselves acquired for a person's private use or consumption, they are supplied in the course of carrying on a business of making a supply of consumer goods available to persons who generally acquire them for private use or consumption; and

(b)   the descriptions of goods the supply of which is made available in the course of that business do not, to a significant extent, include manufactured or imported goods which have not previously been supplied in the United Kingdom.

(6)   A person guilty of an offence under this section shall be liable on summary conviction to imprisonment for a term not exceeding six months or to a fine not exceeding level 5 on the standard scale or to both.

(7)   In this section 'consumer goods' means any goods which are ordinarily intended for private use or consumption, not being—

(a)   growing crops or things comprised in land by virtue of being attached to it;

(b)   water, food, feeding stuff or fertiliser;

(c)   gas which is, is to be or has been supplied by a person authorised to supply it by or under section 6, 7 or 8 of the Gas Act 1986 (authorisation of supply of gas through pipes);

(d)   aircraft (other than hang-gliders) or motor vehicles;

(e)   controlled drugs or licensed medicinal products;

(f)   tobacco.

13.   Prohibition notices and notices to warn

(1)   The Secretary of State may—

(a)   serve on any person a notice ('a prohibition notice') prohibiting that person, except with the consent of the Secretary of State, from supplying, or from offering to supply, agreeing to supply, exposing for supply or possessing for supply, any relevant goods which the Secretary of State considers are unsafe and which are described in the notice;

(b)   serve on any person a notice ('a notice to warn') requiring that person at his own expense to publish, in a form and manner and on occasions specified in the notice, a warning about any relevant goods which the Secretary of State considers are unsafe, which that person supplies or has supplied and which are described in the notice. . . .

(3)   A consent given by the Secretary of State for the purposes of a prohibition notice may impose such conditions on the doing of anything for which the consent is required as the Secretary of State considers appropriate. . . .

(6)   In this section 'relevant goods' means—

(a)   in relation to a prohibition notice, any goods to which section 11 above applies; and

(b)   in relation to a notice to warn, any goods to which that section applies or any growing crops or things comprised in land by virtue of being attached to it.

14.   Suspension notices

(1)   Where an enforcement authority has reasonable grounds for suspecting that any safety provision has been contravened in relation to any goods, the authority may serve a notice ('a suspension notice') prohibiting the person on whom it is served, for such period ending not more than six months after the date of the notice as is specified therein, from doing any of the following things without the consent of the authority, that is to say, supplying the goods, offering to supply them, agreeing to supply them or exposing them for supply.

(2)   A suspension notice served by an enforcement authority in respect of any goods shall—

(a)   describe the goods in a manner sufficient to identify them;

(b)   set out the grounds on which the authority suspects that a safety provision has been contravened in relation to the goods; and

(c)   state that, and the manner in which, the person on whom the notice is served may appeal against the notice under section 15 below.

(3)   A suspension notice served by an enforcement authority for the purpose of prohibiting a person for any period from doing the things mentioned in subsection (1) above in relation to any goods may also require that person to keep the authority informed of the whereabouts throughout that period of any of those goods in which he has an interest.

(4)   Where a suspension notice has been served on any person in respect of any goods, no further such notice shall be served on that person in respect of the same goods unless—

(a)   proceedings against that person for an offence in respect of a contravention in relation to the goods of a safety provision (not being an offence under this section); or

(b)   proceedings for the forfeiture of the goods under section 16 or 17 below, are pending at the end of the period specified in the first-mentioned notice.

(5)   A consent given by an enforcement authority for the purposes of subsection (1) above may impose such conditions on the doing of anything for which the consent is required as the authority considers appropriate.

(6)   Any person who contravenes a suspension notice shall be guilty of an offence and liable on summary conviction to imprisonment for a term not exceeding six months or to a fine not exceeding level 5 on the standard scale or to both.

(7)   Where an enforcement authority serves a suspension notice in respect of any goods, the authority shall be liable to pay compensation to any person having an interest in the goods in respect of any loss or damage caused by reason of the service of the notice if—

(a)   there has been no contravention in relation to the goods of any safety provision; and

(b)   the exercise of the power is not attributable to any neglect or default by that person.

16.   Forfeiture: England and Wales and Northern Ireland

(1)   An enforcement authority in England and Wales or Northern Ireland may apply under this section for an order for the forfeiture of any goods on the grounds that there has been a contravention in relation to the goods of a safety provision.

(2)   An application under this section may be made—

(a)   where proceedings have been brought in a magistrates' court for an offence in respect of a contravention in relation to some or all of the goods of any safety provision, to that court;

(b)   where an application with respect to some or all of the goods has been made to a magistrates' court under section 15 above or section 33 below, to that court; and

(c)   where no application for the forfeiture of the goods has been made under paragraph (a) or (b) above, by way of complaint to a magistrates' court.

(3)   On an application under this section the court shall make an order for the forfeiture of any goods only if it is satisfied that there has been a contravention in relation to the goods of a safety provision.

(4)   For the avoidance of doubt it is declared that a court may infer for the purposes of this section that there has been a contravention in relation to any goods of a safety provision if it is satisfied that any such provision has been contravened in relation to goods which are representative of those goods (whether by reason of being of the same design or part of the same consignment or batch or otherwise).

(5)   Any person aggrieved by an order made under this section by a magistrates' court, or by a decision of such a court not to make such an order, may appeal against that order or decision—

(a)   in England and Wales, to the Crown Court;

(b)   in Northern Ireland, to the county court;

and an order so made may contain such provision as appears to the court to be appropriate for delaying the coming into force of the order pending the making and determination of any appeal (including any application under section 111 of the Magistrates' Court Act 1980 or article 146 of the Magistrates' Courts (Northern Ireland) Order 1981 (statement of case)).

(6)   Subject to subsection (7) below, where any goods are forfeited under this section they shall be destroyed in accordance with such directions as the court may give.

(7)   On making an order under this section a magistrates' court may, if it considers it appropriate to do so, direct that the goods to which the order relates shall (instead of being destroyed) be released, to such person as the court may specify, on condition that that person—

(a)   does not supply those goods to any person otherwise than as mentioned in section 46(7)(a) or (b) below; and

(b)   complies with any order to pay costs or expenses (including any order under section 35 below) which has been made against that person in the proceedings for the order for forfeiture.

EC Proposed Directive on General Product Safety (COM(90) 259 fin. OJ C156/8 27 June 1990)

TITLE I OBJECTIVES, SCOPE AND DEFINITIONS

Article 2

For the purposes of this Directive:

(a)   'product' shall mean any manufactured, processed or agricultural product supplied whether for consideration or not in the course of a business, and whether new, used or reconditioned;

(b)   'safe product' shall mean any product which, during its foreseeable time of use, does not present any risk or only those reduced to such a level, taking account of the product's use, considered as acceptable and consistent with a high standard of protection for the safety and health of persons:

—given its composition, execution, wrapping, presentation and labelling, conditions of assembly, maintenance or disposal, instructions for handling and use and its direct or indirect effect upon or in combination with other products,

—when used for its intended use or in a manner which may reasonably be foreseen, having regard, *inter alia*, to any specific statement made by its supplier or on his behalf in that respect and, in particular, to the normal behaviour of children.

The feasibility of obtaining higher levels of safety or the availability of other products presenting a lesser degree of risk shall not constitute grounds for considering a product to be 'not safe' or 'dangerous';

(c)   'dangerous product' shall mean any product which does not meet the definition of 'safe product' according to point (b) of the present article;

(d)   'supplier' shall mean:

—the manufacturer of the product, when he is established in the Community, and any person presenting himself as the manufacturer by affixing to the product his name, trade mark or other distinctive mark,

—the manufacturer's authorised agent, when the manufacturer is not established in the Community, or, if no such agent exists, the importer of the product,

—distributors and other professionals in the supply chain insofar as their activities may affect the safety properties of a marketed product,

—the commercial supplier of used and/or reconditioned products.

TITLE II GENERAL SAFETY REQUIREMENT

Article 3

1.   Suppliers are under an obligation to place only safe products on the market. Member States shall incorporate in their legislation all necessary measures to ensure that suppliers meet this obligation.

2.   In particular, within the limits of their respective activities, suppliers shall:
—provide the potential user or consumer with the relevant information to enable him to assess the risks presented by a product when such risks are acceptable as such but are not immediately obvious and are not insignificant, and to take precautions against these risks throughout the foreseeable time of use of the product; provision of a warning does not constitute a means of escaping the general safety requirement nor a defence when the product proves to be dangerous,
—adopt appropriate measures to ensure suitable monitoring of the safety of the products, taking account of their particular characteristics, with a view to being properly informed of risks which these products might present, assessing this information and taking appropriate action including, if necessary, recalling the product in question or withdrawing it from the market to avoid these risks.
The measures to be taken to monitor products specifically include, whenever appropriate, marking of the products or product lots in such a way that they can subsequently be identified, sample testing of marketed products and the institution of systematic procedures for assessing and investigating complaints made.
3.   Distributors and other professionals in the supply chain who are not suppliers are required to act with due care in order to contribute to ensuring compliance with the general safety requirement. In particular, within the limits of their respective activities, they shall participate in monitoring the safety of marketed products, for example by passing on information on product risks and cooperating in the action taken to avoid these risks.

Article 4
1.   Suppliers shall be deemed to have complied with the general safety requirement when the product conforms:
—with the specific rules of Community law laying down the health and safety requirements which the product must satisfy in order to be marketed,
—if there are no Community rules, with the specific rules of national law of the member State on whose territory the product is in circulation, such rules being drawn up in conformity with the Treaty and in particular articles 30 and 36 thereof and laying down the health and safety requirements which the product must satisfy in order to be marketed.
2.   In order to assess the conformity of a product with the rules mentioned in paragraph 1, reference shall also be made to national voluntary standards giving effect to a European standard or, when they exist, Community technical specifications or, failing these, safety and health standards for the products concerned drawn up in the member State in which the product is in circulation.
3.   In the absence of any more specific rule, the conformity of a product or category of products with the general safety requirement shall be assessed by reference to the state of the art, to the state of scientific and technical knowledge, having regard to practical feasibility, and to the codes of good practice in respect of safety and health in the sector concerned and to the safety which users or consumers may reasonably expect.
4.   Conformity of a product with the rules mentioned in paragraphs 1 and 2 shall not bar the competent authorities of the member States from taking action to impose restrictions on its being placed on the market or to require its withdrawal from the market where there is evidence that despite such conformity it is dangerous to the health and safety of users or consumers.

9.4   PRODUCT SAFETY AND EUROPEAN COMMUNITY OBLIGATIONS

The influence of the European Community can manifest itself in one of two different ways. The fact that the Community has a consumer protection programme means that Community Regulations taking direct effect on the law of member States may impose general requirements in respect of product safety. Such requirements will be common to all member States of the Community with the result that consumers and traders alike will be subject to the same regime wherever they may find themselves in the European Community. In addition to legislation taking direct effect, the harmonisation programme under articles 100 and 100A of the EEC Treaty (see 3.6.1.2) allows for the adoption of Directives which only take effect after member States have introduced the necessary legislation required to implement such Directives.

In addition to Community initiatives which add to domestic attempts to regulate trading conduct in favour of consumers, regard must also be had to general principles of Community law. In particular, by virtue of the EEC Treaty, domestic regulation must not constitute a quantitative restriction on trade within the community, nor must it have an 'equivalent effect' (art. 30 and see 3.6.2.1 and Weatherill [1988] EL Rev 87).

9.4.1 Community Regulations and Directives

As part of the EC process of positive harmonisation, Regulations in the interest of consumer safety have been prepared. Such Regulations take direct effect as part of English Law (European Communities Act 1972, s. 2(2) and (4) and sch. 2). Thus there are a number of safety regulations which do not owe their existence to the provisions of the Consumer Protection Act 1987 or any of its predecessors, but are based on the provisions of the European Communities Act 1972. Examples include the Classification, Packaging and Labelling of Dangerous Substances Regulations (SI 1984/1244; SI 1986/1922) and the Aerosol Dispensers (EEC Requirements) Regulations (SI 1977/1140; SI 1980/136; SI 1981/1549; SI 1985/1279) amongst others.

A further aspect of the positive harmonisation programme consists of Community Directives which require member States to take appropriate measures to adopt the requirements of the Directive as part of domestic law. Of particular importance in this regard is the proposed general product safety Directive (COM(90) 259 final OJ C156/8 27.6.90) which seeks to oblige suppliers to place only safe products on the market (art. 3.1) and seeks to define the powers which member States should adopt with a view to implementing the general safety requirement (art. 5).

9.4.2 The EEC Treaty, article 30, and domestic consumer safety law

Domestic consumer protection laws are potentially capable of destroying the notion of an internal market within the European Community. Such provisions may be distinctly or indistinctly discriminatory and according to which description applies, the relevant provision will be subject to different rules.

9.4.2.1 Distinctly applicable provisions A distinctly applicable provision amounts to a formal restriction on imports and therefore discriminates between goods coming from other parts of the Community and those which have been produced in the domestic market.

The power of customs and excise officers to detain imported goods for a period of up to two working days so as to allow an enforcement authority to take action (Consumer Protection Act 1987, s. 31(1)) would appear to infringe art. 30 on the ground that it is discriminatory. However, such directly applicable measures may be justified under art. 36 on the ground that they are necessary for the protection of the health and safety of humans (see 3.6.2.2). In this respect, it is essential that the restriction is proportionate to the purpose it is intended to serve and must not be excessively restrictive of inter-Community trade (see *Commission* v *United Kingdom* (case 261/85) [1988] 2 CMLR 11). Thus, a ban on imports may not be justified if a system of checking imported goods can achieve the desired effect.

9.4.2.2 Indistinctly applicable provisions An indistinctly applicable provision does not formally restrict imports, but may have an equivalent effect in the sense that it may have a potentially restrictive effect on trade. It has been seen in 3.6.2.1 that such measures may be justified under the 'rule of reason' in *Rewe-Zentrale AG* v *Bundesmonopolverwaltung für Branntwein* (case 120/78) [1979] ECR 649 (the *Cassis de Dijon* case) on the ground that they are necessary to satisfy mandatory requirements relating to consumer protection.

In relation to product safety, regulations will usually require consumer goods to comply with certain standards and it is quite possible that these standards may differ from requirements which may be imposed by other member States. The second principle in the *Cassis de Dijon* case stipulates that if goods can be lawfully supplied in one part of the Community, an additional restriction imposed by another member State will be presumed invalid, in the absence of a very strong justification.

It is clear that one way in which regulations can comply with the requirements of the *Cassis de Dijon* case is to recognise the principle of equivalence. For example, the Child Resistant Packaging (Safety) Regulations 1986 (SI 1986/758) provide that even where goods fail to comply with British Standards requirements, but satisfy requirements laid down in the exporting member State, they must be admitted. However, there are also some safety regulations which do not contain similar provisions and will therefore potentially contravene art. 30 if they do not recognise the possibility of compliance with requirements applicable to exporters in other member States.

Where regulations appear to infringe art. 30, they may be challenged in the European Court or in national courts and if the challenge is successful, the relevant provision may be declared contrary to the requirements of art. 30. This process of 'negative harmonisation' is destructive (Weatherill [1988] EL Rev 87, 99) since it is piecemeal and dependent on the willingness of individuals to litigate. Instead, it would be preferable to see a detailed programme of positive harmonisation particularly since this would tend to produce a greater degree of certainty in trading and safety standards. Instead, the position which prevails under the *Cassis de Dijon* principle is that standards of safety are dependent on the plethora of different systems which operate throughout the European Community and no one can be entirely sure whether the goods he proposes to export to the United Kingdom will satisfy safety standards or not.

9.5 THE SAFETY AND QUALITY OF FOOD

Regulation of the safety, composition and quality of food has existed for many years and, while the consumer interest in the safety and quality of food is apparent, there is also a public-interest justification for such regulation on the grounds of maintaining standards of public health. Generally, the role of enforcing food law falls to local authority trading standards or consumer protection departments.

The basis of modern food law is now the Food Safety Act 1990, which, despite its misleading title, covers a range of matters relevant to food, including food safety, consumer protection, composition of food, food labelling and the advertising of food. Comprehensive coverage of all these matters is not possible in a book of this nature and the interested reader is directed to titles such as *Butterworths Law of Food and Drugs*; Howells, Bradgate and Griffiths, *Blackstone's Guide to the Food Safety Act 1990* (see also Bradgate and Howells [1991] JBL 320 (July issue)).

For the present purposes, it is proposed to consider the major criminal offences in respect of food safety and quality created by the 1990 Act, local authority follow-up powers of inspection and seizure, food regulations, and defences available to a person charged with the commission of an offence.

The 1990 Act, amongst other things, governs the safety of food. It is therefore important to identify the scope of the Act by defining the term 'food'. The provisions of s. 1(1) make it clear that food includes drink (which includes bottled water, but not that governed by the Water Act 1989), substances of no nutritional value used for human consumption (e.g., food colourings), chewing-gum and ingredients used in the preparation of the foregoing. Furthermore, anything supplied to a consumer which purports to be food will be treated as such (*Meah* v *Roberts* [1978] 1 All ER 97). Thus, a supply of caustic soda instead of lemonade, cannot be defended on the ground that caustic soda is not food. The definition of food excludes live animals, feeding stuffs for animals, controlled drugs and medicines (s. 1(2)).

9.5.1 Injurious food

Under the Food Safety Act 1990, s. 7(1), it is an offence for a person to render food injurious to health with the intent that it shall be sold for human consumption.

9.5.1.1 Injurious to health A central feature of food safety law is the notion of injury to health. In particular, where food is so injurious, the food fails to satisfy the general safety requirement in the Food Safety Act 1990, s. 8 (see 9.5.2) and the enforcement powers of the Act may be invoked (ss. 9 to 13 and see 9.5.3).

An injury to health is defined as an impairment, whether permanent or temporary (s. 7(3)). The Act further provides that in deciding whether food is injurious to health, regard should be had to the probable effect of the food on the health of a person consuming it (s. 7(2)(a)) and the probable cumulative effect of similarly constituted food on the health of a person consuming it in ordinary quantities (s. 7(2)(b)). In other words, it is necessary to consider both the immediate and long-term effects on a hypothetical consumer of consuming food of the kind under consideration.

The wording of s. 7(2) is important, since it does not refer to the consumer who has registered the complaint. Instead, the court must consider the matter from the position of the 'consumer in the Clapham High Street'. Thus, if the complaint is that food has brought on an allergic reaction, it will be necessary for the court to consider whether only a small percentage of consumers would be likely to be affected. Conversely, if an ingredient in cream is harmless to adults, but potentially harmful to invalids and young children, it will be injurious to health (*Cullen* v *McNair* (1908) 72 JP 280) since children and invalids are likely to form a substantial proportion of the consumers of cream.

The reference to 'ordinary quantities' in s. 7(2)(b) means that food will not be regarded as injurious merely because the consumer has over-indulged himself. Furthermore, the wording of s. 7(2)(b) also requires the court to consider the likely effects of the food for the future. For example, some foods may not have an immediate effect but when consumed over a period of time may result in heart disease or some other condition based on continued consumption. Does this mean that chip shops or breweries prepare injurious food (see Howells, Bradgate and Griffiths, *Blackstone's Guide to the Food Safety Act 1990*, pp. 15-16)?

9.5.1.2 Rendering The central feature of s. 7 of the Food Safety Act 1990 is that something must have been done to food to render it injurious to health. Accordingly, s. 7 is aimed at preparers rather than retailers of food.

In order to be guilty of an offence, the person charged must have done some positive act which has resulted in the food becoming injurious to health. Such acts include adding an article to food (e.g., colourants; food sabotage), using an article as an ingredient in the preparation of food, abstracting a constituent from food (e.g., removal by evaporation) and subjecting food to any process or treatment (s. 7(1)(a) to (d)).

The way in which some of these words have been defined means that s. 7 has a very broad scope. In particular, the word 'preparation' is defined as including any form of processing and treatment. In turn, treatment includes subjecting food to heat or cold (s. 53(1)). The reference to processing and treatment would seem to cover not just the final stages of preparing food for human consumption, but also much earlier stages, such as crop spraying and other forms of treatment in the course of growth.

Generally, s. 7 requires a positive act on the part of the food processor, with the result that defects in food resulting from inaction will not fall within its remit. Thus, the natural growth of mould would appear not to amount to rendering food injurious to health, although this will be covered by other provisions of the Act. Similarly, not removing a natural feature of food does not infringe s. 7. Thus the failure to remove natural toxins present in red kidney beans does not amount to the commission of an offence under s. 7.

9.5.2   Food safety requirements

It is an offence to sell, offer for sale, expose or advertise for sale or have in one's possession for the purposes of sale or preparation for sale any food intended for human consumption and which fails to comply with food safety requirements (Food Safety Act 1990, s. 8(1)(a)). Moreover, it is also an offence to deposit with or consign to another any food intended for human consumption which fails to comply with food safety requirements (s. 8(1)(b)). For the purposes of s. 8 where any food which fails to comply with food safety requirements and forms part of a batch or consignment, it is presumed (in the absence of evidence to the contrary) that the whole consignment also fails to satisfy the food safety requirement.

Section 8 has the effect of broadening the range of possible offences capable of being committed in relation to food, but it does not go as far as some would like. In particular, there is no general safety requirement such as that which applies to other consumer goods by virtue of the Consumer Protection Act 1987, s. 10(1) (see 9.3). While food is excluded from the regime created by the 1987 Act, the European Community proposed Directive on general product safety (COM (90) 259 final OJ C156/8 27.6.90; see also 9.3) does apply to food as well as other consumer goods (art. 2(a)). Assuming the Directive is approved in its present form, it would provide a general safety net in respect of all unsafe goods. The important effect of the proposed Directive is that it will impose a positive duty to supply safe food (art. 3). Accordingly, if loopholes are found to exist in the regime created by the 1990 Act, they will be filled by the proposed general safety requirement. For example, if it is the case that the 1990 Act does not apply to a failure to remove harmful toxins naturally present in food, it is possible that such food might be covered by the proposed general safety requirement.

9.5.2.1   Sale etc.   The extended definition of sale for the purposes of the Food Safety Act 1990, s. 8(1)(a) appears to cover almost any sort of supply in the course of a business. Clearly, the wording of the Act does not confine offences to sales within the narrow meaning of the Sale of Goods Act 1979, s. 2. It is also possible for the s. 8 offence to be committed by a person who merely exposes food for sale or stores food items in an area from which they may later be moved for the purposes of sale. The use of the phrase 'offer for sale' would appear to be redundant, since a retailer generally, does not offer to sell anything (*Fisher* v *Bell* [1961] 1 QB 394). However, this defect is compensated for by the other provisions of s. 8(1)(a).

A person can also supply food without being aware that this is the case. For example, food may be supplied by an agent or employee of the owner of the premises from which the food is sold. In such a case the owner is the supplier of the food, but he may be able to raise the statutory due diligence defence (see

s. 21 considered at 3.4.2). Furthermore, the person responsible for the commission of the offence may also be proceeded against under the bypass provisions of s. 20.

9.5.2.2 Depositing and consigning Under the Food Safety Act 1990, s. 8(1)(b), a person commits an offence if he deposits food with or consigns food to another for the purposes of sale or preparation for sale if that food fails to satisfy the food safety requirement. This would appear to be aimed at manufacturers and producers who supply others in the food supply chain. Under previous legislation, the word 'deposit' was given a very broad meaning. For example, meat carried in a cart on its way to premises used for the preparation of food was held to be deposited 'in a place' (*Williams* v *Allen* [1916] 1 KB 425).

9.5.2.3 Human consumption For the purposes of the Food Safety Act 1990, s. 8, no offence is committed unless the food is intended for human consumption. In this respect, there are two important presumptions. First, it is presumed that food commonly used for human consumption is intended for human consumption where it is sold, offered for sale, exposed or kept for sale unless the person charged with the commission of an offence proves the contrary (s. 3(2)). Moreover, where food is found on premises used for the preparation, storage or sale of food, it is presumed, unless the contrary is proved, that it is intended for human consumption (s. 3(3)).

It follows from these provisions that where unsafe food is found on food premises, it is not open to the person charged to argue that the food was not intended for human consumption unless he can prove otherwise. For example, evidence might be called to the effect that the food was to be supplied to a pig farmer for use as animal feed. Similarly, if the person charged has prevented a local authority official from gaining access to food stored on his premises, the prosecution will not fail for want of proof that the food was intended for human consumption (see *Hooper* v *Petrou* [1973] Crim LR 198), since this is presumed in the absence of evidence to the contrary.

9.5.2.4 Food safety The basis of the Food Safety Act 1990, s. 8, offence is that food has failed to comply with the minimum food safety requirement laid down by the 1990 Act. Unsafe food is defined as that which is injurious to health under s. 7 (see 9.5.1), that which is unfit for human consumption and that which is contaminated within the meaning of the Act (s. 8(2)).

9.5.2.4.1 Unfit for human consumption Section 8(2)(b) represents no change in the existing law, with the result that case law relevant to earlier controls on unfit food will be applicable (see Stephenson (1982) 131 NLJ 871).

Food must be more than merely unsuitable for human consumption for the purposes of s. 8(2)(b). Thus pastry contaminated with penicillin mould which is not harmful to human beings (*David Greig Ltd* v *Goldfinch* (1961) 105 SJ 367; *Walker* v *Baxter's Butchers Ltd* [1977] Crim LR 479) is not unfit for human consumption. What is required, instead, is that the food is 'putrid, diseased or unwholesome' (*J. Miller Ltd* v *Battersea Borough Council* [1956] 1 QB 43). Thus if a person prepares bread which contains a toxic, dirty, used bandage (*Chibnall's Bakeries* v *Cope-Brown* [1956] Crim LR 263), or where caustic soda is supplied as lemonade (*Meah* v *Roberts* [1978] 1 All ER 97) the food will not be fit for human consumption.

The distinction between unfit and unsuitable food is now less important than used to be the case, since food which is unsuitable for human consumption due to the presence of some unwanted extraneous material such as mould or a piece of string in a loaf of bread (*Turner & Son Ltd* v *Owen* [1956] 1 QB 48) may be regarded as contaminated for the purposes of s. 8(2)(c). In any case, such food will also be regarded as not of the substance demanded by the consumer (s. 14 and see 9.5.6.2).

9.5.2.4.2 Contaminated food Section 8(2)(c) introduces the entirely new concept of contaminated food. It was clear that there was a loophole in previous legislation where food was unsuitable rather than unfit for human consumption. Food would appear to be contaminated if it is mouldy, rancid, stale or suffers from minor infestation. Likewise, if the food is contaminated with extraneous material such as pesticides or unauthorised additives, it is arguable that s. 8(2)(c) is not complied with.

Section 8(2)(c) requires the food to be so contaminated that it would not be reasonable to expect it to be used for human consumption in that state. The use of the words 'in that state' imply that something may be done to food in order to render it capable of consumption. For example, dates infested with insect excrement can be rendered capable of human consumption if they are processed into brown sauce (*R* v *Archer, ex parte Barrow Lane & Ballard Ltd* (1983) 82 LGR 361).

9.5.3 Enforcement powers

In order to ensure proper enforcement of the provisions of the Food Safety Act 1990, enforcement authorities are given a number of important powers. In particular, there are powers of inspection and seizure, and powers to apply to the court for an improvement notice, prohibition order or an emergency order so as to deal with suspected offenders.

9.5.3.1 Inspection, seizure and destruction Under the Food Safety Act 1990, s. 9(1), an enforcement officer has (at all reasonable times) the power to inspect food intended for human consumption which has been sold or is in the hands of a person for the purposes of supply or preparation for supply. After such an inspection has taken place, an enforcement officer may serve a notice preventing the sale of the food (s. 9(3)(a)(i)) or ordering that the food be removed to a specified place (s. 9(3)(a)(ii)) or requiring the food to be taken immediately before a magistrate so as to secure an order for its destruction (s. 9(3)(b)).

Where food is seized under s. 9(3), the enforcement authority has a maximum of 21 days in which to decide whether the food complies with the food safety requirement (s. 9(4)). If the authority is of the opinion that the food safety requirement has not been satisfied, the food is to be seized and dealt with by the magistrates' court (s. 9(4)(b)). Where the court is of the opinion that the food fails to comply with the food safety requirement, it may order the destruction of the food and require the owner to meet any expenditure incurred in disposing of it (s. 9(6)).

Where an enforcement authority decides to withdraw a notice issued under s. 9(3) or where the magistrates' court decides that the food does not infringe the food safety requirement, the enforcement authority is liable to pay compensation in respect of the depreciation in value of the food resulting from action having been taken (s. 9(7)). This is particularly important where the enforcement authority takes speculative action. While s. 9(1) envisages a prior inspection of food before any further action is taken, it is possible for an enforcement authority to issue a notice under s. 9(3) without a prior inspection, if it appears likely that food may cause food poisoning or any disease communicable to human beings (s. 9(2)). If an enforcement authority acts under s. 9(2) there is the danger that a mistake might be made, in which case, the compensation provisions will come into play.

9.5.3.2 Improvement notices   While the powers of inspection and seizure etc. apply only in relation to unsafe food, there are other enforcement powers which allow other courses of action. An improvement notice may be issued which requires the owner of a food business to comply with regulations made in respect of the processing or treatment of food or for the purposes of securing that food premises are in a hygienic condition (s. 10(1) and (3)). If a person fails to comply with an improvement notice, he commits an offence (s. 10(2)). The definition of a food business is very wide and includes a firm which sells, advertises, delivers, serves, prepares, wraps, labels, transports, stores, imports or exports food (s. 1(3) 'commercial operation'). Furthermore, businesses associated with food sources are also covered (s. 1(3) 'food business'), accordingly, improvement notices could be served on an agricultural business if necessary.

Where an improvement notice is served, it must state the grounds for believing that regulations have not been complied with and what the proprietor has done which amounts to non-compliance. The notice must also state what has to be done to secure compliance with the regulations and must specify the period within which the necessary steps should be taken (s. 10(1)).

9.5.3.3 Prohibition orders   If a person has been convicted of an offence under the food processing and hygiene regulations to which the improvement notice regime applies, an enforcement authority is also empowered to apply to the court for the issue of a prohibition order (Food Safety Act 1990, s. 11(1)(a)). Before a prohibition order is issued, the court must be satisfied that the food business presents a health risk (s. 11(1)(b)). For these purposes, a business presents a health risk if there is a risk of injury to health resulting from the use of any process or treatment, the construction of premises, the use of any equipment or the state or condition of any premises or equipment (s. 11(2)).

Where a health risk is established, a prohibition order must be issued, but the nature of the order will differ according to the nature of the health risk concerned. For example, the prohibition may relate to specified premises, a particular process or method of treatment or the use of certain types of equipment (s. 11(3)), and the order must clearly specify what is prohibited.

Where the enforcement authority is satisfied that a health risk no longer exists, they must issue a certificate, within three days, lifting the order (s. 11(6) and (7)). Furthermore, the person upon whom the order was served may apply for a certificate, in which case the enforcement authority must decide whether there is still a health risk within a period of 14 days (s. 11(7)).

9.5.3.4 Emergency orders Where there is an imminent health risk, the Food Safety Act 1990 confers special emergency powers on enforcement authorities (s. 12(1), (2) and (4)). The relevant procedure consists of the immediate issue of an emergency prohibition notice in terms identical to those which apply to prohibition notices (see s. 11(2) and (3) considered in 9.5.3.3). Alternatively, the enforcement authority can apply to a magistrates' court for an emergency prohibition order (s. 12(2)), but such an order will not be granted unless one day's notice has been given to the proprietor of the food business (s. 12(3)).

Where a prohibition notice has been issued, it will lapse after three days unless an application has been made to the magistrates' court under s. 12(2) for a court order to the same effect (s. 12(7)). Moreover, compensation is payable to the proprietor of the business where the court refuses to grant a prohibition order or where the enforcement authority decides not to apply to the court (s. 12(10)).

In addition to the powers of local authority enforcement officers, the 1990 Act also confers a power of emergency control on the Minister of Agriculture, Fisheries and Food (s. 13(1)). In the light of recent food scares, such a power is an important element in the control of food presenting a substantial health risk. The Act provides that an emergency control order may be made by the Minister in respect of commercial operations relating to food, food sources or contact materials and may be subject to such conditions as the Minister considers appropriate (s. 13(1) and (3)).

9.5.4 Food regulations

Like its predecessors, the Food Safety Act 1990 is largely an enabling statute, allowing for the creation of regulations or orders to deal with specific aspects of food safety and consumer protection (s. 16), compliance with European Community requirements (s. 17), special provisions for particular types of food (s. 18), and the registration and licensing of food premises (s. 19).

Given the number of regulations which already exist in relation to food, the Food Safety Act 1990 provides that these shall continue in force and shall take effect as if made under the 1990 Act (s. 59(3) and sch. 4). In addition to existing regulations, the 1990 Act gives new powers to make regulations which appear to be much stronger than under previous legislation.

9.5.4.1   Food safety and consumer protection   The Food Safety Act 1990, s. 16(1) (see also sch. 1), gives the Minister the power to make regulations in respect of a wide range of matters related to the safety and quality of food. In particular, regulations may be made in respect of the following: the composition of food (s. 16(1)(a)); means of securing that food is fit for human consumption (s. 16(1)(b)); processes or treatments used in the preparation of food (s. 16(1)(c)); hygiene (s. 16(1)(d)); labelling, marking, presenting or advertising food and descriptions which may be applied to food (s. 16(1)(e)) and any other matter which ensures that food complies with the food safety requirement and that the best interests of consumers are protected and promoted (s. 16(1)(f)).

These powers to make regulations are particularly important in the light of developing practices in the food industry. For example, it would be possible to introduce regulations in respect of novel practices such as food irradiation under s. 16(1)(c), on the basis that food irradiation is a form of food treatment or, failing that, as a process. Furthermore, where necessary, such matters can be brought to the attention of consumers by means of regulations made under s. 16(1)(e).

It is also important that the power to make regulations is not merely confined to the food itself, but also covers food sources and contact materials. Regulations in respect of food sources (see s. 1(3)) could relate to matters such as how animals or crops which are a source of food are dealt with. Thus it would be possible to make regulations forbidding the supply of beef from cattle affected by bovine spongiform encephalopathy (BSE) (see also sch. 1, para. 2(1)). The reference to contact materials would take in matters such as containers and other materials in which food is wrapped. Thus, it is possible to make regulations under s. 16(2) which lay down requirements in respect of materials such as cling film which might be harmful if they come into contact with food in specified circumstances, such as during microwave cooking.

The Food Safety Act 1990 also recognises the capacity of the food industry for innovation by conferring on the Minister a power to make regulations in respect of novel foods. These foods include both foods which have not previously been used for human consumption in Great Britain and foods which have only been used for human consumption to a very limited extent. This appears to cover both innovatory foods and those which have existed for years but have not been widely consumed in this country, for example, exotic fruit (see Howells, Bradgate and Griffiths, *Blackstone's Guide to the Food Safety Act 1990*, para. 5.5).

9.5.5   Food quality

While a principal concern of the Food Safety Act 1990 is the matter of public health and safety, there are also provisions which seek to prevent the consumer from being misled over the nature, quality or substance of the food he or she purchases.

The Food Safety Act 1990, s. 14, provides that it is an offence for a person to sell to the purchaser's prejudice any food which is not of the nature or substance or quality demanded by the purchaser (s. 14(1)). The food sold must be intended for human consumption (s. 14(2)) , thus a sale of a cream which is consumed internally, but is in fact intended for external application would not fall within s. 14. It is not a defence that the purchaser acquired the food for the purposes of analysis or examination (s. 14(2)).

9.5.5.1   Sale   If the person charged is to be convicted of the commission of an offence under the Food Safety Act 1990, s. 14, there must have been a sale. Without further explanation, the offence would be confined to the circumstances in which the Sale of Goods Act 1979, s. 2(1), applies. However, for the purposes of the 1990 Act, 'sale' is given an extended definition, so as to include all supplies of food in the course of a business (s. 2(1)), including giving food away as a prize at a place of public entertainment (s. 2(2)(a)) or as part of a promotional exercise (s. 2(2)(b)).

Unlike s. 8, s. 14 does not apply where food is offered or exposed for sale, since s. 14 is concerned with a demand made by the consumer coupled with a judgment about the quality of the food compared with the demand. It follows that it is open to the supplier to refuse to sell to a person he believes may be an enforcement officer. However, due to the extent of the overlap between s. 14 and s. 8, food which is not of the nature, substance or quality demanded will often fail to satisfy the food safety requirement on the ground that the food is contaminated.

9.5.5.2   Nature or substance or quality   The way in which the Food Safety Act 1990, s. 14, is worded creates three separate offences. At one time, the prohibition contained in the equivalent of s. 14 was worded conjunctively (Sale of Food and Drugs Act 1875, s. 6) with the result that the prosecution did not need to distinguish between the three elements of the offence. However, since the Food and Drugs (Adulteration) Act 1928, s. 2(1), the prohibition has been worded disjunctively with the result that the prosecution must specify whether the defendant is charged with selling food which is not of the nature demanded or the substance demanded or the quality demanded by the consumer. Often, a case will fall within more than one category, but if this is so the prosecution can lay more than one information. If the nature of the offence charged is not specified, the prosecution case may be held bad for uncertainty (*Bastin v Davies* [1950] 2 KB 579).

9.5.5.2.1   Nature   Food is not of the nature demanded by the consumer where he is given something not of the variety ordered. For these purposes, it would appear that if there is a breach of the Sale of Goods Act 1979, s. 13, the supplier of the food also commits an offence by not supplying food of the nature demanded. If the consumer asks for lemonade and is supplied with caustic soda (*Meah v Roberts* [1978] 1 All ER 97) an offence is committed under this limb of s. 14. The section is not confined to food which is harmful to health, with the result that an offence is still committed where the consumer does not get what he asked for. Thus, an offence is committed if margarine is supplied as butter or monkfish as scampi (cf. *Preston v Greenclose* (1975) 139 JPN 245) or where 'minced beef' contains a significant amount of meat other than beef (*Shearer* v *Rowe* (1985) 84 LGR 296). Where the food is harmful or contaminated and not of the nature demanded by the purchaser, there will be an overlap with s. 8, since the food safety requirement will not have been complied with (see 9.5.2).

In order to decide whether food is of the nature demanded, it is necessary to consider the way in which it has been described and what the ordinary purchaser would expect. Thus, the description 'butter toffee' implies that the confectionery contains no fat other than butter, with the result that if it contains coconut oil an offence is committed (*Riley Bros (Halifax) Ltd* v *Hallimond* (1927) 44 TLR 238).

9.5.5.2.2 Substance

In the past, food which contained unwanted additives or foreign bodies has been held not to be of the substance demanded by the purchaser. The presence of the unwanted article gives the food a substance to which the customer can reasonably object. It may be asked whether food is of the substance demanded where traces of pesticide or fertiliser are present, not having been washed off prior to sale.

This limb of s. 14 is not complied with where a caterpillar is found in a tin of peas (*Smedleys Ltd* v *Breed* [1974] AC 839), where a beetle is found in a can of strawberries (*Greater Manchester Council* v *Lockwood Foods Ltd* [1979] Crim LR 593) or where penicillin mould has been allowed to grow on a fruit pie (*Watford Corporation* v *Maypole Ltd* [1970] 1 QB 573). In cases of this kind, there is also an overlap with s. 8, in that the food may also be regarded as contaminated.

Food has also been held not to be of the substance demanded where there is a statutory standard for the type of food sold and the food supplied fails to comply with that standard. Thus if regulations require fish cakes to contain at least 35% fish and the defendant supplies a 'mock salmon cutlette' containing only 33% salmon, the item is not of the substance demanded by the consumer (*Tonkin* v *Victor Value Ltd* [1962] 1 All ER 821). In such a case, it can be assumed that a 'mock salmon cutlette' is expected to reach at least the same standard as a fish cake.

Problems may arise where the food contains unwanted additional material which is quite harmless. In such a case, it is necessary to ask whether the purchaser can reasonably object to the presence of the additive. For example, can the consumer reasonably object to the presence of a sterile foil cap in a bottle of milk (*Edwards* v *Llaethdy Merion Ltd* (1957) 107 LJ 138) or a drinking straw in a carton of milk (*Barber* v *Co-operative Wholesale Society Ltd* (1983) 81 LGR 762)? Clearly, the food is not contaminated in such a case, but the consumer nonetheless gets something different in substance to that which he has asked for. On one view, the presence of a sterile foil cap in a bottle of milk does not affect the milk as a substance in the same way that a nail in a boiled sweet does. If the consumer gets what he expects plus something else that comes into his mouth, the food is not of the substance demanded (*Edwards* v *Llaethdy Merion Ltd* (1957) 107 LJ 138 per Lord Goddard CJ). However, with respect, the same can be said of a foil cap which could stick in the throat of a child consumer.

An alternative view is that where the unwanted additional material is harmless, it nonetheless destroys the quality of the thing purchased, even if it does not affect the substance of the food (*Barber* v *Co-operative Wholesale Society Ltd* (1983) 81 LGR 762).

9.5.5.2.3   Quality   Quality should not be confused with description (*Anness* v *Grivell* [1915] 3 KB 685). Thus food of the type requested may be supplied but still fail to comply with the demanded standard of quality. What standard of quality should be achieved will depend on the circumstances of each case. It has been seen that in an action for breach of the contractual implied term about quality in the Sale of Goods Act 1979 (see 7.3.3.3), the standard of quality required will depend on a range of factors, including the price paid and any description applied to the goods. The same is equally true of an action under the Food Safety Act 1990, s. 14, since the price paid for food will reflect on the quality that can reasonably be expected by the consumer. Whether or not food is of the quality demanded is essentially a question of fact with the result that apparently similar cases may result in conflicting decisions on the facts. For example, in *Goldup* v *John Manson Ltd* [1981] 3 All ER 257 minced beef sold cheaply in comparison with better-quality meat and which contained 33% fat was held not to infringe the predecessor of s. 14 in the light of the price at which it was sold, whereas in *T.W. Lawrence & Sons Ltd* v *Burleigh* (1981) 80 LGR 631 a butcher who sold minced beef which contained 30.8% fat was held to be guilty of an offence on the ground that the customer's order implied that meat of a reasonable quality was required.

As in the case of actions under the Sale of Goods Act 1979, a description applied to food is relevant in determining whether the food is of the quality demanded. Thus in *McDonald's Hamburgers Ltd* v *Windle* [1987] Crim LR 200, the defendant displayed a notice explaining the nutritional attributes of their cola and diet cola. A customer asked for diet cola and was supplied with ordinary cola. In the circumstances it was held that the justices were entitled to conclude that the drink supplied was not of the quality demanded. An alternative view of this case is that the cola was not of the nature demanded by the consumer, since what was asked for and what was supplied were different entities.

There appears to be a considerable degree of overlap between the three elements of the s. 14 offence, and an examination of the cases reveals that the courts will rarely strike out an information on the ground that the prosecution have selected the wrong part of s. 14 on which to base their case. Frequently, the words 'substance' and 'quality' seem to be used interchangeably. For example, the presence of foreign objects in food is considered to affect the substance of that food (see 9.5.5.2.2) but it may also affect its quality. Thus a fly in a bottle of milk (*Newton* v *West Vale Creamery Ltd* (1956) 120 JP 318) or a nail in a bag of sweets (*Lindley* v *G.W. Horner & Co. Ltd* [1950] 1 All ER 234) has been held to affect the quality of the food supplied. Likewise, even where the unwanted material is not deleterious, but can reasonably be objected to, it may adversely affect the quality of the food supplied (*Barber* v *Co-operative Wholesale Society Ltd* (1983) 81 LGR 762).

9.5.5.3 Sale to the purchaser's prejudice It is essential that the food supplied should prejudice rather than benefit the purchaser. Without these words, an offence under s. 14 of the Food Safety Act 1990 would be committed every time the supplier gave the consumer more than he had asked for. What is important is that the retailer has supplied the consumer with something inferior to that which could reasonably be expected (*Hoyle* v *Hitchman* (1879) 4 QBD 233 at p. 240 per Lush J).

While prejudice is a requirement, it does not follow that prejudice is confined to cases of actual damage. Thus there is no need to point to pecuniary loss or physical illness resulting from consumption. Instead, it is sufficient that the consumer has asked for one thing and has been given something inferior (ibid.).

Without further qualification, it could be argued that where an enforcement officer purchases food for the purposes of testing, he is not prejudiced since he does not intend to eat the food and it is the local authority that has paid for the food. However, the 1990 Act gets round this problem by stating that it is not a defence that the food was bought merely for analysis or testing (s. 14(2)).

Where the supplier has displayed a notice which adequately brings it home to the consumer that the food is not of the nature, substance or quality demanded, this may affect his liability. A consumer who knows exactly what he is purchasing cannot claim to have been prejudiced. In order to achieve this end, the notice must be very clear in that it must be capable of informing the average consumer that he is not getting what he has asked for (*Rodbourn* v *Hudson* [1925] 1 KB 225).

9.5.5.4 The food demanded Closely associated with the requirement of prejudice is the requirement that the purchaser should have demanded food of a particular nature, substance or quality. If the food does not live up to the consumer's demand, it will ordinarily follow that the supply is to his prejudice in the sense that he has not got what he asked for (*Collins Arden Products Ltd* v *Barking Corporation* [1943] 1 KB 419).

The problem with many consumer purchases is that a detailed demand may not have been made. In such a case, the court may ascertain the requirements of the ordinary consumer by reference to a relevant statutory standard (*Tonkin* v *Victor Value Ltd* [1962] 1 All ER 821). Alternatively, the appropriate standard may be set by reference to the evidence of a public analyst (*T.W. Lawrence Ltd* v *Burleigh* (1981) 80 LGR 631) although it is clear that what the public analyst says is not conclusive (*Goldup* v *John Manson Ltd* [1981] 3 All ER 257).

The fact of a demand will normally be assumed. Thus a purchase in a supermarket nonetheless involves a demand because the consumer picks up goods which correspond with a description represented by the supplier (*Smedleys Ltd* v *Breed* [1974] AC 839).

9.5.6 Defences

9.5.6.1 Reasonable precautions and due diligence Where a person is charged with the commission of an offence under the Food Safety Act 1990, the principal defence available to him is that he has taken all reasonable precautions and has exercised due diligence to avoid the commission of an offence by himself or a person under his control. The elements of this defence are considered in more detail elsewhere (see 3.4.2).

9.5.6.2   Other defences   The Food Safety Act 1990 has failed to re-enact two defences which were previously available to a person charged with the commission of some offences in relation to food. The first of these was the defence of unavoidable consequences which could be pleaded where a person was charged with selling food not of the nature, substance or quality demanded (Food Act 1984, s. 3(2)). The way in which this defence had been interpreted was that an unavoidable consequence of the process of preparation was something that would happen every time food of that kind was prepared. The effect of this interpretation was that the defence became completely unworkable, and it is not surprising that it has been omitted from the defence provisions of the 1990 Act.

The other major omission is that of the 'written warranty' defence which used to exist under earlier legislation (Food Act 1984, s. 102). This defence allowed a person charged with the commission of an offence to plead that his immediate supplier had warranted the food fit for sale for human consumption. The disappearance of this defence is compensated for by the provisions of the Food Safety Act 1990, s. 21(3) and (4), which make a number of relevant presumptions.

By virtue of s. 21(3) it is presumed that a person selling food under his own name or mark has taken reasonable precautions if he has relied on information supplied to him by another person *and* he or some other person has carried out reasonable checks on the food *and* the person charged has no reason to suspect that an offence has been committed. Furthermore, by virtue of s. 21(4), where a person does not sell under his own name or mark (for example, where branded goods are sold) reasonable precautions are assumed to have been taken where the person charged has relied on information supplied to him by another aand he has no reason to suspect that an offence has been committed. The effect of this last presumption is to put the retailer in the same position as he would have been in had the written warranty defence been re-enacted.

9.6   THE SAFETY AND QUALITY OF FOOD - MATERIALS FOR CONSIDERATION

9.6.1   Injurious food

For text see 9.5.1.

Food Safety Act 1990

7.   Rendering food injurious to health
(1)   Any person who renders any food injurious to health by means of any of the following operations, namely—

(a)   adding any article or substance to the food;
(b)   using any article or substance as an ingredient in the preparation of the food;
(c)   abstracting any constituent from the food; and
(d)   subjecting the food to any other process or treatment,
with intent that it shall be sold for human consumption, shall be guilty of an offence.

(2)   In determining for the purposes of this section and section 8(2) below whether any food is injurious to health, regard shall be had—

(a)   not only to the probable effect of that food on the health of a person consuming it; but

(b)   also to the probable cumulative effect of food of substantially the same composition on the health of a person consuming it in ordinary quantities.

(3)   In this part 'injury', in relation to health, includes any impairment, whether permanent or temporary, and 'injurious to health' shall be construed accordingly.

9.6.2   Food safety requirements

For text see 9.5.2.

Food Safety Act 1990

8.   Selling food not complying with food safety requirements

(1)   Any person who—

(a)   sells for human consumption, or offers, exposes or advertises for sale for such consumption, or has in his possession for the purpose of such sale or of preparation for such sale; or

(b)   deposits with, or consigns to, any other person for the purpose of such sale or of preparation for such sale,
any food which fails to comply with food safety requirements shall be guilty of an offence.

(2)   For the purposes of this part food fails to comply with food safety requirements if—

(a)   it has been rendered injurious to health by means of any of the operations mentioned in section 7(1) above;

(b)   it is unfit for human consumption; or

(c)   it is so contaminated (whether by extraneous matter or otherwise) that it would not be reasonable to expect it to be used for human consumption in that state;
and references to such requirements or to food complying with such requirements shall be construed accordingly.

(3)   Where any food which fails to comply with food safety requirements is part of a batch, lot or consignment of food of the same class or description, it shall be presumed for the purposes of this section and section 9 below, until the contrary is proved, that all of the food in that batch, lot or consignment fails to comply with those requirements.

Note:

Is this requirement less far reaching than the general safety requirement of the proposed EC Directive (COM(90) 259 fin. OJ C156/8 27.6.90) which applies to food and is quoted in 9.3?

An important aspect of the food safety requirement is that food should be intended for human consumption. Certain presumptions are made in this regard:

Food Safety Act 1990

3. Presumptions that food intended for human consumption

(1)   The following provisions shall apply for the purposes of this Act.

(2)   Any food commonly used for human consumption shall, if sold or offered, exposed or kept for sale, be presumed, until the contrary is proved, to have been sold or, as the case may be, to have been or to be intended for sale for human consumption.

(3)   The following, namely—

(a)   any food commonly used for human consumption which is found on premises used for the preparation, storage, or sale of that food; and

(b)   any article or substance commonly used in the manufacture of food for human consumption which is found on premises used for the preparation, storage or sale of that food,

shall be presumed, until the contrary is proved, to be intended for sale, or for manufacturing food for sale, for human consumption.

(4)   Any article or substance capable of being used in the composition or preparation of any food commonly used for human consumption which is found on premises on which that food is prepared shall, until the contrary is proved, be presumed to be intended for such use.

A further limb of the food safety requirement is that food should not be unfit for human consumption.

J. Miller Ltd v *Battersea Borough Council*
[1956] 1 QB 43
Queens Bench Division

A bun contained a small piece of metal. Was this food item unfit for human consumption?

LORD GODDARD CJ at p. 47: Section 9 of the [Food and Drugs Act 1938, the predecessor of s. 8 of the Food Safety Act 1990] comes under the heading 'Sale of Unsound Food' and shows, therefore, that it is dealing with the sale of what may be called unwholesome foods. It is the section called into force when a butcher is found to have bad meat, that is to say, meat that is going putrid, exposed in his shop for sale. . . . Moreover, when one is construing an Act of Parliament of this sort one has to use a certain modicum of common sense, and I cannot understand how the magistrate could have thought that a bun containing a small piece of metal could fairly be described as unfit for human consumption. The bun was perfectly good. It had in it this metal which ought not to have been there, and therefore it can be said that metal to the prejudice of the purchaser was in the bun, but that does not make the bun unfit for human consumption.

Note:

Many items of food which are merely unsuitable for human consumption, as opposed to being unfit for human consumption, will now fall within the meaning of contaminated food, thereby covering a case such as *J. Miller Ltd* v *Battersea Borough Council*. What is contaminated seems to depend on what may be done with the food at a later date.

R v Archer ex parte Barrow Lane & Ballard Ltd
(1983) 82 LGR 361
Court of Appeal

Dates imported from Iraq were discovered to suffer from 14% insect infestation, but they were intended for processing into brown sauce.

DONALDSON MR at pp. 365–6: The dates were not 'dessert' dates, being of a different type and place of origin. They were heavily infested with insects which rendered them 'unwholesome for human consumption', to quote the public analyst's certificate. On the other hand, they were not said to be, and it is common ground that they were not, 'unfit for human consumption'. Unfortunately there is no definition of 'unwholesomeness' in the regulations.

The real issue, which was never brought to the attention of the magistrate, arises out of the fact that food may be 'unwholesome' in the context of an untreated use, but 'wholesome', provided that it is thereafter treated. Alternatively it may be 'wholesome' or 'unwholesome' in all normal contexts.

In our judgment regulation 6 should not be construed without regard to the intended use of the food. The regulation in terms applies only to food intended for sale for human consumption. This is a penal regulation which should be construed reasonably but restrictively and it seems to us that 'unfitness for human consumption', 'unsoundness' and 'unwholesomeness' should be judged in the context of the specific use intended. Were it otherwise, fermenting apples intended for the making of cider, which would certainly be unwholesome in the context of their being eaten, could never be imported. This cannot have been intended.

9.6.3   Food quality

For text see 9.5.5.

Food Safety Act 1990

14.   Selling food not of the nature or substance or quality demanded

(1)   Any person who sells to the purchaser's prejudice any food which is not of the nature or substance or quality demanded by the purchaser shall be guilty of an offence.

(2)   In subsection (1) above the reference to sale shall be construed as a reference to sale for human consumption; and in proceedings under that subsection it shall not be a defence that the purchaser was not prejudiced because he bought for analysis or examination.

An essential requirement of s. 14 is that there has been a sale of food. Sale is given a broad definition.

Food Safety Act 1990

2.   Extended meaning of 'sale' etc.

(1)   For the purposes of this Act—
    (a)   the supply of food, otherwise than on sale, in the course of a business; and
   (b)   any other thing which is done with respect to food and is specified in an order made by the Ministers,

shall be deemed to be a sale of the food, and references to purchasers and purchasing shall be construed accordingly.

(2) This Act shall apply—

(a) in relation to any food which is offered as a prize or reward or given away in connection with any entertainment to which the public are admitted, whether on payment of money or not, as if the food were, or had been, exposed for sale by each person concerned in the organisation of the entertainment;

(b) in relation to any food which, for the purpose of advertisement or in furtherance of any trade or business, is offered as a prize or reward or given away, as if the food were, or had been, exposed for sale by the person offering or giving away the food; and

(c) in relation to any food which is exposed or deposited in any premises for the purpose of being so offered or given away as mentioned in paragraph (a) or (b) above, as if the food were, or had been, exposed for sale by the occupier of the premises;

and in this subsection 'entertainment' includes any social gathering, amusement, exhibition, performance, game, sport or trial of skill.

The key features of s. 14 are that food should be of the nature or the substance or the quality demanded by the consumer.

As to the meaning of 'nature' consider the following case.

Meah v *Roberts*
[1978] 1 All ER 97
Queen's Bench Division

Was the supply of caustic soda instead of lemonade a supply of food not of the nature demanded?

WIEN J at pp. 102–5: The information against Meah, Uddin and Ali were first, that they, on 16th July 1975, at the Kashmir Restaurant, sold food in two glasses purporting to contain lemonade intended for but unfit for human consumption in that the glasses contained a solution of caustic soda, contrary to s. 8 of the Food and Drugs Act 1955. The next information in point of time was against Lansley, which alleged that the contravention of the 1955 Act was due to his own act or default. The third information was against Meah, Uddin and Ali to the effect that they sold to the prejudice of the purchaser, Heinz Studer, two glasses of lemonade which were not of the nature of the food demanded by the purchaser, contrary to s. 2 of the 1955 Act. Lastly there was an information against Lansley that the contravention of the 1955 Act was due to the act or default of Lansley and also that Meah, Uddin and Ali had not used all due diligence to secure that the provisions in question were complied with, pursuant to s. 113 of the 1955 Act.

. . . There is a case decided long ago which is in point, namely *Knight* v *Bowers* (1885) 14 QBD 845. That case concerned s. 6 of the 1875 Act, which now has become s. 2 of the 1955 Act. It involved the sale of a drug. The purchaser wished to buy saffron but instead he was sold savin. Saffron at that time was a drug used in the treatment of measles and, as is well known, is also a food colouring agent. Savin on the other hand was a drug improperly used for procuring an abortion. . . .

In the present case in my opinion Meah sold food on the basis that Mr Studer asked for lemonade for his children. It was lemonade that was agreed to be supplied and the waiter genuinely thought he was supplying lemonade. There was an agreement for the sale, and in the circumstances there was, as well, a sale of lemonade, as the justices found, although in fact caustic soda solution was provided. The fact that in pursuance of the sale something different was provided does not alter the fact that, through the waiter, Meah, Uddin and Ali sold lemonade. Clearly, drink (which is 'food') was sold and delivered when Mr Studer asked for lemonade and was provided with liquid that looked like lemonade for which in due course he expected to pay. It could hardly have been a sale of caustic soda solution since that was not requested by the customer. One asks, therefore, what else could have been sold except lemonade. A purported sale of lemonade is sufficient to constitute a sale of 'food' although something quite different was in fact supplied entirely unknown to both the waiter and the customer.

Substance generally covers unwanted extraneous material. The courts have had some difficulty in distinguishing the substance of food from its quality.

Tonkin v *Victor Value Ltd*
[1962] 1 All ER 821
Queen's Bench Division

Was the supply of a 'mock salmon cutlette' containing 33% salmon of the substance demanded?

LORD PARKER CJ at pp. 823–4: The real point in the present case is whether there was enough evidence before the justices to enable them to say, to put it loosely, that the content of fish was so substandard that an offence was established against s. 2 of the (Food and Drugs Act 1955). It has been said in many cases that, if there is no standard fixed by law as to the contents of a particular article, it is for the justices to make up their minds what is the proper standard that should be applied. They can only act on evidence, and the question immediately arises: What evidence will be sufficient to enable them to act? There are many cases in which, although a standard is not fixed by law, the generally accepted view of those in the trade and among analysts is that certain substances should be present in certain fixed proportions. That is quite clear. It is also clear that there may be cases where it can be said, for instance, in the case of an article which has been on the market for years, that it must contain at least a certain percentage, whatever it may be, in other words, a fixed minimum. The question, as I see it, in the present case, is whether there is a third possibility, namely, that the justices are entitled to act if there is evidence that, whatever the true minimum may be, the content of the article is below it.

What happened here was that the public analyst was called. The matter does not rest on his certificate; he was called. According to the case stated:

He accepted the word 'cutlette' as being a small cut of meat or fish and agreed that it could include a compounded article of food. He said that a mock salmon cutlette should contain a substantial amount of fish and that he would say that it was superior to a fish cake. He agreed that no standard was fixed by law for mock salmon cutlettes and that in his view the protein content was deficient.

In connection with that reference to fish cakes, it is to be observed, and, indeed, was found by the justices, that, by the Food Standards (Fish Cakes) Order 1950 (SI 1950/589), a fish cake must contain not less than 35% by weight of fish. In those circumstances, it seems to me that what this public analyst was saying was that 'cutlettes' in certain connections meant a cut of meat or fish; that if that were so, and nobody suggested that it is intended to be that sort of cutlette in the present case, it would contain 100% fish, though not salmon; but that it could include a compounded article of food, that is, fish and something else. He did not say that it was a fish cake, but he said that, in regard to the amount of fish in it, he took the view that it should be superior to a fish cake. It has been suggested that that means superior in some other respect, but in its context here he is clearly saying that it is superior in the sense that it ought to have more fish in it than there is in a fish cake. Therefore, the position really was that he was not saying that this was a fish cake, but that a fish cake, at any rate, had a minimum of 35% of fish, and, in his view, whatever minimum was taken for this form of mock salmon cutlette it should be something greater than 35%. The proved content of these cutlettes was 33%. Accordingly, unless that sort of evidence is not enough to enable the justices to act, an offence was proved.

It may be that different people would take different views on what was the fair minimum content, but I can see no logical reason why evidence that, whatever was the fair minimum, a particular content was below it is not evidence on which the justices can act in deciding whether an offence has been committed under s. 2. . . .

Accordingly, I have come to the conclusion that an offence was proved against the first respondents, and that the case should go back to the justices with a direction that it was proved that the first respondent had contravened s. 2 of the Act, and that they should then go on to consider whether such contravention was due to the act or default of the second respondent.

Barber v *Co-operative Wholesale Society Ltd*
(1983) 81 LGR 762
Queen's Bench Division

Is the supply of milk containing a sterile plastic straw a supply of food not of the substance or quality demanded?

ROBERT GOFF LJ at pp. 766–8: In the course of his judgment, [in *Edwards* v *Llaethdy Meirion Ltd* (1957) 107 LJ 138] as reported in *Bell and O'Keefe on the Sale of Food and Drugs*, 14th ed., p. 39, Lord Goddard CJ said:

I do not think we have ever said that the presence of something in an article of food must necessarily make that food not of the nature, quality or substance demanded by the purchaser. What we have said is that if the complaint is that something has been put in the food which does affect that nature, quality of substance but does not render the food unfit, then it is proper to proceed under section 2 [of the Food and Drugs Act 1955] and not under section 8, which deals with food which is unfit for human consumption. A good illustration is where the sale was of boiled sweets, and when somebody was about to suck one of these sweets, embedded in the sweet was found a nail. In that case it was held by the magistrate that there had been a sale of something which was not of the substance demanded because glucose or sugar, or whatever forms the substance of a sweet, is what you expect, and if you get that plus something which will come into your mouth, like a nail, I think that does affect the matter.

In our judgment, from that decision various conclusions can be drawn. First, the case is concerned with a charge that the goods were not of the substance demanded, not that they were not of the quality demanded. The conclusion was that nothing had happened which affected the milk as a substance. The present case is, of course, concerned with a charge that the goods were not of the quality demanded. Second, the court considered that the question in that case was essentially a question of fact for the justices. The same is undoubtedly true of the present case, though they have, of course, to ask themselves the correct question. Third, Lord Goddard CJ disclaimed the view that 'the presence of something in an article of food must necessarily make that food not of the nature, quality or substance demanded by the purchaser'.

We consider that none of these matters, nor indeed the decision of the court in that case, is inconsistent with the submission of the prosecutor in the present case. In every case concerned with a charge that food has been sold which is not of the quality demanded by the purchaser, it is no doubt true that the question is essentially one of fact for the justices to decide. But, where the case is concerned with the presence of extraneous matter, it is not necessary for the prosecution to prove that the extraneous matter is deleterious. It is sufficient for the prosecution to prove that the presence of the extraneous matter will give rise to the consequence that a purchaser could, in the context of the particular transaction, reasonably object to the presence of that matter in the article of food supplied, though if the presence of the extraneous matter was deleterious, it is difficult to see how in such circumstances the article could be of the requisite quality. If, in the case of *Edwards* v *Llaethdy Meirion Ltd* (1957) 107 LJ 138 the defendants had been charged with selling food which was not of the quality (as opposed to the substance) demanded by the purchaser, we have little doubt that the magistrates would still have acquitted the defendants because they would have been unlikely to hold that a purchaser could have reasonably objected to the presence of an extra milk bottle cap in a bottle of milk.

We therefore answer the question of law as follows. The unexplained presence of a green plastic straw in a bottle of milk will render the milk not of the quality demanded, within the meaning of section 2 of the Food and Drugs Act 1955, if its presence has the effect that the purchaser receives an article which was not, under the relevant transaction, of the quality which he was entitled to expect. This will be so in the present case, not only if the presence of the straw was deleterious to the milk, but also if its presence had the consequence that a purchaser could, in the context of the particular transaction, reasonably have objected to the presence of the straw in the milk.

The fact that food contains too much of a constituent that consumers might reasonably object to may render it not of the quality demanded.

Goldup v *John Manson Ltd*
[1981] 3 All ER 257
Queen's Bench Division

ORMROD LJ at p. 264: If the evidence in the present case is approached in this way the *bare* statement by the analyst 'In my opinion minced beef must not contain more than 25% of fat' is irrelevant since by itself it is not evidence of the quality demanded by the purchaser. The evidence given by the analyst and other witnesses as to the composition of other samples of minced beef is relevant as far as it goes. It proves that most samples of minced beef on sale contain 25% or less of fat which is some evidence of the commercial quality of minced beef. But, in this case, it does not go far enough because there is no indication of whether the samples were sold as first or second quality minced beef, and there is no evidence of the prices charged for the samples. This is particularly important where the cheaper of two qualities is chosen by the purchaser.

The prosecution have to prove that a purchaser of minced beef at 58p per pound is, in effect, demanding minced beef, the commercial quality of which contains significantly less than 33% of fat.

Whether food is of the quality demanded will depend on general consumer expectations, which may differ according to the particular demands of an individual consumer.

T.W. Lawrence & Sons Ltd v *Burleigh*
(1981) 80 LGR 631
Queen's Bench Divisional Court

Does minced beef containing 30.8% fat constitute food not of the quality demanded?

ORMROD LJ at pp. 636–7: In *Goldup* v *John Manson Ltd* [1981] 3 All ER 257, the court went on to point out, at p. 264:

> The prosecution have to prove that a purchaser of minced beef at 58p per pound is, in effect, demanding minced beef, the commercial quality of which contains significantly less than 33% of fat.

The justices came to the conclusion on all the evidence that there had been no breach of section 2 of the Food and Drugs Act 1955, in other words, the quality of mince provided to the consumer was of the quality demanded in that case.

In this case, they have come to the opposite conclusion. They have come to the conclusion that the mince supplied to Mrs O'Leary was not of the quality which she demanded. It is quite clear that in a case like this, the justices were not dealing directly with percentages of anything by way of quality. There are no fixed standards and they had a much more difficult task in this case than in many of these food and drug cases. The justices had to decide: What was the quality that the purchaser demanded? Was the article supplied up to that quality and, finally, was it sold to her prejudice?

In *Goldup* v *John Manson Ltd* this court tried to indicate some of the ways in which the justices can determine the quality which the purchaser was demanding. That must be the first step. On the facts of this particular case, there is no evidence at all of the quality of the mince which Mrs O'Leary was demanding because she ordered the mince either by telephone, or in writing, or by a combination of both. She did not buy the mince in the shop, seeing it on a platter, and she did not specify anything about price. She simply ordered mince. On ordinary principles, the implication of that offer — as it would be strictly in contract terms — would be that she was offering to buy mince of a reasonable quality having regard to the general practice of the trade. The question for the justices was: Was such mince supplied or not?

As to that, the first and most impressive piece of evidence in the case was Mrs O'Leary's own reaction to the mince when she saw it. She is experienced at buying mince and was a regular customer of the defendants. It is quite clear that when she saw it, she thought that it was not right. She thought it looked wrong. In her evidence, she said: 'I was shocked by the colour — a grey colour and too much white fat'. It is a reasonable inference that, rightly or wrongly, she thought that the quality of the mince sold to her was not in accordance with the quality she reasonably expected. That evidence is not at all strong in itself, but, at the same time, it is impressive. She took the mince to the trading standards officer who had it analysed and, on analysis, the fact content was found to be 32.7%. The analyst's observations were as follows: Mince, or minced beef, or minced steak of ordinary commercial quality does not contain fat in excess of 25%. He did the arithmetic and stated that, in his opinion, the sample contained an excess of fat amounting to 30.8%.

This case is not complicated by any question of cheaper quality or anything of that kind because Mrs O'Leary was quite unaware of the price difference. As I see it, it was open to the justices — if they thought it right — to put those two pieces of evidence together (the evidence of Mrs O'Leary and the analyst) and to reach the conclusion that they did.

An essential requirement of the Food Safety Act 1990, s. 14, is that the sale of the food should be to the purchaser's prejudice.

Hoyle v *Hitchman*
(1879) 4 QBD 233
Queen's Bench Divisional Court

MELLOR J at p. 240: What is the meaning of 'prejudice' here? It cannot be confined to pecuniary prejudice, or prejudice arising from the consumption of unwholesome food. The prejudice is that which the ordinary customer suffers, viz. that which is suffered by any one who pays for one thing, and gets another of inferior quality. The official purchaser is to purchase by way of testing whether the prejudice is suffered by the ordinary customer, and he is prejudiced in the same manner. The words 'to the prejudice of the purchaser' are necessary, because if they had not been inserted a person might have received a superior article to that which he demanded and paid for, and yet an offence would have been committed. The words are intended to show that the offence is not simply giving a different, but giving an inferior, thing to that demanded and paid for. It appears to me that the prejudice the Act intends is the general prejudice done to customers. The official personage is made, as it were, an official customer to test what the course of business at the particular shop is.

9.6.4   Defences

For text see 9.5.6. See also 3.4.2 and accompanying materials.

Food Safety Act 1990

21.   Defence of due diligence
(3)   A person satisfies the requirements of this subsection if he proves—
(a)   that the commission of the offence was due to an act or default of another person who was not under his control, or to reliance on information supplied by such a person;
(b)   that he carried out all such checks of the food in question as were reasonable in all the circumstances, or that it was reasonable in all the circumstances for him to rely on checks carried out by the person who supplied the food to him; and
(c)   that he did not know and had no reason to suspect at the time of the commission of the alleged offence that his act or omission would amount to an offence under the relevant provision.
(4)   A person satisfies the requirements of this subsection if he proves—

(a)   that the commission of the offence was due to an act or default of another person who was not under his control, or to reliance on information supplied by such a person;

(b)   that the sale or intended sale of which the alleged offence consisted was not a sale or intended sale under his name or mark; and

(c)   that he did not know, and could not reasonably have been expected to know, at the time of the commission of the alleged offence that his act or omission would amount to an offence under the relevant provision.

CHAPTER TEN

Defective Consumer Services

A frequent cause of consumer complaint is that a service provided by the supplier has not come up to standard. In most instances, the service will have been contracted for, accordingly the consumer's remedies will be dependent on the terms of his contract with the supplier. However, in other instances, the service may be provided otherwise than by way of a contract, for example, medical services provided under the National Health Service. In such a case, the consumer's principal remedies will lie in tort.

While the civil law obligations of the supplier are important, valuable sources of consumer protection can also be found in the form of criminal law regulation of the supply of services (see chapter 11) and in trade association codes of practice voluntarily submitted to by members of the association.

10.1 THE RANGE OF CONSUMER SERVICES AND THE PROBLEMS ENCOUNTERED BY CONSUMERS

Services provided for consumer consumption can come in a variety of forms. Two broad categories can be identified, namely, a service related to the transfer of possession of or ownership in goods or materials or a pure service.

The provision of a pure service requires the expertise or skill of the provider and nothing more. Such services include the professional services of a doctor, a lawyer, a surveyor, a financial adviser or other advice givers. Apart from advice givers, the consumer may also require pure services from the providers of leisure, transport and cleansing services.

Services associated with the supply of goods or materials will normally be provided by a skilled tradesman such as a plumber, electrician or double-glazing contractor, all of whom will use some material article in addition to the skill they exercise. It is important in this context to identify the source of the consumer's complaint. If the product supplied is defective an issue of product liability is raised (see chapters 7 and 8). However, if the manner of installation is the cause of complaint, a defective service has been provided. The other major type of consumer service involves the transfer of possession of goods, without a corresponding transfer of ownership. A typical example of such a service is the contract of hire, for example, the bailment of a rented television for a specified or indeterminate period of time. Important considerations in contracts of this kind are whether the bailor has title to the goods and whether the goods bailed are as described or of the desired quality or fitness. The implied terms relating to description, quality and fitness are almost the same as those implied in a contract for the sale of goods and are considered elsewhere (see 7.3)

Wherever a service is provided, it must be accepted that the service industry has its fair share of cowboys who may be prepared to engage in unfair practices, detrimental to the consumer. The service provider may be guilty of shoddy or late performance, or of overcharging. All of these issues are intimately concerned with the civil liability of the supplier. However, the criminal law, administrative and business self-control may also alleviate the plight of the consumer. Recourse to law may not always be necessary due to the emergence of numerous trade association codes of practice, which may give greater protection to the consumer than is available through the medium of legal controls. In other instances the consumer may be happy to make a complaint to a consumer protection agency and not pursue an action for damages. For example, a complaint to a trading standards authority may result in the prosecution of the provider of a service, particularly where he has given false or misleading information concerning the price, provision or availability of a service. (see chapters 11 and 12).

10.2   CIVIL LIABILITY OF THE SUPPLIER

Consumer services may be provided pursuant to a contract or independently of any such contract. For example, no contract exists between a litigant and a barrister (*Kennedy* v *Broun* (1863) 13 CBNS 677) or between a National Health Service doctor and his patient. Similarly, the purchaser of a house who relies on a building society valuation of the property he proposes to purchase may not have dealt directly with the surveyor who provides the valuation (see *Smith* v *Eric S. Bush* [1989] 2 All ER 514) in which case, no contractual relationship exists. However, in all such cases, the provider of the service will still owe a duty to exercise reasonable care in the provision of the service.

Services provided by way of bailment such as repair, film processing, cleaning and carriage services will often be subject to the terms of a contract which include an implied term to take reasonable care. However, in the case of a gratuitous bailment, the provider nonetheless owes a duty to take reasonable care of the consumer's property. A repairer may also owe a duty of care to a stranger in respect of his failure to effect a safe repair. For example, in *Stennett* v *Hancock* [1939] 2 All ER 578 a garage was liable for negligence where it failed to exercise reasonable care in effecting repairs to the wheel of a vehicle with the result that the wheel flange came loose and struck a pedestrian.

10.2.1 Contractual liability

Normal rules of the law of contract apply to consumer contracts, although in some instances, the application of such rules can present difficulties (see 3.2.1.1). In particular, the consumer must provide consideration. Unlike contracts for the sale of goods, any consideration will suffice for the purposes of a contract for the supply of services (Supply of Goods and Services Act 1982, s. 12(3)).

10.2.1.1 Implied terms under the Supply of Goods and Services Act 1982
The obligations of the parties are represented by the terms of the contract, which may be express terms or may be implied by statute. The Supply of Goods and Services Act 1982 implies a duty on the part of the business supplier to undertake to perform the service with reasonable care and skill (s. 13) and, in the absence of express contractual provision, a duty to perform the service within a reasonable time (s. 14(1)). Furthermore, where the contract does not provide otherwise, there is an implied term to the effect that the consumer will pay no more than a reasonable charge for the service, whether or not the supplier acts in the course of a business (s. 15(1)). It is noticeable that the terms implied in a contract for the provision of services are generally less onerous than those implied in a contract for the sale of goods under which the supplier guarantees the fitness of the goods for the purpose for which the buyer requires them. It has been argued that the standard required of the supplier of consumer services is too low (Stephenson and Clark, National Consumer Council Paper (1985)). However, it may be responded that the person who requests a service will frequently specify the nature and extent of the service he requires (Law Com. No. 156 (Cmnd 9773, 1986), para. 2.24). The response of the Law Commission may, in turn, be criticised on the ground that consumers often fail to specify exactly what they want due to a lack of information on their part. Accordingly, it remains the case that the consumer of services is in a considerably worse position than the consumer of a defective product.

Some services do not fall within the provisions of the Supply of Goods and Services Act 1982. Consistent with the view that the Act gives effect to the common law, a distinction is drawn between a contract of service and a contract for services. It follows that contracts of employment and contracts of apprenticeship do not fall within the provisions of the 1982 Act (s. 12(2)). Other types of service contract may also be excluded from the provisions of the Act, by order of the Secretary of State, so as to give effect to the position at common law before 1982. Thus, exemptions have been made in respect of advocates, company and building society directors and arbitrators (see SI 1982/1771; SI 1983/902 and SI 1985/1) with the effect that the implied term relating to the exercise of reasonable care and skill does not apply to the services provided by such persons.

10.2.1.2 Contracts for services and contracts for work and materials
Many contracts for the provision of a service also involve the supply of goods.

For example, the consumer may engage the services of a plumber to supply and install a bathroom suite. In such a case, it becomes important to distinguish between the supply of goods element in the contract and that part of the contract that relates to the skill exercised by the plumber. If the reason for the consumer's complaint is that the bath is defective, the consumer will be able to invoke the implied terms which relate to the fitness and quality of the goods supplied and which impose a form of strict liability (see 7.3.3 and 7.3.4). However, if the consumer's complaint is that the bath has been badly fitted, his complaint is in respect of the service provided. In such a case, subject to what has been expressly agreed, the supplier of the service is liable only for his failure to exercise reasonable care and skill.

Distinguishing between a contract for the supply of a service and one for the supply of goods is sometimes difficult. Some contracts are primarily contracts for the supply of a service which incidentally involve the supply of a material article. For example, in *Perlmutter* v *Beth David Hospital* (1955) 123 NE 2d 792 the plaintiff, a private patient, was given a blood transfusion with contaminated blood. Expert evidence showed that the contamination was undetectable. The plaintiff claimed that the defendants were strictly liable for breach of the implied term relating to product quality. However, the majority of the court held that the contract was one for the provision of a service and that the defendants would only be liable for a failure to exercise reasonable care (see also *Roe* v *Minister of Health* [1954] 2 QB 66). However, in *Dodd* v *Wilson* [1946] 2 All ER 691 the plaintiff's cattle were harmed as a result of the defendant veterinary surgeon's use of a serum which was not fit for its intended use. The defendant was not negligent but was nonetheless liable for the harm suffered. It is difficult to distinguish these cases and it might be argued that they show scant regard for personal safety compared with the safety of a farmer's cattle. However, a distinction may lie in the fact that a substance such as human blood is not ordinarily regarded as something which is the subject of a commercial transaction (cf. Consumer Protection Act 1987, s. 45(1) and see 8.4.2).

The test employed for distinguishing a supply of goods from a supply of services is to enquire what is the substance of the contract. It is necessary to determine whether the contract is substantially one for the exercise of skill or one which is intended to transfer ownership in goods to the consumer. For example, if a prospective house purchaser engages the services of a surveyor, he will receive a material article in the form of a written report, but the substance of the contract is the skill of the surveyor in surveying the property. Likewise, in *Robinson* v *Graves* [1935] 1 KB 579 a contract for the provision of a service was made where a consumer engaged the services of an artist to paint a portrait, despite the transfer of ownership in the painting. In contrast, a contract for the supply of a meal in a restaurant appears to be a contract for the sale of goods (*Lockett* v *A. & M. Charles Ltd* [1938] 4 All ER 170, see also Supply of Goods and Services Act 1982, s. 12(3)(a)), despite the undoubted skill which goes into the preparation of the meal (see also *Lee* v *Griffin* (1861) 1 B & S 272).

10.2.2 Tortious liability

The non-contractual supplier of a service is not immune from liability as he may owe a duty of care to the consumer of the service. Alternatively, the fault of the supplier may consist of giving misinformation which induces the consumer to enter into a contract with him. In such a case, the misleading information may not be regarded as part of the contract, but the supplier of the service may still be liable for his misrepresentation.

10.2.2.1. Negligence Where there is no contract, the supplier of a service may still be liable for a failure to exercise reasonable care. Thus if the service is provided gratuitously or if the supplier's defective performance foreseeably harms a third party, the supplier may be liable for his negligence. Much will depend on the type of harm suffered by the consumer. As a general rule it is much easier for a negligence action to succeed where the consumer has suffered personal injury or property damage than if the harm is of a financial nature.

Even if there is a contractual relationship between the supplier and the consumer, the consumer may choose to sue for breach of a tortious obligation since it is now established that contractual and tortious duties of care may exist concurrently (see *Midland Bank Trust Co. Ltd* v *Hett, Stubbs & Kemp* [1979] Ch 384; *Forsikringsaktieselskapet Vesta* v *Butcher* [1986] 2 All ER 488 at p. 507; cf. *Groom* v *Crocker* [1939] 1 KB 194 and see also Kaye (1984) 100 LQR 680).

Whether the consumer sues in contract or in tort has practical implications, since different rules on limitation of actions apply whether the action is framed in contract or in tort. Furthermore, there are apparently different rules relating to remoteness of damage and quantification of damages depending on whether the action is framed in contract or in tort.

10.2.2.2 Misrepresentation As with any contract, the supplier of a service may make a number of assertions about his intended performance. Some of these assertions may be treated as express terms of the contract whereas others will amount to representations only. If the representation proves to be false, it may be actionable under the Misrepresentation Act 1967 or under the common law rule concerning negligent misstatements in *Hedley Byrne & Co. Ltd* v *Heller & Partners Ltd* [1964] AC 465.

10.3 CIVIL LIABILITY OF SUPPLIERS – MATERIALS FOR CONSIDERATION

10.3.1 Contractual liability

Supply of Goods and Services Act 1982

12. The contracts concerned

(1) In this Act a 'contract for the supply of a service' means, subject to subsection (2) below, a contract under which a person ('the supplier') agrees to carry out a service.

(2) For the purposes of this Act, a contract of service or apprenticeship is not a contract for the supply of a service.

(3)   Subject to subsection (2) above, a contract is a contract for the supply of a service for the purposes of this Act whether or not goods are also—
   (a)   transferred or to be transferred, or
   (b)   bailed or to be bailed by way of hire,
under the contract, and whatever is the nature of the consideration for which the service is to be carried out.

(4)   The Secretary of State may by order provide that one or more of sections 13 to 15 below shall not apply to services of a description specified in the order, and such an order may make different provision for different circumstances. . . .

13.   Implied term about care and skill
In a contract for the supply of a service where the supplier is acting in the course of a business, there is an implied term that the supplier will carry out the service with reasonable care and skill.

14.   Implied term about time for performance
(1)   Where, under a contract for the supply of a service by a supplier acting in the course of a business, the time for the service to be carried out is not fixed by the contract, left to be fixed in a manner agreed by the contract or determined by the course of dealing between the parties, there is an implied term that the supplier will carry out the service within a reasonable time.

(2)   What is a reasonable time is a question of fact.

15.   Implied term about consideration
(1)   Where, under a contract for the supply of a service, the consideration for the service is not determined by the contract, left to be determined in a manner agreed by the contract or determined by the course of dealing between the parties, there is an implied term that the party contracting with the supplier will pay a reasonable charge.

(2)   What is a reasonable charge is a question of fact.

10.4   THE GENERAL DUTIES OF THE PARTIES TO A SUPPLY OF SERVICES

Where a service is provided by way of a contract, the supplier is subject to a number of implied duties in respect of his performance. Some of these duties will apply to the supplier whether or not there is a contractual relationship between the supplier and the consumer. Additionally, the supplier may also expressly undertake to do more than that which is implied by law. The implied obligations of the supplier include a duty to perform the service with reasonable care and skill, to perform the service within a reasonable time and to charge no more than a reasonable amount. Other factors which may also be relevant are whether personal performance is required and whether the supplier ever guarantees a particular result.

10.4.1   Reasonable care and skill
Whether the action is framed in contract or in tort, the supplier owes a duty to exercise reasonable care in the performance of a service. In a contractual action, the duty is based on the Supply of Goods and Services Act 1982, s. 13, and if

the action is one for negligence at common law, the duty is based on ordinary *Donoghue* v *Stevenson* [1932] AC 562 principles either as a variety of manufacturers' liability or on the basis that the consumer is the supplier's neighbour (see chapter 8).

10.4.1.1 Privity of contract and tortious proximity As a general rule, the duty owed by the supplier will be based on a voluntary assumption of liability, since the relationship between the supplier and the consumer is normally very close, and performance of the service will have been expressly requested. Accordingly, the supplier will be aware of the identity of the person who benefits from the provision of the service. Even if this is not the case, the supplier will usually be aware that someone in the class of persons to which the consumer belongs will rely on the service provided.

In the case of a service provided by way of a contract, a duty of care is implied under the Supply of Goods and Services Act 1982, s. 13. Where a service is provided in a non-contractual setting, the consumer will have to establish that he is sufficiently proximate to the supplier to justify protection in law.

Establishing the necessary relationship of proximity is difficult in cases where the service has not been requested but the consumer has nonetheless relied on the supplier. This problem may arise where one person gives information to another which is then passed on to a third party who detrimentally relies on it, for example where a valuation report by a surveyor is given to a building society in the knowledge that it will be passed on to the purchaser of the surveyed house. In such a case, the surveyor does owe the purchaser a duty to exercise reasonable care, provided he is aware that such a person would almost certainly rely on the valuation (*Smith* v *Eric S. Bush* [1989] 2 All ER 514; *Yianni* v *Edwin Evans & Sons* [1982] QB 438). Furthermore, in this instance, the purchaser will also have paid the building society for the survey, and the society in turn will pay the surveyor for his services which makes the relationship between the parties that much closer.

The duty owed by the surveyor will only extend to those who foreseeably rely on the information. Thus, it would not be reasonable to extend the duty of care to include a friend of the original mortgage applicant to whom the information is later passed.

It would appear that the mortgage valuation cases probably represent the high-water mark of negligence liability for economic loss, since in a line of recent cases involving negligent financial advice, the courts have attempted to define more clearly the very limited circumstances in which the supplier of financial advisory services owes a duty of care to the person who acts on his advice. In *Caparo Industries plc* v *Dickman* [1990] 1 All ER 568 it was held that reasonable foresight of harm on its own is not sufficient to give rise to a duty to take care. It is also essential that there is a very close relationship of proximity between the giver and the recipient of the advice, characterised by reasonable reliance on the advice and that the imposition of a duty of care should be fair and just in the circumstances. Moreover, special regard must be had to the adviser's knowledge of the particular purpose for which the advice is to be used (ibid. at p. 576 per Lord Bridge).

These elements were explained further in *James MacNaughton Paper Group Ltd* v *Hicks Anderson & Co.* [1991] 1 All ER 134 where it was said that regard should be had to the purpose for which the statement was made and communicated, the relationship between the adviser, the advisee and any relevant third party, the size of the class to which the advisee belongs, the knowledge of the adviser and the extent of reliance by the advisee.

The conclusion which follows from these cases is that very rarely will a financial adviser owe a duty of care to a person who relies on his advice, unless the adviser is made fully aware of the nature of the reliance and the transaction the advisee proposes to enter into in reliance on the advice. Thus a company auditor will generally owe no duty of care to a person who relies on audited company accounts to purchase additional shares in the company whose accounts he has audited (*Caparo Industries plc* v *Dickman* [1990] 1 All ER 568). However, a duty of care may be owed by an accountant who negligently prepares accounts to be shown to an identified potential investor (*Morgan Crucible Co. plc* v *Hill Samuel & Co. Ltd* [1991] 1 All ER 148).

Where the consumer commissions building services, the builder will be liable under the terms of his contract with the consumer (see 10.8.3). Whether the builder is also liable for losses suffered by a subsequent purchaser depends on the provisions of the Defective Premises Act 1972 and on the type of loss suffered by the consumer.

If a consumer complains of personal injury or damage to property other than the building itself, the loss is prima facie actionable in tort (see *D & F Estates Ltd* v *Church Commissioners for England* [1988] 2 All ER 992). For these purposes, property damage appears to include damage by one part of a 'complex structure' to another part of the same complex structure (ibid. at p. 1006 per Lord Bridge). Although what constitutes a complex structure is not entirely clear (see 7.5.1).

10.4.1.2 The Required Standard of Care Whether the consumer's action lies in contract or in tort, the same basic standard of care applies. The business supplier of a service has to perform to the standard of the reasonably competent member of the relevant trade (Supply of Goods and Services Act 1982, s. 13; *Bolam* v *Friern Hospital Management Committee* [1957] 1 WLR 582 at p. 586 per McNair J). Accordingly, a jeweller piercing the ears of a consumer is required to reach the standard expected of a reasonable jeweller, not the standard expected of a surgical registrar (*Phillips* v *William Whiteley Ltd* [1938] 1 All ER 566). However, a hairdresser who fails to read instructions on how to use a hair dye before applying it to his client's scalp (*Watson* v *Buckley, Osborne, Garrett & Co.* [1940] 1 All ER 174) or a carpet layer who leaves a carpet in a condition whereby the consumer can trip over an exposed edge (*Kimber* v *William Willett Ltd* [1947] 1 All ER 361) both fail to reach the standard of the reasonably competent. It is a requirement of such cases that the service is provided in a workmanlike and safe manner (*Kimber* v *William Willett Ltd* at p. 362 per Tucker LJ).

A relevant factor considered by the court in determining whether the duty of care has been broken is that of general and approved practice. If the supplier of the service has complied with a standard practice, this may be some evidence that he has exercised reasonable care. However, such compliance should not be regarded as conclusive evidence of the exercise of such care. It may be the case that an established practice has become obsolete and that adherence to it is to be regarded as negligence on the part of the service provider (*Brown* v *Rolls Royce Ltd* [1960] 1 WLR 210).

Since the test applied is objective, it is no defence for the supplier to argue that he has done his incompetent best. The supplier is judged by the standards of the reasonably competent supplier of the type he claims to be. Thus the novice who has just started to supply a service of a particular kind is required to reach the same standard of competence as the supplier with a number of years' experience (*Nettleship* v *Weston* [1971] 2 QB 691).

If the service is not provided in the course of a business, s. 13 of the 1982 Act does not apply, but the private supplier will still be subject to the tortious duty to take reasonable care. However, since the supplier is not acting in the course of a business, the standard he will be expected to adhere to will be lower than that expected of a professional. Nonetheless, he will be expected to reach the standard of a reasonably competent amateur (*Wells* v *Cooper* [1958] 2 QB 265).

It has been argued that the standard of reasonable care and skill is too low a standard for the purposes of consumer services and that it produces uncertainty as to what the consumer can expect from the supplier. However, it would appear that for the time being no changes in the law are likely, since the Law Commission regard the present state of the law as satisfactory. The Law Commission were of the view that the standard of reasonable care is a flexible standard and that decided cases are sufficient guidance on how the test is to be applied in particular instances.

10.4.2. Guaranteeing a result

Since the supplier of a service is ordinarily liable only for a failure to exercise reasonable care, it follows that the supplier will not be deemed to guarantee a particular result. This position holds even for the contractual supplier of services. Unlike the contractual supplier of goods, the supplier of a service is not regarded as an insurer in respect of harm suffered by the consumer. It follows that a solicitor does not warrant the success of proposed litigation and a surgeon does not guarantee that an operation will be successful (*Thake* v *Maurice* [1986] 1 All ER 497). The position in English law differs substantially from Australian law which implies on the part of the supplier of a service a warranty that the service will be reasonably fit for the purpose made known to him by the consumer and that the service is of such quality that it might reasonably be expected to achieve the desired result (Trade Practices Act 1974 (Australia), s. 74(2)).

The contractual supplier of a service can guarantee a result, but this will normally be the result of an express term of the contract. Thus in *G. K. Serigraphics* v *Dispro Ltd* (unreported, CAT 916, 1980) the appellants contracted to stick a laminated surface on printed boards. When the lamination failed to work, the appellants were taken to have agreed expressly to laminate the boards properly. Since they had not done what they had contracted to do, their breach went to the root of the contract.

The problem with express contractual terms is that the consumer must know exactly what he wants and negotiate with the supplier to that end. Unfortunately, the consumer will not always be sure what it is he wants and may not be able to contract for the result he requires. Accordingly, it might be better for the law to imply certain basic standards.

Occasionally, the circumstances of the case may justify the imposition of a standard higher than that of reasonable care, with the result that the supplier of a service may be deemed to have undertaken to produce a particular outcome. In *Greaves & Co. (Contractors) Ltd* v *Baynham Meikle & Partners* [1975] 3 All ER 99 the designers of a warehouse floor were taken to have impliedly warranted that the floor would be reasonably fit for the use of fork-lift trucks. The circumstances showed that the customer had made it clear that such trucks would be used. Furthermore, there had been a warning by the British Standards Institution that traffic vibration could cause cracks in the type of floor recommended by the defendants.

The decision in *Greaves & Co. (Contractors) Ltd* v *Baynham Meikle & Partners* would seem to suggest that design services may fall into a separate category in which the courts are more prepared to imply higher standards on the part of the supplier of the service. Certainly, it is true that a designer supplies an end-product which may be more easily equated with the position of the supplier of goods, thereby justifying a requirement that the design should be reasonably fit for the purpose for which it is intended. In the field of building design services, it is important to relate the designer's obligations to those of the main contractor under his contract with the building owner. In *Independent Broadcasting Authority* v *EMI Electronics Ltd* (1980) 14 BLR 1, the IBA had employed EMI, as main contractors, to design and supply a television mast. BICC were nominated sub-contractors responsible for the design. The IBA had raised doubts about the safety of the proposed design, but they had been assured in a letter sent by BICC to EMI that the mast would not oscillate dangerously. Subsequently, the mast did collapse, due to design faults. In the event, it was held that EMI had warranted the fitness of the mast to the IBA and that BICC had also given the same warranty to EMI. Accordingly, a chain of contractual liability was set up. However, there are also dicta to the effect that where a service only is supplied, a duty to exercise reasonable care alone will arise, but where a chattel is to be delivered there is a strict obligation to ensure that the chattel is fit for its intended purpose, in the absence of an express or implied term negating the liability of the designer. In the circumstances of the IBA case, that warranty would have been given by BICC directly to the IBA (see 14 BLR 1 at pp. 47-48 per Lord Scarman; see also *Samuels* v *Davis* [1943] KB 526).

An important factor in *Greaves & Co. (Contractors) Ltd* v *Baynham Meikle & Partners* was that the supplier knew what the customer required. It would not be reasonable to expect the supplier to comply with the consumer's unstated desires. Thus it is important for the consumer to voice his requirements as these may increase the cost of the service or require the exercise of new skills (*CRC Flooring v Heaton* (8 October 1980 unreported). At the same time, if the consumer engages the services of an expert, he may expect to pay fees representing the skill of the expert. In such a case, it may be reasonable for him to expect a standard of performance in excess of the reasonably competent (*Duchess of Argyll* v *Beuselinck* [1972] 2 Lloyd's Rep 172 at p. 183 per Megarry J).

10.4.3 Personal performance

The Supply of Goods and Services Act 1982, s. 13 provides, *inter alia*, that the supplier will carry out the service. It may be argued that this implies a requirement of personal performance of the service which the supplier has undertaken to supply (see Palmer (1983) 46 MLR 619). If the 1982 Act does incorporate a requirement of personal performance, it would appear to have extended the liability of the supplier as compared with the position at common law where delegation is impliedly permitted, where appropriate (see *Davies* v *Collins* [1945] 1 All ER 247; *Stewart* v *Reavell's Garage* [1952] 1 All ER 1191). While this construction would appear to be possible, the Law Commission (Law Com. No. 156 (Cmnd 9773, 1986), para. 2.25) take the view that s. 13 will not be construed by the courts so as to produce a requirement of personal performance in every case.

10.4.4 Delayed performance

A common consumer complaint is that the work commissioned starts late or takes much longer in performance than was originally anticipated. This is a particular problem in relation to building work including the installation of double-glazing.

   If the supplier has contracted to supply the service on a specified date, failure to comply with that date is a breach of contract which may give the consumer the right to treat his obligation to perform the contract as being at an end. Furthermore, it may be possible to imply an agreed date for performance by reference to a previous course of dealings between the parties. However, in the context of consumer services, particularly those for the supply of expensive building services, it is unlikely that there will be a sufficient degree of regularity to imply the existence of a course of dealing (see also 5.3.3). Whether or not the supplier's breach will have this effect will depend on the ratio quantitatively which the breach bears to the contract as a whole. The supplier's breach may be regarded as insufficiently serious to justify repudiation by the consumer, in which case the breach will be treated as a breach of warranty giving rise to an action for damages only.

   In deciding whether the consumer can treat his obligation to perform as being at an end, it is necessary to determine whether the provision in the contract relating to the time of performance is of the essence of the contract. Generally, time provisions in non-commercial contracts are not treated as being of the essence of the contract, but there are circumstances where this is not so. Time will be of the essence of the contract where the parties have expressly provided for this and where the circumstances of the case suggest that time is of the essence (*United Scientific Holdings Ltd.* v *Burnley Borough Council* [1978] AC 904 at p. 958 per Lord Fraser). Thus if the contract provides for the purchase of shares by a specified date, the time stipulation will be regarded as crucial due to the volatile nature of the subject-matter of the contract (*Hare* v *Nicoll* [1966] 2 QB 130). Furthermore, where a consumer who has been the subject of unreasonable delay gives the supplier reasonable notice requiring performance by a specified date, time will be of the essence of the contract (*Charles Rickards Ltd* v *Oppenheim* [1950] 1 All ER 420). The problem posed by this last rule is that it may be difficult to advise a consumer when he has been the subject of an unreasonable delay as this is a question of fact in each case. If the consumer has contracted for the supply and installation of a central heating system by a specified date and the supplier attempts to perform the work after that date, it may be unreasonable for the consumer to refuse to accept the late performance, in which case he is then in breach of contract.

If the contract does not provide for the time of performance and it is not possible to determine by other means when the service is to be performed, the Supply of Goods and Services Act 1982, s. 14(1), provides that a supplier acting in the course of a business will carry out the service within a reasonable time. What is a reasonable time is a question of fact (s. 14(2)). Therefore, the court will have to consider the nature of the work to be carried out, the availability of the necessary materials for completing the work and the general conditions and customs of the trade under consideration. In deciding whether the supplier is in breach of the implied term, the court will consider what time would have been taken by a reasonably competent tradesman in the particular circumstances of the case under consideration (*Charnock* v *Liverpool Corporation* [1968] 3 All ER 473). The standard required of the supplier is that of the reasonably competent, therefore he will not be liable for delays that are beyond his control. Thus if the delay is due to procrastination or the imposition of unreasonable conditions on the part of the consumer, the supplier will not be in breach of the implied term. Similarly, if the delay is due to external factors beyond the supplier's control, such as a strike by workmen, there will be no breach of s. 14(1) (*Hick* v *Raymond & Reid* [1893] AC 22).

10.4.5 Cost

The amount payable by the consumer for a service provided will depend initially on the terms of his contract with the supplier. It has been observed by the National Consumer Council that when a consumer purchases goods, he will almost always know the price in advance. However, in the case of a supply of services, this will not always be the case (National Consumer Council, *Services and the Law: A Consumer View* (1981), p. 17). Sometimes the supplier will display fixed charges, as do hairdressers, dry cleaners and most entertainment services. However, the supplier of other services may wish to wait to see how much work has to be carried out before valuing the cost of that work. In such a case, the consumer may be surprised at the cost of the service.

If the cost of the service is fixed in advance, generally, the consumer will be bound to pay that amount. Normally, the courts will not mend a bad bargain. However, consumers may only discover at a later stage that the charge is extortionate. Only in rare cases will it be possible to reopen an agreement. For example, in the case of extortionate credit bargains, the Consumer Credit Act 1974, ss. 137 to 140 (see 6.8.3.4) provide for such a power on the part of the court. The Consumer Protection (Cancellation of Contracts Concluded away from Business Premises) Regulations 1987 (SI 1987/2117) implementing the provisions of the EC Council Directive on Doorstep Selling (85/577/EEC 20.12.1985) are also relevant in this regard. The regulations require a trader to give the consumer notice of his right to cancel a contract within seven days of making certain types of contract concluded off trade premises (art. 4(1) and (5)). Further, where the regulations apply, the consumer will be entitled to recover any payments made under the agreement (art. 5(1)). However, it is clear that the regulations do not apply to all contracts for the supply of services. Specific exemptions are given in relation to contracts for the construction or extension of a building (art. 3(2)(a)(iv)), although this would appear not to apply to home improvements involving the installation of goods, such as double-glazing units (ibid.), provided installation has not taken place (art. 7(2)). Furthermore insurance contracts and many contracts for financial services are excluded since provision is made elsewhere for these. In order for the regulations to apply, the consumer must have entered into a contract valued at more than £35 (art. 3(2)(f)) where there has been an unsolicited visit by a trader to a consumer's home or place of work or where the trader has attempted to sell to the consumer goods or services which have not been specifically requested (art. 3(1)). Despite the provisions of these regulations, there are still many contracts which will not be provided for in which the consumer may agree to pay an exorbitant amount and not be able to cancel. For example, wherever the consumer has specifically requested the provision of the service and there has been no unsolicited visit by the trader, an agreed charge will be enforceable against him.

At common law, it may also be possible for the court to construe the contract in such a way as to rewrite the terms of payment (see *Staffordshire Area Health Authority* v *South Staffordshire Waterworks Co.* [1978] 1 WLR 1387 particularly where those terms are onerous. In *Interfoto Picture Library Ltd* v *Stiletto Visual Programmes Ltd* [1988] 1 All ER 348 a contract for the hire of photographic transparencies provided that should the hirer retain photographs for longer than was agreed he should pay £5 per day in respect of each transparency retained. It was considered that the amount charged was excessive and since no steps had been taken to communicate the existence of the onerous provision to the hirer, it would be reasonable to impose a *quantum meruit* payment of £3.50 per transparency per week (see also *J. Spurling Ltd* v *Bradshaw* [1956] 2 All ER 121).

It has been suggested that there should be a discretion on the part of the court to reopen and rewrite consumer contracts in the case of blatant exploitation (Lantin and Woodroffe, *Service Please* (National Consumer Council, 1981), p. 26). However, prospects for reform of the law in this respect appear remote since the Law Commission have concluded that it would not be appropriate to make special provision for consumer services without also making similar provision for supply of goods contracts (Law Com. No. 156 (Cmnd 9773, 1986), para. 4.21).

A difficulty which consumers may encounter is that they have been given an estimate of the cost of work which is subsequently exceeded when the work is completed. An estimate is generally regarded as a prediction which is not binding on the supplier (*Croshaw* v *Pritchard* (1899) 16 TLR 45). One way in which the consumer can protect himself in this respect is to secure a quotation from the supplier. In such a case, the supplier is bound to perform the service for the amount agreed. Thus, even if the work takes longer than was anticipated or if the supplier incurs unexpected costs, the quotation is binding upon him (*Gilbert & Partners* v *Knight* [1968] 2 All ER 248).

If the contract does not provide for the amount payable by the consumer, the Supply of Goods and Services Act 1982, s. 15(1), provides that the consumer will pay a reasonable charge. What is reasonable is a question of fact in each case, but the effect of the section is to order a *quantum meruit* in respect of services rendered (*Way* v *Latilla* [1937] 3 All ER 759). The section will also provide a solution where there is an agreement to pay, but no specific figure has been fixed by the parties. What is a reasonable charge may reflect current market prices. However, this will not always be the case if special consider-ations apply (see *Acebal* v *Levy* (1834) 10 Bing 376).

10.5   THE GENERAL DUTIES OF THE PARTIES – MATERIALS FOR CONSIDERATION

10.5.1   Reasonable care and skill

For the text of the Supply of Goods and Services Act 1982, s. 13 see 10.3.1.

10.5.1.1   Non-contractual duties of care

Smith v Eric S. Bush
[1989] 2 All ER 514
House of Lords

For the facts see 5.8.2.

LORD TEMPLEMAN at pp. 520-522): A valuer who values property as a security for a mortgage is liable either in contract or in tort to the mortgagee for any failure on the part of the valuer to exercise reasonable skill and care in the valuation. The valuer is liable in contract if he receives instructions from and is paid by the mortgagee. The valuer is liable in tort if he receives instructions from and is paid by the mortgagor but knows that the valuation is for the purpose of a mortgage and will be relied on by the mortgagee. . . .

The duty of professional men 'is not merely to use care in their reports. They have also a duty to use care in their work which results in their reports (see (*Candler* v *Crane Christmas & Co.*) [1951] 1 All ER 426 at 432-3 (per Denning LJ)). . . .

In the present appeals the relationship between the valuer and the purchaser is 'akin to contract'. The valuer knows that the consideration which he receives derives from the purchaser and is passed on by the mortgagee, and the valuer also knows that the valuation will determine whether or not the purchaser buys the house.

In *Ministry of Housing and Local Government* v *Sharp* [1970] 1 All ER 1009, . . . Lord Denning MR rejected the argument—

> that a duty to use due care (where there was no contract) only arose when there was a voluntary assumption of liability . . . Lord Reid in *Hedley Byrne & Co. Ltd* v *Heller & Partners Ltd* [1964] AC 465 at 487 and . . . Lord Devlin ([1964] AC 465 at 529) . . . used those words because of the special circumstances of that case (where the bank disclaimed responsibility).

. . . In my opinion the valuer assumes responsibility to both mortgagee and purchaser by agreeing to carry out a valuation for mortgage purposes knowing that the valuation fee has been paid by the purchaser and knowing that the valuation will probably be relied on by the purchaser in order to decide whether or not to enter into a contract to purchase the house.

LORD GRIFFITHS and LORD JAUNCEY OF TULLICHETTLE delivered judgments to the same effect.

LORD KEITH OF KINKEL and LORD BRANDON OF OAKBROOK agreed.

Notes

The relationship between the parties in *Smith* v *Eric S. Bush* was 'akin to contract' but if the relationship is less close, it is less likely that a duty of care will be owed. For example, it is clear that the surveyor would have owed no duty of care to a subsequent purchaser of the house who might have been shown a copy of the report and suffered economic loss. So far as economic loss is concerned, the courts have sought to restrict substantially the circumstances in which it is recoverable. The 'two-stage' test of Lord Wilberforce in *Anns* v *Merton London Borough Council* [1978] AC 728 at pp. 751-2 has been subject to much criticism on the ground that a general test of that nature cannot take into account the wide range of circumstances relevant to whether or not a duty of care should be imposed in respect of economic losses. Instead the House of Lords in *Caparo Industries plc* v *Dickman* [1990] 2 AC 605 has advocated a more cautious approach (per Lord Bridge of Harwich at pp. 617-18):

But since the *Anns* case a series of decisions . . . have emphasised the inability of any single general principle to provide a practical test which can be applied to every situation to determine whether a duty of care is owed and, if so, what is its scope. . . . What emerges is that, in addition to the foreseeability of damage, necessary ingredients in any situation giving rise to a duty of care are that there should exist between the party owing the duty and the party to whom it is owed a relationship characterised by the law as one of 'proximity' or 'neighbourhood' and that the situation should be one in which the court considers it fair, just and reasonable that the law should impose a duty of a given scope upon the one party for the benefit of the other. . . . Whilst recognising, of course, the importance of the underlying general principles common to the whole field of negligence, I think the law has now moved in the direction of attaching greater significance to the more traditional categorisation of distinct and recognisable situations as guides to the existence, the scope and the limits of the varied duties of care which the law imposes.

10.5.1.2 Standard of care

Bolam v Friern Hospital Management Committee
[1957] 2 All ER 118
Queen's Bench Division

The plaintiff alleged negligence on the part of a doctor who had administered electroconvulsive therapy to the plaintiff without first administering a relaxant drug or applying any restraint to the plaintiff to prevent convulsive movements. As a result, the plaintiff suffered a fractured jaw.

McNAIR J at pp. 121-2: How do you test whether this act or failure is negligent? In an ordinary case it is generally said, that you judge that by the action of the man in the street. He is the ordinary man. . . . But where you get a situation which involves the use of some special skill or competence, then the test whether there has been negligence or not is not the test of the man on the top of a Clapham omnibus, because he has not got this special skill. The test is the standard of the ordinary skilled man exercising and professing to have that special skill. A man need not possess the highest expert skill at the risk of being found negligent. It is well-established law that it is sufficient if he exercises the ordinary skill of an ordinary competent man exercising that particular art. . . . Counsel for the plaintiff put it in this way, that in the case of a medical man negligence means failure to act in accordance with the standards of reasonably competent medical men at the time. That is a perfectly accurate statement, as long as it is remembered that there may be one or more perfectly proper standards; and if a medical man conforms with one of those proper standards then he is not negligent. Counsel for the plaintiff was also right, in my judgment, in saying that a mere personal belief that a particular technique is best is no defence unless that belief is based on reasonable grounds.
. . . I myself would prefer to put it this way: A doctor is not guilty of negligence if he has acted in accordance with a practice accepted as proper by a responsible body of medical men skilled in that particular art. . . . Putting it the other way round, a doctor is not negligent, if he is acting in accordance with such a practice, merely because there is a body of opinion that takes a contrary view. At the same time, that does not mean that a medical man can obstinately and pig-headedly carry on with some old technique if it has been proved to be contrary to what is really substantially the whole of informed medical opinion.

10.5.2 Guaranteeing a result

Thake v Maurice
[1986] 1 All ER 497
Court of Appeal

The plaintiffs, a married couple, did not wish to have any more children. The defendant was a surgeon who contracted to carry out a sterilisation by vasectomy on the husband. The appropriate consents were given, but following the operation, Mrs Thake became pregnant. It was contended by the plaintiffs that the defendant had led a reasonable person in the position of the plaintiffs to believe that he had firmly promised that the operation would lead to sterility. On the issue of the alleged 'guarantee', the members of the court differed.

NOURSE LJ at p. 511 (with whom NEILL LJ agreed): The question then is whether the defendant contracted to carry out a vasectomy or to render Mr Thake permanently sterile. The latter alternative necessarily involved a guarantee; in other words, a warranty that there was not the remotest chance, not one in ten thousand, that the operation would not succeed. . . . The contract contained an implied warranty that, in carrying out the operation, the defendant would exercise the ordinary skill and care of a competent surgeon. It did not contain an implied warranty that, come what may, the objective would be achieved. . . . The only question is whether it contained an express warranty to that effect. Would the words and visual demonstrations of the defendant have led a reasonable person standing in the position of the plaintiffs to understand that, come what may, Mr Thake would be rendered sterile and incapable of parenthood?
    . . . In the end the question seems to be reduced to one of determining the extent of the knowledge which is to be attributed to the reasonable person standing in the position of the plaintiffs. Would he have known that the success of the operation, either because it depended on the healing of human tissue, or because in medical science all things, or nearly all things, are uncertain, could not be guaranteed? If he would, the defendant's words could only have been reasonably understood as forecasts of an almost certain, but nevertheless uncertain, outcome. . . . He could not be taken to have given a guarantee of its success.
    I do not suppose that a reasonable person standing in the position of the plaintiffs would have known that a vasectomy is an operation whose success depends on a healing of human tissue which cannot be guaranteed. To suppose that would be to credit him with an omniscience beyond all reason. But it does seem to me to be reasonable to credit him with the more general knowledge that in medical science all things, or nearly all things, are uncertain . . . Where an operation is of modern origin, its effects untried over several generations, would a reasonable person, confronted even with the words and demonstrations of the defendant in this case, believe that there was not one chance in ten thousand that the object would not be achieved? I do not think that he would.

Where a stricter duty is held to exist, it is likely to relate to 'design services'.

Greaves & Co. (Contractors) Ltd v Baynham Meikle & Partners
[1975] 3 All ER 99
Court of Appeal

For the facts see 10.4.2.

LORD DENNING MR at pp. 102-5: Now, as between the owners and the contractors, it is plain that the owners made known to the contractors the purpose for which the building was required, so as to show that they relied on the contractors' skill and judgment. It was therefore the duty of the contractors to see that the finished work was reasonably fit for the purpose for which they knew it was required. It was not merely an obligation to use reasonable care. . . .

The contractors employed a firm of experts, the defendants, . . . structural engineers, to design the structure of the building and, in particular, the first floor of it. There were discussions with them about it. It was made known to them – and this is important – that the floors had to take the weight of stacker trucks. . . . These were to run to and fro over the floors carrying the drums of oil. The structural engineers . . . were given the task of designing the floors for that purpose.

. . . But, after a little time, there was a lot of trouble. The floors began to crack. The men took strong exception to working there. They thought it was dangerous. . . .

What was the cause of this cracking of the floors? The structural engineers said that it was due to the shrinkage of the concrete for which they were not responsible. . . . But the judge did not accept that view. He found that the majority of the cracks were caused by vibration and not by shrinkage. He held that the floors were not designed with sufficient strength to withstand the vibration which was produced by the stacker trucks.

. . . The judge found that there was an implied term that the design should be fit for the use of loaded stacker trucks; and that it was broken. Alternatively, that the structural engineers owed a duty of care in their design, which was a higher duty than the law in general imposes on a professional man; and that there was a breach of that duty.

To resolve this question, it is necessary to distinguish between a term which is implied by law and a term which is implied in fact. A term implied by law is said to rest on the *presumed* intention of both parties; whereas, a term implied in fact rests on their *actual* intention.

It has often been stated that the law will only imply a term when it is reasonable and necessary to do so in order to give business efficacy to the transaction; and, indeed, so obvious that both parties must have intended it. But those statements must be taken with considerable qualification. In the great majority of cases it is no use looking for the intention of both parties. If you asked the parties what they intended, they would say they never gave it a thought; or, if they did, the one would say that he intended something different from the other. So the courts imply – or, as I would say, impose – a term such as is just and reasonable in the circumstances. . . .

Apply this to the employment of a professional man. The law does not usually imply a warranty that he will achieve the desired result, but only a term that he will use reasonable care and skill. The surgeon does not warrant that he will cure the patient. Nor does the solicitor warrant that he will win the case. But, when a dentist agrees to make a set of false teeth for a patient, there is an implied warranty that they will fit his gums: see *Samuels* v *Davis* [1943] KB 526.

What then is the position when an architect or an engineer is employed to design a house or a bridge? Is he under an implied warranty that, if the work is carried out to his design, it will be reasonably fit for the purpose? Or is he only under a duty to use reasonable care and skill? This question may require to be answered some day as a matter of law. But in the present case I do not think we need answer it. For the evidence shows that both parties were of one mind on the matter. Their common intention was that the engineer should design a warehouse which would be fit for the purpose for which it was required. That common intention gives rise to a term implied *in fact*. . . .

In the light of that evidence it seems to me that there was implied in fact a term that, if the work was completed in accordance with the design, it would be reasonably fit for the use of loaded stacker trucks. The engineers failed to make such a design and are, therefore, liable.

If there was, however, no such absolute warranty of fitness, but only an obligation to use reasonable care and skill, the question arises: what is the degree of care required? The judge said:

In the special circumstances of this case . . . it can be said that there was a higher duty imposed on him than the law in general imposes on a medical or other professional man.

I do not think that was quite accurate. It seems to me that in the ordinary employment of a professional man, whether it is a medical man, a lawyer, or an accountant, an architect or an engineer, his duty is to use reasonable care and skill in the course of his employment.

Lord Denning went on to consider the application of the *Bolam* 'reasonable skilled person' test (see 10.5.1.2) and continued at p. 105:

In applying that test, it must be remembered that the measures to be taken by a professional man depend on the circumstances of the case. Although the judge talked about a 'higher duty', I feel sure that what he meant was that in the circumstances of this case special steps were necessary in order to fulfil the duty of care. . . . In this case a new mode of construction was to be employed. The Council of British Standards Institution had issued a circular which contained this note:

The designer should satisfy himself that no undesirable vibrations can be caused by the imposed loading. Serious vibrations may result when dynamic forces are applied at a frequency near to one of the natural frequencies of the members.

Mr Baynham was aware of that note but read it as a warning against resonances, . . . and not as a warning against vibrations in general. So he did not take measures to deal with the random impulses of stacker trucks. There was evidence, too, that other competent designers might have done the same as Mr Baynham. On that ground the judge seems to have thought that Mr Baynham had not failed in the ordinary duty of care. But that does not excuse him. Other designers might have fallen short too. It is for the judge to set the standard of what a competent designer would do. And the judge, in the next breath, used words which seem to me to be a finding that Mr Baynham did fail. It is a key passage:

I do, however, find that he knew, or ought to have known, that the purpose of the floor was safely to carry heavily laden trucks and that he was warned about the dangers of vibration and did not take these matters sufficiently into account. The design was inadequate for the purpose.

It seems to me that that means that Mr Baynham did not take the matters sufficiently into account which he ought to have done. That amounts to a finding of breach of the duty to use reasonable care and skill.

Notes

(1)   Both Browne and Geoffrey Lane LJJ agreed but were at pains to emphasise that the decision laid down no general principle in relation to the obligations and liabilities of professional men.

(2)   How should Lord Denning's views on the implication of 'just and reasonable' terms be read in the light of the House of Lords decision in *Liverpool City Council* v *Irwin* [1977] AC 239?

While the preceding case concerns a business transaction, it would be of considerable benefit to the consumer if a similar approach were to be adopted specifically in relation to consumer services.

Trade Practices Act 1974 (Australia)

74. Warranties in relation to the supply of services

(2) Where a corporation supplies services (other than services of a professional nature provided by a qualified architect or engineer) to a consumer in the course of a business and the consumer, expressly or by implication, makes known to the corporation any particular purpose for which the services are required or the result that he desires the services to achieve, there is an implied warranty that the services supplied under the contract for the supply of the services and any materials supplied in connection with those services will be reasonably fit for that purpose or are of such a nature and quality that they might reasonably be expected to achieve that result, except where the circumstances show that the consumer does not rely, or that it is unreasonable for him to rely, on the corporation's skill or judgment.

(3) A reference in this section to services does not include a reference to services that are, or are to be, provided, granted or conferred under—

(a) a contract for or in relation to the transportation or storage of goods for the purposes of a business, trade, profession or occupation carried on or engaged in by the person for whom the goods are transported or stored; or

(b) a contract of insurance.

10.5.3 Delayed performance

10.5.3.1 Delayed performance in breach of an express contract term

A useful ploy on the part of an aggrieved consumer who believes he has been the subject of unreasonable delay is to put his complaint in writing and demand performance by a specified date.

Charles Rickards Ltd v *Oppenheim*
[1950] 1 All ER 420
Court of Appeal

The defendant agreed to buy a modified Rolls-Royce chassis which was to be delivered by 20 March 1948. The chassis was not available by that date so the defendant pressed for delivery and subsequently on 29 June, gave notice that if it was not delivered within four more weeks he would not accept it. The chassis was made available in October 1948, but the defendant refused to accept it. It was held that he was entitled to take this course of action.

DENNING LJ at pp. 423-4: Time and time again the defendant pressed for delivery, time and time again he was assured that he would have early delivery, but he never got satisfaction, and eventually at the end of June he gave notice saying that, unless the car was delivered by July 25, he would not accept it. The question thus arises whether he was entitled to give such a notice, making time of the essence. . . . [Counsel for the plaintiffs] agrees that, if this is a contract for the sale of goods, the defendant could give such a notice. He accepted the statement of McCardie J in *Hartley* v *Hymans* [1920] 3 KB 475 at p. 495, as accurately stating the law in regard to the sale of goods, but he said that that statement did not apply to contracts for work and labour. He said that no notice making time of the essence could be given in regard to contracts for work and labour. . . .

in my view, it is unnecessary to determine whether it was a contract for the sale of goods or a contract for work and labour, because, whichever it was, the defendant was entitled to give a notice bringing the matter to a head. . . . Adequate protection to the suppliers is given by the requirement that the notice should be reasonable.

The next question, therefore, is: Was this a reasonable notice? Counsel for the plaintiffs argued that it was not. He said that a reasonable notice must give sufficient time for the work then outstanding to be completed, and that, on the evidence in this case, four weeks was not a reasonable time because it would, and did, in fact, require three and a half months to complete it. In my opinion, however, the words of Lord Parker of Waddington in *Stickney* v *Keeble* [1915] AC 386 apply to such a case as the present, just as much as they do to a contract for the sale of land. Lord Parker said at p. 419:

> In considering whether the time so limited is a reasonable time the court will consider all the circumstances of the case. No doubt what remains to be done at the date of the notice is of importance, but it is by no means the only relevant fact. The fact that the purchaser has continually been pressing for completion, or has before given similar notices which he has waived, or that it is specially important to him to obtain early completion, are equally relevant facts.

To that statement I would add, in the present case, the fact that the original contract made time of the essence. In this case, not only did the defendant press continually for delivery, not only was he given promises of speedy delivery, but, on the very day before he gave the notice, he was told by the subcontractors' manager, who was in charge of the work, that it would be ready within two weeks. He then gave four weeks' notice. The judge found that it was a reasonable notice and, in my judgment, there is no ground on which this court could in any way differ from that finding.

Singleton and Bucknill LJ concurred.

10.5.3.2 Delayed performance in the absence of any contractual provision
The Supply of Goods and Services Act 1982, s. 14(1), (see 10.3.1) requires performance within a reasonable time. This merely restates the position at common law.

Charnock v *Liverpool Corporation*
[1968] 1 WLR 1498
Court of Appeal

The plaintiff owned a car which was damaged in a collision caused by the negligence of the driver of the other vehicle, an employee of the first defendant. The car was taken to the second defendants for repair. With the agreement of the plaintiff's insurers, it was understood that an estimate of the cost of repair would be submitted to the insurers by the second defendants and that the insurers would pay the full cost of those repairs. The plaintiff overheard that the second defendants had a lot of warranty work to carry out in their capacity as main dealers for a car manufacturer, but no indication was given that the work on his car would be delayed. In the event, the work on the plaintiff's car took eight weeks when a competent repairer would have taken no more than five weeks to complete the work. The plaintiff was awarded £53 damages in respect of the cost of hiring a replacement car for three weeks.

SALMON LJ at pp. 1505-6: In my view, there was a clear contract to be inferred from the facts between the garage proprietor and the car owner that in consideration of the car owner leaving his car with the garage for repair the garage would carry out the repairs with reasonable expedition and care, and that they would be paid by the insurance company. . . .

The second point is even shorter. The judge found that the garage proprietors broke their contract with the car owner in that they failed to repair the car within a reasonable time. There was ample evidence before him that a reasonable time for carrying out these repairs should not have exceeded five weeks. Since the garage proprietors in fact took eight weeks, they were in breach of their contract. . . . The reason why these garage proprietors were unable to do the work within a reasonable time . . . was that when they took on the work their labour force was very much under strength. Moreover, the holiday period was approaching. Further, and perhaps most importantly, they had an arrangement (which no doubt was commercially of great value to them) with the Rootes group that any warranty work should be given precedence. . . . I cannot see for myself how the fact that they chose to take on the work knowing of the three factors to which I have referred can possibly entitle them to say, 'well, we could have done it within five weeks, . . . but for these three factors which prevented us from doing so'.

The case does not even remotely resemble . . . *Hick* v *Raymond & Reid* [1893] AC 22. That was a case in which the unloading of a cargo was delayed because of a strike which took place long after the contract was made. There was a supervening event which made it impossible for the defendants there to carry out the unloading within the named time. . . . But here there was no supervening event. All the facts were known to the garage owners when they entered into the contract. It seems to me that, if they had wanted to protect themselves against a claim for damages for unreasonable delay, they could and should have warned the car owner that the repairs could not be carried out in the time which is recognised in the trade as the normal and reasonable time for carrying out such repairs.

Appeal dismissed.

10.5.4   Cost

10.5.4.1   Agreed charges   It is clear that exorbitant charges are a cause for concern. If the service provided is financed under a consumer credit agreement, which will often be the case where home-improvement work is carried out, the provisions of the Consumer Credit Act 1974 in relation to extortionate credit bargains may allow the court to reopen the agreement (see 6.8.3.4).

If the agreement is entered into as a result of 'doorstep selling' it too may be cancellable at the option of the consumer under the provisions of the Consumer Protection (Cancellation of Contracts Concluded away from Business Premises) Regulations 1987 (SI 1987/2117). In particular, a breach of these regulations is actionable by the consumer as a breach of statutory duty. Furthermore, in relation to money paid by the consumer, art. 5 provides:

(1) Subject to regulation 7(2) below, on the cancellation of a contract under regulation 4 above, any sum paid by or on behalf of the consumer under or in contemplation of the contract shall become repayable.

(2) If under the terms of the cancelled contract the consumer or any person on his behalf is in possession of any goods, he shall have a lien on them for any sum repayable to him under paragraph (1) above.

By way of qualification to art. 5, art. 7, in relation to return of goods by the consumer after cancellation provides:

(2)   The consumer shall not be under a duty to restore— . . .
   (iv)   goods which, before the cancellation, had become incorporated in any land or thing not comprised in the cancelled contract, but he shall be under a duty to pay in accordance with the cancelled contract for the supply of the goods and for the provision of any services in connection with the supply of the goods before the cancellation.

10.5.4.2 No charge agreed For the text of the Supply of Goods and Services Act 1982 s. 15, see 10.3.

10.6   BUSINESS SELF-REGULATION

It has already been seen that in many instances, legal controls may not be the most appropriate means of dealing with consumer problems and that self-regulating codes of practice promulgated by trade associations may be a better response (see 3.10). The consumer service industry has seen increasing numbers of such codes of practice which are specific to the service to which each code applies. As has been observed, codes of practice can be fashioned to the needs of the particular trade or profession and the needs of the consumers of the service provided. Often, a code of practice will be able to deal with matters which would be extremely difficult to legislate for and because the code is tailor-made for a particular sector of the service market, it will often be more detailed than any legislation could hope to be. However, because adherence to a code of practice is a matter of voluntary choice, it is the case that codes of practice are ineffective in relation to those suppliers who choose not to join a trade association. Furthermore, there is also some doubt as to the effectiveness of codes of practice where the promoting trade association does not possess sufficient powers of enforcement.

In relation to the supply of services, many of the relevant codes of practice contain similar provisions relating to the speed with which the service is provided and the cost of the service. Sometimes, the provisions about cost require the supplier to give a quotation instead of an estimate of likely cost. It is also common to find a requirement that adequate spare parts should be kept in stock and that guarantees should be given in respect of work done. In respect of disputes, it is common to find provision for a conciliation and arbitration scheme. Many codes also contain provisions in respect of exclusion clauses which provide the consumer with greater protection than that given by the Unfair Contract Terms Act 1977.

10.7 BUSINESS SELF-REGULATION – MATERIALS FOR CONSIDERATION

See materials referred to in 3.11.

10.8 SPECIFIC TYPES OF CONSUMER SERVICE

The types of service consumed are many and different considerations apply to different types of service. In selecting varieties of service for more detailed consideration, the choice is likely to be arbitrary, but since the consumer's three major items of expenditure are his house, his car and the family holiday, it is proposed to consider home-improvement services, repair services and holiday law. One particular type of service, namely the provision of credit, is dealt with separately (see chapter 6).

10.8.1 Repair services and other bailments The supply of services to consumers will often involve a bailment relationship. Such a relationship arises wherever the consumer's property is handed over to another for the purposes of safekeeping, repair, processing or carriage. In such instances the service supplier is subject to the general duties which apply to bailees. In some instances, the consumer is also subject to the same duties, for example, where he takes possession of a television under a consumer hire agreement.

10.8.1.1 The supplier as a bailee In most cases of bailment there must be a delivery of goods by the bailor to the bailee (see *Ashby* v *Tolhurst* [1937] 2 KB 242). However, in some instances the delivery may be effected by an intermediary. For example, it may be that goods entrusted to a repairer are passed to another for the purpose of carrying out specialist work.

Generally a bailment will be contractual in nature, but a bailment relationship can arise independently of a contract. Accordingly, a gratuitous bailment relationship can arise despite the absence of consideration. However, this does not mean that the duties of the bailee lie exclusively in the law of tort. It is better to regard bailments as *sui generis* and therefore subject to special rules of their own. In particular, because the bailment relationship is created by the parties themselves, a bailee owes a duty of care to the bailor alone. In contrast, a tortious duty of care is owed to persons generally. The burden of proof in a bailment relationship rests on the bailee. Thus if a garage is entrusted with a consumer's car for repair and the car is stolen, it is for the garage to prove that reasonable care has been exercised (see *Levison* v *Patent Steam Carpet Cleaning Co. Ltd* [1977] 3 All ER 498) or that the failure to take care did not contribute to the consumer's loss (see *Joseph Travers & Sons Ltd* v *Cooper* [1915] 1 KB 73). If the consumer's action were to be regarded as tortious, he would have to prove want of reasonable care on the part of the garage.

The standard of care required of the supplier is the same whether or not the bailment is for reward, namely, a duty to exercise reasonable care and skill appropriate to the relevant circumstances (*Houghland* v *R. R. Low (Luxury Coaches) Ltd* [1962] 1 QB 694). The fact that the service has been paid for may be relevant in that the parties may be said to have raised the standard required of the supplier.

In some instances the consumer may encounter difficulties related to the tort of conversion. As a general rule, the bailee is obliged to return the bailed chattel to the bailor at the end of the period of bailment. However, the bailee may be able to show good cause for not returning the chattel, for example, where the consumer has not paid for the work done by the repairer. In such a case, the repairer may wish to sell the consumer's goods in order to cover the cost of the repairs. Generally, it would be wise for the repairer to reserve a contractual right of disposal because without such express permission, the repairer commits the tort of wrongful interference with goods (Torts (Interference with Goods) Act 1977, s. 2(2)). If this is the case, the bailee is liable for the value of the article at the time of being sued, subject to a deduction in respect of the value of any improvement in the chattel effected by the bailee.

Special provision is made for the sale of bailed goods by the bailee in the Torts (Interference with Goods) Act 1977, s. 12. The Act provides for this right if the bailor is in breach of an obligation to take delivery of the goods or if the bailee, without success, has taken reasonable steps to trace the bailor in order to impose such an obligation. An obligation to take delivery can be imposed on the bailor by serving him with a notice specifying that the goods are ready for collection and stating the amount payable in respect of work done. Concurrently with the service of the notice referred to above, the bailee must also notify the bailor that the goods are to be sold on or after a specified date if delivery is not taken by that date. Where a sale is effected, the bailee is liable to the bailor for the proceeds of sale less the costs of sale and any sum payable to the bailee by the bailor in respect of work done.

10.8.1.2 The consumer as a bailee In some instances the consumer will be a bailee and will therefore be subject to the normal rules that apply to the bailment relationship. The most notable examples of this arise where the consumer hires goods or takes goods pursuant to a hire-purchase agreement. In addition to the ordinary incidents of a bailment relationship, if the bailment is contractual, certain terms relating to the title of the bailor and the description, quality and fitness of the goods bailed are implied into the contract by the Supply of Goods and Services Act 1982, ss. 7 to 10 and the Supply of Goods (Implied Terms) Act 1973, ss. 8 to 11.

10.8.2 Bailment – materials for consideration

10.8.2.1 The supplier as a bailee Generally, a bailment requires a delivery of goods by the bailor to the bailee.

Ashby* v *Tolhurst
[1937] 2 KB 242
Court of Appeal

The plaintiff left his car at a private car park, paid a shilling (5p) and received a ticket from the attendant which stated that the proprietors accepted no responsibility for the safe custody of cars or articles therein and that all cars were left entirely at the owner's risk. When the plaintiff returned to collect his car, he was told by the attendant that he had allowed the plaintiff's 'friend' to take it. In fact the 'friend' had no ticket and forced entry to the car. Negligence on the part of the attendant was admitted but liability was denied.

ROMER LJ at pp. 255-7: . . . In order that there shall be a bailment there must be a delivery by the bailor, that is to say, he must part with his possession of the chattel in question. In the present case there is no evidence whatever of any delivery in fact of the motor car to the attendant on behalf of the defendants. All that the plaintiff did was to leave his car on the car park, paying the sum of 1s. for the privilege of doing so. It is true that, if the car had been left there for any particular purpose that required that the defendants should have possession of the car a delivery would rightly be inferred. If, for instance, the car had been left at the car park for the purpose of being sold . . . or indeed for the purposes of safe custody, delivery of the car, although not actually made, would readily be inferred. But it is perfectly plain in this case that the car was not delivered to the defendants for safe custody. You cannot infer a contract by A to perform a certain act out of circumstances in which A has made it perfectly plain that he declines to be under any contractual liability to perform that act. . . .

It only remains to deal with the suggestion that there was a conversion of the car by the servant of the defendants. Although the car was not delivered to the defendants, I apprehend that the servant acting within his authority might have bound the defendants by an act of conversion if he had purported to deal with the car as the owner. All that is said is that the attendant told the plaintiff . . . that he, the attendant, had given the car to somebody else. It is quite plain that the attendant did not use the word 'given' in its ordinary sense, because the car was not his to give and he knew it. . . . The circumstances in which such a dealing amounts to conversion have been stated by Atkin J, as he then was, in *Lancashire & Yorkshire Railway Co.* v *MacNicoll* (1918) 118 LT 596

It appears to me plain that dealing with goods in a manner inconsistent with the right of the true owner amounts to a conversion . . . providing it is also established that there is an intention on the part of the defendant in so doing to deny the owner's right or to assert a right which is inconsistent with the owner's right.

It is perfectly plain that this attendant did neither the one nor the other.

Sir Wilfrid Greene MR and Scott LJ delivered judgments to the same effect.

On the issue of conversion, to which Romer LJ referred in the previous extract, see now the provisions of the Torts (Interference with Goods) Act 1977 and in particular the bailee's power of sale of goods in his possession under s. 12.

On the assumption that a bailment relationship exists, the principal duty of the bailee is to exercise reasonable care and skill in relation to the goods bailed. Accordingly, the bailee's duty in this respect does not differ from the general duty of care owed by any other supplier of a service. However, the incidence of the burden of proof differs in cases of bailment.

Levison v Patent Steam Carpet Cleaning Co. Ltd
[1978] QB 69
Court of Appeal

The plaintiffs arranged for a £900 carpet to be cleaned by the defendants. When the carpet was collected, Mr. Levison signed a form which stated that the maximum value of the carpet was deemed to be £40 and that all merchandise was accepted 'at the owner's risk. The carpet was never returned, probably because it had been stolen. In the county court, the plaintiffs were awarded £900. The defendants appealed.

LORD DENNING MR at pp. 81–2: Upon principle, I should have thought that the burden was on the cleaners to prove that they were not guilty of a fundamental breach. After all, Mrs Levison does not know what happened to it. The cleaners are the ones that know, or should know, what happened to the carpet, and the burden should be on them to say what it was. . . .

I am clearly of opinion that, in a contract of bailment, when a bailee seeks to escape liability on the ground that he was not negligent or that he was excused by an exception or limitation clause, then he must show what happened to the goods. He must prove all the circumstances known to him in which the loss or damage occurred. If it appears that the goods were lost or damaged without any negligence on his part, then, of course, he is not liable. If it appears that they were lost or damaged by a slight breach - not going to the root of the contract - he may be protected by the exemption or limitation clause. But if he leaves the cause of loss or damage undiscovered or unexplained – then I think he is liable: because it is then quite likely that the goods were stolen by one of his servants; or delivered by a servant to the wrong address; or damaged by reckless or wilful misconduct; all of which the offending servant will conceal and not make known to his employer. . . .

The cleaning company in this case did not show what happened to the carpet. They did not prove how it was lost. They gave all sorts of excuses for non-delivery and eventually said it had been stolen. Then I would ask: By whom was it stolen? . . . In the absence of any explanation, I would infer that it was one of these causes. . . .

Conclusion

I think the judge was quite right in holding that the burden of proof was on the cleaning company to exclude fundamental breach. As they did not exclude it, they cannot rely on the exemption or limitation clauses. I would therefore dismiss this appeal.

Orr LJ and Sir David Cairns agreed.

Appeal dismissed.

Notes

This case involved the application of the doctrine of fundamental breach to an exclusion clause and is one of a number of cases which must be regarded as wrongly decided, now, in relation to the doctrine of fundamental breach. However, it remains good authority for the points it makes about the onus of proof in bailment cases.

10.8.3. Home improvements

A common consumer complaint is that building or other home-improvement work has failed to reach the standard expected by the consumer. The problems encountered by consumers are various, some being extremely serious, others much less important. Sometimes, the basis of the consumer's complaint is a matter of subjective judgment which may render legal controls inappropriate. For example, the consumer may complain that an extension to his house does not blend with the existing structure (see *Home Improvements – A Discussion Paper* (OFT, 1982, para. 6.1.).In the light of this, it may be the case that the use of trade association codes of practice as a means of control is more likely to meet with success, provided some effective means of enforcement of such codes can be found. Other more specific difficulties may arise in determining whether a builder has substantially or only partially fulfilled the obligations under his contract with the consumer. Further grounds for consumer complaint may also emanate from the fact that some suppliers require advance payment in respect of some or all of the work they do. A third set of problems may arise in determining whether a tortious duty of care is owed by the builder and in identifying the appropriate standard of performance required.

10.8.3.1 Partial contractual performance As a general rule English law requires a complete performance before a party to a contract can regard his obligations under the contract as being discharged. Furthermore, if a person has failed to perform his obligations under a contract, it will generally follow that the other party can treat his performance obligations under the contract as being discharged. From this it would seem to follow that a builder will not be able to demand payment for home-improvement work until he has performed in full that which is required of him by the consumer. However, this is not necessarily the case as in English law there is a distinction between entire and severable obligations.

If a contractual obligation is said to be entire, it must be performed completely before the other party is required to pay for that performance. It is said to be a condition precedent to the liability of the recipient of the service that the performance of the other party is complete. Thus in *Sumpter* v *Hedges* [1898] 1 QB 673 the plaintiff agreed to build two houses for the defendant in return for a lump-sum payment of £565. Part of the way towards completion, the plaintiff encountered financial difficulties and informed the defendant that he would not be able to complete the work. In the meantime, the defendant had the houses completed by another contractor. The plaintiff sued to recover the agreed price, but it was held that payment was not due until performance was complete. Furthermore, the plaintiff could not recover on a *quantum meruit* basis in respect of the work he had done as there was no evidence of a voluntary acceptance of any benefit by the defendant.

Where contractual obligations are said to be severable, payment in respect of performance may be due as particular stages of performance are reached. The question which then arises is whether a breach in respect of one stage of performance is sufficiently serious to justify the other party in refusing to make payment in respect of the whole of the defendant's performance. A builder may be able to design a contract which allows for payment as work proceeds subject to the payment of retention moneys on completion of the building work. In such a case there is a series of severable obligations in respect of each stage of the work and an entire obligation to complete the whole of the work in accordance with the terms of the contract.

In *Sumpter* v *Hedges*, the builder's obligation to complete two houses was entire, however, he would not have been disentitled to payment if his breach of contract had been less serious. For example, if the work had been completed a week late (at p. 676 per Collins LJ) the builder would have been entitled to payment in full subject to a deduction in respect of the late completion. Similarly, qualitative defects in the finished product may not be sufficiently serious to allow the consumer to refuse payment. In such a case, there may be an entire obligation in relation to the quantity of work performed, but not in relation to the quality of the work performed (Treitel, *The Law of Contract*, 7th ed. (1987) p. 601). In *Hoenig* v *Isaacs* [1952] 2 All ER 176 the plaintiff had contracted to decorate and furnish the defendant's flat. The work was complete, but the furniture supplied was defective. These defects could be rectified at a cost of £55. It was held that the plaintiff was entitled to payment at the full contract rate of £750 subject to a deduction in respect of the cost of rectifying the defects.

The foregoing does not mean that that if the consumer complains of defective quality in the supplier's performance he will have no grounds for refusing to pay. It may be the case that defects in quality amount to a sufficiently serious breach of contract to justify rescission on the part of the consumer. The principal consideration is whether the consumer has been substantially deprived of the benefit he contracted for. In deciding whether the consumer is entitled to rescind a number of factors will be considered. First, it is necessary to consider whether an award of damages is adequate recompense. The notion of the 'consumer surplus value' (see also 10.8.6.2) may be relevant in this context. Sometimes, the consumer contracts for a benefit which is difficult to value in market terms. If this benefit substantially forms the basis of the contract and is not provided, the consumer may be able to decline to pay for the service. Thus it has been held that a funeral director who negligently constructs a coffin so that it cannot be taken into the funeral service is not entitled to payment (*Vigers* v *Cook* [1919] 2 KB 475).

It is possible that a consumer will place such a value on home-improvement work. However, a further factor must also be considered. The work of the builder is likely to have conferred a substantial benefit on the consumer which will have to be taken into account. The courts will be reluctant to allow a person to refuse payment where he has received such a benefit and is not in a position to restore the benefit to the other party. In the case of home-improvements, the consumer is hardly likely to want to restore double-glazing units to the builder and leave a large hole in his living-room wall!

If the consumer is considered to have accepted the benefit conferred on him by the builder, he will have to pay for the benefit received. However, this will not normally involve paying the full contract price. It is relevant that home-improvement work is carried out on the consumer's own property, since taking possession of one's own property is not automatically regarded as acceptance of the benefit (*Sumpter* v *Hedges* [1898] 1 QB 673). It is not acceptance if the consumer has no real option whether he will take the benefit or not (*Sumpter* v *Hedges* at p. 676 per Collins LJ). This rule is particularly important where the builder's failure to perform causes the consumer to suffer a loss. However, it may also be the case that the failure to perform does not cause any loss or a loss which is substantially offset by the benefit conferred by the incomplete performance. In such a case, the consumer who is able to take advantage of the builder's non-performance may benefit substantially. In *Bolton* v *Mahadeva* [1972] 1 WLR 1009 a contractor agreed to install a central heating system for £560. The system was defective in that it circulated fumes inside the consumer's house and, on average, the house was 10% less warm than it should have been. The defects cost the consumer £174 to repair when the installer had refused to attend to his shoddy performance. The Court of Appeal held that the defects were so great as to constitute non-performance of the contract. The end result was that the consumer had acquired an operative central heating system for £174. However, it was observed that had the contractor been prepared to remedy the defects when asked to do so, the position would have been different.

10.8.3.2 Consumer pre-payments A common feature of the home-improvements sector is that the consumer may be required to make full or partial payment in advance for the work done. The builder can justify such a requirement on the ground that he must purchase materials in advance. However, the building trade is notorious for a high risk of business failure which may leave the consumer who has made a prepayment in the position of an unsecured creditor and with no discernible benefit on his hands. Furthermore, where the consumer makes an advance payment, he may have placed himself in a very weak bargaining position if the work later proves to be defective.

Whether or not the consumer can recover his prepayment will depend on the terms of the contract. In the case of home-improvements, the contract will be one for work and materials and the contractual obligations of the supplier will involve him incurring expenditure before his performance is complete. Because of this, the supplier's right to the payment will be unconditional and the payment will be irrecoverable even though it is not required as security for performance (*Hyundai Heavy Industries Co.* v *Papadopoulos* [1980] 1 WLR 1129). If the supplier has failed to perform at all, the prepayment made by the consumer will be recoverable on the grounds of a total failure of consideration (*Fibrosa SA* v *Fairbairn Lawson Combe Barbour Ltd* [1943] AC 32). If the consideration is regarded as 'whole and indivisible', performance of any part of the thing promised will prevent recovery on the basis of a total failure of consideration. However, the parties may have expressed the intention that the price can be earned incrementally, in which case the consideration may be regarded as divisible, but this will depend on an express term in the contract to this effect.

The fact that the builder has to ask for prepayment may be some indication that he is a credit risk. It has been observed that most builders' merchants will offer one month's credit and that if the consumer is asked for a prepayment, this may indicate that the builder concerned is not considered creditworthy by others in the same sector (*Home Improvements – A Discussion Paper* (Office of Fair Trading, 1982), para. 3.21).

A major risk faced by consumers is that after having made an advance payment, the contractor may become insolvent or a company may cease trading before work is commenced or completed. In such a case, the consumer may be left with little protection and stands a distinct chance of being unable to recover the full amount of his prepayment. Some protection may be found in the form of trade association bonding schemes such as that operated by the Glass and Glazing Federation through their code of ethical practice. Double-glazing contractors who are members of the Federation are required to be covered by a deposit indemnity fund. This gives Federation fund managers the option to ensure that the work is completed at a fair market price, less the value of any deposit paid, or to refund the consumer's deposit.

Consumers are not in the same strong market position to be able to protect their deposit as is possible in business transactions. For example, a business-man who wishes to protect his position in a contract for the sale of goods could insist on reserving title in the goods sold until payment is received (*Aluminium Industrie Vaassen BV v Romalpa Aluminium Ltd* [1976] 1 WLR 676). However, it is unlikely that the consumer would be in a position to insist upon similar protection unless it were to be provided by law.

Suggestions for reform of the law have included one attempt to legislate for 'customers' prepayment accounts' whereby a contractor would be required to hold prepayments on trust in a separate account. The proposal would have prevented the use of the money for business purposes (22 HC Official Report (6th series), cols. 847-9, 28 April 1982). However, such a proposal might work in relation to some prepayments where the work is likely to take some time to complete, but it would be impractical to apply the same rule to services due to be supplied very soon after the consumer's payment. Compulsion and voluntary choice are different matters. A trader who wishes to do so can create a trust in favour of a customer who has made a prepayment by opening a separate trust account, in which case the payment will be protected should the company later become insolvent (*Re Kayford Ltd* [1975] 1 WLR 279; see also Richardson [1985] JBL 456).

10.8.3.3 Duty of care and standard of performance It has been seen that the supplier of a service is ordinarily required to exercise reasonable care and skill. In the case of building work, a higher standard would appear to be appropriate. At common law there is a requirement, based on an implied contractual term, that a builder will carry out work in a good and workmanlike manner with good and proper materials in order to produce a building which is reasonably fit for human habitation (*Hancock* v *B.W. Brazier (Anerley) Ltd* [1966] 2 All ER 901 at p. 903 per Lord Denning MR). As this is a contract term it protects only the person who has dealt directly with the builder and will not avail a subsequent purchaser of the property.

The common law rule has been augmented by the provisions of the Defective Premises Act 1972 which applies not only to the erection of buildings but also to conversions and enlargements (Defective Premises Act 1972, s. 1(1)). The non-excludable duty owed under this Act is strict and extends to every person who acquires an interest in the property, but the Act is also subject to a number of important limitations. In particular, the Act does not apply to dwellings protected by an 'approved scheme' (Defective Premises Act 1972, s. 2) and since most new houses are covered by the approved NHBC scheme, the Act is limited to alterations and conversions (see Spencer (1974) CLJ 307, (1975) CLJ 48). Furthermore, the cause of action is deemed to accrue on completion of the building work and runs for six years from that date (Defective Premises Act 1972, s. 1(5)). Unfortunately many building defects take much longer than six years from the date of completion to reveal themselves, in which case the consumer will be time barred before he realises that any damage has been done.

At one stage, the most important extension of a builder's liability was in the tort of negligence, represented by *Dutton* v *Bognor Regis UDC* [1972] 1 QB 373. Doubts remained about the scope of the duty owed by the builder and the local authority. Subsequent interpretation of the decision in *Anns* v *Merton London Borough Council* [1978] AC 728 has shown that the builder is liable for foreseeable personal injury and property damage suffered as a result of his negligence but that only limited liability exists in respect of economic loss (*D & F Estates Ltd* v *Church Commissioners for England* [1988] 2 All ER 992). The main difficulty is to determine what is property damage and what is economic loss. In *D & F Estates Ltd* v *Church Commissioners for England* the House of Lords held that the cost of repairing a defective building was pure economic loss and therefore generally irrecoverable in the absence of a contractual relationship between the parties. However, the decision is subject to a number of qualifications. If the building is regarded as a complex structure, one part of that structure can cause damage to another part of the same structure. In such a case there is damage to other property (at p. 1006 per Lord Bridge). Furthermore, it would appear to be possible to recover the cost of repair in order to avert a threat of imminent danger to the health or safety of the occupant of the building (at p. 1014 per Lord Oliver; *Department of the Environment* v *Thomas Bates & Son Ltd* [1989] 1 All ER 1075) though, trying to justify this view by reference to what Lord Bridge said in *D & F Estates Ltd* v *Church Commissioners for England* [1988] 2 All ER 992 at p. 1006 may be difficult.

10.8.4   Home-improvements – materials for consideration

10.8.4.1   Partial performance

Sumpter v Hedges
[1898] 1 QB 673
Court of Appeal

For the facts see 10.8.3.1.

COLLINS LJ at pp. 676-7): I think the case is really concluded by the finding of the learned judge to the effect that the plaintiff had abandoned the contract. If the plaintiff had merely broken his contract in some way so as not to give the defendant the right to treat him as having abandoned the contract, and the defendant had then proceeded to finish the work himself, the plaintiff might perhaps have been entitled to sue on a *quantum meruit* on the ground that the defendant had taken the benefit of the work done. But that is not the present case. There are cases in which, though the plaintiff has abandoned the performance of a contract, it is possible for him to raise the inference of a new contract to pay for the work done on a *quantum meruit* from the defendant's having taken the benefit of that work, but, in order that that may be done, the circumstances must be such as to give an option to the defendant to take or not to take the benefit of the work done. It is only where the circumstances are such as to give that option that there is any evidence on which to ground the inference of a new contract. Where, as in the case of work done on land, the circumstances are such as to give the defendant no option whether he will take the benefit of the work or not, then one must look to other facts than the mere taking of the benefit of the work in order to ground the inference of a new contract. . . . The mere fact that a defendant is in possession of what he cannot help keeping, or even has done work upon it, affords no ground for such an inference. He is not bound to keep unfinished a building which in an incomplete state would be a nuisance on his land. I am therefore of opinion that the plaintiff was not entitled to recover for the work which he had done.

A.L. Smith and Chitty LJJ concurred.

Appeal dismissed

Notes
The plaintiff had actually been paid £333 in respect of the completed work, although the judgments make it clear that he was not entitled to a penny of it, accordingly had he been paid nothing, the decision would have been the same. The rule is harsh and can be side-stepped where the court is able to find a contract which imposes severable obligations in relation to the amount of work done.

Hoenig v Isaacs
[1952] 2 All ER 176
Court of Appeal

For the facts see 10.8.3.1. The terms of payment were crucial in that they provided, 'net cash, as the work proceeds, and balance on completion'. The defendant had paid £400 of the £750 due but refused to pay the balance.

DENNING LJ at pp. 180-1): This case raises the familiar question: Was entire performance a condition precedent to payment? That depends on the true construction of the contract. In this case the contract was made over a period of time and was partly oral and partly in writing, but . . . the essential terms were set down in the letter . . . (which) concludes with these words:

The foregoing, complete, for the sum of £750 net. Terms of payment are net cash, as the work proceeds; and balance on completion.

The question of law . . . was whether the plaintiff was entitled in this action to sue for the £350 balance of the contract price. . . . The defendant said that he was only entitled to sue on a *quantum meruit* . . . because he said that the contract price was unreasonably high. . . .

In determining this issue the first question is whether, on a true construction of the contract, entire performance was a condition precedent to payment. It was a lump-sum contract, but that does not mean that entire performance was a condition precedent to payment. When a contract provides for a specific sum to be paid on completion of specified work, the courts lean against a construction of the contract which would deprive the contractor of any payment at all simply because there are some defects or omissions. The promise to complete the work is, therefore, construed as a term of the contract, but not as a condition. It is not every breach of that term which absolves the employer from his promise to pay the price, but only a breach which goes to the root of the contract, such as an abandonment of the work when it is only half done. Unless the breach does go to the root of the matter, the employer cannot resist payment of the price. He must pay it and bring a cross-claim for the defects and omissions, or, alternatively, set them up in diminution of the price. The measure is the amount which the work is worth less by reason of the defects and omissions, and is usually calculated by the cost of making them good. . . . It is, of course, always open to the parties by express words to make entire performance a condition precedent. A familiar instance is when the contract provides for progress payments to be made as the work proceeds, but for retention money to be held until completion. Then entire performance is usually a condition precedent to payment of the retention money, but not, of course, to the progress payments. The contractor is entitled to payment pro rata as the work proceeds, less a deduction for retention money. But he is not entitled to the retention money until the work is entirely finished, without defects or omissions. In the present case the contract provided for 'net cash, as the work proceeds; and balance on completion'. If the balance could be regarded as retention money, then it might well be that the contractor ought to have done all the work correctly, without defects or omissions, in order to be entitled to the balance. But I do not think the balance should be regarded as retention money. Retention money is usually only 10%, or 15%, whereas this balance was more than 50%. I think this contract should be regarded as an ordinary lump-sum contract. It was substantially performed. The contractor is entitled, therefore, to the contract price, less a deduction for the defects.

Somervell and Romer LJJ delivered concurring judgments.

Appeal dismissed.

Notes

(1)   Here the defective performance was not sufficiently serious to go to the root of the contract. However, in some instances a defect in the quality of the work may be so great as to allow the employer to refuse to pay for the work even though it would appear that he has derived a substantial benefit from the work of the contractor. *Bolton* v *Mahadeva* [1972] 1 WLR 1009 was such a case (see 10.8.3.1. for the facts). Cairns LJ at pp. 1011 and 1013 said:

The main question . . . is whether defects in workmanship found . . . to cost £174 to repair - that is, between one third and one quarter of the contract price - were of such a character and amount that the plaintiff could not be said to have substantially performed his contract. . . . In considering whether there was a substantial performance I am of the opinion that it is relevant to take into account both the nature of the defects and the proportion between the cost of rectifying them and the contract price.

(2) The Law Commission *Pecuniary Restitution for Breach of Contract* (Law Com. No. 121, 1983), para. 2.32 have recommended that a party who in breach of contract fails to complete an entire contract but who has also conferred a benefit on the other party should be entitled to some payment, unless the contract provides otherwise. However, one member of the Law Commission (Brian Davenport QC) dissented strongly on this issue, observing that in most commercial building contracts there will be a provision for payment in stages in which case, the problem in *Bolton* v *Mahadeva* will not arise. The note of dissent continued:

> The so-called mischief which the report is intended to correct is therefore likely only to exist in relation to small, informal contracts of which the normal example will be a contract between a householder and a jobbing builder to carry out a particular item of work. Experience has shown that it is all too common for such builders not to complete one job of work before moving on to the next. The effect of the report is to remove from the householder almost the only effective sanction he has against the builder not completing the job. In short, he is prevented from saying with any legal effect, 'Unless you come back and finish the job, I shan't pay you a penny.'. . . If the report's recommendations are implemented, the jobbing builder can leave the site and when the irate and exasperated householder finally brings the contract to an end, send in a bill for the work done up to the time when he abandoned the site. It will then be for the householder to dispute the amount and calculate his counter-claim for damages.

10.8.4.2 Consumer pre-payments

Home Improvements: A Discussion Paper
(Office of Fair Trading, 1982)

3.22 . . . payment in advance for work to be undertaken can be followed by the disappearance of the supplier before the work is started or completed or the trader may become insolvent and go into liquidation before the work is completed. Householders should recognise the possible risks of making payments in advance, before satisfactory completion of the work, which may not be related to any actual costs incurred. They should always approach requests for payment in advance with healthy scepticism and, before agreeing to payment, should satisfy themselves, first that the trader concerned has an established business, secondly, that the advance payment is reasonably related to costs which the trader may be expected to have incurred, and thirdly, that there is every likelihood of the contract being completed.

The problem of disappearing advance payments is one which trade associations have recognised. One way in which the problem can be met is through the use of bonding schemes.

Code of Ethical Practice of the Glass and Glaziers' Federation
(1981)

5.1. It is a requirement of members of this Federation that all those who take deposits from private individuals in relation to glazing work on any private domestic premises shall be covered by the Deposit Indemnity Fund which is known as the GGF Fund Limited and shall take such action as the Rules of the GGF and the Rules of the Fund require.

5.2. If for any reason a member of the GGF is unable to carry out work for which a deposit has been taken, or shows to the Federation that it does not have the financial resources to conclude the work or even to refund the deposit, or any part thereof, then the GGF Fund Limited will ensure that the work is carried out at a fair market price for that work less the value of the lost deposit, or at the discretion of the GGF Fund Limited will repay the deposit.

5.3. This Fund covers contracts of the type described above up to a total value of £6,000, where a deposit has been placed with a member company and it covers deposits of up to 25% on supply and fix contracts, or up to 50% on supply only contracts.

5.4. The Fund is financed entirely by members of the Glass and Glazing Federation and is operated for them by the GGF Fund Limited.

The use of the trust as a means of consumer protection, at present, is a matter of voluntary choice. A company can create a trust in favour of a customer who has made an advance payment, but does not have to.

Re Kayford Ltd
[1975] 1 WLR 279
Chancery Division

MEGARRY J at p. 282: No doubt the general rule is that if you send money to a company for goods which are not delivered, you are merely a creditor of the company unless a trust has been created. The sender may create a trust by using appropriate words when he sends the money . . ., or the company may do it by taking suitable steps on or before receiving the money. If either is done, the obligations in respect of the money are transformed from contract to property, from debt to trust.

10.8.4.3 Duty and standard of care For common law materials on the duty and standard of care owed by the provider of a service generally, see 10.5.

10.8.5 Holidays

The problems encountered by the consumer as a holidaymaker, for the most part, are related to his expectations. The majority of consumer complaints in this respect usually concern lack of enjoyment of the holiday or, in some instances, not getting to the destination on time. For the most part, the consumer's legal remedies will lie in contract, based on a breach of the express or implied terms of his contract, however, important protection is also available through self-regulating codes of practice. Sometimes, the consumer's complaint will be that he has been misled by a statement in a holiday brochure. If the statement is not regarded as a term of the contract, a tortious remedy may still be available in respect of a misrepresentation by the tour operator. Misleading statements in holiday brochures may also result in the operator being guilty of a criminal offence, if the description given is misleading as to the amount payable for a service (see 12.2) or if it is misleading as to the nature or provision of any service, accommodation or facility (see 11.3.2).

10.8.5.1 The obligations of the tour operator   A major difficulty is to determine exactly the scope of the tour operator's liability on his contract with the consumer. Two different views are possible (see Nelson-Jones and Stewart, *Package Holiday Law and Contracts*, 2nd ed. (1989) p. 18; Grant (1991) 141 NLJ 134, 197). One is that since the brochure details what the holidaymaker will get and since the contract is with the tour operator, the tour operator is strictly liable for all damage foreseeably suffered by the consumer in a manner similar to the operation of the implied requirements of quality and fitness in a sale of goods contract. However, tour operators would prefer to see the contract as one for services supplied by a number of independent contractors, for whose actions the tour operator is only liable if he has failed to exercise reasonable care in selecting someone competent. The latter view appears to have been borne out in *Wall* v *Silver Wing Surface Arrangements Ltd* (1981 unreported) in which Hodgson J held that it would be unreasonable to saddle a tour operator with an obligation to ensure the safety of all the components of a package holiday if he has no control over the way in which the hotel owners behave. It would appear to be sufficient for the tour operator to exercise care and skill in making suitable arrangements in selecting hotels and flight operators etc. It follows that if the consumer suffers harm as a result of some negligent act on the part of a hotel employee or due to the state of the hotel in which he stays, the tour operator will not be liable unless he has failed to exercise reasonable care. Thus if a honeymoon couple arrive a day late at their destination due to industrial action, the tour operator is not liable if the delay is beyond anyone's control (*Usher* v *Intasun* [1987] CLY 418). Similarly, if the consumer complains of a cockroach-infested hotel room, the tour operator is only liable if it can be shown that reasonable care has not been exercised in selecting a suitable hotel (*Kaye* v *Intasun* [1987] CLY 1150). Conversely, where it can be shown that the tour operator ought to have realised that he was sending the client to unhygienic conditions, the tour operator should, at least, warn the consumer of the danger (*Davey* v *Cosmos Tours* [1989] CLY 2561).

The position at common law is one which has been widely criticised by consumer organisations who would prefer to see a form of strict liability on the part of tour operators for reasons of convenience. Clearly, it is much easier to proceed against a tour operator based in England than to sue a foreign hotel owner. In one respect, it can be argued that the tour operator may be under a duty to do more than merely exercise reasonable care himself. While tour operators will argue that they are merely required to exercise skill in selecting a suitable contractor to provide holiday services, it can be argued that the Supply of Goods and Services Act 1982, s. 13, renders the tour operator vicariously liable for the defective performance of his delegate (see Grant (1991) 141 NLJ 134, 135-6; *Davies* v *Collins* [1945] 1 All ER 247).

Apart from variations on the meaning of the exercise of reasonable care and skill, there are also dicta which point towards a form of strict liability on the part of the tour operator. For example, it has been said that if a tour operator fails to provide a holiday of the required quality, he is liable in damages (*Jarvis* v *Swans Tours Ltd* [1973] 1 All ER 71 at p. 76 per Edmund Davies LJ). Moreover, in *Cook* v *Spanish Holiday Tours Ltd* (1990) *The Times*, 6 February 1990, the Court of Appeal held that the duty of a tour operator was not merely to book a room, but also to provide the accommodation requested. Thus it appears to follow from this that the tour operator is strictly liable if he fails to provide the full components of the package booked by the customer.

Steps towards a form of strict liability have been taken in the EC Council Directive on package travel, package holidays and package tours (OJ L158/59 13.6.90). The Directive provides that the organiser of a package holiday should be liable for the proper performance of the obligations arising from the contract irrespective of whether those obligations are to be performed by the organiser or others (art. 5(1)). However, this is qualified by a provision to the effect that the organiser is not to be liable where neither he nor another supplier of a service is at fault because the alleged breach of contract is due to the act of the consumer or some third party unconnected with the provision of the service or due to a case of *force majeure* or some other event which could not be foreseen or forestalled (art. 5(2)).

While the Directive does not have to be complied with by member states until the end of 1992, ABTA has already taken steps to amend its Code of Conduct for Tour Operators to comply with the requirements of the earlier proposed Directive (OJ C96/12.4.88, p. 5) on this matter. As a result, there is already a self-imposed regime of strict liability in relation to package tours with departure dates after April 1990. Clause 4.8(i) of the Code provides that it must be a term of all contracts for the sale of foreign inclusive holidays that the tour operator should accept liability for the acts or omissions of its employees, agents, subcontractors and suppliers, resulting in harm other than death, bodily injury or illness. It is clear that this provision also extends to natural events as well as those resulting from the default of the hotelier and that the tour operator will be liable where he has no control over the event giving rise to the complaint. It follows from this that while the law based on the decisions in *Wall* v *Silver Wing Surface Arrangements Ltd*, *Usher* v *Intasun* and *Kaye* v *Intasun* remains the same, consumers in a similar position will now be covered by the Code. Clause 4.8(i) also provides that the protection afforded by it will extend to any person whose name appears on the booking form, thus preventing a privity of contract defence on the part of the tour operator (cf. *Jackson* v *Horizon Holidays Ltd* [1975] 3 All ER 92 below).

In relation to death, bodily injury and illness, clause 4.8(ii) provides that the tour operator must accept responsibility for such harm if caused by the *negligent* acts or omissions of employees, agents and subcontractors etc. provided that they act in the course or scope of their employment. Excluded from this is the act of an air or sea carrier which will be covered by specific transport conventions. There is also a requirement that tour operators should be adequately insured against such liability (Code, cl. 4.8(iv)). While this does not add anything in relation to agents and employees, cl. 4.8(ii) provides protection in excess of the law in relation to the negligent acts or omissions of subcontractors and suppliers. It would appear that the consumer will now have a remedy in a case like *Craven* v *Strand Holidays* (1982) 40 OR(2d) 186 where a holidaymaker was injured when a bus in which he was travelling overturned due to the negligence of the driver. At the time, the tour operator was held not to be liable because it had no control over the bus company and had exercised reasonable care in selecting the company as a subcontractor.

The Code further provides that tour operators will also contract to provide advice, guidance and financial assistance up to a limit of £5,000 per booking to consumers who, while on holiday, suffer illness, injury or death due to a misadventure, not related to the holiday arrangement. The wording of this provision is somewhat ambiguous, and tour operators would be advised to think carefully about the wording of such a contract term so as to avoid construction *contra proferentem* if it were to be tested in legal proceedings. It is intended to mean that tour operators will undertake to provide assistance in the bringing of legal proceedings against the person responsible. However, on its present wording it could be taken to mean that the tour operator will provide up to £5,000 towards the cost of hospital fees incurred by the consumer if he were to fall off a defectively designed motor cycle which has been hired independently of any specific holiday arrangements with the tour operator.

10.8.5.2 Loss of enjoyment An award of expectation damages for a breach of contract is ordinarily related to the standard business expectation of making a profit, however, in the context of disastrous holidays there are other considerations. It may be that what has been provided is worth the money paid for it, in the sense that the value of the flight to the holiday location and the cost of the accommodation provided is equal to the amount paid by the consumer. Even if the court decides that the consumer has only had 'half a holiday' an award of damages based on half the cost of the holiday may not be sufficient compensation for the loss of enjoyment (*Jarvis* v *Swans Tours Ltd* [1973] 1 All ER 71 at p. 72 per Lord Denning MR). The consumer may make a purchase for pleasure or utility conferred which may bear no relation to the price paid (see Harris, Ogus and Phillips (1979) 95 LQR 581). Since there is no question of non-performance, specific performance of the contract is not an appropriate remedy. Similarly, it will not be possible to compensate the consumer by giving reinstatement damages so as to allow satisfactory performance by a third party. Much will depend on what the tour operator's brochure has claimed about the holiday in question and how this has been interpreted by the consumer.

In some instances the tour operator's claims may be interpreted as a misrepresentation, in which case the consumer surplus value may be protected by an award of damages for misrepresentation for loss of enjoyment. In *Chesneau* v *Interhome Ltd* (1983) *The Times*, 9 June 1983 the defendants claimed that a house was in a quiet location near woods with a private swimming-pool and was not part of a holiday complex. In fact, the house was part of a complex and had a shared swimming-pool. Accordingly, the plaintiff found alternative accommodation at an additional cost of £209. The Court of Appeal held that the plaintiff was entitled to recover the additional expenditure plus damages for distress suffered as a result of the defendant's misrepresentation. In other instances, statements in the brochure will be treated as terms of the contract, breach of which will give rise to an action for damages, subject to any purported exclusions or limitations of liability. These terms may be express, being based on matters specifically spelt out in the brochure or they may be implied.

If the tour operator has made specific claims about a particular hotel or resort and these are not complied with, an action for damages may lie for a breach of warranty. Thus if the tour operator contracts to provide accommodation in a four-star hotel within five minutes' walk of a sandy beach and neither of these facilities is available, the consumer will be able to maintain an action for damages. However, the brochure may not be specific in every respect. If the consumer complains of a generally low standard of quality of service, but there are no specific claims in the brochure about the hotel or the service it provides, an action may still lie for a breach of the implied term that the service provided will be reasonable. Whether or not the consumer is successful would appear to depend on the seriousness of the defendant's breach. For example, the unavailability of suitable skis on a skiing holiday (*Jarvis* v *Swans Tours Ltd* [1973] QB 233) or the lack of proper heating in hotel rooms in January (*Adcock* v *Blue Sky Holidays* (13 May 1980 unreported) are serious breaches of contract which will justify damages for disappointment. However, a less serious breach such as the unavailability of a child's cot to a childless couple would hardly justify compensation.

In practical terms, the consumer may be met with a general unwillingness on the part of tour operators to admit liability when a holiday goes disastrously wrong. It can be the case that the operator will hold out until the last minute before offering compensation. One possible argument which may be raised is that the tour operator merely acts as an agent on behalf of the hotel owners (see *Which?*, February 1982, p. 112). However, it is surely the case that it is the tour operator who provides the holiday and therefore acts as principal.

At one time it was thought that damages could not be awarded for distress or injured feelings, however, it is now clear that where the consumer has contracted for a specific form of enjoyment, as is true of holiday cases, an award of damages can be made when the holiday proves to be a disaster (*Jarvis* v *Swans Tours Ltd* [1973] 1 All ER 71).

Where a holiday has been booked by one person on behalf of his family, it is possible that the tour operator can argue that the doctrine of privity of contract prevents the recovery of damages by anyone other than the person making the booking. However, in *Jackson* v *Horizon Holidays Ltd* [1975] 3 All ER 92 the Court of Appeal held that the plaintiff could recover damages in respect of the disappointment suffered by all members of the family. The basis of the decision is in some doubt, but it is still clear that the distress and disappointment suffered by all members of the holiday party is remediable. However, if the consumer suffers specific harm over and above general disappointment, it is clear that such harm must be foreseeable within the principles laid down in *The Heron II* [1969] 1 AC 350. For example, if the consumer suffers from an asthmatic condition which requires special accommodation, it is essential that the tour operator or his agent has been made aware of this at or before the time of contracting (*Kemp* v *Intasun Holidays Ltd* (1987) 7 Tr LR 161).

10.8.5.3 Getting there and back When the consumer has booked a holiday, he can reasonably expect to be transported to and from his destination. However, problems can arise where there is a late alteration to the holiday schedule, where a scheduled flight is overbooked or where the tour operator becomes insolvent.

10.8.5.3.1 Alterations Whether or not alterations to the holiday schedule are permitted will depend on the terms of the contract contained in the standard booking conditions. Many such provisions will amount to limitations of the tour operator's liability and will be dealt with elsewhere. Perhaps the most important type of provision in this respect is one which allows the tour operator to alter itineraries at his discretion. Such a provision must satisfy the Unfair Contract Terms Act 1977 requirement of reasonableness (see also *Anglo-Continental Holidays Ltd* v *Typaldos Lines (London) Ltd* [1967] 2 Lloyd's Rep 61). If the alteration is material or amounts to cancellation of the holiday, the tour operator's breach will amount to non-performance of the contract and the consumer will be entitled to recover any prepayment he has made on the ground of a total failure of consideration. Principles identical to those which apply to prepayments for home-improvement work are relevant here (see 10.8.3.2.).

If the tour operator materially alters holiday arrangements, his conduct may be regarded as a breach of condition and therefore sufficiently serious to allow the consumer to treat his obligation to pay for the holiday as being at an end. In such circumstances, the consumer has two options at common law. He may either accept the breach or waive it and treat the contract as continuing (*Heyman* v *Darwins Ltd* [1942] AC 331; *Johnson* v *Agnew* [1980] AC 367). One difficulty which may face the consumer is whether or not the tour operator's breach is sufficiently serious to allow termination. Clearly, there will be some breaches that go to the root of the contract, but there will be others which may spoil the holiday but may only give rise to an action for damages. For example, if the consumer's flight is delayed due to the fault of the tour operator, but an alternative flight is offered four hours later to a destination 100 miles away from the proposed holiday location, it may be that the consumer must accept the alteration and seek to recover damages in respect of any specific expense incurred and for inconvenience and loss of enjoyment. Failure to accept the alternative offered could be construed as unreasonable conduct amounting to a failure to mitigate loss (*Payzu Ltd* v *Saunders* [1919] 2 KB 581). On the other hand, if the alteration consists of sending the consumer to a totally different holiday resort, it would be unreasonable to expect the consumer to stand for this and a decision to return home might be justified in the circumstances.

In relation to alterations and cancellations, it is the case that the consumer is better protected by the provisions of the ABTA Tour Operators' Code of Conduct (revised July 1989). This deals with the issues of cancellation (cl. 4.3) and material alteration (cl. 4.4) separately. In either event the Code requires the tour operator to offer an alternative comparable holiday or a prompt return of all money paid.

So far as cancellation is concerned, the Code also provides that the tour operator shall not cancel a holiday after the date on which the balance of the price becomes due for reasons other than the outbreak of hostilities, political unrest or other circumstances amounting to *force majeure*. Under cl. 3 of the revised Code certain events over which the tour operator has no control, such as unilateral action on the part of a hotelier making accommodation unavailable, are not to be regarded as *force majeure* events. Furthermore, a strike by the tour operator's own staff is not regarded as sufficient excuse for cancellation. The ABTA guidelines for booking conditions give a definition of cancellation which goes beyond its dictionary definition. Clause 4.3 of the guidelines provides that changing a holiday in such a way that it amounts to the substitution of an entirely different tour will be regarded as a cancellation. Other examples given in the guidelines include the substitution of a resort unreasonably far from that booked by the client, provision of accommodation of an entirely different type to that booked, changes of flight time by more than 24 hours and changes of itinerary omitting the main advertised event or place.

In the case of a material alteration, cl. 4.4 provides that if the tour operator makes such an alteration after a booking, he must give the consumer the choice of an alternative holiday of comparable standard or a full refund of moneys paid. Furthermore, if the alteration is made after the date on which payment of the balance of the price became due, the tour operator is required to pay reasonable compensation. In most cases, the tour operator will itemise, in the brocure, in scale form, the amount of compensation available to the consumer.

The major difficulty is to determine what alterations are to be regarded as material. The code provides little in the way of definition, but the ABTA guidelines for booking conditions, while informal and not binding, provide greater detail in this respect. It is clear from the Code that alterations caused by departure delays resulting from weather or other technical difficulties including industrial disputes are not to be regarded as material (cl. 4.4(v)(a)). Furthermore, changes resulting from overbooking are dealt with separately and must not be regarded as material by the tour operator (cl. 4.4(v)(b)). The guidelines for booking conditions provide that any significant change to the tour not amounting to cancellation will be classified as a material alteration. These are stated to include significant changes of resort, flight changes involving substantial inconvenience and inconvenient changes of airport.

10.8.5.3.2 Overbooking of flights While many package deals will involve transport by means of charter flights, it is sometimes the case that a tour operator will use scheduled flights. A difficulty which can arise is that a consumer who believes he has a confirmed flight booking finds that he is denied access to that flight. The reason this can happen is that many airlines adopt a deliberate policy of overbooking scheduled flights to allow for 'no-shows', namely businessmen who have booked seats on a number of flights knowing that they will use only one of those flights. With a deliberate policy of overbooking, it is clear that there will be occasions on which more passengers will arrive for a flight than can be legally put on board. It is clear that adopting such a policy can result in criminal liability, where the flight operator gives written confirmation of the availability of a seat, but this is no compensation to the disappointed traveller.

An EC Council Regulation (No. 295/91 OJ L36/5 8.2.91) provides for minimum rules on the provision of compensation in such circumstances. The regulation requires an air carrier to formulate a set of rules which it will operate in the event of an overbooked flight (art. 3.1), which should include provision for a call on volunteers prepared to take an alternative confirmed reservation (art. 3.3). Furthermore, special consideration should be given to unaccompanied children and handicapped travellers (art. 3.4).

Where it is necessary to prevent a passenger from boarding a flight on which he is booked, the Regulation gives passengers the choice of reimbursement of the cost of the ticket, re-routing to his final destination at the earliest opportunity or re-routing at a later date at the passenger's convenience (art. 4.1). Irrespective of what choice the passenger makes, he is entitled to the payment of compensation of ECU 150 for flights of up to 3,500 km and ECU 300 for longer flights (art. 4.2). However, where the passenger is re-routed and arrives at his final destintion no more than two hours later on flights of less than 3,500 km (four hours in the case of longer flights), the specified compensation may be reduced by 50% (art. 4.3). In any event, the carrier is not required to pay more than the face value of the passenger's ticket (art. 4.4) and the compensation may be paid in cash or travel vouchers or other services, if the passenger agrees (art. 4.5).

In addition to the provisions in respect of compensation, the Regulation also requires the flight operator to provide a passenger who is denied boarding, free telephone or fax facilities to convey one message, hotel accommodation and refreshments where this proves to be reasonably necessary (art. 6.1).

10.8.5.3.3   Tour operator's insolvency   Where a tour operator or a travel agent becomes insolvent, two principal issues arise. First, the consumer will wish to recover advance payments made if the holiday cannot be taken and secondly, the consumer will wish to be assured of a safe return home, if the insolvency occurs after the holiday has commenced.

Where a tour operator becomes insolvent prior to the commencement of the holiday, it may be the case that the trustee in bankruptcy will arrange for profitable contracts to be performed by another operator. However, it is more likely that most holiday contracts will be terminated prior to the date of performance. Such termination amounts to an anticipatory breach of contract which, if accepted, will entitle the consumer to a full refund. However, as the holidaymaker will be an unsecured creditor of the tour operator, it is unlikely that he will receive in full the amount he has paid.

Greater protection is provided by the travel industry in the form of bonding arrangements made by the Tour Operator's Study Group, the Civil Aviation Authority or the Association of British Travel Agents. In general, if the consumer intends to travel by air, he will be better protected since even if the bond moneys are insufficient to repay all customers, the Air Travel Trust will make good any shortfall and if the Trust is unable to meet that shortfall, the government will step in.

One way in which the consumer can protect himself is by paying for the holiday with a credit card. Under the Consumer Credit Act 1974, s. 75, the creditor is jointly liable to the debtor in respect of the supplier's breach of contract (see 6.4.2.3). The effect of this is that where the consumer has paid the tour operator directly by means of a credit card, the creditor will be bound to satisfy the consumer's claim under s. 75. More difficult, however, is the situation in which the credit card payment has been made to a travel agent. In these cicumstances, it is arguable that the collapse of a tour operator does not amount to a breach of contract on the part of the travel agent, in which case the creditor is justified in rejecting the debtor's claim under s. 75.

Where a tour operator ceases trading during the currency of a holiday, it is of prime importance that the consumer is not left stranded. Again, the travel industry bonding arrangements provide the greatest protection. In some instances where the holiday has been paid for in advance by the now collapsed tour operator, the holiday can continue uninterrupted. Even where this is not the case, the bonding arrangement will be such that any balance due to a hotelier etc. will be paid for. However, this does not stop some hoteliers from demanding immediate payment from the stranded consumer. In such a case, the consumer may be forced to return home early and the bonding arrangement will ensure that a flight is provided. This still leaves the consumer uncompensated in respect of the 'lost' portion of his holiday. Suing the tour operator is not an option, but under the bonding arrangements, the consumer can apply for a partial refund of the cost of his holiday. The order of priorities in which bond moneys are applied is first to ensure that stranded holidaymakers enjoy the remainder of their holiday or are repatriated. Any balance can then be used to make refunds. If the consumer booked his holiday through an ABTA travel agent, the agent may have given a money-back guarantee, in which case the consumer will be reimbursed and the agent will seek to recover that amount under the relevant bonding arrangement. Furthermore, when the EC Directive on package holidays comes into force, it may be that the travel agent will be legally responsible for the improper performance of the contract. art. 5.1 gives member States of the Community the option to impose liability on the 'organiser and/or retailer party'. Furthermore, the Directive requires the responsible party to give evidence of security for the refund of money paid over and for the repatriation of the consumer in the event of insolvency (art. 7).

10.8.6   Holidays – materials for consideration

10.8.6.1   Obligations of the tour operator   A principal concern is whether a tour operator is strictly liable for anything that goes wrong with a holiday or whether the operator is only liable for a personal failure to exercise reasonable care.

Wall v *Silver Wing Surface Arrangements Ltd*
(1981 unreported)

The plaintiff was badly injured as a result of being trapped in a hotel fire and being unable to escape because a fire door had been locked in order to prevent burglars from gaining access to the hotel. The plaintiff sued for breach of an implied contractual term that the plaintiff would be reasonably safe in using the hotel. Hodgson J rejected the plaintiff's argument.

HODGSON J. . . . it is perfectly well known that the tour operator neither owns, occupies or controls the hotels which are included in his brochure, any more than he has control over the airlines which fly his customers, the airports whence and whither they fly and the land transport which conveys them from airport to hotel. . . . If injury is caused by the default of the hotel owners and occupiers . . . the customer will have whatever remedy the relevant law allows. . . .

I would find it wholly unreasonable to saddle a tour operator with an obligation to ensure the safety of all the components of the package over none of which he had any control at all.

The position as it stands under *Wall* v *Silver Wing Surface Arrangements Ltd* will not last long when the provisions of the EC Council Directive on Package Travel (OJ L158/59 13.6.90) are complied with.

EEC Council Directive on Package Travel

Article 5

1.   Member States shall take the necessary steps to ensure that the organiser and/or retailer party to the contract is liable to the consumer for the proper performance of the obligations arising from the contract, irrespective of whether such obligations are to be performed by that organiser and/or retailer or by other suppliers of services without prejudice to the right of the organiser and/or retailer to pursue those other suppliers of services.

2.   With regard to the damage resulting for the consumer from the failure to perform or the improper performance of the contract, member States shall take the necessary steps to ensure that the organiser and/or retailer is/are liable unless such failure to perform or improper performance is attributable neither to any fault of theirs nor to that of another supplier of services, because:

– the failures which occur in the performance of the contract are attributable to the consumer,

– such failures are attributable to a third party unconnected with the provision of the services contracted for, and are unforeseeable or unavoidable,

– such failures are due to a case of *force majeure* such as that defined in article 4(6)(ii) or to an event which the organiser and/or retailer or the supplier of services, even with all due care, could not foresee or forestall.

In the cases referred to in the second and third indents, the organiser and/or retailer party to the contract shall be required to give prompt assistance to a consumer in difficulty.

In the matter of damages arising from the non-performance or improper performance of the services involved in the package, the member States may allow compensation to be limited in accordance with the international conventions governing such services.

In the matter of damage other than personal injury resulting from the non-performance or improper performance of the services involved in the package, the member States may allow compensation to be limited under the contract. Such limitation shall not be unreasonable.

3. Without prejudice to the fourth subparagraph of paragraph 2, there may be no exclusion by means of a contractual clause from the provisions of paragraphs 1 and 2.

4. The consumer must communicate any failure in the performance of a contract which he perceives on the spot to the supplier of the services concerned and to the organiser and/or retailer in writing or any other appropriate form at the earliest opportunity.

This obligation must be stated clearly and explicitly in the contract.

While the obligations imposed under the Directive must be complied with by 31 December 1992, tour operators who are members of ABTA will be subject to a similar regime at a much earlier date, due to the provisions of the ABTA Tour Operator's Code of Conduct.

ABTA Tour Operator's Code of Conduct

4.8 (i) Tour operators shall include as a term of any contract for the sale of their foreign inclusive holidays or tours a provision accepting responsibility for acts and/or omissions of their employees, agents, subcontractors and suppliers. In addition, tour operators shall indicate acceptance of responsibility should the services which the operator is contractually obliged to provide prove deficient or are not of reasonable standards save that tour operators shall not be responsible or accept liability for death, bodily injury or illness caused to the signatory to the contract and/or any other named person on the booking form except as provided by clause 4.8(ii) below. Where the services in question consist of carriage by air or by sea, the tour operator shall be entitled to limit his obligations and liabilities in the manner provided by International Conventions in respect of air or sea carriers.

(ii) A tour operator shall include, as a term of any contract for the sale of foreign inclusive holidays or tours, a provision accepting responsibility for the negligent act and/or omissions of:

(a) his employees or agents, and

(b) his suppliers and subcontractors, servants and/or agents of same whilst acting within the scope of, or in the course of their employment (other than air and sea carriers performing any domestic, internal or international carriage of whatsoever kind) in respect of claims arising as a result of death, bodily injury or illness caused to the signatory to the contract and/or any other of the named persons on the booking.

A tour operator shall indicate that claims under this paragraph shall be subject to English law (or Scottish, where appropriate) in respect of any question of liability or quantum, and all proceedings shall be within the exclusive domain of the English (or Scottish) courts.

(iii) A tour operator shall include as a term of any contract relating to the sale of their foreign inclusive holidays or tours a provision stating that every assistance shall be afforded by them to a client who through misadventure suffers illness, personal injury or death during the period of their holiday arising out of an activity which does not form part of the foreign inclusive holiday arrangement nor an excursion offered through the tour operator. Tour operators shall ensure that such assistance shall take the form of advice, guidance and initial financial assistance where appropriate up to a limit of £5,000 per booking form.

(iv) A tour operator shall ensure that they obtain liability insurance to cover claims made by clients under clause 4.8 of this Code.

10.8.6.2   Loss of enjoyment

D. Harris, A. Ogus and J. Phillips, 'Contract remedies and the consumer surplus'
(1979) 95 LQR 581, pp. 583, 595

The concept of consumer surplus is important in any attempt to measure consumer losses because, unlike firms, consumers make purchases for the pleasure or utility they confer; this utility has no necessary relationship with the price paid, and is of quite a different order from market prices or business profits. It is, of course, difficult to measure utility, but generally economists avoid the conceptual problem by measuring utility in terms of the maximum amount a consumer would pay for a particular purchase. . . .

Consumer surplus may arise from services as well as from the possession of land or goods. Thus a holiday is generally worth more to the tourist than the price he has to pay for it, and the value to the family of wedding photographs exceeds their price. . . .

The common law systems have traditionally been hesitant to award non-pecuniary damages for breach of contract. This may again be attributed to the failure to distinguish between commercial and consumer contracts and to recognise that almost by definition the latter are concerned with the transfer to the promisee of a benefit to be enjoyed rather than a marketable good. But the absence of the award from the reported cases may also be explained by the fact that in most situations it is assumed that the promisee can avoid the loss by obtaining equivalent satisfaction from a substitute. In other words, the problem would arise only where such substitution was not available (as in *Jarvis* v *Swans Tours Ltd* [1973] 1 All ER 71).

Jarvis v *Swans Tours Ltd*
[1973] 1 All ER 71
Court of Appeal

LORD DENNING MR at pp. 72-5: The plaintiff . . . was minded to go for Christmas to Switzerland. . . . He was much attracted by the [brochure] description of Morlialp, Giswil, Central Switzerland. I will not read the whole of it, but just pick out some of the principal attractions:

SWANS HOUSEPARTY IN MORLIALP. *All these Houseparty arrangements are included in the price of your holiday.* Welcome party on arrival. Afternoon tea and cake for seven days. Swiss dinner by candlelight. Fondue party. Yodler evening. Chali farewell party in the 'Alphutte Bar'. Service of representative.

Alongside on the same page there was a special note about ski-packs: 'Hire of Skis, Sticks and Boots . . . 12 days £11.10'.

In August 1969, on the faith of that brochure, Mr Jarvis booked a 15-day holiday with ski-pack. The total charge was £63.45. . . .

The plaintiff went on the holiday, but he was very disappointed. He was a man of about 35 and he expected to be one of a houseparty of some 30 or so people. Instead, he found that there were only 13 during the first week. In the second week there was no houseparty at all. He was the only person there . . . and no one could speak English, except himself. He was very disappointed, too, with the skiing. It was some distance away at Giswil. There were no ordinary length skis. There were only mini-skis, about 3 ft long. . . . In the second week he did get some longer skis . . . but then, because of the boots, his feet got rubbed and he could not continue. . . .

The matter was summed up by the learned judge:

... during the first week he got a holiday in Switzerland which was to some extent inferior ... and, as to the second week he got a holiday which was very largely inferior [to what he was led to expect].

What is the legal position? I think that the statements in the brochure were representations or warranties. The breaches of them give Mr Jarvis a right to damages. It is not necessary to decide whether they were representations or warranties. . . .

The one question in the case is: what is the amount of damages? . . .

It has often been said that on a breach of contract damages cannot be given for mental distress. . . . The courts in those days only allowed the plaintiff to recover damages if he suffered physical inconvenience. . . .

I think that those limitations are out of date. In a proper case, damages for mental distress can be recovered in contract, just as damages for shock can be recovered in tort. One such case is a contract for a holiday, or any other contract to provide entertainment and enjoyment. If the contracting party breaks his contract, damages can be given for the disappointment, the distress, the upset and frustration caused by the breach. I know that it is difficult to assess in terms of money, but it is no more difficult than the assessment which the courts have to make every day in personal injury cases for loss of amenities. Take the present case. Mr Jarvis has only a fortnight's holiday in the year. He books it far ahead, and looks forward to it all that time. He ought to be compensated for the loss of it. . . .

I think the judge was in error in taking the sum paid for the holiday, £63.45, and halving it. The right measure of damages is to compensate him for the loss of entertainment and enjoyment which he was promised, and which he did not get. . . . I think the damages . . . should be the sum of £125. I would allow the appeal accordingly.

Edmund Davies and Stephenson LJJ agreed.

If something more than general distress and disappointment is suffered, ordinary rules on remoteness of damage apply and the tour operator or his agent must be made aware of the possibility of loss at or before the time of contracting.

Kemp v Intasun Holidays Ltd
(1987) 7 Tr LR 161
Court of Appeal

The plaintiff suffered from asthma. His wife booked a holiday and claimed that by way of a passing remark, she had made the defendant's agent aware of the plaintiff's condition. The hotel into which they had been booked was full so they were accommodated elsewhere in inferior accommodation. The family suffered general distress and inconvenience, but also claimed damages in respect of exacerbation of the plaintiff's condition.

KERR LJ at p. 165: The defendants are responsible for all the consequences which they should reasonably have contemplated as liable to flow from their breach of contract. . . .

It is clear that the foreseeable consequences of a breach of contract of this kind . . . will always include any distress, discomfort, disappointment, or . . . 'loss of enjoyment' of the actual holiday in comparison with the contractual holiday which should have been provided. . . . But the responsibility of a tour operator does not necessarily stop there. He must also accept liability for any other consequences which should have been in the reasonable contemplation of the parties if these flowed naturally from his breach and caused additional foreseeable loss or damage. Such liability would equally be within...the first rule in *Hadley* v *Baxendale*. For instance, if the consequence of not providing the contractual accommodation is not merely the loss of its enjoyment . . . but also the fact that the plaintiffs had to sleep out on the beach, with the result that their health suffered in a natural and ordinarily foreseeable way . . . that would be a natural and foreseeable additional consequence which would equally flow from the tour operator's breach.

In relation to 'special losses' Kerr LJ continued, referring to *Cook* v *Swinfen* [1967] 1 WLR 457 where Lord Denning MR said (at p. 461):

Special circumstances, brought home, enlarge the area of foreseeability. . . .
    In these circumstances I think that, just as in the law of tort, so also in the law of contract, damages can be recovered for nervous shock or anxiety state if it is a reasonably foreseeable consequence. So the question became this: when a client goes to a solicitor, is it a reasonably foreseeable consequence that, if anything goes wrong with the litigation owing to the solicitor's negligence, there will be a breakdown in health? It can be foreseen that there will be injured feelings; mental distress; anger; and annoyance. . . . Is it reasonably foreseeable that there may be an actual breakdown in health? I do not think so.

KERR LJ then said of Kemp at p. 167: That illustrates the difference between the foreseeability of the ordinary consequences for which damages are awarded in this kind of case . . . and the special circumstances which must be brought home to a tour operator before damages in respect of injury to health are also to be recoverable. The only possible basis for the latter conclusion is the casual conversation which Mrs Kemp had with one or more of the ladies at Thomas Cook. . . . One can put the matter in many different ways, but there is none whereby this casual conversation can possibly have any contractual consequences for these defendants.

Parker LJ agreed.

10.8.6.3   Alterations and cancellations

ABTA Tour Operators' Code of Conduct

4.3   Cancellation of Tours, Holidays or Other Travel Arrangements by Tour Operators
    (i)   A tour operator shall not cancel a tour, holiday or other travel arrangements after the date when payment of the balance of the price becomes due unless it is necessary to do so as a result of hostilities, political unrest or other circumstances amounting to *force majeure*, or unless the client defaults in payment of such balance.
    (ii)   If a tour operator, for reasons other than hostilities, political unrest or other circumstances amounting to *force majeure*, cancels a holiday, tour or other travel arrangements on or before the date when payment of the balance of the price becomes due, he shall inform agents and direct clients as soon as possible, and shall offer clients

the choice of an alternative holiday of at least comparable standard if available, or of a prompt and full refund of all money paid. Any such refunds shall be sent to agents within 10 clear days and to direct clients within 14 clear days.

(iii)   If a tour operator has to cancel a tour, holiday or other travel arrangements as a result of hostilities, political unrest or other circumstances amounting to *force majeure*, he shall inform agents and direct clients without delay and shall offer clients the choice of an alternative holiday of at least comparable standard, if available, or a prompt and full refund of all money paid. Any such refunds shall be sent to agents within 10 clear days and to direct clients within 14 clear days.

4.4   Alterations to Tours, Holidays and Other Travel Arrangements by Tour Operators

(i)   If a tour operator makes a material alteration to a tour, holiday or other travel arrangement for which a booking has already been made, he shall inform agents and direct clients without delay and shall give clients the choice of either accepting the alteration which must be of at least comparable standard, if available or of receiving a prompt and full refund of all money paid. Any such refunds shall be sent to agents within 10 clear days and to direct clients within 14 clear days.

(ii)   If a tour operator makes a material alteration to a tour, holiday or other travel arrangement after the date when payment of the balance of the price becomes due, he shall also ensure that clients receive reasonable compensation which may be in accordance with a scale of payments. The right to receive compensation and any scale of payments shall be clearly stated in the relevant booking conditions.

(iii)   A tour operator shall not make a material alteration to a tour, holiday or other travel arrangement unless he does so in time to inform agents and direct clients not less than 14 days before the date of commencement of the tour, holiday or other travel arrangements.

(iv)   Where a material alteration is necessary due to hostilities, political unrest or other circumstances amounting to *force majeure*, the above subparagraphs shall not apply. A tour operator shall, however, inform agents and direct clients without delay and shall give clients the choice of either accepting the alteration which must be of at least comparable standard, if available, or of receiving a prompt and full refund of all money paid. Any such refunds shall be sent to agents within 10 clear days and to direct clients within 14 clear days.

(v)   For the purposes of the above subparagraphs material alterations shall not include:

(a)   delays in departures on a tour, holiday or other travel arrangement caused by weather conditions, technical problems to transport, strikes, industrial action or other circumstances beyond the control of the operator;

(b)   changes resulting from overbooking by hotels.

CHAPTER ELEVEN

Advertising Law I –
Misdescriptions of Goods and Services

11.1 THE ROLE OF ADVERTISING

In a modern consumer society, advertising plays a central role in making available to consumers information which the producer of the advertised product wishes the consumer to have. There are a number of criticisms of advertising generally. For example, it is said to promote consumption by playing on emotions, while at the same time providing little useful, objective information for the consumer to use effectively in evaluating the competing claims of rival products. Accordingly, there is the possibility that advertising is capable of inducing an imprudent shopping decision if it encourages a person to buy something he does not want. It may also be argued that producers can use advertising in order to artificially create wants on the part of consumers which the producer can subsequently satisfy with his product (Galbraith, *The Affluent Society*, 4th ed (1984) at p. 129). However, the counter-argument to this is that advertising can encourage production which is important in maintaining a high standard of living and promoting a buoyant economy.

An important effect of misleading advertising is that consumers receive imperfect information or are unable properly to process complex information about a product or service. Since accurate information on matters such as price, quality and the terms of contracting is essential in the promotion of effective competition, regulation of advertising practices is justified.

Whether or not these criticisms are justified, it is undoubtedly the case that advertising is a very powerful tool which if misused can result in the consumer receiving misleading information. Where this is the case, regulation of misleading advertising practices is justified on the ground that it can correct any market failures resulting from the inaccurate information which might otherwise be given to consumers.

The principal controls on advertisers are to be found in the criminal law and in self-regulating codes of practice, although some common law and statutory rules may occasionally be relevant in providing a misled consumer with a remedy in the form of an award of damages.

11.2 CIVIL LAW CONTROLS ON ADVERTISERS

The role of the civil law in controlling advertising practices is limited, but in certain circumstances it may provide a useful source of redress. Some civil law rules are specifically concerned with matters of competition between rival traders and as such do not provide the consumer with any means of redress. For example, some advertising material may infringe a trade mark or constitute a breach of copyright or result in the commission of the tort of passing off. Where a producer engages in comparative advertising he must be careful not to make disparaging remarks about a rival product since this may result in the commission of the tort of slander of goods.

11.2.1 Breach of contract and misrepresentation

The civil law is most likely to be of assistance to the consumer where he is in a contractual relationship with the advertiser. However, given the length of the chain of supply from the producer/advertiser down to the consumer, it is often the case that there is no contract between the advertiser and the consumer due to the operation of the doctrine of privity of contract (see 3.2.1.1). Sometimes it is the case that a collateral contract will be found to exist between the consumer and the advertiser where there is evidence of reliance on advertising material (see 3.2.1.1.2). Furthermore, factual statements made in advertising material, if not terms of a contract, may amount to misrepresentations if they induce the consumer to enter into a contract with the advertiser (see 3.2.1.2).

The difficulty with some advertising material is that it is couched in such terms that it is unlikely to be regarded as a statement of fact. For example, claims to the effect that brand X refreshes the parts of the body that rival products cannot reach or that a particular soap powder washes whiter than white are treated as trade puffs and do not amount to representations capable of giving rise to liability on the part of the advertiser (see *Dimmock* v *Hallett* (1866) LR 2 Ch App 21; *Scott* v *Hansen* (1829) 1 Russ & M 128). However, if the advertisement is more credible and contains statements which may be construed as being factual, liability for misrepresentation may be imposed (see *Smith* v *Land & House Property Corporation* (1884) 28 ChD 7). Thus it might not be wise for an advertiser to claim that dog food prolongs the life of animals that eat it in preference to a rival brand.

There appears to be a general reluctance to allow a commercial promoter to escape liability on the ground that his advertisements amount to nothing more than trade puffery. In such a case, the courts will try to discover an intention to create legal relations on the part of the advertiser (*Esso Petroleum Co. Ltd* v *Commissioners of Customs & Excise* [1976] 1 WLR 1 at p. 6 per Lord Simon). Thus where there is a very precise claim, for example, that a proprietary medicine can cure influenza, the statement is likely to be treated as a contractual term, which could give rise to an action for damages for breach of contract (*Carlill* v *Carbolic Smokeball Co. Ltd* [1893] 1 QB 256).

In other parts of the common law world the position of the advertiser is much clearer. For example, in the USA, there is a general refusal to be bound by a strict application of the doctrine of privity of contract, thereby allowing the consumer to proceed directly against the producer of goods in the event of a misleading statement about his product. In *Randy Knitwear Inc.* v *American Cyanamid Co.* (1962) 181 NE 2d 399, the New York Court of Appeals held that a producer of material used to manufacture children's clothing could be held liable for the loss suffered by the plaintiff when the manufacturer claimed that the material was waterproof. It was clear that there was no direct relationship of privity between the parties, but that was held not to matter since the warranty given by the manufacturer was one effected by means of mass advertising and was ultimately responsible for inducing consumer purchases (see also Trade Practices Act 1974 (Australia), s. 74G).

11.2.2　Negligent misstatement

Where there is no contractual relationship between the advertiser and the consumer, but the consumer has incurred expense through purchasing a product from a retail supplier, there may be the possibility of a negligence action arising out of an alleged negligent misstatement. Liability for such statements lies under the rule in *Hedley Byrne & Co. Ltd* v *Heller & Partners Ltd* [1964] AC 465, but recent explanations of the rule restrict the liability of the maker of the statement. Following the decision of the House of Lords in *Caparo Industries plc* v *Dickman* [1990] 1 All ER 568, a duty of care will only be owed by the maker of a statement where three conditions are satisfied. First, it must be foreseeable that the plaintiff will suffer damage as a result of relying on the statement. Secondly, there must be a close relationship of proximity between the maker of the statement and the person to whom it is communicated and thirdly, it must be just and equitable to impose liability on the maker of the statement (*Caparo Industries plc* v *Dickman* [1990] 1 All ER 568 at pp. 573–4 per Lord Bridge).

Generally, advertising material is communicated to the world at large and there are strong reasons for doubting whether a misleading advertisement will give rise to a successful action for damages for negligent misstatement. While it may be foreseeable that a consumer will suffer damage as a result of relying on a statement contained in advertising material, it does not necessarily follow that there will be a sufficiently close relationship of proximity between the consumer and the advertiser or that it will be just and equitable to impose liability.

It would appear that in deciding whether the maker of a statement is to be liable in negligence for the consequences of the plaintiff's reliance on that statement, six criteria must be considered (*James McNaughton Paper Group*

Ltd v *Hicks Anderson & Co.* [1991] 1 All ER 134 at pp. 144-5 per Neill LJ). These are (1) the purpose for which the statement was made; (2) the purpose for which the statement was communicated; (3) the relationship between the maker of the statement, the recipient of the information and any relevant third party; (4) the size of any class to which the recipient of the information belongs; (5) the state of knowledge of the maker of the statement; and (6) reliance by the recipient of the information.

Because advertisements are directed to a large class of people it is likely that the courts may be reluctant to impose a duty of care on advertisers for fear of opening the floodgates of litigation. Moreover, it might be difficult to argue that the advertiser is always aware of the particular manner in which the consumer will rely on the information given to him. However, it is to be hoped that this does not result in a general rule to the effect that manufacturers' promotional material can never give rise to liability, particularly since advertisements are specifically intended to induce consumer purchases (see Borrie, *Development of Consumer Law and Policy*, p. 31; cf. *Lambert* v *Lewis* [1980] 2 All ER 978 p. 1003 per Stephenson LJ).

A major difficulty in this area is that, in its present form, the law of contract is badly equipped to deal with complaints about misleading advertising where the courts continue to adhere to the doctrine of privity of contract. At the same time, while developments in the tort of negligence in the 1970s and the early 1980s, for example, the 'two-stage' test in *Anns* v *Merton London Borough Council* [1978] AC 728 and *Junior Books Ltd* v *Veitchi Co. Ltd* [1983] 1 AC 520 were a judicial response to paper over the cracks in the law of contract, recent authorities suggest a return to the traditional role of the tort of negligence. In particular, the use of negligence as a means of compensating for economic losses is now subject to considerable restrictions on policy grounds and it is doubtful how far the consumer will be able to seek recompense in respect of expenditure incurred in reliance on a misleading manufacturer's advertisement in the absence of statutory intervention in favour of the consumer.

11.3   ADVERTISING AND THE CRIMINAL LAW

Given the ineffectiveness of the civil law as a means of controlling misleading claims made in advertising material and given that prevention is normally regarded as better than cure, statutory intervention in the form of regulatory criminal offences has become necessary. This was particularly the case since many misleading practices are capable of producing information deficiencies on the part of consumers. Accordingly, legislation might tend to encourage high standards of truthfulness on the part of traders, thereby helping consumers to make better informed choices when they made a purchase. The best known incursion into this area can be found in the Trade Descriptions Act 1968, which is concerned not simply with advertising *per se* but also with unfair trading practices generally.

11.3.1   Misdescriptions of goods

For some time, Parliament has recognised the need to protect consumers and honest traders alike against the misleading practice of misdescribing goods supplied in the course of trade. The earliest legislation of this type was to be found in the Merchandise Marks Acts 1887 to 1953, but the present controls are now to be found in the Trade Descriptions Act 1968, a more overtly consumer protectionist statute than its predecessors.

The 1968 Act creates two major criminal offences of strict liability, namely, that of applying a false trade description to goods in the course of a trade or business (s. 1(1)(a)) and supplying or offering to supply in the course of a trade or business any goods to which a false trade description is applied (s. 1(1)(b)).

11.3.1.1 Conditions of application of section 1

For the purposes of both parts of s. 1 of the Trade Descriptions Act 1968, there must be a trade description (see 11.3.1.4) which is false to a material degree (see 11.3.1.5) and which relates to goods. Goods include ships, aircraft, things attached to land and growing crops (s. 39(1)).

The wording of s. 1 makes it clear that the offences created only apply to a person who acts in the course of a business (see 1.1.2). Accordingly, it is not intended to apply to private suppliers, particularly where they do not deal with a view to profit. However, where the act or default of an individual employee results in the commission of an offence by his employer, the employer may plead that act or default as a defence (s. 24(1)(a) and see 3.4.2.2) and the individual employee may be prosecuted instead (s. 23 and see 3.4.2.2.3).

While the person charged, in most cases, is likely to be a retail or other business supplier, the wording of s. 1 does not specifically require this. Clearly s. 1(1)(b) is exclusively concerned with supplies or purported supplies, but s. 1(1)(a) is concerned with applying a false trade description to goods. There is nothing in s. 1(1)(a) that specifies that the person applying the description need necessarily supply the goods *to* a consumer, since the offence can be committed by 'any person'. Thus an offence under s. 1(1)(a) may be committed by a person who buys in the course of a business, such as an antique dealer, a second-hand car dealer (*Fletcher* v *Budgen* [1974] 1 WLR 1056) or by a third party who has an interest in the disposition of the goods in the course of trade (*Fletcher* v *Sledmore* [1973] RTR 371). Presumably, a commission agent who makes false representations about the goods he has authority to sell would also have a sufficient interest to commit an offence under s. 1(1)(a).

In contrast, it would appear that a person with no interest in the subsequent transaction does not commit an offence where he makes a misleading statement about goods which the consumer subsequently purchases, since the statement is not associated with a supply of goods. Thus if a garage mechanic refuses to give an MOT certificate because he wrongly believes the car tested is not roadworthy, no offence is committed because the statement does not relate to a supply of goods (*Wycombe Marsh Garages Ltd* v *Fowler* [1972] 1 WLR 1156).

Offences under the Act can be committed by a company. For these purposes, the actions of a senior company officer such as the managing director or company secretary will be treated as the actions of the company itself, but there is nothing to prevent the individual officer forming part of the directing mind and will of the company from being prosecuted as well (s. 20(1)).

11.3.1.2   Applying a false trade description   Under s. 1(1)(a) of the
Trade Descriptions Act 1968 it is an offence for a person to apply a false trade
description to goods. The meaning of the word 'applies' is also relevant to
s. 1(1)(b) since a supplier of goods will only be guilty of an offence under that
provision if a trade description has been applied to the goods which are the
subject-matter of the prosecution.

On a literal interpretation, any application of a trade description to goods
would appear to be sufficient for the purposes of the 1968 Act. However, the
judicial approach to the interpretation of this word has involved an examination of the mischief which the 1968 Act and its predecessors, the Merchandise
Marks Acts 1887 to 1953 were designed to prevent. Accordingly, it has been
held that the application of the trade description must be associated with a
supply of goods. Thus a false statement made after a sale of goods has been
effected does not amount to the commission of an offence since it is incapable
of inducing a purchase (*Hall* v *Wickens Motors (Gloucester) Ltd* [1972] 1 WLR
1418; see also *Wycombe Marsh Garages Ltd* v *Fowler* [1972] 1 WLR 1156
considered at 11.3.1.1).

The word 'applies' is given a statutory definition in the Trade Descriptions
Act 1968, s. 4, which covers a comprehensive list of methods of application. By
virtue of s. 4(2) the statement does not have to be in permanent form, since an
oral statement will suffice, although in this last respect, the time-limit for
bringing a prosecution is shorter than in the case of a permanent description
(s. 19(4); cf Magistrates' Courts Act 1980, s. 127).

11.3.1.2.1   Marking, affixing and attaching the description   A person applies a
description to goods if, in any manner, he marks them with it or affixes or
attaches it to the goods, their packaging or anything supplied with the goods
(s. 4(1)(a)). This would clearly cover descriptive labels attached to goods such
as a description of shoes manufactured from man-made materials as being
made of leather (*Haringey London Borough Council* v *Piro Shoes Ltd* [1976]
Crim LR 462). Since the definition also covers things supplied with goods, a
description contained in an invoice, an order form (*R* v *Ford Motor Co. Ltd*
[1974] 1 WLR 1220) or an instruction leaflet, provided it is read before
purchase, will also amount to the application of a trade description. The
reference to applying a description 'in any manner' would cover a description
other than by way of a written or oral statement. Thus a misleading pictorial
illustration or an active attempt to disguise a defect (see *Cottee* v *Douglas Seaton
(Used Cars) Ltd* [1972] 1 WLR 1408 at p. 1417 per Milmo J) would suffice for
this purpose.

11.3.1.2.2   Placing the goods with a description   A person also applies a
description to goods if he places them in, on or with anything to which a
description has been applied (s. 4(1)(b)). Thus a dairy supplier who puts his
milk in bottles embossed with the name of another dairy applies a description
to the milk (*Donnelly* v *Rowlands* [1970] 1 WLR 1600; see also *Stone* v *Burn*
[1911] 1 KB 927). Section 4(1)(b) also covers the act of placing the marked
object with the goods. Thus a trade description has been applied where a petrol

filling station is prominently marked with signs indicating that a particular brand of petrol is sold there, but the garage in fact sells another brand (*Roberts v Severn Petroleum & Trading Co. Ltd* [1981] RTR 312).

11.3.1.2.3 Using a description in relation to goods   A trade description is also applied when it is used in any manner likely to be taken to refer to the goods (s. 4(1)(c)). For the purposes of s. 4(1)(c) a person must be aware of the description applied in order to have used it in relation to the goods (*Newham London Borough Council* v *Singh* [1988] RTR 359).

Section 4(1)(c) would appear to cover general statements displayed in a shop window, which on a reasonable interpretation may be taken to refer to goods on display inside the shop (Lawson, *Advertising Law* (1978), p. 206). It may also apply to cases in which a description is contained in a document such as a trade journal (*Rees* v *Munday* [1974] 1 WLR 1284) or an order form or invoice which is not physically supplied with the goods purchased (see *R* v *Ford Motor Co. Ltd* [1974] 1 WLR 1220; *Routledge* v *Ansa Motors (Chester-le-Street) Ltd* [1980] RTR 1).

11.3.1.2.4 The position of advertisers   A person who publishes an advertisement which contains a false trade description may also be said to use the description in relation to the goods. This conclusion is confirmed by the provisions of the Trade Descriptions Act 1968, s. 5. This states that if an advertisement is used in relation to a class of goods, it shall be taken to refer to all goods in that class, whether or not they are in existence at the time of publication, for the purpose of deciding whether an offence has been committed under s. 1(1)(a) (s. 5(2)(a)) and where a person both supplies goods and publishes the advertisement, whether an offence is committed under s. 1(1)(b) (s. 5(2)(b)).

The provisions of s. 5 apply to advertisements, catalogues and price lists (s. 39(1)) which may have been in circulation for some time and may become out of date, with the result that the advertisement may be accurate in respect of some goods, but not others. In order to counteract this possibility, s. 5(3) provides that the court should have regard to matters such as the form and content of the advertisement, the time, place, manner and frequency of the advertisement and matters which make it unlikely that the person receiving the goods would think of them as forming part of the class referred to. Thus the fact that a customer has relied on an out-of-date advertisement and that the advertisement has been recently published but the goods purchased are old stock may be considered in deciding if an offence is committed by the advertiser.

A further consideration in relation to advertisements is that the advertiser may publish material supplied to him by another. In these circumstances, provided the advertiser has taken reasonable precautions and has acted with due diligence, a defence of reliance on information supplied by another will be available to him (s. 24(1) and see 3.4.2.2.2). Furthermore, the innocent advertiser also has a defence of innocent publication under s. 25.

11.3.1.2.5 Compliance with the customer's order A trade description may be applied where a consumer orders goods using a trade description and goods are supplied which fail to comply with that description (s. 4(3)). Thus if the consumer orders a pair of 'all-leather shoes' and is supplied with shoes with a man-made sole, a trade description has been applied. Similarly, a customer who orders a 1975 model and is supplied with a car in fact manufactured in 1972, a trade description is applied (*Routledge* v *Ansa Motors (Chester-le-Street) Ltd* [1980] RTR 1). It has been observed that there may be occasions when a supplier or manufacturer cannot guarantee that goods will comply with the requirements of the customer and that an offence may be committed due to s. 4(3) (*Review of the Trade Descriptions Act 1968* (Cmnd 6628, 1976), para. 170). However, this problem will be averted where the discrepancy is insignificant since in order to attract liability, the trade description must be false to a material degree (s. 3; *Review of the Trade Descriptions Act,* para. 172), furthermore, if there is any doubt, the trader could disassociate himself from the description with a suitable statement to that effect (*Review of the Trade Descriptions Act 1968,* para. 173 and see also *Newham London Borough Council* v *Singh* [1988] RTR 359).

11.3.1.3 Supplying or offering to supply goods to which a false trade description is applied The Trade Descriptions Act 1968, s.1(1)(b), makes it an offence for a person acting in the course of a business to supply or offer to supply goods to which a false trade description has been applied. The offence created by s. 1(1)(b) is committed passively by a retailer who supplies goods which have been misdescribed by another, accordingly the offender may be described as merely irresponsible as opposed to the offender under s. 1(1)(a) who may be described as unscrupulous (*Newman* v *Hackney London Borough Council* [1982] RTR 296).

11.3.1.3.1 Supply The word 'supply' is not defined in the Act, but it is clear that the defendant must have provided the consumer with something whether by way of sale or part-exchange (*Davies* v *Sumner* [1984] 3 All ER 831), pursuant to a hire-purchase contract or by way of gift in a promotional exercise. It has been held that a supply involves any form of distribution (*Cahalne* v *London Borough of Croydon* (1985) 149 JP 561, 565 per Stephen-Brown LJ). Thus a contract of hire is a form of supply, even if property in the goods does not pass to the consumer. However, the supply must be of a commercial nature with the result that a supply of goods by a private club to one of its members will not ordinarily fall within the scope of s. 1(1)(b) (*John* v *Matthews* [1970] 2 QB 443).

11.3.1.3.2 Offering to supply Without further qualification, these words would be insufficient to allow the conviction of a retailer since the position at common law is that a retailer does not, generally, offer to sell goods displayed for sale on his premises (see *Fisher* v *Bell* [1961] 1 QB 394), nor does an advertisement stating that goods are available for supply ordinarily amount to an offer to supply (see *Partridge* v *Crittenden* [1968] 1 WLR 1204) since in both cases, the supplier merely makes an invitation to treat.

The Trade Descriptions Act 1968 avoids this conclusion by providing that a person who exposes goods for supply or has goods in his possession for the purposes of supply is deemed to offer to supply them (s. 6). It follows from this that there does not need to be a purchase in order that a prosecution may be mounted under s. 1(1)(b). For example, an enforcement officer will be able to bring proceedings if goods to which a false trade description has been applied are displayed for sale on retail premises (*Stainthorpe* v *Bailey* [1980] RTR 7).

11.3.1.3.3   Awareness of the falsity of the description   Since the offence created by s. 1(1)(b) consists of supplying goods which have been misdescribed by someone else, there is always the danger that a retailer may be convicted of an offence when he is unaware of the falsity of the description. If the supplier has taken reasonable precautions and has acted with due diligence, he may be able to rely on the general defences provided in s. 24(1) (see 3.4.2). In addition to these defences, where the defendant is charged with the commission of an offence under s. 1(1)(b) only, he may also plead that he did not know and could not with reasonable diligence have ascertained that the goods did not conform to the description applied to the goods (s. 24(3)).

The defence in s. 24(3) is essentially one of excusable ignorance and does not raise the same issues as the general defences in s. 24(1). One view of s. 24(3) is that it ought to be confined to latent defects in goods (*Naish* v *Gore* [1971] 3 All ER 737) and that it should have no application to representations about goods, since the truth or falsity of these can be discovered. Generally, if the representation takes the form of a false odometer reading, the defence is unlikely to succeed since it is almost certainly possible to discover the falsity of such a representation with the exercise of due diligence (*Lewis* v *Maloney* [1977] Crim LR 436).

It would appear that for the purposes of s. 24(3), it is necessary for the defendant to show that he did not know of the facts constituting the offence charged and that he could not with reasonable diligence have ascertained that the goods did not conform to their description (*Barker* v *Hargreaves* [1981] RTR 197 at p. 202 per Donaldson LJ). Proof that reasonable precautions have been taken is entirely irrelevant (ibid.). Thus if a car suffers from a latent corrosion defect, which is not immediately discoverable, the defence may be available (ibid.).

11.3.1.4   Trade descriptions   It is central to the regime created by the Trade Descriptions Act 1968 that the goods in respect of which the defendant is charged with the commission of an offence should have been subject to a false trade description.

The essence of a trade description is that it is factual in nature, thereby allowing the court to determine whether it is true or false. It follows that a statement, the truth of which is not capable of precise ascertainment, will not be regarded as a trade description. Thus, a promise to the effect that a central heating system will operate silently is not a trade description because it is not a factual statement (*R* v *Lloyd* 13 February 1976 unreported)). It has also been stated, in another context, that the Act was never intended to make a criminal offence out of what is really a breach of warranty (*Beckett* v *Cohen* [1972] 1 WLR 1593 at pp. 1596-7 per Lord Widgery CJ).

A consequence of this is that what amounts to a misrepresentation at common law will probably also amount to a trade description for the purposes of the Trade Descriptions Act 1968, accordingly statements of opinion and intention and mere puffs generally, will not fall within the ambit of s. 2 (cf. 11.3.1.4.4).

The Trade Descriptions Act 1968, s. 2, seeks to provide a comprehensive list of what is capable of amounting to a trade description. It has been observed already that one of the drawbacks of this approach is that advertisers may develop claims in respect of goods which do not fall within the list of prohibited statements and that it might be better to introduce a general duty to trade fairly, an aspect of which would be the prohibition of the use of any misleading statement (see 3.12). It is true that s. 2 does not adequately deal with a number of potentially misleading statements in respect of goods which have come to light since the draftsman's attempt to define a trade description (see 11.3.1.4.11).

Section 2 defines a trade description as an indication direct or indirect of any of the following matters:

(a) quantity, size or guage;
(b) method of manufacture, production, processing or reconditioning;
(c) composition;
(d) fitness for purpose, strength, performance, behaviour or accuracy;
(e) any physical characteristics not included in the preceding paragraphs;
(f) testing by any person and results thereof;
(g) approval by any person or conformity with a type approved by any person;
(h) place or date of manufacture, production, processing or reconditioning;
(i) person by whom manufactured, produced, processed or reconditioned;
(j) other history, including previous ownership or use.

11.3.1.4.1 Quantity, size or gauge (s. 2(1)(a)) For the purposes of the Act, quantity includes matters such as height, length, width, capacity, weight, volume and number (s. 2(3)).

11.3.1.4.2 Method of manufacture, production, processing or reconditioning (s. 2(1)(b)) This covers statements to the effect that consumer goods have been made or processed in a particular manner, such as 'home-grown' or 'hand-made'. Whether this provision would apply to a claim that eggs are 'free-range' is possibly doubtful, although the word 'production' is probably broad enough to cover the matter and in any case either s. 2(1)(e) or (j) might also apply.

11.3.1.4.3 Composition (s. 2(1)(c))   This would certainly cover statements concerning the materials from which an article is made, for example, a statement to the effect that bread is made with wholemeal grain, that a knife is made of Sheffield steel or that the contents of a specified package include sardines (*Lemy* v *Watson* [1915] 3 KB 371) would fall within s. 2(1)(c). A manufacturer who claims to produce 'vegetable lard' also represents the composition of his product since the word 'lard', without further qualification denotes the use of pig fat (*Wolkind* v *Pura Foods Ltd* (1988) 85 LGR 782).

Section 2(1)(c) also appears to go further than the ingredients from which a thing is made and may also include parts missing from goods intended to be supplied as a package. For example, if goods are described in an advertisement and the customer is wrongly told that he will receive something identical to the description (*Cavendish Woodhouse Ltd* v *Wright* (1985) 149 JP 497; *Denard* v *Smith* (1990) *Guardian*, 21 August 1990), a factual statement relating to composition may have been made. Similarly, if a customer is told that he will receive a free gift when he purchases a particular item, this too may relate to the composition of the package (*British Gas Corporation* v *Lubbock* [1974] 1 WLR 37). However, it might be better to regard these cases as falling within the residual category covered by s. 2(1)(e) if s. 2(1)(c) is properly confined to materials from which a product is made (*British Gas Corporation* v *Lubbock* at p. 43 per May J).

11.3.1.4.4 Fitness for purpose, strength, performance, behaviour or accuracy (s. 2(1)(d))   The matters listed here are all of a qualitative nature, which is inevitably likely to produce problems, since the required quality of goods will depend on a range of factors including the price paid for the goods. Where a car dealer makes an extravagant statement about the physical performance of a second-hand car, s. 2(1)(d) may apply. Thus to describe an unroadworthy vehicle as beautiful, as a good little runner or as having a good engine would appear to amount to the application of a trade description relating to the quality of its performance (see *Robertson* v *Dicicco* [1972] RTR 431; *Furniss* v *Scholes* [1974] Crim LR 199). The question to consider is what interpretation would the ordinary man place on the words used in the description (*Kensington & Chelsea London Borough Council* v *Riley* [1973] RTR 122).

These statements appear to be remarkably similar to trade puffs which do not attract liability for misrepresentation in the civil law and which did not attract criminal liability in *Cadbury Ltd* v *Halliday* [1975] 1 WLR 649. Perhaps they illustrate a deep-seated public distrust of the ability of the motor vehicle trade to control their less scrupulous members.

Less difficulty has been encountered in respect of objectively quantifiable statements about performance. Thus to describe a watch as waterproof when it leaks (*Sherratt* v *Geralds The American Jewellers Ltd* [1970] Crim LR 302) or to state that a microscope is capable of magnifying up to 455 times when its maximum useful magnification is 120 times (*Dixons Ltd* v *Barnett* (1988) 8 Tr LR 37) is to misrepresent the performance capabilities of the article to which the description is applied.

11.3.1.4.5 Other physical characteristics (s. 2(1)(e))   In case anything has been omitted from the list of physical characteristics in s. 2(1)(a) to (d), s. 2(1)(e) provides a general safety net in relation to such physical characteristics. It would appear that statements relating to component parts supplied with goods sold, such as free gifts (*British Gas Corporation* v *Lubbock* [1974] 1 WLR 37) or a car to which additional accessories such as a tool kit or a sun-roof are fitted, are best explained as relating to physical characteristics not covered by the earlier paragraphs of s. 2(1).

11.3.1.4.6 Testing by any person and the results thereof (s. 2(1)(f))   The wording of this paragraph seems to require a statement to the effect that goods have been tested *and* that they have passed the test. Thus a bare statement that a car has been 'AA tested' without a further indication that the test has been passed would probably not be sufficient. This is considered to be a defect in the Act and it has been proposed that where there is a reference to testing, it should be presumed, in the absence of a statement to the contrary, that there is an indication that the test has been passed (*Review of the Trade Descriptions Act 1968* (Cmnd 6628, 1976), para. 129).

A statement to the effect that a car has an MOT certificate would fall within this paragraph since the granting of the certificate is conditional on the goods having satisfied Ministry of Transport requirements. In this latter event the seller of the car would be guilty of an offence, but the content of the certificate is not to be taken as a trade description applied by the garage providing the certificate since it clearly states that it is not to be relied on (*Corfield* v *Sevenways Garage Ltd* [1985] RTR 109) and in any event the statement is not associated with a supply of goods.

11.3.1.4.7 Approval by any person or conformity to a type approved by any person (s. 2(1)(g))   A statement to the effect that goods conform to British Standards requirements (*Downland Bedding* v *Retail Trading Standards Association* (1959) *The Times*, 17 January 1959), or merely displaying the 'Kitemark' would fall within this provision. Similarly, a claim to the effect that goods are approved by a particular body such as the AA or a trade union would also suffice. It may also be the case that the use of the trade mark of a manufacturer with a national reputation can be said to imply conformity with a type approved by another person (*Durham Trading Standards* v *Kingsley Clothing Ltd* (1990) 9 Tr LR 50), although this does appear to stretch the wording of s. 2(1)(g) somewhat and it would be better to treat such cases as falling within s. 2(1)(i).

False representations of royal approval (s. 12) and claims that goods have been supplied to another person (s. 13) constitute the commission of offences in their own right.

11.3.1.4.8 Place or date of manufacture, production, processing or reconditioning (s. 2(1)(h))   A description of a commodity as a 'Norfolk king turkey' (*Beckett* v *Kingston Bros (Butchers) Ltd* [1970] 1 All ER 715) or 'Havana cigars' (*R* v *Butcher* (1908) 99 LT 622) would appear to fall within s. 2(1)(h). But conventional descriptions arising out of trade usage probably do not. Thus frozen Yorkshire puddings or Cheddar cheese are not required to be produced only in the area their name suggests.

The paragraph also covers false statements about the date of manufacture. Thus a car registered in 1975 but manufactured in 1972 cannot be sold as a new 1975 model (*Routledge* v *Ansa Motors (Chester-le-Street) Ltd* [1980] RTR 1). Even a qualified statement of the age of a vehicle may not be sufficient to escape liability. Thus it would be unwise for a car dealer to state that the approximate year of manufacture of a vehicle is 1971 when he is not entirely sure how old the car is (*R* v *Coventry City Justices, ex parte Farrand* [1988] RTR 273).

11.3.1.4.9 Person by whom manufactured, produced or reconditioned (s. 2(1)(i))   It may be important to the consumer that he purchases a product made by a nationally recognised producer. Thus a trade description is applied where a petrol filling station advertises its product as Esso petrol when it is another brand (*Roberts* v *Severn Petroleum & Trading Co. Ltd* [1981] RTR 312; see also *Durham Trading Standards* v *Kingsley Clothing Ltd* (1990) 9 Tr LR 50). In these cases, the inference was that the advertised brand was being supplied, but if it follows from this that where a name is printed on goods it indicates that they have been manufactured by the person named, many suppliers of 'own-brand' products would be in serious difficulties.

11.3.1.4.10   Other history including previous ownership or use (s. 2(1)(j)) The majority of cases which have fallen within this paragraph have involved inaccurate odometer readings on motor vehicles (*Tarleton Engineering Co. Ltd* v *Nattrass* [1973] 1 WLR 1261; *R* v *Hammertons Cars Ltd* [1976] 1 WLR 1243), but other matters relating to the past history of goods made available for supply will also be relevant. For example statements to the effect that goods are 'shop-soiled', 'salvaged' or 'fire-damaged' stock would appear to relate to the past history of the goods in question. Similarly, false statements about the number of previous owners of a car fall within s. 2(1)(j) (*R* v *Inner London Justices, ex parte Wandsworth London Borough Council* [1983] RTR 425).

11.3.1.4.11   Matters not covered by s. 2(1)   one of the major drawbacks of a closed list of prohibited statements is that there will be circumstances in which a statement is apt to mislead but which does not fall within any of the listed categories of trade description. For example, it has been held that an assertion that goods are worth a particular amount or represent extra value cannot amount to trade descriptions as the assertion is not factual and is therefore incapable of precise ascertainment (*Cadbury Ltd* v *Halliday* [1975] 1 WLR 649). The matter of value is one on which people will express different opinions. However, it is at least arguable that a reasonable person might regard a statement such as 'extra value' as implying 'extra chocolate for the same price' and might therefore fall within s. 2(1)(a) (Stephenson, *The Criminal Law and Consumer Protection* (1984), p. 17). The matter is now largely academic since value and worth claims are covered by the misleading pricing provisions in the Consumer Protection Act 1987, ss. 20 and 21 (see 12.2).

Other matters which may not be covered by s. 2(1) and which may give a misleading impression include indications of the identity of the supplier or distributor of goods (see *Review of the Trade Descriptions Act 1968* (Cmnd 6628, 1976), para. 126); statements concerning the commercial standing of the manufacturer, supplier or distributor of goods, such as the ability to provide an after-sales service (ibid., para. 125) and false statements about the content of printed and recorded materials (ibid., para. 128).

11.3.1.5 Implied trade descriptions The Trade Descriptions Act 1968, s. 2(1) provides that a statement in respect of one of the listed matters may be made directly or indirectly, but this still requires an express written or oral statement to have been made about the goods to which the description applies. It would appear that in addition to express statements, a trade description may also be implied from the conduct of the defendant. Support for this view can be gleaned from the Act itself which extends the definition of a trade description to include anything likely to be taken as an indication of a matter listed in s. 2(1) (s. 3(3)).

The fact that there may be liability for an implied trade description is borne out by the large number of falsified odometer reading cases. In each of these, there is strictly no express statement, but the courts have had no difficulty in applying the provisions of the 1968 Act to them. Similarly, cars may be repaired in such a way that they tell a lie about themselves (*Cottee* v *Douglas Seaton (Used Cars) Ltd* [1972] 1 WLR 1408 at p. 1416 per Lord Widgery CJ). However, taking this principle too far might be dangerous since it would also apply to restorers of antiques and artistic works, whose job it is to ensure that their work is not easily detectable (ibid. at p. 1415 per Lord Widgery CJ).

It follows from this that there must be a positive statement on the part of the defendant in order to give rise to liability (ibid.), with the result that no offence is committed where the defendant remains silent on a particular matter relating to the goods in question. However, it would appear to be the case that a person can give an indirect indication of a matter listed in s. 2(1) by way of an opinion where the person to whom the statement is directed is a private individual (*Holloway* v *Cross* [1981] 1 All ER 1012), but no offence would necessarily be committed if the communication was to another trader (*Norman* v *Bennett* [1974] 1 WLR 1229 at p. 1233 per Lord Widgery CJ).

11.3.1.6 Falsity

11.3.1.6.1 False to a material degree By virtue of s. 3(1) of the Trade Descriptions Act 1968 a false trade description is one which is false to a material degree. This definition is based on the requirement that the description must be of such substance that it is capable of inducing a purchase (Molony Report on *Consumer Protection* (Cmnd 1781, 1962), para. 634). Thus a statement which amounts to nothing more than a trade puff will not be treated as a false trade description on the basis that such statements are not capable of inducing a purchase (see *Cadbury Ltd* v *Halliday* [1975] 1 WLR 649, cf. *Robertson* v *Dicicco* [1972] RTR 431).

Where a statement is capable of verification, it will attract liability only if it is false to a material degree. This suggests that a statement can be technically false, but if it is not likely to mislead anyone, no offence is committed. Thus, a dairyman who supplies milk in bottles embossed with the name of another dairy, but which are sealed by means of a silver-foil cap, embossed with the name of the dairyman himself commits no offence because no one is likely to be misled by the trade description and since the words on the foil cap can be regarded as an accurate description of the milk (*Donnelly* v *Rowlands* [1970] 1 WLR 1600). The test applied appears to be objective, in that it is necessary to consider whether a reasonable consumer would have been misled, accordingly, if the statement is objectively misleading, it does not matter that the actual consumer has not been misled (*Chidwick* v *Beer* [1974] Crim LR 267; *Dixons Ltd* v *Barnett* (1989) 8 Tr LR 37 at p. 41 per Bingham LJ).

A statement may also be false to a material degree not by virtue of what it says, but by virtue of what it leaves out. For example, if the defendant tells only half the truth, the omission may render the description false to a material degree. For example, to describe a motor vehicle manufactured in 1972 but registered in 1975 as a new 1975 model is a materially false statement since an average person would take the description to mean that the vehicle was manufactured in 1975 (*Routledge* v *Ansa Motors (Chester-le-Street) Ltd* [1980] RTR 1 at p. 5 per Kilner Brown J). However, to call a car new when it has suffered superficial damage which has been repaired using new parts does not amount to the commission of an offence (*R* v *Ford Motor Co. Ltd* [1974] 1 WLR 1220). In such a case, the description falls within the principle *de minimis non curat lex*, but if the damage to the car had been more serious, it is possible that repairs would have been so extensive that to call the vehicle 'new' would have been misleading.

It is clear from the cases so far considered that whether or not a description will be held to be false to a material degree will depend on the context in which the words are used (*R* v *Anderson* [1988] RTR 260 at p. 266 per Waterhouse J). For example, if what has been done to a 'new' car is likely to diminish its value (such as registering it in the name of the dealer), the description 'new' may be regarded as false (ibid.).

The language used by the defendant will also matter. For example, one word taken on its own may be materially false, but if it is qualified by other words it may become accurate. For example, the word 'lard', implies the presence of pig fat, but the words 'vegetable lard' imply a completely different commodity particularly when statements on the packaging make a virtue of the fact that 100% vegetable oils are used (*Wolkind* v *Pura Foods Ltd* (1987) 85 LGR 782).

11.3.1.6.2 Literally true statements In addition to the basic rule on the materiality of the statement, the Trade Descriptions Act 1968 provides further that a literally true but misleading statement, namely, one which is likely to be taken by the average man (*Southwark London Borough Council* v *Elderson* (1981) unreported)) for an indication of a matter listed in s. 2(1), is deemed to be false (s. 3(2)). Thus if a car is described as 'beautiful' when it is in poor mechanical condition, an offence is committed since there is a statement which is misleading about a matter listed in s. 2(1)(d) (*Robertson* v *Dicicco* [1972] RTR 431). Similarly, if a car dealer advertises a vehicle as having had one owner, but does not state that the one owner was a leasing company which had leased the car to a number of different users, s. 3(2) renders this a false indication of a matter covered by s. 2(1)(j) (*R* v *Inner London Justices, ex parte Wandsworth London Borough Council* [1983] RTR 425).

11.3.1.6.3   Misleading statements not amounting to a trade description   By virtue of s. 3(3), a statement which is not a trade description within s. 2(1) can still attract liability if it is false to a material degree and is likely to be taken as an indication of one of the matters listed in s. 2(1). For example, s. 2(1) seems to require a statement of fact with the result that s. 3(3) is the more appropriate provision to apply to misleading estimates of the mileage accumulated by a motor vehicle (*Holloway* v *Cross* [1981] 1 All ER 1012).

11.3.1.7   Disclaimers of liability   Although not mentioned in the Trade Descriptions Act 1968, a practice has developed, with judicial approval (*Waltham Forest London Borough Council* v *T. G. Wheatley (Central Garage) Ltd* [1978] RTR 157 at p. 162 per Lord Widgery CJ), of disclaiming liability in respect of the falsity of trade descriptions. The practice has been most prevalent in the second-hand car trade in relation to inaccurate odometer readings, although examples can also be found in other areas of trade.

11.3.1.7.1   The legal status of disclaimers   The use of disclaimers is relevant to, although not directly analogous with, the general defences contained in s. 24(1) (see 3.4.2). In particular, it has been held that the use of a disclaimer by a car dealer who is not sure that an odometer reading is accurate is an example of taking reasonable precautions (*Zawadski* v *Sleigh* [1975] RTR 113 and see 3.4.2.1.1). However, it may be argued that this is not desirable, as it might encourage the use of blanket disclaimers as an alternative to taking time to check the accuracy of descriptions applied to goods before the time of sale (Borrie (1975) Crim LR 662 at pp. 667-9).

A disclaimer is not a defence to liability in the sense that it is not a form of confession and avoidance. Instead, it has been held that it is better to regard an effective disclaimer as displacing any inference which arises from the initial trade description (*R* v *Hammertons Cars Ltd* [1976] 1 WLR 1243 at p. 1248 per Lawton LJ) and that it amounts to saying, 'I am not making any representations at all' (*Wandsworth London Borough Council* v *Bentley* [1980] RTR 429).

Because of the judicial emphasis placed on displacing the inference arising from the initial trade description, a practice grew up, again with judicial approval, of 'zeroing' odometer readings so that the customer could not possibly regard the reading as accurate. However, what this judicial acceptance failed to appreciate was that by returning the reading to zero, the car dealer was in fact applying a description himself, with the result that he might be charged with the commission of an offence under s. 1(1)(a) (*R* v *Southwood* [1987] 1 WLR 1361).

One consequence of the decision in *R* v *Southwood* is that, as a general rule, a disclaimer cannot be used where the defendant is charged with the commission of an offence under s. 1(1)(a), since it would be illogical to allow a person to assert that a statement is false and then claim that because the customer knows the statement is false, no description has been applied (*R* v *Southwood* at p. 1370 per Lord Lane CJ). On the other hand, it is well established that a disclaimer may be used by a person charged with the commission of an offence under s. 1(1)(b), since he is not the person who has applied the description to the goods and may not have any means of discovering the inaccuracy of the description.

11.3.1.7.2 The form and content of disclaimers Since the most frequent use of disclaimers has been in relation to car odometer readings, the commonest form of disclaimer is a notice displayed on or near the car to which it applies. However, there is also something akin to a disclaimer where a trader qualifies what amounts to a false description with words which correct what would otherwise create a false impression. For example, the word 'lard' might ordinarily imply a product made of pig fat, but if the finished product is described as 'vegetable lard', with a clear statement to the effect that it is made of 100% vegetable oils, there is no false trade description (*Wolkind* v *Pura Foods Ltd* (1987) 85 LGR 782). It is suggested that this type of case is better dealt with on the basis that the description is not false to a material degree (see 11.3.1.6.1) rather than by reference to rules on disclaimers. The problem with applying the disclaimer doctrine to a case such as this is that the person who seeks to rely on the disclaimer is also the person who has applied the description to the goods and on the basis of *R* v *Southwood* [1987] 3 All ER 556, the defendant should not be allowed to disclaim liability in respect of a self-applied description.

If a disclaimer is to be effective, it must be as bold, precise and compelling as the trade description itself and must be communicated at or before the time of supply (*Norman* v *Bennett* [1974] 1 WLR 1229 at p. 1232 per Lord Widgery CJ), so as to nullify the effect of the false trade description. Thus, very clear words are required and it would be insufficient for the trader to use words such as 'may be incorrect' (*R* v *King* [1979] Crim LR 122). Similarly, disclaimers in small print or made by way of a casual remark during a conversation will not suffice (*R* v *Hammertons Cars Ltd* [1976] 1 WLR 1243).

11.3.2 Misdescriptions of services, accommodation and facilities

The modern consumer is just as much concerned with the quality and safety of the services she or he consumes as with the goods she or he buys. Indeed, the purchase of many consumer goods will also involve making arrangements for services in the form of a maintenance agreement. The civil law obligations of the supplier of a service have already been considered (see chapter 10), but it is also important to ensure that the consumer is not misled by inaccurate statements made about the services she or he contracts for.

The Trade Descriptions Act 1968, s. 14, went beyond the recommendations of the Molony Committee on Consumer Protection (Cmnd 1781, 1962, para. 5) in providing for misdescriptions of services, accommodation and facilities. In recognition of the fact that s. 14 broke new ground, the liability imposed on suppliers was less stringent than that which applied to the supplier of goods in that Parliament included a limited requirement of *mens rea*. This requirement may not have been based solely on sympathy for the service industry, since it has been admitted subsequently that any assessment of the quality of services involves a very subjective element (*Review of the Trade Descriptions Act 1968* (Cmnd 6628, 1976), paras 43-49).

11.3.2.1 Conditions of application of section 14 Not all misdescriptions of services are covered by the provisions of the Trade Descriptions Act 1968, s. 14, since there is a detailed list of the matters in respect of which an offence may be committed (s. 14(1)(i) to (v) and see 11.3.2.4). Furthermore, there is a *mens rea* requirement as to parts of the offences created (see para. 11.3.2.2.).

These matters apart, s. 14(1) provides that it is an offence for any person acting in the course of a trade or business to make a prohibited statement. It follows that, as in the case of s. 1, an offence may be committed by any person, whether he be the supplier of the service or not, provided he acts in the course of a trade or business (see 1.1.2). Thus an offence may be committed by someone who is not the supplier, but has an interest in the outcome of the transaction entered into by the consumer (*Bambury* v *Hounslow London Borough Council* [1971] RTR 1 and see 11.3.1.1).

The 1968 Act does not specifically state that a business includes the activities of a profession (cf. Unfair Contract Terms Act 1977, s. 14; Sale of Goods Act 1979, s. 61(1)). For the purposes of s. 14, this is likely to be important as many services are provided in a professional capacity and it should follow that such services fall within the scope of the section. It has been held that s. 14 is capable of applying to false statements concerning qualifications since such an indication is likely to be taken to refer to the quality of the service provided (*R* v *Breeze* [1973] 1 WLR 994) which would seem to suggest that s. 14 ought to apply to the provision of professional services.

For the purposes of both parts of s. 14, a statement must have been made. One obvious example of making a statement arises when it is communicated to another person (*R* v *Thomson Holidays Ltd* [1974] 1 All ER 823), but it does not follow that an offence is only committed when the statement is read by another person (*Wings Ltd* v *Ellis* [1984] 3 WLR 965 at p. 981 per Lord Scarman). It is possible for a statement to be made without it being communicated to another. For example, a statement is made when it is published, when brochures are posted in bulk to travel agents, when a message is passed on by telephone, when information is posted to clients and when the information is read by the person to whom it is communicated (*Wings Ltd* v *Ellis* [1984] 3 WLR 965 at p. 971 per Lord Hailsham LC).

Since s. 14 is not concerned with statements that induce a contract (cf. *Hall* v *Wickens Motors (Gloucester) Ltd* [1972] 3 All ER 759 in relation to s. 1), it does not matter that the offending statement is made after the conclusion of the relevant contract (*Breed* v *Cluett* [1970] 2 QB 459). Thus, a mechanic who makes a false statement about the work he has carried out on his client's car may still be guilty of an offence under s. 14 even where he has already been paid for the work he has done.

Where a person is charged with the commission of an offence under s. 14, the general defences in s. 24 may be pleaded. However, because of the *mens rea* requirement, considered below, it seems unlikely that these defences will be of much use. If a defendant is shown to have recklessly made a statement or if he knows that a statement made by himself is false, it is likely to be difficult to establish that reasonable precautions have been taken and that due diligence has been exercised (cf. *Sunair Holidays Ltd* v *Dodd* [1970] 1 WLR 1037; *Wings Ltd* v *Ellis* [1984] 3 WLR 965).

11.3.2.2 The mens rea requirement
It is clear from the wording of the Trade Descriptions Act 1968, s. 14(1) that knowledge of the falsity of the offending statement or recklessness in the making of the offending statement are alternative requirements.

11.3.2.2.1 Knowledge of the falsity of a statement   At first sight, the wording used in s. 14(1)(a) would appear to suggest a *mens rea* offence. However, the House of Lords in *Wings Ltd* v *Ellis* [1985] AC 272 has held that the offence created is, in fact, one of 'semi-strict' liability. The important issue is that while the defendant must have knowledge of the falsity of the statement he makes, that knowledge may exist at any time and does not have to exist at the time the statement is first published.

Section 14(1)(a) does not make it an offence to knowingly make a false statement, it merely requires that the defendant should have made a statement and that, at some time subsequently, the defendant knew the statement was false. In *Wings Ltd* v *Ellis* tour operators published and distributed to travel agents a 1981/82 winter brochure which incorrectly indicated that a hotel in Sri Lanka was air-conditioned. The mistake was discovered in May 1981 and all Wings' staff and associated agents were notified. Furthermore, all clients who had already booked that holiday were informed of the position. However, no erratum slip was produced and the complaint which gave rise to the prosecution came from someone who booked the advertised holiday in January 1982. At that stage Wings were aware of the error, although they had not been aware of the falsity of the statement at the time the brochure was published. Since the appellants had made a statement in their brochure and since they knew it was false when they were notified of the absence of air-conditioning facilities in the hotel, an offence was committed. Moreover, further offences are also committed every time the brochure is read and relied upon by a person who wishes to do business with the person making the statement.

It follows from the reasoning employed in *Wings Ltd* v *Ellis* that if the person charged is unaware of the falsity of his statement at the time it is relied on by a customer, no offence is committed under s. 14(1)(a). Thus a sleeping partner who has not been kept informed of events by an active partner may not be convicted under s. 14(1)(a) (*Coupe* v *Guyett* [1973] 2 All ER 1058).

11.3.2.2.2   Recklessness   The offence created by s. 14(1)(b) is that of reckless-ly making a statement which is false. A statement is made recklessly if it is made regardless of whether it be true or false and regardless of whether the maker had reasons for believing it might be false (s. 14(2)(b)). This definition clearly encompasses recklessness as defined in *Derry* v *Peek* (1889) 14 App Cas 337 (in the sense of a fraudulent misstatement) but it also goes beyond this in the sense that dishonesty need not be proved. For example, it has been held that the prosecution need only show that the person charged did not have regard to the truth or falsity of his statement. It is not necessary to establish that the defendant deliberately closed his eyes to the truth (*MFI Warehouses Ltd* v *Nattrass* [1973] 1 WLR 307 at p. 313 per Lord Widgery CJ).

It is necessary that the defendant is reckless at the time of the commission of the offence, which is the time the statement is made. Thus, if the defendant's statement is true at the time of making, no offence is committed if later events cause a change of circumstance (*Sunair Holidays Ltd* v *Dodd* [1970] 1 WLR 1037). However, this view must be considered in the light of the House of Lords interpretation of when a statement is 'made' in *Wings Ltd* v *Ellis* [1985] AC 272: see 11.3.2.1).

The state of mind required by s. 14(1)(b) is generally to be found by way of inference, but if it is shown that a statement is known to be false at the time of making and no steps are taken to correct it, recklessness can be inferred (*Yugotours Ltd* v *Wadsley* (1988) 8 Tr LR 74).

Generally, what happens after the defendant has recklessly made a statement will be irrelevant to the question of liability. Thus if the defendant apologises for his mistake and tries to make up for the falsity of his statement this will not affect his liability for the commission of an offence, but it may be a relevant consideration in mitigation of sentence (*Cowburn* v *Focus Television Rentals Ltd* [1983] Crim LR 563).

11.3.2.3   The meaning of services, accommodation and facilities

11.3.2.3.1   Services   The Trade Descriptions Act 1968 at various points makes a clear distinction between goods and services. One result of this is that the term 'service' when given its natural meaning does not, except in very rare cases, embrace the supply of goods (*Newell* v *Hicks* [1984] RTR 135). Generally, a service involves doing something for somebody (*Newell* v *Hicks* at p. 148 per Robert Goff LJ).

11.3.2.3.2   Accommodation   It is clear from the number of cases involving inaccurate statements in tour operators' brochures that s. 14 embraces statements about short-term holiday accommodation. But it does not follow from this that any statement about property falls within the 1968 Act. In particular, inaccurate statements related to the disposition of land or an interest in land fall outside the scope of the 1968 Act (*Review of the Trade Descriptions Act 1968* (Cmnd 6628, 1976, para. 70). However, misleading statements about real property abound and it was suggested in the *Review* that false statements made in the course of a business prior to the exchange of contracts should be included within the regime of the 1968 Act (paras 81-90).

No government action has been taken in this respect, but it would appear that the prospects for reform of the law are good. A private member's Estate Agents (Property Misdescription) Bill 1991 (Bill No. 25) has got to the stage of a second reading, apparently with the blessing of the government. The Bill proposes the creation of a strict liability offence (subject to a due diligence defence: clause 2(1)) of making in the course of an estate agency business a false or misleading statement about a 'prescribed matter' (cl. 1(1)). Prescribed matters are those specified by order of the Secretary of State (cl. 1(6)(d)). Presumably the sort of matters which can be expected to be covered will include measurements and other physical characteristics of the property. It would also be wise to include some reference to the description of the location so that Battersea is not described as South Chelsea. Other aspects of location are also important, such as proximity to specified amenities and attractions.

As the Bill stands, at present, it applies only to estate agents, but there is no logical reason why it should not also apply to other professionals, such as solicitors, particularly if the 'one-stop property shop' takes off in the future. Likewise, as drafted, the Bill will not cover statements made by builders who market their own property.

The Bill covers only statements in respect of private residential property (cl. 1(3)), but there is no reason why it should not also extend to misdescribed commercial property as well.

11.3.2.3.3 Facilities It would appear that the word 'facility' should be construed *eiusdem generis* with the words 'service' and 'accommodation' with the result that a representation that a retailer is willing to supply goods should not be treated as a facility (*Westminster City Council* v *Ray Alan (Manshops) Ltd* [1982] 1 WLR 383). Accordingly a closing-down sale held at a shop which does not close down cannot be described as a facility.

A facility may be described as something which is made available to customers to use if they are so minded (*Westminster City Council* v *Ray Alan (Manshops) Ltd* [1982] 1 WLR 383 at p. 386 per Ormrod LJ). It has also been held that while the word 'facility' is capable of a very broad interpretation, for the purposes of penal statutes, it should be construed narrowly to mean that the trader is prepared to provide his customers with the wherewithal to do something for himself (*Newell* v *Hicks* [1984] RTR 135 at p. 148 per Robert Goff LJ). Accordingly, the provision of a car park or a swimming-pool constitutes the provision of a facility. However, it appears that where a retailer displays a credit card logo on his premises he indicates that he is prepared to provide a service. Where a trader offers a refund if goods can be purchased cheaper elsewhere, it appears that he does not offer a facility (*Dixons Ltd* v *Roberts* (1984) 82 LGR 689; cf. Consumer Protection Act 1987, s. 21 and see 12.2).

11.3.2.4 Statements covered by section 14 In order to secure a conviction, the prosecution must show that a false statement has been made in respect of one of the matters listed in s. 14. For these purposes a statement is false if it is false to a material degree (s. 14(4)). It follows from this that, as in the case of prosecutions under s. 1, the courts will apply the *de minimis* principle and ignore trifling departures from the truth.

In order to broaden the scope of the prohibition in s. 14, it is further provided that anything likely to be taken for a statement in respect of services etc., if false, shall be treated as such (s. 14(2)(a)). For example, in *R v Clarksons Holidays Ltd* (1972) 57 Cr App R 38, the offending 'statement' was an artist's impression. Strictly a picture is not a statement, but it can be taken to refer to the accommodation provided.

It has been seen that if the defendant's statement relates to what has been done already or what he is doing at present, it is a statement of fact and is covered by s. 14 (*Breed v Cluett* [1970] 2 QB 459 and see 11.3.2.1). Under s. 14, considerable difficulties have been experienced in relation to tour operators' claims in brochures about holiday accommodation. Such statements may amount to nothing more than a warranty which may give rise to an action for breach of contract, but do not give rise to criminal liability under the 1968 Act. The mischief aimed at by s. 14 is the factually false or misleading statement.

It follows from this that if a tour operator predicts what will be available at a foreign holiday resort because the accommodation is undergoing improvements at the time he prepares his brochure, no offence is committed by the tour operator if the statements prove to be inaccurate because of the failure of the hotel owner to provide what has been predicted (*R v Sunair Holidays Ltd* [1973] 1 WLR 1105; see also *Beckett v Cohen* [1972] 1 WLR 1593). In such cases, the statement relates to the future and cannot be said to be true or false at the time of making (*R v Sunair Holidays Ltd* [1973] 1 WLR 1105 at p. 1109 per McKenna J).

In some instances, a promise may imply a factual statement, in which case it may result in a successful conviction. For example, it may be possible to imply that the person making the forecast believes his prediction will come true (*R v Sunair Holidays Ltd* and see also *British Airways Board v Taylor* [1976] 1 WLR 13 at p. 17 per Lord Wilberforce). Similarly, if the circumstances of the case are such that the defendant knows that it is possible that his 'promise' cannot be fulfilled, the statement may be treated as one of fact. For example, if an airline confirms the availability of a seat on a specified flight at a time when the airline operates a deliberate overbooking policy, there are bound to be circumstances in which a passenger holding a confirmed booking will be denied the right to board. In such a case, the airline may be guilty of an offence under s. 14(1)(a) (*British Airways Board v Taylor* [1976] 1 WLR 13).

The list of matters in respect of which a false statement may be made, either recklessly or with knowledge of its falsity, include the following:

(a) the provision in the course of any trade or business of any services, accommodation or facilities;

(b) the nature of any services, accommodation or facilities provided in the course of any trade or business;

(c) the time at which, manner in which or persons by whom any services, accommodation or facilities are so provided;

(d)   the examination, approval or evaluation by any person of any services, accommodation or facilities so provided; or

(e)   the location or amenities of any accommodation so provided.

11.3.2.4.1   The provision of any services, accommodation or facilities (s. 14(1)(i))   It would appear that the word 'provision' cannot be taken to refer to anything other than the fact of providing services etc. Thus s. 14(1)(i) will not extend to cover statements relating to the terms on which services are provided, such as their price (*Newell* v *Hicks* [1984] RTR 135 at p. 149 per Robert Goff LJ). If a different interpretation were to be placed on s. 14(1)(i), this would render redundant the remaining matters referred to in s. 14, since all matters relating to services would be covered by the one sub-paragraph.

Generally, statements which relate to the provision of a service will inform the customer what is provided. For example, s. 14(1)(i) will apply to statements which describe the features of hotel accommodation, such as whether it has a swimming-pool and bedrooms with terraces (*R* v *Clarksons Holidays Ltd* (1972) 57 Cr App R 38). Similarly, if a builder gives an indication of how the finished product will look (*Beckett* v *Cohen* [1972] 1 WLR 1593) or if an airline reserves a seat for a passenger (*British Airways Board* v *Taylor* [1976] 1 WLR 13) a statement is made about the provision of a service.

11.3.2.4.2   The nature of any services, accommodation or facilities (s. 14(1)(ii))   This appears to cover statements in respect of the quality of the service provided. Thus statements to the effect that a hotel provides a 'good, efficient service' will relate to the nature of a service (R v *Clarksons Holidays Ltd* (1972) 57 Cr App R 38).

11.3.2.4.3   The time at which and the manner in which or the persons by whom any services, accommodation or facilities are provided (s. 14(1)(iii))   This would appear to cover an airline reservation which stipulates the time of the flight and claims that a dry cleaner offers a 24-hour service.

11.3.2.4.4   The examination or approval by any person of any services, accommodation or facilities (s. 14(1)(iv))   Statements to the effect that a hotel or restaurant is 'AA and RAC Approved' or is listed in the Egon Ronay Guide fall within this provision.

11.3.2.4.5   The location or amenities of any accommodation (s. 14(1)(v))   It may be that this provision is redundant in that it may well overlap completely with s. 14(1)(i) (*Sunair Holidays Ltd* v *Dodd* [1970] 1 WLR 1037). Statements to the effect that holiday accommodation has a balcony with a sea view and a swimming-pool relate to the amenities of the accommodation, but these are matters which also relate to the provision of the accommodation. Perhaps, s. 14(1)(v) goes further in that the reference to location and amenities may include statements about the locality in which a hotel is to be found which may not necessarily be covered by s. 14(1)(i).

11.3.2.5   Reform of Section 14   It has been observed that s. 14 of the Trade Descriptions Act 1968 was enacted without the benefit of proposals from the Molony Committee on Consumer Protection. Since its enactment, s. 14 has revealed a number of deficiencies which were outlined in the *Review of the Trade Descriptions Act 1968* (Cmnd 6628, 1976). As has been noted one of the most serious criticisms of s. 14 is that the reference to accommodation appears not to include false statements related to residential property sales (see 11.3.2.3.2).

Section 14 does not cover all descriptions of services to be provided, since some statements of this kind relate to the future. However, statements of this kind are misleading (see *Beckett* v *Cohen* [1972] 1 WLR 1593) and can persuade the consumer to contract with one person rather than another. On this basis, the review document concluded that there should be a new offence of supplying services which do not comply with a description given of them (Cmnd 6628, paras 96-8). It was also suggested in relation to future statements that if the truth or falsity of the statement can be tested, it should be an offence to make a false statement about the future supply of services and that it should be an offence to make statements about services where the maker of the statement has no intention of supplying such services (Cmnd 6628, para. 104).

Because the use of the criminal law in relation to the misdescription of services was novel in 1968, it was considered more appropriate to introduce a *mens rea* requirement. However, in the interests of consistency with other provisions in the Trade Descriptions Act 1968, it was proposed that s. 14 offences should impose strict liability, subject to the operation of the general defences in s. 24.

11.4   ADVERTISING AND THE CRIMINAL LAW – MATERIALS FOR CONSIDERATION

11.4.1   Misdescriptions of goods

For text see 11.3.1

Trade Descriptions Act 1968

Prohibition of false trade descriptions
1.   Prohibition of false trade descriptions
   (1)   Any person who, in the course of a trade or business,—
      (a)   applies a false description to any goods; or
      (b)   supplies or offers to supply any goods to which a false trade description is applied;
shall, subject to the provisions of this Act, be guilty of an offence.
   (2)   Sections 2 to 6 of this Act shall have effect for the purposes of this section and for the interpretation of expressions used in this section, wherever they occur in this Act.

2.   Trade description
   (1)   A trade description is an indication, direct or indirect, and by whatever means given, of any of the following matters with respect to any goods or parts of goods, that is to say—

(a) quantity, size or gauge;

(b) method of manufacture, production, processing or reconditioning;

(c) composition;

(d) fitness for purpose, strength, performance, behaviour or accuracy;

(e) any physical characteristics not included in the preceding paragraphs;

(f) testing by any person and result thereof;

(g) approval by any person or conformity with a type approved by any person;

(h) place or date of manufacture, production, processing or reconditioning;

(i) person by whom manufactured, produced, processed or reconditioned;

(j) other history, including previous ownership or use.

(2) The matters specified in subsection (1) of this section shall be taken—

(a) in relation to any animal, to include sex, breed or cross, fertility and soundness;

(b) in relation to any semen, to include the identity and characteristics of the animal from which it was taken and measure of dilution.

(3) In this section 'quantity' includes length, width, height, area, volume, capacity, weight and number. . . .

3. False trade description

(1) A false trade description is a trade description which is false to a material degree.

(2) A trade description which, though not false, is misleading, that is to say, likely to be taken for such an indication of any of the matters specified in section 2 of this Act as would be false to a material degree, shall be deemed to be a false trade description.

(3) Anything which, though not a trade description, is likely to be taken for an indication of any of those matters and, as such an indication, would be false to a material degree, shall be deemed to be a false trade description.

(4) A false indication, or anything likely to be taken as an indication which would be false, that any goods comply with a standard specified or recognised by any person or implied by the approval of any person shall be deemed to be a false trade description, if there is no such person or no standard so specified, recognised or implied.

4. Applying a trade description to goods

(1) A person applies a trade description to goods if he—

(a) affixes or annexes it to or in any manner marks it on or incorporates it with—

(i) the goods themselves, or

(ii) anything in, on or with which the goods are supplied; or

(b) places the goods in, on or with anything which the trade description has been affixed or annexed to, marked on or incorporated with, or places any such thing with the goods; or

(c) uses the trade description in any manner likely to be taken as referring to the goods.

(2) An oral statement may amount to the use of a trade description.

(3) Where goods are supplied in pursance of a request in which a trade description is used and the circumstances are such as to make it reasonable to infer that the goods are supplied as goods corresponding to that trade description, the person supplying the goods shall be deemed to have applied that trade description to the goods.

5. Trade descriptions used in advertisements

(1) The following provisions of this section shall have effect where in an advertisement a trade description is used in relation to any class of goods.

(2) The trade description shall be taken as referring to all goods of the class, whether or not in existence at the time the advertisement is published—

(a)   for the purpose of determining whether an offence has been committed under paragraph (a) of section 1(1) of this Act; and

(b)   where goods of the class are supplied or offered to be supplied by a person publishing or displaying the advertisement, also for the purpose of determining whether an offence has been committed under paragraph (b) of the said section 1(1).

(3)   In determining for the purposes of this section whether any goods are of a class to which a trade description used in an advertisement relates regard shall be had not only to the form and content of the advertisement but also to the time, place, manner and frequency of its publication and all other matters making it likely or unlikely that a person to whom the goods are supplied would think of the goods as belonging to the class in relation to which the trade description is used in the advertisement.

6.   Offer to supply
A person exposing goods for supplying or having goods in his possession for supply shall be deemed to offer to supply them.

11.4.1.1   Applying a false trade description   An application of a trade description which is not associated with a supply of goods will not attract liability under the Trade Descriptions Act 1968.

Wycombe Marsh Garages Ltd v *Fowler*
[1972] 1 WLR 1156
Queen's Bench Division

The defendants examined a car to determine whether it was qualified to receive a MOT test certificate. As a result of their testing they stated, falsely, that the car suffered from defects which would justify refusal of a certificate. Did this amount to the application of a false trade description?

LORD WIDGERY CJ at pp. 1160-1: the prosecution based their case primarily on [the Trade Descriptions Act 1968, s. 2(1)(f)]. They said that there had here occurred an indication with respect to 'testing by any person and results thereof', and went on to say that it was a false indication. For my part, I think that approach based on (f) was not soundly based. It seems to me that what is struck at under (f) is a person providing goods and falsely pretending that they have been tested in some way when they have not, or falsely pretending that the result of a particular test was in a form which it was not. . . .

It seems to me that one must have regard here to the undoubted mischief which prompted the passing of this Act and so far as the Act deals with goods the mischief was that goods might be provided by sale or otherwise with a misleading trade description attached to them.

11.4.1.2   Supplying goods to which a false trade description has been applied   Because of the broad definition of supply in the Trade Descriptions Act 1968, s. 6, there is no need for a contract of sale to be concluded.

Stainthorpe v *Bailey*
[1980] RTR 7
Queen's Bench Division

MICHAEL DAVIES J having cited s. 6 continued at pp. 15–16: In my view, on the facts as found by the justices, there can be no question whatsoever but that the defendant was exposing goods for supply and also indeed that he had the goods, namely, the motor van, in his possession for supply. That seems to me to be supported by the brief conversation he had with Mr Fricker and supported by the terms of the advertisement in the evening paper which quite plainly was offering for sale that very same vehicle.

I find the justices' reasons which I have just read, namely, that the vehicle was not at the place of business and that there was nothing to indicate to members of the public that it was for sale and that there ought to have been an opportunity, before it could be said that there was such an offer, for the defendant to complete a preliminary conversation — presumably on the telephone — quite insufficient and wholly irrelevant to the matter which the justices had to decide. I find nothing in the case which justifies their finding that section 6 did not catch the facts here and in my judgment they were in error in that regard in respect of the third information.

Where a person is charged with the commission of an offence under s. 1(1)(b), he has a specific defence:

Trade Descriptions Act 1968

24. Defence of mistake, accident, etc.

(3)   In any proceedings for an offence under this Act of supplying or offering to supply goods to which a false trade description is applied it shall be a defence for the person charged to prove that he did not know, and could not with reasonable diligence have ascertained, that the goods did not conform to the description or that the description had been applied to the goods.

As to the effect of this defence consider:

Barker v Hargreaves
[1981] RTR 197
Queen's Bench Division

DONALDSON LJ, having cited the Trade Descriptions Act 1968, s. 24(1) (see 3.4.2) and s. 24(3), continued at pp. 202–3: There is a very clear distinction between the two subsections. Under subsection (1) it is necessary for the defendant to prove that he took all reasonable precautions and exercised all due diligence to avoid the commission of 'such an offence', that is to say, an offence under the Act. Subsection (3), on the other hand, is directed to the particular offence and it says that it is a defence to prove that he did not know of the facts constituting the particular offence and could not with reasonable diligence have ascertained that the goods did not conform to the description, again pointing to the particular complaint.

When it comes to section 24(3) it is a different defence because it relates to the specific defects which were found in the vehicle and form the basis of the charge. Those are the corrosion defects. But, unlike under section 24(1), where he can rely on information received from other people, when it comes to section 24(3) it is no answer that he was misled by others. What he has to do is to show that it was a latent defect, that is to say, a defect which could not with reasonable diligence have been ascertained.

11.4.1.3 Trade descriptions
Trade descriptions are statements of fact, not warranties or promises, which may or may not come true. See further *Beckett v Cohen* [1972] 1 WLR 1593 extracted at 11.4.2.

11.4.1.4 Implied trade descriptions The Trade Descriptions Act 1968 does not apply only to obviously misleading statements.

Holloway v *Cross*
[1981] RTR 146
Queen's Bench Division

The defendant wished to sell a car which he believed had a falsified odometer reading. A prospective purchaser enquired as to the mileage and the defendant expressed an opinion which later proved to be incorrect.

DONALDSON LJ, explaining the defence argument at pp. 150–1: The purchaser was interested to find out, since the matter was in doubt, what was the opinion of the defendant as to the mileage of the car. Taking the facts as a whole, the purchaser knew perfectly well that the defendant did not know what the mileage was. . . . In my judgment that is an undue simplification. If it is a valid argument in relation to section 2(1) and that the words, taken in the circumstances in which they were used, do not fall within 2(1) — which, I may say, is somewhat debatable, bearing in mind that 2(1) relates to an indication 'direct or indirect' — it seems to me almost clear beyond argument that if this was not a trade description it was likely to be taken by the purchaser as an indication of the history of the car and, of course, if so taken was false to a material degree.

There cannot have been any point in asking the opinion of the seller as to the mileage which it seemed to have done, except with a view to obtaining an indication of what its mileage was in fact.

11.4.1.5 Falsity The *de minimis* rule applies to the Trade Descriptions Act 1968 since only those statements which are false to a material degree will attract liability.

Donnelly v *Rowlands*
[1970] 1 WLR 1600
Queen's Bench Division

The defendant supplied milk in bottles embossed with the name of another dairy, but also fitted a foil cap which bore his own name. Had he applied a false trade description or did he supply goods to which a false trade description was applied and was the description false?

LORD PARKER CJ at p. 1603: As I see it, the justices here approached the matter by looking at the whole of the description on the bottles. The whole of the description on the bottle consisted of the wording on the foil cap and the embossed wording. What I think the justices were saying was: if you look at the whole thing, the falsity contained in the embossed words on the bottles was not a falsity to a material degree bearing in mind the accuracy of the trade description on the foil cap.

In my judgment that is a possible approach, though for my part I find it quite unnecessary to go to those lengths. It seems to me here that such trade description as there was was not false to any degree. The words on the foil cap were an accurate trade description of the milk, and in their context the words on the bottle did not refer to the milk which had already been accurately described, but merely conveyed, as the fact was, that it was a bottle belonging to the person whose name was embossed. Looked at in that way, which is the ordinary way that any member of the public would look at it, there was no falsity here at all in the trade description.

Note

The defendant was charged with the commission of an offence under s. 1(1)(b), but did he apply a false trade description? In this case, did the correction on the foil cap amount to a disclaimer of liability? If it did, can a disclaimer be used in respect of a self-applied description? See further 11.3.1.7.

A statement may also be false to a material degree by virtue of what it does not say (see s. 4(3), above) and consider:

Routledge v *Ansa Motors (Chester-le-Street) Ltd*
[1980] RTR 1
Queen's Bench Division

For the facts see 11.3.1.6.1.

KILNER BROWN J, having cited the Trade Descriptions Act 1968, s. 3(3), continued at pp. 5–6: The short point is that this was in fact a 1972 vehicle, and, although it was registered for the first time in 1975, it was false to describe it as a 1975 vehicle. In particular, the test which ought to be applied and the question which the justices should direct themselves to consider is the impression which is given by the words used to the reasonable man, the purchaser in a given case.

The justices, in my view, misdirected themselves largely due to the fact that a contention on behalf of the defendants that there was no case to answer invited them to approach the matter on the basis that the authorities showed that a vehicle could correctly be described as new until it had been registered and the subject of a retail sale. A contention was further put that, the vehicle having been first registered on 1 August 1975, it could lawfully be described as a 1975 vehicle since newness dates from the first retail use of the vehicle and not from its date of manufacture. . . .

The question that the justices should have asked themselves did not concern the newness; it did not concern the fact that it had not been used between 1972 and 1975, but would an average customer be likely to believe, on reading those words, that 1975 was the year of manufacture? That question they never posed to themselves. That was, in my judgment, the proper question which they should have posed to themselves. In the circumstances, in my view, it is quite clear that the answer to the question which is put to this court for consideration is that they did not come to a correct determination in law.

11.4.1.6 Disclaimers of liability For text see 11.3.1.7.

In order that a disclaimer of liability should be effective, it must be very clear in its effect.

Norman v *Bennett*
[1974] 1 WLR 1229
Queen's Bench Division

LORD WIDGERY CJ at p. 1232: I think that, where a false trade description is attached to goods, its effect can be neutralised by an express disclaimer or contradiction of the message contained in the trade description. To be effective any such disclaimer must be as bold, precise and compelling as the trade description itself and must be as effectively brought to the notice of any person to whom the goods may be supplied. In other words, the disclaimer must equal the trade description in the extent to which it is likely to get home to anyone interested in receiving the goods.

To be effective as a defence to a charge under section 1(1)(b) of the [Trade Descriptions Act 1968] any such disclaimer must be made before the goods are supplied. In sales over the counter, sale and supply are all one transaction: but in the case of, for example, second-hand cars there may be a significant interval between the striking of the bargain and delivery of the goods, and it is at delivery that supply takes place for the purposes of this legislation.

The preceding case related to a charge under s. 1(1)(b), but can a person apply a false description and then disclaim liability?

R v *Southwood*
[1987] 1 WLR 1361
Court of Appeal

LORD LANE CJ at pp. 1369–70: The decision in *R* v *Hammertons Cars Ltd* [1976] 1 WLR 1243 is certainly binding upon us so far as section 1(1)(b) is concerned. It is not open to us, in the light of that decision, to hold that a disclaimer has no effect when the defendant is charged with supplying a motor vehicle with a false trade description. We take the view, however, that there is a proper distinction to be drawn between the two paragraphs.

Apart from the reasons advanced by the Crown Court judge and also by the Divisional Court in *Newman* v *Hackney London Borough Council* [1982] RTR 296, there is the following consideration. Section 24(3) protects the defendant charged under section 1(1)(b) who did not know about any misdescription and could not have discovered it by the exercise of reasonable diligence. It does not cater for the defendant who has exercised diligence and as a result of that diligence has discovered that the odometer displays a false reading. There must be some method whereby he can protect himself. He should not be in a worse position than the man who is protected by section 24(3). The answer seems to lie in section 24(1)(b). That section must mean that it is a defence to show that the defendant took all reasonable precautions and exercised all due diligence to avoid — or, one must add, to attempt to avoid — the commission of an offence under the Act. Thus the defendant who by making inquiries discovers the falsity of a reading would no doubt be able to protect himself by frankly disclosing the result of his inquiries in such a way that any purchaser would be in the same state of knowledge as the dealer himself.

Turning from section 1(1)(b) to section 1(1)(a), could the same considerations apply to the dealer who has actually falsified the instrument? It seems to us to be absurd to suggest that the actual falsifier could, by any stretch of the imagination, be said to have taken all reasonable precautions to attempt to avoid the commission of an offence merely by issuing a disclaimer, however expressed. By his initial actions in falsifying the instrument he has disqualified himself from asserting that he has taken any precautions, let alone all reasonable precautions.

11.4.2   Misdescriptions of services, accommodation and facilities

For text see 11.3.2.

Trade Descriptions Act 1968

14.   False or misleading statements as to services, etc.

(1)   It shall be an offence for any person in the course of any trade or business—

    (a)   to make a statement which he knows to be false; or

    (b)   recklessly to make a statement which is false;

as to any of the following matters, that is to say,—

    (i)   the provision in the course of any trade or business of any services, accommodation or facilities;

    (ii)   the nature of any services, accommodation or facilities provided in the course of any trade or business;

    (iii)   the time at which, manner in which or persons by whom any services, accommodation or facilities are so provided;

    (iv)   the examination, approval or evaluation by any person of any services, accommodation or facilities so provided; or

    (v)   the location or amenities of any accommodation so provided.

(2)   For the purposes of this section—

    (a)   anything (whether or not a statement as to any of the matters specified in the preceding subsection) likely to be taken for such a statement as to any of those matters as would be false shall be deemed to be a false statement as to that matter; and

    (b)   a statement made regardless of whether it is true or false shall be deemed to be made recklessly, whether or not the person making it had reasons for believing that it might be false.

(3)   In relation to any services consisting of or including the application of any treatment or process or the carrying out of any repair, the matters specified in subsection (1) of this section shall be taken to include the effect of the treatment, process or repair.

(4)   In this section 'false' means false to a material degree and 'services' does not include anything done under a contract of service.

11.4.2.1   The *mens rea* requirement   Section 14 of the Trade Descriptions Act 1968 requires the false statement to have been made either knowingly or recklessly.

As to the meaning of 'knowingly' consider the following:

Wings Ltd v *Ellis*
[1984] 3 WLR 965
House of Lords

For the facts see 11.3.2.2.1.

LORD SCARMAN at pp. 980–2: . . . it is now necessary to determine the proper construction to be put upon the words of section 14(1)(a). The necessary ingredients of the offence as formulated in the subsection are that: (1) a person in the course of a trade or business (2) makes a statement (3) which he knows to be false (4) as to the provision in the course of trade or business of any services, accommodation, or facilities. The respondent submits that the essence of the offence is knowingly making a false statement. The appellant submits that it suffices to prove that the statement was made on a person's behalf in the course of his business and that its content was false to the knowledge of the person carrying on the business.

My lords, I accept the appellant's construction as correct. First, it advances the legislative purpose embodied in the Act, in that it strikes directly against the false statement irrespective of the reason for, or explanation of, its falsity. It involves, of course, construing the offence as one of strict liability to the extent that the offence can be committed unknowingly, i.e. without knowledge of the act of statement: but this is consistent with the social purpose of a statute in the class to which this Act belongs. And the strictness of the offence does no injustice: the accused, if he has acted innocently, can invoke and prove one of the statutory defences. Secondly, the appellant's submission has the advantage of following the literal and natural meaning of the words used. The subsection says not that it is an offence knowingly to make the statement but that it is an offence to make the statement.

Respondent's counsel, however, in support of his submission made a number of telling points. None of them is, in my judgment, strong enough to overcome the difficulties in his way. First, he relied on the general principles governing the interpretation of the provisions of a criminal statute. They are, however, for the reasons already developed, not applicable to this statute. Secondly, he submitted that he who makes a statement must as a matter of common sense know that he is making it. This is not so, however, when one is dealing, as in this statute, with statements made in the course of a trade or business. It would stultify the statute if this submission were to be upheld. Thirdly, he contrasted the wording of section 14(1)(a) with (b). Section 14(1)(b) provides that it should be an offence 'recklessly' to make the false statement. The inference arises, therefore, that the offence under section 14(1)(a) requires proof of a deliberate false statement. This, with respect, I believe to be his best point, but it cannot prevail against all the indications to which I have referred in favour of the interpretation put upon (a) by the appellant.

But this is not the end of the respondent's case. There remains the question: did the respondent make any statement at all as to the air-conditioning of the hotel bedroom on 13 January when Mr Wade read it? The respondent's submission was that such a statement was made only once, on publication of the brochure in May 1981. The importance of the question is not only that the prosecution pinned its case to 13 January 1982 but that in May 1981 the company did not know the statement was false whereas in January 1982 it did know it was false.

This submission was not open to the respondent company before the justices or in the Divisional Court. The Court of Appeal had decided in *R* v *Thomson Holidays Ltd* [1974] QB 592 that a new statement is made on every occasion that an interested member of the public reads it in a brochure published by a company engaged in attracting his custom. The court considered that communication is the essence of statement. My lords, I think *Thomson's* case was correctly decided, even though I do not accept the totality of the court's reasoning. A statement can consist of a communication to another: and in the context of this Act and the circumstances of this class of business I have no hesitation in accepting the court's view that communication by an uncorrected brochure of false information to someone who is being invited to do business in reliance upon the brochure is 'to make a statement' within section 14(1)(a). But there can be statements which are not communicated to others. It was unnecessary for the Court of Appeal to hold that communication was of the essence, and to that extent only I think the court erred.

The respondent's case that the company only made one statement, i.e. on publication of the brochure, is as fallacious in its way as is the view of the Court of Appeal that without communication there is no statement. I have no doubt that a statement as to the air-conditioning in the hotel was made when the brochure was published. But further statements to the same effect were made whenever persons did business with the company on the strength of the uncorrected brochure which so far from being withdrawn continued to be the basis on which the company was inviting business.

There is no injustice in this being the effect of the statute. If the company believed that there was no default on its part when the false description was communicated to Mr Wade, it should have admitted that the offence was committed and called evidence to establish a section 23 or section 24 defence. Instead, the company chose to argue that no offence had been committed at all, an argument which for the reasons I have given, I believe to be unsustainable.

Accordingly, I hold that the respondent company did make a statement as to the air-conditioning to Mr Wade on 13 January 1982.

For these reasons I would make answer to the certified point of law as follows. A statement which was false was made by the respondent company in the course of its business when it was read by Mr Wade, an interested member of the public doing business with the respondent company upon the basis of the statement. The offence was committed on that occasion because the respondent company then knew that it was false to state that the hotel accommodation was air-conditioned. The fact that the company was unaware of the falsity of the statement when it was published as part of the brochure in May 1981 is irrelevant. If the company believed it was innocent of fault, it was open to it to prove lack of fault. It did not do so.

What is recklessness for the purposes of s. 14(1)(b)?

MFI Warehouses Ltd v *Nattrass*
[1973] 1 WLR 307
Queen's Bench Division

LORD WIDGERY CJ at p. 313: The only reference to this question in authority upon this particular section is to be found in Lord Parker CJ's judgment in *Sunair Holidays Ltd* v *Dodd* [1970] 1 WLR 1037. There, after reading the section, Lord Parker CJ observed, at p. 1040:

> In other words, this by statute is importing the common law definition of 'recklessly' as laid down in *Derry* v *Peek* [1889] 14 App Cas 337, and adopted ever since.

It does not appear that this dictum was essential to the decision in the case with which Lord Parker CJ was concerned and there is no reason to suppose that there had been argument upon it. For these reasons I would be disinclined to accept Lord Parker CJ's words as being the final pronouncement on this question, and think that it behoves this court to look into the matter again. I am supported in this view by a comment made by Roskill LJ in giving the judgment of the court in *R* v *Clarksons Holidays Ltd* [1972] Crim LR 653: it was not necessary for him to express any final view on the point but he indicated his impression that Lord Parker CJ's observation would not be accepted if the matter were fully argued. That the word 'reckless' may have more than one meaning in law is apparent from a consideration of the judgment of Salmon J in *R* v *Mackinnon* [1959] 1 QB 150 and the judgment of Donovan J in *R* v *Bates* (1952) 36 Cr App R 175. I am inclined to think that it was the fact that the word 'reckless' has more than one meaning which prompted the draftsman to give a special definition of that word in the Act with which we are presently concerned, and I think, therefore, that we should approach the problem of construction by having regard to that definition rather than to preconceived notions of what the word 'reckless' should mean. I have much sympathy with the view of Salmon J that where a criminal offence is being created and an element of the offence is 'recklessness', one should hesitate before accepting the view that anything less than '*Derry* v *Peek* recklessness' will do. On the other hand, it is quite clear that this Act is designed for the protection of customers and it does not seem to me to be unreasonable to suppose that in creating such additional protection for customers Parliament was minded to place upon the advertiser a positive obligation to have regard to whether his advertisement was true or false.

I have accordingly come to the conclusion that 'recklessly' in the context of the Act of 1968 does not involve dishonesty. Accordingly it is not necessary to prove that the statement was made with that degree of irresponsibility which is implied in the phrase 'careless whether it be true or false'. I think it suffices for present purposes if the prosecution can show that the advertiser did not have regard to the truth or falsity of his advertisement even though it cannot be shown that he was deliberately closing his eyes to the truth, or that he had any kind of dishonest mind. If I had taken the contrary view I would have held that the facts found in this case would not support the conviction.

The Trade Descriptions Act 1968 is concerned with statements of fact, not promises or warranties.

Beckett v *Cohen*
[1972] 1 WLR 1593
Queen's Bench Division

The defendant agreed to build a garage for a client and promised that the work would be completed within 10 days and that the garage would resemble that of a neighbour. Neither promise was fulfilled.

LORD WIDGERY CJ at pp. 1596–7: If before the contract has been worked out the person who provides the service makes a promise as to what he will do, and that promise does not relate to an existing fact, nobody can say at the date when that statement is made that it is either true or false. In my judgment Parliament never intended or contemplated for a moment that the Act of 1968 should be used in this way to make a criminal offence out of what is really a breach of warranty.

However, in some cases a person can make a statement about the future, knowing that it cannot become true.

British Airways Board v *Taylor*
[1976] 1 WLR 13
House of Lords

For the facts see 11.3.2.4.

LORD WILBERFORCE at pp. 17–18: My lords, the distinction in law between a promise as to future action, which may be broken or kept, and a statement as to existing fact, which may be true or false, is clear enough. There may be inherent in a promise an implied statement as to a fact, and where this is really the case, the court can attach appropriate consequences to any falsity in, or recklessness in the making of, that statement. Everyone is familiar with the proposition that a statement of intention may itself be a statement of fact and so capable of being true or false. But this proposition should not be used as a general solvent to transform the one type of assurance with another: the distinction is a real one and requires to be respected, particularly where the effect of treating an assurance as a statement is to attract criminal consequences, as in the present case. As Lord Widgery CJ said in *Beckett* v *Cohen* [1972] 1 WLR 1593, 1596, it was never intended that the Act of 1968 should be used so as to make a criminal statement out of what is really a breach of warranty. . . .

But there is a special feature about cases under the Trade Descriptions Act 1968 which alters the nature of the court's approach. In section 14, the section which describes the offence charged against the British Airways Board, it is provided, by subsection (2)(a), that for the purposes of the section

anything (whether or not a statement as to any of the matters specified in the preceding subsection) likely to be taken for such a statement as to any of those matters as would be false shall be deemed to be a false statement as to that matter.

So the crucial question, in relation to the letter of August 14, 1973, is whether it was likely to be taken (sc. by the addressee) for a statement as to the time at which the service was provided. Whether it was so likely is thus a question of fact to be found.

. . . it is an essential feature of the Act that, when it has to be considered whether descriptions or statements are misleading, it is the meaning which they are likely to bear to the person or persons to whom they are addressed that matters, and not the meaning which they might, on analysis, bear to a trained legal mind. A similar approach was taken by MacKenna J (delivering the judgment of the Court of Appeal (Criminal Division) in *R* v *Sunair Holidays Ltd* [1973] 1 WLR 1105, 1113).

In the present case the justices made the following relevant findings:

(a)   'That the passenger ticket, the earlybird certificate and the letter of August 14, 1973, separately and together contained an implied statement of an existing fact' (paragraph 6(g)):

(b)   'That a passenger in possession of the passenger ticket would believe that such a ticket stated a fact, namely a place had been reserved for him or her on the flight specified and *at the time* so specified. Further, that the earlybird certificate would only serve to reinforce in the mind of a passenger that such a place was available on the flight so specified and at the time specified. The letter of August 14, would similarly reinforce a passenger's view that a certain fact existed (by implication) namely that he would fly in an aeroplane from London to Bermuda on August 29, 1973, on the flight and time specified' (paragraph 6(h)).

(c)   'The statement contained in the letter was false and made recklessly since in view of the appellant's admitted policy a reservation on the flight could not be confirmed at the date of the letter as it was always possible that Mr Edmunds would be off-loaded. It followed that no reservation had been made in the sense that an ordinary person would take it to mean i.e., a certain booking. This was especially so in view of the circumstances in which the letter was written' (paragraph 18(b)).

In my opinion these were findings which the justices were entitled to make. And the essence of them is that the letter, taken together with the ticket and the earlybird certificate would be taken as a statement that Mr Edmunds had a certain booking, which statement, in view of the overbooking policy, was untrue, since his booking, though very likely to be a firm one, was exposed to a risk — small but, as events proved, real — that it might not give him a seat on the aircraft. I think that the justices were entitled to find that this would be taken as a statement of fact, rather than as a mere promise that Mr Edmunds would be flown on the day and at the time specified, and that they did so find.

11.5   ADVERTISING AND INJUNCTIVE RELIEF

In addition to the Trade Descriptions Act 1968, the European Community has also turned its attention to misleading advertising in the form of its Misleading Advertising Directive (84/450/EEC 10.9.84) which has been implemented in the United Kingdom in the form of the Control of Misleading Advertisements Regulations 1988 (SI 1988/915). The regulations do not create any new criminal offences, but they do allow the Director General of Fair Trading to seek an injunction to restrain the publication of advertisements to which the regulations apply and which are considered to be misleading under the definition given in the regulations.

For the purposes of the regulations, an advertisement is misleading if, *inter alia*, it deceives or is likely to deceive persons to whom it is addressed or whom it reaches and is likely to affect the economic behaviour of such persons (art. 1(2)).

The regulations are designed to apply to the majority of advertisements, although there is a specific exception in the case of investment advertisements and advertisements in respect of certain matters dealt with under the Financial Services Act 1986, part V (art. 3). That the regulations are a 'safety net' is clear from the provisions of art. 4 which specifies that in the event of a complaint to the Director General of Fair Trading, the complainant may be required to establish that all other means of dealing with the complaint have been employed and have failed to deal adequately with it (art. 4(3)). Accordingly, if the matter can be dealt with by means of action under a relevant code of practice, such action should be allowed to take its course.

Where it is clear to the Director that all other avenues have been exhausted and that the advertisement is misleading, he may bring proceedings for an injunction, including an interlocutory injunction, against any person who appears to be concerned with the publication of the advertisement (art. 5). Where such proceedings are brought, the court may grant an injunction on such terms as may appear appropriate to the circumstances of the case, provided the advertisement appears to the court to be misleading.

Where an injunction is granted, it may relate not only to the advertisement in respect of which the complaint has been received, but also to any advertisement in similar terms or one which is likely to convey a similar impression (art. 6(2)). Furthermore, an injunction may still be granted where evidence has been called to the effect that no loss has been caused to anyone (art. 6(5)(a)) or that the publisher did not intend the advertisement to mislead (art. 6(5)(b)).

Generally, the onus lies on the publisher to adduce evidence which will justify the refusal to grant an injunction. Thus, if the publisher can prove that his advertisement is factually accurate (art. 6(3)), or if he calls evidence of the matters referred to in art. 6(5), the inference is that an injunction will not be granted (see generally *Director General of Fair Trading* v *Tobyward Ltd* [1989] 2 All ER 266).

CHAPTER TWELVE

Advertising Law II – Sales Promotion

All manufacturers and suppliers will want to promote their products in a way that will increase sales. A common promotion practice is the publication of claims about the price at which goods or services are supplied, since consumers will often make a purchase if they think they are getting good value for money. If such price campaigns are to be considered acceptable by the law and by relevant codes of practice, it is essential that they do not mislead the consumer. Other techniques employed as a means of promotion include so-called 'free' competitions, which may infringe rules on lotteries and prize competitions and are also governed by rules in codes of practice.

12.1 BASIC PRINCIPLES OF SALES PROMOTION PRACTICE

The British Code of Sales Promotion Practice (1984) supervised by the Code of Advertising Practice Committee lays down a number of basic principles for the guidance of the advertising and sales promotion industry. It is the responsibility of the promoter of a particular campaign to ensure that the requirements of the code are complied with and if the promotion is considered to contravene the code, the promoter will be required to make such changes as are considered appropriate and to pay compensation to consumers who have been adversely affected, where it appears suitable to do so (British Code of Sales Promotion Practice, para. 1.4). Furthermore, if the promoter fails to take action when requested to do so, he will be the subject of adverse publicity (ibid.).

The primary general principle stipulated by the code is that all sales promotions should be legal, decent and honest. In particular, this means that a sales promotion campaign should deal fairly and honourably with consumers and should not seek to abuse their trust or take advantage of their lack of experience or knowledge (para. 4.4) and should not be a cause of avoidable disappointment (para. 4.5).

A premium is placed on truthfulness and the code requires all promotions to avoid misleading those to whom they are addressed (paras 4.8 and 5.4.1) and if called upon to do so, the promoter must be able to immediately substantiate any claim made in advertising material (paras 4.9 and 5.4.2).

12.2 PRICE INDICATIONS AND COMPARISONS

The history of the regulation of price claims dates back to the Trade Descriptions Act 1968, s. 11, the provisions of which were subsequently augmented by the Price Marking (Bargain Offers) Orders (SI 1979/364, 633 and 1124). The unfortunate effect of the former was that it was too limited in its scope and there were numerous misleading statements about price which were not covered by its provisions. The Bargain Offers Orders were very badly drafted with the result that enforcement authorities were never too sure whether to mount a prosecution and the business community could not be sure that what appeared to be perfectly legitimate advertising practices would not infringe their provisions. Furthermore, there were still a number of apparently misleading practices which remained lawful because of the poor drafting of the orders.

To meet these criticisms, sections 20 to 26 of the Consumer Protection Act 1987 introduce an entirely new regime based on a general offence of misleading pricing (s. 20(1)) supplemented by the Code of Practice for Traders on Price Indications (Department of Trade. 1988) indicating what statements are to be regarded as misleading and what is acceptable (s. 25) and a rule-making power which will allow the Secretary of State to regulate the circumstances in which and the manner in which specified price indications may be made and to identify those indications which may be regarded as misleading (s. 26).

The offences created by s. 20 consist of giving an indication which is misleading (s. 20(1)), which includes an indication that the price payable for goods (see s. 45(1)), services (see s. 22), accommodation (see s. 23) or facilities (see ss. 22 and 23) is lower than the amount actually charged by the supplier. The Act also applies to indications which, although initially true, later become misleading (s. 20(2)).

12.2.1 The Code of Practice and the regulations

Some difficulties have arisen over the status of the Code of Practice and proposed regulations. The Consumer Protection Act 1987 provides that a contravention of the Code may be relied on as evidence of the commission of an offence under s. 20 and for the purposes of negativing a defence (s. 25(2)(a)). It also provides that compliance with the requirements of the Code may be taken as evidence that no offence has been committed or that the person charged has a defence (s. 25(2)(b)). The final wording of s. 25(2) represents a victory for the consumer protection lobby, since the original intention of the government was to make compliance with the Code an absolute defence. The effect of the present provisions, however, is to create an element of uncertainty in relation to the question of criminal liability.

The Code of Practice also lists a number of practices which have been recognised as misleading for some time. Consumer groups, representatives of enforcement authorities and the Retail Consortium have argued, with some justification, that such recognised practices should be governed directly by regulations which render them unlawful. However, it would appear that the government is resisting such a move (see Bragg (1988) 51 MLR 210, 211). If such practices are not declared illegal, it follows from the provisions of s. 25(2) that contravention of the Code of Practice is merely evidence of the commission of an offence.

12.2.2 Liability for the commission of an offence under section 20

The offences created by the Consumer Protection Act 1987, s. 20, possess some common elements. In particular, the offender must act in the course of a business and there must be an indication of price given to a consumer.

12.2.2.1 Business activities The general rules on what constitutes a business activity will apply (see 1.1.2), but it would appear that because of the words, 'business of his' the only person who may be guilty of an offence is the person who runs the business. Thus it would seem to follow that if the act or default of a junior employee results in the commission of an offence by the employer and the employer can prove that he has taken reasonable precautions and has acted with due diligence (s. 39(1) and see 3.4.2), there will be no prospect of a successful prosecution since the employee does not run the business (see s. 40(1); cf. *Whitehead* v *Collett* [1975] Crim LR 53 under Trade Descriptions Act 1968, s. 11).

If a person does act in the course of a business of his, it does not matter that he acts in a secondary capacity, since s. 20(3)(a) applies the provisions of s. 20(1) and (2) to price indications made by an agent. Thus, commission agents selling goods or property on behalf of the owner may be guilty of an offence under the Act where they give a misleading indication of the price at which the goods or property is sold.

12.2.2.2 Consumer An offence under the Consumer Protection Act 1987, s. 20, is committed where a misleading indication is given to any consumer. A consumer is defined as a person who might wish to be supplied with goods or services (s. 20(6); see further 1.1.3) with the result that a car dealer who falsely understates the value of a second-hand car with a view to buying it cheaply from a consumer commits no offence, since the misleading indication is not related to a supply *to* a consumer. If the same statement is linked to a part-exchange deal, it is arguable that it would then fall within the provisions of s. 20, since it would then be partly related to the supply of the new car (Bragg (1988) 51 MLR 210, 214)

12.2.2.3 Price The misleading indication must relate to a price, which is defined as meaning the aggregate (or the method of calculating the aggregate) of the sums required to be paid by the consumer (Consumer Protection Act 1987, s. 20(6)). Accordingly, if a mandatory payment requirement (such as the VAT element) is omitted from the price quoted, an offence is committed (see also s. 21(1)(c)).

A matter which raises some difficulty is whether a price includes an estimate or a quotation. Since a quotation is an unconditional offer to supply at the price quoted (*Gilbert & Partners* v *Knight* [1968] 2 All ER 248) it will relate to a price, and an offence will be committed if the quotation is not adhered to. However, an estimate is not a fixed price, and is not capable of acceptance as an offer to supply at the price stated (*Croshaw* v *Pritchard* (1899) 16 TLR 45) with the result that the supplier could make a reasonable charge (Supply of Goods and Services Act 1982, s. 14). On this basis, it is difficult to see how an inaccurate estimate can be regarded as an indication of price (cf. Merkin, *A Guide to the Consumer Protection Act 1987*, p. 95), unless estimates can be taken as a 'method which will be applied' (s. 20(6)(b)).

12.2.3 Misleading indications about the price at which goods, services etc. are available

The Consumer Protection Act 1987, s. 20(1) applies to misleading indications about the price at which goods or services etc. are available. While this will apply to a very wide range of misleading statements, it would appear that if the indication relates to something which is not available, no offence is committed. Thus, the indication 'Special Offer Widgets only 50p' would not amount to the commission of an offence if Widgets are not stocked on the premises concerned. However, if the promotional offer relates to 'free' goods supplied with a specified purchase, the Trade Descriptions Act 1968, s. 1, may apply (*Denard* v *Smith* (1990) *Guardian*, 21 August 1990 and see 11.5.1.4.3).

Furthermore, if the price indication is given in a post-contractual invoice it cannot relate to the availability of the goods, particularly if a different price indication was given at the time of contracting (*Miller* v *F.A. Sadd & Son Ltd* [1981] 3 All ER 265). Accordingly, if such an indication does not relate to the price at which the goods are available, it would appear that s. 20 also fails to apply in such circumstances (see Merkin, *A Guide to the Consumer Protection Act 1987*, p. 93).

The wording of s. 20(1) specifies that the indication may be about availability generally or from particular persons. It follows from this that a misleading indication in respect of the price charged by the advertiser himself or that charged by another trader or traders generally will fall within the prohibition. Thus inaccurate indications such as 'Was £50, now £40' or 'Joe Bloggs' price £30' or 'West End price £60' will offend against s. 20(1). In this respect, it should be observed that s. 20 is concerned with indications rather than comparisons, so that the reference to 'Joe Bloggs' price' does not have to involve a comparison between the advertiser's price and that charged by Joe Bloggs.

12.2.4   Indications which become misleading

By virtue of the Consumer Protection Act 1987, s. 20(2), an indication which is initially true but which later becomes misleading may result in the commission of an offence if it is reasonable to expect some consumers to rely on it subsequently and the person giving the indication has not taken all reasonable steps to prevent consumers from relying on it. For example, if a tour operator stipulates in its annual brochure that a price for a self-catering holiday is inclusive of additional charges, but subsequently discovers that the owner of the accommodation proposes to make additional charges on site, the tour operator would need to take reasonable action (as to which see Code of Practice for Traders on Price Indications, paras 3.4.2 and 3.4.3) to inform clients who had read the brochure before the operator was informed of the change (for other manifestations of s. 20(2) see Code of Practice, paras. 3.2 and 3.3).

Where a person has already entered into a contract in reliance on a statement of this kind but is not due to make payment until a later stage and the position as to price subsequently changes, the trader is advised to cancel any such transaction (Code of Practice, para. 3.1.1).

12.2.5   Misleading

The cornerstone of the pricing regime created by the Consumer Protection Act 1987 is the definition of 'misleading'. Earlier attempts at the control of misleading price indications were tied to a supply or an offer to supply goods, however, s. 20(1) refers simply to 'an indication which is misleading'. Accordingly, it will be sufficient that a misleading statement about a price is displayed or published. Accordingly, a price display in a supermarket window which does not accord with the price printed on the goods on the shelves will amount to the commission of an offence and there will be no need to consider whether the offer price or the shelf price is the price to be charged (cf. *J. Sainsbury Ltd* v *West Midlands County Council* (1982) 90 ITSA Monthly Review 58).

The definition of the word 'misleading' is to be found in s. 21, which has to be read in conjunction with the Code of Practice for Traders on Price Indications which, without specifically identifying which parts of s. 21 apply, does give guidance on what type of price indications should not be used.

Section 21(1) provides that in order to determine whether an indication is misleading, it is necessary to consider what is conveyed by the indication and what those consumers to whom it is addressed might reasonably infer from it or any omission from it.

The fact that an omission may give rise to liability is important, since this places the onus on the promoter to ensure that his price indications are as explicit as possible. Thus if the price indication does not reveal that it is only available to old-age pensioners or is limited to the first 100 purchases made in the shop, or that a promotional offer on a three-piece suite applies only to suites of a particular colour (*Sweeting* v *Northern Upholstery Ltd* (1982) 2 Tr LR 5) it is misleading by virtue of what it omits.

The opening words of s. 21(1) import both objective and subjective elements. What is conveyed by the indication is presumably to be judged objectively. It is also necessary to consider what might reasonably be inferred from the indication by those consumers to whom it is addressed. If a consumer places an unusual interpretation on a particular indication, it may be regarded as misleading, provided it is not an unreasonable interpretation (*Doble* v *David Greig Ltd* [1972] 1 WLR 703 at p. 710 per Forbes J) . Thus, if a price is stated exclusive of VAT and the purchaser reasonably believes that the price stated is that which he will have to pay, an offence is committed, because what is important is not the amount which the seller seeks to obtain, but the effect of the price indication on the mind of the person to whom goods or services are being offered (*Richards* v *Westminster Motors Ltd* [1976] RTR 88 at p. 93 per Waller J). It does not follow from this that an offence will necessarily be committed in similar circumstances if the supply is to another trader, since a fellow member of the motor vehicle trade might be aware of the practice of quoting VAT exclusive prices (ibid).

Section 21(1) goes on to identify five instances in which an indication is to be regarded as misleading. These are:

(a)   that the price is less than in fact it is;

(b)   that the applicability of the price does not depend on facts or circumstances on which its applicability does in fact depend;

(c)   that the price covers matters in respect of which an additional charge is in fact made;

(d)   that a person who in fact has no such expectation—

(i)   expects the price to be increased or reduced (whether or not at a particular time or by a particular amount); or

(ii)   expects the price, or the price as increased or reduced, to be maintained (whether or not for a particular period);

(e)   that the facts or circumstances by reference to which the consumers might reasonably be expected to judge the validity of any relevant comparison made or implied by the indication are not what in fact they are.

12.2.5.1   Indications that the price is less than in fact it is (s. 21(1)(a)).
This amounts to a re-enactment of the offence created by the Trade Descriptions Act 1968, s. 11(2), subject to the caveat that it is not confined to a supply or an offer to supply, but covers any indication (see 12.2.5). It follows from this wording that an offence is committed where a consumer is misled about the amount he will have to pay for goods, services, accommodation or facilities.

Since s. 21(1)(a) includes the offence created by s. 11(2) of the 1968 Act, the case law under that provision remains relevant. Established contraventions of s. 11(2) included overcharging where a price list has been displayed (*Whitehead* v *Collett* [1975] Crim LR 53); quoting a price applicable only to cash sales (*Read Bros Cycles (Leyton) Ltd* v *Waltham Forest London Borough Council* [1978] RTR 397); indicating a reduced price which applies only to a limited range of goods (*North Western Gas Board* v *Aspden* [1975] Crim LR 301; Code, para. 2.2.2) and quoting a VAT exclusive price (*Richards* v *Westminster Motors Ltd* [1976] RTR 88).

In respect of VAT exclusive prices, the Code of Practice gives useful guidance to traders, stipulating that where they deal with private consumers, prices should always include VAT (para. 2.2.6). Prices may be indicated exclusive of VAT where the preponderance of business is with trade customers, but if consumer customers also frequent a trader's premises, there should be a clear indication that prices exclude VAT (para. 2.2.7). Moreover, special provision is made for suppliers of professional services and for building work where the final charge may be uncertain. For example, an estate agent is advised to either quote a fee which includes VAT or to state 'fee $1\frac{1}{2}\%$ of purchase price plus $17\frac{1}{2}\%$ VAT' (para. 2.2.8).

Since VAT rates can change, there is the possibility that a trader may commit an offence where his statement of charges later becomes misleading. In these circumstances, the trader is advised to make the change clear to the consumer before he is committed to buying goods affected by the change (Code, para. 3.5.1).

If the trader displays goods in a particular form, but supplies them in a different state, any price indication must state that the price indicated does not apply to the goods in the state they are displayed. Thus, a supplier of furniture in kit form should make it clear that the price advertised does not apply to ready-assembled furniture (Code, para. 2.2.3).

There is also special advice for suppliers who make an additional charge for postage and packaging or for delivery. Such traders are advised to make consumers aware of any such additional charges before they are committed to buy (Code, paras 2.2.4 and 2.2.5). If there is any doubt about what the charge might be, it will be sufficient to state that, for example, current Post Office rates apply.

Retailers may also be faced with problems emanating from promotional material printed on goods supplied by the manufacturer. These 'flash offers', which may either offer a reduction in price or may offer additional goods free of charge or at a reduced rate should be complied with by the retailer in order to avoid the commission of an offence (Code, para. 1.7.1). Furthermore, since the test of what is misleading is based on the reasonable interpretation of the particular consumer reading the price indication, any ambiguity in the flash offer will be construed against the retailer (*Doble* v *David Greig Ltd* [1972] 1 WLR 703).

The provisions of the Trade Descriptions Act 1968 applied only to price indications in respect of goods, but the Consumer Protection Act 1987 applies also to indications in respect of services. In this field, there are a number of matters which require further consideration. For example, restaurants and hotels may sometimes elect to require customers to pay a mandatory service charge. In such a case, that charge must be clearly displayed where it can be seen by customers before they place their order (Code, para. 2.2.10). Charges for holidays may differ according to the time of year when they are taken, but it is common practice for the likes of travel agents to display a range of different holidays and their respective costs. In these circumstances, it is important that the consumer understands what he will get for the price paid. Thus, travel agents are advised that consumers should be made fully aware of the basic price for a holiday and what is included in the price. Furthermore, details of optional extras and their cost should also be provided (Code, para. 2.2.12).

Some tradesmen, such as plumbers and electricians may wish to impose a call-out charge. If this is the case, the supplier is advised to ensure that the consumer is made aware of such charges prior to the supply of the service (Code, para. 2.2.17).

12.2.5.2 Prices dependent on facts which have not been made clear (s. 21(1)(b)) Arguably such indications may also amount to an indication that the price of goods is less than in fact it is. For example, advertising a promotional offer which is only available in respect of goods of a particular colour (*Sweeting* v *Northern Upholstery Ltd* (1983) 2 Tr LR 5) might come within either provision. Other price indications which would appear to fall within this provision include promotional offers which require a purchase by a specified date or in conjunction with another purchase. Thus an indication that consumers will be supplied with a free garden hose with every lawnmower purchased will fall within this provision if there is an unstated condition that the offer is only available on purchases above a specified amount.

12.2.5.3 Indications that the price includes matters in respect of which an additional charge is made (s. 21(1)(c)) Again there would appear to be a certain element of overlap with s. 21(1)(a), in that a failure to include a mandatory additional charge (such as VAT) in the price stated may fall within both provisions. Section 21(1)(c) also appears to cover offers of free goods, where there is a charge for postage (Code, para 1.10.4; and see Bragg (1988) 51 MLR 210, 217; Howells (1990) 7 Tr Law 194).

12.2.5.4 Indications that the price is to be increased, reduced or maintained at its present level (s. 21(1)(d)). A price indication is misleading if it suggests that a price is to be increased, when the person giving the indication has no such expectation. Moreover, an indication will still come within s. 21(1)(d) whether or not the amount of the price rise is specified and whether or not the date of the intended rise is stated. It would appear that the seasonal bout of predictions about the content of the Chancellor of the Exchequer's Budget speech, heralded by notices to the effect that customers should 'Buy now to beat the Budget' could well fall within this provision, if there is no expectation that prices will rise. Section 21(1)(d) will also cover the 'everlasting sale', namely the situation in which a retailer displays a sale notice, in the knowledge that prices will not change for some considerable time (see *Westminster City Council* v *Ray Alan (Manshops) Ltd* [1982] 1 All ER 771).

Under the Price Marking (Bargain Offers) Order 1979 (SI 1979/364) as amended), price comparisons were permitted if the price compared was one charged in specified different circumstances. One of the more dubious examples of this, which escaped a successful prosecution was the NYPM (next year's price maybe), but misleading indications of this kind would now fall within s. 21(1)(d), on the assumption that the trader has no expectation that a different price will be charged.

These provisions have particular importance in relation to introductory offers and after-sale or after-promotion prices. For these purposes, the guidance given to traders in the Code of Practice is that a promotion should not be called an introductory offer unless the trader intends to continue to offer to sell the product at a higher price after the expiry of the offer period (Code, para. 1.3.1). Moreover, where a comparison is made with a future price, the exact nature of the price used as the basis for comparison should be explained. Misleading abbreviations such as ASP (after-sale price) or APP (after-promotion price) should be avoided (Code, para. 1.2.4).

The reference to intended price reductions is presumably to cover the situation in which a retailer uses a price indication which encourages customers to buy immediately when the retailer expects prices to fall in the future. The paragraph also applies to indications which suggest that a price is to be maintained at a particular level, whether or not for any particular period, when the retailer has no such expectation. This appears to cover statements to the effect that prices will remain at a particular level for a limited period only, when the retailer has not prepared any plans for a change in price.

The effect of s. 21(1)(d) is to render a person criminally liable for a false statement about his intention. The main difficulty which is likely to be encountered in this respect is that it will be necessary to prove, some time after the event, that a person did or did not have a particular intention. This is likely to be no mean feat!

12.2.5.5 Comparisons with another price or value where the facts on which the comparison is based are not stated (s. 21(1)(e))

For the purposes of ss. 21(1)(e) and 21(2)(e), a comparison is defined as a comparison of the price or a method of determining that price with another price or value or any method of calculating such a price or value (whether express or implied and whether past, present or future) (s. 21(3)). The wording of s. 21(3) is very wide, and it is difficult to imagine any price comparison which escapes the net it creates.

The Code of Practice gives general guidance on the use of comparisons. In particular, it advises traders not to leave the customer guessing and to avoid the use of language which suggests that a comparison is being made (Code, para. 1.1.1). One feature of the previous law was the widespread use of seemingly meaningless abbreviations for prices used as the basis for comparison, some of which were bogus. Examples included the RRP (recommended retail price), the MRP (manufacturer's recommended price), the RAP (ready-assembled price), the SOP (special order price) the ASP (after-sale price) and the NYPM (next year's price maybe). One feature of the Code of Practice is that abbreviations of this kind should be avoided on the ground that they cause confusion.

The Code of Practice is not concerned solely with comparisons with other prices. It also advises traders not to make comparisons with a claimed value of a product or that goods or services are worth a particular amount (Code, para.

1.8). Such claims were prevalent under previous legislation, but the difficulty with the word 'value', is that it has a different meaning to different people.

12.2.5.5.1 Previous selling prices A common basis for price comparison is the previous price charged by the person giving the price indication. Provided the comparison is not misleading, there is no objection to its use, but past practices arising out of the unfortunate wording of previous legislation resulted in the development of a number of abuses.

Generally, the trader is advised to state both his present selling price and the higher previous price used as the basis for comparison (Code, para. 1.2.1). Without further qualification, this requirement would still allow the use of 'stale' prices charged many years ago and those charged by chain stores in another retail outlet (see *Westminster City Council* v *Ray Alan (Manshops) Ltd* [1982] 1 All ER 771) from being used as the basis for comparison.

In order to defeat such misleading practices, the Code of Practice states that the previous price referred to in the indication should be the last price charged and that the goods, service, accommodation or facility should have been available in the outlet at which the indication is given for at least 28 consecutive days in the six months preceding the publication of the indication (Code, para. 1.2.2). Unlike the provisions of the Trade Descriptions Act 1968, s. 11(1), in this respect, the onus of proving compliance with the requirements of the Code lies on the trader rather than on the prosecution. In this sense, the Code provisions act as a defence rather than as a definition of the substantive offence.

An exception to the 28 days in the past six months rule is provided for in the case of food and other short-shelf-life goods, for which the Code requires the previous price used as the basis for comparison to be the last price charged for products of that kind (Code, para. 1.2.4).

In some cases, it may not be possible to comply fully with the requirements of para. 1.2.4 of the Code of Practice. If this is the case, the Code provides further that goods can be sold in contravention of its provisions if the advertiser gives a full and unambiguous explanation. Accordingly, it is possible for a trader to state that a product has only been available at the higher price for a period of 10 days or that the higher price was charged in a specified number of retail outlets owned by the group giving the price indication. Furthermore, where such a comparison is made, it must be fair and meaningful (Code, para. 1.2.3). It would appear that outrageous departures from the basic requirements of the Code of Practice will be deterred by market forces - if the trader has to give explicit details of what he is doing consumers will realise that they are being misled. However, it is suggested that past practice indicates that notices of this kind are probably not read by the majority of consumers and even if they are, they may not be fully understood.

If a trader wishes to make a series of reductions on a product line that is not selling well, the 28-day rule does not apply to intermediate price reductions and, unless a full explanation of the nature of the series of reductions is given, the highest price in the series must comply with the 28-day rule and all other prices, including the current selling price must be stated (Code, para. 1.2.6). Thus, it will be necessary for the price indication to state ~~£30~~, ~~£20~~, ~~£15~~, £10.

12.2.5.5.2   Recommended prices   A further practice widely used in the past has been to compare a current selling price with one recommended by a manufacturer. However, there have been difficulties resulting from the use of bogus recommendations and genuine manufacturers' recommendations set at an unreasonably high level for the benefit of preferred trade customers. To clarify matters, the Code of Practice provides that the price must be one recommended by the manufacturer as the sale price to consumers; the trader must deal with the manufacturer on commercial terms and the price should not be significantly higher than the price at which the product is sold generally (Code, para. 1.6.3).

Generally, abbreviations should not be used, but the Code is prepared to countenance the use of the initials 'RRP' as an indication of a recommended retail price, but terms such as 'list price' should not be used unless there is a clear indication of whose list price is used as the basis for comparison.

12.2.5.5.3   Other traders' prices   At one stage, comparisons with another trader's product might have been regarded as 'knocking copy', thereby being discouraged as an advertising practice, however, in a more competitive environment, such comparisons have become more prevalent.

In order to avoid misleading comparisons with a price charged by someone else, the Code provides that the person giving the indication should only engage in such a practice if he knows that the price quoted is accurate and up to date; that the name of the other trader and the premises at which the price is charged are clearly identified and that the price relates to products which are substantially similar to those offered by the person giving the price indication (Code, para. 1.5.1). Furthermore, if there are any differences between the products compared, these should be identified in the price indication.

A practice frequently used in the past has been the claim that if a product can be purchased elsewhere at a lower price than that charged by the person giving the price indication, the difference will be refunded. Attempts were made to fit these into the regime created by the Trade Descriptions Act 1968, s. 14, in relation to services, but the courts found difficulty in treating an indication of a charge made as a facility or a service (*Dixons Ltd* v *Roberts* (1984) 82 LGR 689).

Under the Consumer Protection Act 1987, such statements are permitted, but not in relation to 'own-brand' products which cannot be purchased elsewhere, unless the offer extends to equivalent products stocked by others (Code, para. 1.5.2). Furthermore, if there are conditions attached to the offer to the effect that the product must be purchased in a particular area, these must be made clear to the consumer.

12.2.5.5.4   Comparisons with prices charged in different circumstances   The Code of Practice lists the most familiar comparisons with a price charged in different circumstances. These include the price charged for a different quantity of the goods subject to the price indication (10p each - 30p for 4); the price charged for goods in a different condition (shop-soiled £5 - when new £20); the price charged for different availability, for example, special order prices; the price charged for goods in a totally different state (ready-assembled price £75 - self-assembly kit price £45) and the price charged for special groups of people (pensioners £5 - others £10).

The main problem encountered under the Trade Descriptions Act 1968 and the Price Marking (Bargain Offers) Order was that there was no requirement that the trader should have been prepared to do business at the price used as the basis for comparison. Thus in the case of special order prices, it was perfectly lawful to use as the basis for comparison the price that would have been charged for the dress in the violent shade of puce and lime green that few people would ever consider buying and which had never been stocked in any case. To avoid this problem the Code requires the trader to have the product available in the different quantity, condition etc. at the price stated (Code, para. 1.4.2).

Where the price for goods in perfect condition is used as the basis for comparison, the Code recognises that the goods may not be available in their perfect form, but goes on to require the trader to identify the nature of the price of those goods. In other words, the trader is required to say whether the price of the goods in perfect condition is the previous selling price of the person giving the indication, that of another trader or a recommended retail price (Code, para. 1.4.3). In each case, the price indication has to comply with the guidelines applicable to such comparisons.

If a trader wishes to compare a price with the price for those goods when in a different state, he is required to have a reasonable proportion (stated to be about one third) of the goods in that different state available for supply at the price quoted (Code, para. 1.4.4). Thus it will not be possible to stock a single item at a ludicrously high price so as to give a basis for price comparisons.

12.2.6 Defences

12.2.6.1 Defences specific to section 20 In addition to the general defence of taking reasonable precautions and acting with due diligence in s. 39 (see further 3.4.2.1), the Consumer Protection Act 1987 provides for a number of other defences to possible pricing offences.

It is a defence to show that a price indication complies with regulations made by the Secretary of State (s. 24(1)). Furthermore, if a misleading indication of price is given in editorial material, it is a defence for the publisher to show that the indication was not contained in an advertisement (s. 24(2)). It follows from this that a magazine article comparing prices charged by retailers for particular commodities would not constitute the commission of an offence under s. 20, if it cited inaccurate information on presently charged prices.

A person who, in the course of business, publishes advertising material supplied to him by others is also able to raise the defence that at the time of publication, he did not know and had no reasonable grounds for suspecting that the publication would involve the commission of an offence (s. 24(3)). If there are facts which the publisher could not reasonably be expected to know, such as the price previously charged by the person giving the indication or the price charged by another retailer, the defence will protect the publisher of the advertising material. However, the publisher can reasonably be expected to be aware of the provisions of the Code of Practice, with the result that the s. 24(3) defence would not be available where he publishes an advertisement which compares a selling price with an amount the product is worth.

Where a person indicates a recommended price for goods, services, accommodation or facilities and a third party supplies the advertised materials at a higher price than that recommended, the person making the recommendation is able to raise a defence, provided he does not indicate the availability of the product from himself and it is reasonable to assume that the product will be mainly sold at the recommended price (s. 24(4)). Thus if a car manufacturer advertises nationally, indicating a recommended price for a particular type of vehicle, no offence is committed by the manufacturer where a dealer sells at a higher price than that stated in the advertisement, if the price is one recommended to all franchised dealers. One difficulty which has arisen in the past, is the practice of recommending a bogus retail price to a small number of preferred retailers. In such a case, the s. 24(4) defence would not be available since it is not a price recommended to the majority of retailers. One of the more serious implications of this defence is that while the manufacturer has a defence in the circumstances outlined, the retailer charging the higher price commits no offence because he has given no indication. Accordingly, there may be scope for avoiding liability altogether under s. 20 through collusion between manufacturers and retailers.

12.2.6.2 Disclaimers While a disclaimer does not provide a defence, it does have the effect of negativing the liability of a person giving a misleading indication. The principal use of the disclaimer doctrine has been in relation to offences under the Trade Descriptions Act 1968, s. 1, and is considered in more detail elsewhere (see 11.3.1.7).

For the purposes of the Trade Descriptions Act 1968, s. 1, a disclaimer of liability, generally, will not be available in respect of a self-applied description (*R* v *Southwood* [1987] 3 All ER 556). Since all price indications are descriptions of the price charged by the person giving the indication, it should follow from this that a disclaimer in general terms ought to be ruled out by the courts. It is difficult to imagine circumstances in which a person may legitimately use a price comparison based on currently available information and subsequently claim that any false impression which might be created should the indication prove to be inaccurate should be ignored. Even if disclaimers of liability are to be permitted, they will have to comply with the requirement that they should be as bold, precise and compelling as the initial price indication (*Norman* v *Bennett* [1974] 3 All ER 351). Given the likely effect of most price indications on the mind of consumers, the disclaimer would have to be so powerful in effect that any benefit derived from the price indication might be negated.

12.3 PRICE INDICATIONS AND COMPARISONS – MATERIALS FOR CONSIDERATION

For text see 12.2.

Consumer Protection Act 1987

PART III MISLEADING PRICE INDICATIONS

20. Offence of giving misleading indication

(1) Subject to the following provisions of this part, a person shall be guilty of an offence if, in the course of any business of his, he gives (by any means whatever) to any consumers an indication which is misleading as to the price at which any goods, services, accommodation or facilities are available (whether generally or from particular persons).

(2) Subject as aforesaid, a person shall be guilty of an offence if—

(a) in the course of any business of his, he has given an indication to any consumers which, after it was given, has become misleading as mentioned in subsection (1) above; and

(b) some or all of those consumers might reasonably be expected to rely on the indication at a time after it has become misleading; and

(c) he fails to take all such steps as are reasonable to prevent those consumers from relying on the indication.

(3) For the purposes of this section it shall be immaterial—

(a) whether the person who gives or gave the indication is or was acting on his own behalf or on behalf of another;

(b) whether or not that person is the person, or included among the persons, from whom the goods, services, accommodation or facilities are available; and

(c) whether the indication is or has become misleading in relation to all the consumers to whom it is or was given or only in relation to some of them. . . .

(6) In this part—

'consumer'—

(a) in relation to any goods, means any person who might wish to be supplied with the goods for his own private use or consumption;

(b) in relation to any services or facilities, means any person who might wish to be provided with the services or facilities otherwise than for the purposes of any business of his; and

(c) in relation to any accommodation, means any person who might wish to occupy the accommodation otherwise than for the purposes of any business of his;

'price', in relation to any goods, services, accommodation or facilities, means—

(a) the aggregate of the sums required to be paid by a consumer for or otherwise in respect of the supply of the goods or the provision of the services, accommodation or facilities; or

(b) except in section 21 below, any method which will be or has been applied for the purpose of determining that aggregate.

21. Meaning of 'misleading'

(1) For the purposes of section 20 above an indication given to any consumers is misleading as to a price if what is conveyed by the indication, or what those consumers might reasonably be expected to infer from the indication or any omission from it, includes any of the following, that is to say—

(a)   that the price is less than in fact it is;

(b)   that the applicability of the price does not depend on facts or circumstances on which its applicability does in fact depend;

(c)   that the price covers matters in respect of which an additional charge is in fact made;

(d)   that a person who in fact has no such expectation—

(i)   expects the price to be increased or reduced (whether or not at a particular time or by a particular amount); or

(ii)   expects the price, or the price as increased or reduced, to be maintained (whether or not for a particular period); or

(e)   that the facts or circumstances by reference to which the consumers might reasonably be expected to judge the validity of any relevant comparison made or implied by the indication are not what in fact they are.

(2)   For the purposes of section 20 above, an indication given to any consumers is misleading as to a method of determining a price if what is conveyed by the indication, or what those consumers might reasonably be expected to infer from the indication or any omission from it, includes any of the following, that is to say—

(a)   that the method is not what in fact it is;

(b)   that the applicability of the method does not depend on facts or circumstances on which its applicability does in fact depend;

(c)   that the method takes into account matters in respect of which an additional charge will in fact be made;

(d)   that a person who in fact has no such expectation—

(i)   expects the method to be altered (whether or not at a particular time or in a particular respect); or

(ii)   expects the method, or that method as altered, to remain unaltered (whether or not for a particular period); or

(e)   that the facts or circumstances by reference to which the consumers might reasonably be expected to judge the validity of any relevant comparison made or implied by the indication are not what in fact they are.

(3)   For the purposes of subsections (1)(e) and (2)(e) above a comparison is a relevant comparison in relation to a price or method of determining a price if it is made between that price or that method, or any price which has been or may be determined by that method, and—

(a)   any price or value which is stated or implied to be, to have been or to be likely to be attributed or attributable to the goods, services, accommodation or facilities in question or to any other goods, services, accommodation or facilities; or

(b)   any method, or other method, which is stated or implied to be, to have been or to be likely to be applied or applicable for the determination of the price or value of the goods, services, accommodation or facilities in question or of the price or value of any other goods, services, accommodation or facilities.

22.   Application to provision of services and facilities

(1)   Subject to the following provisions of this section, references in this part to services or facilities are references to any services or facilities whatever including, in particular—

(a)   the provision of credit or of banking or insurance services and the provision of facilities incidental to the provision of such services;

(b)   the purchase or sale of foreign currency;

(c)   the supply of electricity;

(d)   the provision of a place, other than on a highway, for the parking of a motor vehicle;

(e)   the making of arrangements for a person to put or keep a caravan on any land other than arrangements by virtue of which that person may occupy the caravan as his only or main residence.

(2)   References in this part to services shall not include references to services provided to an employer under a contract of employment.

(3)   References in this part to services or facilities shall not include references to services or facilities which are provided by an authorised person or appointed representative in the course of the carrying on of an investment business. . . .

23.   Application to provision of accommodation etc.

(1)   Subject to subsection (2) below, references in this Part to accommodation or facilities being available shall not include references to accommodation or facilities being available to be provided by means of the creation or disposal of an interest in land except where—

(a)   the person who is to create or dispose of the interest will do so in the course of any business of his; and

(b)   the interest to be created or disposed of is a relevant interest in a new dwelling and is to be created or disposed of for the purpose of enabling that dwelling to be occupied as a residence, or one of the residences, of the person acquiring the interest.

(2)   Subsection (1) above shall not prevent the application of any provision of this Part in relation to—

(a)   the supply of any goods as part of the same transaction as any creation or disposal of an interest in land; or

(b)   the provision of any services or facilities for the purposes of, or in connection with, any transaction for the creation or disposal of such an interest.

(3)   In this section—

'new dwelling' means any building or part of a building in Great Britain which—

(a)   has been constructed or adapted to be occupied as a residence; and

(b)   has not previously been so occupied or has been so occupied only with other premises or as more than one residence,

and includes any yard, garden, out-houses or appurtenances which belong to that building or part or are to be enjoyed with it;

'relevant interest'—

(a)   in relation to a new dwelling in England and Wales, means the freehold estate in the dwelling or a leasehold interest in the dwelling for a term of years absolute of more than 21 years, not being a term of which 21 years or less remains unexpired;

(b)   in relation to a new dwelling in Scotland, means the *dominium utile* of the land comprising the dwelling, or a leasehold interest in the dwelling where 21 years or more remains unexpired.

24.   Defences

(1)   In any proceedings against a person for an offence under subsection (1) or (2) of section 20 above in respect of any indication it shall be a defence for that person to show that his acts or omissions were authorised for the purposes of this subsection by regulations made under section 26 below.

(2)   In proceedings against a person for an offence under subsection (1) or (2) of section 20 above in respect of an indication published in a book, newspaper, magazine, film or radio or television broadcast or in a programme included in a cable programme service, it shall be a defence for that person to show that the indication was not contained in an advertisement.

(3)   In proceedings against a person for an offence under subsection (1) or (2) of section 20 above in respect of an indication published in an advertisement it shall be a defence for that person to show that—

(a) he is a person who carries on a business of publishing or arranging for the publication of advertisements;

(b) he received the advertisement for publication in the ordinary course of that business; and

(c) at the time of publication he did not know and had no grounds for suspecting that the publication would involve the commission of the offence.

(4) In any proceedings against a person for an offence under subsection (1) of section 20 above in respect of any indication, it shall be a defence for that person to show that—

(a) the indication did not relate to the availability from him of any goods, services, accommodation or facilities;

(b) a price had been recommended to every person from whom the goods, services, accommodation or facilities were indicated as being available;

(c) the indication related to that price and was misleading as to that price only by reason of a failure by any person to follow the recommendation; and

(d) it was reasonable for the person who gave the indication to assume that the recommendation was for the most part being followed.

(5) The provisions of this section are without prejudice to the provisions of section 39 below. . . .

Code of Practice for Traders on Price Indications

PART 1: PRICE COMPARISONS
1.1   Price comparisons generally

1.1.1   Always make the meaning of price indications clear. Do not leave consumers to guess whether or not a price comparison is being made. If no price comparison is intended, do not use words or phrases which, in their normal, every day use and in the context in which they are used, are likely to give your customers the impression that a price comparison is being made.

1.1.2   Price comparisons should always state the higher price as well as the price you intend to charge for the product (goods, services, accommodation or facilities). Do not make statements like 'sale price £5' or 'reduced to £39' without quoting the higher price to which they refer.

1.1.3   It should be clear what sort of price the higher price is. For example, comparisons with something described by words like 'regular price', 'usual price' or 'normal price' should say whose regular, usual or normal price it is (e.g. 'our normal price'). Descriptions like 'reduced from' and crossed out higher prices should be used only if they refer to your own previous price. Words should not be used in price indications other than with their normal everyday meanings.

1.1.4   Do not use initials or abbreviations to describe the higher price in a comparison, except for the initials 'RRP' to describe a recommended retail price or the abbreviation 'man. rec. price' to describe a manufacturer's recommended price (see para. 1.6.2 below).

1.1.5   Follow the part of the code (ss. 1.2 to 1.6 as appropriate) which applies to the type of comparison you intend to make.

1.2   Comparisons with the trader's own previous price
General

1.2.1   In any comparison between your present selling price and another price at which you have in the past offered the product, you should state the previous price as well as the new lower price.

1.2.2 In any comparison with your own previous price:

(a) the previous price should be the *last* price at which the product was available to consumers in the previous six months;

(b) the product should have been available to consumers at that price for at least 28 consecutive days in the previous six months; and

(c) the previous price should have applied (as above) for that period at the *same* shop where the reduced price is now being offered.

The 28 days at (b) above may include bank holidays, Sundays or other days of religious observance when the shop was closed; and up to four days when, for reasons beyond your control, the product was not available for supply. The product must not have been offered at a different price between that 28-day period and the day when the reduced price is first offered.

1.2.3 If the previous price in a comparison does not meet one or more of the conditions set out in para. 1.2.2 above:

(i) the comparison should be fair and meaningful; and

(ii) give a clear and positive explanation of the period for which and the circumstances in which that higher price applied.

For example 'these goods were on sale here at the higher price from 1 February to 26 February' or 'these goods were on sale at the higher price in 10 of our 95 stores only'. Display the explanation clearly, and as prominently as the price indication. You should *not* use general disclaimers saying for example that the higher prices used in comparisons have not necessarily applied for 28 consecutive days.

Food, drink and perishable goods

1.2.4 For any food and drink, you need not give a positive explanation if the previous price in a comparison has not applied for 28 consecutive days, *provided* it was the last price at which the goods were on sale in the previous six months and applied in the same shop where the reduced price is now being offered. This also applies to non-food perishables, if they have a shelf-life of less than six weeks.

Catalogue and mail order traders

1.2.5 Where products are sold only through a catalogue, advertisement or leaflet, any comparison with a previous price should be with the price in your own last catalogue, advertisement or leaflet. If you sell the same products both in shops and through catalogues, etc., the previous price should be the last price at which you offered the product. You should also follow the guidance in paras 1.2.2(a) and (b). If your price comparison does not meet these conditions, you should follow the guidance in para. 1.2.3.

Making a series of reductions

1.2.6 If you advertise a price reduction and then want to reduce the price further during the same sale or special offer period, the intervening price (or prices) need not have applied for 28 days. In these circumstances unless you use a positive explanation (para. 1.2.3):

the highest price in the series must have applied for 28 consecutive days in the last six months at the same shop: and

you must show the highest price, the intervening price(s) and the current selling price (e.g. '~~£40~~, ~~£20~~, ~~£10~~, £5')

1.3 Introductory offers, after-sale or after-promotion prices

Introductory offers

1.3.1 Do not call a promotion an introductory offer unless you intend to continue to offer the product for sale after the offer period is over and to do so at a higher price.

1.3.2   Do not allow an offer to run on so long that it becomes misleading to describe it as an introductory or other special offer. What is a reasonable period will depend on the circumstances (but, depending on the shelf-life of the product, it is likely to be a matter of weeks, not months). An offer is unlikely to be misleading if you state the date the offer will end and keep to it. If you then extend the offer period, make it clear that you have done so.

Quoting a future price

1.3.3   If you indicate an after-sale or after-promotion price, do so only if you are certain that, subject only to circumstances beyond your control, you will continue to offer identical products at that price for at least 28 days in the three months after the end of the offer period or after the offer stocks run out.

1.3.4   If you decide to quote a future price, write what you mean in full. Do not use initials to describe it (e.g. 'ASP', 'APP'). The description should be clearly and prominently displayed, with the price indication.

1.4   Comparisons with prices related to different circumstances

1.4.1   This section covers comparisons with prices:

(a)   for different quantities (e.g. '15p each, 4 for 50p');

(b)   for goods in a different condition (e.g. 'seconds £20, when perfect £30');

(c)   for a different availability (e.g. 'price £50, price when ordered specially £60');

(d)   for goods in a totally different state (e.g. 'price in kit form £50, price ready-assembled £70'); or

(e)   for special groups of people (e.g. 'senior citizens' price £2.50, others £5').

General

1.4.2   Do not make such comparisons unless the product is available in the different quantity, conditions, etc. at the price you quote. Make clear to consumers the different circumstances which apply and show them prominently with the price indication. Do not use initials (e.g. 'RAP' for 'ready-assembled price') to describe the different circumstances, but write what you mean in full.

'When perfect' comparisons

1.4.3   If you do not have the perfect goods on sale in the same shop:

(a)   follow s. 1.2 if the 'when perfect' price is your own previous price for the goods;

(b)   follow s. 1.5 if the 'when perfect' price is another trader's price; or

(c)   follow s. 1.6 if the 'when perfect' price is one recommended by the manufacturer or supplier.

Goods in a different state

1.4.4   Only make comparisons with goods in a totally different state if:

(a)   a reasonable proportion (say a third (by quantity)) of your stock of those goods is readily available for sale to consumers in that different state (for example, ready assembled) at the quoted price and from the shop where the price comparison is made; *or*

(b)   another trader is offering those goods in that state at the quoted price and you follow s. 1.5 below.

Prices for special groups of people

1.4.5   If you want to compare different prices which you charge to different groups of people (e.g. one price for existing customers and another for new customers, or one price for people who are members of a named organisation (other than the trader) and another for those who are not), do not use words like 'our normal' or 'our regular' to describe the higher price, unless it applies to at least half your customers.

1.5 Comparisons with another trader's prices

1.5.1 Only compare your prices with another trader's price if:

(a) you know that his price which you quote is accurate and up-to-date;

(b) you give the name of the other trader clearly and prominently, with the price comparison;

(c) you identify the shop where the other trader's price applies, if that other trader is a retailer; and

(d) the other trader's price which you quote applies to the same products – or to substantially similar products and you state any differences clearly.

1.5.2 Do not make statements like 'if you can buy this product elsewhere for less, we will refund the difference' about your 'own-brand' products which other traders do not stock, unless your offer will also apply to other traders' equivalent goods. If there are any conditions attached to the offer (e.g. it only applies to goods on sale in the same town) you should show them clearly and prominently, with the statement.

1.6 Comparisons with 'recommended retail price' or similar

General

1.6.1 This section covers comparisons with recommended retail prices, manufacturers' recommended prices, suggested retail prices, suppliers' suggested retail prices and similar descriptions. It also covers prices given to cooperative and voluntary group organisations by their wholesalers or headquarters organisations.

1.6.2 Do not use initials or abbreviations to describe the higher price in a comparison *unless*:

(a) you use the initials 'RRP' to describe a recommended retail price; or

(b) you use the abbreviation 'man. rec. price' to describe a manufacturer's recommended price.

Write all other descriptions out in full and show them clearly and prominently with the price indication.

1.6.3 Do not use a recommended price in a comparison unless:

(a) it has been recommended to you by the manufacturer or supplier as a price at which the product might be sold to consumers;

(b) you deal with that manufacturer or supplier on normal commercial terms. (This will generally be the case for members of cooperative or voluntary group organisations in relation to their wholesalers or headquarters organisations); and

(c) the price is not significantly higher than prices at which the product is generally sold at the time you first make that comparison.

1.7 Preprinted prices

1.7.2 Make sure you pass on to consumers any reduction stated on the manufacturer's packaging (e.g. 'flash packs' such as '10p off RRP').

1.7.2 You are making a price comparison if goods have a clearly visible price already printed on the packaging which is higher than the price you will charge for them. Such preprinted prices are, in effect, recommended prices (except for retailers' own-label goods) and you should follow paras 1.6.1 to 1.6.4. You need not state that the price is a recommended price.

1.8 References to value or worth

1.8.1 Do not compare your prices with an amount described only as 'worth' or 'value'.

1.8.2   Do not present general advertising slogans which refer to 'value' or 'worth' in a way which is likely to be seen by consumers as a price comparison.

1.9   Sales or special events

1.9.1   If you have bought in items specially for a sale, and you make this clear, you should not quote a higher price when indicating that they are special purchases. Otherwise, your price indications for individual items in the sale which are reduced should comply with s. 1.1 of the code and whichever of ss. 1.2 to 1.6 applies to the type of comparison you are making.

1.9.2   If you just have a general notice saying, for example, that all products are at 'half marked price', the marked price on the individual items should be your own previous price and you should follow s. 1.2 of the code.

1.9.3   Do not use general notices saying, e.g. 'up to 50% off' unless the maximum reduction quoted applies to at least 10% (by quantity) of the range of products on offer.

1.10   Free offers

1.10.1   Make clear to consumers, at the time of the offer for sale, exactly what they have to buy to get the 'free offer'.

1.10.2   If you give any indication of the monetary value of the 'free offer', and that sum is not your own present price for the product, follow whichever of ss. 1.2 to 1.6 covers the type of price it is.

1.10.3   If there are any conditions attached to the 'free offer', give at least the main points of those conditions with the price indication and make clear to consumers where, before they are committed to buy, they can get full details of the conditions.

1.10.4   Do not claim that an offer is free if:

   (a)   you have imposed additional charges that you would not normally make;

   (b)   you have inflated the price of any product the consumer must buy or the incidental charges (for example, postage) the consumer must pay to get the 'free offer'; or

   (c)   you will reduce the price to consumers who do not take it up.

PART 2: ACTUAL PRICE TO CONSUMER

2.1   Indicating two different prices

2.1.1   The Consumer Protection Act makes it an offence to indicate a price for goods or services which is lower than the one that actually applies, for example, showing one price in an advertisement, window display, shelf marking or on the item itself, and then charging a higher price at the point of sale or checkout.

2.2   Incomplete information and non-optional extras

2.2.1   Make clear in your price indications the full price consumers will have to pay for the product. Some examples of how to do so in particular circumstances are set out below.

Limited availability of product

2.2.2   Where the price you are quoting for products only applies to a limited number of, say, orders, sizes or colours, you should make this clear in your price indication (e.g. 'available in other colours or sizes at additional cost').

Prices relating to differing forms of products

2.2.3   If the price you are quoting for particular products does not apply to the products in the form they are displayed or advertised, say so clearly in your price indication. For example, advertisements for self-assembly furniture and the like should make it clear that the price refers to a kit of parts.

Postage, packing and delivery charges

2.2.4 If you sell by mail order, make clear any additional charges for postage, packing or delivery on the order form or similar document, so that consumers are fully aware of them before being committed to buying. Where you cannot determine these charges in advance, show clearly on the order form how they will be calculated (e.g. 'Post Office rates apply'), or the place in the catalogue, etc. where the information is given.

2.2.5 If you sell goods from a shop and offer a delivery service for certain items, make it clear whether there are any separate delivery charges (e.g. for delivery outside a particular area) and what those charges are, before the consumer is committed to buying.

Value added tax
(i) Price indications to consumers

2.2.6 All price indications you give to private consumers, by whatever means, should include VAT.

(ii) Price indications to business customers

2.2.7 Prices may be indicated exclusive of VAT in shops where or advertisements from which most of your business is with business customers. If you also carry out business with private consumers at those shops or from those advertisements you should make clear that the prices exclude VAT and:
    (i)   display VAT-inclusive prices with equal prominence, or
    (ii)   display prominent statements that on top of the quoted price customers will also have to pay VAT at [$17\frac{1}{2}\%$] (or the current rate).

(iii) Professional fees

2.2.8 Where you indicate a price (including estimates) for a professional fee, make clear what it covers. The price should generally include VAT. In cases where the fee is based on an as-yet-unknown sum of money (for example, the sale price of a house), either:
    (i)   quote a fee which includes VAT; or
    (ii)   make it clear that in addition to your fee the consumer would have to pay VAT at the current rate (e.g. 'fee of $1\frac{1}{2}\%$ of purchase price, plus VAT at [$17\frac{1}{2}\%$]').
Make sure that whichever method you choose is used for both estimates and final bills.

(iv) Building work

2.2.9 In estimates for building work, either include VAT in the price indication or indicate with equal prominence the amount or rate of VAT payable in addition to your basic figure. If you give a separate amount for VAT, make it clear that if any provisional sums in estimates vary then the amount of VAT payable would also vary.

Service, cover and minimum charges in hotels, restaurants and similar establishments

2.2.10 If your customers in hotels, restaurants or similar places must pay a non-optional extra charge, e.g. a 'service charge':
    (i)   incorporate the charge within fully inclusive prices wherever practicable; and
    (ii)   display the fact clearly on any price list or priced menu, whether displayed inside or outside (e.g. by using statements like 'all prices include service').

Do not include suggested optional sums, whether for service or any other item, in the bill presented to the customer.

2.2.11   It will not be practical to include some non-optional extra charges in a quoted price; for instance, if you make a flat charge per person or per table in a restaurant (often referred to as a 'cover charge') or a minimum charge. In such cases the charge should be shown as prominently as other prices on any list or menu, whether displayed inside or outside.

Holiday and travel prices

2.2.12   If you offer a variety of prices to give consumers a choice (for example, paying more or less for a holiday depending on the time of year or the standard of accommodation), make clear in your brochure – or any other price indication – what the basic price is and what it covers. Give details of any optional additional charges and what those charges cover, or of the place where this information can be found, clearly and close to the basic price.

2.2.13   Any non-optional extra charges which are for fixed amounts should be included in the basic price and not shown as additions, unless they are only payable by some consumers. In that case you should specify, near to the details of the basic price, either what the amounts are and the circumstances in which they are payable, or where in the brochure, etc. the information is given.

2.2.14   Details of non-optional extra charges which may vary (such as holiday insurance), or of where in the brochure, etc. the information is given should be made clear to consumers near to the basic price.

2.2.15   If you reserve the right to increase prices after consumers have made their booking, state this clearly with all indications of prices, and include prominently in your brochure full information on the circumstances in which a surcharge is payable.

Ticket prices

2.2.16   If you sell tickets, whether for sporting events, cinema, theatre, etc. and your prices are higher than the regular price that would be charged to the public at the box office, i.e. higher than the 'face value', you should make clear in any price indication what the 'face value' of the ticket is.

Call-out charges

2.2.17   If you make a minimum call-out charge or other flat-rate charge (for example, for plumbing, gas or electrical appliance repairs, etc. carried out in consumers' homes), ensure that the consumer is made aware of the charge and whether the actual price may be higher (e.g. if work takes longer than a specific time) before being committed to using your services. . . .

PART 3: PRICE INDICATIONS WHICH BECOME MISLEADING AFTER THEY HAVE BEEN GIVEN

3.1   General

3.1.1   The Consumer Protection Act makes it an offence to give a price indication which, although correct at the time, becomes misleading after you have given it, if:

(i)   consumers could reasonably be expected still to be relying on it; and

(ii)   you do not take reasonable steps to prevent them doing so.

Clearly it will not be necessary or even possible in many instances to inform all those who may have been given the misleading price indication. However, you should always make sure consumers are given the correct information before they are committed to buying a product and be prepared to cancel any transaction which a consumer has entered into on the basis of a price indication which has become misleading.

3.1.2 Do not give price indications which you know or intend will only apply for a limited period, without making this fact clear in the advertisement or price indication.

3.1.3 The following paragraphs set out what you should do in some particular circumstances.

3.2 Newspaper and magazine advertisements

3.2.1 If the advertisement does not say otherwise, the price indication should apply for a reasonable period (as a general guide, at least seven days or until the next issue of the newspaper or magazine in which the advertisement was published, whichever is longer). If the price indication becomes misleading within this period make sure consumers are given the correct information before they are committed to buying the product.

3.3 Mail order advertisements, catalogues and leaflets

3.3.1 Paragraph 3.2.1 above also applies to the time for which price indications in mail order advertisements and in regularly published catalogues or brochures should apply. If a price indication becomes misleading within this period, make the correct price indication clear to anyone who orders the product to which it relates. Do so before the consumer is committed to buying the product and, wherever practicable, before the goods are sent to the consumer.

3.4 Selling through agents

Holiday brochures and travel agents

3.4.1 Surcharges are covered in para. 2.2.15. If a price indication becomes misleading for any other reason, tour operators who sell direct to consumers should follow para. 3.3.1 above; and tour operators who sell through travel agents should follow paras 3.4.2 and 3.4.3 below.

3.4.2 If a price indication becomes misleading while your brochure is still current, make this clear to the travel agents to whom you distributed the brochure. Be prepared to cancel any holiday bookings consumers have made on the basis of a misleading price indication.

3.4.3 In the circumstances set out in para. 3.4.2, travel agents should ensure that the correct price indication is made clear to consumers before they make a booking.

3.5 Changes in the rate of value added tax

3.5.1 If your price indications become misleading because of a change in the general rate of VAT, or other taxes paid at point of sale, make the correct price indication clear to any consumers who order products. Do so before the consumer is committed to buying the product and, wherever practicable, before the goods are sent to the consumer.

12.4 LOTTERIES AND PRIZE COMPETITIONS

Games and competitions have been used for many years as a means of sales promotion. The number of such competitons is considerable including those which require substantial thought and skill down to those dependent on pure chance, such as newspaper bingo. While such games are useful as a means of sales promotion they may be regarded as illegal either because they amount to an illegal lottery (Lotteries and Amusements Act 1976, s. 1) or because they constitute an unlawful prize competition (Lotteries and Amusements Act 1976, s. 14).

Apart from the legal controls on lotteries and prize competitions, considered below, there is also business self-control in the form of the British Code of Sales Promotion Practice (BCSPP) which among other things requires a clear but uncomplicated explanation of the rules of the competition and conditions of entry (BCSPP, para. 6.2.2) and makes special provision for the availability of results (BCSPP, para. 6.2.3). In relation to prize competitions, the duration of the competition should be clearly stated and the chances of winning should not be exaggerated (BCSPP, para. 6.2.4).

12.4.1 Lotteries

See Merkin [1981] LMCLQ 66.

In historical terms, one of the main reasons for exercising controls over lotteries as a means of sales promotion was that their promotion tended to offend Victorian morality on the ground that they amounted to a form of gambling. In particular, it was seen to be immoral that a person should be able to get something for nothing and since there was no other means of control, the lottery laws were drafted into use (*R* v *Crawshaw* (1860) Bell CC 303).

The present regime for the purposes of lotteries is now contained in the Lotteries and Amusements Act 1976 which lays down a general rule to the effect that all lotteries not permitted by the Act are unlawful (s. 1). Permitted lotteries include small lotteries (s. 3), private lotteries (s. 4) and societies' lotteries (s. 5). Small lotteries include those organised at school fêtes where participation is confined to those who attend the fête and in which no money prizes are given. Private lotteries consist of those organised by a society for the benefit of its members. Societies' lotteries cover those registered promotions on behalf of an organisation set up for charitable, sporting or other purposes not for private gain. Since lotteries designed to increase sales do not fall within any of these categories, they are potentially unlawful.

It now remains to consider the definition of a lottery, which is to be derived from common law rules, in the absence of a statutory definition. For these purposes, a lottery appears to have three essential elements in that it must amount to a distribution of prizes dependent on chance under which the customer has given some payment for the chance of winning a prize (*Imperial Tobacco Ltd* v *Attorney-General* [1980] 2 WLR 466 at p. 473 per Viscount Dilhorne).

Other matters such as fraud on the part of the promoter and profit made by the promoter have also been considered to be relevant in the past, but can probably be disregarded. Accordingly, the three main elements in the definition of a lottery are distribution, payment and chance. Of these, distribution has not given rise to any difficulty of definition, provided something of value, whether it be money, some material article or anything else to which a value can be ascribed is given as a prize (*Director of Public Prosecutions* v *Bradfute & Associates Ltd* [1967] 2 QB 291 per Lord Parker CJ at p. 296). However, some difficulties have arisen in relation to the meaning of payment and chance resulting from a battle between the courts and competition promoters seeking to find ways of defeating the lottery laws.

If promoters could find a way of devising a completely free competition or one which was not dependent solely on chance but which nonetheless promoted sales, the battle was won.

12.4.1.1 Payment If competitors are required to make some sort of a payment for the prize they receive, the promotion will amount to a lottery. This remains the case even if the promoter does not actually make any direct profit from the promotion, since it will be assumed that a profit is made through an increase in custom (*Taylor* v *Smetten* (1883) 11 QBD 207).

If the customer is required to pay an entry fee, the promotion is clearly a lottery, but the same is true where the customer has to make a purchase in order to become a participant. Thus if a retailer sells packets of tea which have a printed coupon on the packaging which may be redeemed for a prize, the promotion is a lottery on the ground that the purchase price of the packet of tea covers the aggregate cost of the tea and the prize (*Taylor* v *Smetten* (1883) 11 QBD 207). Likewise, if a newspaper runs a competiton of chance, a condition of entry to which is proof of purchase of the newspaper, the promotion is a lottery (*Stoddard* v *Sagar* [1895] 2 QB 474).

To get round the payment rule, promoters devised competitions which did not impose a mandatory requirement of purchase, but nonetheless hoped that extra custom would follow. Even this did not escape the attention of the courts, since in *Willis* v *Young* [1907] 1 KB 448 it was held that even though there was no requirement of payment, in practice the promotion resulted in a 20% increase in sales of a newspaper. The essential nature of the promotion was to increase sales with the result that the lottery laws extended to cover both gambling and genuine cases of offering free gifts (cf. contra *Express Newspapers plc* v *Liverpool Daily Post & Echo plc* [1985] 3 All ER 680).

The rule in *Willis* v *Young* was subsequently undermined in a series of cases in the 1960s and 1970s which did not overrule the earlier decision, but left the matter very unclear. For example, it was held that a free bingo game in a public house which undoubtedly increased sales was not financed by the drinks purchased by customers (*McCollom* v *Wrightson* [1968] AC 522). Similarly, a competition organised by a national brewery which involved giving an envelope containing the competition to anyone who requested one involved no payment, even though most of those who took part would be customers of the promoter (*Whitbread & Co. Ltd* v *Bell* [1970] 2 All ER 64). The conflict between *Willis* v *Young* and *Whitbread & Co. Ltd* v *Bell* was considered by the House of Lords in *Imperial Tobacco Ltd* v *Attorney-General* [1980] 2 WLR 466 in which the respondents had run a 'spot-cash' promotion by printing 265 million cards which entitled winning participants to a prize ranging from a packet of cigarettes to £100,000. 262.25 million of these cards were inserted in packets of cigarettes manufactured by the respondents and the remaining 2.25 million cards were available to the public either from Imperial Tobacco or over the counter in some shops. It was held that the scheme was a lottery since those customers who entered the competition using the cards inserted in packets of the cigarettes had paid for both entry to the competition and the cigarettes, but this decision ignored the 2.25 million cards available to anyone. If the proportion of free cards had been much greater, the House of Lords might have been forced to consider the true position of these 'mixed' competitions (see Lawson, *Sales Promotion Law* (1987), p. 11), instead of just sweeping the matter under the carpet.

12.4.1.2 Chance   If a competiton does involve a payment, it can still avoid the lottery laws if its outcome is not dependent on pure chance. If customers have no idea how or when a prize will be awarded, the promotion must be dependent on pure chance and will be regarded as a lottery (*Howgate* v *Ralph* (1929) 45 TLR 426). The essence of a game of skill is that there is something a competitor can do to influence the result, and it seems that only minor merit or skill will be sufficient for these purposes. Thus forecasting the result of a horse-race involves skill since those with better knowledge of horse-racing are considered more likely to win (*Stoddard* v *Sagar* [1895] 2 QB 474). Similarly, if the competition can be won by detailed research it will not be a lottery (*Hall* v *Cox* [1899] 1 QB 198), but a requirement of observation alone is probably not enough to escape the application of the lottery laws (*Hall* v *McWilliam* (1901) 85 LT 239 – counting spots).

Even if skill is involved, the lottery laws may still apply if the exercise of that skill does not determine the outcome of the competition. Accordingly, the promoter must judge the competitors on the skill they have used and must not judge it simply on the basis of a pre-set result picked at random. Thus in *Coles* v *Odhams Press Ltd* [1935] All ER 598 the competition involved skill in filling in a crossword grille, but there were many different ways of completing the grille. Successful participants were those who used the solution selected by the promoter. Accordingly, competitors were required to 'take blind shots at a hidden target' (at p. 601 per Lord Hewart CJ).

If the competition involves a mixture of luck and skill, much will depend on the extent to which the skill or the chance determines the outcome. If a contestant is not required to exercise any skill until he has had the luck to obtain a winning coupon, the competition is more likely to be regarded as a lottery (*Director of Public Prosecutions* v *Bradfute & Associates Ltd* [1967] 1 All ER 112).

12.4.2   Prize Competitions

The exercise of a minimal degree of skill takes a competition outside the scope of the lottery laws. Since a prediction of the outcome of a horse race was said to involve skill on the part of competitors and therefore, was not illegal as a lottery, the Lotteries and Amusements Act 1976, s. 14 was enacted to deal specifically with prize competitions.

Under s. 14 it is unlawful for a newspaper or business to promote trade by means of a competition which offers prizes resulting from forecasting (s. 14(1)(a)) or in which success does not depend to a substantial degree on the exercise of skill (s. 14(1)(b)).

While s. 14(1)(a) applies to forecasting the result of a horse-race, it also covers other forms of forecasting. Thus predicting the outcome of sporting or other events the result of which is uncertain would also fall within this provision. However, it would appear that a 'spot-the-ball' competition is not covered by s. 14(1)(a) because it involves trying to pinpoint the position of a ball rather than guessing the deliberations of the panel of experts called upon to decide where the ball was positioned. In any case, it might be difficult to regard the position of a football or the predictions of a panel of experts as 'the result of an event' (*News of the World Ltd* v *Friend* [1973] 1 All ER 422).

It may also be argued that pinpointing the position of a football involves the exercise of skill, but this is only relevant to cases falling within s. 14(1)(b) since skill is not a relevant factor in s. 14(1)(a) (*News of the World Ltd* v *Friend*).

The main difficulty with s. 14(1)(b) is that 'substantial skill' is required to render the competition lawful, but the requirement of skill has not been the subject of direct judicial scrutiny. It must mean more than just the absence of luck, otherwise s. 14 would not differ from the requirements of the lottery laws. However, in *Witty* v *World Service Ltd* [1936] Ch 303, the court, having decided that a competition which required participants to use their geographical knowledge to identify photographs of parts of the United Kingdom was not a lottery, failed to consider whether the competition required the exercise of substantial skill. But this does not help to decide whether individual research or the use of native wit constitutes the exercise of substantial skill.

Neither branch of s. 14 mentions an element of payment and it is almost certainly the case that the provisions of s. 14 will apply whether participants have been required to pay for entry or not (*Imperial Tobbacco Ltd* v *Attorney-General* [1980] 2 WLR 466).

12.5 LOTTERIES AND PRIZE COMPETITIONS – MATERIALS FOR CONSIDERATION

For text see 12.4.

Lotteries and Amusements Act 1976

1. Illegality of lotteries
All lotteries which do not constitute gaming are unlawful, except as provided by this Act.

14. Prize competitions
(1) Subject to subsection (2) below, it shall be unlawful to conduct in or through any newspaper, or in connection with any trade or business or the sale of any article to the public—
  (a) any competition in which prizes are offered for forecasts of the result either—
    (i) of a future event; or
    (ii) of a past event the result of which is not yet ascertained, or not yet generally known;
  (b) any other competition in which success does not depend to a substantial degree on the exercise of skill.

(2) Nothing in subsection (1) above with respect to the conducting of competitions in connection with a trade or business shall apply in relation to sponsored pool betting or in relation to pool betting operations carried on by a person whose only trade or business is that of a bookmaker.

(3) Any person who contravenes this section shall, without prejudice to any liability to be proceeded against under section 2 above, be guilty of an offence.

(4) In this section 'bookmaker', 'pool betting' and 'sponsored pool betting' have the meanings assigned to them by section 55 of the Betting, Gaming and Lotteries Act 1963.

For an examination of the issues raised by these sections consider the following extract.

Imperial Tobacco Ltd v Attorney-General
[1981] AC 718
House of Lords

For the facts see 12.4.1.1.

VISCOUNT DILHORNE at pp. 735, 736, 737–8, 739:
Was the Spot Cash scheme an unlawful lottery?
In this connection one can ignore the cards which were or were to be distributed but were not to be inserted in the packets of cigarettes. They formed a very small proportion of the total. We are concerned only with the distribution of the 260 million cards in the packets of Players King Size cigarettes.

Section 1 of the Lotteries and Amusements Act 1976 declares that all lotteries which do not constitute gaming are, except as provided by that Act, unlawful lotteries. The Spot Cash scheme does not come within any of the exceptions. The Act does not define a lottery nor does any other Act.

In *Whitbread & Co Ltd* v *Bell* [1970] 2 QB 547 Lord Parker CJ, with whose judgment the other members of the court agreed, said, at p. 555:

Nowhere in the history of lotteries or in this Act is there a statutory definition of a lottery. At least it consists of the distribution of prizes by chance, that is to say, cases where there is no element of skill whatever on the part of the participant. . . . It is clear, however, and indeed admitted, that that is not a complete definition. . . .

There is, so far as I know, no case of a successful prosecution for running a lottery which has not involved some payment or contribution by the participants, and indeed the trend of authority has all been the other way. There must be some payment or contribution, if not towards the prizes themselves, at any rate towards funds, i.e. profits, out of which prizes are provided.

. . .

There are no doubt many cases in which the money paid by participants contributes to the prizes and in such cases if the distribution of the prizes is by chance, it is easy to conclude that it is a lottery. Proof that the money so contributed goes into a fund out of which the prizes are paid may not be so easy and if such proof is necessary, then it would be easy to avoid the conclusion that there was a lottery by arranging that the prizes came from an independent source. . . .

The respondents say that as no more was paid for a packet with a card in it than was paid for a packet of the same cigarettes, no part of the price paid was attributable to the card and so there was no payment for the chance.

The appellant contended that where payment for an article, albeit at the normal price, is necessary to obtain the chance, that in law amounts to payment for a chance. . . .

In my view none of them lend support to the view that for a lottery to be unlawful, where the chance is obtained with something else, it must be shown that the price is 'loaded' and that part of it is attributable to the chance. . . .

The facts of *Taylor* v *Smetten* (1883) 11 QBD 207 bear some resemblance to those of this case. There packets of tea were sold at 2s. 6d. a packet. Each packet had in it a coupon entitling the purchaser to a prize, the prizes varying in character and value. Delivering the judgment of the court, Hawkins J said, at p. 211:

> There can be no doubt that the appellant in enclosing and announcing the enclosure of the coupon in the packet of tea, did so with a view to induce persons to become purchasers and realise a profit to himself; and, although it was admitted by the respondent that the tea was good and worth all the money, it is impossible to suppose that the aggregate prices charged and obtained for the packages did not include the aggregate prices of the tea and the prizes.

The court held that there was a lottery. This decision was not based on any presumption that the price of the tea was 'loaded' so as to include the price of the chance. It was clear in that case, and indeed accepted, that a purchaser bought for 2s. 6d. a packet of tea and a chance of winning a prize. . . .

Lord Denning MR thought that the mistaken view of the courts for 70 years was noticed in *McCollom* v *Wrightson* [1968] AC 522. I must confess my inability to find anything in the speech of Lord Hodson, with which the other members of the House agreed, to that effect. Lord Hodson said it was unnecessary to consider whether *Willis* v *Young* [1907] 1 KB 448 was rightly decided. In that case numbered medals were distributed free among members of the public. The holders of winning numbers won a prize. The winning numbers were published in a newspaper. It was not necessary to buy a paper to win a prize. This operation was designed to increase and did increase the circulation of the paper.

Although no payment was made for the medal, it was held that those who received the medals contributed collectively sums of money which constituted the fund from which the profits of the paper were drawn 'and also the money for the prize winners came'.

In this case too, I do not find it necessary to consider whether that case was rightly decided. I doubt if it was. It may have led to Lord Parker CJ's reference in the *Whitbread* case [1970] 2 QB 547 to contributions towards funds out of which prizes are provided. However this may be, that case is of no assistance in the present case.

I do not find in any of the other cases to which Lord Denning MR referred any criticism or rejection of what I take to be the *ratio decidendi* of the cases he thought wrongly decided.

That *ratio* I take to be that where a person buys two things for one price, it is impossible to say that he had paid only for one of them and not for the other. The fact that he could have bought one of the things at the same price as he paid for both, is in my view immaterial. . . .

Was the Spot Cash scheme an unlawful competition?
It has long been the law that for there to be a lottery, the distribution of the prizes must solely depend on chance. If the winning of a prize involved the exercise of any skill, then it was not a lottery. Ingenious schemes were devised which closely resembled lotteries but which were not unlawful on account of some degree of skill being required. In the Betting and Lotteries Act 1934 this loophole was stopped and now section 14 of the Act

of 1976, a consolidation Act, makes it an offence for any person to conduct 'in connection with any trade or business or the sale of any article to the public' a competition in which success does not depend to a substantial degree on the exercise of skill.

The section does not define 'competition'. It was submitted for the appellant that all lotteries are competitions and that a lottery conducted in connection with a trade or business or the sale of any article to the public consequently contravenes the section.

I do not think that this can be right. Apart from the improbability of Parliament ever intending to enact that all unlawful lotteries should be competitions coming within this section and so making a person who committed a criminal offence in conducting a lottery also guilty of an offence under this section, the legislative history appears to me to show that the net was being spread to catch schemes which due to the exercise of skill were not caught by the provisions as to lotteries. That leads me to the conclusion that a competition to come within the section must be one which involves the exercise of some degree of skill. If it is a substantial degree, then no offence is committed. I can find nothing in the section to suggest that only competitions which the competitor must pay to enter are within the section and I disagree with Lord Denning MR as to this but I agree with him in holding that it was wrong in the *Whitbread* case [1970] 2 QB 547 to hold that there was an unlawful competition.

As to the meaning of skill, consider the following extract.

Merkin, 'Prize competitions – the lottery of legality
[1981] LMCLQ 66, pp. 74-5

5. *Chance*

The definition of lottery originally adopted by the courts – the distribution of prizes by chance – soon came to be taken to mean that where distribution was not by chance but by skill the scheme ceased to be a lottery. Rather surprisingly, in the light of their interpretation of payment, the courts from the beginning adopted a view of skill generous in the extreme. In the words of Humphreys J in *Moore* v *Elphick* [1945] 2 All ER 155 (emphasis added):

If merit or skill plays *any* part in determining the distribution, there has been no lottery

the only qualification on this being that the

merit or skill must be real skill which has some effect.

. . .

The skill required by competitors under the first limb has never been fully defined. This has clearly been the correct approach for the real issue is the absence of pure luck, the antithesis of which may be wider than 'skill' as commonly recognised. As a result there has been no need to determine whether, for example, knowledge acquired by experience or latent ability are skill, for they are clearly not luck. The skill required by the entrants need not be substantial in terms of intellectual demand, nor in terms of proportion to chance – minimal skill in either sense will do. Further, it is irrelevant that no entrant has exercised any skill at all for the test is whether skill could have been used. Some examples will show how easy it has been for advertisers to satisfy this limb: selecting the winners of horse races or football matches requires skill; word competitions of various kinds do not rest on pure luck; competitions involving research or simply calculation are skilful, although simple observation without more is not. The only cases which are arguably incorrectly decided under this limb concern competitions requiring entrants to put a number of factors in order of public popularity, to be assessed by the choices of all entrants, held to be lotteries but probably involving the modicum of skill required for legality.

Index